CONTRI

FO

GENEALOGIES OF THE FIRST SETTLERS

OF THE

ANCIENT COUNTY OF ALBANY,

From 1630 to 1800.

BY

PROF. JONATHAN PEARSON.

CLEARFIELD

Reprinted for
Clearfield Company, Inc. by
Genealogical Publishing Co., Inc.
Baltimore, Maryland
1998, 2000, 2003

Originally published: Albany, New York, 1872
Reprinted: Genealogical Publishing Co., Inc.
Baltimore, 1976, 1978, 1984
Reprinted from a volume in the George Peabody
Department of the Enoch Pratt Free Library
Baltimore, Maryland
Library of Congress Catalogue Card Number 76-20241
International Standard Book Number 0-8063-0729-3
Made in the United States of America

A

KEY TO THE NAMES OF PERSONS

OCCURRING

In the Early Dutch Records of Albany and Vicinity

PREFACE.

The student who searches the early Dutch records meets with many difficulties, none of which are more vexatious than their personal names. The majority of the First Settlers ordinarily used no surnames, some evidently had none. In these cases individuals were often distinguished by personal peculiarities, trades, &c., which, though sufficient for the time, give little or no aid to one tracing the pedigree of a family. It is only after great familiarity with the early writings and a careful noting of the use of surnames as they are sometimes subscribed to wills, conveyances, and other important papers that any connection can be established between a first settler and his later descendants.

But while many individuals had no surnames whatever apparently, a few families had two or more. Marcelis Janse Van Bommel was farmer of the burger and tapster's excise of liquors in Beverwyck many years. Some of his children took *Marcelis* as their surname, others *Van Iveren*; without a knowledge of this fact it would be quite impossible for his descendants to trace back their pedigree to him. A similar case occurred in the Albany branch of the Bratts. In the passage over from Holland one child was born at sea in a storm and he was named Storm Van Derzee, which epithet he and his descendants have since used as a surname.

It was not uncommon for the same individual to have two or more surnames and to use them indifferently. Jan Barentse Wemp [Wemple] was sometimes called Poest; he had a mill on the Poesten-kil which perhaps derived its name from him rather than from the Dutch word *poesten*. After his death in 1663 his widow Maritie Myndertse married Sweer Teunise. He had two surnames, Van Velsen and Van Westbroeck. Jan Fort of Niskayuna had the following *aliases:* Jan La Fort, Jan Vandervort and Jan Libbertee.

The change in the spelling and pronunciation of names is likewise a source of considerable embarrassment. Who would recognize the ancient Du Trieux (pronounced Du Troo) in the modern Truax, or Beaufils in Bovie, or Barrois in Barroway, or finally the familiar name of Jones in such laughable disguises as TSans, TJans, and Shawns.

The system of nomenclature in common use among the early Dutch settlers consisted in prefixing the child's to the father's Christian name, terminating in *se* or *sen;* in baptism but one name was usually given; the patronymic was used by custom in all cases, and in the absence of a surname was sometimes adopted as such. Thus the children of Rutger Jacobsen (Van Schoenderwoert or Van Woert) were respectively Margaret *Rutgers*, Engel *Rutgers*, and Harmen *Rutgers*, and *Rutgers* was subsequently assumed as the family name. The two sons of the First Settler Wynant Gerritse (Vander Poel) were Melgert *Wynantse* and Gerrit *Wynantse*. The First Settler, Harmen Tomase Hun (Van Amersfort) had a son named Tomas *Harmense* and a daughter Wyntie *Harmense*. The First Settlers Philip and David Schuyler, were more commonly called Philip and David *Pieterse*, being sons of Pieter Schuyler.

Occasionally two patronymics were used, as Samuel Arentse Samuelse Bratt; i. e., Samuel Bratt the son of Arent, who was the son of Samuel.

The use of surnames gradually increased among the Dutch from the time the Province was occupied by the English in 1664, and after the first quarter of the following century few names were written without the addition of a family name.

The following list is intended to serve as a key to such surnames as are occasionally or almost constantly omitted in the ancient Dutch Records of Albany and Schenectady. It is as nearly full as the compiler, after a somewhat careful reading of these documents, can make it. The names of persons without surnames, or if having them were not entered in those records, will not of course be found here; unfortunately these are somewhat numerous. Another embarrassment in the identification of persons arises from the fact, that some bear the same Christian name. When such cases occur in the following list, the dates annexed will sometimes aid in solving the difficulty. Thus the surname of Jacob Abrahamse, found in documents dating 1665-84, was Vosburg *alias* Kuyper; in those of date 1705, it was Van Deusen. But where there is little or no difference in the dates this help fails, and all is left to conjecture.   J. P.

SCHENECTADY, OCT. 18, 1870.

1

NAMES.

ABELSE. [1680–4.
Hendrick Abelse Riddershalve or Riddenhaas,

ABRAHAMSE.
Abraham Abrahamse Schuyler, 1709.
Christina Abrahamse Schuyler, 1709.
David Abrahamse Schuyler, 1709.
Dirck Abrahamse Schuyler, 1709.
Engeltie Abrahamse Van Densen, 1700.
Gerrit Abrahamse Lansing, 1728.
Jacob Abrahamse Kuyper | Same (?) 1665–84.
Jacob Abrahamse Vosburgh |
Jacob Abrahamse Van Deusen, 1705.
Jacobus Abrahamse Schuyler, 1709.
Melchert Abrahamse Van Deusen, 1683–1705.
Willem Abrahamse Tietsoort, 1686.
Teuwis Abrahamse Van Deusen, 1700.

ADAMSE.
Aaltie Adamse Dingman, 1700.

ADRIAANSE.
Gysbert Adriaanse Van Bunick, 1638.
Jacob Adriaanse Van Utrecht, 1630.
Jacob Adriaanse Soogemakelyck, or Van Woggelum, 1638–55.
Jacob Adriaanse Raedemacker, 1653.
Pieter Adriaanse Soogemakelyck, *alias*, Gemakelyck or Van Woggelum, 1681.

AERTSE.
Brant Aertse Van Slichtenhorst.
Jacob Aertse Wagenaar, 1642.
Jan Aertse Van Bergen op Zoom, 1677.
Wouter Aertse Van Nieukerck, 1660.

AHASUERUSE.
Dirck Ahasueruse Roseboom, 1749.

ALBERTSE.
Andries Albertse Bratt, *alias* De Sweedt, 1674–82.
Barent Albertse Bratt, 1670–1700.
Dirk Albertse Bratt, 1678–9.
Eve Albertse Bratt.
Engeltie Albertse Bratt.
Engeltie Albertse Slingerland, 1725.
Gisseltie Albertse Bratt.
Harmen Albertse Vedder, 1659.
Jacob Albertse Planck, 1634.
Jan Albertse Bratt, 1677–85.
Jan Albertse Planck, 1631.
Johannes Albertse Slingerland, 1725.
Lambert Albertse Van Neck, 1659–62.
Storm Albertse Bratt, *alias* Van der Zee, 1663–97.
Teunis Albertse Slingerland, 1725.
Thomas Albertse Slingerland, 1725.
Willem Albertse Van Munichendam, 1654.
Wouter Albertse Van den Uythoff or Wytenhoff, 1663–74.

ANDRIESSE.
Albert Andriesse Bratt or De Noorman, 1630–82.
Andries Andriesse Gardenier.
Andries Andriesse Huygh, 1705.
Anna Andriesse Huygh, 1705.

ANDRIESSE.
Annatie Andriesse Casparus, 1700.
Arent Andriesse Bratt, 1664.
Arent Andriesse Van Frederickstadt, 1636.
Ariaantie Andriesse Scherp, 1699.
Arien Andriesse Gardenier.
Burger Andriesse Huygh, 1705.
Cathalina Andriesse Huygh, 1705.
Catryna Andriesse De Vos, 1664–91.
Claas Andriesse De Graaf, 1682.
Cornelia Andriesse Scherp, 1703.
Cornelis Andriesse Huygh, 1705.
Engeltie Andriesse Witbeck, 1683.
Geertruy Andriesse Van Doesburgh, 1661.
Geertruy Andriesse Dochter, 1679.
Gysbert Andriesse Scherp, 1700–2.
Hendrick Andriesse Van Doesburgh, 1654–64.
Jacob Andriesse Gardenier.
Jan Andriesse DeGraaf, 1650–9.   [lingh, 1664.
Jan Andriesse Iersman (Irishman) Van Dub-
Jan Andriesse Douw, *alias* Kuyper, 1646–86.
Johannes Andriesse Schaap, 1695.
Johannes Andriesse Witbeck, 1706.
Johannes Andriesse Huygh, 1705.
Jochem Andriesse Huygh, 1705.
Lambert Andriesse Huygh, 1705.
Margarita Andriesse Huygh, 1705.
Maria Andriesse Huygh, 1705.
Willem Andriesse Rees, 1672.

ANTONISSEN.
Cornelis Antonissen Van Slyck, *alias* Broer Cornelis, 1641–57.
Adam Antonissen Swart, 1690.

ARENTSE.
Andries Arentse Bratt, 1695.
Benony Arentse Van Hoeck, 1700.
Dirk Arentse Bratt, 1685.
Engeltie Arentse Slingerland, 1713.
Gerrit Arentse Slingerland, 1713.
Leendert Arentse Graw, 1689.
Rutger Arentse Schoemaecker, 1679.
Rebecca Arentse Vedder, 1715.
Samuel Arentse Bratt, 1685.
Sara Arentse Slingerland, 1715.
Teunis Arentse Slingerland, 1715.

ARIE.
Johannes Arie Oothout, 1756.

ARISSEN.
Joris Arissen or Aertse Vander Baest, 1670–90.

ARNOUTSE.
Lysbet Arnoutse Viele, 1699.
Maria Arnoutse Viele, 1684.

BALTUSE.
Catrina Baltuse Van Benthuysen, 1720.
Elizabeth Baltuse Van Benthuysen, 1720.
Jacobus Perreker (Parker ?) Baltuse Van Benthuysen, 1720.
Johannes Baltuse Van Benthuysen, 1720.

BARENTSE.

Andries Barentse Coeymans, 1695.
Annatie Barentse Van Rotmers, 1662.
Antony Barentse Bratt, 1682.
Ariaentie Barentse Coeymans.
Cornelis Barentse Ditmarse, 1692.
Dirk Barentse Bratt. 1682-3.
Frans Barentse Pastoor. 1654-61.
Geertruy Barentse Van Dwingeloo, 1662.
Jan Barentse Wemp, 1645-61.
Jan Barentse Kunst, 1662.
Jan Barentse Dulleman, 1661-2.
Jan Barentse Poest (*alias* Wemp ?) 1664-7.
Jan Barentse Timmerman, 1660.
Jannetie Barentse Coeymans.
Johannes Barentse Bratt, 1692.
Pieter Barentse Coeymans.
Pieter Barentse Cool, 1687.
Reinier Barentse Van Iveren.
Samuel Barentse Coeymans.
Teunis Barentse Cool, 1687.
Tys Barentse Schoenmaker Van Edam, 1636.

BASTIAENSE.

Jacob Bastiaense DeWit, 1700.
Jan Bastiaense Van Gudsenhoven, 1658-65.
Harmen Bastiaense Visscher or De Vyselaer,
Hester Bastiaense Visscher, 1700.   [1675-83.

BRANTSE.

Cornelis Brantse Van Nieuwkerck, 1664.
Evert Brantse Van Amersfort.

CARELSE.

Hans Carelse Noorman, 1673.

CARSTENSEN.

Carsten Carstensen Noorman or Van Norwe-
gen, 1658-79.

CASPARSE.

Agnietie Casparse Conyn, 1703-21.
Caspar Casparse Conyn, 1721.
Collette Casparse Winne, 1783.
Commertie Casparse Conyn, 1721.
Elizabeth Casparse Conyn, 1721.
Eva Casparse Conyn, 1721.
Isaac Casparse Halenbeek, 1706.
Jan Casparse Halenbeek, 1725.
Janneke Casparse Conyn, 1701.
Leendert Casparse Conyn, 1721.
Maritie Casparse Conyn, 1721.
Pieter Casparse Conyn, 1721.
Ragel Casparse Conyn, 1721.
Willem Casparse Halenbeek, 1729.

CHRISTOFFELSE.

David Christoffelse Davidts.
Joris Christoffelse Davidts, 1673.

CLAESE.

Adriaen Claese Vryman, 1654.
Anna Claese Vander Bogart, 1724.
Barber Claese Groesbeeck, 1695-1707.
Carsten Claese Timmerman, 1658.
Cornelis Claese Van den Bergh, 1651-1701.
Feitie Claese Van Schaick, 1696.
Frans Claese Van der Bogart, 1724.
Gerrit Claese Kulerman, 1670.
Gerrit Claese Vau Nieukerck, 1662.
Gysbert Claese Van Amsterdam, 1636.
Jacob Claese Egmont, 1683.
Jacob Claese Groesbeeck, 1707.
Jacob Claese Van Woert, 1736.   [1658-64.
Jan Claese Bakker Van Oosanen or Oostrand,

CLAESE.

Jesse Claese Degraaf, 1699.
Johannes Claese Groesbeck, 1701-3.
Lourens Claese Van Schaick, 1695-1700.
Lourens Claese Van der Volgen, 1720.
Lourens Claese Tolk, 1702.
Pieter Claese Kaye Van Oostzanen, 1661-3.
Pieter Claese Bout, 1659.
Rebecca Claese Groesbeeck, 1707.
Ryck Claese Van Vranken, 1684.
Stephanus Claese Groesbeeck, 1707.
Symon Claese Turck, 1664.
Tjerck Claese Dewit, 1663.
Willem Claese Groesbeeck, 1681-1707.

COENRAETSE.

Hans Coenraetse Backer, 1674.   [1660.
Hans or Jans Coenraetse Van Neurenburgh,
Hendrick Coenraetse Van Bon, 1660.
Jacob Coenraetse Ten Eyck, 1732.

CORNELISE.

Ackes or Jacques Cornelise Van Slyck, 1663-7.
Adriaen Cornelise Van Vespen, 1671.
Adriaen Cornelise Van Bersingeren, 1642.
Arnout Cornelise Viele, 1661-91.
Claes Cornelise Van den Bergh, 1660-2.
Claes Cornelise Van Voorhout, 1642-62.
Claes Cornelise Swits, 1663.
Cornelis Cornelise Vernoy, 1667.   [Vosje.
Cornelis Cornelise Van Schoenderwoert, *alias*
Cornelis Cornelise Bogart, 1660.
Cornelis Cornelise Van Voorhout, 1642-64.
Cornelis Cornelise Van der Hoeven, 1676-82.
Cornelis Cornelise De Vos, 1653-7.
Cornelis Cornelise Viele, 1661-83.
Cornelis Cornelise De Boer, 1659-61.
Cornelis Cornelise Slyck, 1659.
Cornelis Cornelise Van Sterrevelt, 1657-62.
Cornelia Cornelise Van den Bergh, 1714.
Dirck Cornelise Van Vechten, 1709.
Dirck Cornelise Duyster, 1626.
Eldert Cornelise Tymesen, 1709.
Geertie Cornelise Van den Bergh, 1714.
Gerrit Cornelis Van Nes, 1697.
Gerrit Cornelise Van den Bergh, 1714-19.
Goosen Cornelise Van den Bergh, 1714.
Gysbert Cornelise Wesop, 1667.
Gysbert Cornelise Bogart, 1661-86.
Gysbert Cornelise Van Wesp *op de Berg* or
    Aende Berg, 1645-1667.
Gysbert Cornelise Van den Bergh, 1714.
Isaac Cornelise Swits, 1664-90.
Jacques Cornelise Van Slyck, 1663-7.
Jacob Cornelise Vos or Bogart, 1683-97.
Jacob Cornelise Van der Bogart, 1685-95.
Jacob Cornelise Schermerhoorn, 1742.
Jan Cornelise Van Nes, 1697.
Jan Cornelise Van der Hoeven, 1681-5.
Jan Cornelise Van Houten, 1640.   [men, 1634.
Jan Cornelise Buys changed to Jan Jansen Da-
Jan Cornelise Van Hoesen, 1681.
Jan Cornelise Roodt, 1670-91.
Jan Cornelise Kleyn, 1660.
Jan Cornelise Timmerman, 1660.
Jan Cornelise Vyselaer, *alias* Gow, 1660-1702.
Jan Cornelise Van der Heyden, 1660-4.
Jannetie Cornelise Van Schaick, 1703.
Hendrick Cornelise Van Nes, 1697.
Hendrick Cornelise Van Buren, 1662.
Hendrick Cornelise Maasen, 1663.

CORNELISE.
Maas Cornelise Van Buren, 1662.
Maes Cornelise Koperslager, 1675.
Maritie Cornelise Mingael, 1666.
Maritie Cornelise Van den Bergh, 1714.
Maria Cornelise Muller, 1702.
Marten Cornelise Van Ysselstein, 1661–8.
Marten Cornelise Vlas, 1681.
Marten Cornelise Van Buren, 1662–1703.
Matthias Cornelise Van den Bergh, 1714.
Pieter Cornelise Van Munichendam, 1636.
Pieter Cornelise Viele, 1670.
Pieter Cornelise De Jongh, 1659.
Poulus Cornelise Van Flensburgh, 1671.
Poulus Cornelise Van Abcoude, 1660.
Roeloff Cornelise Van Houten, 1638.
Ryer Cornelise Soesbergen, 1660.
Salomon Cornelise Van Vechten, 1698–1700.
Seger Cornelise Van Voorhout, 1642–62.
Styntie Cornelise Van Buren, 1672.
Teunis Cornelise Slingerland, 1659–70.
Teunis Cornelise Spitsbergen, 1663–75.
Teunis Cornelise Van der Poel, 1661–87.
Teunis Cornelise Van Rossum, 1662.
Teunis Cornelise Van Vechten, 1637–83.
Teunis Cornelise Swart, 1661.
Tobyas Cornelise Van Buren, 1662–1703.
Tryntie Cornelise Van den Bergh, 1714.
Weyntie Cornelise Bosch, 1690.
Willem Cornelise Coster or Koster, 1643.
Willem Cornelise Van den Bergh, 1706.
Wynant Cornelise Van den Bergh, 1714.

COSTERSE.
Jan Coster or Costerse Van Aecken 1659–77.

CRISTYSSEN or CHRISTIAANSE. [1636.
Cristen Cristyssen Noorman Van Vleckburgh,

DANIELSE.
Arent Danielse Van Antwerpen, 1720.
Daniel Danielse Van Antwerpen, 1699.
Jan Danielse Van Antwerpen, 1720.
Johannes Danielse Fort, 1736.
Pieter Danielse Van Antwerpen, 1720.
Pieter Danielse Van Olinda, 1669.
Symon Danielse Van Antwerp, 1699–1720.

DAVIDTSE.
Andries Davidtse Christoffelse Davidts, 1700.
Pieter Davidtse Schuyler, 1683–96.
Thomas Davidtse Kikebel, 1682.

DIRKSE.
Abraham Dirkse Van Vechten, 1699.
Adriaen Dirkse De Vries, 1654.
Andries Dirkse Bratt, 1727.
Anna Dirkse Goes, 1732.
Anna Dirkse Van Vechten.
Annatie Dirkse Bratt, 1727.
Annatie Dirkse Van Vechten, 1687.
Benjamin Dirkse Van Vechten, 1739.
Catalyntie Dirkse Ten Broeck.
Catalyntie Dirkse Bratt, 1727.
Christina Dirkse Ten Broeck.
Cornelia Dirkse Ten Broeck.
Dirk Dirkse Keyser, 1658.
Dirk Dirkse Vanderkarre, 1694.
Elisabeth Dirkse Bratt, 1727.
Elisabeth Dirkse Ten Broeck.
Elsie Dirkse Ten Broeck.
Fytie Dirkse Van Vechten, 1687–1704.

DIRKSE.
Geertruy Dirkse Ten Broeck.
Harmen Dirkse Van Vechten, 1793.
Jan Dirkse Vinhaeghen, 1663.
Jan Dirkse Van Eps, 1664–84.
Jan Dirkse Van Bremen, 1648–62.
Jan Dirkse Engelsman Van Amersfort, 1638.
Jannetic Dirkse Van Vechten, 1687.
Johannes Dirkse Bratt, 1727.
Johannes Dirkse Goes, 1732.
Johannes Dirkse Ten Broeck.
Johannes Dirkse Van Vechten, 1687.
Johannes Dirkse Van der Heyden, 1729.
Lena Dirkse By, 1704.
Luykas Dirkse Goes, 1732.
Lydia Dirkse Ten Broeck.
Lysbet Dirkse Van Eps, 1668–81.
Maria Dirkse Bratt, 1727.
Michael Dirkse Van Vechten, 1689.
Neeltie Dirkse Van Vechten, 1687.
Philip Dirkse Van Vechten, 1739.
Samuel Dirse Van Vechten, 1687.
Samuel Dirkse Ten Broeck.
Sara Dirkse Van Vechten, 1687.
Symon Dirkse Pos, 1630–44.
Takel Dirkse Van Heemstraaten, 1700.
Teunis Dirkse Van Vechten, 1638–1704.
Tobias Dirkse Ten Broeck.
Wyntie Dirkse Van Vechten, 1687.

DOUWESE.
Gillis Douwese Fonda, 1654.
Jan Douwese Fonda, 1681.

EGBERTSE.
Anthony Egbertse Bratt, 1753.

EVERTSE.
Ephraim Evertse Wendel, 1690.
Evert Evertse De Goyer, 1664.
Hanse Evertse Kuyper, 1725.
Jacob Evertse Kuyper, 1725.
Jan Evertse Schoenmaker, 1661–5.
Johannes Evertse Kuyper, 1725.
Johannes Evertse Wendel, 1720–36.
Robert Evertse Wendel, 1690.
Susanna Evertse Wendel, 1690.
Tys Evertse De Goyer, 1664–8.

FRANSE.
Aaltie Franse Pruyn, 1683–1700.
Abraham Franse Van Aalsteyn, 1700.
Claas Franse Van de Bogart, 1699–1720.
Elsie Franse Clauw or Klauw, 1683–1700.
Gerritie Franse Hardick, 1737.
Henrick Franse Clauw or Klauw, 1686–1705.
Jan Franse Hardick, 1737.
Jan Franse Van Hoesen, 1659–1703.
Jaunetie Franse Clauw or Klauw, 1695.
Jurrian Franse Clauw or Klauw, 1699.
Maria Franse Clauw or Klauw, 1700.
Sara Franse Hardick, 1737.
Tierck Franse Van der Bogart, 1720.
Tryntie Franse Van der Bogart, 1724.
Volkje Franse Hardick, 1737.
Willem Franse Hardick, 1737.
Wyntie Franse Clauw or Klauw, 1683.

FREDERICKSE.
Carsten Frederickse Van Iveren, 1663.
Claas Frederickse Van Petten, 1664–8.
Myndert Frederickse Van Iveren, 1675–1704.
Salomon Frederickse Bouw or Bosch, 1689.

FREDERICKSE.
Willem Frederickse Van Leyden, 1642.
Willem Frederickse Bout, 1654–83.

GERBERTSE or HERBERTSE.
Eldert or Elbert Gerbertse Cruiff, 1654–86.

GERRITSE.
Abraham Gerritse Spoor, 1719.
Adriaan Gerritse Papendorp, 1682–7.
Aeltie Gerritse Lansing.
Ann Gerritse Spoor, 1719.
Annetie Gerritse Lansing, 1694.
Barent Gerritse Van den Bergh, 1700–5.
Barentie Gerritse Paus, 1683.
Claas Gerritse Van Vranken, 1705.
Cornelia Gerritse Spoor, 1719.
Cornelis Gerritse Greeff, 1661.
Cornelis Gerritse Van Schoenderwoert, 1642.
Cornelis Gerritse Van den Bergh, 1700.
Elisabeth Gerritse De Honneur, 1679–82.
Elbert Gerritse Lansing, 1693.
Geertruy Gerritse Van den Bergh, 1699.
Geertruy Gerritse Van Schoonhoven, 1701.
Goosen Gerritse Van Schaick, 1637–75.
Gerrit Gerritse Lansing, 1702–1742.
Grieta Gerritse Van Vranken, 1700.
Grietie Gerritse Van Vechten, 1683.
Gysbert Gerritse Van Brakel, 1699–1709.
Gysbertie Gerritse Lansing.
Hendrick Gerritse Van Meulen, 1671–80.
Hendrick Gerritse Verwy or Van Wie, 1689.
Hendrick Gerritse Van Nes, 1736.
Hendrick Gerritse Lansing, 1747.
Hilletie Gerritse Lansing.
Jacob Gerritse Van Schaick, 1756.
Jacob Gerritse Van Laer, 1670–5.
Jacobus Gerritse Brouwer, 1676.
Jacobus Gerritse Van Vorst, 1671–89.
Jan Gerritse Van Marcken, 1661–75.
Jan Gerritse Van Oldenburgh, 1662.
Jannetie Gerritse Papendorp.
Jannetie Gerritse Van Nes.
Johannes Gerritse Spoor, 1719.
Johannes Gerritse Lansingh, 1730.
Johannes Gerritse Roos, 1695.
Johannes Gerritse Van Vechten, 1692–1700.
Lucas Gerritse Wyngaart or Backer, 1670–93.
Maria Gerritse Van den Bergh, 1702.
Maria Gerritse Spoor, 1719.
Maritie Gerritse Lansing, 1694.
Marten Gerritse Van Bergen, 1630–96.
Pieter Gerritse Kleyn, 1671.
Reyer Gerritse Lansing, 1747.
Roeloff Gerritse Van der Werken, 1700.
Teunis Gerritse Verwey, 1666.
Volkert Gerritse Van Vechten, 1681.
Willem Gerritse Van Nes.
Willem Gerritse Spoor, 1719.
Willem Gerritse Van den Bergh, 1752.
Wynant Gerritse Van der Poel, 1654–99.

GEURT.
Geertruy Geurt Van Schoonhoven, 1700.
Hendrik Geurt Van Schoonhoven, 1700.
Hendrikje Geurt Van Schoonhoven, 1700.
Jacobus Geurt Van Schoonhoven.
Jacomyntie Geurt Van Schoonhoven, 1700.
Margaret Geurt Van Schoonhoven, 1700.

GILLISE.
Jan Gillise Kock, 1657.

GOOSENSE.
Aert Goosense Van Twiller, 1661–84.
Antony Goosense Van Schaick, 1681.
Geertruy Goosense Van Schaick, 1681.
Gerrit Goosense Van Schaick.
Sybrant Goosense Van Schaick, 1681–42.

GREGORY.
Nicolaas Gregory Hillebrant, 1658.

GYSBERTSE.
Cornelis Gysbertse Van den Bergh, 1683–1714.
Frederick Gysbertse Van den Bergh, 1662.
Gerrit Gysbertse Van den Bergh, 1683–1700.
Gerrit Gysbertse Van Brakel, 1699.
Teunis Gysbertse Bogaerdt, 1658.
Willem Gysbertse Van den Bergh, 1683–1795.

HANSE or HANSEN.
Andries Hanse Scherp, 1674–84.
Andries Hanse Huygh, 1679–1705.
Andries Hanse Barhydt or Barheit, 1692–99.
Andries Hanse Van Sweden (Scherp?), 1663.
Carel Hanse Toll, 1720.
Hendrikie Hanse Dreeper, 1694.
Jan Hanse Barheit, 1701.
Jeronimus Hanse Barheit, 1685–1700.
Johanna Hanse Barheit, 1705.
Rachel Hanse Toll or Van Toll, 1697.

HARMENSE.
Ariaentie Harmense Visscher, 1701.
Bastiaen Harmense Visscher, 1683–1703.
Cornelis Harmense Knickerbakker, 1708.
Dirkie Harmense Weevers, 1678.
Evert Harmense Knickerbakker, 1708.
Frederick Harmense Visscher, 1699.
Cornelia Harmense Knickerbakker, 1708.
Harmen Harmense Van Gansevoort, 1664–75.
Hester Harmense Visscher, 1683,
Jan Harmense Backer, 1658–83.
Jan Harmense Weendorp, 1663.
Jan Harmense Van Turick, 1664.
Jannetie Harmense Knickerbakker, 1708.
Johannes Harmense Visscher, 1693–1709.
Johannes Harmense Knickerbakker, 1708.
Maria Harmense Visscher, 1700.
Myndert Harmense Van der Bogart, 1683–1706.
Maritie Harmense Lieversen, 1683.
Nanning Harmense Visscher, 1683–1711.
Pieter Harmense Knickerbakker, 1708.
Sara Harmense Visscher, 1691–5.
Tierck Harmense Visscher, 1696–1722. [1706.
Thomas Harmense Hun Van Amersfort, 1662–
Wyntie Harmense Van Hun, 1681.
Lourens Harmense Knickerbakker, 1708.

HELMERSE.
Catharina Helmerse Otten, 1703.
Jan or Johan Helmerse Van Baasle, 1642.
Jan Helmerse, *alias* Jan De Bock, 1657–60.

HENDRICKSE.
Adam Hendrickse Vrooman, 1683.
Bartholomew Hendrickse Vrooman, 1786.
Claas Hendrickse VanUtrecht, or Schoonhoven,
Coenraet Hendrickse Burger, 1700. [1654–60.
Cornelise Hendrickse Van Es or Nes, 1643.
Cornelis Hendrickse Van Buren, 1701.
Dirk Hendrickse Bye, *alias* De Sweedt, 1675–80.
Dirk Hendrickse Van Gottenburgh, 1663.
Eva Hendrickse Vrooman, 1691.
Geesie Hendrickse Van Wye, 1700.

HENDRICKSE.

Gerrit Hendrickse Van Rys or Reis, 1663.
Guert Hendrickse Van Schoonhoven, 1681–1700.
Hendrick Hendrickse Van Harstenhorst, 1662.
Isaac Hendrickse Burger, 1706.
Jacob Hendrickse Ten Eyck, 1733.
Jacob Hendricke Sibinck, 1655–65.
Jacob Hendrickse Lery, 1663.
Jacob Hendrickse Varrevanger, 1661.   [1654.
Jacob Hendrickse Maet, *alias* Van Loosereght,
Jan Hendrickse Van Bael, 1659–79.
Jan Hendrickse Bruyns, 1662–1701.
Jan Hendrickse Van Salsbergen, 1673–1700.
Jan Hendrickse Vrooman, 1683–93.
Jan Hendrickse Bout, 1706.
Jan Hendrickse Van den Bergh, 1683–8.
Jan Hendrickse Roothaer, 1662.
Jannetie Hendrickse Van Doesburgh, 1698.
Jannetie Hendrickse Van Wie, 1704.
Johannes Hendrickse Roseboom, 1704.
Johannes Hendrickse Ten Eyck, 1733.
Marten Hendrickse Verbraeck, 1668.
Marten Hendrickse Hamelward, 1638.
Marten Hendrickse Beeckman, 1661.
Mayke Hendrickse Van den Bergh, Graef, 1684.
Philip Hendrickse Brouwer, 1660–4.
Pieter Hendrickse De Haas or Hans, 1683–99.
Rutger Hendrickse Van Soest, 1630.
Seger Hendrickse Van Soest, 1630.

HERBERTSE, or HARPERTSE.

Abraham HarpertseVan Deusen, 1736. [1640–65.
Andries Herbertse Constapel Van der Blaas,

HERTGERS.

Pieter Hertgers Van Vee, 1645–62.

ISAACKSE.

Abraham Isaacse Ver Planck, 1667.
Abraham Isaacse Fonda, 1747.
Annatie Isaacse Van Deusen.
Arent Isaacse Van Hoeck, 1658–63.
Baatha Isaacse Van Deusen.
Cornelia Isaacse Van Deusen, 1740.
Cornelia Isaacse Van Deusen, 1740.
Douwe Isaacse Fonda, 1732.
Gerrit Isaacse Lansing. 1747.
Elizabeth Isaacse Van Deusen, 1740.
Helena Isaacse Van Deusen, 1740.
Isaac Isaacse Van Deusen, 1740.
Johannes Isaacse Van Deusen, 1740.
Maritie Isaacse Van Deusen, 1740.
Mattheus Isaacse Van Deusen, 1740.
Sarah Isaacse Van Deusen, 1740.
Tryntie Isaacse Van Deusen, 1740.

JACOBSE.

Aeltie Jacobse Gardenier, 1683.
Albert Jacobse Gardenier, 1677–85.
Andries Jacobse Gardenier, 1680–97.
Caspar Jacobse Halenbeek.   [1661–1707.
Claas Jacobse Groesbeeck *alias* Van Rotterdam,
Cornelis Jacobse Schermerhoorn, 1700.
Cornelis Jacobse By, 1659.
Cornelis Jacobse Van Oostsanen, 1661.
Gerrit Jacobse Schout or Shout, 1697–1701.
Gerrit Jacobse Lansing, 1734.
Harmen Jacobse Wendel, 1749.
Harmen Jacobse Bambus, 1657.
Helena Jacobse Schermerhoorn, 1700.
Hendrick Jacobse Beeckman, 1746.   [1742.
Herbert or Harpert Jacobse Van Deusen, 1683–

JACOBSE.

Jacob Jacobse Elkens, 1618.
Jacob Jacobse Schermerhoorn, 1700.
Jan Jacobse Van Noortstrant, 1677–87.
Jan Jacobse Gardenier or Flodder, 1685–95.
Jannetie Jacobse Schermerhoorn, 1700.
Johannes Jacobse Glen, 1699–1704.
Johannes Jacobse Eversen, 1744.
Johannes Jacobse Lansingh, 1751.
Josine Jacobse Gardenier, 1696.
Luycas Jacobse Schermerhoorn, 1700.
Magtelt Jacobse Schermerhoorn, 1700.
Neeltie Jacobse Schermerhoorn, 1700.
Pieter Jacobse Vosburgh, 1657.
Pieter Jacobse Van Iinsborgh, 1663,
Pieter Jacobse Borsboom, 1662.
Pieter Jacobse Clockluyer, 1661.
Pieter Jacobse Marius, 1663–90.
Reyer Jacobse Schermerhoorn, 1678–96.
Rutger, Rut or Ruth Jacobse Van Schoender-
    woert or Van Woert, 1636–63.
Symon Jacobse Schermerhoorn, 1683–1705,
Samuel Jacobse Gardenier, 1681.
Teunis Jacobse Bierdrager, 1661.
Teunis Jacobse Van Schoenderwoert, 1640.
Willem Jacobse Van Deusen, 1683–1731.
Wybrecht Jacobse Dochter, 1661.

JACOBUSE.

Johannes Jacobuse Lansing, 1742.

JANSE.

Abraham Janse Van Aelsteyn, 1700.
Adriaen Janse Appel,*alias* Van Leyden, 1656–83.
Adriaen Janse Croon, 1700.
Adriaen Janse Van Ilpendam, 1656.
Adriaen Janse De Vries, 1656.
Adriaen Janse Van Duynkerken, 1660.
Aeltie Janse Wemp, 1663.
Albert Janse Van Amsterdam, 1642.
Albert Janse Ryckman, 1671–8.
Andries Janse Witbeck, 1683–1700.
Anna Janse Mebie, 1716.
Anna Janse Van Hoesen, 1694.
Anna Janse Goes, 1697.
Barbar Janse Goewey, 1702.
Barent Janse Van Ditmars, 1685.
Barent Janse Bratt, 1681.
Barent Janse Bal, 1660.
Barent Janse Wemp, 1662–83.
Bastiaen Janse Crol, 1630–41.
Casparus Janse Bronck, 1738.
Catharina Janse Van Hoesen, 1694.
Claas Janse Stavast, 1672–84.
Claas Janse Van Rotterdam, 1654.
Claas Janse Van Baren, 1663–78.
Claas Janse Van Boekhoven, 1662–99.
Claas Janse Nykerk, 1634.
Claas Janse Ruyter, 1638.
Claas Janse Van Breda, 1639.
Claas Janse Van Warlwyck, 1642.
Cornelis Janse Cuyper, 1634.
Cornelis Janse Damen, 1634.
Cornelia Janse Gardenier, 1702.
Daniel Janse Van Antwerpen, 1660–92.
Dirk Janse Croon, 1660.
Dirk Janse Smit, 1660.
Dirk Janse Van Edam, 1636.
Dirk Janse Goes, 1697–1700.
Evert Janse Cuyper, 1681–1725.
Evert Janse Wendell, 1658–74.

JANSE.

Evert Janse Kleermaker, 1633.
Frans Janse Pruyn, 1661-86.
Geertruy Janse Witbeck, 1683-1702.
Geertruy Janse Lansing, 1695.
Gerrit Janse Cuyper, 1662.
Gerrit Janse Stavast, 1673-8.
Gerrit Janse Herttenbergh, 1664.
Gerrit Janse Van Kulenbergh, 1681.
Gerrit Janse Ruyting, 1690.
Gerrit Janse Lansing, 1657.
Gerrit Janse Roos, 1695.
Hans Janse Van Rotterdam, 1638.
Harmen Janse Turkyen, 1681.
Harmen Janse Ryckman, 1667.
Harmen Janse Bos, 1666.
Harmen Janse Scheel, 1658.   [1702.
Harmen Janse Knickerbakker Van Wye, 1682-
Harmen Janse Solsbergen, 1706.
Harmen Janse Van Bommel, 1685.
Harmen Janse Metselaer, 1718.
Harmen Janse Lyndrayer, 1681.
Helmer Janse Jeroloman, 1702.
Hendrick Janse, *alias* Ribbide, 1664.
Hendrick Janse Van Fewide, 1685.
Hendrick Janse Oothout, 1683.
Hendrick Janse Van Salsbergen, 1699-1705.
Hendrik Janse Reur, 1658.
Hendrik Janse Damen. 1634.
Hendrick Janse Witbeck, 1696-1703.
Hendrick Janse Looman, 1661.
Hendrick Janse Van Wytert, 1657.
Hendrick Janse Westerkamp, 1667.
Hendrick Janse Roseboom, 1662.
Hendrick Janse Van der Vin, 1654.
Isaac Janse Van Arnham, 1699.
Isaac Janse Van Aelsteyn, 1700.
Jacob Janse Gardenier or Flodder, 1638-95.
Jacob Janse Van Campen, 1649.   [1636-83.
Jacob Janse Schermerhoorn Van Amsterdam,
Jacob Janse Van Noortstraut, 1638-86.
Jacob Janse Hap or Stoll, 1630-61.
Jacob Janse Loockermans, 1659.
Jacob Janse Van Hoesen, 1684.
Jacob Janse Stoutenbergh, 1646.
Jan Janse Myndertse, 1629.
Jan Janse Ouderkerk " *Smalle Kuyper* " 1681.
Jan Janse Flodder or Gardenier, 1642-1702.
Jan Janse Van Arnhem.
Jan Janse Van Eeckelen, 1661-7.
Jan Janse Bleecker, 1666-1732.
Jan Janse Kromenborch, 1657.
Jan Janse Van Otten, 1657.
Jan Janse Oothout, 1660-88.
Jan Janse Van Rotterdam, 1662-90.
Jan Janse Noorman, 1673-96.
Jan Janse Van Salsbergen, 1683.
Jan Janse Damen, 1634.
Jan Janse Van Otterspoor, 1658.
Jan Janse Molenaer, 1695.
Jan Janse Yoncker, 1703.
Jan Janse Goes, 1697-1700.
Jan Janse Van Haarlem, 1697.
Jan Janse Post, 1683.
Jan Janse Van Bremen, 1646.
Jan Janse Van St. Obin, 1657.
Jochem Janse Bakker, 1665.
Johannes Janse Witbeck, 1683.
Johannes Janse Lansing, 1749.
Johannes Janse Van Hoesen, 1694.

JANSE.

Jonas Janse Bronck, 1738.
Jonatan Janse Witbeck, 1703.
Joseph Janse Van Zandt, 1753.
Judick Janse Goes, 1697.
Judic Janse Van Hoesen, 1683.
Jurriaen Janse Van Hoesen, 1674-1703.
Jurriaen Janse Groenwout, 1662-86.
Lammert Janse Van der Laen, 1661.
Leonard Janse Bronck, 1738.
Lena Janse Gardenier, 1702.
Lucas Janse Witbeck, 1692-1700.
Lucas Janse Van Salsbergen, 1693.
Lysbet Janse Goewey, 1702.
Lysbet Janse Witbeck, 1683.
Lysbet Janse Bognert, 1699.
Magtelt Janse Post, 1695.
Marcelis Janse Van Bommel, 1659-1700.
Maria Janse Van Hoesen, 1694.
Maritie Janse Witbeck, 1698.
Matthys Janse Goes, 1690.
Maurits Janse Van Broeckhuysen, 1636.
Mayke Janse Goes, 1697.
Michael Janse Van Brookhuysen, 1636.
Myndert Janse Wemp, 1672-7.
Neeltie Janse Damen, 1634.
Paulus Janse Van Gertruydenburgh, 1642.
Philip Janse Bronck, 1738.
Pieter Janse Bosch, 1689.
Pieter Janse Van Stockholm, 1658.
Pieter Janse Lamaker, 1659.
Pieter Janse Van Hoorn or De Boer, 1661.
Pieter Janse Loockermans, 1656-79.
Pieter Janse Vrooman, 1706.
Reindert Janse Hoorn, 1659.
Rem Janse Smit.
Richart Janse Van Den Bergh, 1702.
Roeloff Janse Van Frederikfort, 1662.
Sara Janse Van Bremen, 1703.
Sara Janse Witbeck, 1698.
Simon Janse Turk, 1659.   ;[84.
Steven Janse Conninck, or Timmerman, 1654-
Stoffel Janse Abeel, 1659-84.
Styntie Janse Van Hoesen, 1694.
Symon Janse Post, 1695.
Symon Janse Romeyn, 1658-62,
Teuntie Janse Goes, 1697-1702.
Thomas or Tomas Janse Mingael, 1656-9.
Tomas Janse Schipper, 1660.
Tomas Janse De Boer, 1661.
Tryntie Janse Van Bristede, 1636.
Tys Janse Goes, 1697.
Volkert Janse Douw, 1681-1700.
Volkert Janse Van Hoesen, 1694.
Willem Janse Damen, 1634.
Willem Janse Halenbeck, 1707.
Willem Janse Slyckoten, 1661.
Willem Janse Schutt or Dommelaer, 1657-65.
Willem Janse Stoll, 1654-61.

JERONIMUS.

Wouter Jeronimus Barheit, 1713.

JILLISE, or GILLISE.

Douwe Jillise Fonda, 1674-99.
Hendrick Jillise Meyer, 1676.
Pieter Jillise Metselaer, 1657.

JOCHEMSE.

Lambert Jochemse Van Valkenburgh, 1693.
Maria Jochemse Van Valkenburgh, 1700.

JOCHEMSE.
Rachel Jochemse Ketelhuyn, 1690.

JOHANNESE.
Abraham Johannese Wendel, 1691.
Catalyntie Johannese Wendel, 1691.
Elizabeth Johannese Wendel, 1691.
Elsie Johannese Wendel, 1691.
Ephraim Johannese Wendel, 1691.
Evert Johannese Wendel, 1691.
Isaack Johannese Wendel, 1691.
Jacob Johannese Wendel, 1691.
Jacob Johannese Van der Heyden, 1755.
Johannes Johannese Lansing, 1748-55.
Johannes Johannese Wendel, 1655-91.
Luykas Johannese Wyngaert, 1726-54.
Maritie Johannese Wendel, 1691.
Pieter Johannese De Garmeau, 1753.
Sara Johannese Wendel, 1691.
Susanna Johannese Wendel, 1691.

JONASSE.
Volkert Jonasse Douw, 1709.

JOOSTE.
Jacob Jooste Van Covelens, 1662.

JORISSEN.
Hans Jorrissen Houten, 1633.

JURRIAENSE.
Daniel Jurriaense Rinckhout, 1704.
Eefie Jurriaense Rinckhout, 1704.
Fytie Jurriaense Van Hoesen, 1699.
Jan Jurriaense Post, 1667.
Jan Jurriaense Becker, 1669-99.
Jan Jurriaense Hogan, 1730.
Jannetie Jurriaense Rinckhout, 1704.
Teunis Jurriaense Rinckhout, 1704.
Willem Jurriaense Backer, 1637-50.

LAMBERTSE.
Cornelis Lambertse Van Doorn, 1642.
Gerrit Lambertse Van Valkenburgh, 1683.
HendrickLambertse Bont or Bint, *alias* Sassian.
Jan Lambertse Van Bremen, 1661-6.
Jannetie Lambertse Van Valkenburgh, 1683.
Jochem Lambertse Van Valkenburgh,1683-1703.
Maritie Lambertse Loockermans, 1682.

LATYN.
Johan Latyn Verduyn, 1636.

LEENDERTSE.
Caspar Leendertse Conyn, 1683-1721.
Lysbert Leendertse Conyn, 1704.
Philip Leendertse Conyn, 1683-1703.
Philip Leendertse Van der Grist, 1658.
Sander Leendertse Glen, 1639-1660.

LOURENSE. [erent.
Claas Lourense Van der Volgen, *alias* Van Purm-
Cornelis Lourense Van Wurmdrink, 1709.
Johannes Lourense Van Alen, 1706.
Pieter Lourense Van Alen, 1709.

LUYKASE.
Claas Luykase Wyngaert, 1700-4.
Evert Luykase Backer, 1677.
Gerrit Luykase Wyngaert, 1701-6.
Jacobus Luykase Wyngaert, 1701-20.
Jan Luykase Wyngaert, 1689-1704.
Luykas Luykase Van Hoogkerke, 1686-1705.
Luykas Luykase Wyngaert, 1709.
Lysbet Luykase Wyngaert, 1700.
Marya Luykase Wyngaert, 1709.
Pieter Luykase Coeymans, 1683-92.

MAESSE.
Catalyntie Maesse Van Buren, 1733.
Cornelis Maesse Van Bloemendael, 1706-83.
Cornelis Maesse Van Buren, 1631.
Hendrick Maesse Van Buren, 1733.
Jacob Maesse Van Bloemendael, 1733.
Johannes Maesse Van Bloemendael, 1728.
Johannes Maesse Van Buren, 1733.

MARIUS.
Jacob Marius Groen, 1709.

MARTENSE.
Aert Martense Doorn, 1686.
Annatie Martense Cregier, 1734.
Barent Martense Van Buren, 1742.
Catalina Martense Van Buren, 1703.
Cornelia Martense Van Buren, 1703.
Cornelis Martense Potter, 1659.
Cornelis Martense Van Buren, 1703.
Cornelis Martense Van Isselsteyn, 1705.
Cornelis Martense Van Aelsteyn, 1703.
Elisabeth Martense Cregier, 1734.
Geertruy Martense Cregier, 1734.
Gerrit Martense Van Bergen.
Hendrick Martense Van Coppenhoegen, 1659.
Hendrick Martense Beeckman, 1673-95.
Jan Martense Wever or De Weever, 1689-94.
Jannetie Martense Van Bergen, 1683.
Johannes Martense Beeckman, 1682.
Johannes Martense Smit, 1683.
Magdalena Martense Van Buren, 1703.
Maria Martense Van Buren, 1703.
Maria Martense Cregier, 1734.
Marten Martense Cregier, 1734.
Marten Martense Van Buren, 1703.   [maker.
Myndert Martense Van Bergen (or Raam-
Paulus Martense Van Benthuysen, 1666-1703.
Paulus Martense Van Rynsburgh, 1662.
Pieter Martense Van Buren, 1703.
Willem Martense Huis or Hues, 1658-72.
Willem Martense Moer, 1665.

MATEUWESE.
Jan Mateuwese Van Deursen, 1696.

MATTYSE.
Coenraad Mattyse Hoogteling, 1688.

MEESE.
Hendrick Meese Vrooman, 1670-5.
Jacob Meese Vrooman, 1683-92.
Pieter Meese Vrooman, 1657-83.
Pieter Meese Hoogeboom, 1701.

MELGERTSE OR MELCHERTSE.
Abraham Melgertse Van Der Poel, 1710.
Ariaentie Melgertse Van Der Poel, 1710.
Catharina Melgertse Van Deusen, 1691-1703.
Coatie Melgertse Van der Poel, 1683.
Maria Melgertse Van der Poel, 1710.
Melgert Melgertse Van der Poel, 1710.
Rachel Melgertse Van der Poel, 1710.
Ruth Melgertse Van Deusen, 1700-3.
Trinke Melgertse Van der Poel, 1710.
Wynant Melgertse Van der Poel, 1710.

MICHIELSE.
Jan Michielse Van Edam, 1637.

MYNDERTSE.
Burger Myndertse (Smit), 1708.
Frederick Myndertse Van Iveren, 1707.
Harmen Myndertse Van der Bogart, *alias* Har-
manus A Boghardij, 1646.

MYNDERTSE.
Hendrick Myndertse Roseboom, 1728–36.
Jan Myndertse Wemp, 1699.
Johannes Myndertse Van Iveren, 1707.
Neeltie Myndertse (Smit), 1703.
Reinier Myndertse Van Iveren (Smit), 1707.

NICOLAASE.
Maria Nicolaase Ripse [Van Dam ?] 1683.
Pieter Nicolaase Van Nordinge, 1637.

PAULUSE.
Marten Pauluse Van Benthuysen, 1697–1705.

PHILIPSE.
Dirk Philipse Conyn, 1708.
Gysbert Philipse Velthuysen, 1654.
Jan Philipse Muller, 1663.
Leendert Philipse Conyn, 1687–1706.
Philip Philipse Demoer, 1693–99.

PIETERSE.
Abraham Pieterse Vosburgh, 1653–74.
Adam Pieterse Winne, 1684.
Adriaen Pieterse Van Alkmaer, 1653.
Aert Pieterse Tack, 1661–1.
Allette Pieterse Winne, 1688.
Antje Pieterse Borsboom, 1693.
Antje Pieterse Quackenbos, 1685.
Arent Pieterse Coeymans, 1636.   [1636–1701.
Barent Pieterse Coeymans, alias Molenaer,
Cornelia Pieterse Van OLinda, 1693.
Cryn Pieterse Van Seventer, 1659.
Daniel Pieterse Winne, 1684.
David Pieterse Schuyler, 1660–73.
David Pieterse Coeymans, 1636.
Francois Pieterse Winne, 1674–84.
Frans Pieterse Clauw or Klauw, 1662–1700.
Jacob Pieterse Coeymans, 1636.
Jacobus Pieterse Winne, 1684.
Jan Pieterse Mebie, 1603.
Jan Pieterse Mulder, 1660–1.
Jan Pieterse Bronck, 1669–77.
Jan Pieterse Kleermaker, 1660.
Jan Pieterse Van Woggelum, 1682.
Jannetie Pieterse Vosburgh, 1683.
Jillis Pieterse Meyer or Timmerman, 1660–76.
Johannes Pieterse Van Alen, 1689–1706.
Johannes Pieterse Quackenbos, 1683–90.
Killiaen Pieterse Winne, 1684.
Livinus Pieterse Winne, 1684.
Luycas Pieterse Coeymans, 1661–85.
Lucas Pieterse Houtsager (Coeymans), 1660.
Maria Pieterse Loockermans, 1677.
Marten Pieterse Winne, 1684.
Mattys Pieterse Vrooman, 1684.   [84.
Mees or Meeuwes Pieterse Hoogeboom, 1661–
Nathaniel Pieterse Van Leyden, 1661.
Philip Pieterse Schuyler, 1656–72.
Pieter Pieterse Lansing, 1736.
Pieter Pieterse Van Woggelum, 1671–87.
Pieter Pieterse Root or Roode, 1661–71.
Pieter Pieterse Lassen, 1659–81.
Pieter Pieterse Winne, Jr., 1676–84.
Pieter Pieterse Van Netten, 1658.
Reinier Pieterse Quackenbos, 1683–89.
Reyntien Pieterse Barroquier, 1654.
Teunis Pieterse Suidam, 1705.
Teunis Pieterse Temper, 1657–60.
Tomas Pieterse Winne, 1684.
Walrave Pieterse Claerhout, 1659.
Willem Pieterse Slyck, 1685.

PIETERSE.
Willem Pieterse Van Alen, 1689.
Wouter Pieterse Quackenbos, 1676–99.

REYERSE.
Gerrit Reyerse Lansing, 1693.

RIPSE.
Claas or Nicolaas Ripse Van Dam, 1658–1700.

ROELOFFSE.
Aaltie Roeloffse Van der Werken, 1700.
Albert Roeloffse Van der Werken, 1708.
Gerrit Roeloffse Van der Werken, 1702–5.
Hendrick Roeloffse Van der Werken, 1702–8.
Jan Roeloffse De Goyer.
Maritie Roeloffse Van der Werken, 1698.

ROLANTSEN.
Adam Rolantsen Van Hamelwart, 1638.

RUTSE.
Johannes Rutse Bleecker, 1749.

RYCKSE.
Gerrit Ryckse Van Vranken.
Maas Ryckse Van Vranken.

RYNDERTSE OR REINDERSE.
Arent Reinderse Smit, 1645.
Barent Rynderse Smit, 1668–77.
Claas Reinderse Mynderse, 1706.

SALOMONSE.
Jacob Salomonse Goeway, 1683.
Jan Salomonse Goewey, 1683–1702.

SAMUELSE.
Francis Samuelse Pruyn, 1752.
Jacob Samuelse Pruyn, 1752.
Johannes Samuelse Pruyn, 1752.

SANDERSE.
Catryntje Sanderse Glen, 1695.
Jacob Sanderse Glen, 1672–86.
Johannes Sanderse Glen, 1699.
Sander Sanderse Glen, 1693.

SEGERSE.
Cornelis Segerse Van Voorhout, 1642–62.

SICKELSE.
Zacharias Sickelse Van Weenen, 1659.

STEVENSE.
Cornelis Stevense Mulder or Muller, 1682–1709.
Abraham Stevense Croat, 1637–58.

STOFFELSE.
Jan Stoffelse Abeel, 1682.

STORM.
Wouter Storm Bratt, or Van der Zee, 1699.

SYBRANTSE.
Anthony Sybrantse Van Schaick, 1686–1704.
Catharina Sybrantse Van Schaick, 1686.
Gerrit Sybrantse Van Schaick, 1686.
Goosen Sybrantse Van Schaick, 1686.

SYMONSE.
Adriaen Symonse Boer, 1661.
Adriaen Symonse Bet, 1661.
Gerrit Symonse Veeder, 1699–1720.
Helmer Symonse Veeder, 1715.
Jacob Symonse Klomp Barroquier, 1653–4.
Johannes Symonse Veeder, 1699–1742.
Pieter Symonse Veeder, 1699.
Pieter Symonse Michiels Van Oostsanen, 1661–4.
Symon Symonse Groot, 1654–62.
Volkert Symonse Veeder, 1699–1720.

2

TAKELSE.

Dirk Takelse Heemstraaten, 1701-6.
Tryntje Takelse Heemstraaten, 1722.

TERSSEN.

Jan Terssen Van Franiker, 1635.

TEUNISE.

Adriaen Teunise Vanderbilt, 1640.
Anna Teunise Metselaer, 1685.
Arent Teunise Van Luyten, 1642.
Claas Teunise Uylenspiegel, 1645.
Cornelia Teunise Van Deusen, 1700.
Cornelia Teunise Verwey, 1694.
Cornelis Teunise Bos or Bosch, 1631-67.
Cornelis Teunise Van Westbroeck or Bos, 1663-6.
Cornelis Teunise Van Vechten, 1669-1705.
Cornelis Teunise Van Slyck, 1661-8.
Cornelis Teunise Hoogeboom, 1661-3. [1631-61.
Cornelis Teunise Van Breuckelen or Brakelen,
Cornelis Teunise Van Merkerk, 1637.
Cornelis Teunise Mulder or Muller, 1703-6.
Cornelis Teunise Swart, 1680-5.
Cornelis Teunise Slingerland, 1705.
Dirk Teunise Van Vechten, 1676-1705.
Dirkje Teunise Metselaer, 1685.
Egbert Teunise Metselaer, 1685.
Esaias Teunise Swart, 1686-91.
Eva Teunise Van Schoenderwoert, 1709.
Gerrit Teunise De Reus, 1631.
Gerrit Teunise Van Slyck, 1738.
Gerritje Teunise Metselaer, 1685.
Gerrit Teunise Van Vechten, 1676-1747.
Jacob Teunise Quick, 1661-89.
Jacob Teunise De Looper, 1656.   [1683-1730.
Jacob Teunise Van Schoenderwoert or Woert,
Jacob Teunise Kay, 1676.
Jan Teunise De Paep, 1660.
Jan Teunise Van Deusen, 1695-6.
Jannetie Teunise Van Vechten, 1683.
Johannes Teunise Mingael, 1685.   [94.
Jurriaen Teunise Tappan or Van Tappan, 1671-
Jurriaen Teunise Glazemaecker, 1658-67.
Maritie Teunise Metselaer, 1685.
Marten Teunise Metselaer or Demetselaer, 1685.
Pieter Teunise Van Bronswyck, 1684-6.
Pietertie Teunise Van Vechten, 1700.
Robert (?) Teunise Van Deusen, 1695-1700.
Sweer Teunise Van Velsen or Van Westbroeck, 1664-90.   [83.
Teunis Teunise Metselaer or Demetselaer, 1658-
Willempie Teunise Metselaer, 1685.
Willempie Teunise Bratt, 1701.

TEUWISSE.

Cornelis Teuwisse Mulder, 1709.
Harpert Teuwisse Van Deusen, 1712.
Jan Teuwisse Van Deusen, 1696.
Robert Teuwisse Van Deusen, 1700.

TOMASE.

Gabriel Tomase Stridles.
Harmen Tomase Hun Van Amersfort, or Van Hun, 1661-1700.
Johannes Tomase Mingael, 1681-1701.
Johannes Tomase Wyngaerd, 1702.
Luykas Tomase Witbeck, 1746.
Maritie Tomase Mingael, 1664.
Pieter Tomase Mingael, 1683-1700.

TYMENSE.

Reynier Tymense Van Edam, 1636.

TYSSEN.

Cornelia Tyssen Van der Heyden, 1700.
Cornelia Tyssen Goes (?), 1683.
Jacob Tyssen Van der Heyden, 1653-89.
Jan Tyssen Goes, 1677-1732.
Jurriaen Tyssen Van Amsterdam, 1654.

VOLKERTSE.

Andries Volkertse Douw, 1690-1701.
Catryntie Volkertse Douw, 1700.
Dirk Volkertse Van Veghten, 1747.
Dorothea Volkertse Douw, 1700.
Ephraim Volkertse Van Veghten, 1747.
Grietie Volkertse Douw, 1701.
Hendrick Volkertse Douw, 1700.
Johannes Volkertse Douw, 1747.
Johannes Volkertse Van Veghten, 1747.
Jonas Volkertse Douw, 1681-1700.
Margaret Volkertse Van Veghten, 1747.
Symon Volkertse Veeder, *alias* De Bakker, 1654-67.

WESSELSE.

Anna Catharina Wesselse Ten Broeck, 1723.
Christina Wesselse Ten Broeck, 1723.
Cornelis Wesselse Ten Broeck, 1723.
Dirk Wesselse Ten Broeck, 1663-1705.
Jacob Wesselse Ten Broeck, 1723.
Jochim Wesselse Backer, 1633-1683.

WILLEMSE.

Claas Willemse Van Coppernol, 1676-1702.
Cornelis Willemse Van den Bergh, 1670-1706.
Dirk Willemse Van Slyck, 1687.
Gerrit Willemse Oosterum, 1631.
Gerrit Willemse Van den Bergh, 1728-42.
Gerrit Willemse Groesbeek, 1746.
Gysbert Willemse Van den Bergh, 1708.
Hendrick Willemse Backer, 1657-85.
Jan Willemse Schoon, 1661.
Jan Willemse Scuth, 1646.
Jannetie Willemse Van Slyck, 1688.
Maritie Willemse Groesbeeck, 1746.
Nicolaas Willemse Groesbeeck, 1746.
Pieter Willemse Van Slyck, 1689-92.
Roeloff Willemse Van Heerden, 1662.
Teunis Willemse Van Woutbergh, 1677.
Teunis Willemse Boots, 1684.
Tryntie Willemse Van Slyck, 1688-94.
Wynant Willemse Van den Bergh, 1701-6.

WYBESSE.

Jan Wybesse Van Harlingen, 1662.
Jan Wybesse Spoor, 1685-98.

WYNANTSE.

Catalina Wynantse Van den Bergh, 1749.
Catarina Wynantse Van den Bergh, 1749.
Gerrit Wynantse Van der Poel, 1683-91.
Maria Wynantse Van den Bergh, 1749.
Melgert Wynantse Van der Poel, 1671-1710.
Volkert Wynantse Van den Bergh, 1749.
Volkie Wynantse Van den Bergh, 1749.
Willem Wynantse Van den Bergh, 1749.

YSBRANTSE.

Jan Ysbrantse Timmer, 1662.

CONTRIBUTIONS

FOR THE

Genealogies of the First Settlers of Albany.

———•◦•———

In offering to the curious the following contributions for the family history of Albany county, it may be expected that the compiler should briefly indicate the character of the people, the extent of territory occupied, the sources and deficiencies of information, and the peculiar difficulties of the work.

The site of the present city of Albany was first occupied as a trading post in 1614. After the charter of the Privileged West India Company, in 1621, Fort Orange was built, around which clustered the little hamlet occupied by the servants and factors of the Company, who claimed and exercised the entire Indian trade. Hence colonization was not encouraged, contrary to the provisions of the charter, by which they were bound to "advance the peopling of those fruitful and unsettled parts:" the greed of gain swallowed up all other interests. At length the evil became so apparent and so forcibly presented to the notice of the Directors in Amsterdam, that they were obliged to seek a remedy. On the 7th day of June, 1629, under the title of "Freedoms and Exemptions" concession was made to Patroons to plant colonies in New Netherland.

From the haste with which the Directors in Holland proceeded to avail themselves of the privileges thus granted, one might almost suspect this charter was granted for their special profit and gratification. The failure of the West India Company and the Patroons in fulfilling the requisitions of their charters relating to the colonization of the new province and the encouragement of agriculture, became so apparent in 1638 as to call for the interference of the States-General, and after the agitation and rejection of many projects the Directors were induced to proclaim free trade and free lands to private persons under what they conceived necessary restrictions. This measure had a happy effect in stimulating immigration to New Netherland from the mother country.

The population of New Netherland, at the beginning of Stuyvesant's administration (1647), is variously estimated at from 1,000 to 3,000; at its close in 1664 it was about 10,000. The Dutch had held the province fifty years, and this was the result of their attempts to colonize it. Its natural advantages both for trade and agriculture were unequaled by any like portion of the continent. The nation which had redeemed its own country from the ocean, which had conquered its freedom from the Spanish yoke, and led all European nations in foreign trade was just the people to found a new empire on these shores. The Dutch character was not wanting in the requisite energy, perseverance and pluck ; but it was the system of government, persevered in against protests and petitions, that was chiefly at fault.

The population of Fort Orange at this early period can not be exactly known ; that it was small may be justly inferred from several facts : First. The church built in 1643 was 34 ft. by 19 ft. and contained but nine *banken* (benches) for the worshipers : yet this house served the little community until 1656. Second. A Jesuit missionary who visited the village in 1646 mentions that it contained then but ten thatched cottages. Third. The number of settlers shown by the Van Rensselaer papers as having been sent over to the *Colonie* up to 1664 is only 210.* It is not to be supposed that all those persons who were attracted to Fort Orange by its happy location for Indian traffic, were either tenants or servants of the Patroon of Rensselaerswyck, or were even under his manorial jurisdiction. Fort Orange and the little hamlet which clustered around its walls for safety were always claimed by the West India Company as under their exclusive authority. This claim, however, was strenuously resisted by the Patroon. Hence originated that memorable and almost bloody contest for power between those obstinate, hard-headed officials, Gov. Stuyvesant and Commissary Slichtenhorst.

The Dongan charter of 1686, however, quieted further questions of jurisdiction : Albany became a city one mile wide on the river and 13½ miles long. All outside of these limits belonged to the *Colonie*.

The early population of Fort Orange and Beverwyck, though almost pure Dutch at first, was changeable : after a few years spent in traffic with the Indians some returned to *Patria :* some retired to New Amsterdam (New York), whilst others passed beyond the limits of the *Colonie* and purchased lands at Kinderhook, Claverac, Catskill, Coxsackie, Niskayuna, Half Moon, and Schenectady.

The conquest of the province by the English in 1664 introduced a new element into the population ; the sheriff of the county, clerk of the village and city, and officers and soldiers of the garrison were mainly English or New Englanders : a few of these intermarried with Dutch maidens and became permanent citizens. Later, another nationality was introduced : through the bounty of Queen Anne some thousands of Palatines were sent over in 1708–22 ; they settled at East and West Camps on the Hudson, and afterwards in the Schoharie valley, and at German Flats on the Mohawk.

* *O'Callaghan's History of New Netherland.*

Unt l 1661 the powers of the magistrate of Fort Orange extended south to the Esopus (Kingston). By the division of the province into counties in 1683, Albany county comprised all the territory north of Dutchess and Ulster on both sides of the river, and the village of Albany was regarded as the fountain of authority both in church and judicial matters by the scattered inhabitants of this great region.

The Albany church founded about 1640 was the only one north of Esopus having a permanent ministry until long after 1700, save that of Schenectady : and as all young children in early times were christened in the church and their names entered in the *Doop Boek*, these ancient baptismal records have a peculiar value and interest to the genealogist. Unfortunately the records, previous to 1684, are wanting ; from that date onward they are complete.

The following pages contain the names of all children baptized and recorded in this church from 1684 to 1800 posted and arranged in families. Large additions have also been made from other sources, among which are the wills, deeds, mortgages, marriage and other contracts, powers of attorney, proceedings of magistrates, &c., found in the offices of the county and city clerks : the early records and papers in the secretary of state's office, the most of which have been fully calendared by Dr. O'Callaghan ; and Mr. Munsell's *Annals* and *Historical Collections of Albany.* These sources of information are by no means exhausted : the patient antiquarian has still ample room for gleaning in the same fields, and new ground for research in family papers, records in family bibles, and more especially in those of the *Colonie* belonging to the Van Rensselaer family.

Although these contributions are not to be regarded as full pedigrees of the families named, down to 1800, they are as complete in most cases for the first three or four generations as they are ever likely to be made from documentary evidence. Considering the great interest awakened periodically among the descendants of Anneke Janse and the real or imaginary connection which most of the ancient Dutch families of the valley of the Hudson, claim with that noted lady, it might reasonably be supposed that their pedigrees would long before this have been clearly established. In some cases this is the fact, but it is to be feared that through tradition or something worse a large element of fiction has been introduced into many genealogies, which it is hoped may in part be removed by the facts hereafter stated.

The *Schenectady Families* occasionally referred to in the following pages is a work in manuscript similar to this, relating to Schenectady and the valley of the Mohawk.

GENEALOGIES.

ABBREVIATIONS used in the following pages: Ch: children; b., born; bp., baptized; m., married; a., aged; d., died.

Aarnout (See Arnold).

Abbot (Ebbet), James, and Lena Sting. Ch: Johannes, b. Feb. 4, 1767.

ABBOT, William, and Margaret (*Mary*), Jackson; m. Nov. 30, 1777. Ch: Jane, b. Oct. 8, 1779; Margaret, b. Nov. 6, 1781; Nancy, b. June 20, 1783.

Abeel, Stoffel Janse: master carpenter; in Beverwyck in 1653; Feb. 3, 1655, he was aged about 32 years; his wife was Neeltie Janse Croon; Dec. 4, 1670, made his will in which he mentions the following children: Magdalena, then aged 17, and already married; Maria, aged 14; Johannes, aged 11, and Elizabeth.

ABEEL, Johannes, m. Catalina Schuyler, April 10, 1694; merchant; removed to New York city about 1696, but returned; mayor of Albany, 1694–5 and 1709–10: his gravestone dug up near the 2d Dutch Church, had the following inscription:

"Here lies the body of John Abeel who departed this life ye 28th day of Jany., 1711, and in the 44 year of his age.
Dient begin van wel te leven
Gingh der weer den Hemel waert
Uyt den Hemel was gegeven
Storf maar verliet de Aert."

Ch: Neeltie, bp. in Albany, April 14, 1695; Christoffel, bp. in New York, Dec. 16, 1696; Catalina, bp. in New York, Oct. 23, 1698; Neeltie, bp. in Albany, March 30, 1701; Jannetie, bp. in Albany, June 6, 1703; David, bp. in Albany, April 29, 1705, m. Maria Duyckink of New York, Feb. 4, 1726.

ABEEL, Christoffel, and Margarita Bries, m. Sept. 23, 1720. Ch: Joannes, bp. April 8, 1722, "an alleged lunatic;" Anthony, bp. Jan. 22, 1724; Anthony Bries, bp. April 11, 1725; David, bp. Aug. 13, 1727; Catharina, bp. Dec. 13, 1729; Rutgart, bp. Feb. 5, 1732; Cathalyna, bp. June 9, 1734; Jacobus, bp. Jan. 26, 1736; Maria, bp. April 27, 1740.

ABEEL, David, Jr., m. Neeltie Van Bergen "Van Katskil," July 2, 1752. Ch: Annatie, bp. March 1, 1753.

ABEEL, Jacobus, m. Egbertie (*Abigail*) Van Buren, "Van Papsknee" Nov. 18, 1757. Ch: Margarita, bp. Aug. 27, 1758; Willem, bp. Nov. 21, 1761; Christoffer, b. Aug. 22, 1764; Cornelis, b. Feb. 13, 1767; Margarita, b. July 3, 1769; Hendrik, Jan. b. 4, 1772; Cathalyna, bp. July 17, 1774; Margarita, b. July 22, 1779.

Abel, Jacob, and Elizabeth Humbert. Ch: Johan Hendrik, bp. Jan. 13, 1754.

ABEL, Andries, m. Annatie (*Johanna*), Marshall, Aug. 24, 1771. Ch: Hendrick, b. May 25, 1772; Annatie, b. June 19, 1774; Johannes, b. Jan. 1, 1777; Andries, b. March 12, 1779; Elizabeth, b. April 6, 1784; Geertruy, b. Oct. 7, 1788; Peter, b. April 25, 1793.

Abrahamse (see Tietsoort), Anthony, and Catrina...... Ch: Johannes, bp. Feb. 10, 1712; Neeltie, bp. Nov. 22, 1719; Lydia, bp. July 2, 1721.

ABRAHAMSE, Johannes, m. Catharyna Schians, Aug. 14, 1739. Ch: Anthony, bp. March 23, 1740; Christiaan, bp. Jan. 24, 1742.

Acker, Joost, and Margarita Wever. Ch: Nicolaas, b. Jan. 7, 1762; Margarita, b. Dec. 3, 1765.

ACKER, Hendrick, and Margarita Land. Ch: Albert and Michael, b. April 16, 1783.

Ackerman, Gilbert, and Rachel De Garmo, m. Feb. 14, 1799. He d. Oct. 11, 1834, æ. 66 y. 10 mo.: She d. Aug. 10, 1827, in her 54th yr. Ch: Jacob, b. Oct. 22, 1799; Richard, b. April 6, 1800; Elizabeth, b. April 14, 1802.

Ackerson, John, and Maria...... Ch: Cornelis, b. May 30, 1728.

ACKERSON, John, and Engeltie Vrooman. Ch: Adam, b. May 19, 1769.

ACKERSON, Cornelis, m. Rebecca Van Santvoord, March 2, 1770. Ch: Margarita, b. June 11, 1771; Willempie, b. June 2, 1773.

Adams, James, m. Margarita Hegeman, "Van Neskatha" Nov. 12, 1752. Ch: Willem, bp. July 29, 1753; Albertus, bp. Oct. 23, 1755; Albertus, bp. Sept. 11, 1757.

ADAMS, John, and Mary...... Ch: Elizabeth, bp. June 23, 1765.

ADAMS, Willem, and Hester Willis (*Willson*). Ch: Margarita, b. July 8, 1776; Maria, b. Jan. 19, 1790.

ADAMS, Peter C., and Catalina Van Bergen. Ch: William Van Bergen, b, Dec. 6, 1796.

Adriaensen, Van Veere, Maryn, a noted freebooter who came to Beverwyck in 1631 and afterwards figured disreputably in Gov. Kieft's time in New Amsterdam,—*O' Callaghan's Hist. N. N.*

ADRIAENSEN, Gysbert, Van Bunick, came out to Beverwyck in 1638 in the "Key of Calmar.—*O' Callaghan's Hist. N. N.*

ADRIAENSEN, Jacob, Van Utrecht, at Beverwyck in 1639 to 1657, perhaps the same as as Jac. Adr. Soogemakelyk, *alias* Van Woggelum.

ADRIAENSEN, Rut or Rutger. Held a patent for a lot in Beverwyck in 1652, which he sold to Frederick & Henderick Gerritse.

Aertse, Rut, [perhaps the same as the last,] in 1674 owned a house next to that of Pieter Clairbout on north side of State street between James street and Broadway.

AERTSE, or Aerse, Wouter, Van Nieukerck, sashmaker, a soldier in the W. I. Company's service in Director Kieft's time; in 1678 he bought of Sweer Theunise Van Velsen a lot on the west corner of Broadway and Van Tromp street.

AERTSE, Jacob, and Sarah Pels. Ch: Jacob, bp. Feb. 20, 1695.

Aherrin, James, and Mary Haines. Ch: Susanna Haines, bp. July 16, 1779.

Albertsen, Hendrick came out a second time in 1642 with his wife Geertruy Dries and her brother Hendrick Dries, Van Driesbergen. He was the first ferry master; died in 1648 or 1649.— *O'Callaghan's Hist. N. N.*

Albrecht, Hendrick, and Elizabeth Folent (*Foland*). Ch: Johannes, bp. Aug. 6. 1749; Eva, bp. Sept. 29, 1751; Anna, bp. Nov. 11, 1753; Philip, bp. Sept. 28, 1755; Helena, bp. Jan. 15, 1758; Jacob, b, Oct. 11, 1763; Hendrick, b. Oct. 10, 1765; Frederic, bp. April 10, 1768.

Albrecht, Johannes, and Rosina Buis or Briesch, m. Jan. 31, 1779. Ch: Hendrick, bp. March 5, 1780.

Allen, John, and Eleanor Sullivan. Ch: John, bp. Jan. 22, 1758.

Allen, David, and Jennet Stewart. Ch: Alexander, bp. March 26, 1779: John, b. April 27, 1780 ; James, b. March 26 , 1782.

Allen, James, and Mary Halenbeck. Ch: William, b. May 4, 1795.

Allertsen, Frans, cooper, at Beverwyck in 1638, afterwards at New Amsterdam.

Amory, John, m. Neeltie Staats, Nov. 9, 1769. Ch: Elizabeth. bp. June 28, 1772.

Anderson, Walter, and Ann.... Ch: Christian, bp. June 24, 1758.

Andrew, Thomas, and Rachel Ostrander, of Halve Maan. Ch: Sara, b. July 3, 1773.

Andriese, Arent (Van Frederickstadt) came to Beverwyck in 1636; perhaps the same as Ar. And. Bratt, which see.

Andriese, Jan, "de Iersman Van Dublingh" *alias* Jantie [Johnny.] He settled in Beverwyck before 1645; afterwards at Catskil where he bought land of Pieter Bronck; in 1657 he was complained of by Hans de Vos for selling brandy to the Indians at Catskil. He died in 1664. His bouwery contained 69 morgens besides a lot for a homestead.

Anthony, Israel, and Elizabeth Van Arnhem. Ch: Alida, b. March 16, 1788.

Anthonyse, Egbert, and...... Ch: Barent, b. May 10, 1684.

Any, David, and Anna Maria...... Ch: Jacob, bp. May 13, 1764.

Appel, Adriaen Janse, from Leyden; 1654 received a patent for a lot at Beverwyck on condition that the house to be erected thereon be not an ordinary tippling house but an inn for travelers; 1656 he sued Marcelis Janse for the loss of an anker of brandy by drawing it with violence through the streets ; 1676-86 he was one of the four school-masters of Albany. He resided for a time at New Amsterdam. He had two sons, Johannes and Willem, who at different times resided at Schenectady, Albany and New York; at the former place they were both wounded by the French and Indians in their attack upon the village Feb. 9, 1690.

Appelstouwn [Appelton ?] John, "geboren tot Leicester in oude England," m. Annatie Casparus, Oct.11, 1701. Ch: Johannes, bp. March 29, 1702.

Archard [Orchard ?] Matthew, and Elizabeth Murphy. Ch: Rachel, bp. July 25, 1790.

Archer (Archel) and Mary ..... Ch: Mary, born in Feb. in Kinderhook and bp. March 11, 1722 (Athens Luth. Ch.); Sara, bp. Feb. 16, 1726.

Ariaen, Meester (Doctor), was in Beverwyck in 1665.

Arissen, Gerrit, and wife...... Ch: Arien, bp. Sept. 9, 1683.

Armstrong, John, and Catryna De Garmo. Ch: Catharina, bp. Dec. 12, 1730; Maria, bp. Nov. 25, 1733.

Arnold (Arnout), Jacob of Normanskil; first wife Margriet Arnold. Ch: Isaac, bp. Dec. 26, 1742; second wife Anna Mook, m. Nov. 10, 1751. Ch: Jacob, bp. April 26, 1752; Margarita, bp. Dec. 16, 1753; Elizabeth, bp. July 18, 1756; Johannes, b. June 5, 1762; Hendrik, b. Oct. 26, 1765.

Arnold, Johannes, and Annatie Hillebrand. Ch: Annatie, b. Feb. 23, 1766.

Arnold, Elias, and Geertruy Groesbeeck. Ch: Annatie, b. July 22, 1779; Gysbert, b. July 26, 1781; Elizabeth, b. March 4, 1784; Elizabeth, b. June 6, 1785; Neeltie, b. March 12, 1789; Gerrit, b. June 18, 1791; Maria, b. Oct. 27, 1793.

Arnold, Hendrick, and Jannetie Van Alstyne. Ch: Jacobus, b. Nov. 1, 1786; Caty, b. May 22, 1790.

Arnold, Isaac, of the Hellenberg, and Gerritie Huyck. Ch: Margarita, b. Aug. 12, 1790.

Arnold, Isaac, and Sophia Philips. Ch: Elizabeth, b. Dec. 28, 1794; Catharine, b. Jan. 23, 1799.

Arnot, John, and Mary Walley, m. Jan. 21, 1794. Ch: Jacob, bp. April 12, 1802.

Arnoud (see Arnold), Johannes, and Elizabeth Bries (Buis, Buisch). Ch: Ariaantie, bp. April 19, 1778; Hendrik, b. Jan. 8, 1780; Pieter, b. May 29, 1784; Jacobus, June 19, 1790.

Atkinson, Peter, and Ann Griffin. Ch: Isabella, b. Nov. 14, 1777.

Auringer, Marten, and Christina Sheer. Ch: Elizabeth, b. Nov. 28, 1778.

Auringer, Marten, and Maria Buis. Ch: Margarita, b. June 13, 1789.

Austin, Aaron, and Elsie Austin. Ch: Cornelis, b. Oct. 3, 1782.

Austin, Robert, and Mary Parks. Ch: Matthew, b. Feb. 21, 1799 ; Penelope, b. Dec. 3, 1800.

Baart, Harmes, and Anna...... Ch: Lodewyk, b. March 6, 1767.

Babbington (Bebbington), Samuel, and Elsie.. Lieut. Babbington petitioned for and obtained, in 1715, a parcel of land on the Beaver's kil near widow Doretee Casparse Halenbeck's land. This afterwards passed to Evert Wendel. He was appointed sheriff in 1717. Ch: Sara, bp. Oct. 14, 1716; Elizabeth, bp. Oct. 7, 1722.

Bachus, Backis (See Bockes).

Backer (See Bakker).

Badt (Beth), Willem of Schenectady, and Elizabeth Van Vorst, m. Aug. 31. 1739. Ch : Thomas, bp. June 1, 1740. (See *Schenectady Families*).

Bailey, Thomas, and Olive Hall. Ch: Sarah, b. Sept. 7, 1782.

Bakker (Backer). See Evert Luykase and Jochem Wesselse.

Bakker (Backer), Hendrick De, at Beverwyck in 1642; Vander Donck says he killed at one shot 11 grey geese out of a large flock ; 1660 he was fined 12 guilders and costs for bringing in a load of hay on Sunday about the third tolling of the bell.

Bambus, or Bamboes, Harmen Jacobse, in Beverwyck in 1656; he fled from the place in 1657 to escape imprisonment for debt, and his sloop, Eikenboom, and other property were attached at the suit of Rutger Jacobsen. Having concealed himself at Esopus he was there shot by an Indian in 1658 and his body was carried to New Amsterdam for burial.

Bamnitz, James, and Francyntie Cahoen. Ch : Jacobus, b. Aug. 23, 1767. "Dese zyn van de Presbyterianen en daarom zonder getuygen."

Bancker (Bancken), Gerrit, was in New Amsterdam before 1655; two years later he was in Beverwyck, where he continued to reside till his death, which took place before the 27th Feb., 1691. His home lot was on the south side of Yonker (now State) street the third east of Pearl as it then existed. His wife was Elizabeth Dirkse Van Eps, sister of Jan Van Eps, one of the first settlers of Schenectady. After the death of her husband Mrs. Bancker removed to New York and engaged in trade. She died the 3d of July, 1693, aged 70 years, leaving a large property for the time to her son Evert. Ch : Evert, b. Jan. 24, 1665 ; Anna, who m. Johannes De Peyster of New York, Sept. 21, 1688.

Bancker, Evert, son of Gerrit B., was a merchant in Albany, but retired to his farm in Guilderland during the latter part of his life : he was buried on the 10th July, 1734 : 1692 he was a justice of the peace ; 1695-6 and 1707-9 mayor of Albany ; he m. Elizabeth Abeel, daughter of Stoffel Janse Abeel, Sept. 24, 1686 ; she was born March 23, 1671, and was buried March 20, 1734. His home lot in Albany was on the south side of Yonker (now State) street next east of his father's, and 4th east of Pearl street as it then existed. He made his will March 13, 1734, proved July 31, 1734, in which he gave to his son Johannes £50 "provided he continue to live with me till my decease or till I dispose of my farm where I now live." He mentions the following children who are to share alike in his estate: Christoffel, Willem, Jannetie, Adriaan, Gerardus and Johannes. Ch : Gerardus, b. Feb. 11, 1688 ; Neeltie, b. March 1, 1689 ; Gerardus, b. June 12, 1691 ; Elizabeth, b. July 29, 1693 ; Christoffel, b. Oct. 27, 1695 ; Anna, b. at New York, Oct. 3, 1697 and d. Oct. 2, 1706 ; Willem, b. Oct. 28, 1699 ; Jannetie, b. Aug. 28, 1701 ; Adrianus, b. Oct. 10, 1703 ; Gerardus, b. April 1, 1706 ; Anna, b. June 12, 1708 and d. May 30, 1709 ; Johannes, b. March 15, 1710, and d. April 30 ; Johannes (see his father's will).

Bancker, Christopher, of New York, son of the above, m. Elizabeth Hooglant in New York, Oct. 16, 1719. Ch : Adriaan, bp. in New York, July 3, 1720.

Bancker, Adriaan, of New York, m. G. Elizabeth Van Taerling in New York, Jan. 30, 1729.

Bancker, Gerrit or Gerardus, m. Maria DePeyster in New York, Oct. 31, 1731. Ch : baptized in Albany ; Anna, Sept. 3, 1732 ; Evert, Aug. 10, 1734 ; Elizabeth, May 9, 1736 ; Johannes, Feb. 22, 1738.

Bancker, Willem, and Annatie Veeder, m. in Schenectady, Dec. 17, 1726. Ch : baptized in Schenectady : Evert, Dec. 13, 1727 ; Thomas Brouwer not registered ; Elizabeth, July 16, 1732 ; Catharina, Oct. 6, 1734 ; Neeltie, Dec. 21 (?), 1737 ; Annatie, Aug. 16, 1740 ; Jannetie, March 25, 1744 ; Evert, Sept, 21, 1746.

Bancker, Johannes, and Magdalena Veeder. Ch : baptized in Schenectady ; Elizabeth, June 7, 1735 ; Gerrit, Feb. 27, 1737.

Bancker, Johannes, and Geertruyd Jacobi, m. April 19, 1778. Ch : Henry, b. Feb. 9, 1779 ; Margarita, bp. Oct. 27, 1780. [See *Schenectady Families.*]

Bankly, Jonathan, and Orsel Bankly. Ch : Thomas, bp. April 4, 1736.

Barentse, Willem, and Lysbeth Sickels. Ch : Willem, bp. Aug. 11, 1691.

Barheit, Jeronimus Hanse,and Rebecca Evertse, m. April 9, 1684. Ch : Margriet, bp. Oct. 4, 1685 ; Wouter, bp. Aug. 4, 1691. He made will Aug. 22, 1716, proved Feb. 23, 1722-3 in which he speaks of his wife Rebecca, son Wouter and one daughter.

Barheit, Andries Hanse, "yeoman of ye Great Flatt neer Coxhacky;" had a lot of land next to Pieter Bronck's farm. Perhaps the same as "Andries Hanse de Sweedt, dwelling at Kinderhoek" in 1675. His wife was Geertie or Gerritje Teunis, daughter of Teunise Teunise de Metselaer. She was not living in 1699 when Egbert Teunise [her brother ?] became guardian of her four children. Ch : Johannes, bp. Feb. 8, 1685 ; Geertruy, bp. Oct. 13, 1689 ; Barent, bp. Oct. 15, 1693.

Barheit, Wouter, and Rachel Winne, m. March 28, 1715. He was buried Jan. 8, 1732. Ch : Hieronimus, bp. Feb. 12, 1716 ; Teuntie, bp. Sept. 1, 1717 ; Margarita, bp. May 15, 1720 ; Margarita, bp. May 5, 1723 ; Tytje, bp. May, 16, 1725.

Barheit, Wouter, and Cornelia..... Ch : Wonter, bp. April 18, 1717.

Barheit, Willem, and Catalyna Barheit. Ch : Dirk, bp. Oct. 1, 1725.

Barheit, Wouter,and Rachel Barheit. Ch : Anna Maria, bp. March 3, 1737 ; Eva, bp. Dec. 23, 1739.

Barheit, Hieronimus, and Sara...... Ch : Elizabeth, bp. July 31, 1743.

Barheit. Walter P., and Catharine McGee. Ch : James, b. Sept. 14, 1795.

Barheyt, Johannes, m. 1st Catharina Gilbert, July 6, 1701. Ch : Johannes, bp. May 16, 1703 and settled in Schenectady ; Cornelia, bp. Oct. 6, 1706 ; Hieronimus, bp. March 20, 1709, and settled in Schenectady ; Barentje, bp. Oct. 14, 1711 ; Willem, bp. July 10, 1715 : m. 2d Catalyna Dingman, March 23, 1718. Ch : Alida, bp. Oct. 25, 1719 ; Adam, bp. 6, 1723.

Barreith (See Barret).

Barringer (See Berringer).

Barret (Berrit), Robert, and Wyntie Janse. She was buried Nov. 23, 1746. Ch : Margriet, bp. Dec. 4, 1689 ; Tammus, bp. March 25, 1692 ; Maria, bp. June 17, 1694 ; Sara, bp. Nov. 26, 1696 ; William, bp. Jan. 18, 1699 ; Magdalena, bp. Aug. 31, 1701.

Barret, Robert, m. Maria Martin, April 25, 1738. He was buried Oct. 12, 1756, and she on the 18 Dec., 1754. Ch : Maria, bp. Sept. 17, 1738 ; Judith, bp. Aug. 31, 1740 ; Thomas, bp. Nov. 7, 1742, and died Dec. 6, 1813, aged 72 years ; Elizabeth, bp. Jan. 18, 1747.

Berrit, Thomas, and Barentje Spoor ; m. Dec. 27, 1713 ; in 1719 widow Barentje Spoor had a lot 30 by 100 on the west corner of Hudson and Pearl streets. Ch : Robert, bp. Nov. 29, 1714 ; Anna Maria, bp. Sept. 23, 1716 ; Margarita, bp. March 8, 1719.

Berrit, William, of Schenectady, m. Catalina Bratt of same place in 1725. Ch : Robert, bp. July 23, 1727. [See also *Schenectady Families.*]

Barrington, Lewis, 1st wife Jane White. Ch: James White, b. Oct. 11, 1778: 2d wife Margaret Adams. Ch: Annatie, b. April 13, 1782; Jacob Pruin, b. April 13, 1784; Anna, b. Nov. 31, 1788; Lewis, b. March 31, 1790; Margaret, b. May 1, 1792.

Barrois (Barroa, Barroway, Berwar, Berwee), Antoine, and...... Ch: Anna, bp. May 3, 1685.

BARROIS, Charles, "geboren tot Mont Real in Canada en nu wonende in de Co. Ulster," m. Aaltie Roeloffse Van der Werke, June 7, 1707. Ch: Antje, bp. Feb. 15, 1708; Jacobus, bp. Oct. 23, 1709; Antoine, bp. Oct. 14, 1711; Maria, bp. Sept. 9, 1722.

BARROIS (?) (Borrowell, Borreway), William, and Elizabeth Salsbury. Ch: Casparus, b. Nov. 23, 1782; Hester, b. Jan. 25, 1784; David, b. March 10, 1786.

Bartel, Johannes, and Elizabeth Houex. Ch: Lucretia, b. Jan. 16, 1778.

Barth (Beth?), Thomas, and Maria...... Ch: Elsie, bp. Nov. 25, 1721; Wyntje, bp. May 24, 1724; Magdalena, bp. June 19, 1726.

Baschasche, Henry, and Sophia Magdalena.... Ch: John, bp. Nov. 19, 1749.

Bassett (Bessidt), Michael (Mynkell), son of Michael B. of New York and b. Jan. 21, 1705, and Lybetje Schermerhorn, m. April 18, 1728. Ch: Michael, bp. Aug. 10, 1728; Lena, bp. Dec. 12, 1731; Cornelis, bp. Aug. 14, 1734; Lena, bp. Nov. 19, 1735; Lena, bp. May 14, 1738; Michael, bp. Sept. 28, 1740; Michael, bp. Oct. 25. 1741; Jannetie, bp. Aug. 28, 1743; Cornelis, bp. Sept. 8, 1745; Cornelis, bp. Jan. 24, 1748; Annatie, bp. Nov. 4, 1750.

BASSETT, Michael, m. Maritie Van Vranken, Dec. 12, 1767. Ch: Elizabeth, b. March 20, 1768; Susanna, b. April 28, 1770; Cornelis, bp. May 30, 1773; Geertruy, b. May 5, 1776; Gerrit, bp. May 9, 1779; Michael, b. Aug., 1784; Nicolaas, b. May 19, 1787.

BASSETT, Cornelis, and Engeltie Cool. Ch: Elizabeth, b. Jan. 5, 1770.

BASSETT, D.D. Rev. John. He was ordained at Albany, June 28, 1787, as coadjutor of Do. Westerlo, resigned his office in 1805; and died at Bushwick, L. I., Aug. 29, 1824, in his 59th year. On the 19th May, 1795, he married Ann Hun; she died at Penn Yan, Oct. 17, 1848, aged 86 years. Ch: Eleanor, b. July 29, 1796; Elizabeth, b. April 16, 1798; Maria, b. Dec. 18, 1800; John, b. Nov. 8, 1802.

Batblado (Patblado), James, m. Sara Bath, Jan. 30, 1739. Ch: James, bp. Feb. 15, 1741.

Bates, John, and Mary Butler. Ch: Catharina, b. Jan. 1777.

Bath (Beth?), James and Margarita...... Ch: David, bp. May 26, 1723.

Baxter (see De Baxter), Willem, and Martha Baxter, "op de Halve maan." Ch: Martha, b. Nov. 23, 1768.

Beasely, John, m. Lydia Van Benthuysen, Nov. 1, 1723. Ch: Henry, bp. June 7, 1724; Johanna, bp. March 13, 1726.

Beasley, Hendrik, and Maria Noble. Ch: Johannes, bp. Aug. 26, 1753.

Beaufils (see Bovie).

Becker (Bekker), Jan Jurrianse, in 1656 was clerk at Fort Casimir (on the Delaware); 1660 degraded from his office, fined and banished from South river for selling liquor to Indians; same year had leave to keep school at New Amsterdam; 1663 was inhabitant of Greenbush; afterwards notary public and schoolmaster for the youths at Beverwyck and "esteemed very capable that way, while Jacob Jooste Covelens was allowed for ye teaching of ye younger children." He made his will the 3d Aug., 1694, in which he speaks of son Johannes, and daughter Martina (wife of Willem Hogan), who was made administratrix of his estate, Dec. 16, 1697.

BECKER, Johannes, Jr., and Anna Van der Zee. Ch: Mariken, bp. Nov. 15, 1685; Hilletje, bp. Jan. 23, 1689; Johannes, bp. Aug. 4, 1691; Hilletje, bp. Sept. 10, 1693; Storm, bp. Jan. 19, 1696; Gerrit, bp. Oct. 9, 1698; Elizabeth, bp. June 8, 1701; Albertus, bp. Dec. 25, 1703; Annatie, bp. May 5, 1706; Pieter, bp. Sept. 26, 1708.

BECKER, Hans Jurriaensen, and Cornelia Claese, 1686 to 1696; Cornelia Van Schaick, 1698. Ch: Johannes, bp. Oct. 10, 1686; Claas, bp. May 6, 1694; Coenraet, bp. Feb. 18, 1696; Arent, bp. Jan. 16, 1698.

BECKER, Johannes, and Cornelia Uzile, m. Oct. 15, 1714. Ch: Anna, bp. Dec. 11, 1715; Cornelia, bp. Nov. 17, 1717; Johannes, bp. Dec. 27, 1719; Pieter, bp. Dec. 31, 1721; Storm, bp. Jan. 18, 1724.

BECKER, Johannes, and Sara Van Arnhem, m. Oct. 14, 1717. Ch: Johannes, bp. Feb. 1, 1719; Abraham, bp. Feb. 3, 1720; Cornelia, bp. Aug. 13, 1721; Isaac, bp. March 13, 1723; Nicolaas, bp. Nov. 8, 1724; Cornelis, bp. Sept. 4, 1726.

BECKER, Gerrit (Gerardus), and Ariaantje Vanderkar, m. Oct. 23, 1726. Ch: Anna, bp. Jan. 14, 1728; Dirk, bp. June 14, 1730; Tytje, bp. April 27, 1735.

BECKER, Albertus, and Catharina Van der Zee, m. Jan. 17, 1733; Wouter, bp. July 18, 1736.

BECKER, Abraham, and Elizabeth Van der Zee, m. July 17, 1740. Ch: Johannes, bp. in Schenectady, Aug. 26, 1744; Sara, bp. May 22, 1752; Gerardus and Catarina, bp. Sept. 18, 1757; Catarina, bp. Oct. 15, 1758 or 9 (?).

BECKER, Dirk (written Gerrit Dirkse in 1755), and Eva Hogen, m. May 11, 1755.; Gerrit, bp. Oct. 17, 1756; Maria, b. Feb. 8, 1760.

BECKER, Arent, and Antje Van Woert, m. June 11, 1763. Ch: Gerrit, b. Jan. 4, 1764; Catharina, b. Oct. 25, 1765; Jannetie, b. April 26, 1771.

BECKER, Arent, and Margaret Balsing. Ch: Sara, b. Feb. 12, 1764; Frederick, b. April 22, 1769.

BECKER, Wouter, and Annatie De Ridder, m. Feb. 25, 1764. Ch: Albertus, b. March 29, 1765; Catharina, b. May 10, 1770.

BECKER, Hannes, and Annatie..... Ch; Catharina, b. Feb. 14, 1768; Johannes, bp. July 22, 1770.

BECKER, Pieter, and Anna Acker (Ackerson), both of Saratoga, 1773. Ch: Elizabeth, b. April 7, 1771; David, b. June 16, 1773.

BECKER, Gerrit, and Marytie Wynkoop, m. April 16, 1780. Ch: Eva, b. Jan. 6, 1781; Evert, b. Nov. 10, 1782; James, b. Oct. 20, 1791.

BECKER, Storm, and Elizabeth Clute. Ch: Albertus, b. Nov. 12, 1795. [Gen. Storm A. Becker, d. April 10, 1828 in Schoharie, aged 64.]

Beebe, James and Lydia Larroway. Ch: Thomas, b. Sept. 2, 1799.

[**Beekman,** Marten, and Susanna (?). Ch: Johannes; Hendrick; Metie (?) wife of Cornelis Cornelis Van der Hoeven.]

BEECKMAN, Johannes Martense, smith, made his will Dec. 16, 1728, proved Dec. 2, 1732, in which he speaks of wife Eva and all the children written below except Ariaantie. He was buried Sept. 30, 1732. His first wife was Machtelt Jacobse Schermerhorn. Ch: Johannes, bp. Jan. 27, 1684: Jacob, bp. Aug. 12, 1685 and was buried March 23, 1739; Susanna, bp. Sept. 25, 1687; Helena, bp. Jan. 13, 1689. His second wife was Eva Vinhaeghen, m. Oct. 26, 1692; Ch: Johannes, bp. May 20, 1694; Marten, bp. Sept. 8, 1695; Maria, bp. April 11, 1697; Johanna, bp. Nov. 20, 1698; Johannes Janse, bp. Jan. 8, 1701, and was buried Feb. 26, 1741; Alida, bp. Nov. 29, 1702; Neeltie, bp. May 27, 1705; Hendrik, bp. March 30, 1707; Jannetie, bp...... ; Neeltie, bp. Oct. 27, 1710, and was buried July 9, 1752; Ariaantie, bp. Aug. 29, 1714.

BEECKMAN, Hendrick Martense of Schotac, and Annetie Quackenbos. Ch: Susanna, bp. March 7, 1686; Lydia, bp. June 2, 1689; Hendrick, bp. June 5, 1692; Maritie, bp. Jan. 9, 1695; Pieter, bp. July 25, 1697; Magdalena, bp. Oct. 5, 1701.

BEECKMAN, Jacob, and Debora Hansen, m. Dec, 18, 1715. He was buried March 23, 1739: she, the 12th Dec. 1745. Ch: Machtelt, bp. Oct. 30, 1715: Hendrick, bp. May 4, 1718, buried Sept. 9, 1746: Effie, bp. June 19, 1720; Johannes, bp. Nov. 4, 1722; Debora, bp. Oct. 2, 1726; Johannes, bp. Aug. 12, 1733.

BEECKMAN, Johannes, Jr., in 1720 he had a lot on or near the south corner of Pearl and Steuben streets. He was buried Oct. 26, 1756. His first wife was Esther Wendel, m. Jan. 15, 1714. Ch: Johannes, bp. June 8, 1717; Jannetie, bp. Nov. 15, 1719; Elsie, bp. July 29, 1622. His second wife was Sara...... (the wife of Johannes B., was buried Aug. 28, 1746). Ch: Eva, bp. Aug. 30, 1730; Johannes, bp. Oct. 30, 1732; Catharyna, bp. Aug. 29, 1736; Eva, bp. July 8, 1739; Margrietje, bp. Aug. 30, 1741; Johannes, bp. March 18, 1744.

BEECKMAN, Marten, and Geertruy Visscher, m. Dec. 28, 1721. Ch: Johannes, bp. March 11, 1722; Tjerk Harmense, bp. Aug. 9, 1724; buried June 24, 1726; Femmetie, bp. Sept. 10, 1727; Henricus, bp. Sept. 7, 1729; Eva, bp. Feb. 13, 1734.

Beekman, Hendrik and Annatie Swits; he was buried Dec. 3, 1755. Ch: Johannes, bp. Nov. 8, 1738; Hester, bp. Oct. 18, 1741; Cornelis, bp. Sept. 25, 1743; Marten, bp. Jan. 10, 1746; Isaac, bp. Sept. 3, 1749; Eva, bp. Nov. 12, 1752.

BEEKMAN, Johannes, and Debora Van Schaick. Ch: Jacob, bp. Sept. 26, 1749. [Johannes J. Beekman and Gerritie Van Schaick were m. Jan. 29, 1761.]

BEEKMAN, Johannes and Maria Nicoll, m. Feb. 13, 1754. Ch: Tjerk Harmense, bp. Oct. 23, 1755.

BEEKMAN, Hendrick, Jr., and Catryna (?) Cuyler. Ch: Catrina, b. May 15, 1760.

BEEKMAN, Johannes Jacobse, and Maria Sanders; he was mayor of Albany, 1783-6, and died Dec. 17, 1802: she died Nov. 2d, 1704, aged 54 y. 22 d. Ch: Debora, b. Nov. 26, 1763; Barent Sanders, b. May 2, 1767; Machtel, b. Nov. 21, 1768; Sara, b. Dec. 9, 1771; Evje, b. July 24, 1774; died Dec. 6, 1792; John Sanders, b. Aug. 23, 1781; died Jan. 14, 1782 (?).

BEEKMAN, Gerardus, "van New York" and Anna Douw, m. June 3, 1761. Ch: Petrus Douw, b. Sept. 2, 1762, and died Feb. 23, 1835; Hannah, widow of Peter Douw Beekman, d. April 3, 1849, aged 83. Jacobus, b. Dec. 29, 1766; Gerardus, b. Aug. 5, 1767; Anna, b. Sept. 16, 1769; died, Oct. 3, 1821; Maria, b. Aug. 18, 1773; Gerardus, b. Oct. 27, 1775.

BEEKMAN, Johannes M., and Elizabeth Douw, m. Jan. 21, 1764. Ch: Marten, b. Nov. 15, 1767; Petrus, b. Aug. 19, 1769; Marten, b. May 5, 1772; Petrus, b. March 15, 1775.

BEEKMAN, Johannes H., and Hendrikie Van Buren Ch: Hester, April 18, 1768; Leendert, June 24, 1777; Annatie, Nov. 29, 1780.

BEEKMAN, Christopher, and Maria Thownan. Ch: Nicolaas, b. July 6, 1780.

Beecraft (Bickroft), Willem, and Sara...... Ch: Jonathan, bp. Oct. 28, 1748.

BEECRAFT, Thomas, and Mary Bunt. Ch: Thomas, bp. Aug. 28, 1748.

Beely (see Bailey).

Beem, John, and Sarah Jenkins (?). Ch: Adam, bp. Jan. 3, 1794.

Beers, Adam, and Catharina Frieer. Ch: Neeltie, b May 13, 1763.

Beesinger (see Peesinger).

Beint, Edward, and Nanny...... Ch: Edward, bp. Nov. 30, 1760.

Bekker (see Becker).

Bell (Bill), Jan, and Rachel Abrahamse. Ch: Lydia, bp. March 7, 1738; Anthony, bp. Jan. 20, 1740; John, bp. Jan 12, 1753. Jan Bell, "Weduwnaer Van Klaverac" m. Mary Burnham, "Weduwe Van Albanie" April 6, 1753

BELL, John and Margarita Souper (Duper). Ch: Johannes, b. July 22, 1764; Ebbetie, b. Aug. 19, 1766; Wyntie, b. Sept. 30, 1768; Gerrit, bp. Feb. 24, 1771.

BELL, William, and Ann Wallis. Ch: Ann, b. May 26, 1776.

BELL, Stephen, and Elizabeth Kidney. Ch: William, b. Aug. 22, 1776; Roeloff, b. Feb. 16, 1781.

BELL, Samuel, and Jane McChesney (McChesnut). Ch: Maria, b. Aug. 28, 1778; John, b. July 5, 1779.

BELL, James, and Mary McCarly. Ch: James, b. Jan. 22, 1778.

Belvil (Belleville), Franciscus, and Neeltie Abrahamse, m. April 24, 1739. Ch: Catharyn, bp. July 15, 1739. Jacobus, bp. Oct. 18, 1741; Anna, bp. May 13, 1744.

Bembo, Jan Van Lingen, a soldier in the W. I. Company's service at Fort Orange in 1656-8.

Ben, David, and Annatie Garner. Ch: Sara, b. May 1, 1764; Hugo, Dec. 22, 1766: James, Oct. 2, 1768.

Bender, Christiaan, and Elizabeth...... Ch: Christina, b. Oct. 16, 1764.

Bendingh (see Bordingh).

Bengburn (see Pangburn).

Bennet, Ephraim of Colonie, and Geertruy Bloemendal, m. June 8, 1772. Ch: Johannes, b. Nov. 29, 1773; Rebecca, b. Sept. 6, 1776; Thomas, b. May 14, 1780.

Benoit (Benneway, Bennewe) Pierre, "Van Rochelle," and Henderikie Van Schoonhoven, m. Dec.

14, 1696. Ch: Pierre, bp. Sept. 19, 1697; Marie, bp. Nov. 30, 1698; Margarita, bp. Aug. 16, 1702; Geurt and Jacob, twins, bp. June 24, 1705; Gerrit B., was buried July 8, 1741; Martha, bp. Aug. 3, 1707.

BENOIT, Pierre, and Anna Fort, m. March 7, 1723. Ch: Hendrikie, bp Jan. 18, 1724; Margarita, bp. Nov. 26, 1725; Petrus, bp. Sept. 7, 1729; Maria, bp. Nov. 15, 1730; Eva, bp. May 9, 1736; Johannes, bp. Aug. 31, 1740.

Bennoit (Bennewe), Jacob (Jacobus), 1st wife Catharyna...... m. Aug. 1, 1732. Ch: Catharina, bp. July 9, 1732; 2d, w. Elizabeth.... Ch: Peter, bp. May 9, 1736; 3d wife, Elsie. Ch: Martha, bp. May 22, 1743; Geurt, bp. July 7, 1745.

BENNOIT (Bennewe), Vincent (Finschen), and Annetie Bovie. Ch: Geurt, bp. Jan. 25, 1756; Pieternelle, bp. Aug. 14, 1757.

BENNOIT (Bennewe), Petrus, and Maria Fort, m. Nov. 10, 1759. Ch: Jacomyntie, bp. Nov. 7, 1761; Johannes, b. March 2, 1772.

Bensen (Benson, Bensingh, Bensick), Sampson, was an inhabitant of New York (New Amsterdam), as early as 1649, and made his will July 20, 1726, proved Feb. 23, 1731 [at what age ?]. He had children Dirk, deceased at the date of his will; Herman, Sampson, Robert, also deceased, Henricus, daughter Palo (?) deceased, Elizabeth, wife of Egbert Van Borsum, and Catalina.— *Genealogy of the Bergen Family.*

BENSEN, Dirck, a carpenter, was an inhabitant of Beverwyck, 1653–60, when he was deceased and soon after his widow Catalyn Bercx, m. Harmen Thomase Hun from Amersfort. In 1663 she and H. T. H. made a joint will at which time the following children of Dirck Bensen by Catalyna Bercx were living; Dirck, æ. 13 yrs. ; Sampson, æ. 11 y. ; Johannes, æ. 8 yrs. ; Catarina, æ. 6 yrs. ; Maria, æ. 4 yrs.

BENSEN, Sampson, and Tryntie Matheuse. Ch: Sampson, bp. April 13, 1684; Robert, bp. Jan. 1, 1686; Willem, bp. Oct. 30, 1687; Elizabeth, bp Sept. 13, 1689; Johannes, bp. July 3, 1692; Helena, bp. Feb. 14, 1694; Maria, bp. Feb. 5, 1696.

BENSEN, Dirk, in 1684, master of an open boat called the Eendraght plying between New York and Albany. He died prior to 1721. 1st wife Tytje...... She died about 1732. Ch: Eva, bp. Feb. 3, 1686; Rachel, b. April 13, 1689; Eva, bp. in New York, March 19, 1693; Dirk, bp. in New York, 1696; Tysje or Tytje, bp. in New York Sept. 13, 1699. 2d wife, Jannetie Van De Water, m. in New York, Nov. 10, 1707.

BENSEN, Johannes, and Lysbeth Matheuse (Teuwisse). Ch: Cataline, bp. Oct. 7, 1688; Mattheus, bp. Feb. 1, 1693; Catrine, bp. Sept. 15, 1695; Maria, bp. in New York June 18, 1699; Johannes, bp. in New York, May 29, 1701; Benjamin, bp. in New York March 22, 1704.

BENSON (Benton), Dirck, and Maritie Wyngaart, m. March 24, 1765. Ch: Samuel, bp. Jan. 26, 1766; Gerrit, b. Aug. 28, 1767; Johannes, b. March 3, 1769; Willem, b. Oct. 23, 1770; Abraham, b. April 30, 1773; Catharina, b. April 11, 1775; Dirck, Dec. 31, 1777; Christina, b. May 2, 1779; Christina, b. May 21, 1780; Gysbert, b. July 2, 1782; Catharina, b. April 23, 1784; Maria, b. Nov. 8, 1786.

BENSEN, John, of Colonie, and Cathalyna Van Alstyn, m. June 10, 1770. Ch: Lena, b. Nov. 10, 1781.

BENSEN, Samuel, and Mary Nicolson. Ch: Richard, b. Jan. 8, 1792; Mary, b. March 15, 1798.

BENSEN, Gerrit of Schenectady and Dolly (Dorothea) Hoffman, m. in Schenectady Dec. 2. 1793. Ch: Mary, b. Dec. 23, 1795; Gilbert, b. Nov. 9, 1796.—[See *Schenectady Families.*]

BENSEN, Abraham, and Sarah Hagadorn (Augerdon, Hoogeboom). Ch: Mary, b. May 9, 1796; Margaret, b. Sept. 28, 1797; Catharina, b. June 9, 1800; Robert, b. Oct. 20, 1808; Emeline, b. June 15, 1810; Christina, b. Feb. 25, 1813; Charlotte Amelia, b. Oct. 26, 1815.

BENSEN, Dirk, and Helen Lowe. Ch: Maria, b. June 15, 1796.

BENSEN, Gerrit, and Margaret..... Ch: Catharine Brinckerhoff, b. Dec. 19, 1809.

Bent (see Bout).

Berher, Hendrick, and Sophia..... Ch: Maria, Barbara, b. June 13, 1761.

Berkley, Hendrik; and Anna Coaglar Ch: Anna Catharina, b. July 3, 1779.

Bernard, Joost, and Christina Hemmer. Ch: David, bp. June 7, 1752.

BERNARD, Frederic, and Sophia Zeel. Ch: Elizabeth, b. Dec. 8, 1770.

Bernhard, Jacob, and Anna...... Ch: Sofia, b. Aug. 16, 1762.

Bernhart (Bernard), Johannes, and Christina Huyck (Hubet). Ch: Johannes, bp. March 28, 1755; Jacob, b. Jan. 31, 1762.

Berringer (Barringer) Zacharias and Anna Fallor (Feller). Ch: Marytje, b. April 26, 1767; Margarita, b. Sept. 11, 1770; Christina, b. June 6, 1779.

BERRINGER, Jurriaan (George) and Elizabeth Beem (Boehm, Pean). Ch: Catharina, bp. Sept. 1, 1771; Adam, b. Jan. 29, 1776; Coenraad, b. Sept. 2, 1778; Margarita, b. Dec. 22, 1781; Annatie, b. Jan. 22. 1784; Willem, b. Jan. 28, 1787; Eleanor, b. June 1, 1790.

BERRINGER, Hans, and Annatie Valentine. Ch: Philip, b. May 14, 1780.

BERRINGER, David, and Mary Barbara Heiner. Ch: Johannes, b. July 16, 1784; Catharina, b. March 9, 1786; Jacob, b. March 5, 1788; Frederic, b. Sept. 26, 1790; Eve, b. Aug. 26, 1793.

BERRINGER, Philip, and Catharine Meyer, m. May 17, 1785. Ch: Maria, b. Nov. 30, 1786; Jacob, b. Oct. 5, 1787.

BERRINGER, Jacob, and Catharine Heiner: Ch: Philippus, b. Dec. 2, 1786; Jeremias, b. March 16, 1790; Rebecca, b. Aug. 14, 1792.

Berrit (see Barret).

Berry, William, and Elizabeth Roseboom. Ch: Maria, bp. June 29, 1759.

BERRY, John, 1st wife Catharine Pikket; 2d wife Elizabeth Muchmore. Ch: Marytje, b. Jan. 29, 1774; John, b. July 27, 1778; Maria, b. March 18, 1781.

BERRY, John, and Catharine Harbeck. Ch: Maria Charlotte, b. Jan. 25, 1795; Helen Augusta, b. Oct. 3, 1798; Joanna Catharina, Oct. 8, 1801.

Berwee, Berwey (see Barrois).

Bessidt (see Bassett).

Beth (see Badt and Barth).

Bet or Bats (see Boer).

Bevee (see Bovie).

Bevier, Abraham of Esopus, and Rachel Vernoy. Ch: Louis, bp. Feb. 1, 1708.

Beurum, Jacob, and Sara Bronck. Ch: Agnietie, bp. June 11, 1749.

Blanchard, James, and Margaret DePeyster. Ch: Joseph DePeyster b. May 31, 1783.

Blackney, John, and Mary McCay. Ch: Mary, b. Nov. 11, 1780.

Bleecker, Jan Janse, came from Meppel province of Overyssel in 1658. He was b. in 1641, d. Nov. 21, 1732 and was buried in the church on the 24th Nov. He was by trade a blacksmith, later a trader. He was recorder of the city, 1696–99 ; Justice of the peace, 1797 ; member of the Provincial Assembly 1698–1700; Mayor 1700–1 ; He m. Margariet Rutse, dau. of Rutger Jacobsen Van Schoenderwoert, Jan. 2, 1667. She was b. 1647 and d. 1733. Ch : Johannes, b. 1668; Rutger, Nicolaas, Catharine, Jane, Margaret; Hendrick, bp. April, 1686 ; Rachel, bp. Nov. 14, 1688 ; Maria, bp. Feb. 7, 1692.

Bleecker, Johannes, Jr. Recorder of Albany, 1700 ; Mayor and member of the General Assembly, 1701–2. He was carried away captive to Canada in 1686 ; returned Oct. 23, 1687 : Acted as Indian interpreter. He made his will Dec. 18, 1738, his wife and all his children save Hendrik then living ; d. Dec. 20, 1738, and buried in the church on the 23d. He owned a lot, 1720, on the west corner of North Pearl and Maiden Lane which run through to Chapel street. He m. Anna Coster, dau. of Hendrick Coster, Oct. 29, 1693. Ch : Johannes, bp. Aug. 26, 1694 ; Geertruy, bp. Nov. 15, 1696, she m. Abraham Wendell ; Hendrik, bp. Sept. 8, 1699 ; Nicolaas, bp. Sept. 20, 1702; Hendrik, bp. June 2, 1706 and d. Oct. 21, 1724, among the Senecas ; Margarita, b. April 8, 1712 ; Jacob, b. March 1, 1715 and d. 1747 ; Anthony, bp. Jan. 11, 1718.

Bleecker, Rutger, Recorder 1725 ; Mayor, 1726–8 ; buried in the church Aug. 5, 1756; m. Catalyna Schuyler, dau. of David I. Schuyler and widow of Jan Abeel, May 26, 1712. She was buried in the church, Oct. 25, 1747. Ch : Johannes, bp. Feb. 8, 1713, m. Elizabeth, dau. of Barent Staats ; Margarita, bp. Oct. 8, 1714, m. Edward Collins ; Jacobus, bp. Dec. 9, 1716 ; Myndert, bp. July 3, 1720.

Bleecker, Johannes, Jr. 1st wife, Janneke Ten Eyck, m. Dec. 13, 1724. The was buried May 10, 1757. She d. Dec. 12, 1738. Ch. Johannes, bp. Aug. 22, 1725. Geertie, bp. March 5, 1727 ; Jacob, bp. Sept. 22, 1728, d. Oct. 5, 1802, æ. 74 y. 3d. Johannes, bp. May 9, 1731, and d. June 19, 1811, æ. 80 y. ; Geertruy, bp. Oct. 2, 1733. 2d wife Eva Bries, m. Jan. 10, 1741. She was buried Dec. 4, 1752. Ch: Anna, bp. March 7, 1742 ; Catharina, bp. Oct. 19. 1744.

Bleecker, Nicolaas, Jr., son of Johannes B., and Anna Coster, m. Margarita Roseboom, April 10, 1728. He was buried in the church Jan. 4, 1751. Ch. Aug. 16, 1794, æ. 88 y. 3 m. 16 d. Ch: Hendrik, b. 1729, m. Catalina Cuyler ; Gerritie, bp. Aug. 30, 1730; Gerritie, bp. June 4, 1735; Anna, bp. Aug. 15, 1737. Johannes, bp. Aug. 26, 1739 ; Nicolaas, bp. April 25, 1742, died unmarried ; Gerritie, bp. Feb. 21, 1748.

Bleecker, Johannes Ruth (Rutgerse), m. Elizabeth Staats, Aug. 5, 1748. He was a surveyor, d. 1800. Ch: Rutger, bp. July 5, 1745, m. Catharine Elmendorf; Barent, bp. June 5, 1748; Barent, bp. Nov. 18, 1750 ; Barent, bp. Nov. 12, 1752, buried Nov. 5, 1756; Jacobus, bp. Oct. 23, 1755 ; Catalina, bp.

Oct. 15, 1758; Barent bp. June 9, 1760, m. Sarah Lansing, dau. of Gerrit Lansing, had no ch; Johannes, b. Oct. 4, 1763, d. Dec. 29, 1833, æ. 70, buried from 50 North Pearl street.

Bleecker, Jacob, son of Johannes, m. Margaret Ten Eyck, Jan. 6, 1745; he was buried July 14, 1747. She was b. 1715, and d. 1777. Ch; Jacob, b. July 22, 1747.

Bleecker, Hendrick, Jr., and Catalyntie Cuyler. Ch : Margarita, bp. Nov. 23, 1755, m. Harmanus Ten Eyck ; Nicolaas, bp. Jan. 22, 1758, m. Neeltie Staats ; Hendrik, bp. Oct. 2, 1763, d. Nov. 11, 1837; Johannes, b. May 11, 1766; Catharina, b. Feb. 3, 1769, m. James Van Ingen ; Johannes, b. May 18, 1772.

Bleecker, Johannes Johannese, and Gerritje Van Schaick : he died June 6 (13, 19), 1811, in his 81st year. Ch: Tanneke, b. Oct. 15, 1763, m. Isaac Truax ; Anna, b. Nov. 29, 1766; Johannes, b. Nov. 8, 1768; m. Anna Van Alen, had no children ; Anna, b. May 25, 1771, d. Sept. 3, 1811, unmarried ; Sybrand, b. Nov. 5, 1773, d. April 29, 1814, *sine prole*; Jacob, b. Dec. 13, 1776, unmarried.

Bleecker, Rutger, and Catharina Elmendorf; he died March 17, 1831. Ch: John, b. Dec. 20, 1771, m. 1st, Eliza Bridgen; 2nd, Hetty Lynn; Peter Edmund, b. Sept. 9, 1774; Elizabeth, b. at Schenectady 1777, m. Pieter Brinckerhoff, of New York, she d. in Albany, July 25, 1868 in her 91st y. ; Maria, b. Sept. 18, 1780, m. Morris S. Miller of Utica; and d. March 9, 1850, in Utica; Blandina, b. Oct. 1, 1783; m. Charles E. Dudley; Sarah Rutger, b. Jan. 16, 1788. At the baptism of this child the father was deceased.

Bleecker, Jacob Jacobse, and Elizabeth Wendell, dau. of Harmanus I. Wendell, m. Feb. 18, 1776: he d. Nov. 30, 1806 in his 62d year. She d. March 14, 1818, in her 65th year. Ch. Jacob, b. March, 2, 1777, d. 10 Sept. 1804, unmarried ; Harmanus, b. Oct. 9, 1778 ; Harmannus, d. Oct. 24, 1779, m. Sebastiana Cornelia Mentz, and d. July 19, 1849, without issue.

Bleecker, Johannes J., and Ann Elizabeth Schuyler, m. in New York, March 29, 1769. Ch: Abeltje, b. June 5, 1776.

Bleecker, Johannes N., and Margarita Van Deusen ; he d. Oct. 23, 1825, æ. 86 (87), she d. April 13 1794, æ. 47 y. 8 m. 23d. Ch: Margarita, b. April 30, 1776, m. John Van Schaick; Margarita, b. Feb. 10, 1778, m. Mary Storm, and d. Jan. 28, 1808, in his 30th y. ; Ariaantje, b. April 1, 1780, m. Rev. John B. Romeyn, and d. in New York, Oct. 22, 1825 ; Gerritie, b. Nov. 26, 1781; Elizabeth, b. March 12, 1784, m. Rev. Jacob Brodhead ; Annatie, b. April 2, 1786, and d. Oct. 14, 1794 ; Nicolaas, b. Jan. 6, 1788; Nicolaas, b. Nov. 12, 1789.

Bleecker, Jacobus (James), and Rachel Van Santen, m. Nov. 18, 1782; Rachel, widow of James B., d. March 22, 1837, æ. 79. Ch ; Sara, b. Aug. 1783; Sara, b. March 24, 1785; Cathalina, b. Dec. 22, 1787 ; Gerrit Van Santen, b. Aug. 2, 1790.

Bleecker, Nicolaas, and Neeltie Staats : she was buried Dec. 6, 1831, from No. 288 North Market st. Ch : Hendrik, b. Aug. 19, 1784, d. at Canajoharie Feb. 9, 1823, æ. 39 ; Debora, b. Nov. 4, 1786 ; Gerrit, b. Aug. 28, 1788; Gerrit, b. Oct. 19, 1789 ; Debora, b. Sept. 1, 1791; Harmanus, b. Jan. 7, 1793; Catalina, July 14, 1796 ; Catalina, b. Sept. 25, 1797 ; Catharina, b. Jan. 10, 1800.

BLEECKER, Johannes, and Jane Gilliland. Ch; Elizabeth, b. Feb. 2, 1787; Charlotte, b. Feb. 15, 1789; Margarita, b. May 7, 1791.

BLEECKER, Barent, and Sarah Lansing, m. Dec. — 1787, he d. June 1, 1840, æ. 80. She d. Oct. 12, 1831, buried from 317 North Market street. Ch; Elizabeth, b. Aug. 4, 1793.

BLEECKER, John, and Elizabeth Van Rensselaer; Elizabeth the widow of John B., d. March 29, 1841, æ. 73. Ch: Stephen Van Rensselaer, b. Jan. 5, 1803, d. April 16, 1827 in his 24th yr.

Bloemendaal, Johannes Maase, had house lot on east corner of Columbia and North Pearl streets. Jan Maasen, Jr., was buried Dec. 17, 1756; m. 1st, Rebecca Fonda, Sept. 4, 1718. Ch: Maas, bp. May 31, 1719; Joannes, bp. March 1, 1721; Cornelis, bp. Dec. 2, 1722; Maria, bp. Aug. 16, 1724; Pieter, bp. Feb. 16, 1726; Jacomyna, bp. Aug. 10, 1728. 2d wife, Sara. Ch: Maas, bp. Nov. 7, 1731; Albertus, bp. Dec. 14, 1735.

BLOEMENDAAL, Jacob Maase, and Sara Gardenier, m. Feb. 5, 1731. He was buried June 4, 1755; she, the 6th of March, 1752. Ch: Maas, bp. Aug. 19, 1733; Cornelis, bp. March 22, 1741.

BLOEMENDAAL, Pieter, and Christina De La Grange, m. Dec. 6, 1751; she was buried Oct. 15, 1756. Ch: Johannes, bp. Nov. 12, 1752; Engeltie, bp. Sept. 29, 1754.

BLOEMENDAAL, Albertus, and Maria Ostrander, m. May 25, 1756; he died July 4, 1818, in his 82d y. She was buried Oct. 7, 1756. Ch: Sara, bp. Oct. 3, 1756; buried Oct. 15, 1756. 2d wife Ann Harssen (Herser), m. Aug. 13, 1763; she died Nov. 18, 1797, æ. 56 y. 8m. 13d. Ch: Jacob, b. Feb. 22, 1764; Sara, b. Feb. 11, 1766; Bernardus, b. Dec. 25, 1767; m ..... Shanklin, d. April 12, 1822; Catharina, b. Aug. 2, 1770; Jacob, b. Oct. 18, 1772; Aaltie, b. Sept. 28, 1773; Maria, b. March 23, 1776; Maria, b. March 26, 1779; Anna, b. Nov. 20, 1781; Elizabeth, b. March 16, 1785.

BLOEMENDAAL, Maas, Jr., and Helena Schermerhorn. Ch: Jacob, bp. Jan. 21, 1759; Sara, b. July 13, 1766; Engeltie, b. May 15, 1768: Gerritie, b. Jan. 21, 1775.

BLOEMENDAAL, Maas, and Catharina Steenberg. Ch: Pieter, b. April 7, 1764; Rachel, b. March 30, 1769.

BLOEMENDAAL, Jacob, and Margarita Roller (Ruller). She died March 20, 1847 æ. 83 y. Ch: Maas, b. July 26, 1783; Andries, b. March 28, 1786; Johannes, b. April 3, 1790; Jacob, b. Feb. 1, 1793; Gerrit, Aug. 19, 1795; Elizabeth, b. March 10, 1798; Helena, b. June 9, 1801; Alida, b. Dec. 26, 1803.

BLOEMENDAAL, Johannes and Catharina Sharp, m. March 24, 1784. Ch: Rachel, b. June 27, 1784; Maas, b. Oct. 10, 1785; Juriaan, b. Feb. 26, 1789; Cornelia, b. Oct. 23, 1790; Maria, b. Dec. 1, 1793.

BLOEMENDAAL, Cornelis, and Lena Reisdorp, m. May 18, 1784. Ch: Maas, b. Nov. 3, 1787; Lourens, b. Feb. 16, 1790; Cornelis, b. May 15, 1793.

BLOEMENDAAL, Pieter, and Barbara Sharp, m. Feb. 11, 1787. Ch: Maas, b. Oct. 22, 1787; Catharine, b. July 27, 1793.

Blom, Hendrik, and Elizabeth Gardenier, m. Dec. 9, 1743. Ch; Albertus, bp. Oct. 21, 1744; Maria, bp. July 26, 1746.

Bloodgood, Abraham, and Elizabeth Van Valkenburgh. He was grandson of Francis Bloetgoet of Flushing, L. I , and d. Feb. 7, 1807, æ. 65; his widow Elizabeth, d. July 21, 1823, æ. 78. Ch: Francis, b. June 12, 1775; James, b. Jan. 10, 1778; Lynd (?), b. Dec. 25, 1781; Joseph, b. Aug. 17, 1783; Rachel, b. May 7, 1786; Maria, b. Feb. 12, 1790.

BLOODGOOD, James, and Lydia Van Valkenburg; he d. May 4, 1799, æ. 64 y. She d. Jan. 8, 1811, in her 78th y. Ch: Eva, b. March 27, 1777.

Bockes (Backis, Bacchus), Pieter, and Eva Maria Miller. Ch: Anna, bp. May 29, 1752; Johannes, bp. Aug. 25, 1754. Elizabeth, bp. March 18, 1757; Catarina, bp. April 22, 1759.

BOCKES (Bacchus), Pieter, Jr., and Anna Vegen. Ch: Catrina, bp. Aug. 25, 1754

BOCKES (Bacchus), Baltus, and Barber Coen, m. Jan. 13, 1757. Ch: Johannes, bp. Feb. 26, 1758: Catharina, bp. May 3, 1767.

BOCKES (Backes), Hannes, and Barbara ...... Ch: Margarita, b. Aug. 5, 1769.

Boeringley, Philip, and Catharina Meyer. Ch: John, b. Sept. 19, 1791.

Boets (see Bots).

Bofie, or Boffy (see Bovie).

Bogardus (Bogart), Anneke (Annetie) Janse.[*] This celebrated character came to Rensselaerwyck, in 1630 with her husband Roeloff Jansen who acted as assistant *bouwmeester* for the Patroon at a salary of 180 guilders. Five or six years after, the family was found at New Amsterdam where Roeloff received a patent in 1636, for 31 morgens (62 acres) of land lying along the East river between the present Warren and Christopher streets. About this time he d., and in the year 1637 or 1638 his widow married Domine Everhardus Bogardus or Bogart, the first settled minister of New Netherland. Ten years later she again became a widow and so continued until her death which took place in 1663 at Albany, to which place she had returned after the death of her second husband in 1647. Her property consisted chiefly of the Domine's Bouwery above mentioned, and was divided by her will equally among her three daughters and five sons. By her first husband, whom she married in Holland, she had, First: Sarah Roeloffse who married Surgeon Hans Kierstede, June 29, 1642. After his death she married Cornelis Van Borsum of Brooklyn ferry, Sept. 1, 1669; and later Elbert Elbertsen of New York, July 18, 1683. She came from Amsterdam with her parents in 1630, and became a great proficient in the Indian tongue; in 1664 she acted as interpreter in the treaty made by Stuyvesant with the River Indians. She died in 1693. Second: Catrine Roeloffse. She married Lucas Rodenburg vice director of Curaçoa, who d. about the y. 1656. Her second husband was Johannes Van Brugh, who was a prominent merchant and magistrate of New Amsterdam, and served in the common council several years after the English accession. They were married March 29, 1658. He d. in New York at an advanced age about 1699. His widow survived him. Their children were, Helena, wife of Teunis DeKay, m. May 26, 1680; Anna, wife of Andries Grevenraet;

[*] She is said to have been the daughter of Tryn Jansen, midwife at New Amsterdam and connection by marriage of Govert Loockermans. *Dutch MSS.*, III, 55; *O'Callaghan's History New Netherland,* I, 142.

Pieter ; Catharina wife of Hendrick Van Rensselaer of Albany ; Johannes ; and Maria, wife of Stephen Richard. Third : Sytje. She married Pieter Hartgers Van Wee who came over in 1643, and first settled in Beverwyck as one of the magistrates of the court of Fort Orange in 1654. He d. in Holland in 1670 leaving two daughters in Beverwyck. Fourth : Jan. At the date of his mother's will in 1663 he was unmarried. In 1665, he accidentally killed one Gerrit Verbeck with a gun, for which he was acquitted by the governor in form. Soon after he removed to Schenectady where with his wife he was slain by the French and Indians in the great massacre of 1690, leaving no children. By her second husband, Do. Bogardus, Anneke Janse had four children. Willem ; Cornelis, bp. in New York, Sept. 9, 1640 ; Jonas, bp. Jan. 4, 1643, and Pieter bp. April, 2, 1645.

BOGARDUS, Willem, of New Amsterdam, and Wyntie Sybrantse, m. in New Amsterdam, Aug. 29, 1659. In 1656, he was appointed clerk in the Secretary's office in New Amsterdam, and in 1687 postmaster of the province. Ch : baptized in New York ; Everhardus, bp. Nov. 2, 1659 ; Sytje, bp. March 16, 1661 ; Anna, bp. Oct. 3, 1663, m. Jacob Brouwer, of Gowanus ; Cornelia bp. Aug. 25, 1669 ; Everhardus bp. Dec. 4, 1675, m. Anna Dally in New York June 3, 1704, had a son Willem bp. there Jan. 7, 1705 ; Maria, bp. Sept. 14, 1678 ; Lucretia, bp. Sept. 14, 1678 ; Blandina, bp. Sept. 13, 1680. About 1686, Willem Bogardus m. his second wife, Walburga DeSille, widow of Frans Cregier, son of Capt. Martinus Cregier.

BOGARDUS, Cornelis, and Helena Teller, dau. of Willem Teller of Albany. He lived in Albany, where he d. in 1666, leaving one son Cornelis, who m. Rachel DeWit, and d. Oct. 13, 1707.

BOGARDUS, Pieter, mariner. He resided in Albany till near the close of his life, when he removed to Kingston, where he d. in 1703. In 1673, he was one of the magistrates of the town, and in 1690, was commissioned with others to treat with the Five Nations and to look after the defence of the town. He made his will Feb. 3, 170½. His wife was Wyntie Cornelis Bosch, dau. of Cornelis Teunise Bosch and Maritie Thomas Mingael who afterwards m. Jurriaen Janse Groenwout in 1664. Ch : Evert ; Shibboleth ; Hannah, b. Jan. 22, 1679, m. Pieter Bronck ; Maria, m. Johannes Van Vechten of Schaghticoke ; Anthony ; Rachel, bp. Feb. 13, 1684 ; Ephraim, bp. Aug. 14, 1687 ; Petrus, bp. April 30, 1691.

BOGARDUS, Cornelis ; he was schoolmaster in Albany in 1700 ; soon after with his wife Ragel Tjerckse DeWit he removed to Kingston his wife's native place.* He d. Oct. 13, 1707. Ch : Jenneken, bp. in New York May, 13,1694; Ragel, bp. in Albany April 27, 1701, and was buried there Feb. 13, 1757; Cornelis.

BOGARDUS, Shibboleth, and Ann...... his wife. His house 1720–37 was on the north corner of James and Steuben streets. He was buried on the 26th of Sept., 1747, his wife on May 25, 1747. Ch : Pieter, bp. March 4, 1711, he was buried Oct. 21, 1756; Jacob, bp. in New York, Aug. 31, 1712; Ephraim, bp. in New York, Nov. 21, 1714; Wyntje, bp. April 21, 1717; Catryna, bp. Dec. 6, 1718; Shibboleth, bp. Oct. 2, 1720; Cornelia, bp. July 1, 1722; Ephraim, bp. Feb. 12, 1724; Ephraim, bp. Oct. 2, 1726, and buried Aug. 6, 1745.

*"Cornelis et Ragel Bogardus abierunt mense Augusto 1790 cum testamento Kingstown." *Albany Church Records.*

BOGARDUS, Anthony, and Jannetie Knikkelbakker, "weduwe Van Henrik Lansing," m. March 6, 1709. He was buried in Albany April 17, 1744. Ch : Wyntie, bp. in New York, Sept. 1, 1710 ; Marya, bp. Feb. 10, 1712; Pieter, bp. May 21, 1716; Cornelis, bp. Aug. 3, 1718; Cornelia, bp. Oct. 11, 1719; Evert, bp. June 10, 1722, and buried July 33, 1746 ; Anna, bp. Feb. 17, 1725.

BOGARDUS, Ephraim, and Agnietie De Garmo, m. Sept. 23, 1720. Ch : Petrus, bp. April 10, 1721 ; Catharina, bp. Sept. 16, 1722 ; Wyntie, bp. March 8, 1724 ; Ephraim, bp. Aug. 7, 1726 ; Jacob, bp. July 14, 1728 ; Catharina, bp. Feb. 18, 1730 ; Maria, bp. May 7, 1732 ; Anna, bp. Oct. 6, 1734.

BOGARDUS, Petrus, and Sara......, his wife. Ch : Egbert, bp. Sept. 27, 1724 ; Cornelis, bp. May 22, 1727 ; Anneke, daughter of Pieter Bogardus, was buried Sept. 20, 1747.

BOGARDUS, Shibboleth, and Catarina (Elizabeth) Van der Werken, m. Nov. 10, 1750. Ch : Shibboleth, bp. March 1, 1752; Maria, bp. Aug. 26, 1753; Anna, bp. March 28, 1756.

Bogaart, Pieter, and Rebecca Fonda. She was buried Feb. 5, 1754. Ch : Jannetie, bp. Oct. 14, 1711 ; Jacob, bp. July 22, 1716 ; Peter, bp. Sept. 14, 1718; Rebecca, bp. April 10, 1721; Abraham, bp. Dec. 18, 1723 ; Madalena, bp. Jan. 9, 1725.

BOGAART, Jan, of Kinderhook, and Catryna Van Wie, m. April 5, 1707. Ch : Marritie, bp. April 5, 1713.

BOGAART, Isaac, and Hendrikie Oothout, m. Nov. 25, 1725. Ch : Jacob, bp. Aug. 7, 1726 ; Hendrik, b. Oct. 26, 1729, and died June 28, 1821, æ. 92 y. ; Jacob, bp. Jan. 14, 1733 ; Jacob and Catharina, bp. Sept. 22, 1734 ; Isaac, bp. June 14, 1741.

BOGAART, Benjamin, and Anna Halenbeck, m. Feb. 20, 1727. Ch : Jannetie, bp. June 9, 1727 ; Dorothea, bp. Dec. 2, 1729 ; Maria, bp. Aug. 13, 1732 ; Rachel, bp. Nov. 10, 1734 ; Jacob, bp. Jan. 12, 1736 ; Anna, bp. Sept. 9, 1739 ; Magdalena, bp. Dec. 5, 1742 ; Anna, and Isaac, bp. Jan. 12, 1746.

BOGAART, Douwe, and Willempie Bratt, m. Dec. 7, 1739. Ch : Maria, bp. Oct. 5, 1741 ; Rebecca, bp. Jan. 26, 1743 ; Barent, bp. Jan. 4, 1745 ; Magdalena, bp. Feb. 28, 1748 ; Rachel, bp. May 24, 1750 ; Willempie, bp. June 26, 1757.

BOGAART, Jacob, Jun., and Maria Yates, m. Oct. 24, 1741. Ch : Rebecca, bp. Aug. 8, 1742 ; Catalyntie, bp. June 17, 1744 ; Pieter, bp. Jan. 10, 1746 ; Pieter, bp. Dec. 25, 1747 ; Anneke, bp. Oct. 22, 1749 ; Christopher, bp. Feb. 2, 1752 ; Christopher, bp. March 8, 1754 ; Jacob, bp. March 7, 1756 ; Jacob, bp. Nov. 30, 1760 ; Jacob, b. May 14, 1762 ; Maria, b. Nov. 17, 1763.

BOGAART, Hendrick J., m. 1st Engeltie Van Schaick, June 29, 1751. Henry I. Bogart died June (Jan.) 27, 1821. Ch : Dorothea, bp. May 3, 1752 ; Jannetie, bp. July 4, 1755. Henry I. Bogaart, md. 2 ; Barber Marcelis (1759 ?), Barbara Bogart, d. Oct. 3, 1816, æ. 88 yrs. 1 mo. Ch : Hendrikie, b. Feb. 29, 1760 ; Johannes, b. Sept. 5, 1761 ; Johanna, b. Nov. 18, 1763 ; Isaac, b. Sept. 7, 1765 ; Gerrit, b. March 9, 1777.

BOGAART, Abraham, and Marytie Bassett. Ch : Pieter, bp. July 7, 1754 ; Rebecca, bp. June 15, 1755 ; Annatie, b. Jan. 8, 1765.

BOGAART, Pieter P., and Barber Van Vranken. Ch: Pieter, bp. Feb. 25, 1759; Pieter, bp. Dec. 11, 1760; Rebecca, b. Nov. 14, 1764; Rykert, b. July 22, 1766; Rykert, b. Sept. 20, 1769.

Bogaard, Jacob, and Catalyntie Schuyler. He was buried April 6, 1725. Ch: Jannetie, bp. March 4, 1711; Alida, bp. June 2, 1713; Pieter, bp. Sept. 18, 1715; Maria, bp. Nov. 17, 1717; Maria, bp. March 8, 1719; Catalyna, bp. July 16, 1721.

Bogart (Bogaart, Bogert), Cornelis, and Cornelia Le Maître his first wife. Ch: Jannetie, bp. Feb. 18, 1705; on the 8th of Oct., 1707, he m. Dorothea Oothout. Ch: Jannetie, bp. Jan. 25, 1708; Hendrick, bp. Oct. 30, 1709; Catharina, bp. Feb. 10, 1712; Rachel, bp. March 6, 1715; Hendrick, bp. Sept. 28, 1718; Hendrick, bp. July 5, 1724. Cornelis Bogart was buried July 29, 1755.

BOGART, Myndert, and Neeltie Palmentier. Ch: Helena, bp. Oct. 12, 1707.

BOGART, Pieter J., and Saartie Van Schaick, m. Jan 2, 1773. Ch: Jacob, b. Aug. 13, 1773; Jacob, b. July 27, 1775; Mazyke, bp. Sept. 28, 1777; Gosen, b. Sept. 28, 1779; Annatie, b. May 5, 1784; Rebecca, b. May 7, 1788.

BOGART, Isaac, and Cathalyntie Hun, m. Dec. 1, 1773; Harmen, b. Oct. 13, 1774; Isaac, b. Sept. 18, 1776; Jannetie, b. Oct. 11, 1782. Isaac Bogart, died Sept. 27, 1818.

BOGART, Barent, and Alida Van den Bergh. Ch: Agnietie, b. Oct. 6, 1775; Willemple, bp. Jan. 11, 1778; Cornelia, b. July 29, 1780, and died Jan. 31, 1806, æ. 25 y. 6m. 2d.; Douwe, b. May 30, 1783; Alida, b. Aug. 19, 1788, died Nov. 20, 1815, æ. 27 y. 3m. 1d.; Alexander Hamilton, died Oct. 1, 1826, æ. 21y. 9m. 15d.; Agnes, died Dec. 15, 1818, æ. 6y. 2m. 8d.

BOGART, Christoffel, and Rebecca Winne. Ch: Jacob, b. Oct. 20, 1779; Jellis, b. May 14, 1782; Maria, b. Aug. 4, 1790.

BOGART, John, and Catharina Ten Broeck. Ch: Hendrik, b. April 22, 1788; Sara, b. Feb. 22, 1790. John Bogart, and Christiana Vought. Ch: Henrietta, b. Nov. 28, 1797; Isaac, b. Dec. 31, 1811; Philip Grandin Augustus, b. Aug. 31, 1814. [Capt. John Bogart, d. May 22, 1853, aged 92.]

BOGART, Isaac H., and Catalina Visscher, m. Jan. 31, 1799. He died Sept. 22, 1841, aged 76 years, 15 days. She died April 10, 1845, aged 74 years 2 months 14 days. Ch: Engeltie, b. Nov. 27, 1789; John Henry, b. Aug. 31, 1809.

Bogert, Gerrit, and Margaret Nixon, m. Jan. 8, 1795. Ch: Magdalena Maria, b. Jan. 30, 1796; Barbara, b. May 21, 1799; Alexander Hamilton, b. Dec. 17, 1804; William Henry Laurentius, b. Nov. 28, 1810.

BOGERT, Jacob P., and Alida Bloemendaal. Ch: Peter, b. Oct. 4, 17??; Peter and Sarah, b. Aug. 21, 1801.

Bogl, Pierre, and Emmetie Claase. Ch: Marie, bp. Jan. 10, 1686; Emmetie, bp. Sept. 6, 1691.

Bont, see also Bout. Hendrik Lambertse, and wife .... before the massacre (1690), he owned a bouwery at Schenectady, called *Poversen's Landeryen,* which he sold afterwards to Douwe Aukes, and removed to Klaverak. Ch: Catalyntie, bp. April 28, 1686.

BONT, Jan Henrikse, of Claveraec, m. Jennetie Scharp, Jan. 20, 1704. Ch: Henderik, bp. at Schenectady, June 18, 1704; Matthys, bp. Jan. 13, 1706; Geesie, bp. Jan. 19, 1708.

BONT, Henderick, and Jannetie Evertse. Ch: Evert, bp. April 30, 1710.

BONT, Anthony, and Wyntie Bogardus ...... Ch: Ephraim, bp. Feb. 19, 1749.

Bonting, James, and Neeltie, his wife . .... Ch: Anna, bp. Sept. 15, 1732.

Boogh (see Bouw).

Boom (Boam), Johannes, and Maria Geertruy. .. ..his wife. Ch: Margriet, bp. June 14, 1740. Maria, bp. Feb. 28, 1742; Hendrick, bp. Jan. 1, 1744. Johannes Boom a "High Dutchman" was buried July 22, 1745.

BOOM, Johannes, and Ann Burger. Ch: Abraham, bp. Jan. 1, 1742.

BOOM, Mattheus, and Maria Hilten, m. April 25, 1752. Ch: Johannes, bp. Aug. 2, 1752. Mattheus Boom, and Josina Seger. Ch: Nicolaas, bp. May 4, 1755; Catrina, bp. June 3, 1759; Johannes, bp. July 12, 1761; Nicolaas, b. Nov. 23, 1763; Wyntie, b. Nov. 16, 1766; Magdalena, b. March 6, 1769; Margarita, b. July 30, 1771; Elizabeth, b. Oct. 27, 1772; Jacob, b. Jan. 21, 1775; Matthias, bp. Dec. 14, 1777.

BOOM, Abraham, and Dorothea Cunnigam. Ch: Annatie, b. Dec. 6, 1764; Margarita, b. April 21, 1765; Johannes, b. Jan. 1, 1767; Elizabeth, b. Sept. 8, 1769; Maria, b. Oct. 30, 1771; Geertruy, b. July 4, 1773.

BOOM, Johannes, and Annatie Brouwer; m. Sept. 13, 1783. Ch: Nicolaas, b. July 13, 1786; [Johannes Boom and Sybil Johnson were m. July 8, 1781. Johannes Boom d. Jan. 14, 1832, æ. 84.]

Boon, Francis, a French trader among the Indians settled in Albany about 1654. Ten years later he removed to New York. He married Lysbet Cornelise Van Voorhoudt, widow of Gysbert Cornelise Van Wesep. On the 28 Feb., 1697, he married Catharina Blanck, widow, in New York. A son Jacob was bp. in New York, June 6, 1666.

Boonards, Christiaan, and Annatie Freelich. Ch: Lydia, b. Dec. 11, 1780.

Bordingh (Bendingh) Claas, a trader in New Amsterdam in 1647, was in Beverwyck in 1654. His widow, Susanna Marsuryn, lived in Pearl St., New York, in 1686. He had ten children baptized in N. Y.

Borgat (see Burghart).

Borghsal, Samuel, and Cornelia, ... his wife. Ch: Mary, bp. July 26, 1724.

Borhans (see Burhans).

Born (see Burn).

Bort, James, and wife Margariet .... Ch: Elizabeth, bp. Nov. 5, 1721.

Bos (Bosch, *alias* Van Westbroeck) Cornelis Teunise, it is said, came to Beverwyck in 1631 as servant or *bouwknecht* to Cornelis Maase Van Buren. His wife was Maritie Tomase Mingael, who after his death in 1666 married Jurriaen Janse Groenwout. He owned considerable real estate in the village. At his death he had one daughter, Wyntie, living. He was accused frequently before the court, of slander and backbiting; in 1657 by Do. Schaets; in 1658 of having defamed the honorable court; and again in 1659, for which he was fined 1,200 guilders and banished for 12 years; next year he was again arraigned for a similar offence against Willem Teller.

Bos, Pieter Janse, and Susanna Barentse .... his wife, m. 1688. Ch: Eytie, bp. March 24, 1689; Jan, bp. Aug. 4, 1691; Jenneken, bp. in N. Y. Dec. 17, 1693; Sara, bp. in N. Y. June 20, 1697.

Bos (Bosch), Gysbert, and Hester Ryck [Ryckse Van Vranken (?)] his wife. Ch: Rachel, b. March 12, 1762; Marytie, b. Jan. 24, 1766; Rebecca, b. Sept. 13, 1768; Hester, b. July 16, 1771; Pieter, b. Aug. 13, 1777.

Boschee (see Bozee).

Boskerk, Joseph, and Susanna (Santje) Wendel. Ch: Hendrick, b. Dec. 24, 1770; Lea, b. Oct. 27, 1771; Lourens, b. Nov. 19, 1773; Gerrit, b. March 26, 1775; Lea, b. March 13, 1778; Gerrit, b. April 26, 1782.

Bots (Boets, Burch), William, and Maria Christiaanse, m. Feb. 9, 1740. Ch: Sara, bp. Sept. 21, 1740; Anna, bp. Aug. 31, 1746; Anna, bp. Sept. 4, 1748; Maria, bp. Dec. 30, 1753.

Bout, Willem Frederickse, in Beverwyck as early perhaps as 1642. In 1657 and after he kept a public house, and was farmer of the excise of wine, beer, &c.

Bout (or Bent), Pieter, a brickmaker, in Beverwyck 1655; brought an action against Pieter Jacobse Borsboom in 1657, for breach of contract in refusing to make bricks for him.

Bouts, Geertie, in Beverwyck, 1655-66; in 1690, her adopted son, Stephen, was carried away captive from Schenectady at time of the massacre.

Bouw (Boogh), Salomon Frederickse, and Anna Bratt, m. Jan. 1, 1686. Ch: Frederick, bp. Sept. 12, 1686; Barent, bp. Feb. 24, 1689.

Bovie (Bofie, Bouphi, Bovier, Bevier, Beaufils; the last is the proper and original spelling of this name), Matthys (Matthew), and Catharine Barrois (Barro, Barwee), his first wife. Ch: Catarina, bp. Feb. 12, 1690; Maria, bp. Sept. 8, 1699; Anna, bp. in Schenectady, Jan. 18, 1702; Catrina, bp. in Schenectady, Jan. 7, 1705; Antoine, bp. Nov. 2, 1707; Philip, bp. Oct 30, 1710; Francois, bp. May 25, 1713. Matthew Bovie's second wife was Maria .... Ch: Gerrit, bp. Sept. 23, 1716; Catryna, bp. Oct. 25, 1719; Gerrit, bp. May 3, 1722; Ulderick, bp. Jan. 8, 1724; Margarita, bp. Oct. 24, 1725; Anna, bp. June 4, 1727; Claes, bp. Jan. 15, 1729; Philip, bp. Oct. 13, 1732.

Bovie (Boffy), Claas, and Cornelia Pieterse Brouwer, m. Sept. 24, 1714. Ch: Petrus, bp. March 31, 1717; Catryna, bp. March 8, 1719; Rykert, bp. Jan. 11, 1721; Henrik, bp. March 3, 1723; Mattheus, bp. Aug. 16, 1725; Abraham, bp. Oct. 20, 1728; Philip, bp. Aug. 2, 1730; Jacob, bp. July 2, 1732. Claas (Frans?) Bovie and Magtelt Van Vranken were m. Feb. 7, 1735. Perhaps this was the marriage of *Frans* B. below.

Bovie, Anthony, and Catharina Van der Werken. Ch: Catharina, bp. Aug. 23, 1729; Gerrit, bp. Feb. 3, 1731; Maria, bp. May 20, 1733; Antie, bp. April 13, 1735; Jannetie, bp. Dec. 23, 1737; Mattheus, bp. Sept. 9, 1739; Adriana, bp. June 14, 1741; Anneke, bp. May 29, 1743; Marytie, bp. Nov. 8, 1747. Catreen Bovie was buried Dec. 19, 1747.

Bovie, Frans, of "Connestigeoune," and Magtel Van Vranken: the bans were declared in Schenectady, Jan. 18, 1735; probably m. Feb. 7, 1735; (see *Claas* B. above) ...... Ch: Elizabeth, bp. in Schenectady, June 13, 1736; Mattheus, bp. Oct. 22, 1738; Geertruy, bp. June 24, 1741; Carel, bp. June 24, 1744.

Bovie, Ryckert, and Marytie Huyck, m. Sept. 5, 1743. Ch; Nicolaas, bp. in Schenectady, Aug. 26, 1744; Geertie, bp. Jan. 31, 1748; Sara, bp. June 31 (*sic*), 1750; Cornelia, bp. April 7, 1754; Maria, b. May 15, 1762; Annatie, b. Jan. 24, 1768.

Bovie, Gerrit, of Hoosic, and Ariaantie Brouwer, m. Sept. 7, 1754. Ch: Anthony, bp. Dec. 21, 1755; Maria, bp. Dec. 30, 1761; Petrus, bp. April 15, 1764.

Bovie, Matthias, Jr., of "Nestougjoone," and Baata Vander Heyden, m. in Schenectady, Oct. 11, 1760. Ch: Baatje, bp. May 31, 1761; Geertruy, b. Feb. 2, 1766; Catharina, bp. Sept. 11, 1768; Rachel, bp. Sept. 6, 1772; Rachel, b. Nov. 15, 1776; Elizabeth, b. June 8, 1784.

Bovie, Matthias, and Maria Wendel. Ch: Catharina, b. Oct. 31, 1764; Annatie, b. Oct. 29, 1765.

Bovie, Philip, and Geertruy Van den Bergh. Ch: Mattheus, bp. Sept. 15, 1765; Matthias, bp. Sept. 11, 1768. Philip Bovie and Eva Sharp were m. Dec. 15, 1775.

Bovie (Bevee), Matthias, and Elizabeth Lansing, m. March 6, 1790. Ch: Philip, b. Sept. 16, 1790; Geertruy, b. March 6, 1800; Ann and Catharine, b. Aug. 18, 1802. "Ann is the elder by two hours than Catharine," inserted (in the *Doop Boek*) by desire."

Bower, Nicolaas, and Annatie Bartel. Ch: Philip, b. Sept. 2, 1787.

Bowman, Andries, and Lea Oosterhout. Ch: Rebecca, bp. Oct. 25, 1780.

Bowman, Benjamin, and Christina Dowland (Downey). Ch: Andrew, b. April 15, 1799; Benjamin, b. July 11, 1800.

Boyd, James, and Jane McMaster. Ch: Robert, bp. April 2, 1777; Agnes, b. Jan. 5, 1779; John, b. June 15, 1780.

Boyd, Alexander, and Elizabeth Becker (Bocker), Ch: John, b. July 28, 1784; Peter, b. Aug. 25, 1795.

Boyd, John, and Christina Van Deusen. Ch: James, b. July 7, 1790.

Boyd, Hugh, and Catharine Staats, m. Jan. 14, 1796. Ch: Ann, b. Jan. 6, 1797.

Braale, Alexander, and Elizabeth Cavel. Ch: Mary, b. Oct. 10, 1779.

Bradford, Rev. John Melancthon, D.D., and Mary Lush his wife. He was ordained and installed minister of the First Reformed Dutch church of Albany the 11th of August, 1805; was dismissed in Oct. 1820, and died March 25, 1826. Ch: Louisa Ridgeley, b. Nov. 4, 1808; Stephen Lush, b. March 25, 1810; Mary Elizabeth, b. July 10, 1811; Johannes Melancthon, b. Nov. 14, 1813; Alexander Warfield, b. Feb. 21, 1815; Lydia Stringer Lush, b. June 6, 1819.

Bras (Brash), Johannes, and Lena Shafner. Ch: Sofia, b. June 11, 1779; Johannes, b. March 10, 1784; Sara, b. April 2, 1786; Abraham, b. Jan. 4, 1788.

Bratt. Two brothers of this name, Arent Andriese, and Albert Andriese, were among the early settlers of Albany. The former settled in Schenectady with his family in 1662, and became the progenitor of the families of this name in that city and vicinity; the latter remained in Albany. [NOTE. Some of the Bratts belonged to the Lutheran Church of Albany, whose ancient records are lost. Such children as were christened there, will not be found here.]

BRATT, Albert Andriese, de Noorman, had a farm and mill on the Norman's kil, which took its name from him. In 1672, his son Barent succeeded him in the occupation of the mill, and in 1677 Teunis Slingerland, his son-in-law, succeeded to the lease of his farm. He died, according to Dr. O'Callaghan, the 7th June, 1686, " een van de oudste en eerste inwoonders der Colonie Rensselaerswyck." His first wife was Annetie Barentse Van Rotmers, who was deceased in 1662. On the 24th Oct., 1670, the governor gave an order for the separation of Albert Andriese and Geertruy Vosburgh because " strife and difference hath arisen between them." His children, all by his first wife probably, wefe Barent; Eva, the wife first of Antony de Hooges, and second of Roeloff Swartwout of Esopus; Storm *alias* Storm Albertse Vanderzee; Engeltie, wife of Teunis Slingerland of Onisquathaw; Gisseltie, wife of Jan Van Eechelen; Andries; Jan; Dirk.

BRATT, Barent Albertse, lived in 1700 without the North Gate just west of the Main Guard, near or on the east corner of Steuben street and Broadway, and had frequent warnings from the Common Council not to fence in certain grounds there belonging to the city. All his children were born before 1684, as their names are not found in the church records extant. The following came to maturity and had families: Antony, Dirk, Johannes, Daniel.

BRATT, Dirk Albertse, was living in Albany as late as 1678; his children if he had any, have not been met with in the records of the Dutch church.

BRATT, Jan Albertse (of Catskil, 1720), and Geesie (Goesie Goschie) Janse, (Dirkse?). Ch: Johannes, bp. Feb. 3, 1684; Andries and Pieter, twins, bp. Jan. 10, 1686; Barent, bp. Sept. 11, 1687; Pieter, bp. Nov. 11, 1689; Storm, bp. Jan. 12, 1690; Elaje, bp. July 21, 1692; Roeloff, bp. Jan. 17, 1694; Margaret, bp. Jan. 22, 1696; Pieter, bp. Jan. 16, 1698, m. Christina Bowman; Johannes, bp. July 5, 1702. The three following baptisms are recorded in the *Doop-boek* of the ancient Lutheran Church of Loonenburgh (Athens); Magdalena, b. " op de Flakte," Mar. 15, 1704, and bp. in the Lutheran church of Albany, June 5, 1704; Jochem or Joachim, b. " on the Flat" July 24, and bp. in the Lutheran church of New York, Sept. 4, 1706; Gosetje, b. " op de Flakte Loonenburgh," and bp. " op Klinkenberg," June 6, 1708.

BRATT, Dirk Arentse, was son of the first settler Arent Andriese B., of Schenectady; m. to Maria Van Eps in 1684, by Reinier Schaets, son of Do. Schaets, and magistrate at Schenectady. Dirke Arentse settled in Niskayuna. Ch: Lysbeth, bp. Feb. 3, 1686; Johannes, bp. Aug., 27, 1693; Catalijntie, bp. Oct. 9, 1695, m. Willem Barret; Anna, bp. Aug. 11, 1696; Maritie, bp. Sept. 7, 1701, m. Ryckert Van Vranken; Andries, bp. Oct. 12, 1707; Dirk, bp. Oct. 30, 1710. All the above children are mentioned in their father's will made Jan. 16, 1727. See *Schenectady Families.*

BRATT, Samuel Arentse of Schenectady, brother of the above, and Susanna Jacobus Van Slycke. Ch: Margriet, bp. April 25, 1686; Hanna, bp. June 5, 1692. See *Schenectady Families.*

BRATT, Antony (Barentse?) and Willempie Tunise Bratt, m. Dec. 9, 1685: chamberlain of the city, sexton and voorlezer of the church. On May 13, 1702, he was about 45 years of age. Ch: Lea and Rachel twins, bp. April 2, 1686; Barent, bp. May 5, 1687; Teunis, bp. Feb. 16, 1690, was appointed chamber-

lain of the city instead of his father, Feb. 14, 1712; Antony, bp. Dec. 23, 1692; Dirk, bp. March 31, 1695; Benjamin, bp. May 1, 1698; Egbert, bp. Feb. 16, 1701; Egbert, bp. July 26, 1702; Johannes, bp. July 22, 1705; Daniel, bp. Aug. 15, 1708.

BRATT, Dirk Barentse, and Anna Teunise, m. Sept. 12, 1686. Ch: Susanna, bp. Dec. 30, 1686; Egbertje, bp. May 15, 1692; Anthony; Dirk.

BRATT, Claas, and Lysbet Willemse. Ch: Isaac, bp. .... 1691.

BRATT, Johannes Barentse, and Maria Ketelhuin, m. May 7, 1693. Capt. Johannes Bratt had a lot on the north corner of Maiden Lane and Broadway in 1711. He was deceased in 1714. His widow, Maria, was living in 1726. Ch: Susanna, bp. Dec. 3, 1693; Jochem, bp. Aug. 4, 1695; Susanna, bp. July 4, 1697; Bernardus, bp. Jan. 7, 1700; Anna, bp. Oct. 3, 1701; Bernardus, bp. Aug. 29, 1703; Johannes, bp. April 29, 1705; Margarita, bp. June 29, 1707; Anthony, bp. June 26, 1709; his wife was buried Oct. 18, 1754.

BRATT, Andries Albertse, de Sweed, *alias* de Noorman; in 1683 he owned a saw mill on the Wynantskil; In 1730 had a lot on the east side of Pearl street between Beaver and Hudson streets. His first wife was Cornelia Teunise Verwey (Van Wie, Vernoy). Ch: Annetje, bp. Dec. 17, 1694; Maritie, bp. Aug. 1, 1697; Effie, bp. Jan. 7, 1700; Teunis, bp. Jan. 27, 1703; Barent, bp. April 7, 1706. His second wife was Wyntie Rosa, the bans were proclaimed Sept. 18, 1708; she was buried Dec. 24, 1742. Ch: Maria, bp. Sept. 11, 1709; Hillege, bp. June 30, 1718; Margarita, bp. April 3, 1720; Albert, bp. Feb. 28, 1722; Geertruy, bp. May 3, 1724; Catharina, bp. Jan. 2, 1725

BRATT, Daniel (Barentse?), and Elizabeth Lansing, m. April 18, 1697. Ch: Susanna, bp. Oct. 31, 1697; Elizabeth, bp. Sept. 3, 1699; Gerrit, bp. Jan. 21, 1702; Bernardus, bp. Sept. 24, 1704; Maria, bp. April 20, 1707; Henricus, bp. Dec. 18, 1709; Antony, bp. Aug. 7, 1713. He married his second wife, Wyntje Bogardus, April 17, 1732. Ch: Antony bp. Dec. 10, 1732; Jannetie, bp. March 3, 1734; Willempie, bp. May 18, 1735. He was buried June 8, 1740.

BRATT, Arent, of Schenectady and Jannetie Vrooman, m. Oct. 14, 1704. Ch: Johannes, bp. Jan. 5, 1709; Magdalena bp. June 21, 1713. See *Schenectady Families.*

BRATT, Storm [See also Vanderzee] and Sophia, his wife. Ch: Maria, bp. May 24, 1713; Jan, bp. July 26, 1717; Cornelia, bp. June 7, 1719; Adriaan, bp. March 25, 1722.

BRATT, Barent (Janse?) Jr., and Maria Rykman, m. Dec. 28, 1714. Ch: Willempie, bp. Dec. 18, 1715; Rachel, bp. Oct. 10, 1718. He m. Elizabeth Marselis, Aug. 1, 1730. Ch: Barber, bp. May 19, 1731. Barent Janse Bratt was buried Jan. 6, 1744.

BRATT, Pieter (son of Jan Albertse B.), and Christina Bowman, m. Feb. 3, 1716. Ch: Jan, bp. Oct. 12, 1716, m. Susanna Segers; Adriaen, bp. May 14, 1721; Adam, bp. Dec. 21, 1723; Maria, bp. May 8, 1726.

BRATT, Anthony, and Rebecca Vander Heyden, m. July 22, 1716. Ch: Willempie, bp. June 30, 1718; Ariaantje, bp. March 1, 1721; Antony, bp. Sept. 29, 1723; Teunis, bp. Nov. 26, 1725; Cornelia, bp. June 3, 1728; Daniel, bp. Nov. 22, 1730; Daniel, bp. Sept. 8, 1734; Johannis, bp. Sept. 21, 1737.

BRATT, Dirk, Jr., and Cornelia Waldron, m. Sept. 6, 1719. Ch: Anthony, bp. Feb. 3, 1720; Tryntie, bp.

Dec. 17, 1721; Pieter, bp. June 7, 1724; Johannes, bp. July 3, 1726; Willempie, bp. July 7, 1728; Willempie, bp. June 21, 1731; Teyntie, bp, May 21, 1732; Engeltie, bp. Jan. 8, 1735; Willempje, bp. June 5, 1737; Anthony, bp. July 31, 1738; Willempje, bp. Oct. 26, 1740. Dirk Bratt, Jr., made his will Dec. 16, 1763, proved June 17, 1767, in which he speaks of his wife Cornelia, son Pieter, daughter Tryntie, wife of Jacob De Foreest, and daughter Engeltie, deceased.

BRATT, Akes and Margarita Clute, m. Nov. 6, 1721. Ch: Samuel, bp. Jan. 7, 1722.

BRATT, Benjamin, and Madalena (Magdalena) Ryckman, m. Nov. 27, 1720. Ch: Maria, bp. Jan. 28, 1722; Anthony, bp. June 16, 1723; Willempie, bp. March 27, 1726; Nelletie, bp. June 16, 1728; Anthony, bp. Nov. 7, 1731.

BRATT, Egbert, and Elizabeth Lansing. Ch: Willempie, bp. May 5, 1723; Hendrick, bp. Oct. 4, 1724; Hendericus, bp. Nov. 7, 1725; Anthony, bp. Jan. 29, 1727; Jannetie, bp. Sept. 7, 1729; Hendricus, bp. Dec. 29, 1732; Willempie, bp. Oct 31, 1736; Johannes, bp. Oct. 19, 1740; Johannes, bp. Jan. 4, 1745.

BRATT, Jochem, of "Schachtekook," and Neeltie Groesbeeck, m. Dec. 3, 1732. Ch: Maria, bp. May 27, 1733; Elizabeth, bp. Jan. 18, 1735.

BRATT, Johannes, and Margarita Van Franken, m. Feb. 10, 1732. Ch: Barber, bp. Jan. 29, 1735; Elizabeth, bp. Oct. 3, 1736; Alida, bp. April 16, 1738; Cathalyna, bp. May 4, 1740; Dirk, bp. Sept. 20, 1741; Dirk, bp. June 15, 1743.

BRATT, Barnardus, in 1737, with Gerrit Bratt occupied a lot on South Pearl Street, west side, at the foot of Gallows Hill. On Jan. 17, 1735, he m. Catharyna Van Vechten. Ch: Daniel, bp. Sept. 12, 1736; Johannes, bp. Sept. 3, 1738; Maria, bp. Sept. 21, 1740; Maria, bp. June 23, 1742; Elizabeth, bp. in Schenectady, Dec. 25, 1744; Gerrit Teunise, bp. Feb. 21, 1748; Hendricus, bp. Nov. 4, 1750.

BRATT, Barent A., and Annatie ...., his wife. Ch: Cornelia, bp. Aug. 14, 1737; Anna, bp. Jan. 10, 1739; Engeltie, bp. March 7, 1742.

BRATT, Gerrit, and Maria Ten Eyck, m. Sept. 15, 1736. Ch: Elizabeth, bp. Sept. 11, 1737. [Geurt Bratt and Elizabeth Kam, m. Sept. 15, 1737.]

BRATT, Hendricus, and Rebecca Van Vechten, m. Oct. 4, 1739. Ch: Elizabeth, bp. Oct. 5, 1740; Alida, bp. April 4, 1742; Susanna, bp. Nov. 30, 1746. Hendrick Bratt was buried July 13, 1746.

BRATT, Abraham, and Lydia .... his wife. Ch: Christina, bp. May 24, 1741.

BRATT, Bernard, and Margarieta Williams, m. Oct. 30, 1740. Ch: Johannes, bp. Aug. 16, 1741; John B. Bratt, d. Sept. 9, 1822, æ. 81 y. 1 m. 23 d. ; Agnietie, bp. July 10, 1743.

BRATT, Adriaan, of Niskitha, and Zelia Van Zanten (Zandt), m. Oct. 7, 1738, she was buried Oct. 11, 1754. Ch: Anthony, bp. Oct. 4, 1741; Joseph, bp. Aug. 14, 1743; Adriaan, bp. April 21, 1745; John, bp. March 13, 1748; Albert, bp. Dec. 2, 1750; Jan. bp. Oct. 13, 1754. Adriaan Bratt, widower, m. Lydia Van Alsteyn, Jan. 15, 1757. Ch: Celia, bp. Oct. 16, 1757; she married Lucas Taylor; Eva (b. about 1760), m. John Henry Miller; Geurt, b. Feb. 27, 1762; Jochem, b. May 4, 1765; Andries, b. Aug. 29, 1767; Wyntie, b. Oct. 8, 1769, she m. Abraham Hop.

BRATT, Anthony D., and Christina De La Grange. Ch: Elizabeth, bp. Feb. 14, 1742; Johannes, bp. July 1, 1744; Eytie, bp. April 18, 1747; Annatie, bp. March 25, 1750.

BRATT, Jan, and Catharina Fonda, m. Oct. 19, 1740. Ch: Wyntie, bp. June 20, 1742; Johannes, bp. Oct. 16, 1743; Jan, bp. Nov. 16, 1746; Wyntie, bp. Oct. 15, 1749.

BRATT, Adam, and Lydia Segers, m. Jan. 9, 1741. Ch: Gerrit, bp. Feb. 6, 1743; Pieter, bp. Oct. 19, 1744; Maria, bp. Aug. 3, 1746; Susanna, bp. May 8, 1748; Staats, bp. March 11, 1750.

BRATT, Jan Pieterse, and Susanna Segers, m. July 31, 1742. Ch: Christina, bp. May 29, 1743; Maria, bp. July 8, 1744; Pieter, bp. Dec. 25, 1746; Gerrit, bp. in Schenectady, July 30, 1749; Christina, bp. April 9, 1752; Johannes, bp. July 7, 1754; Lidia, bp. Aug. 22, 1756; Myndert, b. Nov. 3, 1758; Engeltie, b. April 7, 1762; Sannatie, b. Jan. 24, 1765.

BRATT, Dirk, Jr., and Marytie .... his wife. Ch: Johannes, bp. Aug. 24, 1746; Wyntie, bp. Aug. 19, 1750.

BRATT, Albert, and Anna Carel, m. Nov. 24, 1743. Ch: Andries, bp. in Schenectady, Oct. 7, 1744; Catharina, bp. April 24, 1748; Wyntie, bp. March 31, 1751; Catarina, bp. Nov. 11, 1753; Jan and Hendrick, bp. June 12, 1757.

BRATT, Anthony A., and Wyntie Bogardus. Ch. Rebecca, bp. Jan. 18, 1747; Ephraim, bp. Jan. 6, 1751. The wife of Anthony A. Bratt was buried June 26, 1751, her child was buried July 7, 1751.

BRATT, Bernardus, and Eva Toll (widow Van Patten, of Schenectady), m. in Schenectady, Dec. 23, 1748. Ch: Maria, b. in Schenectady, June 4, 1749, and "obiit ante baptism." Nicolaas, b. in Schenectady, July 8, 1750, Jochem, bp. Sept., 15, 1757; Rebecca, bp. Oct., 4, 1761. In 1780 Bernardus Bratt had a house and lot at the South Ferry.

BRATT, Anthony Egbertse, and Maria Van Alsteyn. Ch: Jacob, bp. Dec. 24, 1752; Elizabeth, bp. Dec. 9, 1753; Pieterje, bp. Sept. 12, 1756; Jacob, b. July 7, 1760.

BRATT, Samuel A., and Annatie Manzen. Ch: Johannes, bp. Sept., 22, 1754.

BRATT, David, of Niskitha, and Tryntie Langh, m. Dec. 6 1754. Ch: Storm, bp. Jan. 18, 1756; Baartje, bp. April 23, 1758.

BRATT, Adriaan, widower, and Maritie McKans, m. March 23, 1753. Ch: Pieter, bp. April 22, 1754; Alida, bp. Sept., 12, 1756; Maria, bp. Dec., 24, 1758; Annatie, bp. Feb., 1, 1761; Andries, b. April 10, 1763.

BRATT, Dirk, widower, Van Nistagioene and Catarina Hybelaar, "geboren in Sweden," m. Dec. 6, 1753. Ch. Margarita, bp. March 30, 1755.

BRATT, Daniel Bernarduse, and Willempie Bratt, m. May 7, 1756. Ch: Catarina, bp. July 4, 1756; Daniel, bp. Sept. 24, 1758; Wyntie, bp. Jan. 31, 1762; Daniel, b. March 12, 1764; Marytie, b. Feb. 26, 1767; Johannes, bp. March 17, 1772.

BRATT, Albert, and Magdalena Lang. Ch: Storm, bp. July 4, 1756; Sophia, bp. Sept. 24, 1758; Christian, b. Jan. 13, 1763; Johannes, b. Jan. 25, 1768.

BRATT, Teunis, and Catalyntje Van Ness, m. July 24, 1756. Ch: Rebecca, bp. June 19, 1757; Rebecca, bp. June 3, 1759; Hendrick, bp. Jan. 1762; Anthony, b. July 6, 1765; Johanna, b. June 31 (sic), 1769; Johannes, b. Oct. 22, 1772; Adriantie, b. Sept. 23, 1775; Johanna, bp. Oct. 22, 1777.

BRATT, Gerrit, of Niskatha, and Lena Hooghteling, m. Nov. 1, 1764. Ch: Lydia, b. Sept. 3, 1765 ; Cornelia, b.. Sept. 27, 1767; Christina, b. Nov. 26, 1769; Coenraad, b. April 3, 1774.

BRATT, Anthony, and Mollytie Van Deusen, m. Feb. 4, 1764. Ch: Egbert, b. Feb. 11, 1765.

BRATT, Arent, and Jannetie Hoghing (Hogen), m. March 30, 1766. Ch: Annatie, b. July 15, 1766 ; Jannetie, b. March 10 (?), 1769 ; Johannes, b. March 30, 1771 ; Isaac, b. July 4, 1773 ; Johannes, bp. Oct. 3, 1779 ; Willem, b. Feb. 2, 1782 ; Simon Veder, b. April 5, 1785 ; Hannah, b. June 27, 1794.

BRATT, Johannes A., and Maacke Fonda, of the *Colonie*, m. Sept. 12, 1765. Ch : Anthony, b. July 22, 1766 ; Aaltie, b. Aug. 13, 1767; Aaltie. b. Jan. 13, 1771 ; Aaltie, b. Nov. 4, 1773 ; Rebecca, b. Dec. 14, 1776.

BRATT, Baltus, of the Colonie, and Elizabeth Foller (Rosina Follet, Fuller), m. May 11, 1765. Ch : Catharina, b. Dec. 5, 1766 ; Nicolaas, b. May 23, 1767 ; Jacob, b. April 14, 1769 ; Margarita, b. June, 23, 1771 ; Rosina, b. Dec. 8, 1781 ; Marytie, b. July 8, 1783.

BRATT, Storm, and Dorothea Van Alsteyn of Niskatha, m. Feb. 15, 1766. Ch : Catharina, b. Feb. 4, 1767.

BRATT, Pieter, and Vrouwtje Arhart, widow, m. in New York, June 26, 1766. Ch : Dirk, b. Oct. 14, 1767, Johannes, b. July 20, 1771 ; Franciscus, b. Feb. 15, 1773 ; Engeltie, b. Feb. 1, 1777 ; Engeltie, b. June 19, 1779 ; Anthony, b. Feb. 11, 1781.

BRATT, Johannes E., and Gerritie Lansing, m. July 31, 1767. Ch : Gerrit, b. March 8, 1768.

BRATT, Adam (Adriaan ?) and Maria McKans. Ch : Lydia, b. April 19, 1769 ; Margarita, b. Nov. 21, 1770.

BRATT, Andries, of Niskatha, and Annatie Van Aerkar, m. Feb. 4, 1769. Ch: Annatie, b. April 20, 1770 ; Hendrick, b. Aug. 23, 1777 ; Nicolaas, b. July 17, 1780 ; John, b. Oct. 9, 1785.

BRATT, Pieter, of Niskatha, and Margarita Fry, m. Dec. 16, 1769. Ch : Adam, b. Oct. 12, 1770 ; Alida, b. July 22, 1780 ; Gerrit, b. June 14, 1783.

BRATT, Pieter T., of the Colonie, and Jannetie Springsteen, m. June 10, 1770. Ch: Santje, b. April 7, 1771 ; Christina, b. May 16, 1788 ; Janse, b. Oct. 26, 1789.

BRATT, Joseph, of Niskatha, and Wyntie .... m. Oct. 27, 1770. Ch : Hadriaan, b. Sept. 14, 1771.

BRATT, Willem, of Niskatah, and Ariaantie Moak, m. June 31, (*sic*) 1770. Ch : Jacob, b. Aug. 10, 1771.

BRATT, Johannes, and Margarita Daath. Ch : Catharina, b. Feb. 4, 1773.

BRATT, Hendrick (Hendrikus), and Annatie David (Davies, Davidson). Ch: Bernardus, b. Dec. 13, 1774 ; Johannes, b. Sept. 18, 1777 ; Daniel, b. Sept. 24, 1779 ; (Daniel B. d. July 16, 1847, aged 67 y. 9 m. 23 d., and Ann Bloomingdale, wife of Daniel B., b. Nov. 20, 1781, d. June 24, 1822, a. 40 y. 7 m. 4 d.) ; Gerrit Theunise, b. Aug. 24, 1783 ; Hendricus, b. Dec. 4, 1785; Jacobus, b. Sept. 3, 1787 ; Catharina, b. Feb. 14, 1790.

BRATT, Albert, and Elizabeth Chambers. Ch : Magdalena, b. July 5, 1775.

BRATT, Johannes, and Sara Wendell. Ch : Anthony, b. Aug. 26, 1779 ; Anthony, b. Sept. 8, 1780 ; Hendrick Wendell, b. May 5, 1783 ; Theunis, b. Jan. 10, 1786.

BRATT, Staats, and Maria Segers. Ch: Susanna, b. Feb. 7, 1779.

BRATT, Hendrick, and Maritie Arnold. Ch: Albert b. June 15, 1779.

BRATT, Anthony E., and Alida Hoghing (Van Schaack), m. April 8, 1773. Ch: Egbert, b. March 8, 1777.

BRATT, Daniel, and Christina Beekman, m. June 29, 1777. Ch : Anthony, b. Dec. 9, 1778 ; Nicolaas, b. Dec. 23, 1780 ; Christina, b. Sept. 12, 1782 ; Margarita, b. June 8, 1785 ; John, b. Feb. 12, 1792.

BRATT, Hendricus, and Maria Eights, m. May 9, 1776. Ch : Anthony, b. Oct. 12, 1783. On Nov. 29, 1785, Hendricus B., m. Elizabeth Van den Bergh. Ch : Theunis b. May 13, 1787; Theunis, b. May 17, 1789 ; Catharine, b. Dec. 3, 1797.

BRATT, Johannes F., and Wyntie Bratt, m. March 10, 1785. Ch : Johannes, b. May 30, 1786 ; Johannes, " in huis gedoopt wegens ziekte " Aug. 13, 1787 ; Franciscus.

BRATT, Anthony T., and Geertje Van den Bergh, m. April 8, 1787. Ch : Theunis, b. July 3, 1788 : Annatie, b. March 18, 1791 ; Catalyntie, b. Sept. 18, 1794.

BRATT, Adriaan, and Maritie Arnhout. Ch : Maritie, b. Dec. 11, 1792.

BRATT, Nicolaas, and Lucy Britton. Ch : Baltus, b. Oct. 19, 1793.

BRATT, Adam, and Annatie .... his wife. Ch : Margaret, b. Nov. 17, 1793.

BRATT, John, and Margaret Winne. Ch : Catalina, b. Feb. 22, 1795.

BRATT, Isaac, and Elizabeth Van Deusen, m. Dec. 31, 1795. Ch : Jane, b. Jan. 6, 1797 ; Lea, b. Aug. 27, 1799 ; Annatie. b. May 23, 1802 ; John, b. Nov. 21, 1804; Elizabeth, b. June 14, 1807 ; Aaron, b. March 10, 1810 ; Isaac, b. Oct. 1, 1812 ; Isaac, b. Jan. 24, 1815.

BRATT, Bernardus, and Margaret Dyke (Night). Ch : John, b. Sept. 17, 1799 ; Daniel, b. Jan. 9, 1802.

BRATT, Pieter A., and Catalina Van Everen. Ch : Catalina, b. Jan. 15, 1798 ; Gerrit Van Iveren, b. April 1, 1800.

Brazee, Willem, and Elizabeth Salsbury. Ch : Willem, b. May 25, 1776.

Breem, Adam, and Catherina Freer. Ch : Catharina, June 26, 1765.

Breeze, see Bries.

Bressie, and Brezie, see Brussy.

Brewster, see Bruster.

Brice, John, and Caty Lotteridge. Ch : Mary, b. Feb. 23, 1792.

Bries (Briesch, Breeze), Hendrick, shoemaker. His wife, Maria, after his death m. .... Lookermans. He had a son Anthony.

BRIES, Anthony, and Catrine Ryckman, m. Sept. 21, 1692. He made his will Nov. 22, 1703, in which he speaks of the following children and father-in-law, Albert Ryckman. He died Nov. 22, 1704. Ch : Maria, bp. Aug. 25, 1693 ; Neeltie, bp. March 17, 1795; Hendrick, bp. Oct. 31, 1697 ; Catharina, bp. Jan. 5, 1700 ; Margareta, bp. Sept. 28, 1701 ; Eva, bp. Oct. 17, 1703.

BRIES, Wilhelm, and Catrina Janse. Ch : Benjamin, bp. .... 1694.

BRIES, Hendrik, and Wyntie Van Vechten, m. Jan. 13, 1726. Ch : Anthony, bp. Feb. 22, 1727 ; Maria, bp. Jan. 12, 1729; Johannes, bp. Oct. 24, 1730, buried July 13, 1756; Maria, bp. Oct. 1, 1732; Antony, bp. June 3, 1734; Catharina, bp. April 4, 1736; Neeltie, bp. March 18, 1739, m. Douwe Fonda; Hendrik, bp. April 4. 1742; Gerrit Theunisse, bp. Jan. 25, 1744; Albert, bp. Nov. 16, 1746. (Hendrick Bries was buried at Papsknee, Sept. 22, 1753.)

BRIES, Anthony, and Catharyntie Yates. Ch: Hendrick, bp. Nov. 30, 1760; Johannes, b. Aug. 5, 1764; Gerrit Theunise, b. Sept. 3, 1767; Christoffel, b. Nov. 6, 1770; Johannes, b. July 22, 1774: Antony, b. March 12, 1780.

BRIES, Hendrick, and Ariaantje Vinhagel. m. May 11, 1766. Ch: Johannes, b. July 21, 1766; Jacobus, b. April 13, 1768.

BRIES (Breeze), Gerrit T., and Geertruy Groesbeeck. Ch : Wyntie, b. Aug. 24, 1775 ; Sara, b. Nov. 18, 1778 ; Alida, b. July 6, 1784.

Brinckerhoff, Isaac, and Sophia Quackenbush. Ch: Rachel Maria, b. Nov. 25, 1793.

BRINCKERHOFF, John, and Geertruy Schuyler, m. Sept. 25, 1796. He d. March 10, 1835, aged 61 y. 7 mo. 7 d. She d. Feb. 23, 1826, aged 53 y. 7 mo. 13 d. Ch : Richard, b. Oct. 7, 1797; Abraham Schuyler, b. Sept. 12, 1799; Isaac, b. Dec. 22, 1801; John, b. Feb. 5, 1804; Martin Beeckman, b. June 11, 1806 ; Cornelius, b. June 10, 1808 ; Eve Maria, b. July 23, 1811.

Broadhurst, Jonathan, " jong man van Derington in Engelandt'" and Catalyntie Bensing " weduwe van Reinier Schaets," m. April 23, 1696. He was sheriff of Albany Co. 1701-3. Ch : Samuel, bp. Sept. 1, 1700.

Brockhols, Capt. Anthony. He was senior officer and commander of the military under the governor. He m. Susanna Schrik, step-dau. of Willem Teller, sen., May 2, 1681. They had a son Anthony, bp. in Albany, Aug. 14, 1687; his other ch. were bp. in New York.

Brodhead, Daniel, and Hester Wyngaard, m. Sept. 21, 1719. Ch: Thomas Garton, bp. Aug. 25, 1723; Gerrit Lucas, bp. Oct. 25, 1724; Richard, bp. April 3, 1726 ; Ann, bp. Oct. 1, 1727.

Brogdon, John, and Margaret Kelly. Ch : Joseph, bp. Oct. 26, 1778.

Bromly, John, and Sara (Zelia)..... Ch : Willem, bp. Feb. 28, 1722; Maria, bp. May 17, 1724; Judy, bp. June, 19, 1726.

Brommily, William, and Lena Boom, m. June, 1, 1742. Ch: Johannes, bp. Oct. 1, 1743; Johannes, bp. Sept. 8, 1745; Simon, bp. Feb. 19, 1749; Samuel, bp. Aug. 4, 1751 ; Samuel, bp. Oct. 14, 1753 ; Willem, bp. March 6, 1757.

Bronck, Pieter, brewer of Beverwyck as early as 1645, where he owned several house lots and a brewery, which he sold in 1662, and bought lands at Coxsackie, upon which he settled. In 1665, his farm consisted of 176 morgens, besides a calf pasture of 6 morgens. His wife was Hilletie Tyssinck. Of their children there were two sons, Jan and Pieter.

BRONCK, Jan, of Catskil (Coxsackie), where he probably built a mill in 1670, the following iron work for which he purchased from Albert Andriese Bratt of Albany, " een groote ysere krnck met een heughel en een ysere spil met een Rontsel en een bequam kruys tot de Spil, etc." He made his will Sept. 9, 1738, proved Oct. 6, 1742, in which he speaks of the following 5 sons only. His wife was Commertje Leendertse Conyn. Ch: Pieter, eldest son ; Antje,

bp. Feb. 21, 1686; Jonas, bp. April 28, 1689; Philip, bp. Sept. 20, 1691; Philip, bp. Sept. 7, 1692; Helena. bp. April 28, 1695; Caspar, bp. July 12, 1697; Leonard.

BRONCK, Pieter, of Katskil, 1720 (Coxsackie), and Antje (Hanna) Bogardus, dau. of Pieter B., m. Nov. 17, 1705 [April 2, 1705, according to a Bogardus bible.] Ch : Pieter, bp. Sept. 1, 1706; Pieter, b. Nov. 10, 1707; Jan, b. Sept. 17, 1709; Ephraim, b. Jan. 5, 1712 ; Maria, b. May 30, 1713; Anthony, b. March 8, 1715 ; Commertie, b. May 6, 1717; Wyntie, b. March 5, 1719.

BRONCK, Leendert (Leonard), of Catskil, and Anna De Wandelaer, m. Feb. 26, 1717. Ch : Jan, bp. July 14, 1723 ; Sara, bp. May 30, 1725; Commertie, bp. Sept. 10, 1727; Catharina, bp. Sept. 7, 1729.

BRONCK, Philip, and Sara .... his wife. Ch : Commertie, bp. Oct. 11, 1724 ; Wyntie, bp. May 1, 1726 ; Philip, bp. April 16, 1731.

BRONCK, Jonas, and Antje Conyn, m. Nov. 5, 1721. Ch : Jan, bp. Oct. 25, 1724 ; Philip, bp. Oct. 2, 1726 ; Commertie, bp. April 19, 1731.

BRONCK, P. Jr., and R. Bronck. Ch: Johannes, bp. Sept. 7, 1735.

BRONCK, Jan (son of Pieter B. and Hanna Bogardus), and Lydia Van den Bergh, m. 1741. Ch : Hanna, b. June 21, 1743, m. Richard Vanden Bergh, Dec. 24, 1763 ; Rykert, bp. April 21, 1745; Pieter, bp. Jan. 18, 1747.

BRONCK, Pieter C., and Elizabeth Van Wie. Ch : Annatie, b. Nov. 3, 1788.

BRONCK, Henry, and Sara Osterhout. Ch: Mary, b. March 28. 1790 ; Catharine, b. March 27, 1792.

Brooks (Brocks, Broecks), Jonathan, and Rebecca Tattem (Tatton), m. April 13, 1727. In 1729 he had a lot on west side South Pearl St., at the foot of Gallows Hill. Ch: Elizabeth, b. June 4, 1727 ; Ann, bp. Jan. 22, 1737 ; Maria, bp. Feb. 4, 1739; Catarina, bp. Aug. 6, 1749. [Jonathan Brooks, d. April 3, 1829, a. 91 y.]

BROOKS (Brocks), Josua, and Geertie Bons. Ch : Jan (John), bp. Dec. 24, 1738 ; William, bp. May 15, 1748.

BROOCKS (Brocks), Pieter, and Francyntje Wendell, m. Nov. 7, 1771. Frances, w. of Pieter B., d. April 25, 1818, a. 65 y. 6 m. 5 d. Ch : Jonathan, b. Aug. 13, 1772; Rebecca, bp. Oct. 15, 1775 ; Johannes, b. Nov. 11, 1777; Susanna, b. March 11, 1779 ; Pieter, b. May 3, 1780.

BROOKS, Jonathan, and Elizabeth Bratt. Ch : Rebecca, b. Oct. 16, 1774 ; Johannes, b. May 14, 1779.

BROOKS, Jonathan, and Angelica Brooks. Ch : Rachel, b. Sept. 25, 1811.

Brouwer, Philip Hendrickse, brewer. He was in Beverwyck as early as 1655, where he owned a house lot and brewery. He became one of the original proprietors of Schenectady in 1662; the following year he accidentally shot Claas Cornelise Swits there. He died in 1664. His wife's name was Elsie Tjerk. It is not probable that he left any children.

BROUWER, Willem, in 1655, owned property in New Amsterdam; was in Beverwyck in 1657; and was buried Aug. 3, 1663, when the following entry is made in the deacon's book: " Tot die begraevenisse van Willem Brouwer, 40 guilders 15 (stuivers)." His son Hendrick settled early in Schenectady and it is not known that he left any other children.

BROUWER, Hendrick Willemse of Schenectady, and Maritie Pieterse Borsboom " weduwe Van Teunis Karstense beide Van Schenectade," m. March 26, 1692. Ch : Johannes, bp. Feb. 12, 1693 ; Henrik, bp. Dec. 25, 1706. See *Schenectady Families.*

BROUWER, Jacob, and Maria Bovie, m. April 6, 1717. Ch : Catryna, bp. Dec. 29, 1717 ; Nelletie, bp. March 13, 1720 ; Petrus, bp. April 29, 1722 ; Antje, bp. June 7, 1724 ; Mattheus, bp. Jan. 15, 1727 ; Lena, bp. March 30, 1729 ; Lena, bp. May 9, 1731 ; Maria, bp. Oct. 7, 1733 ; Ariaantje, bp. March 8, 1738 ; Catarina, bp. Sept. 28, 1740 ; Mattheus, bp. Aug. 7, 1743.

BROUWER, Nicolaas, and Marytie Boom, m. July 15, 1757. Ch : Cornelis, bp. Oct. 9, 1757 ; Johannes, bp. Jan. 6, 1760 ; John Brouwer, d. Sept. 30, 1844, a. 85 ; Willem, b. March 29, 1763, William Brouwer, d. Jan. 21, 1831, a. 68 y. and was buried from 210 S. Pearl st. ; Annatie, and Maria twins, b. Aug. 5, 1765 ; Annatie, b. March 18, 1769.

BROUWER, Mattheus, and Annatie Ouderkerk. Ch : Catharina, b. April 1, 1772.

BROUWER, Cornelis, and Elizabeth Visbach, m. May 15, 1773. He lived on the site of the Female Academy and d. April 13, 1828, a. 90 y. Ch : Hester, b. June 17, 1775 ; Elizabeth, b. Sept. 31 (*sic*) 1776 ; Cornelis, b. Nov. 6, 1778 ; Annatie, b. Jan. 7, 1781 ; Jacob, b. Dec. 9, 1782 ; Maria, Nov. 18, 1784.

BROUWER, Nicolaas, and Sara Drake. Ch : Cornelia, b. April 8, 1775.

BROUWER, Johannes, and Marytje DeWever, m. Feb. 14, 1780. Mary, w. of John Brouwer, d. March 31, 1823, a. 68 y. 5 mo. 22d. Ch : Maria, b. Nov. 5, 1780, Mary, dau. of Jno. B. and w. of Jas. Cameron, d. June 18, 1835, a. 54 y. 7 mo. 12 d. ; Abraham, b. July 3, 1782 ; Nicolaas, b. April 5, 1784 ; Willem, b. Feb. 23, 1786 ; Johannes, b. Nov. 24, 1787, and d. in N. Y., March 3, 1836, a. 48 y. ; Annatie, b. Sept. 19, 1789 ; Cornelius, b. July 18, 1791 ; Robert Ray, b. June 24, 1793 ; Dirk Van Schelluyne, b. June 18, 1796 ; Catharine, b. July 6, 1800.

BROUWER, Cornelis, and Cathalyntje McManny (McManus) m. June 4, 1780. Ch : Nicolaas, b. Oct. 7, 1780 ; Maria, b. May 16, 1787.

BROUWER, Gerrit, and Antje Seger, m. May 12, 1780. Ch : Wyntje, b. June 4, 1782 ; Ariaantje, b. April 16, 1784 ; Maria, b. Sept. 18, 1786.

BROUWER, Willem, and Mary Marschalk. He d. Jan. 21, 1831, a. 68 y. Ch : Charlotte, b. Sept. 19, 1788. Willem B. m. Margarita Van Zandt. Jan. 30, 1792. Margaret, widow of William B., d. Oct. 3, 1845, a. 78. Ch : Maria, b. Dec. 21, 1793 ; Elizabeth, Aug. 4, 1798 ; William, b. Nov. 18, 1800 ; Ann, b. March 13, 1811.

Brown, Robert, and Maria Hujes (Hughs ?) Ch : Thomas, bp. Dec. 20, 1693.

BROWN, Thomas, and Jane Mordan. Ch : John, b. Sept. 10, 1778. Thomas Brown, and Sarah Fairchild. Ch : Jannetie, b. Nov. 13, 1781.

BROWN, John, and Margaret Wilson. Ch : Margaret, b. Dec, 17, 1778.

BROWN, William, and Jane (De) Ridder (Read), m. April 26, 1778. Ch : John, bp. July 6, 1778.

BROWN, William, and Mary Cadogan, m. Aug. 25, 1776. Ch : Catharine, b. March 5, 1779.

BROWN, Charles. F., and Mary C. Ramsey. Ch : Rosina Catharine, b. Oct. 24, 1783.

BROWN, Jacob, and Dinah Van Everen. Ch : Margaret, b. Dec. 30, 1799,

Brownlow (Bromlee), David, and Elspie Aikens. Ch : David, b. March 1, 1797 ; Robert, b. July 28, 1799.

Bruce, Daniel, and Jean Wilson. Ch : Mary, bp. Dec. 10, 1758.

BRUCE (Brous) Thomas, and Elizabeth ..... Ch : Elizabeth, b. July 7, 1767.

Bruin, Casparus, and Catharina Groesbeck, Ch : Alida, Dec. 11, 1773.

Brunt, Edward, and Margaret Kerkenaar. Ch : Wilhelmus, b. Dec. 24, 1794.

Brussy, Christoffel, and Christine Claas (Styntje Nicolaase). Ch : Cornelis and Michael, twins, bp. July 2, 1686 ; Margariet, bp. May 16, 1690 ; Maria, bp. Dec. 27, 1691 ; Geertruy, bp. Jan. 14, 1694.

BRUSSY (Bressy), Nicolaas, "wonende in de county Ulster," and Catelyntje Bont, " Geboren tot Schannechtady, nu wonende dan Claverac," m. Aug. 17, 1706. Ch : Christoffel, bp. June 15, 1707 ; Gabriel, bp. Jan. 15, 1709.

BRUSSY, Andries, of " Koxhakki," and Engeltie Clauw, m. July 13, 1707. Ch : Christoffel, bp. Jan. 26, 1709.

BRUSSY (Bruzy, Brezie), William, and Catharine Van Deusen, m. Nov. 24, 1776. Ch : Christina, Sept. 21, 1779.

Bruster (Brewster), Benjamin, and Margarija, Goey. Ch : Pieter, b. April 21, 1780.

Bruyn (De Bruyn), Jan Hendrickse. In 1678, in answer to the sheriff forbidding to trade with the Indians on the ground that he was a New Yorker, he alleged that he had been a burgher of Albany for upwards of 20 years ; notwithstanding, the court adjudged that he should be prohibited from trade because he had not kept fire and light in Albany for one whole year. Bruyn protested. He dealt largely in real estate in Albany.

Bruyns, Hage, of Smallandt, m. Anneke Janse, of Holsteyn, March 28, 1653 ; the same year he bought a lot in New Amsterdam. In 1656 he owned a lot in Beverwyck.

BRUYNS, Hage, of Esopus, son of the above, b. Nov. 22, 1654. m. Geesie Schurmans in New York, Dec., 10, 1681. In 1686, his widow lived in King street, New York.

Bryan, John, and Catharine .... Ch : Anna and Mary, bp. Aug. 9, 1747 ; Ann, bp. Dec. 18, 1748.

Buckhout, James, and Margaret Brett. Ch : Acinah, b. Oct. 14, 1790.

Buckley, Marten, and Isabel Wilson. Ch : Catarina, bp. Jan. 15, 1749. Marten B., and Catarina Oothout. Ch : Annatie, bp. Nov. 4, 1750 ; Adriaan, bp. Nov. 24, 1751 ; Marten, bp. June 24, 1753. Marten B., and Rachel Redlof. Ch : Marten, bp. Feb. 25, 1759.

Buisscher, (Butcher ?) Harmen, and Sara Wyngaart. Ch : Lucas, bp. Jan. 21, 1750.

Bulsen (Bulsing, Bunsing), Hendrick, and Cathalyna Goewey. Ch : Cornelis, bp. March 18, 1732 ; Salomon, bp. Jan. 6, 1734 ; Salomon, bp. April 18, 1735 ; Benjamin, bp. March 2, 1740 ; Alexander, bp. Dec. 5, 1742 ; Alida, bp. Sept. 8, 1745 ; Johannes, bp. July 10, 1748 ; Gerardus, bp. Aug. 30, 1752 ; Alida, bp. Aug. 1, 1756.

BULSEN, (Bulsing), Salomon, and Geertruy Clute. Ch: Hendrick, b. Sept. 18, 1762; Ariaantje, b. Sept. 15, 1764; Cathalyntje, b. Feb. 15, 1767; Pieter, b. Jan. 7, 1770; Cornelis. b. Jan. 31, 1772; Alida, b. Jan. 13, 1777; Elizabeth, b. June 21, 1779.

BULSEN, Cornelis, and Annatie Consaul (Gonsalus) m. Dec. 21, 1761. Ch: Cathalyntje, b. Dec. 19, 1763; Sara, b. Oct. 6, 1764; Hendrik, b. Sept. 20, 1766; Johannes, b. Feb. 1, 1769; Alida, b. June 30, 1771; Joseph, b. Feb. 10, 1774; Francyntie, b. June 11, 1777.

BULSEN, Alexander, and Aaltie (Alida) Oothout, m. May 5, 1765. Ch: Hendrick, b. Jan. 24, 1766; Maayke, b. Oct. 10, 1767; Cornelis, b. Dec. 4, 1768; Maayke, b. Jan. 5, 1771; Salomon, b. Feb. 6, 1773; Johannes, b. March 27, 1775; Cathalyntie, b. April 14, 1777; Alexander, b. June 22, 1779; Abraham, b. Aug. 27, 1781; Aaltie, b. April 3, 1784; Maria, b. Jan. 17, 1786.

BULSEN (Bulsing), Hendrick, and Cornelia (Neeltie) Marus, m. Dec. 11, 1768. Ch: Cathalyntie, bp. Oct. 8, 1769; Annatie, b. Feb. 21, 1775; Hendrik, b. April 3, 1779; Jannetie, b. Feb. 3, 1782. Hendrik Bulsing and Maria Moor. Ch: Elizabeth, b. Aug. 14, 1790.

BULSEN (Bulsing), Hannes, and Molly Wilson, m. Dec. 26, 1774. Ch: Cathalyna, b. Dec. 7, 1776: Anna, b. April 17, 1777; Marytje, b. Sept. 2, 1778; Marytje, b. March 9, 1780; Jane, b. July 9, 1784.

BULSEN (Bulsing), Benjamin, and Elizabeth Moor. Ch: Johannes, b. Sept. 15, 1779; Catharina, b. March 11, 1783.

BULSEN, Henry, and Catharine Cate (Kerk). Ch: Nicholas, b. Dec. 22, 1796; Elizabeth, b. May 3, 1798.

BULSEN, Peter, and Rachel Smith, m. June 5, 1796. Ch: Elizabeth, b. July 15, 1796.

Burch, see Bots.

Burgaart (Burger, Burghart, Burgart, Borgat), Coenraadt Hendrickse of Claverac, 1704, of Kinderhook, 1720. He was eldest son of Hendrick Coenraedtse Burgaart or Burger, and Marya Janse Franse Van Hoesen. He had a brother Jan, in 1704. His wife was Geesje Hendrickse Van Wye (Verwey). Ch: Marietje, bp. Feb. 27, 1698; Henderick, bp. May 12, 1700; Styntje, bp. Jan. 4, 1702; Ytie, bp. Jan. 8, 1704; Jan, bp. Jan. 13, 1706; Coenraat, bp. Jan. 18, 1708; the following are recorded in the Register of the Lutheran church, in Athens; Gerrit, b. April 27, "op Klinkenberg," 1709; Petrus, b. at Kinderhoek, July 15, 1711, and bp. at Klinkenberg, Feb. 1, 1712; Jacobus, b. April 27, and bp. at Klinkenberg, May 1, 1715; Ari, b. Dec. 14, 1720, at Kinderhoek and bp. at Klaverack, Jan. 15, 1721.

Burger (Borgaart), Jan, of Kinderhook, and Katharina Van Wie. Ch: Hendrick, bp. June 29, 1707; Coenraad, bp. April 25, 1709; Eltje, b. April 3, "op Klinkenberg" and bp. at same place in the Lutheran church, April 22, 1711; Teunis, bp. Aug. 27, 1715; Gerrit Hendrikse, bp. Oct. 11, 1719.

BURGER, Coenraad, and Catharina Mook. Ch: Coenraad, bp. Feb. 20, 1780.

Burgert, Hendrick, Jr., and Catarina Huyck. Ch: Anna, bp. Jan. 14, 1748.

Burghart (Burger), Isaac Hendrickse, and Judic Janse Hoes. Ch: Alida, bp. Sept. 4, 1698; Henrick, bp. June 30, 1706.

BURGHART, Petrus, and Eva Huyck. Ch: Lambert, bp. Dec. 29, 1751.

Burghes, Thomas, and Mary Geyel (?). Ch: John, Dec. 14, 1781.

Burhans (Borhans), Barent, and Margaret Janse. Ch: Magdalena, bp. Jan. 8, 1706.

BURHANS, Johannes, and Tempe Van Northen. Ch: Lena, b. Sept. 2, 1777. Mrs. Temperance, w. of John Burhans, d. in Westerlo, Sept., 1815, a. 72.

BURHANS, Hendrikus, and Tempe (Temperance) Du Mond. Ch: Willem, b. Aug, 2, 1781: Margaret, b. Feb. 2, 1783; Henry, b. April 1, 1790.

Burk, John, and Elizabeth Reimsnyder. Ch: Margarita, b. Nov. 4, 1780.

BURK (Burrick), John J., and Margarita Bears. Ch: Willem, b. Jan. 21, 1782.

BURK, Christiaan, and Tabitha Chisson. Ch: Zacharia, b. July 12, 1788; Rachel, b. Oct. 20, 1790.

Burn (Born), Samuel, and Magdalena (Helena) Pruyn, m. Feb. 25, 1740. Ch: Frans, bp. Jan. 4, 1741; Jannetje, bp. July 4, 1742; Margarieta, bp. May 13, 1744; Jacomyntje, bp. April 25, 1746; Samuel, bp. March 6, 1748; David, bp. May 26, 1751; Alida, bp. July 14, 1753; Catalyntje, bp. May 18, 1755.

BURN, Jan, and Lena .... Ch: Willem, bp. May 27, 1750.

BURN, Hannes, and Geesie Smitt. Ch: Maria, b. July 31, 1768.

Burns, John, and Lydia Burch. Ch: Robert, Feb. 20, 1796.

Burnside, James, and Debora Janse. Ch: Margaret, bp. July 22, 1759.

BURNSIDE, Peter, and Maria De Lange. Ch: Elizabeth, bp. Feb. 13, 1776.

BURNSIDE, Thomas, and Ariaantie Ten Eyck. Ch: Margarita, b. Feb. 6, 1776; Andries, b. July 9, 1778: Jane, b. Nov. 9, 1781; James, b. Aug. 29, 1783; Ariaantje, b. March 12, 1786.

BURNSIDE, William, and Mary Hudson. Ch: William, b. Feb. 25, 1777.

BURNSIDE, James, and Catharina Warren. Ch: Elizabeth, b. Nov. 26, 1781.

Burr, Aaron, and Theodosia Bartow, m. 1782. Ch: Theodosia Bartow, b. June 21, and bp. July 28, 1783. Mrs. Burr was the widow of Col. Prevost of the British army. Her daughter m. Joseph Alston of South Carolina in Jan., 1801, and was lost at sea early in Jan., 1813.

Burt, Benjamin, and Elizabeth Hoghels. Ch: Catharina, b. Oct. 19, 1770.

Burton, John, and Elizabeth Yoll. Ch: John Edward, bp. Nov. 15, 1756.

BURTON, Hannes, and Elizabeth Pest. Ch: Philip, b. Sept. 25, 1765.

Bush, George, and Mary Magee. Ch: Abraham, b. May 25, 1795.

Bussing, Cornelis, and Christina .... Ch: Baltus, bp. Feb. 1, 1769.

BUSSING (Bushing), Timotheus and Jannetie (Jane) Crosby. Ch: William, b. April 29, 1777; Sara, bp. April 12, 1778; Harmen, bp. Oct. 19, 1779; Ann, b. April 5, 1782: Isaac, b. June 7, 1784. (Timothy Bussing d. in Bethlehem March 24, 1831, in his 90th year).

Butler, Edmond, and Nancy Tilson. Ch: Anantie, b. Feb. 14, 1776.

4*

Buys, Jan, and Hendrikje Damen (?). Ch: Johannes, bp. Nov. 1, 1685. See New York Baptisms, 1711–14, in *Valentine's Manual*, 1864.

Buys (Buis), Jacob, and Gouda Annis. Ch: Jan, b. April 18, 1779; Jacob B., and Catharine Oothout. Ch: Johannes, b. Dec. 25, 1782.

Buyse, John, and Anne Rutherford. Ch: Eleanor, b. Sept. 1, 1790; John, b. July 22, 1793.

Byvanck (Byvang), Johannes, of Oldenzeel, Holland, b. in 1634; in Albany, 1665; m. 1st, Bolitje Evertse Duyching in New York, Oct. 24, 1666. Ch: Hendricus, bp. Feb. 20, 1684; Gerrit, bp. March 17, 1686; Maria, bp. Feb. 12, 1688. Jan Byvanck, widower, m. Sara Frans, widow, in New York, Nov. 3, 1692, he had several children bp. in New York, 1702–5.

Caarn, Hendrick, and Catryna .... Ch: Anna, bp. March 10, 1717.

Caghill, Cornelius, and Hanna Russell. Ch: Daniel, b. Aug. 12, 1780.

Caillier, see Collier.

Caldwell (Colwell), James, and Elizabeth Barents. Ch: George, b. Aug. 6, 1778.

Cambefort (Comfort), of Schenectady, 1690, and Niskayuna, 1720; owned land on the north side of the Mohawk river "Boven Kaquarrioone" (Hoffman's Ferry), which he sold in 1694 to Carel Hanse Toll. His first wife was Antje Raal. Ch: Geraldus, bp. May 11, 1690, and probably settled in New York. His second wife was Ariaantie Uldrick, widow of Gerrit Claase of Albany, m. Oct. 16, 1692.

CAMBEFORT (Comfort), Geraldus of New York; was a cooper and had his shop burned there in 1733, but by "the timely assistance of the inhabitants and *Fire Indians*," his house was saved. He m. Catharine Burger, in New York, March 24, 1713. Ch: bp. in New York; Annatie, bp. Sept. 28, 1714; Catharina, bp. Aug. 18, 1717.

Campbell, Moses, and Elizabeth Combes. Ch: Margaret, bp. Sept. 9, 1759.

CAMPBELL (Kimmel), Pieter, and Maria .... Ch: Pieter, Dec. 30, 1770.

CAMPBELL (Kemmel), Archibald, and Christina Starenberg. Ch: Archibald, b. April 8, 1778.

CAMPBELL, Robert, and Sara McDavid. Ch: Margaret, bp. April 1, 1779; Robert, b. March 27, 1781.

CAMPBELL, Alexander, and Mary McMillen (McMuller). Ch: John, b. May 24, 1779; Angus, b. April 13, 1781.

CAMPBELL, Price, and Margaret Clark. Ch: Alexander, b. April 15, 1776; Margaret, b. Feb. 1, 1778; William, b. Dec. 4, 1780; Catharine, bp. Dec. 18, 1781.

CAMPBELL, Alexander, and Catharine Steel. Ch: William, b. April 13, 1781.

Canada, Guy, and Margaret Patterson. Ch: Sarah, b. March 16, 1795.

Cane, William, and Elizabeth Dox. Ch: William Abraham, b. Nov. 5, 1778.

Canker, Jan F., and Johanna Wyser. Ch: Maria, bp. Aug. 5, 1754.

Canner (Conner), Wm., and N. Canner. Ch: Sara Rachel Regina, bp. Dec. 30, 1761.

Canton, Richard, and Catrina Baquena (?). Ch: Elizabeth, b. June 28, 1789.

Cardigan, Hugh, and Catharine Miller. Ch: Barnabas, bp. Aug. 27, 1749.

Carkner, see Kirchner.

Carr, William, and Sara Wilson. Ch: Benjamin, b. July 13, 1777; James, b. Oct. 25, 1779.

Carter, William, and Ann Gasley. Ch: Patty, b. Oct. 20, 1778; Samuel, b. Oct. 5, 1790; Ward, b. May 18, 1797.

Cartridge, Robert, and Elizabeth Hopjer. Ch: Archibald, bp. July 23, 1749.

Cartwright, Richard, "an esteemed merchant," d. in Canada, Oct. 1794 a. 73 yrs. m. Ann Beesley. Ch: John, bp. July 12, 1747; Susanna, bp. Aug. 7, 1748.

Casemay, Patrick, and Mary Craig. Ch: Jean, bp. Jan. 30, 1757.

Casparse (Carstense?) Van Ivere, Warner, and Anna Pruyn. Ch: Casparus, bp. Aug. 1. 1697; Alida, Aug. 6, 1704.

Casper, Johannes, and Elizabeth .... Ch: Gerrit, bp. Jan. 22, 1744.

Casparus, Valentine, and Rebecca Snyder. Ch: Margarita, b. Oct. 14, 1783; Jacob, b. March 19, 1786.

CASPARUS, Martinus, and Catharine Countryman. Ch: Abraham, b. Nov. 24, 1799.

Casselman, Pieter, and Elizabeth Weasen. Ch: Christiaan, bp. Oct. 27, 1751.

Cassiday, Lucas, and Rachel Cool. Ch: Ralph, Jan. 2, 1778.

Cetin, Edward, and Isabel Marshall. Ch: Samuel, bp. Dec. 25, 1747.

Chace, William, and Mary Stone. Ch: Mary Ann, bp. Aug. 22, 1759.

Chambers, Abraham Gaasbeck, stepson of Thomas Chambers, *alias* Clabbort of Esopus, m. Sara Bayard in New York, Aug. 26, 1703. Ch: Blandini, bp. Jan. 6, 1706.

CHAMBERS, Lourens (Leonard), and Fanny Thiff (Kief). Ch: Lourens, bp. July 28, 1778; Mary, b. Oct. 18, 1781.

CHAMBERS, David, and Margarita Van der Werken. Ch: Albert, b. Feb. 15, 1779.

CHAMBERS, Hendrik, and Rachel Van Santen (Zandt) m. April 4, 1779. Ch: Edward, b. June 20, 1780.

Chapman, William, and Elizabeth Lambert. Ch: John William, b. Jan. 13, 1798; Elizabeth, b. March 9, 1800.

Charles, George, and Mary Price. Ch: William, b. May 2, 1797; Stephen, b. Sept. 15, 1799; Maria, b. March 29, 1803; Sara Ann, b. Feb. 5, 1806; Eleanor, b. Jan. 6, 1809; Elizabeth, b. Sept. 30, 1811; George, b. May 28, 1814.

Chesney, Alexander, and Jane McMolly. Ch: Mary, b. Jan. 20, 1776.

Chisholm, James, and Eve McCloud, m. Nov. 8, 1797. Ch: Margery, b. Aug. 18 1798.

Christiaanse, Christiaan; 1671, he brought a morgen and a half of land at Schenectady of Paulus Janse; 1694 he sold his house and lot there. His son Christiaan remained in Schenectady. His wife was Maritje Ysbrantse Elders. Ch: Neeltie, bp. Nov. 11, 1685; Elizabeth, bp. July 11, 1693; Daniel, bp. April 11, 1697; Christiaan; Johannes.

CHRISTIAANSE, Johannes, of Half Moon, 1720, "geboren tot Schannechtede en wonende tot Oonistagioene," m. Neeltie Cornelise, June 30, 1709. Ch: Marytje, bp. July 3, 1709; Elizabeth, bp. March 11, 1716; Sara, bp. Nov. 15, 1718; Johannes, bp. Feb. 26, 1724; Christiaan, bp. Jan. 1, 1726; Neeltie, bp. Jan. 5, 1729; Cornelis, bp. Aug. 13, 1732. (Jan Christiaanse was buried Nov. 16, 1746).

Christie, Gabriel, and Sarah Stevenson. Ch: Napier, bp. Sept. 16, 1758.

Christman, Nicholas, and Maria Christman, m. April 10, 1780. Ch: Frederick, b. Oct. 27, 1780.

CHRISTMAN, Hans, and Cath. Dochsteder. Ch: Pieter, b. Nov. 28, 1780.

Cittene, see Kidney.

Claas, Johan Pieter, and Clara Margarita Curtin (Kortjen, Curteen, Courdin), m. April 22, 1758. Ch: Anna, bp. May 6, 1759; Susanna, bp. March 1, 1761; Johannes, "6 weken oud," bp. May 22, 1763; Johan Pieter, b. April 25, 1766; Andries, b. Oct. 29, 1768; Marytje, bp. March 10, 1771; Nicolaas, b. Oct. 16, 1775; Catharina b. Oct. 13, 1778.

CLAAS, Pieter, and Annatie Van Esis. Ch: Margaret, b. Jan. 5, 1793.

Claerbout, Pieter, voorzanger in the church, was in Beverwyck in 1659, probably had departed or deceased before 1674. He had a daughter Ariaentie, bp. in New York, April 7, 1658, and a son Walraeff Pieterse Claerbout.

CLAERBOUT, Walraeff, Pieterse, a trader in Beverwyck, in 1659. He m. Emmetie Hendrickse, June 10, 1668, in New York. He was then said to be of Haerlem and she of Manhatans. He had a daughter Belitie, bp. in New York, Jan. 16, 1669.

Clapper, Pieter, and Margaret House. Ch: Nicolaas, b. June 16, 1787.

Clark (Klerk), Roeloff, and Lena.... Ch: Hilletie, bp. Nov. 6, 1726; Helletie, bp. May 7, 1732; Elizabeth, bp. Aug. 27, 1738.

CLARK, Patrick, and Cornelia Waldron. Ch: Nelly, bp. Feb. 26, 1749; Martin, bp. Nov. 4, 1750; Elizabeth, bp. Nov. 10, 1751; Maria, bp. March 11, 1753; Tryntje, bp. Sept. 15, 1754; Susanna, bp. Oct. 3, 1756; John, bp. Aug. 27, 1758; Cornelia, b. April 29, 1762; Paulus, b. Nov. 10, 1767; Engeltie, b. Dec. 18, 1767.

CLARK, Alexander, and Nancy Grant. Ch: Caty, bp. Jan. 17, 1779; Elizabeth, b. Aug. 29, 1789.

Clauw (Klauw), Frans Pieterse, carpenter, in Beverwyck as early as 1656, of Kinderhook, 1683, had two sons, Hendrick and Jurriaan. He was called the *Kint Van Weelden*, but in 1680 lived at Kinderhook in great poverty. *Sluyter's and Dankers' Tour.*

CLAUW, Hendrick Fransen, and Cornelia Andriesse Sharp, m. Oct. 14, 1685. Ch: Frans, bp. Nov. 7, 1686; Elizabeth, bp. July 8, 1688; Jannetje, bp. May 25, 1693; Andries, bp. June 28, 1696; Maria, bp. July 10, 1698; Gysbert, bp. Nov. 3, 1700; Pieter, bp. Aug. 8, 1703; Gerrit, bp. Oct. 14, 1705; Hendrick, bp. July 11, 1708.

CLAUW, Jurriaen Fransen, of Kinderhoek, 1720, and Maria Janse .... Ch: Frans, bp. June 1, 1701; Rachel, bp. June 13, 1703; the following were bp. in the Lutheran church at Athens.: Lea, b. "op Kinderhoek," Jan. 20, 1705, bp. "op Klinkenberg," June 10, 1705; Maria, b. "op Kinderhoek" Nov. 15, 1708; Johannes, b. "op Kinderhoek," Feb. 1, 1711; Willem, b. "op Kinderkoek," Aug. 20, 1716.

CLAUW, Hans Jurriaense and Anna Catharina.... Ch: Jacob, b. Sept. 22, 1722, and bp. at Claverack, "22 naar Trin."

CLAUW, Hendrick, and Rebecca.... Ch: Hendrik, bp. Oct. 6, 1734; Johannes, bp. Sept. 22, 1736; Frans, bp. Dec 17, 1738. [Caspar Clauw d. in Athens, Sept. 28, 1828, a. 95 y.]

CLAUW, Gysbert, and Wyntie (Neeltie) Scherp. Ch: Hiltje, bp. July 1, 1739; Lourens, bp. Aug. 16, 1741; Gysbert, bp. May 29, 1748; Johannes, bp. July 14, 1751.

CLAUW, Willem, and Christyntie Huyck, m. Feb. 3, 1739 Ch: Mayke, bp. Jan. 23, 1740; Rachel, bp. May 29, 1752.

CLAUW, Pieter, and Johanna .... Ch: Mattheus, bp. Jan. 11, 1741.

CLAUW, Frans, and Catalyntje Bording. Ch: Engeltie, bp. Oct. 3, 1748.

CLAUW, Hendrick, and Elizabeth Hollenbeck. Ch: Gysbert, bp. Oct. 7, 1768.

CLAUW, Lourens, and Annatie Bord. Ch. Gysbert, bp. April 14, 1771.

Claver, Johan Nicolaas, and Susanna Merriday (Merideth), m. Aug. 1, 1767. Ch: William, b. Aug. 4, 1768; Johannies, b. June 25, 1770; Maria, b. July 18, 1772; Elizabeth, b. Aug. 1, 1774; Hilletie, b. Dec. 5, 1776; Catharina, b. April 10, 1798.

CLAVER, William, and Catharine Schuyler. Ch: Mary, b. April 23, 1791; Mary Schuyler, b. Aug. 13, 1792; Charlotte, b. Jan. 29, 1797.

Clement, Jacobus, in 1755 the second interpreter to the Indians; m. Jannetie Van Woert, Feb. 27, 1743. Ch: Marie, bp. Feb. 6, 1747; Nicolaas, bp. Oct. 23, 1748; Nicolaas, bp. Dec. 2, 1750.

CLEMENT, Johannes, and Rachel Redliff (Radcliffe), m. Dec. 30, 1753. Ch: Annatie, bp. Jan. 1, 1755.

CLEMENT, Nicolaas, and Rachel DeGarmo. Ch: Sara, b. Dec. 12, 1777.

Clemerger (Clemison, Clemisher, Clemisham) Daniel (*alias* Dennis Clevison), and Rachel Milton. Ch: John, b. Nov. 31 (*sic*), 1785; Hendrik, b. Dec. 16, 1787; Rachel, b. June 2, 1790; William, b. Sept. 1, 1796; George, b. Jan. 18, 1800.

Clinton, Joseph of Hellenbergh, and Mary Brouwer. Ch: David, b. Aug. 18, 1790.

Clum, Thomas, and Margarita Davies. Ch: Thomas, bp. Nov. 3, 1779.

Clute (Cloet), Capt. Johanne (Jans), came to Beverwyck about 1656 from Neurenbergh, was a trader, and considerable land-holder, at Loonenburgh, Niskayuna, Albany &c. He had good credit with the Indians. It is not known that he had any family. On his death, his property passed to his Nephew Johannes Clute, the boslooper.

CLUTE, Johannes, of Niskayuna, nephew of the preceding, m. Bata Slichtenhorst. Ch: Jacob (?); Alida, bp. Sept. 14, 1684; Elizabeth, bp. March 16, 1687; Gerardus, bp. Aug. 4, 1689; Margarita, bp. July 11, 1693; Gerardus, bp. in New York, Jan. 1, 1697; Johannes, bp. Aug. 12, 1700; Anna; Bata, bp. in Schenectady May 7, 1704. Johannes Clute was buried at Niskayuna, Nov. 26, 1725.

CLUTE, Frederick, of Half-Moon 1720, came from Kingston about 1703, and bought land of Johannes Clute at Niskayuna. What relationship existed between them is not known. He m. Francyntje Du-

Mont or DuMond. Ch: Jacob (?); Sara, bp. Feb. 19, 1707; Magdalena, bp. June 26, 1709; Pieter, bp. April 20, 1712; Walraven or Waldron. See *Schenectady Families*.

CLUTE, Jacob, of Canistagioene 1720, and Geertruy Van Vranken, m. April 12, 1707. Ch: Gerrit, bp. Jan. 4, 1708; Gerrit. bp. July 10, 1709; Elizabeth, bp. Feb. 10, 1712; Ariaantje, bp. May 1, 1715; Bata, bp. Aug. 18, 1717; Johannes, bp. Nov. 15, 1719; Petrus, bp. Aug. 12, 1722; Nicolaas, bp. May 30, 1725.

CLUTE, Waldron (Walraven), and Anna..... Ch: Antje, bp. Oct. 21, 1722; Frederic, bp. March 8, 1724; Evert and Francyntje, bp. Feb. 27, 1726; Nicolaas, bp. July 7, 1728; Maria, bp. March 28, 1730; Willem, bp. Oct. 10, 1731.

CLUTE, Johannes, and Anna .... Ch: Johannes, bp. Sept. 15, 1728; Alida, bp. July 2, 1731; Lysbeth, bp. April 15, 1733; Barber, b. April 27, 1735; Barber, bp, Feb. 15, 1738; Bata, bp. Nov. 18, 1739; Anna, bp, Feb. 14, 1742; Gerrit, bp. March 11, 1744.

CLUTE, Jacob, and Maria Brouwer, m. Nov. 16, 1727. Ch: Nelletie, bp. Oct. 13, 1728; Fredericus, bp. Feb. 22, 1730; Pieter, bp. Oct. 31, 1731; Francyntie, bp. Oct. 2, 1733; Johannes, bp. June 14, 1735.

CLUTE, Gerrit (Gerardus), and Machtelt Heemstraat, m. May 28, 1725. Ch: Catie, bp. Dec. 31, 1732; Gerardus, bp. Oct. 19, 1735; Jacobus, bp. Jan. 18, 1736; Bata, bp. Nov. 5, 1738; Elizabeth, bp. Jan. 21, 1741; Maritie, bp. May 1, 1743; Claartje, bp. May 5, 1745. Gerardus Clute was buried July 27, 1746.

CLUTE, Gerrit, and Marite Heemstraat, m. Sept. 22, 1732. Ch: Dirk, bp. Feb. 5, 1738; Geertruy, bp. June 22, 1740; Gerrit, bp. Nov. 7, 1742; Gerardus, bp. June 17, 1750.

CLUTE, Pieter, and Adriana (Ariaantje). Ch: Geertruy, bp. June 1, 1470; Francyntie, bp. in Schenectady, Feb. 20, 1743; Nicholas, bp. May 13, 1744; Elizabeth, bp. July 26, 1746; Pieter, bp. Nov. 4, 1750; Rachel, bp. April 12, 1752.

CLUTE, Johannes, Jr., and Sarah Van Arnhem, m. Sept. 27, 1752. Ch: Johannes, bp. Sept. 9, 1753; Alida, bp. in Schenectady, Mar. 9, 1755; Alida, bp. Feb. 6, 1757; Anna, bp. April 1, 1759; Elizabeth, bp. Jan. 24, 1762; Abraham, b. Jan. 11, 1764; Gerrit, b. Feb. 20, 1765; Abraham, b. May 16, 1767; Sara, May, 25, 1769; Abraham, April 16, 1773; Wouter, b. April 11, 1775. (John J. Clute, formerly of New York, d. in Albany, Feb. 24, 1836, a. 84 y.).

CLUTE, Johannes, and Jannetje Ouderkert, m. Oct. 6, 1753. Ch: Jacob, bp. April 7, 1754; Wyntie, bp. Aug. 31, 1755; Johannes, bp. May 6, 1759; Elizabeth, b. Sept. 23, 1765; Abraham, bp. Nov. 12, 1771.

CLUTE, Frederick, of Niskayuna, and Magtel Quackenbos, m. in Schenectady May 22, 1742. Ch: Abraham, bp. Sept. 22, 1754; Willem, bp. May 14, 1758. See *Schenectady Families*.

CLUTE, Nicholas, of Saratoga, and Ariaantje (De) Ridder, m. Nov. 2, 1754. Ch: Evert, bp. Aug. 31, 1755; Gerrit, bp. Nov. 6, 1757; Annatje, bp. June 19, 1760.

CLUTE, Johannes G., and Catarina Lansing. Ch: Gerardus, bp. Sept. 21, 1755; Abraham, bp. Jan. 22, 1758; Dirk, b. April 19, 1760.

CLUTE, Frederick, of Saratoga, and Maria (De) Ridder, m. 2, Nov. 1754. Ch: Maria, bp. Dec. 28, 1755; Maria, bp. Jan. 28, 1759; Gerrit, bp. March 8, 1761; Annatie, b. Nov. 10, 1765; Annatie, bp. Oct. 21, 1770.

CLUTE, Nicholaas, and Claartje Clute. Ch: Bata, bp. March 4, 1761; Catharina, b. Jan. 30, 1763.

CLUTE, Jacob, and Maayke Lansing, m. June, 12, 1761. Ch: Gerardus, b. Jan. 23, 1763; Hendrick, b. Oct. 27, 1765; Dirk, b. July 15, 1768.

CLUTE, Jacob, and Janneke Steenbergen, m. in Schenectady, July 4, 1765. Ch: Marytje, b. Jan. 23, 1768.

CLUTE, Gerrit (Gerardus), and Sara Abel. Ch: Jacobus, b. Aug. 9, 1776; Adam, bp. in Schenectady, Sept. 16, 1781.

CLUTE, Dirk, and Rachel Lansing. Ch: Jacob, b. Oct. 13, 1785; Abraham, b. Oct. 31, 1787; Gerrit, Oct. 18, 1789.

CLUTE, Gerrit, and Elizabeth Kane, m. Nov. 20, 1791. Ch: John, b. Aug. 28, 1792; Johanna, b. Jan. 1, 1794; William, b. Nov. 1, 1795; Ann, b. March 3, 1798; Rebecca, b. April, 5 1800; Pieter Kane, b. June 3, 1806; Cornelia Ann, b. March 19, 1810. (Elizabeth, widow of Gerrit Clute, d. Sept. 20, 1850, in her 85th y.)

CLUTE, Gerrit, and Bata Bovie. Ch: Charles, b. Oct. 21, 1804.

Clyne, See Klein.

Cobes, Ludovicùs, born in Herentals in Brabant; was court messenger in Beverwyck as early as 1656; notary public in Albany, and in 1677 secretary of Schenectady, where he died. His only daughter m. Johannes Klein.

Coenraads, Philip, and Franz Clomb (Fromy Clumm). Ch: Franz, b. Oct. 11, 1763; Adam, b. Dec. 20, 1766.

Coeny, William, and Elizabeth King, m. Sept. 15, 1777. Ch: Catharina, bp. July 22, 1778

Coeymans, Pieter. Ch: Barent the miller (*De Molenaer*); David : Arent; Jacob ; Lucas ; Dirkje, wife of Cornelis Vos, deceased, 1665; Geertruy, w. of Abraham Vosburgh. These brothers came to Rensselaerwyck in 1636 from Utrecht.—*See O'Callaghan's Hist. N. Netherlands*, I, 435.

Coeymans, Barent Pieterse, the miller, bought a large tract of land at the place called by his name. His w. was a daughter of Andries DeVos. His Ch: were Andreas, who moved to Raritan, N. J. He had two Ch: bp. in New York; Johanna, Nov. 9, 1716; and Mayke, March 23, 1720; Samuel, b. Aug. 3, 1670; Pieter; Ariaantje, b. Oct. 19, 1672; Jannatie; and Geertie, wife of Jacob Ten Eyck.

Coeymans, Lucas Pieterse, *de houtsager*, and Ariaantie ... Ch: Jannetje, bp. Oct. 19, 1684. He and Jan Cornelise Vyselaer in 1675, bought of Sweer Teunise Van Veesen a saw mill called the Poesten mill, on what is now called the Poesten kil, on the east bank of the Hudson over against Stoney Point (*Steene Hoeck*).

Coeymans, Pieter Barentse, and Elizabeth Greveraad, m. Oct. 5, 1713. Ch: Mayke, bp. Oct. 19, 1714, m. Andreas Witbeck; Elisabeth, bp. Oct. 27, 1716, m. Jacob Van Alen; Pieter Bar. Coeymans, m. Charlotte Amelia Drawyer, his second wife. Ch: Gerritje, bp. Oct. 21, 1722, m. John Barclay; Anne Margaret, bp. April 11, 1725, m. Pieter Ten Eyck; Charlotte Amelia, b. Dec. 24, 1727, m. Johannes Bronck, (Pieter Coeymans was buried on Beeren island, April 30, 1744). (Died at Coxsackie, April 22, 1828, Mrs. Charlotte McCarty, wid. of late Gen. McCarty, and granddau. of Pieter Coeymans, in her 88th year).

ARIAENTJE COEYMANS.

From portrait in possession of Barent Ten Eyck.

Oldest House in Coeymans, built by Ariaentje Coeymans,
early in the last century.

Colbrecht (Colebridge), Willem, and Esther Van Duzen, m. Nov. 15, 1777. Ch: Stephen, b. Oct. 19, 1781; Hugh Bennys, b. Nov. 6, 1783; William, b. March 9, 1790.

Coldin, John, and Alida Van Wurmer. Ch: John, b. Aug. 11, 1780

Collen, William, and Elizabeth Bratt. Ch: Elizabeth, b. June 9, 1779.

Colwell, Joshua, and Annatie Broadin. Ch: Rebecca, b. Aug. 14, 1779.

Collier (Caillier, Caljer), Jochem, and wife Madalena (?) of New Amsterdam. Ch: Jeurgie, bp. in N. Amst., March 13, 1644; Jacobus, bp. in New Amsterdam, Feb. 9, 1653; Hans (?); Michiel; Jurriaan. In 1660 Jochem Caljer was not living; his wid. was then the wife of Gysbert Theunisse. In 1660 she sold her late husband's lot on South William Street, New Amsterdam, and in 1663 another lot in Stone street.

COLLIER (Caillier), Michiel, of Coxhackie, 1720, and Fitje Jurriaense Van Hoesen. Ch: Magdalena, bp. July 17, 1688; Jochem, bp. June 8, 1690; Folkie, bp. Oct. 23, 1692; Jurriaan, bp. May 26, 1695; Johannes, bp. April 9, 1699; Caspar, bp. Jan. 4, 1702; the following from the Athens Lutheran Church Records; Jacob, b. "op de Flakte" bp. in the Albany Lutheran Church, June 11, 1704; Isaac, b. "op de Flakte" June 16, 1706, and bp. in Lutheran Church, in New York. Sept. 4, 1706; Isaac, b. Sept. 22, "op de Flakte Loonenburgh" and bp. "op Klinkenberg" Dec. 6, 1711.

COLLIER (Caillier), Juriaan, of Kinderhook, 1683, and Lysbeth ...... Ch: Dorethee, bp. May 19, 1689. Juriaan C. was 32 years old in 1676.

COLLIER (Caljer) Caspar, and Rachel .... Ch: Catharine, bp. March 15, 1741.

COLLIER (Caillier), Jochem, and Christina Vosburg, m. June 16, 1721. Ch: Michiel, bp. May 6, 1722; Johannes, bp. Sept. 18, 1737.

COLLIER, George, and Cataline O'Brien, m. Sept. 7, 1793. Ch: Cataline, b. April 13, 1797; Margaret, b. Oct. 4, 1801.

Collins, Lieut. John, attorney-at-law, 1720, m. Margarita Schuyler. Ch: Edward, bp. July 30, 1704, attorney-at-law, mayor of Albany, 1733, m. Margarita Bleeker, buried "in church," March 29, 1753. Lieut. John Collins, d. April 13, 1728. His wife survived him.

COLLINS, Andrew, and Charlotta M. Hart. Ch: William, b. May 30, 1782.

Collinson, John, "geboren tot London in oude Engeland," and Rebecca Bratt, "weduwe Van Claas Bogaart," m. March 20, 1703. Ch: Johannes, bp. Dec. 19, 1703.

Colwell, see Caldwell.

Comfort, see Cambefort.

Compston (Comestone, Connystead, Cumpston, Comptton), Edward. m. first, Mary Van Schaick, May 24, 1778. Ch: John Henry, b. Feb. 4, 1780; Andrew Van Schaick, b. Aug. 24, 1781; Andrew Van Schaick, b. Aug. 29, 1783; Samuel, b. Aug. 18, 1784; Samuel, b. Sept. 30, 1789. He m. secondly, Mary Bratt. Ch: Alida, b. July 20, 1796. Major Edward Cumpston, a Revolutionary officer, formerly of Albany, d. in Auburn, Aug. 22, 1825, a. 72 y.

Conchlin, Joseph, "op de Halve Maan" and Rebecca Robinson. Ch: Johannes, bp. Nov. 19, 1768.

Conckkel, Frederick, and.... Ch: Pieter, bp. Feb. 19, 1758.

Coneel (Conel), John, "a soldier," in Albany, 1666; removed to Catskil about 1678, and bought land there of Capt. Jan Clute and Harmen Gansevoort, not living in 1706, when his widow, Margaret, owned a lot in Maiden Lane.

Congel, Uzra, and Mary Hungerford. Ch: Job, b. Nov. 19, 1780.

Conger, Reuben, and Lena De Voe, m. May 10, 1780. Ch: Hilletje, b. May 9, 1781.

Conklin, William, and Jane Brouwer. Ch: Nicolas, b. May 10, 1777.

Connel, Edward, and Sara Polton (Pówlton, Proeltenny, Bolton ?). Ch: Catharina, b. Oct. 7, 1776; Daniel, bp. July 21, 1779; Maria, b. Oct. 25, 1782.

Connelly, William, and Elizabeth Kelly. Ch: Sera, "4 maand oud," bp. Feb. 11, 1764.

Consaul and Consaulus, see Gonsaulus

Constable, Charles, and Mary Ashley, m. Jan. 2, 1722. Ch: Patrick, bp. Dec. 2, 1722.

Constapel (gunner), Andries Herbertsen, Van der Blaes, was in New Amsterdam till 1654, when he removed to Beverwyck. He owned considerable real estate in the village and vicinity, among which was half the island opposite to Fort Orange, which after his death, in 1662, was sold to Jeremiah Van Rensselaer. In 1662, he killed one Segar Cornelise Van Voorhout in self-defense. His wife was Annatie Jurriaensen. Ch: bp. in New York, Jan, July 25, 1649, and Johannes, Sept. 3, 1651. It is not known that any of his children survived him.

Conyn, Leendert Philipse, was in Beverwyck, as early as 1655, d. in 1704, m. Agnietie.... Ch: Philip, Caspar and Jacob (?).

CONYN, Philip Leendertse, of Coxhackie, 1720. m. Wyntie Dirkse. Ch: Leendert, b. Sept. 9, 1683; Dirk, bp. April 19, 1685; Agniete, bp. Feb. 6, 1687; Antie, bp. Jan. 27, 1689; Feytie, bp. Jan. 15, 1693; Philip, bp. Jan. 29, 1694; Saartie, bp. July 17, 1698; Johannes, bp. June 15, 1701.

CONYN, Caspar Leendertse, of Claverac, 1720, made will March 3, 1720-1, proved June 7, 1727, in which he mentions wife Alecta and all the following children except Tanna. He m. Alette (Alecta) Winne. Ch: Anna, bp. Jan. 6, 1684; Tanne, bp. Dec. 28, 1684; Leendert, bp. March, 1687; Anganietie, bp. May 12, 1689; Pieter, bp. June 28, 1691, deceased, 1721; Casparus, bp. Dec. 31, 1693; Marietie, bp. Jan. 1, 1696; Lysbeth, bp. Dec. 25, 1697; Commertie, bp. May 12, 1700; Racheltie, bp. Dec. 28, 1701; Eva, bp. June 3, 1705.

CONYN (Conynen) Jacob, and Marytie.... Ch: Johan, bp. July 21, 1700.

CONYN, Dirke Philipse, and Rachel Andriesse of Bergen, N. J. Bans proclaimed in Albany, Sept. 16, 1707, m. in New York, Oct. 24, 1707. Ch: Weintie, bp. Aug. 1, 1708.

CONYN, Leendert, of Kinderhook, 1720, and Emmetie.... Ch: Elbertie, bp. Jan. 10, 1714; Agnietie, bp. Oct. 6, 1717; Philip, bp. May 15, 1720; Lourens, bp. June 10, 1722.

CONYN, Pieter, and Alida De Wandelaer, m. Nov. 13, 1714. Ch: Sara, bp. Oct. 9, 1715; Pieter, bp. May 26, 1717.

CONYN, Leendert, and Hendrikje Cool, m. Jan. 15, 1714. Ch : Petrus, bp. Jan. 8, 1721.

CONYN, Philip, of Coxhackie, 1720, and Catharina .... Ch : Philip, bp. June 7, 1724; Jannetie, bp. April 17, 1726; Leendert, bp. Jan. 22, 1730 ; Jeremias, bp. Jan. 21, 1739.

CONYN, Philip, of Coxhackie, 1750, and Commertie Bronck, m. June 12, 1750. Ch : Philip, bp. Jan. 17, 1753.

Cool, Pieter Barentse of manor of Livingston, 1720, m. Hendrikje Janse, in New York, Nov. 3, 1680. P. B. Cool " weduwnaer van Hendrikje Janse en Janneke Dingman jonge dochter beyde van Kinderhoek " were m. in Albany, 1688.... Ch : Hendrick, bp. July 10, 1687; Henrik, bp. Oct. 5, 1707 ; Pieter, bp. April 30, 1710.

COOL, Lambert, and Maritie Kidney, m. Dec. 30, 1743. Ch : Johannes, bp. April 19, 1745 ; Engeltie, bp. July 24, 1748 ; Roeloff, bp. May 24, 1750 ; Rachel, bp. July 12, 1752.

COOL, Pieter, and Alida Dingmanse. Ch : Hendrickie, bp. Aug. 26, 1752.

COOL, Johannes, and Annatie Daniels. Ch : Maria, b. Oct. 2, 1771 ; John Daniels, b. Oct. 31, 1773 ; Geertruy, b. Sept. 28, 1777 ; Pemberton, bp. Feb. 20, 1780.

Coons, see Koens.

Cooper (Couper), Obadiah, and Cornelia Gardenier. He was buried May 6, 1742, she, April 17, 1748. Ch : William, bp. Oct. 5, 1718 ; Obadia, bp. Oct. 9, 1720; Sara, bp. Oct. 21, 1722 ; Elizabeth, bp. Aug. 23, 1724 ; Jacob, bp. April 17, 1726 ; Abraham, bp. Feb. 21, 1728 ; Maria, bp. Nov. 9, 1729 ; Cornelia, bp. June 6, 1733 ; Cornelis, bp. Dec. 12, 1735.

COOPER (Couper), John, and Elizabeth.... Ch : Cornelia, bp. March 8, 1740 ; Samuel, bp. Sept. 27, 1741.

COOPER (Couper), Thomas, and Elizabeth Van Buren (Duren), m. Oct. 4, 1742. She was buried Sept. 11, 1748. Ch : Obadiah, bp. Nov. 6, 1743 ; Obadiah, bp. Oct. 19, 1744 ; Jannetie, bp. Jan. 12, 1746 ; Elizabeth, bp. Oct. 23, 1748.

COOPER (Couper), Obadiah, and Maria Fonda, m. March 4, 1743. Ch : Cornelia, bp. Jan. 11, 1744 ; Pieter, bp. Jan. 12, 1746.

COOPER, Jacob, and Josina Orchard. Ch : Cornelia, bp. Dec. 6, 1748 ; Maria, bp. Aug. 26, 1750 ; Obadiah, bp. Nov. 12, 1752 ; Annatje, bp. Dec. 9, 1753 ; Sara, bp. Aug. 29, 1756 ; Obadiah, bp. March 18, 1759 ; Thomas, b. March 2, 1768.

COOPER, Abraham, and Catarina Ostrander, m. March 22, 1752. Ch : Elizabeth, bp. May 29, 1752 ; Obadiah, bp. Sept. 22, 1753 ; Cornelia, bp. Sept. 8, 1754 ; Maria, bp. Sept. 12, 1756 ; Rebecca, bp. Nov. 2, 1760 ; Obadiah, b. Sept. 30, 1763 ; Lea, b. Sept. 4, 1764 ; Catharina, b. Sept. 21, and bp. Sept. 23, 1766, the mother being then dead.

COOPER, Christiaan, and Anna Margarita Strong. Ch : Coonraad, b. Sept. 5, 1768; Hendrick, b. July 13, 1778. [Christiaan Cooper and Catharine Deerstyne, m. May 28, 1793.]

COOPER, Obadiah, and Annatie (Hannah) Van den Bergh, m. May 27, 1769. She d. June 21, 1801, a. 50 y. 3 m. 15 d. Ch : Elizabeth, b. July 1, 1770 ; Elizabeth, b. July 11, 1775 ; Cornelia, b. Nov. 6, 1777 ; Jannetie (Caroline ?) b. Sept. 1, 1781, Caroline d. Oct. 15, 1837, a. 56 ; Cathalyna, b. March 20, 1785 ; Margarita, b. Nov. 28, 1787 ; Rachel, b. Aug. 13, 1791.

COOPER, Wilhelmus, and Marytje Beronger (Anna, M. Berringer). Ch : Christiaan, b. July 2, 1784 ; Elizabeth, b. Nov. 1, 1787 ; Frederick, b. March 27, 1790.

COOPER, Pieter, and Anna Strong (Strnck), m. July 18, 1783. Ch : Elizabeth, b. Aug. 8, 1784 ; Johannes, Jan. 19, 1786 ; Hendrick, March 18, 1788 ; Annatie, b. March 14, 1790.

COOPER, William, and Maria Hilton. Ch : Sarah Hilton, b. Sept. 7, 1784.

COOPER, Obadiah F., and Lena Albrecht, m. June 8, 1781. Ch : Cornelia b. May 22, 1786 ; Cornelia, b. Nov. 16, 1788.

COOPER, Thomas, and Lea Cooper, m. Sept. 6, 1786. Ch : Catharina, b. March 15, 1787.

COOPER, Paulus (same as last ?) and Lea Cooper. Ch : Abraham, b. May 10, 1789.

Copes, Isaac, and Mary McLean. Ch : Mary, bp. June 25, 1758.

Copley, Calvin, and Rachel Winne. Ch : Charles, b. Oct. 17, 1795.

Cornelise, Jesse, and Maria,.... his w. Ch : Petrus, bp. June 2, 1717.

CORNELISE, Jephta, and Christina Martense, m. April 30, 1716. Ch : Johannes, bp. April 3, 1720.

Cornick (Cowneck), Jonathan, and Margaret Perry. Ch : Elizabeth, b. May 24, 1797 ; Catharine, b. Sept. 13, 1799.

Corsel, Jacob, and Catharina his wife. Ch : Jacob Hendrick, bp. May 3, 1761 ; Catharina Margarita, bp. Jan. 2, 1763.

Cortney, John, first wife, Bregje Segers ; second wife, Mary Teeser. Ch : Thomas, bp. Aug. 5, 1778 ; Judikje, b. Aug. 12, 1780 ; John, b. June, 1791.

Coster (Koster), Hendrick, m. Geertje Goosense Van Schaick, After his death in 1678 she married Johannes Lansingh Ch : Anthony, eldest son ; Goosen ; Gerritje, wife of Johannes Roseboom ; Antje, wife of Johannes Bleeker.

COSTER, Anthony, baker, and Elizabeth Ten Broeck, m. Dec. 15, 1698. He was buried in the church, Feb. 6, 1753 ; she, on the 3d May, 1757. Ch : Henderick, bp. Sept. 3, 1699, buried in the church, Sept. 17, 1745 ; Christiana, bp. Dec. 15, 1700 ; Geertruytje, bp. July 28, 1706 ; Ephraim, bp. Sept. 23, 1716.

Costigan, Francis, and Jane Hagerman. Ch : Grace, b. Nov. 16, 1797 ; Isaac, b. Nov. 7, 1799 ; John, b. May 4, 1801 ; Sarah, b. Oct. 1, 1806 ; Arma, b. Sept. 15, 1807.

Cowper, see Cooper.

Courtnie (Courtir), John, born in Ireland, and Marytje Vander Linde, widow of Jan Oliver, m. Aug. 3, 1735. Ch : Elisabeth, bp. Jan. 25, 1736 ; John, bp. Feb. 12, 1744.

Cowenhoven, Samuel, and Catelyntje Wyngaart. Ch : Samuel, bp. Dec. 17, 1758.

Crane, Josiah, Jr., and Carolina Walters. Ch : Maria Catharina, b. Sept. 23, 1783.

Cranker, Indlow (?), and Neeltie DeGarmo. Ch : Sara, b. Dec. 15, 1780.

Crannel (Grennel, Crellen, Crenel), William, and Margarita Bennewe (Bennoit), m. June 4, 1726. Ch : Robert, bp. July 10, 1726 ; Petrus, bp. Feb. 10, 1728 ; Petrus, bp. Jan. 9, 1732 ; William Winslow, bp. Jan. 28, 1739.

Crannell, Robert, and Ariaantje Bovie, m. Nov. 13, 1748. Ch: William Winslow, bp. Sept. 26, 1749, d. Dec. 27, 1828, a. 80 y. ; Mattheus, bp. Aug. 4, 1751 ; Petrus, bp. Nov. 14, 1756; Petrus, bp. March 11, 1759.

CRANNELL, John, and Johanna McManna. Ch: Mary, bp. Sept. 13, 1757.

CRANNELL, Pieter, and Catarina Egmont. Ch: Margarita, bp. Oct. 15, 1758 ; Annatie, b. Dec. 5, 1762 ; Sara Winselo (Winslow), b. Dec. 30, 1766 ; Jacob, b. Sept. 10, 1769 ; Willem, b. Sept. 18, 1771.

CRANNELL, John, and Volkie Van Alsteyn, m. Jan. 29, 1757. Ch: William, bp. Dec. 18, 1757 ; Isaac, bp. Jan 4, 1760: Martin, b. Aug. 22, 1762; Robert, b. Nov. 17, 1764; Marytie, b. Feb. 6, 1767; Margarita, b. Dec. 21, 1770; Robert, bp. May 17, 1772.

CRANNELL (Crenel), Hendrik and Jacomyntie Bloemendaal. Ch: Maas, b. Feb. 23, 1768 ; Margarita, b. Nov. 24, 1769; Cornelis Cadmus, b. Dec. 30, 1772 ; Rebecca, b. April 5, 1774 ; Robert, b. June 17, 1776 ; Johannes, b. March 22, 1779 ; Petrus, b. May 10,1781.

CRANNELL, William Winselo (Winslow), and Marytje Eman, m. Jan. 9, 1780. He d. Dec. 27, 1828, æ. 80 y. She d. Oct. 28, 1825. Ch: Ariaantie, b. Dec. 27, 1780; Mattheus, b. Nov. 9, 1784; Maria, b. Dec. 4, 1789 ; Mary, b. Nov. 13, 1790.

CRANNELL, Martin, and Caty Brokus. Ch: Baltus, b. Oct. 27, 1790.

CRANNELL, Isaac, and Mary (Maris), Morris, m. Nov. 24, 1789. Ch: Folkie, b. Oct. 29, 1790.

CRANNELL, Nicholas, and Gerritie Van den Bergh. Ch ; Robert, b. June 17, 1793; Wynant, b. Oct. 9, 1796; Matthew, b. Sept. 9, 1800; Mary, b. June 31 (*sic*), 1802.

Creddisch, J., and Cornelia Buscher. Ch: John, bp. June 29, 1734.

Creeve (*Creere*), Thomas (Tam), and Jannetie.... his w. Ch: Neeltje, bp. June 28, 1684; Johannes, bp. May 4, 1686 ; Johannes, bp. June 16, 1689.

Cregg (Gregg ?), John and, Sara.... his wife. Ch: Catharine, bp. June 22, 1781.

Cregier (Kregier), Capt. Martyn. He was the first burgomaster of New Amsterdam ; a fearless and skillful military leader and an exemplary magistrate. Retiring from the city he settled on a plantation in Niskayuna, a portion of which is still held by his descendants, and there ended his days in the early part of 1713 (?) (*O'Callaghan's Hist. N. Netherland*, II, 554). His children were, Martyn, Frans, Catharina, and perhaps others. Frans was b. at Borcken in Holland ; he settled as a merchant at New Castle on the Delaware, and was deceased in 1666, when his father and brother-in-law, De Sille, administered on his estate. He m. Walburga De Sille of Maestricht, Holland, Feb. 29, 1660, in New Amsterdam ; after his death she m. Willem Bogardus. Catharina Cregier m. Nicasius De Sille, May 26, 1655, in New Amsterdam ; in 1686 she was a widow and resided in Broad street.

CREGIER (Kregier), Martyn, Jr., m. Jannetje Hendrickse Van Doesburgh, daughter of Maritie Damens, by her 2d husband. Hendrick Andriese Van Doesburgh, in Albany, Oct. 11, 1671. He was public clerk in New Amsterdam, from 1646 to 1661: probably removed to Albany about 1685; owned a lot inherited from his mother-in-law on the east side of North Pearl a little south of Steuben street; made his will

Jan. 12, 1702; proved March 3, 1711¾, in which he speaks of his w. Jannetje and all the children below written ; d. Jan. 21, 1702. His wife made her will Aug. 22, 1734, proved June 10, 1741, and mentions all the children except Johanna ; was buried in Niskayuna, Aug. 28, 1734. Ch: Martin; Elizabeth wife of Daniel Van Olinda ; Maria, w. of Johannes (?) Vreelandt ; Annatie, w. of Victor Becker; Johanna, bp. in Albany, Sept. 19, 1686; Samuel, bp. in New York, July 23, 1690 ; Geertruy, bp. in Albany, July 9, 1693, m. Ulderick Van Vranken.

CREGIER, Samuel and Geertruy Visscher, m. May 20, 1716, of Halfmoon, 1750. He d. Sept. 1777, aged 88 y., and was buried in Albany. His wife was buried in Albany, Sept. 9, 1754. Ch: Jannetje, b. Feb. 20, 1717; Martynus, b. Feb. 3, 1719 ; Dirkie, b. July 24, 1721; Bastiaan, b. Nov. 5, 1723 ; Anna, b. April 11, 1726; Marya, b. March 30, 1728 ; Abram, b. Jan. 20, 1730 ; Geertruy, b. Feb. 18, 1731 ; Hester, b. Sept. 11, 1733.

CREGIER, Martinus, (son of Marten, Jr.), vintner, and Margaret Van Dolsen, m. in New York, July 29, 1702. She and the following children were living in New York in 1741. John, Vintner and w. Anne ; Henry, mariner: Martinus, mariner ; Jane, spinster ; Margaret, widow of Burdett Fleetwood, mariner.

CREGIER, Martinus, and Sara Van Vranken. Ch: Geertruy, bp. Aug., 2, 1752; Elizabeth, bp. June 23, 1754 ; Maria, bp. Oct. 24, 1756.

CREGIER, Bastiaan m 1st, Maria Fonda, d. Jan. 13, 1759 ; 2d, Derickie Visscher, both of Niskayuna, Jan. 12, 1765. He d. Dec.. 17, 1795, aged 72 y., 1 m. 9d. His w. Dirckie, d. Aug. 2, 1795, a. 60 y., 4 m. 3 d. Ch: Samuel, b June 22, 1769; Teunis, b. Jan., 31, 1771; Martinus, b. Feb. 23, 1775 ; Isaac, b. July 17,1777.

CREGIER, Martinus, and Cathlyntie, [De] Foreest. Ch: Sara, b. Nov. 15, 1780.

CREGIER, Martinus, and Eva Vanden Bergh. Ch: Dirkie, b. Sept. 4, 1800 ; Sebastian, b. Nov. 17, 1802, and d. in Niskayuna, May 8, 1870, in 69th year.

CREGIER, Samuel, and Mary Fairchild. Ch: Dirkie, b. Oct. 25, 1800 ; Ann Maria, b. Feb. 25, 1803.

Cremer (Krimer, Cramer), Jacob. and Maria Barbara. Ch: Georgius Matthias, bp. Nov. 21, 1761.

CREMER, Jurriaen and Margarita .... Ch: Petrus, b. Feb. 21, 1767 ; Laurens, b. March 30, 1769.

Crevel, see Cribel.

Crever, Johannes and Marytje Kelmer. Ch: David, b. Oct. 9, 1771.

Cribel (Gruwel, Grewel, Crevel, Cruel), Francis, and Ann Palsin (Balsing, Baltz). Ch: Jellis, bp. Dec. 11, 1757 ; Catarina, bp. Oct. 21, 1758 ; Elizabeth, bp. April 13, 1766; Hendrik, b. April 3, 1764 ; Annatie, bp. May 29, 1768; Martinus, b. June 15, 1770.

Cromwell, Jacobus, of Schenectady, and Maria Philipse m. in Schenectady, Sept. 26, 1703. Ch : Stephanus, bp. March 6, 1709. See also *Schenectady Families.*

Crook, see Kruck.

Croon, Dirk Janse, was appointed magistrate of Beverwyck in 1655, and again in 1658 ; 1660 superintendent of wells ; in 1663, *Juffrouw* Maria Wessels, of New Amsterdam, claimed the half of his property on account of breach of promise. In 1664, he was probably in Amsterdam, Holland.

Crozier, Johannes, and Agnes Darrich. Ch: James, b. Nov. 10, 1778.

Cruiselaar, Silvester, and Maria Shram. Ch: Johannes, b. March 5, 1785.

Cruiff, see Gerbertse.

Crum, John and Catharine Rudolff. Ch: John Rudolff, b. May 2, 1792.

Cry, Lourens, and Anna Margarita.... Ch: Philip Frederick, bp Jan. 30, 1770.

Cumming, Daniel, and Elizabeth (Abigail), Grant. Ch: Nancy, bp. Nov. 19, 1775; Margaret, April 18, 1779.

Cummings, Cornelis, and Hannah Swells. Ch: Margaret, b. May 22, 1778.

CUMMINGS, John, and Isabella McCay. Ch: Mary, b. Dec. 15, 1781.

Cunningham, Henry, and Margaret.... Ch: Margaret, bp. Dec. 13, 1747.

Cuyler (Coeyler, Coyler), Henderick, tailor, born in 1637, came to Albany about 1664, and bought a lot on the hill, on east side of North Pearl street near State, in 1680 he owned a lot on the south side of State street, west of Pearl "near ye Fort," which after his death passed into the possession of his son-in-law, Pieter Van Brugh. In 1675 he made his brother Reynier, "*cnoopemaecker tot Amsterdam*," his attorney to receive certain property of Pieter Nicolaas Gouverneur. He was deceased in 1691, and his wife Anna.... in 1703. Ch: Johannes, eldest, b. in 1661; Abraham; Maria, bp. in New York, March 13, 1678, and was licensed to marry John Crugger of New York, March 2, 1703; Anna, m. Myndert Schuyler; Sara, m. Pieter Van Brugh of New York, Nov. 2, 1688.

CUYLER, Johannes, trader, b. in 1641, eldest son of Hendrik Cuyler, admitted freeman of New York city 1696, mayor of Albany, 1725-6; he had a lot on east side ol Pearl street second south of Steuben extending to James street. He m. Elsje Ten Broek, Nov. 2, 1684. She was buried in the church, April 14, 1746. Ch: Anna, bp. Nov. 29, 1685; Christina, bp. Sept. 25, 1687; Christina, bp. Dec. 4, 1689, buried in the church, Nov. 20, 1755; Hendrick, bp. Jan. 10, 1692; Sara, bp. Oct. 22, 1793; Elsje, bp. Aug. 25, 1695; Cornelis, bp. in New York, Feb. 14, 1697; Johannes, bp. Feb. 19, 1699; Maria, bp. Nov. 25, 1702; Elizabeth, bp. May 13, 1705; Rachel, bp. Sept. 21, 1707; Rachel, bp. Nov. 27, 1709.

CUYLER, Abraham, trader, m. Caatje Bleeker, Nov. 17, 1689. He was buried in the church, July 14, 1747; she d. April 8, 1734. Ch: Hendrick, b. in New York, Dec. 22, 1690; Grietje, bp. Oct. 26, 1692; Anna, bp. April 14, 1695, d. Nov. 17, 1709; Johannes, b. June 21, 1698; Sara, bp. April 28, 1700; Maria, b. March 30, 1703, d. Feb. 16, 1722; Sara, bp. Oct. 6, 1706; Catharina, bp. Feb. 18, 1709; Abraham, b. Dec. 27, 1713; Nicholaas, b. June 27, 1716.

CUYLER, Hendrick, Jr., m. Margarita Van Deusen, Dec. 1, 1722. Ch: Catharina, bp. July 14, 1723; Cathrina, bp. June 6, 1725; Elizabeth, bp. Sept. 25, 1726; Abraham, bp. May 25, 1729; Catalyna, bp. Aug. 22, 1730; Abraham, bp. Aug. 5, 1733.

CUYLER, Johannes A., m. Catharina Wendel, Oct. 28, 1727. He was buried Oct. 27, 1746; she was buried in the church, April 14, 1746. In 1729, he had a house lot on the east corner of Broadway and Steu-

ben St. Ch: Elsie, bp. Sept. 15, 1728; Harmanus, bp. May 3, 1730; Johannes, bp. Sept. 21, 1731; Abraham, bp. Sept. 3, 1732; Catharina, bp. May 12, 1734; Cornelis, bp. Oct. 19, 1735; Anna, bp. Sept. 5, 1736; Margarita, bp. Ap.r 20, 1740; Jacob, b. Sept. 28, 1741; Jacob, bp. Jan. 10, 1746, d. in Coxsackie, Oct.2, 1823.

CUYLER, Cornelis, m. Catharina Schuyler, Dec. 9, 1726. In 1730 he had a house lot on south side of Steuben street, the fourth west of Chapel street. Ch: Johannes, bp. Jan. 29, 1729; Elizabeth, bp. Aug. 8, 1731; Philip, bp. Aug. 29, 1733; Hendrik, bp. Aug. 22, 1735; Elsie, bp. April 10, 1737, buried in the church, July 2, 1752; Margarieta, bp. Dec. 10, 1738; Cornelis, b. Oct. 31, 1740; Abraham, b. April 11, 1742 (Col. Abraham Cuyler, died at Yorkfield, Canada, Feb. 5, 1810, a. 68); Dirk, bp. May 12, 1745.

CUYLER, Abraham, Jr., m. Jannetie Beeckman, May 5, 1744. Ch: Catharina, bp. Jan. 10, 1745.

CUYLER, Abraham, m. Catharine Wendel, April 1, 1762. Ch: Hendrick, b. Jan. 30, 1763; Jacob, b. March 1, 1765; Margarita, b. Feb. 2, 1768; Helena, b. Dec. 3, 1770; Hendrick, b. July 15, 1773.

CUYLER, Nicolaas, merchant, m. Maria Schuyler, May 11, 1745. She was buried at the Flats, Feb. 3, 1750. Ch: Catharine and Susanna, bp. Jan. 10, 1746; Abraham, bp. Nov. 20, 1748.

CUYLER, Cornelis, Jr. and Annatie Wendel. Ch: Catharina, b. Jan. 4, 1764.

CUYLER, Abraham C., m. Jannetie Glen, April 10, 1764. He was mayor of Albany, 1770-8, and d. in Yorkfield, Canada, Feb. 5, 1810, a. 68 years. Ch; Cathalina, b. June 17, 1765; Jacob, b. Aug. 15, 1766; Elizabeth, b. Dec. 5, 1767; Cornelis, b. July 7, 1769; Jacob Glen, b. Aug. 20, 1773.

CUYLER, Philip, and Sarah.... Ch: Cathalyna Sophia, b. Jan. 19, 1766.

CUYLER, Jacob, and Lydia Van Vechten, m. March 5, 1764. He d. June 5, 1804, a. 62 y. 6 m. Ch: Johannes, b. Aug. 14, 1766, d. Aug. 7, 1811, a. 45 y.; Dirk, b. Oct. 9, 1767, d. March 31, 1800, a. 32 y. 5 m. 22 d.; Catharina, b. June 22, 1770; Jacob, b. Nov. 21, 1772; Glen, b. Feb. 18, 1775; Tobias Van Vechten, b. Nov. 4, 1777; Cornelis, b. May 7, 1780.

CUYLER, Abraham N. and Margarita Wendell. Ch: Nicolaas, b. April 13, 1765; Catharina, b. and bp. "*op desen dag,*" Feb. 27, 1771; Maria, b. Feb. 15, 1773; Elizabeth, b. Dec. 12, 1775; Robert, b. Sept. 9, 1777; Jeremie, bp. March 8, 1782.

CUYLER, Harmanus, and Elizabeth Van Bergen. Ch: Johannes, b. May 29, 1774.

CUYLER, Cornelis, and Jannetie Yates. Ch: Joseph, b. Aug. 20, 1779; Cornelis, Aug. 15, 1781; Cornelis, b. Feb. 15, 1783; Maria, b. Feb. 22, 1785.

CUYLER, John C., and Hannah Mayley. He d. Oct. 25, 1828, in his 63 year. Ch: Caty, b. ....12, 1788; John Mayley, b. Nov. 25, 1796; Augustus, b. Jan. 7, 1799; William Tremper, b. Dec. 21, 1801; Catharine Mayley, b. Feb. 6, 1807.

CUYLER, John J., m. Jennet Wray, Feb. 6, 1789; she died, Nov. 16, 1789, a. 20 y. 1 m. 26 d. Ch: George Wray, bp. Nov. 15, 1789.

CUYLER, Jacob A., and Rebecca Kane (Cane). Ch: William, b. April 14, 1790; Elizabeth, b. Feb. 1, 1792; Abraham, b. Aug. 8, 1796; Abraham, b. March 15, 1798; Philip Stephen Van Rensselaer, b. Nov. 17, 1799; Henry, b. May 3, 1803; Henry, b. March 23, 1804.

Cuyler, John T., and Mary Vernor. Mary Vernor, relict of John Cuyler, and daughter of John and Eve Vernor, d. July 20, 1846, a. 70 y. 9 m. 14 d. Ch: Vernor, b. June 19, 1799; Peter Schuyler, b. July 28, 1801.

Cuyler, Glen, and Mary Forman Ledyard. Ch: Benjamin, Ledyard, b. Sept. 18, 1797; Richard Glen, b. July 2, 1799.

Damen, Maritie, owned a house and lands at Niskayuna, and a house and lot in Pearl street, Albany. By her first husband, Dirk Van Eps, she had two children : Jan Dirkse Van Eps, who settled in Schenectady, and Lysbet who married Gerrit Bancker, of Albany, and by her second husband, Hendrick Andriese Van Doesburgh; she had a daughter, Jannetie, who m. Marten Cregier, Jr., of Albany and Niskayuna; finally in 1664 she m. Cornelis Van Nes.

Daniels (Danielson), Charles, and Elizabeth.... Ch: Margarita, bp. March 2, 1737; Dirk, bp. Nov. 23, 1740.

Daniels, John, m. Geertruy Hilton, June 6, 1752. Ch: Anna, bp April 22, 1753. [John Daniels was buried Dec. 12, 1754.]

Daniels, Hendrick, m. first, Maria Northen. Ch: Jannetie, "oud 7 weken," bp. April 5, 1765. He m. second, Molly McGuyer (McYoung, McCoul). Ch: Abraham, b. Aug. 24, 1767; Margarita, b. Sept. 1, 1772; Elizabeth, b. May 3, 1776.

Daniels (Danielson), Johannes of Halve Maan, and Jannetie Leen (Dennison). Ch: Johannes, bp. Feb. 7, 1770; Pieter, b. March 17, 1771; Margarita, b. July 11, 1773; David, b. Oct. 3, 1774.

Daniels, Johannes, and Sofia Hilton. Ch : Johannes, b. March 10, 1781.

Daniels, Jacob, and Maria Riddel. Ch : Pieter, b. Oct. 30, 1784.

Danielson, see Daniels.

Dareth, see Dret.

Dark, Carel, of Steen Rabie, and Margarita Barent (Borns). Ch: Coenraad, b. Nov. 1, 1767; Elizabeth, b. April 4, 1771.

Dark (Dirk), Anthony, m. Anna Barbara Brussin. Oct. 28, 1771. Ch: Margarita, b. Nov. 22, 1774.

Dauchsi, see Dox or Doxsi.

Davenport, John of Schaagtcokook, and Hendrickis Bennewe (Benoit). Ch : Jacob,b. July 27,1763.

Davidts, Christoffel (Kit), a native of England, b. in 1616; in 1650 lived on a farm at *Dominie's hoeck* now called Van Wie's point. 1656 received a patent for 36 morgens of land at Esopus about a (Dutch) mile inland from the North river; 1663 asks permission to reenter on land from which he had been driven by Indians at Esopus. His wife was Cornelia, dau. of Andries De Vos of Beverwyck. She died in 1657, leaving at least two children : Joris Christoffelse, and David Christoffelse. The latter with wife and four children were massacred by the French and Indians at Schenectady, Feb. 9, 1690.

Davids, Davis, Davies, Davie.

Davids, Thomas, and Maicke (Mary)....Ch : Thomas, bp. Aug. 26, 1722; David, bp. Sept. 13, 1724.

Davie (Davis), John, m. Elizabeth Wyngaard, Jan. 11, 1747. Ch: Daniel, bp. Aug. 28, 1748; Maria, bp. March 11, 1750; Nancy, bp. Oct. 7, 1751; Jacobus, bp. Nov. 11, 1753; Jacobus, bp. Aug. 27, 1755; Catalina, bp Feb. 26, 1758; Johannes, b. July

31, 1762; Pieter, b. March 10, 1764; Cathalyntje, b. Sept. 12, 1766; Cathalyntie, b. Aug. 21, 1769; Jacobus, b. Feb. 1, 1772.

Davis, Edward (Ned), m. Jannetie Duret (Droit), Jan 8, 1763. Ch: Cornelia, b. Oct. 27, 1763; Johannes, b. Sept. 8, 1765; Cornelius, bp. Sept. 27, 1767; Rachel, b. July 15, 1770; Annatie, June 22, 1773; Elias,b. Dec. 29,1775; Cornelis,b. Aug. 14,1778.

David, William, and Ruth North. Ch: Francis, bp. May 3, 1779.

David (Davies), Pieter, m. Elizabeth Colwell (Colrill, Caldwell), July 22, 1784. Ch: John, b. Sept. 7, 1784; Maria, b. Aug. 14, 1786; Cathalina, b. Nov. 22, 1784; Elizabeth, b. March 28, 1793; Ann, b. June 7, 1795; James, b. Aug. 9,1798; Joseph Caldwell, b. March 12, 1800.

Dauser, Caspar, and Elizabeth.... Ch: Eva, b. June 8, 1771.

Dawson (Daason), Volkert, and Geertruy Hilton. Ch : Barent b. Oct. 26,1765; Ryckert, b. Oct. 25, 1765; Maria, b. and bp. Dec. 25, 1769; Ariaantje, b. Dec. 11, 1771; Willem, b. Aug. 2,1778.

Deal, William, and Caty McGahary. Ch : Jane, b. July 11, 1778.

Dean, George, m. Annatie Van Deusen, in New York, July 3, 1765. Ch: Abraham, b. April 13, 1766; Abraham, Oct. 8,1770; Abraham and Rachel, b. Jan. 31, 1773.

Deane, Stuart, m. first Pietertje Bratt. Ch: Maria, b. Sept. 29, 1778; Anthony, b. Dec. 20, 1780; Pieter, b. Oct. 23, bp. Dec. 14, (the mother then being dead), 1783. He m. second, Margaret Wheaton. Ch: Abraham, b. Aug. 30. 1790. [Capt. Stuart Deane, a famous Albany navigator, d. Aug. 5, 1836, a. 90 y.]

DeBacker, see Backer.

DeBoy, see Dubois.

DeBruyn, see Bruyn.

DeCamp, Mathias, and Mary Mollens. Ch: Jenny, b. March 18, 1777.

DeCarmau, see DeGarmo.

DeDeckere, Johan (Jan), was appointed vice director and secretary of New Orange, June 21, 1665, and remained in this office one year, returning to New Amsterdam in 1656; subsequently he became a member of the council. He had a son Jacobus, bp. in New York, Nov. 17, 1658.— *O'Callaghan's Hist. N. N.*, II, 304.

Decker (Dekker) Jan, and Tuysje.... Ch: Lourens, Feb. 2, "op de flakte Loonenburgh" and bp. there March 9, 1712. *Luth. Church Rec. Athens.*

Decker (Dekker), Gerhard and Geertruyd.... Ch: Christoffel, b. at Tachkanick, Sept. 3, 1720.

DeDuytscher, Roeloff, and Jannetie Brussy (Brissi, Bressy). Ch: Christina, bp. Aug. 8, 1703; Christoffel, bp. July 15, 1705. Johannes, bp. Jan, 25, 1708.

DeForeest, Hendrick, from Utrecht, an early settler of New Amsterdam. He owned a bouwerie on Manhattan island and 100 morgens of land at Haerlem. After his death in 1638 his wife, Geertruy Bornstra, m. Andries Hudde. Hendrick DeF. left two sons, Johannes and Isaac. The former m. Susanna Verlet June 8, 1673. They lived in Beaver street, New Amsterdam. Isaac Deforest, from Utrecht, was a brewer. He received a patent for 50 morgens of land on Man-

5

hattan island in 1647 ; in 1656, he was weighmaster ; married Sara DuTrieux [now Truax] in New Amsterdam, June 9, 1641, and had 14 children baptized in New Amsterdam, of whom *Philip* bp. July 28, 1652, settled in Beverwyck.

DeForeest, Philip, cooper, of Manor Rensselaerswyck, m. Tryntje Kip in New York, Jan. 5, 1676. He was buried in Albany, Aug. 18, 1727. Ch : Sara, bp. in New York, Jan. 2, 1678 ; Susanna, bp. in Albany, April 1, 1684 ; Metje, bp. July 25, 1686 ; Isaac, bp. Feb. 20, 1689 ; Jesse, bp. Jan. 13, 1692 ; Catrina, bp. Nov. 25, 1694 ; Johannes, bp. Sept. 12, 1697 ; David, bp. Sept. 8, 1700 ; Abraham, bp. Feb. 21, 1703.

DeForeest, David, m. Abigail Van Aalsteyn, Nov. 8, 1718. Ch : Philip, bp. Feb. 21, 1719 ; Philip, bp. May 1, 1720; Jannetje, bp. March 11, 1722 ; Martin, bp. May 14, 1724 ; Catharina, bp. Sept. 15, 1728 ; Susanna, bp. Sept. 26, 1731 ; Maria, bp. April 21, 1734; Jacob, bp. March 3, 1737.

DeForeest, Jesse, m. Neeltje Quackenbos, Aug. 22, 1718; was buried Sept. 27, 1756. Ch : Catryna, bp. May 31, 1719 ; Philip, bp. Oct. 14, 1720 ; Cornelia, bp. Feb. 20, 1723 ; Wouter, bp. Nov. 14, 1725 ; Isaac, bp. Sept. 29, 1728 ; Catharina, bp. May 20, 1731 ; Neeltie, bp. Oct. 21, 1733 ; Sara, bp. Aug. 8, 1736 ; Marytie, bp. March 16, 1740.

DeForeest, Johannes, m. Maria Quackenbosch, Oct. 12, 1725; was buried June 13, 1754. Ch : Catarina, bp. June 4, 1727 ; Wouter, bp. Nov. 17, 1728 ; Cornelia, bp. Sept. 7, 1729 ; Cornelia, bp. Nov. 1, 1730, was buried Oct. 17, 1754 ; Philip, bp. Nov. 7, 1731 ; Philip, bp. Dec. 24, 1732 ; Philip, bp. Dec. 21, 1733 ; Wouter, bp. Nov 26, 1735 ; Philip, bp. March 13, 1737 ; Sara, bp. June 4. 1738 ; Johannes, bp. Nov. 11, 1739 ; Johannes, bp. March 15, 1741.

DeForeest, Abraham, m. Rebecca Symonse Van Antwerpen, March, 27, 1832. Ch : Catharina, bp. March 11, 1733 ; Maria, bp. May 23, 1736 ; Symen, bp. Feb. 17, 1739 ; Sara, bp. Feb. 14, 1742 ; Cathalyna, bp. Dec. 14, 1743 ; Sara, bp. Aug. 5, 1750 ; Rebecca, bp. July 24, 1757.

DeForeest, Philip, Jr. (son of Jesse), m. Maria Bloemendal, May 4, 1745. Ch : David, bp. June 7, 1747 ; Johannes, bp. Aug. 18, 1751 ; Rebecca, bp. July 22, 1753.

DeForeest, Philip, m. Rachel Van Ness. Ch : Catarina, bp. May 28, 1749 ; Catalina, bp. Dec. 8, 1751 ; Jesse, bp. June 30, 1754 ; Jesse, bp. Aug. 22, 1756 : Neeltie, bp. Oct. 1, 1758 ; Annatie, bp. Feb. 22, 1761.

DeForeest, Marten, and his two brothers, Philip and Jacob, lived on adjoining farms in what is now North Greenbush. He m. Tanneke Winne. Ch : Catrina, bp. Sept. 15, 1751 ; Peter, bp. April 15, 1753 ; David, b. Aug. 31, and bp. Sept. 21, 1775 ; Philippus, bp. Jan. 15, 1758 ; Willem, b. Feb. 29, bp. April 13, 1760 ; Catharina, b. May 6, 1762 ; Rachel, b. March 23, 1764 ; Jannetje, b. Sept. 14, 1766 ; Marytje, b. Jan. 29, 1769 ; Jacob, b. May 28, 1771 ; Daniel, b. Ang. 4, 1774.

DeForeest, Wouter, m. first, Engeltie Bratt, Sept. 14, 1754. Ch : Jesse, bp. Nov. 24, 1754 ; Dirk, bp. Feb. 6, 1757 ; Dirk, bp. Jan. 4, 1761. He m. second, Alida Clute, Aug. 20, 1763. Ch : Johannes, b. April 1, 1765 ; Philip, b. July 9, 1767 ; Annatie, b. April 26, 1769 ; Annatie, b. Aug. 14, 1770 ; Isaac, b. Aug. 17, 1772 ; Neeltie, b. Jan. 15, 1774 ; Johannes, b. April 5, 1776.

DeForeest, Isaac, m. Alida Fonda, April 14, 1753. Ch : Neeltie, bp. Aug. 24, 1755 ; Jesse, bp. June 25, 1759 ; Jesse, b. May 25, 1762 ; Alida, b. Aug. 21, 1765 ; Maria, b. April 19, 1769.

DeForeest, Jacob, m. Tryntje Bratt, July 24, 1756. Ch : David, bp. Aug. 13, 1758 ; Abigail, b. April 4, 1762 ; Dirk, b. June 10, 1764 ; Pieter Bratt, b. Sept. 3, 1766 ; Catharina, b. April 13, 1768 ; Johannes, b. June 5, 1776.

DeForeest, Jacob, bp. April 1, 1773 ; Engeltie, b. June 5, 1776.

DeForeest, Simon, of " Halve Maan," m. Mary McGinnis, June 5, 1761. Ch : Rebecca, b. July 3, 1762 ; Sara, b. March 15, 1764 ; Annatie, b. July 23, 1767 ; Dorothea, b. July 29, 1771.

DeForeest, Philip, and Maayke Van den Bergh. Ch : Rachel, b. Dec. 23, 1769.

DeForeest, David, of " Colonie," m. Elizabeth Witbeck, May 26, 1770. Ch : Philippus, b. March 7, 1771 ; Lucas, b. March 25, 1773 ; Maria, b. March 20, 1775 ; Geertruy, b. Dec. 13, 1778 ; Rebecca, b. Aug. 8, 1782, m..... Reed of New York ; Abraham Witbeck, b. Sept. 30, 1786 ; John, b. July 25, 1789.

DeForeest, Pieter, of " Colonie," m. Pietertje Van Aalsteyn, June 4, 1775. Ch : Cathalina, b. July 4, 1776 ; Marten, b. Nov. 29, 1778 ; Reinier, b. July 8, 1781 ; Cathalyntje,· bp. May 27, 1786 ; Tanneke, b. May 12, 1790.

DeForeest, Philip, m. Annatie Van Deusen, June 7, 1778. Ch : Marten, b. July 23, 1779 ; Christiana, Aug. 24, 1781 ; Wilhelmus, b. Sept. 22, 1784 ; Tanneke, b. Jan. 7, 1787. [Philip W. De Foreest d. Aug. 19, 1800, a. 42 y. 1 m. 9 d.]

DeForeest, Jesse, m. Rebecca Van Santen, Aug. 1, 1779. Ch : Wouter, b. Nov. 21, 1780 ; Engeltie, b. Feb. 12,1785 ; Maria, b. Nov. 1,1786 ; Dirk, b. March 2, 1788 ; Hetty, b. Oct. 12, 1789 ; Catalina, b. Aug. 12, 1795.

DeForeest, Johannes, and Elbertie Van Aalsteyn. Ch : Philip, b. Feb. 21, 1780 ; David, b. July 6, 1783.

DeForeest, Dirk, m. Rebecca Bratt, Jan. 14, 1781. Ch : Teunis, b. July 24, 1781 ; Wouter, b. Nov. 23, 1783 ; Engeltie, b. April 22, 1785 ; Cathalyntie, b. May 10, 1788 ; Henry, b. Nov. 27, 1797 ; Walter, b. June 10, 1800.

DeForeest, David (son of Marten) m. Rachel, Vander Heyden, Feb. 27, 1780. Ch : Janneke, b. May 12, 1782 ; Johannes, b. May 18. 1785, d. Jan., 1857. [David De Foreest d. April, 1835.]

DeForeest, William, m. Abigail (De) Foreest, March 16, 1783. Ch : Marten, b. Sept. 1, 1784.

DeForeest, David, m. Susanna Fonda, Dec. 25, 1779. Ch : Wouter, b. March 31, 1787 ; Pieter, b. July 25, 1789 ; Abraham, b. Oct. 20, 1790 ; Stephen, b. Jan. 5, 1801.

DeForeest, Dirk, and Maria Fonda. Ch : John, b. Nov. 17, 1787 ; David, b. Dec. 26, 1790.

DeForeest, John J., and Barbara Van Aalsteyn. Ch : John, b. Aug. 27, 1791.

DeFort, see Fort.

Defreeze, Douwe Aukes, b. 1640, was an innkeeper at Schenectady. On the 9th Feb., 1690, his wife, two children and negro servant Francyn, were massacred by the French and Indians. Douwe Aukes *jong man van Schenegtade en Maria Viele weduwe van* Matthys Vrooman, were m. in Albany, Feb. 4, 1685. Ch : Margariet, bp. March 21, 1686.

DeGarmo, De Garmeaulx, De Charmau, *alias* Villeroy.

DeGarmeaulx, *alias* Villeroy, Pierre, "Pieter the Frenchman" was in Albany as early as 1665, Peter Villeroy a Frenchman, laborer, could not take the oath of allegiance, &c., in 1699, because he was a Papist. He was buried March 6, 1741. His wife was Caatje Vander Heyden, sister of Dirk V. D. H. Ch: Anna, bp. Oct. 15, 1684; Marie, bp. May 23, 1686; Jacobus, bp. March 29, 1689; Agniet, bp. March 20, 1692; Johannes, bp. April 6, 1694; Matthieu, bp. June 1, 1696; Dirk, bp. Oct. 2, 1698; Abraham, b. April 3, 1702; Jillis, bp. March 22, 1704.

DeGarmo, Johannes, m. Egbertie Visscher, Oct. 9, 1719. In 1734, his house was on the north side of Steuben street, a little west of James street. Ch: Pieter, bp. May 8, 1720; Bastiaan, bp. Aug. 12, 1722; Jacob, bp. Jan. 26, 1724, buried Aug. 12, 1746; Dirkje, bp. March 13, 1726.

DeGarmo, Mattheus, and Rebecca.... Ch: Pieter, bp. Jan. 24, 1722; Johannes, bp. Nov. 3, 1723; Johannes, bp. Sept. 20, 1724; Catharina, bp. Jan. 8, 1727; Hester, bp. July 27, 1729; Hester, bp. Dec. 25, 1731; Mattheus, bp. Feb. 21, 1734; Abraham, bp. Jan. 21, 1739; Jacobus, bp. June 21, 1741; Sara, bp. Oct. 27, 1743.

DeGarmo, Jillis, m. Rachel Evertsen, Jan. 9, 1731. Ch: Catharina, bp. July 2, 1731; Jacob, bp. Nov. 19, 1732; Johannes, bp. Feb. 9, 1735; Catharyna, bp. May 28, 1738; Jillis, bp. Jan. 8, 1749.

DeGarmo, Pieter, and Sara Gardenier. Ch: Rebecca, bp. Oct. 25, 1747; Nicolaas, bp. July 2, 1749; Rachel, bp. March 3, 1751; Rachel, bp. Feb. 23, 1752; Catarina, bp. Feb. 3, 1754; Nicolaas, bp. Aug. 31, 1755; Nicolaas, bp. Sept. 18, 1757; Neeltie, bp. Aug. 19, 1759; Hester, b. Feb. 22, 1763.

DeGarmo, Pieter, m. Geertruy Kregier, "Van Nistigioene," Sept. 27, 1752. Ch: Johannes, bp. Dec. 22, 1754; Geertruy, bp. April, 9, 1758; Samuel, b. April 15, 1790; Geertruid, b. May 17, 1763; Bastiaan, b. Feb. 22, 1766; Martinus, b. Sept. 27, 1769.

DeGarmo (Charman), Johannes, m. Anna Kittel, Oct. 27, 1751. Ch: Rebecca, bp. Nov. 10, 1754; Joachim, bp. Nov. 14, 1756; Joachim, bp. June 17, 1759; Mattheus, bp. April 6, 1761.

DeGarmo, Jacob, of Albany, m. Fytje Becker of Niskitha, May 19, 1758. Ch: Cathrina, b. May 19, 1760; Ariaantje, b. Apr. 29, 1763; Eva, b. Aug. 4, 1768; Rachel, b. Aug. 26, 1772; Gerrit, b. June 10, 1775.

DeGarmo, Pieter, and Lena Bomp. Ch: Sara and Mattheus, twins, b. Dec. 31, 1767; Johannes, b. Aug. 20, 1769.

DeGarmo, Johannes, and Margarita Wendell. Ch: Pieter, b. May 28, 1782; Martinus, b. May 25, 1788.

DeGarmo, Gerrit, m. Cornelia Cooper, Jan. 10, 1799. He d. Dec. 19, 1809, a. 34 y. 5 m. 9 d. She d. June 30, 1818, a. 39 y. 9 m. 9 d. Ch: Jacob, b. Oct. 11, 1799; Annatie, b. Aug. 6, 1801; Cornelius Van den Bergh, b. April 28, 1803; Benjamin, b. March 31, 1806, and d. April 25, 1807.

DeGoyer, see Jan Roeloffse.

DeGoyer. Tys Evertse, 1664 planter in Colony Rensselaerwyck; had a brother Evert Evertse master carpenter in Amsterdam, Holland. His father and mother, Evert Tysse and Grietje Janse deceased, formerly lived at Naerden.

DeGraaf, Andries, a brickmaker, was an inhabitant of New Amsterdam in 1661. Jan Andriese, his son, was also a brickmaker and lived in Beverwyck in 1655. He was fined 500 gl. with two others for selling liquor to the Indians in 1658. With one Hoogeboom he went to New Amsterdamin 1661 and commenced the making of bricks.

DeGraaf, Claas Andriese, b. 1628, settled early in Schenectady where his descendants are found to this day. He m. Lysbet Willemse Brouwer (sometimes called Rinckhout). She d. Nov. 18, 1723. Of 10 children only the following were bp. in Albany. Isaac, bp. Aug. 4, 1691; Antje, bp. Aug. 27, 1693. (*See also Schenectady Families*).

DeGraaf, Jesse, son of Claas, m. Aaltie Akkermans (Helston, Hennion) in New York, Oct. 20, 1705. Ch: Claas, bp. Dec. 25, 1706; Elizabeth, bp. April 30, 1710; Aaltie, bp. Oct. 31, 1714.—*See also Schenectady Families.*

DeGraaf, Jan, and Geertruy..... Ch: Anna, bp. April 20, 1712.

DeHaen, Isaac, a trader in Beverwyck, 1663-4.

D'Hinsse, Jacob, a surgeon in Beverwyck, 1654-67. In 1654, he received a patent for two lots of land at Fort Casimer on the Delaware river. In 1657, he brought an action against Thomas Powelson [Powell,] of Beverwyck for fees; the defendant answered that the plaintiff was engaged to attend his family for two beavers ($6.40) a year; plaintiff insisted that such an agreement referred only to sickness from natural causes, not to cases of wounds willfully inflicted; and the case was put over. D'Hinsse had a lot on east side of Broadway, just south of State St.

DeHooges, Anthony, came to New Netherland in 1641, and next year succeeded Arent Van Curler as superintendent of the Colony Rensselaerswyck, and town clerk. His lot in Beverwyck, was on the north corner of Beaver St. and Broadway. He died about 1656. His wife Eva Albertse Bratt, after his death, m. Roeloff Swartwout of the Esopus in 1657. DeHooges left the following Ch: all living in 1657: Maricken, Anneken, Catarina, Johannes, Eleanora, being minors, they probably removed with their mother to Esopus.

DeHulter, Johan, with his wife Johanna De Laet, dau. of Johannes De Laet, embarked for New Netherland in May, 1653, from Amsterdam, in the vessel called the *Graef*, with different families, taking with them a number of free men, among whom were several mechanics, as one extraordinary potter [*Steenbakker*, brickmaker], who intended to settle either in the colony or other convenient place. Mrs. DeHulter, through her father, inherited one-tenth of the colony Rensselaerwyck which she received in a conveyance of the land lying between the Poesten and Wynant's kil from Jeremiah Van Rensselaer in 1674. This land her second husband, Ebbingh, conveyed to Jurriaen Theunise in 1676, who afterwards conveyed it to Philip Pieterse Schuyler. De Hulter died about 1657 and his widow m. Jeronimus Ebbingh of Esopus, Feb. 22, 1658-9 in New Amsterdam. After the death of her first husband, Mrs. D. H. removed to Esopus and settled upon a patent of land there, consisting of 500 acres, which she obtained in 1657, at the same time selling out her property in Beverwyck. A pantile bakery, established by her husband, formed a part of this property.

Dekker, Jan, and Tysje Bogert. Ch : Jacob, bp. April 13, 1707 ; Marytje. bp. Oct. 17, 1708.

Decker. Simeon, and Cornelia.... Ch : Abraham, b. Dec. 28,1796.

De La Grange, Johannes, a Huguenot, is said to have emigrated from La Rochelle, France, about 1656, settled in New Amsterdam, and left 4 sons : *Johannes ; Omie ; Isaac ;* and *Jacobus.*

De La Grange, Johannes, b. 1658, d. at Bergen, N. J., May, 6, 1742. He left two sons : *Johannes,* and Christiaan. [Johannes La G. m. Ytie Croesvelt, Sept. 28, 1697, in New York.]

De La Grange, Johannes, b. 1706, d. at Elizabethtown, N. J., Nov. 5, 1782, leaving one son : *Johannes.*

De La Grange, Johannes, b. Aug. 28, 1733, d. Sept. 19, 1798. He had 'a son Johannes, who d. in Union, Broome Co., N. Y., in 1866.

De La Grange, Omie, came to Albany, 1665, [this name is usually written *Omy* in the old records, but it is claimed by some of the family that it should be *Omie,*] son of Johannes the first settler ; he was a trader, and besides owning several lots in Albany, bought of John Hendr : Vrooman in 1686, one-half of Van Bael's Patent on the Norman's kil and with Johannes Symonse Veeder, in 1716, bought the other half. Many of his descendants occupy portions of these lands in the towns of New Scotland and Guilderland. Omie De La G. m. Annetie De Vries. Ch : Johannes ; *Omie ;* Christiaan, admitted freeman in New York, 1734 ; Isaac, bp. April 28, 1686 ; Christina, bp. Oct. 10, 1688 ; Jacobus, bp. April 23, 1692.

De La Grange, Omie, Jr., lived on the Van Bael Patent, m. Elsie Van Loon March 28, 1697 : having no children living he left his property to his nephews Bernardus, Johannes, and Omie.

De La Grange, Johannes (son of Omie), lived on the Van Bael Patent, had Ch : Johannes : Christiaan ; Annatie ; Margaret, and Christina.

De La Grange, Isaac (son of Omie), m. Maria .... Ch : Omie ; Isaac ; Coenraad ; Grietje, m. Johannes Look ; Antje, m. Anthony Quackenbush ; and Maria, bp. Oct. 17, 1730.

De La Grange, Jacobus (son of Omie), lived on the Patent at the Normans kil, m. Engeltie Veeder in Schenectady, Oct. 24, 1717. Ch : Susanna, bp. in Schenectady, Sept. 25, 1719 ; *Barnardus,* bp. in Schenectady. March 11, 1721 ; Susanna, bp. in Schenectady, Sept. 15, 1723, m. Jacob Jacobsen ; Antie, bp. in Albany, April 21, 1728 ; m. Johannes Evertsen ; Debora, bp. in Schenectady Aug. (?) 1729, m. Philip Teunise ; Johannes ; Omie Arie, b. Nov. 12, 1738 ; *Myndert ;* Christina, m. Johannes Bloemendal.

De La Grange, Bernardus (son of Jacobus), a lawyer, lived in New Brunswick, N. J., m. ....., Warrington ; in 1776 ; moved with his family to England ; d. Dec. 10, 1797. Ch : James Brazier, b. 1760 ; Susannah, m. John Wadman.

De La Grange, James Brazier, d. 1822, leaving one son James Warrington, who m. Harriet Demarest of Waterford, N. Y., and now lives in England.

De La Grange, Myndert (son of Jacobus), lived on the Patent at the *Swarte* kil, m. Helena A. Swits, March 5, 1769 ; Engeltie, bp. in Schenectady : Jan. 14. 1770 ; Neeltie, bp. in Schenectady, June 16, 1771 ; James, bp. Jan. 19, 1777 ; Ann, who m. Aaron Van Patten.

De La Grange, James (son of Myndert), lived on the Patent at the *Swarte* kil, m. Hester Vanderzee, d. 1825. Ch ; Myndert ; Hester ; Margaret ; and Eve.

De La Grange, Arie (son of Jacobus), a surveyor, m. Maria Van Antwerp, in Schenectady, Feb. 18, 1762. He d. April 2 (6), 1798 ; his wife d. Feb. 6, 1801, a. 58 y. 4 m. 2 d. Ch : Jacobus, b. Jan. 22, 1763 ; Maria, b. Aug. 2, 1765 ; Maria, Aug. 23, 1766 ; Gerrit, b. June 15, 1771 ; Gerrit, b. Nov. 21, 1777, d. Dec. 19, 1777.

De La Grange, Jacobus (son of Arie), m. first, Annatie Visscher (b. Dec. 25, 1763, d. Aug. 20, 1794), Feb. 10, 1784 ; secondly, Maria McCrea (b. Feb. 2, 1771, d. June 15, 1856), Feb. 15, 1796 ; Capt James La G. d. Feb. 16, 1827, in his 65th year. Ch : Arie, b. Dec. 4, 1784, d. 1811 ; Gerrit, b. Sept. 17, 1787, d. Jan. 17, 1863, a. 75 y. ; James, b. Oct. 21, 1789, d. Sept. 1, 1828 ; Alida, b. Sept. 28, 1791, d. Aug. 11, 1793 ; Myndert, b. May 28, 1793, d. May 26, 1794 ; Mary Ann, b. Sept. 23, 1797, d. April 13, 1848 ; Susannah, b. March 20. 1799, d. Sept. 3, 1800 ; John, b. Oct. 27, 1800, d. Nov. 12, 1846 ; Susannah, b. Oct. 27, 1802, m. Peter V. Shankland, and d. March 6, 1838 ; William, b. July 2, 1804, d. Feb. 23, 1869 ; Stephen, b. Dec. 21, 1806, d. Nov. 5, 1807 ; Stephen, b. Oct. 14, 1808, d. Sept. 25, 1813 ; George, b. June 1, 1810 ; Stephen McCrea, b. May 10, 1815.

De La Grange, Gillis [son of Christiaan], and Jenneken Adriaense Molenaar. Ch : Christyntje, bp. Sept. 24, 1693 ; Elisabeth, bp. Oct. 6, 1695 ; Anna, bp. in Schenectady, Dec. 29, 1700 ; Christiaan, bp. July 25, 1703.

De La Grange, Christiaan, and Marytje Evertsen. Ch : Anna, bp. March 20, 1748.

De La Grange, Omy, m. Marytje Van Brakelen, Oct. 2, 1743. Ch : Marytje, bp. March 12, 1749.

De La Grange, Johannes, and Elizabeth Mcnoy. Ch : Metje, b. Feb. 24, 1762,

De La Grange, Coenraad, m. Annatie (De) La Grange, Oct. 8, 1768. Ch : Maria, b. Aug. 7, 1778.

(De) La Grange, Johannes, and Maria Knoll. Ch : Christiaan, bp. Oct. 3, 1779.

(De) La Grange (Granzy), Christiaan, and Elizabeth Freeman. Ch : Engeltie. b. Dec. 11, 1786 ; Jannetie, b. May 25, 1790. (See also *Schenectady Families*)

(De) La Grange, Pieter, and Judith Maas [Bloemendaal]. Ch : Jelles, bp. Aug. 16, 1798.

De La Grange, Jacob, m. Ariaantje Truax, May 4, 1783. Ch : Ann, b. Oct. 23, 1790.

De Lamater, Claude, and Christiana .... Ch : Christiana, bp. Feb. 12, 1717.

De Lamater, Evert, m. Mary Cole, Oct. 20, 1795. Ch : John Cole, b. Aug. 3, 1795.

Delamont, Jacob, died March 14, 1719, aged 81 years, leaving two sons : Jan, who settled in Schenectady ; and Marten, of Schaghticoke.

Delamont, Marten Jacobse, of "Schadtkooke " m. Lysbeth Viele, Nov. 14, 1702. Ch : Pieter, bp. Oct. 1, 1703 ; Catharina, bp. April 20, 1707 ; Catharina, bp. Oct. 31, 1708 ; Pieter, bp. Oct. 7, 1711 ; Abraham, bp. Feb. 10, 1717.

DeKoning, Jan, and Geertruy Janse. Ch : Margariet, bp. June, 26, 1709

DeLaWarde, Jan, came over from Antwerp in 1662; besides a lot in Albany and land in Niska-yuna he owned an island in the Mohawk river above Schenectady, for which in 1698, he acknow-ledged to have received satisfaction from Joris Aertse Vander Baast, some years previously. He died in Albany, Jan. 28, 1702.

DeLavil (perhaps DeLaval), see Donnowa.

DeLaval, Capt. Thomas, a trader in New York and Albany, 1668–82, owned one or more houses in Albany ; 1670, mayor of New York and commissioned one of the council ; 1677, farmer of the weighhouse for 6500 guilders ; d. 1682, his son John his executor.

Dellius (Van Dell), Godefridus.... Ch : Jeane, bp. Oct. 25, 1685 ; Jean Allette, bp. Dec. 23, 1687. He came to Albany in 1683, as assistant minister to Domine Schaets and left in 1699, on account of his connection with the extravagant land grants ob-tained from the Indians. His salary for the first three years was 900 guilders *Hollands geldt* ($360) and for the next four years 400 pieces of eight ($400).

DeLong, James, and Margariet.... Ch : Mar-gariet, bp. March 7, 1736.

DeLooper, Jacobus Teunise, 1657, had an affray with Frans Barentse Pastoor ; 1658, quarrelled with Jan Roeloffse [Anneke Janse's son,] drew his knife and wounded him before the door of Jan De Wever ; same year he was schout or constable of the village.

DeMaecker, Pieter, a house carpenter ; in 1655 he owned a lot in New Amsterdam ; in 1657 the iron work which he furnished for the church at Be-verwyck was accepted for his subscription towards its erection. He returned to Amsterdam, Holland, about 1659, when he authorized the sale of his lot in Beverwyck.

De Manse, Adam, and Jannetie De Voy (Voe?) Ch : Catrina, bp. Nov. 24, 1751.

DeMarchal, Willem, a trader in Beverwyck, 1662.

DeMess, Benjamin, and Rachel.... Ch : Hester, bp. April 22, 1716.

DeMetselaer, see Metselaer.

DeMoer, Philip Philipse, and Elizabeth Ganse-voort. Ch : Sander, bp Jan. 24, 1686 : Jacob, bp. Aug 27, 1693. (See also *Schenectady Families*).

DeVysselaer, see Visscher.

Dennison, J., and Elizabeth.... Ch : Alexan-der, bp. Nov. 19, 1729

Dennison, Hugo, "Van Nieuw York," m. Rachel Vanden Bergh, Oct. 8, 1757. Ch : Jacobus, b. May 14, 1762 ; John, b. July 22, 1778. [Hugh Denniston, innkeeper, 1780.—*Hist. Coll. Albany*, I, 312.]

Dennison, James, and Lena (Hanna) Lansing. Ch : June 10, 1783 ; Rachel, b. Dec. 31, 1786.

Denniston, Isaac, and Eleanor Visscher She d. March 26, 1835, a. 71 y. Ch : [Elizabeth] no name given in baptismal register of the church, born Sept. 18, 1789, m. Col. Samuel Connord, and d. Feb. 8, 1865, a. 76 y. ; Hugh, b. Aug 15, 1793, d. March 30, 1852, a. 57 y.; Susanna, b. June 15, 1795 ; Margaret, b. July 24, 1802, d. July 23, 1823, a. 29 y. ; Sarah, w. of James Gourlay, Jr., d. Aug. 26, 1828.

Denniston, Gerrit Visscher, and Eleanor Visscher. Ch : Gerrit Visscher, b. April 27, 1791.

Denny, John, and Penella Lydie.... Ch : Lydia, b. Oct. 11, 1778.

DeNoorman, see Noorman and Bratt.

DePeyster, Johannes, grandson of Abraham De Peyster of New York, and born Jan. 14, 169¾, m. Anna Schuyler, Nov. 24, 1715. She was buried in the church Sept. 16, 1750. He was mayor of Albany, 1729–31 and 1732–3. Ch : Anna, bp. March 31, 1723, m. Volkert P. Douw ; Rachel, bp. May 30, 1728, m. Tobias Ten Eyck ; Myndert Schuyler, bp. March 6, 1834 ; Myndert Schuyler, bp. Sept. 2, 1739.

DeRemer, Pieter, and Elsie Barrington (Barb-ington). Ch : Elsie, b. May 3, 1777 ; Sara, b. Aug. 16, 1781.

Derham, Stephen, and Susanna Cool. Ch : Cath-arina, b. Oct. 22, 1780.

DeRham, see Rham.

DeRidder (Ridder), Evert, schoolmaster, m. Anna Van Nes (Esch) .... 1688. Ch : Annetie, bp. April 14, 1689 ; Gerrit, bp. Aug. 17, 1691 ; Maria, bp. Nov. 20, 1692 ; Gerrit, bp. Jan. 6, 1695 ; Hendrick, bp Jan. 17, 1697 ; Catrine, bp. March 19, 1699 ; Cor-nelis, bp. July 20, 1701 ; Killian, bp. Dec. 25, 1703 ; Rachel, bp. April 28, 1706 ; Simon, bp. Nov. 3, 1710 ; Marytje, bp. Jan. 18, 1713.

DeRidder, Gerrit, m. Anna Vanden Bergh, Jan. 3, 1722. Ch : Antje, bp. March 17, 1723 ; Susanna, bp. March 6, 1725 ; Maria, bp. Feb. 12, 1727 ; Antje, bp. June 21, 1729 ; Catharina, bp. Feb. 1, 1730 ; Ariaan-tje, bp Jan. 23, 1732 ; Rachel, bp. Feb. 5, 1738 : Ma-ria, bp. Feb. 26, 1744.

DeRidder, Cornelis, m. first, Susanna Vanden Bergh, Nov. 23, 1725. Ch : Antie, bp. Aug. 28, 1726 ; Susanna, bp. Sept. 3, 1727. He m. secondly, Ger-ritie Van Hoesen, July 7, 1733. Ch : Waters, bp. Dec. 2, 1733 ; Evert, bp. Jan. 11, 1741. [Cornelis DeRid-der was buried April 28, 1844.]

DeRidder, Hendrick, and Anna.... Ch : Geertie, bp. Oct. 10, 1731 ; Evert, bp. Feb. 21, 1735 ; Hen-drick Van Nes, bp. Jan. 9, 1740 ; Antje, bp. Sept. 26, 1742 ; Hendrick Van Nes, bp. June 3, 1744.

DeRidder, Simon, and Hilletie.... Ch : Anna, bp. Oct. 27, 1734.

DeRidder, Kiliaan, and Hilletie.... Ch : Wouter, bp. April 17, 1737.

DeRidder, Evert, and Marytje.... Ch : Johannes, bp. Dec. 31, 1738.

DeRidder, Wouter, and Anneke Vanden Bergh. Ch : Simon, bp. Feb. 1, 1761 ; Simon, b. Oct. 4, 1763 ; Simon, b. Dec. 18, 1765 ; Anneke, bp. Jan. 3, 1768 ; Jannetje, b. Aug. 27, 1770.

Derrith, see Dret.

DuFour (Foy, Voe, Fou, etc.), Jean, of " Halve maan," " *geboren tot* N. Y., *en wonende aan Bloe-mendal*," m. Catharina Vander Werken, May 11, 1706 ; Jan DeVoe was buried July 27, 1746. His wife was buried July 1, 1746. Ch : Jean, bp. Feb. 19, 1707 ; Geertruy, bp. Sept. 26, 1708 ; Geertruy, bp. Nov. 5, 1710 ; Jannetie, bp. Dec. 25, 1714 ; Wil-lem, bp. Sept. 23, 1716 ; Marretie, bp. Aug. 3, 1718 ; Isaac, bp. Dec. 11, 1720 ; Jannetie, bp. Jan. 20, 1723 ; Catharina and Ariaantje, bp. Sept. 26, 1725.

DeVoe (Vous), Jan, m. Fytje Vanderkar, May 17, 1735. Ch : Jan. bp. July 16, 1737 ; Lena, bp. Oct. 21, 1744 ; Catarina, bp. April 9, 1749 ; Dirk, bp. Nov. 12, 1752 ; Willem, bp. Aug. 17, 1755.

DeVous, Roeloff, m. Elizabeth Goeldin, Oct. 23, 1741. Ch : Jan, bp. Sept. 19, 1742 ; Maria, bp. Feb.

17, 1745 ; Catharina, bp. Aug. 23, 1747 ; Jan, bp. Dec. 18, 1748 ; Samuel, bp. May 5, 1751. Willem , bp. April 20, 1755 : Catharina, bp. June 5, 1757 ; Willem, bp. Jan. 6, 1760.

De Voe (Voy), Isaac, of " Halve Maan," m. Maritie Van Olinda (de Linden,) Aug. 19, 1750. Ch : Catarina, bp. Dec. 24, 1752 ; Martinus, bp. Dec. 22, 1754 ; Jan, bp. Nov. 20, 1757 ; Jannetie, bp. Nov. 9, 1760 ; Isaac, 4 *weeke oud*, bp. June 5, 1763 ; Gerardus, b. April 14, 1766.

De Voe, Johannes, and Maria Keller. Ch ; Coenraet, bp. March 14, 1753 ; Johannes, bp. April 30, 1758 ; Jacob, bp. July 19, 1761 ; Daniel, b. Sept. 15, 1770.

DeVoe (Tevoe), Johan Ernst, [perhaps the same as last] and Maria Keller. Ch : Abraham, bp. May 11, 1755.

DeVoe, Jurian, first wife Anna Kelder (Catharina Keller). Ch : Anna Margarita, bp. May 29, 1761 ; Anthony, b. March 3, 1764. Second, w. Elizabeth Dunning. Ch : Elizabeth, b. May 27, 1768 ; Maria, b. Feb. 20, 1771.

DeVoe, Daniel, and Catharina.... Ch : Annatje, b. Feb. 16, 1762.

DeVoe, Johannes, and Magdalena File, Ch : Isaac, b. Feb. 25, 1773 ; Maria, b. Feb. 24, 1778 : Celia, b. July 25, 1788.

DeVoe, Johannes, and Margarita Redly. Ch : Heiltje, b. May 25, 1777.

DeVoe, Jan, m. Annatie Connor, Sept. 10, 1778. Ch : Elizabeth b. June 18, 1779 ; Maria, b. April, 15, 1781.

De Vos, Andries, was in Beverwyck, as early as 1640, and magistrate in 1648 ; he owned the land north of Steuben and west of Pearl streets, extending across the *Vossen kil ;* besides this he owned and sold divers other lots as late as 1675. His wife (name unknown) and one child d. in March, 1665 ; he had at least three other children : a daughter who m. Barent Pieterse Coeymans, Cornelia, who m. Christoffel Davidts, and d. 1657 ; and Catalyntie who m. three husbands : 1st : Arent Andriese Bratt, by whom she had six children ; 2d, Barent Janse Van Ditmars, who was killed at Schenectady, Feb. 9, 1690; and 3d, Claas Janse Van Boekhoven, whom she survived, and died in Schenectady, in 1712.

DeVos (Vos, Vosje), Cornelis, Van Schoenderwoert, was in the service of the W. I. Company in Beverwyck, in 1652-7, and owned several houses and lots. He m. Dirckie Pieterse Coeymans, sister of Barent Pieterse C., who in 1665, when her effects were sold to pay her funeral expenses. Soon after he returned to Holland.

DeVries, Adriaen Dirckse, owned a lot in Beverwyck in 1654, which he exchanged with Wynant Gerritse [Vander Poel] ; complained of Harmen Herpertse and Seger Cornelise for blowing horns and ringing bells before his door and at him in presence of his neighbors ; 1661 gave power of attorney to Jan Bast : Gudsenhoven to collect 50 rix dollars for him in Holland on account of his son Dirk Adriaense who was supposed to be dead. One Adriaen Dirckse from Maersen (perhaps the above) m. Maritie Lievens, widow in New Amsterdam, July 23, 1745.

De Wandelaer, Johannes, from Leyden, Holland, trader, m. Sara Schepmoes of New York, March 17, 1672. He bought and sold divers lots in Albany, the last of which was on the east corner of State and Chapel streets which he purchased of Jan Thomase in

1678. He made his will June 20, 1705, and speaks of the following Ch : except Abraham and Pieter, but not of his wife. In 1702 he was a merchant in New York. Ch : Andries, eldest son, probably settled in N. Y., where he had a son bp April 2, 1704 ; Abraham bp. March 22, 1685 ; Sara, bp. April 3, 1687 ; Catarina, bp. Aug., 17 1689 ; Anna, bp. Feb. 7, 1692 ; Pieter, bp. Nov. 19, 1693 ; Alida, bp. Dec. 18, 1695 ; the three following were probably born in New York, Johannes ; Adriaen ; Pieter.

DE WANDELAER, Johannes, Jr., of Schaatkooke ; his house lot in 1714, was on the west corner of Broadway and Maiden Lane ; he also owned land in Schaahkook e which he sold to the city of Albany, in 1718, for £240. He m. Lysbeth Gansevoort, April 6, 1701. Ch : Sara, bp. July 20, 1701 ; Harmen, bp. Nov. 25, 1702 ; Johannes, bp. Oct. 22, 1704 ; Rebecca, bp. Sept. 29, 1706 ; Andries, bp. Dec. 15, 1708 ; Angenietje, bp. March 4, 1711 ; Pieter, bp. Sept. 20, 1713 ; Maria, bp. Dec. 25, 1715 ; Harmen, bp. Feb. 16, 1718 ; Adriaan, bp. May 19, 1722.

DE WANDELAER, Pieter, first wife, Ariaantie Van Vechten : she and her child d. and were buried in March, 1751. Ch : Johannes, bp. July 31, 1748 ; Barent, bp. March 11, 1750. His second wife, Anna (Bogardus) Van Vechten, widow, he m. March 10, 1753. Ch : Elizabeth, bp. Dec. 16, 1753 ; Johannes, bp. April 25, 1756, [Mr. John De W., of Palatine, d. Aug. 16, 1824, a. 69 y.] ; Johannatje, b. June 7, 1763

DE WANDELAER, Johannes G., m. Gerritje Gansevoort, May 14, 1777. Ch : Pieter, b. May 4, 1778 ; Maria, b. Dec 1, 1779 ; Harmen, b. Sept. 10 , 1781.

De Wever (Wever), Jan Martense, 1657, owned a house and lot and resided at Beverwyck until about 1664, when he became a tenant of Volkert Janse Douw and Jan Thomase, on the island *Schotack*, and was forbidden to proceed with the cultivation of the island by the Heer Rensselaer. In 1671, he and his wife Dirckie Harmense bought a farm behind Kinderhook where they resided in 1678.

De Weever (Weever). Abraham and Ann Kerni (Carnin, Kernin, Kerner, Kernel). Ch : Catarina, bp. Oct. 23, 1748 : Annatie, bp. March 25, 1750 ; Cornelis, bp. Feb. 23, 1752 ; Maritie, bp. Sep., 22. 1754 ; Margarita, bp. Jan. 23, 1757 ; Magdalena, bp. Sept. 19, 1762 ; Abraham, b. July 4, 1765 ; Abraham, b. July 21, 1766 ; Willem, bp. May 15, 1769. [Mr. Abraham Wever, d. March 23, 1809, a. 100 y. and Mr. Peter Wever of Ancram, d. Feb. 26, 1832, a. 99 y. 10 m.]

DeWilleger, Simon, and Jane Coon. Ch : Ann, b. Oct. 27, 1791.

DeWinter, Bastiaen, a native of Middleburgh, Holland, came to Schenectady about 1662. Falling sick, in 1670 he sold his house lot in Schenectady, together with his bouwery on the *Groote Vlachte* to Jan Lahatie, Joris Aertse Van der Baast, and Elias Van Guysling, with the intention of returning to Holland, but died before doing so. In 1678, the Dutch church of Albany claimed and probably obtained his property for the use of the poor. He seems to have left no heirs in this country.

DeWitt, Tjerck Claase, from Zunderland, Holland, 1661 he had one brother-in-law, Jan Albertse [Bratt ?] in Beverwyck, and another named Pieter Janse, in Oosterbemus in East Friesland, Holland ; T. C. DeW. in 1661 had land there inherited from his father from which he was receiving rents. He owned land at Esopus where he became a permanent resident about 1660. 1663 he was ordered to be punished at Esopus for opposing authority. He sold his house and lot in Albany in 1666. He m. Barber Andriese from Amsterdam, Holland, on April 24, 1656, in New Amsterdam.

DeWit, Jacob Bastiaanse, "weduwnaer Van Barber Gysbertse " m. Saartje Janse " weduwe Van Jan Jacobse Gardenier," Sept. 10, 1695. Ch: Annatie, bp. Jan. 7, 1700.

DeWit, Bastiaan, of Kinderhook, and Margarita Pearson (Pearse). Ch: Barbara, bp. Jan. 13, 1706.

DeWit, William, and Hester Dykman. Ch: Thomas, b. Feb. 27, 1779 ; Maria, b. June 1, 1781.

Diamond, William M., and Rebecca Wendell. Ch: Thomas, b. June 3, 1797 ; Mary Ann, b. Oct. 22, 1801 ; John Wendell, b. May 18, 1799 ; Alida Wendell, b. Nov. 27, 1803 ; Sarah, b. Nov. 22, 1806.

Dickinson, Charles, and Elsie Lansingh. Ch: Cornelia, b. Sept. 26, 1788.

Diel, Bastiaan, and Catharina Ruyter. Ch: Petrus, bp. April 8, 1757 ; Margarita, bp. Oct. 18, 1761.

Dillon, Hugh, and Judith Dunagoe. Ch: Mary, bp. Aug. 9, 1747.

Dingman, Adam, born in Haerlem in Holland, residing in Greenbush 1663 ; bought a farm 1677 in Kinderhoeck of his father-in-law, Jacob Janse Gardenier ; m. Aeltie Jacobse Gardinier ; in 1683 they made a joint will ; on March 20, 1720–21 he made a separate will in which he speaks of sons and daughters (not by name) and son-in law Pieter Cool. Ch: Jacob ; Janneke, w. of Pieter Barents Cool ; Josyntie, bp. Sept. 28, 1684 ; Garrit, bp. Jan. 16, 1687.

Dingman, Jacob, of Kinderhook, and Eva Swartwout. Ch: Adam, bp. Jan. 7, 1700 ; Johannes, bp. Feb. 13, 1704 ; Eefje, b. Sept. 17, 1706 ; Gerardus, bp. Jan. 9, 1709.

Dingman, Gerrit, of Kinderhook, m. Cornelia Gardenier, Sept. 22, 1714. Ch: Maria, bp. April 19, 1719 ; Elizabeth, bp. July 26, 1724.

Dingman, Johannes, and Marytje Muller, Ch: Geesje, bp. Dec. 17, 1749.

Dingman, Abraham, and Lena (Lea) Salsbury. Ch: Jacob, b. Feb. 4, 1785 ; Margarita, b. Nov. 11, 1788.

Dingman, John, and Catalina Springer. Ch: Philip, b. July 10, 1795.

Dobel, William, and Christina…. Ch: Catharina, b. Jan. 29, 1767.

Dole, James, m. Antje Van Santvoord, July 22, 1767. Ch: Staats Van Santvoord, b. August 6, 1768.

Dole, William, and Catharina McGurah. Ch: Jane, b. Dec. 4, 1775.

Donaldson, Irck (Isaac?) and Margaret Richey. Ch: William, b. Oct. 25, 1778.

Donnowa, (Dunnevan, De Lavil), Jan and Hopie (Hope), Hunt. Ch: William, bp. Feb. 22, 1738 ; Mary, bp. Oct. 16, 1743 ; Geertruy, bp. April 11, 1747.

Donneway, James, m. Elsie Smith, Nov. 20, 1768. Ch: Marytje, b. Aug. 9, 1769 ; John, b. May 27, 1771 ; Maria, b. Jan. 18, 1774 ; Geertruy, b. Dec. 11, 1775 ; Geertruy, bp. Oct. 17, 1777 ; Thomas, b. Aug. 16, 1779 ; Willem, b. March 23, 1782 ; Geertruy, b. Aug. 15, 1784 ; Catharina, b. Nov. 10, 1786 ; Margarita, b. March 5, 1789.

Dool, George, and Catharina Seger. Ch: Alexander, b. Sept. 6, 1778.

Dorscher, Volkert, and Geertruy Hilten. Ch: Barent, bp. Nov. 21, 1761.

Douw, Capt. Volkert Janse, from Frederickstadt was in Beverwyck 1638–1686. His house lot was on the west corner of State street and Broadway, property still owned by the family. He was a trader and brewer, and in connection with Jan Thomase dealt largely in real estate. Their brewery, situated on the east half of the Exchange block and extending to the river, they sold in 1675 to Harmen Rutgers, son of Rutger Jacobsen. In 1663, they bought of the Indians *Schotack* or *Apjen's* [Little Monkey's] island and the main land lying east of it. He also owned *Constapel's* island lying opposite Bethlehem, half of which in 1677, he sold to Pieter Winne. In 1672, he owned Schutter's island below Beeren island, which he sold to Barent Pieterse Coeymans. He m. Dorotee Janse from Breestede, Holland, April 19, 1650, in New Amsterdam. She was sister of Rutger Jacobsen's wife, and d. Nov. 22, 1781. He was deceased in 1686. He had the following sons : Jonas the eldest ; Henderick ; Volkert ; and probably Andries ; all of whom grew to maturity and had families.

Douw, Jan Andries, bought a house in Albany in 1678, and remained there until about 1690, when he removed to New York ; whether or how related to Volkert above is not known. His wife's name was Catryn…. Ch: Margriet, bp. Aug. 10, 1684 ; Elsie, bp. June 2, 1689 ; Adriaan, bp. in New York, June 22, 1691 ; Maria, bp. in New York, June 17, 1694 ; Maria, bp. in New York, Dec., 20, 1696.

Douw, Jonas Volkertse, of Manor Rensselaerswyck, m. first, Magdalena Pieterse Quackenbos, Nov. 14, 1682 ; and secondly, Catrina Van Witbeck, widow of Jacob Sanderse Glen, April 24, 1696. On the 7 Oct. 1736, he " in den Heer onslape op een Donderdag omtrent te 2 ure namiddag en 'Smaendags begraven na dat hy vier weken sick gewest is." He was buried in Greenbush. Ch: Maritie, bp. Oct. 19, 1684 ; Volkert, b. Nov. 14, 1686, and d. April 17, 1711 ; Dorothee, b. June 22, 1689 ; Pieter, b. March 24, 1692, and d. Aug. 21, 1775.

Douw, Andries, of Manor Rensselaerswyck ; in 1684, he was master of the open boat *John* plying between Albany and New York. He m. first, Effie Hanse ; secondly, Lydia De Meyer ; and thirdly, Adriana Vandergrift in New York. Feb. 24, 1708. Ch: Johannes, bp. Oct. 10, 1686 ; Catharina, bp Nov. 26, 1704 ; Catharina, bp. in New York, Dec. 19, 1708 ; Rynier, bp. in New York, Nov. 5, 1710 ; Volkert, bp. April 3, 1713.

Douw, Henderick, of Manor Rensselaerswyck, m. Neeltie Myndertse (Van Yvere) "weduwe Van Marten Gerritse Van Bergen," Oct. 3, 1697. He was buried May 18, 1751. Ch: Volkert, bp. June 26, 1698 ; Volkert, bp. Sept. 3, 1699 ; Dorothea, bp. March 23, 1701 ; Pietertje, bp. Aug. 16, 1602 ; Johannes, bp. June 25, 1704 ; Neeltie, bp. Nov. 27, 1709.

Douw, Volkert, of Manor Rensselaerswyck, m. Margareta Van Tricht, Nov. 16, 1701. She was buried Jan, 1752 ; he was buried Sept. 2, 1753. Ch: Dorothea, bp. Aug. 16, 1702 ; Abraham, bp. Nov. 17, 1706 ; Johannes, bp. Jan. 12, 1709 ; Elizabeth, bp. Oct. 24, 1711 ; Margarita, bp. April 14, 1717.

Douw, Andries, and Lidia … Ch: Anna, bp. Jan. 22, 1716 ; Wilhelmus, bp. April 11, 1718 ; Johannes, bp. April 22, 1722.

Douw, Petrus, m. Anna Van Rensselaer, dau. of Hendrick V. R., Oct. 8, 1717. He d. Aug. 21, 1775, a. 83 y. 5 m. 8 d. ; she d. April 3, 1756, a. 60 y. 2 m. 3 d. Ch : Magdalena, b. Aug. 1, 1718 ; Volkert, b. March 23, 1720 ; Hendrik, b. April 13, 1722 ; and d. Dec. 17, 1756, a. 34 y. 8 m. 3 d. ; Catharina, b. March 23, 1724, and d. Jan. 1, 1811, a. 86 y. 9 m. 8 d. ; Maria, b. Dec. 25 (Bible), bp. Nov. 25 (Church Records), 1725, w. of Johannes Gansevoort, and d. Aug. 17, 1759, a. 33 y. 7 m. 12 d. ; Margarita, b. Oct. 2 (Bible), bp. Sept. 7 (Church Records), 1729 ; Anna, b. Feb. 20 (Bible), bp. Feb. 5 (Church Records), 1732 ; Elizabeth, b. Dec. 1, 1733 ; Rachel, b. Feb. 27, 1736, d. Aug. 4, 1806, a. 70 y. 5 m. 3 d.

Douw, Abraham, m. Lyntie Winne, Jan. 6, 1730. She was buried Nov. 6, 1749. Ch : Elsie, bp. Aug. 22, 1731 ; Volkert, bp. Dec. 16, 1733 ; Pieter, bp. Nov. 2, 1735 ; Margrietje, bp. Nov. 23, 1740. [Abraham Douw and Catharina Lansing, m. Nov. 23, 1761.]

Douw, Volkert, Junior, and .... Ch : Henricus, bp. Aug. 6, 1732 ; William, bp. Oct. 26, 1735 ; Johannes and Abraham, bp. Oct. 5, 1740. [Henry Douw buried at Greenbush, Dec. 20, 1756.]

Douw, Volkert Pieterse, m. first, Anna De Peyster, May 20, 1742 ; and secondly, Marytje Cadwees [in 1762]. He was mayor of Albany, 1761–70 ; d March 20, 1801, a. 80 y. 11 m. 14 d. Ch : Anna, bp. March 27, 1743 ; Rachel, bp. Feb. 17, 1745 ; Myndert Schuyler, bp. Dec. 14, 1746 ; Magdalena, bp. Oct. 23, 1748 ; Magdalena, bp. May 27, 1750 ; Catarina, bp. Nov. 10, 1751 ; John De Peyster, bp. Jan. 25, 1754 ; Johannes De Peyster, bp. Jan. 25, 1756 ; d. Feb. 26, 1835, buried from his residence in State street ; Maria, bp. Oct. 19, 1760 ; Lyntje, b. June 13, 1763.

Douw, Johannes V., and Jannetie Bogaart. Ch : Volkert, bp. Aug. 12, 1742 ; Dorothe, bp. Oct. 24, 1742 ; Volkert, bp. May 27, 1744 ; Cornelis, bp. Sept. 8, 1745 ; Cornelis, bp. Nov. 16, 1746 ; Margarieta, bp. Oct. 23, 1748 ; Margarieta, bp. Oct. 22, 1749 ; Volkert, bp. Nov. 18, 1750.

Douw, Volkert A., and Annatie Wendell, m. Nov. 19, 1757. Ch : Johannes, bp. Sept. 17, 1758.

Douw, Andries, m. Catharina [De] Foreest, Jan. 23, 1767. Ch : Volkert, b. Feb. 26, 1768 ; Rachel, bp. June 31, (*sic*) 1770 ; Aaltie, b. Dec. 2, 1772 ; Rachel, b. May 25, 1775, d. Dec. 23, 1838, a. 63 y. 6 mo. 28 d. ; Volkert, b. Jan. 1, 1778, d. Nov 1, 1813, a. 35 y. 10 m. ; Annatie, b. Dec. 24, 1781.

Douw, Pieter Winne, m. Ryckie Van Schaick, July 21, 1762. Ch : Abraham, b. Aug. 19, 1764 ; Sybrand, b. March 25, 1767 ; Lyntje, b. May 17, 1778 ; Lyntje, b. Oct. 26, 1779.

Douw, Cornelis, m. Catharina Van Schaick, June 6, 1773. Ch : Jannetie, b. July 11, 1774 ; Johannes, b. Aug. 18, 1776 : Jannetie, b. March 11, 1781, Alida, b. June 16, 1784.

Douw, John DePeyster, m. first Debora Beekman, dau. of Jno. Jas. B., Dec. 23, 1787 ; secondly, Margaret Livingston in [1796] ; thirdly, Catharine D. Gansevoort, Jan. 22, 1811. He d. Feb. 22, 1835, a. 80 y. His first w. Debora, d. July 23, 1791, a. 27 y. 7 mo. 27 d. ; Catharine, wid. of Jno. D'P. D., d. April 13, 1848. Ch : Folker Pieter, b. April 10, 1790 ; Ann DePeyster, b. Jan. 31, 1797 ; Margaret Livingston, b. Nov. 26, 1798 ; Louisa, b. July 11, 1801 ; John De Peyster, b. Dec. 16, 1812 ; Mary, b. Sept. 3, 1815 ; Catharine Louisa, b. Sept. 10, 1817.

Douw, Sybrant, m. Lyntje Ten Eyck, March 31, 1794. He d. March 14, 1809 ; she d. Feb. 2, 1836, a. 66 y. Ch : Abraham, b. Oct. 10, 1794 ; Hendrick Ten Eyck, b. May 4, 1798.

Downal, John, and Lydia Donnan. Ch : William, b. Aug. 4, 1774.

Downall, Andrew, and Catharine Thompson. Ch : Christiaan, b. Dec. 17, 1778.

Downing, P. and Sarah ..... Ch : Sara, bp. Dec. 3, 1732.

Doxie, Dox, Dauchsi.

Doxie, Samuel, of Schaatkooke, "geboren in lang Eylandt," m. first, Barber Janse Goewey, Sept. 1, 1699 ; secondly, Lysbeth Bas (Janse), ... 29, 1707. Ch : Maria, bp. Dec. 2, 1702 ; Maria, bp. Dec. 31, 1704 ; Johannes, bp. Dec. 15, 1706 ; Alida, bp. Jan. 8, 1710 ; Thomas, bp. Feb. 10, 1712 ; Pieter, bp. May 24, 1713 ; Jacob, b. Jan. 27, 1720 ; Johannes, bp. April 12, 1723 ; Margarita, bp. Sept. 3, 1727 ; Johannes, bp. June 14, 1729.

Doxie (Doxs), Pieter, m. Geertruy Du Fou (Voe, Vou, Voow), May 23, 1736. Ch : Elizabeth, bp. May 15, 1737 ; Jan, bp. July 2, 1738 ; Samuel, bp. April 20, 1740 ; Maritie, bp. Oct. 16, 1743 ; Isaac, bp. Aug. 25, 1745 ; Pieter, bp. Jan. 3, 1748.

Doxs, Abraham, m. Rebecca Marselis, Jan. 14, 1742. Ch : Petrus, bp. Oct. 24, 1742, before the revolutionary war a skipper on the North river, d. at Benton, Yates Co., N. Y., in 1831, in his 90th y. ; Elisabeth, bp. April 8, 1744.

Dox, Thomas, and Elizabeth Van Woert (Becker). Ch : Samuel, bp. March 25, 1750 ; Pieter, bp. July 12, 1752 ; Maria, bp. Sept. 11, 1757.

Dox, Isaac, of Halve Maan, m. Lena De Voe, Nov. 15, 1766. Ch : Geertruy, b. Jan. 19, 1767 ; Jan, b. Nov. 11, 1771 ; Fytje, b. Dec. 30, 1777.

Dox, Jan, of Halve Maan, m. Marytje DeVoe, Nov. 26, 1771. Ch : Pieter, b. Feb. 26, 1772 ; Elisabeth, b. Aug. 17, 1774 ; Elisabeth, b. July 10, 1776 ; Pieter, b. Sept. 28, 1778.

Dox, Pieter, and Catalyntie Lansing. Capt. Pieter Dox, a soldier of the Revolution, d. at Hopeton, Yates Co., N. Y., Nov. 28, 1831, a. 89 y. Ch : Abraham, b. June 7, 1780 ; Wyntie, b. July 26, 1782, d. at Geneva, Feb. 10, 1826 ; Gerrit Lansing, b. May 13, 1784, appointed Postmaster of Albany after his brother's death ; in 1816, d. at Waterloo, Aug. 2, 1847, a. 62 ; Pieter, b. Sept. 27, 1785, Postmaster at Albany, d. Nov. (21) 27, 1815 ; Jacob, b. Dec. 18, 1787, d. at Geneva, Jan. 15, 1823, a. 36 y. ; Myndert Marselis, b. Jan. 6, 1790.

Dox, Pieter, m. Nancy Rendell, April 8, 1781. Ch : Thomas, b. Oct. 7, 1783 ; William, b. Nov. 24, 1785 ; Peter, b. Sept. 17, 1796.

Dret (Dareth, Derith, Droit, Duret), Jan, from Utrecht, m. Ryckie Van Dyck from same place, Nov. 1, 1654, in New Amsterdam. Soon after, he came to Beverwyck where he remained till his death in May, 1669. His name often appears in the Records as the buyer and seller of lots.

Dret, Jan, m. M. (Anna) DeVoe (Du Fou), Aug. 15, 1735. Ch : Jan, bp. Jan. 25, 1736 ; Rachel, bp. June 19, 1737 ; Catharyna, bp. June 17, 1739 ; Jannetie, bp. March 15, 1741 : Tobias, bp. Dec. 8, 1742 ; Isaac, bp. July 7, 1745 ; Rachel, bp. Sept. 11, 1748

DRET (Derith, Duret), John, m. first, Sara Revison (Levingston), May 22, 1763 ; and secondly, Nelly Duret in [1771]. Ch : Johannes, b. Oct. 17, 1763 : Isaac, b. Sept. 17, 1765 ; Tobias, b. Sept. 1, 1767 ; Rachel, b. Aug. 10, 1772 ; Annatie, b. Oct. 6, 1781.

Driesbach, Joost, and Caty Hooghstrasser. Ch : Elizabeth, b. July, 1793 ; Catharine, b. Aug. 15, 1795 ; Simon, b. Nov. 12, 1797.

Droit, see Dret.

Dubois, Jacobus, of Esopus, and Susanna Leg. Ch : Pieternella, bp. Jan. 25, 1708.

DUBOIS, Solomon, of Esopus, and Tryntje Gerritse. Ch : Cornelis, bp. Feb. 1, 1708.

DUBOIS (DeBoy), Salomo, and Ariaantje.... Ch : Hendrikus, b. March 23, 1775 ; Rebecca, b. May 18, 1777 ; Johannes, b. July 17, 1779.

Duer, William, and Catharina Alexander. Ch : John, b. Oct. 7, 1782.

Du Four, Du Fou ; Du Foy ; see De Voe.

Dulvebach, Christiaan, m. Cathalyna (Ann) De Foreest, June 25, 1764. Ch : Johannes, bp. Sept. 16, 1764 ; Rebecca, bp. Jan. 25, 1767 ; Abraham, b. Feb. 24, 1769.

Dulleman, Jan Barentse, baker, from Zwoll, Holland, in Beverwyck in 1661. His father Barent Barentse Van Ernst and mother Beertie Janse Dullemans, were both deceased in 1663.

Du Moree, Pieter, in 1676, owned land behind Kinderhoek.

Dunbar (Tumbarr), John, m. first, Bata Winne ; and secondly Maria Van Hoesen, April 1, 1724. He was b. Aug. 31, and d. May 7, 1736, in Schenectady. In 1714 he was associated with Rev. Thomas Barclay and Col. Peter Matthews in building the Episcopal church in Albany. In 1730, he removed to Schenectady where he resided on the south corner of Front and Church streets. He made his will April 13, 1736, wife not living, speaks of the following Ch : Robert ; John ; Mary ; Catharine ; Willempie ; and Alexander. He was a vintner or " taffering ceeper." Ch : bp. in Albany, Robert, Nov. 20, 1709 ; Jannetie, May 17, 1724 in Schenectady, Anna, Jan. 7, 1733 ; Alexander, Nov. 17, 1734.

DUNBAR (Tumbaar), Robert, m. Cornelia Spoor, Oct. 8, 1732. Ch : John, bp. April 8, 1733 ; Maria, bp. May 12, 1734 ; Gerrit, bp. Nov. 9, 1735 ; Maria, bp. May 27, 1739 ; Levinus, bp. March 14, 1742 ; Wilhelmus, bp. July 15, 1744.

DUNBAR (Tumbaar, Ten Baar), John, m. Helen Gerritse Lansing, April 19, 1755. Ch : Robert, bp. June 27, 1756 ; Eytje, bp. Feb. 11, 1759 ; Cornelia, bp. April 12, 1761.

DUNBAR (Ten Baar) Gerrit, and Cathalyntie Bratt (Bat). Ch : Cornelia, bp. Dec. 27, 1761 ; Margarita, b. Jan. 3, 1764 ; Maria, b. Sept. 28, 1766 ; Johannes, b. May 3, 1769 ; Margarita, b. Nov. 1, 1772 ; Robert, b. Dec. 1, 1776.

DUNBAR (Ten Baar), Lavinus, m. Margarita Hansen, Oct. 15, 1767. Ch : Robert, b. Dec. 10, 1767 ; Cornelia, o. Jan. 11, 1770 ; Robert, b. June 9 1772 ; Geertruy, b. Oct. 2, 1777.

DUNBAR (Ten Baar), Willem, m. Elizabeth Van Deusen, June 9, 1770. He d. July 10, 1825, a. 81 y. 1 mo. 22 d. She d. June 4, 1822, a. 73 y. 5 mo. 13 d. Tryntje, b. Nov. 26, 1770 ; Robert, b. June 19, 1773.

[Gen. Robert D., Jr., d. June 30, 1837, a. 64] ; Arent, b. April 27, 1776 ; Arent, b. Nov. 6, 1778, d. April 4, 1806, a. 28 y. 4 m. 28 d. ; Cornelia, b. Sept. 21, 1785.

DUNBAR, Robert, m. Annatie Slingerland, Nov. 27, 1780. Ch : Johannes, b. May 24, 1782 ; Cornelius, b. June 16, 1802.

DUNBAR, Jacob, and Margaret Crannel. Ch : Jacob, b. Feb. 24, 1791.

DUNBAR, Philip, and Susanna Angus McIntosh. Ch : Angus, b. July 22, 1795 ; Margaret, b. May 5, 1797.

Dunnevan, see Donnowa.

Duret, see Dret.

DuTrieux, or Du Triu ; see Truax.

Duyvendorp, Johannes, and Elizabeth.... Ch : Jacob, bp. April 6, 1740.

Dyckman, Jan, came to New Netherland in 1651, as book keeper, and to Beverwyck in 1654, as *commies*, which office he filled one year when he was disabled by insanity. He d. in Sept., 1672. His wife, Maria Bosyns, d. in 1676. They left two sons, Cornelis, b. 1647, and Johannes, who was b. 1662.

DYCKMAN, Johannes, of Benthem, Holland, m. Magdalena Tourneurs, of Midwout, June 15, 1673, in New York. Ch : baptized in New York, Daniel, bp. Dec. 3, 1673 ; Maria, bp. April 26, 1676 ; Gerrit, bp. April 6, 1678 ; Magdalena, March 27, 1680 ; Jan, bp. May 6, 1682 ; Grietie, bp. Jan. 11, 1685 ; Johannes, bp. in Albany, May 11, 1690 ; Jacob, bp. in New York, July 11, 1692.

DYCKMAN, Cornelis, of Niskayuna, 1685. Ch : Claas, bp. Feb. 23, 1690 ; Geertie, bp. in New York, July 18, 1694 ; Elizabeth, bp. in New York, Sept. 7, 1701.

Easterly, Thomas, m. Baata Van Woert, Dec. 8, 1779. Ch : Elisabeth, b. Aug. 27, 1780 ; Maria, b. July 16, 1782 : Thomas, b. March 7, 1783 ; Theunis, b. April 26, 1786 ; Catharina, b. Jan. 14, 1788 ; Martinus, b. Feb. 4, 1790 ; Charlotte, b. April 28, 1792.

Easton, John, and Janet Rutherford. Ch : James, b. Jan. 16, 1779.

Eaton, John, and Christiana McArthur. Ch : Barbara, b. July 27, 1796.

Ebbet, see Abbot.

Ecker, Thomas, and Elizabeth.... Ch : Marytje, bp. Oct. 2, 1720.

Edigh, Jacob, and Margaret York. Ch : Susanna, b. Sept. 23, 1790,

EDIGH (Ebigh, Eadick), Christopher, and Sophia Radley. Ch : Margaret, b. Nov. 18, 1792 ; John Radley, b. March 11, 1799.

Edich (Ettich), Frederick, and Geertruy Smith. Ch : Catharine, b. April 19, 1793.

Edurson (?) Thomas, and Christina. ... Ch : Willem, bp. July 3, 1763.

Egbertse, Barent, probably son of Egbert Teunise Metselaer or de Metselaer, m. Maria DeGarmean, Aug. 26, 1704 ; she was buried Jan. 9, 1725. Ch : Egbert Teunise, bp. Jan. 13, 1705 ; Pieter, bp. Sept. 19, 1708 ; Maritie, bp. Feb. 10, 1712 ; Catrina, bp. Jan. 23, 1715 ; Susanna, bp. April 6, 1718 ; Jacob, bp. Sept. 13, 1724. June 1, 1727, Barent Egbertse being about to marry Elsie La Grange, widow of Omy La Grange, dec'd, and dau. of Jan Van Loon, covenants to respect her rights in all property now owned or which may hereafter become hers.

EGBERTSE, Benjamin, probably a son of Egbert Thunise Metselaer or de Metselaer, and Annetje Visscher. She was buried Oct. 22, 1753. Ch: Egbert Teunise, bp. March 4, 1711; Marretje, bp. Feb. 21, 1714; Femmetie, bp. Jan. 16, 1717; Lena, bp. May 22, 1720.

EGBERTSE, Teunis, m. Engeltie Beekman, Feb. 28, 1716. Ch: Maretie, bp. July 15, 1716; Neeltie, bp. June 30, 1718; Susanna, bp. March 13, 1720; Lena, bp. Oct. 22, 1721; Egbert, bp. June 16, 1723; Lena, bp. Aug. 30, 1725; Anna, bp. Oct. 1, 1727; Maria, bp. Jan. 4, 1730; Lena, bp. March 11, 1733; Marten and Jacob, bp. June 3, 1736.

Egbertsen, Egbert B., m. first, Rachel ....; and secondly, Maria (Malli, Molly?) Lente (Linch). Ch: Barent, bp. Aug. 10, 1728; John, bp. Feb. 25, 1731; Petrus, bp. March 18, 1733; Rebecca, bp. April 13, 1735; Maria, bp. Dec. 12, 1739. The following are the second wife's Ch: Abraham, bp. July 6, 1743; Annatie, bp. April 25, 1746; Anthony, bp. July 10, 1752, d. Jan. (24) 23, 1833, a. 80; Jacob Visscher, bp. Jan. 29, 1758.

Egberts, Jacob, and Mary Kuis. Ch: Mary, bp. Sept. 26, 1749.

Egbertsen, Marten, m. Josina Schermerhorn, Jan. 28, 1772. Ch: Johannes, b. Jan. 26, 1778.

Eger, Johannes, and Catharina Young. Ch: Johan Nicolaas, b. March 22, 1763.

EGER, Nicolaas, Jr., and Geertruy Young. Ch: Elisabeth, b. July 1, 1763.

Eggelheymel, Hans Nicolaas, and Margarita. .... Ch: Hans Pieter, bp. Oct. 21, 1753.

Egmont, Jacob Claese, and .... Ch: Nicolaas, bp. April 13, 1684; Jacob, "geboren nae des Vaders doodt," bp. Dec. 27, 1685.

EGMONT, Jacob, in 1726, bought a lot of the city on the east corner of Pearl and Hudson streets; m. Anna Lansing, Oct. 19, 1716, was buried May 25, 1734. Ch: Elsie, bp. Jan. 28, 1718; Maria, bp. Nov. 8, 1719; Jacob, bp. Feb. 28, 1722; Gerrit, bp. May 5, 1723; Nicolaas, bp. Oct. 11, 1725; Catharina, bp. Nov. 19, 1727; Evert, bp. June 21, 1729; Johannes, bp. March 14, 1731; Catharina, bp. Sept. 17, 1732.

EGMONT, Jacob, m. Maria Lewis, Jan. 29, 1744. Ch: Annatie, bp. Feb. 17, 1745; Mary, bp. Aug. 14, 1748; Rachel, bp. June 7, 1752; Catarina, bp. May 7, 1758.

Eiby, Hannes, and Margarita Heenes (Heener). Ch: Anna, "geboren voor 7 weken" bp. Aug. 18, 1765; Juriaan, b. Oct. 21, 1766.

Eights, Abraham, and Catharina Brooks (Broecks). He d. Jan. 10, 1820, a. 74 y. She d. June 9, 1829, a. 80 y. Ch: Abraham, b. Oct. 21, 1771; [Dr. Jonathan E. b. 1773, d. Aug. 10, 1848, a. 75; Alida Wyncoop, his widow, d. May 15, 1849, a. 77 y.]; Rebecca, b. Dec. 23, 1777; Maria, b. Jan. 18, 1780; Elizabeth, b. Feb. 19, 1782; Rachel, b. May 7, 1784; Rachel, b. Jan. 21, 1786.

Eivry (Avery?), Thomas, and Elizabeth .... Ch: Thomas, bp. Nov. 23, 1760.

Elleth (Rylleth, Telleth, Ellis?), Nathaniel and Margarita .... Ch: Neth: Ealeweth, bp. Feb. 23, 1724; Anna, bp. Nov. 14, 1725; Jen, bp. Sept. 24, 1727; John, bp. Feb. 23, 1729.

Ellis, Frederick .... Ch: Nathaniel, bp. Sept. 25, 1687.

Elmendorf, Coenraad, "jong man Van Kingston en Ariaantie Gerritse weduwe Van Cornelis Martense Van Bueren," m. June 28, 1693. He m. secondly, Blandina Kierstede, mother of Jenneke, bp. Jan. 6, 1706.

Elmendorp, Jacob, Jr., and Lea Bloemendal. Ch: Coenraad, b. Sept. 25, 1781.

Elvendorf (Elmendorff?), Jonathan, and Margaret Fetter. Ch: John Fetter, b. March 9, 1792.

Elmendorff, Peter Edmund, and Eliza Van Rensselaer. He was an eminent lawyer and lived on the west side of Pearl street, third house north of the Female Academy, which his w. inherited from her mother, Maria Sanders, dau. of Robert Sanders and w. of Philip Van Rensselaer. This lot descended to her dau. Maria, w. of Peter Sanders. Peter E. Elmendorf d. May 15, 1835, a. 70 y.; she d. April 26, 1835 a. 58. Ch: Sarah, b. Dec. 31, 1793 (?); Maria, b. March 26, 1796; Edmund Peter, b. July 21, 1803; John Van Rensselaer, b. April 18, 1807; Catharine, b. Jan. 26, 1809; Edmund Peter, b. Nov. 24, 1813.

Emry, John, and Neeltie Staats. Ch: Maria, b. July 26, 1770.

Engels (English), Nathaniel, and Ida ... Ch: Margariet, bp. Dec. 28, 1735; Margariet, bp. March 8, 1738.

Ensign, Ezekiel, and Abigail Gibbs. Ch: Allen, bp. Jan. 21, 1778.

Erhart, Johannes, and Christina Wies. Ch: Willem, bp. May 9, 1756.

Erl (Earl?), William, and Ann .... Ch: William, bp. Oct. 27, 1761.

Ering, Samuel, and Saartje Oostrander. Ch: Catharina, b. July 5, 1773.

ERING, Hannes, and Elisabeth Wolff. Ch: Catharine, b. June 11, 1778.

Ertienberger (Ertberger), Daniel, and Regina Cath: Leonard (Leonling, Leenerien). Ch: Christoffel, b. March 17, 1765; Regina, b. Dec. 31, 1769; Daniel, b. Dec. 18, 1771.

Ertyberger, Jacob, and Lois Hungerford. Ch: Elizabeth, b. Sept. 6, 1798.

Erwin, John, m. Mary Thomson (McMillen), July 6, 1778. Ch: Margaret, bp. June 6, 1779.

Esmy (Ismy), Thomas, and Elizabeth Palmatier. Ch: Petrus, b. May 24, 1775; Isaac Hegeman, b. July 4, 1779.

Esselsteyn, Van Esselsteyn, Ysselsteyn.

ESSELSTEYN, Marten Cornelise, one of the first settlers of Schenectady on Oct. 23, 1668, he sold his bouwery to Claas Frederickse Van Petten and Cornelis Viele, and removed to Claverack. On Jan. 12, 1676-7, Marten Cornelise, b. in the city of Ysselsteyn, and Mayke Cornelise "b. in Barrevelt," both living in Claverack, made their joint will. He was not living in 1705. They had one son, Cornelise Martense.

ESSELSTEYN, Cornelis Martense of Claverack, and wife Cornelia Vandenbergh (Vredenbergh). He made his will June 21, 1740, proved Jan. 16, 1748-9, then spoke of wife Cornelia and Ch: Willem, eldest son, David; Jacob; Johannes; Isaac; Baata, w. of .... Van Deusen. The following were bp. in Albany: Tobias, Aug. 3, 1690; Abraham, Jan. 8, 1704; David, Oct. 28, 1705, who made his will Jan. 15, 1747-8, ... proved Jan. 17, 1748-9, in which he speaks of his mother; left his property to his brothers Johannes, Willem, Jacob and sister Baata.

Esselsteyn, (Iselsteyn), Willem and Feytie..... Ch: Jannetie, bp. Jan. 18, 1721.

Evans, Thomas, and Elizabeth ..... Ch: Mary, bp. Jan. 20, 1737.

Evertse, Jan, master shoemaker in Beverwyck, 1661-7. [This family were probably Lutherans.]

Evertse, Dirk and .... Ch: Aaltie, bp. in New York, June 29, 1663; Jannetie, bp. in New York, Aug. 31, 1664; Hendrick, bp. in New York May 8, 1667; Grietie, bp. in New York, May 5, 1672; Fytie, bp. in New York, Nov. 22, 1676; Hendrikie, bp. in New York, May 1, 1680; Richardt, bp. in Albany, Feb. 24, 1684; Evert, bp. Feb. 3, 1686; Arent, bp. Jan. 25, 1688; Arent, bp. March 17, 1689.

Everson, Benjamin, and Antje .... Ch: Tjerk Harmense, bp. April 20, 1712.

Evert Janse, kuyper (the cooper), perhaps son of Jan Evertse above; had a lot on east corner of Maiden Lane and Broadway in 1706, afterwards occupied by his son Johannes Evertse; made his will, April 8, 1725, proved Dec. 28, 1733, in which he speaks of sons Johannes Evertse, the eldest; Jacob; and Hans [who was buried in Lutheran church yard, Dec. 12, 1741.] He also had a son Abraham, bp. July 14, 1686. His wife was Maria ..... He was buried in the Lutheran churchyard, Nov. 8, 1726.

Evertse, Johannes, m. Barentje Bruyn, July 28, 1712. She was buried Feb. 5, 1752. [Jan Evertse, a cooper, lived in 1717, on east corner of Broadway and Maiden Lane.] Ch: Maria, bp. Oct. 8, 1713; Alitha, b. Dec. 26, 1714, was bp. in the Lutheran church, Jan. 1, 1715; Evert, bp. May 10. 1716.

Evertse, Johannes, m. Elizabeth Bouman, July 24, 1722. [Maria, wife of Johannes Everts, was buried Feb. 11, 1728.]

Evertse, Jacob, was buried Jan. 11, 1755. His wife, was Elizabeth.... Ch: Evert, b. at Coxsackie " de week voor Pinxter van dit jaer " and bp. in the Lutheran church at Klinkenberg, May, 26, 1706; Anna Maria, b. in the beginning of May, and bp. in the Lutheran church at Albany, May 23, 1708; Rachel, b. Nov. 8, 1710, and bp. in the Lutheran church, Feb. 4, 1711; Johannes, b. March 30, and bp. in the Lutheran church, April 15, 1716; Rebecca, bp. in the Dutch church, Sept. 21, 1718; Anna Maria, b. March 3, and bp. in Lutheran church April 8, 1721; Jacob, bp. Sept. 20, 1724, in the Dutch church.

Everts, Evert, and Marytje.... Ch: Johannes, bp. April 6, 1740.

Evertsen, Johannes, and Susanna La Grange. Ch: Bernardus, bp. Nov. 1, 1747; Evert, bp. Jan. 22, 1749; Elizabeth, bp. Feb. 17, 1751; Engeltie, bp. March 3, 1756; Hendrick, bp. March 8, 1761; Christina, b. March 13, 1763.

Evertsen, Nicolaas, and Elizabeth Vander Kar. Ch: Fytje, bp. July 29, 1750.

Evertse, Marten, and Catarina Steur. Ch: Johannes, bp. Aug. 19, 1753.

Evertsen, Barnardus, m. Martina (Maritie) Hoghen, July 8, 1771. He d. Jan. 24, 1802, a. 54 y. 2 m. 22 d.; she d. May 8, 1807, a. 57 y. 7 m. 4 d. Ch: William, b. Feb. 12, 1778, d. Jan. 18, 1798, a. 19 y. 11 m. 6 d.; Johannes, b. July 8, 1780, d. Nov. 17, 1832, a. 52 y.; Maria, b. Sept. 6, 1782; Jacob, b. July 21, 1784, d.

June 18, 1800, a. 15 y. 10 m. 28 d.; Engeltie, b. Nov. 3, 1789, d. March 22, 1799, a. 9 y. 7 m. 22 d.; Jane, bp. April 26, 1792.

Evert (Evertsen), John, m. Nancy Howard, Jan. 16, 1777. Ch: Margarita, bp. Nov. 21, 1779; Engeltie, b. Oct. 13, 1783.

Evertsen, Evert, m. Elizabeth Goewey, July 10, 1779. Ch: Susanna, b. June 13, 1780; Catharina, b. Feb. 28, 1782; Catharina, b. Jan. 18, 1784; Jacob, b. Jan. 19, 1790; Gerrit, b. June 6, 1792; Ann, b. July 20, 1797; Bernardus, b. May 10, 1799; Gerrit, b. Oct. 27, 1801.

Evertsen, Johannes, and Jennet White. Ch: Jacob Truex, b. Sept. 2, 1780.

Evertsen, Hendrik, m. first, Hendrikie Winne, Sept. 2, 1783; secondly, Cornelia Slingerland, Aug. 9, 1795. [Henry Evertsen, d. July 9, 1814, a. 53 y. 3 m. 6 d.] Ch: Susanna, b. June 2, 1784; John, b. March 20, 1789, d. July 5, 1834, in 45th y.; Fikie, b. March 5, 1792; Henrikie, b. April 3, 1796; Hendrikie, b. Oct. 19, 1797; Isaac, b. June 6, 1800; Henry, b. March 26, 1803.

Evertsen, Jacob, and Hannah Slingerland. He d. July 12, 1829, a. 62 y. 11 m. 23 d. Ch: Johannes, b. Nov. 5, 1789; Christina, b. Oct. 22, 1793; Jacob, b. March 31, 1796; Maria, b. Jan. 3, 1802; Abraham Truax, b. June 14, 1807.

Exeen, Alexander, and Catharyntje Waldron. Ch: Johannes, b. Aug. 11, 1776.

Eyter, Anthony, and Wyburgha.... Ch: Pieter, bp. Jan. 26, 1755.

Fairchild (Feerquil), Joseph (Jesse), and Marytje Gerritsen. Ch: Isaac, bp. Aug. 6, 1775; Rebecca, b. May 31, 1777; Susannah, b. July 19, 1779.

Fairlie, Major James, and Maria Yates. He was for 30 years clerk of the Circuit Court of New York city where he died Oct. 10 (?), 1830, at his residence, 41 Cortland street. Ch: Robert, b. June 25, 1796; Louisa, b. in New York Aug. 7, and bp. in Albany, Oct. 30, 1798.

Falkner, Domine Justus, and w. Gerritje. He was a Lutheran minister and officiated from 1704 to .... at various places from Albany to Long Island. He resided chiefly at Loonenburgh (Athens) or at a place near by called *Klinkenbergh.* In 1720 he lived at Claverack on *Preuwen hoeck.* Ch: Sara Justa, his 2d dau. b. May 2, 1720 at Loonenbergh.

Fallon, Patrick, and Margaret .... Ch; Eleanor, bp. Feb: 24, 1748; Margaret, bp. March 12, 1749.

Fallor, Zacharias, and Femmy De Foy. Ch: Zacharias, b. Sept. 14, 1777.

Fannine, Matthew, m. Mary Patrick, Jan. 15, 1724. Ch: Onar, bp. July 5, 1724.

Farquson (Farguson), Collin (Connel), and Mary McCarn. Ch: John, b. Sept. 2, 1776; Robert, bp. Jan. 29, 1779.

Farguson, Patrick, and Anna Forbes. Ch: Elisabeth, b. Nov. 20, 1777.

Farguson, Duncan, and Isabella Emerson. Ch: Isabella, bp. June 8, 1778.

Fatten, Francis Mark, and Catharine V. D. Groesbeeck. Ch: John, b. Dec. 13, 1799; Catharine Groesbeek, b. Oct. 23, 1801; William Groesbeek, b. Sept. 8, 1802.

Faulkner, William, and Margareta Anderson. Ch: Jenet and Isabel, b. May 11, 1778.

Feero, Hendrik, and Maria Van Vredenburg. Ch: Abraham, b. May 7, 1775; Catharina, b. May 14, 1779; Elias, b. Dec. 22, 1786; Rachel, b. March 11, 1789.

Feero, Christiaan, m. Catharina Levison, March 28, 1779. Ch: David, b. June 12, 1781; Maria, b. May 19, 1783; Pieter and Margarita, b. Nov. 23, 1786.

Fero, Petrus, m. Jannetie Van Deusen, Dec. 18, 1785. Ch: David, b. Aug. 3, 1786; Lea, b. Dec. 15, 1788; Cornelis, b. Sept. 16, 1789.

Feil (Fyle), Johan Melchior (Melchert), and Elisabeth Rickart, (Hansing, Hursinger, Hansinger). Ch: Elisabeth, bp. May 31, 1761; Maria, b. March 18, 1763; Catharina, b. May 7, 1764; Isaac, b. "in May," bp. July 13, 1766; Jacob, b. June 5, 1768; Magdalena, b. April 4, 1771; Melchert, b. May 3, 1773.

Ferguson, or Farquson, see Farguson.

Fester, Johannes, and Catharina .... Ch: Johannes, bp. Dec. 6, 1761.

Fetterly, Peter, and Hannah Borsley. Ch: Frederic, b. April 9, 1791.

Fierse, Pieter, and Mary Hunter. Ch: Catharine, b. Jan. 29, 1786.

Filman, Richard, and Sara Marll. Ch: Richard, bp. Dec. 6, 1778.

Fine, John, cooper, "Van Waterfort in Yrlandt," m. first, Jopje Claase Van Slyck (Schaak), June 4, 1696; and secondly. Alida Janse Gardenier, dau. of Jan Jacobse, G. of Kinderhook, Aug. 13, 1699. Ch: Willem, bp. Feb. 13, 1698; Catharine, bp. Dec. 29, 1700, was buried, Nov. 12, 1735; Jan, bp. Oct. 8, 1702.

Finke, Hendrik, and Annatie Cocks. Ch: Johannes, b. Dec. 3, 1776.

Finkelbach, Adam, and Helena Finger. Ch: Hannah, b. March 28, 1792.

Finky, Johannes, and Maria Luyts. Ch: Elizabeth, b. Oct. 20, 1776; Elizabeth, b. Aug. 16, 1778.

Fisher (see Visscher).

Flamisham, Dennis, and Rachel Milton. Ch: William, b. Dec. 13, 1794.

Flamsborough, see Flansburgh.

Flansburgh, Vlensburgh.

FLANSBURGH (Flamsborough), Peter, m. Maritie, Becker, Dec. 24, 1783. Ch: Sophia, b. July 12, 1791. [Peter Flansburgh and Frankse Van den Bogart " Van Niskatha," m. July 24, 1790].

Flat, Patrick, and Eleanor Viele. Ch: Patrick, bp. Nov. 26, 1749.

Flemming, James, m. Magdalena Gardenier, March 4, 1738. Alexander, bp. Dec. 17, 1738; John, bp. Jan. 7, 1741.

Flensburgh, Mattheus. m. Maria Van Zanten, Feb. 12, 1716. He had a lot near the "Horse Guard blockhouse;" corner of Hudson and Green streets in 1718; was buried June 8, 1739. Ch: Joannes, bp. Nov. 4, 1716; Catryna, bp. Aug. 24, 1718; Joseph, bp. Oct. 14, 1720; Margarita, bp. Dec. 2, 1722; Anthony, bp. Nov. 29, 1724; Margarita, bp. Feb. 12, 1727; Catharina, bp. May 25, 1729; Catharina, bp. Jan. 23, 1732 (?); Annatie, bp. July 7, 1732; David, bp. March 19, 1737.

FLENSBURGH, Daniel, m. Johanna Yates in New York, July 20, 1717. He was buried Aug. 24, 1725. Ch: Johannes, bp. June 30, 1718; Anna, bp. April 23; 1721; Margarita, bp. Jan. 8, 1723; Margarita, bp. Oct. 4, 1724.

FLENSBURGH, Johannes, m. Cornelia Hooghteling, Aug. 22, 1741. Ch: Mattheus, bp. May 23, 1742; Lena, bp. Feb. 12, 1744; William, bp. Sept. 28, 1745; Daniel, bp. May 29, 1752; Daniel, bp. Nov. 3, 1754; Maria, bp. June 19, 1757; Petrus, bp. Jan. 28, 1759; David, bp. May 3, 1761; Lena, b. Oct. 28, 1765; Maria, bp. March 15, 1769.

FLENSBURGH, Anthony, m. Anna Radcliffe (Redley), May 18, 1752. Ch: Margarita, bp. March 11, 1753; Lambert, bp. Oct. 23, 1755; Annatje, bp. Feb. 11, 1759; Rachel, bp. May 2, 1765; Mattheus, b. Aug. 13, 1768.

FLENSBURGH, Joseph, and Elizabeth Veeling (Veeder). Ch: Johannes, bp. March 10, 1754; James, bp. Jan. 4, 1756.

FLENSBURGH, Mattheus, m. Christina Schever (Snyder, Schneider), Dec. 17, 1762. Ch: Johannes, " 4 *weken oud*" bp. June 26, 1763; Andries, b. May 26, 1765; Willem, b. Jan. 21, 1767; Cornelia, b. April 24, 1775; Daniel, b. Aug. 2, 1778; Cornelia, b. Dec. 10, 1782; Adam, b. March 20, 1784.

FLENSBURGH, Willem, and Christina Boeckes (Bakkes, Bacches). Ch: Cornelia, b. Sept. 14, 1768; Coenraad, b. May 1, 1769; Marytje, b. July 3, 1770; Lena, b. July 9, 1777; Eva, b. March 17, 1782; Mattheus, b. July 3, 1784; Gerrit, b. April 16, 1787.

FLENSBURGH, David, m. Maria Smith, Aug. 17, 1782. Ch: Cornelia, b. March 17, 1783; Elizabeth, b. Sept. 16, 1787.

FLENSBURGH, John M., m. Catharine Bekker (Baker), July 11, 1785. Ch: Jacob, b. May 4, 1788; Elizabeth, b. June 11, 1790; Matthew, b. Oct. 26, 1792.

FLENSBURGH (see Flansburgh).

Fletcher, John, and Syntje Seger. Ch: Annatie, bp. Nov. 5, 1780.

Flinn, James, and Jannetie Vrooman. Ch: Abraham, b. Aug. 18, 1774; Pieter, bp. June 30, 1780.

FLINN, Johannes, and Catharine Keesselbery. Ch: John, b. Nov. 14, 1779.

Flint, Robert, and Johanna (Susanna), ... in 1735 he had a lot on Gallows Hill. Ch: Adam, bp. Nov. 23, 1735; Alexander, bp. Nov. 6, 1737.

Flipse Frederick, carpenter in 1663, of Amsterdam in New Netherland, wife Margarita Hardenbroeck.

Flodder, see Gardenier.

Florid (Floyd), James, and Margarita Seger. Ch: Margarita, bp. March 14, 1781.

Follett, Charles, and Mary Bloodgood. Ch: Francis, b. March 5, 1768; Joseph, b. Jan. 10, 1779.

Follinsby (Volansby), George, and Jannetje Van Valkenburg. Ch: Johannes and Catarina, bp. May 10, 1752.

Follansbee (Vollansby), Jeroom, m. Elizabeth Witbeck, Dec. 25, 1777. Ch: George, b. March 1, 1778.

Fonda, Jillis Douwese, was in Beverwyck as early as 1654, his wife was Hester ....; in 1666 a suit was brought against her for removing Lodovicus Cobes' wife's petticoat from the fence; defendant said plaintiff pawned the article for beaver; put over; 1664 Hester Douwse assisted by her son Douw Gillise and daughter Greetien Gillise sold to Jan Coster Van Aecken two distiller's kettles for 400 gl. seewant. She was then probably a widow. In 1666 Hester Douwse was the widow of Barent Gerritse.

FONDA, Douw Jillese, and Rebecca.... He owned land at *Lubberde land* (Troy) in 1676, d. Nov. 24 (27), 1700. Ch: Jan. b. 1668; Jillis; Isaac, bp. March 9, 1684; Rebecca, bp. March 17, 1786; Anna, bp. Feb. 2, 1690; Claas (?).

FONDA, Jillis, gunstocker of Schenectady, m. Rachel Winne, Dec. 11, 1695. Ch: Douwe, bp. Aug. 23, 1696; Tanneken, bp, March 9, 1698. See *Schenectady Families.*

FONDA, Johannes, of manor Rensselaerwyck, m. Maritje Loockermans, Dec. 5, 1694, he was buried June 26, 1740. Ch: Rebecca, bp. May 10, 1696; Pieter, bp. Nov. 7, 1697; Maria, bp. Jan. 7, 1700; Douwe, bp. Sept, 28, 1701; Johannes, bp. Nov. 7, 1703; Catharina, bp. Jan. 23, 1706; Abraham, bp. Jan. 18, 1708; Lena, bp. Oct. 28, 1710; Geertruy, bp. Feb. 21, 1714.

FONDA, Isaac, m. Alida Lansing, dau. of Hendrick and Elisabeth L., Dec. 30, 1707. She was buried March 23, 1748. Ch: Douw, bp. July 24, 1709; Elisabeth, bp. in New York, July 4, 1711; Rebecca, bp. Feb. 21, 1714; Henderick, bp. July 15, 1716; Abraham, bp. Aug. 10, 1718; Maria, bp. June 4, 1721; Isaac and Jacob, bp. June 31 [30], 1723.

FONDA, Claas, m. Annetie Marselis, Nov. 16, 1716. She was buried Sept. 5, 1751. Ch: Rebecca, bp. April 14, 1718; Gysbert, bp. Sept. 25, 1720; Douwe, bp. Feb. 2, 1724; Elisabeth, bp. May 13, 1727; Barber, bp. Nov. 9, 1729; Douwe, bp. Nov. 27, 1732.

FONDA, Pieter, m. Maritie Beeckman, March 7, 1724. She was buried Nov. 5, 1744. Ch: Maria, bp. June 7, 1724; Catalyna, bp. Nov. 7, 1725; Lena, bp. Oct. 8, 1727; Rebecca, bp. Nov. 9, 1729; Johannes, bp. March 4, 1733; Johannes, bp. Oct. 12, 1735.

FONDA, Douw Isaacse, m. Aaltje Onderkerk, dau. of Isaac O. and Mayke Van Nes, March 2, 1727. He had a lot on east side of Pearl, corner of Columbia, opposite Johannes Maas Van Bloemendaal's, in 1736. Ch: Isaac, bp. Jan. 17, 1728; Maria, bp. Jan. 4, 1830; Jan, bp. Jan. 10, 1731; Alida, bp. Oct. 7, 1733; Maria, bp. Aug. 13, 1735; Mayke, bp. Oct. 21, 1737; Mayke, bp. Jan. 14, 1739; Isaac, bp. April 15, 1744.

FONDA, Douw, m. A. Van Nes, Oct. 29, 1732. Ch: Abraham, bp. March 25, 1733; Maria, bp. Aug. 13, 1735; Hendrikje, bp. March 1, 1738; Jacob, bp. March 29, 1741; Rebecca, bp. April 15, 1744.

[It is not easy to distinguish the children belonging to the above two Douw Fondas, by the church register. The above distribution is the best that could be made by the compiler.]

FONDA, Abraham, and Elbertje (Hendrikje) Van Alen. Ch: Jan. bp. March 23, 1735; Stephanus, bp. Aug. 11, 1736; Stephanus, bp. April 16, 1738; Petrus, bp. March 8, 1740; Laurens, bp. Jan. 10, 1742; Abraham, bp. Jan. 18, 1744; Elbertje, bp. Dec. 27, 1747.

FONDA, Johannes, and M. .... Ch: Jan, bp. Sept. 5, 1736. [The w. of Johannes Fonda was buried at the Patroon's June 12, 1755.]

FONDA, Hendrik, m. first Anna Van Vechten, Feb. 17, 1739; secondly, Catharina Groesbeek [1745]. Ch: Alida, bp. Aug. 31, 1740; Isaac, bp. May 12, 1745; Elisabeth, bp. Oct. 25, 1747; Isaac, bp. Jan. 13, 1751; Geertje, bp. June 15, 1755; Johannes, bp. Aug. 27, 1758; Johannes, b. Feb. 19, 1760.

FONDA, Abraham Isaacse, m. Maria Van Schoonhoven, Sept. 8, 1743. Ch: Alida, bp. Feb. 17, 1745; Jacobus, bp. Dec. 25, 1746; Alida, bp. July 30, 1749;

Isaac, bp. May 22, 1752; Susanna, bp. April 3, 1757; Abraham, bp. Oct. 7, 1759; Abraham, bp. Oct. 14, 1759.

[The baptism of this last child seems to have been entered twice in the Church Register.]

FONDA, Isaac Isaacse, and Cornelia (Cordelia) De Foreest. Ch: Alida, bp. April 16, 1749; Neeltie, bp. Nov. 18, 1750; Isaac, bp. May 6, 1753; Jesse, bp. Aug. 3, 1755; Jesse, b. Feb. 14, 1760.

FONDA, Douwe, and Aaltje Van Buren. Ch: Elisabeth, bp. Jan. 13, 1751; Rebecca, bp. Dec. 14, 1755.

FONDA, Johannes, m. Elisabeth Ouderkerk, Dec. 10, 1750. Ch: Eldert, bp. April 28, 1751; Aaltje, bp. June 14, 1752; Helena, bp. May 12, 1754; Douw, bp. July 6, 1755; Isaac, bp. Jan. 16, 1757; Johannes, bp. June 11, 1758; Abraham, bp. Oct. 15, 1759 (?); Jacob, bp. May 3, 1761; Annatje, *oud* 4 *Weken* bp. Dec. 27, 1762; Pieter, b. March 28, 1764; Cornelius, b. April 12, 1766; Willem, b. July 23, 1768; Douwe, b. Aug. 17, 1771.

FONDA, Isaac D., and Susanna (Saintje) De Foreest. Ch: Abigail, bp. Sept. 9, 1753; Douwe, bp. Oct. 13, 1754; David, bp. Jan. 16, 1757; Douwe, bp. Aug. 26, 1759; Johannes, bp. April 6, 1761; Abigail, b. May 28, 1766; Phillipus, b. May 30, 1768; Aaltje, b. July 8, 1770.

FONDA, Gysbert, m. Elsie Douwe, Oct. 6, 1753. She d. July 24, 1823, a 92 y., at 320 North Market St. Ch: Nicolaas, bp. Dec. 21, 1755; Leyntje, bp. April 23, 1758; Lyntje, bp. Sept. 29, 1761; Nicolaas, bp. Oct. 9, 1764; Nicolaas, b. Sept. 29, 1768; Nicolaas, b. 1770, d. Feb. 27, 1797, a. 27y. 4m. 23d.; Abraham, b. April 5, 1773.

FONDA, Johannes, m. Dirkie Winne, March 18, 1757. Ch: Maria, bp. Nov. 13, 1757; Pieter, bp. July 15, 1759; Rachel, b. Aug. 18, 1760; Pieter, b. June 13, 1763; Daniel, b. Jan. 18, 1769; Cathalina, b. March 5, 1771; Willem, b. Jan. 9, 1773; Johannes, b. April 2, 1775; Tanneke, b. June 21, 1780.

FONDA, Jan, m. Eegie Vander Zee, Jan. 5, 1759. Ch: Susanna, bp. March 9, 1760; Susanna, b. Dec. 8, 1762; Wouter, b. June 4, 1764; Elisabeth, b. May 16, 1766; Maria, b. June 2, 1768; Johannes, b. July 20, 1770; Wyntje, bp. Aug. 2, 1772; Johannes, b. Aug. 5, 1776.

FONDA, Isaac, m. Rebecca Groesbeck, Jan. 1, 1766. [Isaac Fonda m. Sara Wynkoop, Nov. 22, 1779.] Ch: Douwe, b. Dec. 7, 1767; Jannetje, b. Nov. 16, 1769; Wouter, b. Dec. 13, 1771; Alida, b. Feb. 21, 1773.

FONDA, Jacob, m. Dirkie Visscher, Dec. 10, 1768. Ch: Douwe, bp. Aug. 28, 1769; Harmen, b. Aug. 9, bp. Aug. 21, 1771; Harmen, b. Oct. 11, 1773.

FONDA, Abraham D., m. Hendrikje Lansing, Aug. 20, 1771. Ch: Douwe, b. Sept. 2, 1772; Sara, b. Nov. 7, 1773; Aaltie, b. March 28, 1775; Douwe, b. Oct. 13, 1776; Anneke, b. Jan. 1, 1779; Anna, b. Oct. 13, 1781.

FONDA, Isaac J. (Junior), m. Antje Van Santvoord, April 11, 1779. Ch: Isaac, b. Dec. 6, 1780, d. at Cohoes, Dec. 6, 1859, a. 80 y.; Cornelis, b. Sept. 12, 1781; Jesse, b. April 27, 1786; Jacob, b. March 11, 1790.

FONDA, David, and Catharina Ten Broeck. He d. Aug. 3, 1805, a. 48 y. 6 m. 22 d. Ch: Susanna, b. Jan. 11, 1781; Johannes Ten Broeck, b. Feb. 15, 1782; Elizabeth, b. Nov. 7, 1783; Isaac, b. Aug. 30, 1785; Tobias, Feb. 20, 1787; Johannes, b, Nov. 19, 1788; Mary, b. July 2, 1790.

FONDA, Johannes H., and Alida (Aaltie), Levison. Ch: Hendrik, b. Feb. 5, 1783; Maria, b. Dec. 15, 1786; Catharina, b. July 2, 1788.

FONDA, Douwe and Machtel Lansing. Ch: Lansing, b. March 21, 1789. [Douw F. m. Matilda Beekman, Nov. 22, 1794, and d. May 17, 1833, a. 74 y. 1 mo. 6 d. She was b. Nov. 21, 1768, d. Oct. 3, 1837.]

FONDA, Johannes (J. Jun ?), m. Cornelia Hun, Oct. 19, 1783. Ch: Sara, b. June 5, 1784; Isaac, b. March 7, 1786; Maria, b. July 3, 1788; William, b. Aug. 27, 1791; Cornelia, b. Aug. 4, 1797.

FONDA, Jacobus (James), m. Willempie Bogert, Aug. 30, 1783. Ch: Maria, b. Feb. 7, 1784; Willempie, b. Feb. 9, 1785; Abraham, b. Aug. 28, 1786; Abraham, b. March 18, 1788; Rebecca, b. Jan. 3, 1790; Alida, b. Aug. 22, 1791; Abraham, b. March 10, 1793; Douw Bogert, b. Feb. 23, 1795; Isaac, b. Nov. 1, 1796; Magdalena, b. Sept. 25, 1798, d. Feb. 20, 1838, in 41st yr.

FONDA, Abraham, H. (?), and Penina Petteson. Ch: Isaac, b. Oct. 17, 1785.

FONDA, Walter, and Catrine Fort. Ch: Egje, bp. Oct. 19, 1788.

FONDA, William, and Susanna Halenbeck. Ch: [name omitted], b. Aug. 20, 1795; Cornelia, b. Feb. 17, 1797; William, b. Oct. 28, 1800.

FONDA (?) (Sardy), Eliahan (?), and Rachel Hun. Ch: Catalina, b. March 25. 1797.

Foot (Food), James, and Elizabeth Williams. Ch: Margaret, bp. Nov. 3, 1779; John, bp. Sept. 27, 1784.

Foot, Asa, m. Caty (Catharine), Davis (David), Jan. 19, 1790. Ch: Ephraim, b. Nov. 6, 1790; Henry, b. Feb. 7, 1799; Elizabeth, b. Aug. 31, 1801; James, b. Dec. 18, 1803.

Forbellot. Ch: and Uz....Ch: Ann, bp. Oct. 5, 1733.

Foreest and Forrest, see DeForeest.

Forseight (Forsyth ?), Alexander, m. Mary Fraser, Dec. 10, 1776. Ch: Jane, b. Oct. 24, 1777.

Forster, Jacobus (Jacob), and Jenneth Jenkins. Ch: Jacobus, bp. Nov. 12, 1771; Johannes, b. Sept. 17, 1776; Peter, b. June 3, 1793.

Foster, James, and Elizabeth Clinton. Ch: Nancy, b. July 5, 1803; Clinton, b. Nov. 25, 1804.

Fort, Jan, Orangien (of Fort Orange ?), widower, m. Marie Grande, in New Amsterdam, Nov. 24, 1641.

FORT (La Fort, Vander Vort, Libertee), of Niskayuna, and Margriet Rinckhout. He made his will Nov. 3, 1706, proved Oct. 3, 1707, in which he makes mention of the following Ch: Anna; Johannes; Abraham; Nicolaas; Jacob; Mary; Daniel, bp. Sept. 1, 1687; Isak, bp. Sept. 3, 1699.

FORT (Le Fort), of Half Moon, 1720, m. Gerritie Vanden Bergh, Oct. 23, 1709. Ch: Margarita, bp. April 30, 1710; Margriet, bp. Feb. 10, 1712; Teuntje, bp. Sept. 27, 1713; Johannes, bp. Sept. 18, 1715; Ariaantje, bp. April 28, 1717; Eva, bp. Dec. 21, 1718; Gerrit, bp. Sept. 18, 1720; Margarita, bp. June 24, 1722; Isaac, bp. June 28, 1724.

FORT, Jan, of Nistigieone, and Rebecca Danielse Van Antwerpen. Ch: Joannes, bp. Oct, 12, 1713; Maria, bp. April 7, 1715; Margarita, bp. Jan. 21, 1728. (See *Schenectady Families*).

FORT, Abraham, of Schaagkooke, 1720, and Anna Barber Clute. Ch: Frederick, bp. April 9, 1721. See *Schenectady Families*.

FORT (De Fort) Jacob (Jacobus), of Half Moon, 1734, m. first, Sara De Wandelaer, Jan. 14, 1726; and secondly, Maritie Oosterhout [1750.] Ch: Elisabeth, bp. April 23; 1727; Johannes, bp. Jan. 12, 1729; Abraham, bp. Feb. 3, 1731; Margarita, bp. March 24, 1734; Harmen, bp. Jan. 8, 1737; Leendert, bp. July 6, 1744; Abram, bp. May 19, 1751; Elisabeth, bp. Nov. 3, 1753.

FORT, Isaac, of Schachtekooke, 1751, m. first, Jacomyna Viele, Sept. 7, 1729; secondly, Sara Viele of Stillwater, July 7, 1751. Ch: Margarita, bp. in Schenectady, Feb. 13, 1732; Maria, bp. Jan. 8, 1735; Johannes, bp. Oct. 16, 1736; Maria, bp. May 13, 1739; Gerritje, bp. May 29, 1757; Louis, bp. May 6, 1759; Johannes, bp. Sept. 6, 1761.

FORT, Johannes, of Genistagioene, m. Maria Van Vranken, in Schenectady, Nov. 24, 1750. Ch: Nicolaas, bp. Jan. 14, 1753. See *Schenectady Families*.

FORT, Abraham, m. first, Sara Van Woert, Nov. 18, 1752; secondly, Eva Bennewe (Benoit), July 1, 1758. Ch: Margarita, bp. Dec. 30, 1753; Sara, bp. Jan. 6, 1760; Jacob, b. May 22, 1763; Annatie, bp. Jan. 30, 1767.

FORT, Frederick, and Debora Van .... Ch: Elisabeth, bp. April 15, 1753.

FORT, Harmen, and Rebecca Van Woert. Ch: Hendrikie, bp. June 7, 1761; Sara, b. Jan. 11, 1763; Jacob, b. July 12, 1764; Margarita "*in huis gedoopt*," June 9, 1766; Margarita, bp. in Schenectady, Sept. 4, 1768; Annatie, bp. June 17, 1770; Marytje, b. Dec. 18, 1772.

FORT, Gerrit, and Catharina Van Aalsteyn. Ch: Cornelia, b. Aug. 15, 1763.

FORT, Simon, of Onostoungjoone, m. Annatie Vranken, in Schenectady, Oct. 22. 1762. Ch: Ryckert, b. Aug. 12, 1766. See *Schenectady Families*.

FORT, Johannes, and Elizabeth Quackenbush. Ch: Isaac, b. June 25, 1768; Petrus, b. Sept. 4, 1777.

FORT, Nicolaas, and Catharine Van den Bergh. Ch: Abraham, b. April 18, 1783.

Frank, Nicolaas, and Elizabeth Fonda. Ch: John, b. June 17, 1787; Catharina, b. March 22, 1790; James, b. March 22, 1803.

FRANK, John, and Isabella Eesbester (Isbister). Ch: John, bp. March 18, 1792; Isaac Van Arnhem, b. Oct. 28, 1796; Ann, b. Oct. 10, 1798.

Fraser, James, and Mary .... Ch: Jean, bp. Oct. 24, 1758.

Frederick, Jacob, and Christina Metiker. Ch: Maria Magdalena, b. Sept. 21, 1771.

Frederickse, Carsten, Van Ieveren, master smith. He and his brother Myndert Frederickse (See *Myndertse*), had their smith shop on the north corner of Broadway and Spanish (now Hudson) street, and owned also a lot on north corner of Broadway and State street. His wife was Tryntje Warners. They made a joint will, July 1, 1689, in which they speak of their four children. Margaret, a. 20 y.; Warner, a. 15 y.: Anna Marytje, a. 12 y., who owned the lot on north corner of Broadway and State street, in 1714, and was buried Sept. 18, 1728; Magdaleentje, a. 9 y.

Freehold, Abraham, and Catarina..... Ch: Catarina, bp. June 24, 1759.

Freelich, Marten, and Anna Maria Hagedorn. Ch: Christoffer, b. April 12, 1764.

Freeman, Mark, and Frances..... Ch: Elizabeth, bp. June 19, 1759.

FREERMAN, Dominie Barnhardus, minister at Schenectady, 1700-5, m. Margarita Van Schaick in New York, Aug. 25, 1705. He d. in 1841, and she Jan. 18, 1738. Their dau. Anna Margarita, m. her cousin David Clarkson, son of the secretary of the province.

Freet, Abraham, and Jannetje Hetcher. Ch: Frederick, b. Sept. 13, 1764.

Frets, Jacob, and Margareta Ernstpets. Ch: Johannes, bp. Feb. 20, 1757.

Frey, Jacob, and Alida Barheit. Ch: Johannes, bp. Sept. 8, 1754.

Freydach, Henderick, and Christina Deppen. Ch: Johannes, bp. Nov. 10, 1754.

FREYDACH, Coenraad, and Christina Debt. Ch: Coenraad "oud 6 weken," bp. Dec. 19, 1762; Abraham, b. Oct. 1, 1764.

Friday, Philip, and Hannah Bussing. Ch: Mary b. Aug. 11, 1797. See Vrydag also.

Frielinghuysen, Dominie Theodorus, came to Albany in 1746, as pastor of the church, his first recorded baptism was on the 20th of July, the last was on Oct. 14, 1759. He sailed from New York on Oct. 10 (?) 1759, for Holland, from whence he never returned. His wife was Elizabeth Sims. Ch: Eva, bp. Dec. 5, 1756; Eva, bp. Sept. 10, 1758.

Fry, Michael, of Halve Maan m. Engeltie Vanderkar, Feb. 2, 1762. Ch: Dirck, "geb: voor 3 weken," bp. Aug. 5, 1764.

Fryer, Isaac, and Elizabeth.... In 1720 he had a lot on north corner of Pearl and Hudson streets, 35 by 120 ft. and in 1730 another lot on north side of Hudson street the 5th east from Pearl. He was buried "in the English church" Aug. 3, 1755. Ch; William, bp. March 11, 1722; Lydia, bp. Nov. 10, 1723; Isaac, bp. Nov. 25, 1725; Lydia, bp. Nov. 12, 1727; Catharine, b. 1731, d. Oct. 3, 1791, a. 60 y. 2 m. 3 d.

Fryer, John, and Annatie Van Zanten. Capt. John Fryer, d. July 23, 1784, a. 64 y. Ch: Sarah, bp. Dec. 6, 1747; Sarah, bp. Nov. 26, 1749; Sarah, bp. Feb. 23, 1752.

FRYER, John, m. Elizabeth Van Woert, March 2, 1759. Ch: John, bp. Oct. 15, 1758 (9?): Annatie, bp. Jan 17, 1762; Jacob, b. Oct. 9, 1764: Elizabeth, b. Jan. 10, 1766; Eldert, b. Jan. 4, 1768; Josina, b. March 4, 1770; Lena, b. Sept. 27, 1772; Christina, b. Jan. 13, 1775; Willem, b. Oct. 27, 1777.

FRYER, Willem, and Hanna Ferrel. Ch: Isaac, b. March 6, 1762.

FRYER, Abraham, and Jannetie Hetril, Ch: Annatie, b. Nov. 14, 1762; Maria, b. Oct. 19, 1767.

FRYER, Isaac, and Elizabeth Hilten. He d. June 13, 1802: a. 68 y. 5 m. 19 d. ; She d. Sept. 27, 1794, a. 57 y. 10 m. 28 d. Ch: Willem, b. Nov. 15, 1764 d. Dec. 27, 1815, a. 51 y. 16 d. ; Anny, b. Feb. 6, 1776.

FRYER, Johannes, and Catharina Kennryk. Ch: Johannes, b. March 3, 1766, d. Dec. 16, 1815, a. 49 y. 15 d.

FRYER, Johannes, and Mary Follewyzer. Ch: John, b. Oct. 11, 1784; Maria, b. April 14, 1786; John, b. June 18, 1788; Annatie, b. Oct. 3, 1790; Elisabeth, b. Sept. 2, 1793.

FRYER, Isaac Isaacse, m. Catharina Van Wie, Oct. 8, 1784. He d. May 10, 1831, a. 64 y., and she d. May 3, 1850, a. 85 y. Ch: Sara, b. Feb. 9, 1787.

FRYER, Jacob, m. Agnietje (Annatie, Hannah), Muller, Dec. 25, 1787. Ch: Philip, b. July 14, 1788; Annatie, b. Feb. 10, 1790; Geertruy, b. Jan. 16, 1792; John, b. Nov. 21, 1793; Elisabeth, b. March 5, 1796; Agnes, b. March 26, 1800; Jacob Van Voorst, b. May 11, 1802.

FRYER, Eldert, and Helena Melger (McGee). Ch: John, b. Dec. 26, 1795 ; John, b. Aug. 20, 1797; James, b. Feb. 29, 1799; William, b. July 4, 1801; Elisabeth, b. Aug. 21, 1803; Alexander, b. May 17, 1807; Elijah Samuel, b. Jan. 9, 1809.

FRYER, Matthew, and Susanna Carles. She d. April 18, 1855, a. 91 y. Ch: Judith, b. March 17, 1794; Elisabeth, b. Oct. 4, 1795; Isaac Bogert, b. Oct. 18, 1801.

Fuller, James, and Jane Kert. Ch: William, b. Sept. 28, 1779.

FULLER, William, and Rebecca Forgess. Ch: Samuel, b. June 18, 1783 ; William, b. March 10, 1785.

Fulsom, John, m. Elisabeth File (Viele ?) July 18, 1781. Ch: Anna, b. Aug. 26, 1782; Elisabeth, b. Jan. 8, 1785.

Furt (Fiur), Roeloff, and Barbara Koen. Ch: Adam, bp. Dec. 25, 1748 ; Margarita, bp. April 28, 1751.

Furtle, Stephen, and Maria Graham. Ch: Sara, b. April 25, 1779.

Fyle, see Feil.

Gaaf, John, and Immetie .... Ch: John, bp. July 3, 1726.

Gaffers, Reuben (William), and Maria Furrie. Ch: Barbara, b. March 5, 1793 ; William Matthias, b. Jan. 14, 1791.

Gaignen, Francois, m. Ariaantje Janse, June 3, 1688. Ch: Agniet, bp. Sept. 8, 1689.

Gansevoort (Van Gansevoort, so written by himself), Harmen Harmense, brewer in Beverwyck as early as 1660; In 1677, bought of Poulus Martense Van Benthuysen the lot on south corner of Broadway and Maiden Lane, which is still owned by his descendants. He m. Maritie Leendertse Conyn; she was buried Jan. 7, 1743. Ch: Leendert, bp. Sept. 19, 1683; Rachel, bp. June 20, 1686; Lydia, bp. July 20, 1690; Rebecca, bp. July 9, 1693; Hendrick, bp. Sept. 27, 1696, was buried Sept. 27, 1746.

GANSEVOORT, Leendert, m. Catrina De Wandelaer, May 11, 1712. He d. Nov. 30, 1763; she d. Aug. 16, 1767. He resided on the Stanwix Hall lot. Ch: Harmen, bp. April 20, 1712; Hendrick, bp. Aug. 19, 1716; Sara, bp. Dec. 28, 1718; Johannes, b. April 3, 1719 (Bible), bp. April 7, 1721; Maria, bp. June 9, 1723, buried Oct. 3, 1739; Pieter, bp. July 25, 1725; Elsie, bp. Sept. 17, 1727, buried, March 20, 1753; Agnietie, bp. Feb. 4, 1730.

GANSEVOORT, Harmen, m. Magdalena Douw, May 6, 1740. He d. March 7, 1801, a. 88 y. 7 m. 17 d.; she d. Oct. 12, 1796, a. 78 y. 2 m. Ch: Sara, bp. June 17, 1741; Petrus, bp. Jan. 16, 1743; Anna, bp. Oct. 19, 1744; Anna G., relict of C. D. Wynkoop, d. Aug. 9, 1794, a. 49 y. 10 m. 3 d. ; Catarina, bp. Oct. 25, 1747; Petrus, bp. July 16, 1749; Leendert, bp. July 14, 1751; Hendrick, bp. Sept. 22, 1753; Hendrick, bp. June 5, 1757; Catarina, bp. Oct. 15, 1758.

GANSEVOORT, Johannes, m. first, Maria Douw, dau. of Petrus Douw, Dec. 2 (church record) Nov. 29 (Bible), 1750, she d. Aug. 17, 1759; m. secondly, Effie Beekman, Sept. 9, 1764, she d. Sept. 9, 1798, and was buried at the *Hooghe Bergh.* He d. Nov. 28, 1781, a. 62 y. Ch: Catarina, bp. June 9, 1751; Leendert, bp. Jan. 14, 1753; Leendert, b. June 3, 1754, and d. Dec. 16, 1834, in 81st y.; Annatie, bp. July 31, 1757; Catharina, b. Oct. 24, 1765, and d. Nov. 11, 1766.

GANSEVOORT, Pieter, m. Gerritje Ten Eyck, Jan. 7, 1752. She was dau. of Jacob Ten Eyck, d. July 31, 1782. Dr. Pieter G., d. March 17 (19), 1809, a. 83 y. 8 m. Ch: Maria, bp. Dec. 3, 1752, d. Aug. 1, 1841, a. 89 y. 8 m.; Coenraad, bp. July 14, 1754; Gerritje, bp. April 8, 1757; Catarina, bp. March 18, 1759, and d. April 14, 1802, a. 42 y.; Coenraad, bp. March 15, 1761, and d. Aug. 9, 1829, a. 68 y. 5 m., his widow d. in Holmdell, N. J., Jan. 11, 1850, a. 82 y.; Elsie, b. Oct. 12, 1762; Elsie, b. Aug. 28, 1764, and d. May 14, 1824, a. 60 y.; Anna, b. March 13, 1766; Leendert, b. March 12, 1768, and d. Nov. 20, 1803, a. 35 y.; Hendrik and Margarita, bp. June 27, 1770.

GANSEVOORT, Leendert, Junior, m. Hester Cuyler, May 14, 1770. He d. at Whitehall, Aug. 26, 1810; She d. March 28, 1826, a. 77 y. Ch: Magdalena, b. Feb. 26, 1771; Catharina, bp. Sept. 14, 1772; Abraham Cuyler, b. July 23, 1775; Magdalena, b. Aug. 17, 1777, m. Jacob Ten Eyck, and d. May 14, 1863, a. 86 y.; Catharina Cuyler, b. July 24, 1789.

GANSEVOORT, Pieter, Junior, m. Catharina Van Schaick, Jan. 12. 1778. Brig. Gen. Pieter G., U. S. A., d. July 2, 1812, a. 62 y. 11 m. 16 d., Catharine his widow, d. Dec. 30, 1830, a. 79 y.; Ch: Harmen, b. Sept. 12, 1779; Wessel, b. Nov. 23, 1781, d. at Danby, Vt., Aug. 7, 1863. a. 80 y.; Leendert, b. Oct. 15, 1783; Petrus, b. Dec. 18, 1786; Pieter, b. Dec. 22. 1788; Maria, b. April 6, 1791.

GANSEVOORT, Leendert, Junior, m. Maria Van Rensselaer, dau. of Col. Kilian V. R., at the age of 17 y. on the 17th of April, 1777. He d. Dec. 16, 1834, and was buried at *Wolven Hoek.* She d. April 2, 1842. Ch: Maria, b. Feb. 17, 1778, m. Abm. Hun; Ariaantie, b. Aug. 26, 1780, and d. Dec. 7, 1839, a. 59; Catharina Douw, b. May 9, 1782; Elizabeth Richards, b. April 2, 1784, m. T. Ross in 1811, and d. Sept. 7, 1830; Johannes, b. March 30, 1786; ... a son, b. June 22, 1788 "lived one hour;" Rachel Douw, b. Nov. 9, 1790; "it is remarkable that my wife (Maria Van Rensselaer) was the first child baptized by Dominie Westerlo, and this daughter of hers the last one baptized by him during a ministry of thirty years;" Eefie, b. Nov. 25, 1793, m. Jacob H. Ten Eyck, and d. May 25, 1833; Ann Van Rensselaer, b. Sept. 27, 1795, d. Nov. 6, 1806; Elsie, b. Feb. 11, 1797, and d. Aug. 17, 1798; Rensselaer b. Feb. 8, 1799; Dr. Rensselaer G. d. in Louisiana, Oct. 19, 1839, a. 39 y.; Elsie, b. Nov. 8, 1801, m. R. M. Cuyler, July 21, 1830.

GANSEVOORT, Leonard H., and Mary Ann....... Ch: Peter, b. Aug. 26, 1810; Guert, b. June 27, 1812; Catharine, b. April 27, 1814; Leonard, b March 14, 1816; Frances, b. Sept. 23, 1818.

Gantz, George, and Jane Neal. Ch; Rosina, bp. April 17, 1791.

Gardenier (*alias* Flodder), Jacob Janse, a carpenter in Beverwyck as early as 1638; in 1656, he owned the north side of Wall street from William street to Pearl street, which he divided into lots and sold by his agent Sander Leendertse Glen; he early

bought land in Kinderhook together with the *Goyer's* kil opposite or near *Apje's* island or Schotack. His immediate descendants very generally settled in that vicinity. His first w. was Josyna ..., who d. Feb., 1669; he afterwards m. Barentje Stratsmans, widow of Hans Coenraatse; in 1688, she was again a widow with ten children by her first husband and five by her second, all living. The estates of the two fathers were then divided among these 15 children. The following children of Jacob Janse Gardenier arrived to mature age and had families: Jan; Samuel; Andries; Hendrick; Albert; Aeltie, who m. Adam Dingman.

GARDENIER, Albert Jacobse, and Maritie .... He was a carpenter in Albany in 1677. Ch: Josyntje, bp. Jan. 25, 1685; Lysbeth, bp. March 27. 1687; Barber, b. Jan. 8, 1690; Cornelia, bp. in New York, June 14, 1693; Hermanus, bp. in New York, Jan. 8, 1696.

GARDENIER (Flodder), Jan Jacobse, millwright of Kinderhook, in 1720; his wife was Sara Janse Van Bremen. By his will made Sept. 24, 1689, it appears that he then had six children living; his widow administered on the estate June 21, 1695. In 1697 there were the following Ch: Josyntje, w. of Edward Wheeler; Ariaantje, w. of John Woodcock; Alida; Jacob, b. in 1681; Helena, bp. Feb. 13, 1687; Jan, bp. May 12, 1689; Cornelia, bp. Oct. 11, 1691.

GARDENIER, Samuel, of Kinderhook, and Helena Dirkse (Hendrickse) Bye (Bey, Beyst). Ch: Dirk, bp. March 23, 1690; Jacob, bp. April 16, 1692; Josina, bp. Dec. 31, 1693; Henderick, bp. Jan. 22, 1696; Saartje, bp. Sept. 3, 1699; Lysbeth, bp. May 19, 1702; Samuel, bp. June 18, 1704; Engeltie, bp. Jan. 19, 1707; Hendrik, bp. Oct. 30, 1709.

GARDINIER, Andries Jacobse of Kinderhook, m. Eytie Ariaanse (Ariese) weduwe van Henderick Gerritse Van Wyen, Nov. 13, 1692; made a will July 1, 1704; proved Aug. 13, 1717, in which he speaks of my brother Samuel and the following Ch: Andries, bp. Oct. 22, 1693, m. Sara Van Woert, Aug. 22, 1714; Jacob, bp. May 26, 1695; Aric, bp. Aug. 14, 1698.

GARDENIER, Henderick, and Neeltie Claase. He d. about 1694; in 1695 his widow m. Johannes Ouderkerk. He owned a house lot adjoining easterly the parsonage lot of the Dutch Church in Schenectady. Andries Gardenier and Cornelis Claese, administered on his estate, April 7, 1695. Ch: Claas; Andries; Joryna; Henderick, bp. March 11, 1694.

GARDENIER, Claas, m. Rachel Winne, Aug. 13, 1713. Ch: Hendrik, bp. Nov. 17, 1714; Adam Winne, bp. Sept. 22, 1717; Neeltie, bp. Dec. 28, 1718; Anneke, bp. May 15, 1720; Andries, bp. June 9, 1723; Rachel, bp. Jan. 2, 1726; Jacob, bp. Feb. 21, 1728.

GARDENIER, Hendrik, m. Margarita Van Woert, May 30, 1718. Ch: Neeltie, bp. Nov. 22, 1719; Jacob, bp. Dec. 25, 1720; Neeltie, bp. June 17, 1722; Hendrik, bp. April 23, 1727.

GARDENIER, Andries, m. first, Josyna Gardenier, Dec. 31, 1715. Ch: Eytje, bp. Oct. 2, 1720. He m. secondly, Sara .... Ch: Neeltie, bp. Nov. 13, 1731.

GARDENIER, Jacob, m. Anna (Johanna) Tippen, Oct. 30, 1724. Ch: Helena, bp. Sept. 5, 1725.

GARDENIER, Samuel, m. Barentje Barheit (Bareith), June 11, 1736. Ch: Samuel, bp. July 10, 173 7; Catharina, bp. June 17, 1739; Cornelia, bp. Nov. 6, 1748; Johanna, geboren May 10, bp. July 1, 1753.

GARDENIER, Hendrik N., m. Eva Van Valkenburgh, July 11, 1740. Ch : Rachel, bp. July 19, 1741 ; Nicolaas, bp. April 27, 1746; Elisabeth, bp. May 1, 1748 ; Jacobus, bp March 25, 1750; Cornelis, bp. March 15, 1752; Hendrick, bp. April 7, 1754.

GARDENIER, Hendrick H., m. first, Maria Dingman; secondly, Maria Goewey, May 20, 1755. Ch : Samuel, bp. May 20, 1744; Helena, bp. Jan. 7, 1750; Hendrik, bp. April 4, 1756.

GARDENIER, Adam Winne, and Jannetie .... Ch : Martha, bp. Oct. 25, 1747.

GARDENIER, Andries, and Catarina DeGarmo. She was buried Oct. 29, 1756. Ch : Rebecca, bp. Dec. 22, 1751 ; Hester, bp. Aug. 29, 1754.

GARDENIER, Andries H., of Albany, m. first, Margarita, Goewey (Houwy) Jan. 12, 1754. Ch : Henderick, bp. Oct. 20, 1754 ; Alida, bp. April 4, 1756 ; he m. secondly, Sara Hanse (Hansen). Ch : Hendrick, b. May 16, 1760 ; Filipp, b. March 14, 1762 ; Geertruid, b. Jan., 1764 ; Margarita, b. Nov. 26, 1765 ; Hendrik, b. April 17, 1768; Philip, b. April 1, 1770; Andries, b. April 7, 1772; Annatie, b. Sept. 28, 1777; Neeltie, b. March 29, 1779.

GARDENIER, Philip, m. Elisabeth Van Schaaick, April 28, 1792. Ch : Maria, b. Oct. 17, bp. Oct. 2 (*sic*), 1795 ; Sarah, b. Feb. 5, 1798.

GARDENIER, Henry A., and Henrietta Van Everen. Ch : John, b. Aug. 25, 1797 ; George, b. Dec. 11, 1800.

GARDENIER, Henry A. (same as last ?), and Harriet. Ch : Catharine and Margaret, b. Dec. 11, 1812.

Gardner, Thomas Champion, m. Willempie Bogert, Nov. 26, 1798. Ch : Douwe, b. Aug. 18, 1799 ; Thomas, b. July 28, 1801; Mary, b. March 16, 1803; Cornelia, b. Dec. 25, 1807; Cornelia, b. June 25, 1808.

Gates, John, of Halve Maan, m. Geertruy Van Vranken, March 21, 1779. He d. Sept. 9, 1825, a. 75 y. 10 m. 6 d. ; she d. May 8, 1839, a. 85 y. Ch : Elizabeth. b. July 25, 1781 ; Joseph, b. Oct. 12, 1782 ; Gerrit b. May 28, 1785; Hanna, b. Jan. 26, 1787 ; John, b. Oct. 31, 1788, and d. Jan. 24, 1810.

GATES, John, and Catharine Van Vranken. Ch : Cornelius, b. Sept. 23, 1797.

Gebbus (Gibbs ?), Willem, and Maria Forry. Ch : Hendrick, b. Nov. 14, 1785.

Gebhard (Gibhart, Geefhart), Johann (Hannes) Caspar, m. Elizabeth Seger, Oct. 5, 1741. Ch : Joseph, bp. April 4, 1742 ; Anna, bp. Aug. 10, 1746.

Gerbertsen (Cruiff), Elbert (Albèrt), b. at Hilversen in Gooyland, Holland, m.Tryntje Janse, widow of Jan Janse Ryckman ; in 1663 they made a mutual will but do not speak of any children. He was a sawyer and had a house and two saw-mills at Bethlehem. He seems to have been a violent and quarrelsome man, given to abuse and defamation. He died in 1675.

Gerritse.

REYER ELBERTSE, (Albertse) ; his wife, Maritie Barentse, had been the widow of Gerrit Van Schaick, and mother of Goosen Gerritse Van Schaick. In 1653, he had a patent for land on the *Third* or *Fossen* kil bounded south by Columbia street and east by Broadway, a portion of which was afterwards owned by theVan Schaick family. He left two sons : Arien Reyerse ; and Gerrit Reyerse.

GERRIT Reyerse, son of Reyer Elbertse, born in Utrecht, m. Annatie Janse of Amsterdam, in New York, April 11, 1665. He was a trader in company

with his half brother Goosen Gerritse Van Schaick. He made his will Feb. 15, 1693 - 4, and was deceased before 1700. Ch : Elbert ; Johannes ; Reyer ; Annatie ; Maritie, m. Harpert Jacobse Van Deusen.

GERRITSE, Elbert, m. Maria Pruyn, July 2, 1693. He was buried in the church Nov. 18, 1750, his w. Maritie, was buried Aug. 21, 1731. Ch : Anna, bp. May 6, 1694; Alida, bp. Jan. 12, 1696; Alida, bp. June 1, 1701; Gerrit, bp. April 30, 1704; Henrik, bp. Dec. 18, 1709.

GERRITSE, Reyer, m. Geertruy Lansing, April 23, 1704. He was buried Oct. 21, 1752; she was buried April 25, 1754. He made a will Aug. 10, 1747....proved Nov. 4, 1752; in it he mentions no children but speaks of " my nephew Henderick Gerritse son of Elbert Gerritse, my cousin [nephew] Gerard Groesbeck son of Stephanus Groesbeck, my cousins [nephews] John, Gerrit, Peter and Philip, Lansing, and of my brother [in-law] John Lansing."

GERRITSE, Frederick, and Lysbeth Carstense, Ch : Folkie, bp. June 30, 1689 ; Styntje, bp. June 7, 1691.

GERRITSE, Huybert, m. Maria Lansing, Dec. 20, 1693. Ch : Lysbeth, bp. July 29, 1694.

Gerritsen, Jan (Johannes), m. Christina Pruyn, May 8, 1706. Ch : Gerrit, bp. April 6, 1707.

GERRITSEN, Jan (probably the same as last), and Maritie .... Ch : Anna, bp. March 30, 1713; Maria, bp. May 30, 1717; Gerrit, bp. Dec. 16, 1722. Jan Gerritsen was buried in the church, Nov. 12, 1725.

GERRITSEN, Frederick, and Maria Tuck (Tok, Toch, Dock). Ch : Rachel and Annatie, bp. March 11, 1750; Ann Gerritsen, d. June 26, 1848 a. 97 : Henderick, bp. Jan. 6, 1754; Elizabeth, bp. Nov. 6, 1757; Elizabeth, bp. March 18, 1759; Catharina, b. July 27, 1762.

Garritsen, Abraham, and Jane Francisco. Ch : Altie, b. Aug. 26, 1790.

Gevick (see Hevick and Heven).

Gibhert (see Gebhard).

Gibson, David, and Maria .... Ch : James, b. Aug. 2, 1777.

GIBSON, Collin, and Ellen Story. Ch : Mattheus, b. Jan. 7, 1778.

Gilbert, John, baker, and Cornelia Van den Bergh, dau. of Arent V. D. B. Jan Gilbert, d. May 11, 1707. Ch : Maria, bp. May 24, 1685 ; Anna, bp. Sept. 2, 1694 ; Arent, bp. Aug. 1, 1697.

GILBERT, Peter M. and Margarita Smith. Ch : Sara, bp. June 12, 1785.

Gilchrist, William, and Hester Nelson. Ch : John, b. April 28, 1777.

Gillespie (Gillaspy), Niel, and Mary Jackson. Ch : Daniel, b. Oct. 2, 1781.

Gilliland (Gillilon), William, and Anna Doff (?). Ch : Ann, bp. Aug. 17, 1757. William Gilliland m. Elizabeth Phagen, Feb. 8, 1759 ; and Mary Steward, July 10, 1765.

Ginning, Jacob, and Christiana Passagie. Ch : Jacob, b. April 25, 1799.

Giver, John, and Magdalena Schermerhorn. Ch : William, b. March 4, 1792

Glen, Sander Leendertse, was a servant of the West India Company at Fort Nassau in 1633 ; received a grant of land there 1651 ; also received a patent for a lot in Smits' Valey, New Amsterdam in 1646, which he sold in 1660 ; was then called *coop-man* of Beverwyck. In 1665, he obtained a patent for lands in Schenectady, which land, he called *Nova Scotia*, and became his permanent residence. He owned real estate in divers parts of Albany, and was a considerable trader with the Indians. His wife was Catalyn Doncassen or Dongan, sister of Willem Teller's first wife and perhaps of Pieter Lookerman's wife. Ch : Jacob ; Sander, b. 1647 ; Johannes, b. Nov. 5, 1648. Sander Leendertse Glen, d. 1685. See *Schenectady Families.*

GLEN, Jacob Sanderse, eldest son of Sander Leendertse Glen, trader of Albany, where he died Oct. 2, 1685, as appears by the following entry in the deacon's book. "In Albanie, Oct. 2. Anno 1685, is myn broeder Jacob Sanderse [Glen] dieiaken in den here ontslapen s'naghs ontrent een winnigh naer 2 uren tussen vriday en Saterdagh." In 1680 he owned a house lot on the south side of State street the second west from Pearl street, which afterwards passed to Harmanus Wendel who married his daughter Anna. His wife Catharina Van Witbeck after his death married Jonas Volkertse Douw, April 24, 1696. Ch : Johannes, b. 1675 ; d. 1707 ; Anna, b. 1677, and m. Harmanus Wendel ; Jacob, b. 1679, only son living in 1707 ; Helena, bp. Nov. 21, 1683, living unmarried in 1707 ; Sander, bp. Nov. 15, 1685, and not living in 1707. See *Schenectady Families.*

GLEN, Johannes Sanderse, "weduwnaar van Annatie Peek" m. Diwertje Wendel, "Weduwe Van Meindert Wemp," June 21, 1691. She d. April 10, 1724. Ch : Jacobus, bp. Jan. 1, 1692. See *Schenectady Families.*

GLEN, Sander, m. Rebecca Swits, Dec. 18, 1714, several children were baptized in Schenectady.

GLEN, Johannes, Jr., m. Jannetje Bleecker, Dec. 11, 1698. Ch : Catharina, bp. Sept. 8, 1699 ; Jacob Sanderse, bp. in Schenectady, Oct. 17, 1703 ; Johannes, bp. Feb. 26, 1703 ; made his will Sept. 20, 1769.... proved March 31, 1770 ; gave half his estate to the four children of his late brother Jacob, viz., John, Hendrick, Cornelis and Jannetie Cuyler, w. of Abraham Cuyler ; and the other half to the 4 children of his sister Catharina, late w. of Johannes Cuyler, viz. Elsie, w. of Barent Ten Eyck, John Cuyler Jr. ; Cornelis Cuyler, Jr., and Jacob Cuyler.

GLEN, Jacob, m. Elizabeth Cuyler, Dec. 29, 1732. He had a lot on west corner of Steuben and Chapel street, was buried in the church April 16, 1746. Ch : Jannetie, bp. Nov. 11, 1733 ; Johannes, bp. July 2, 1735 ; Elsie, bp. April 8, 1737 ; Hendrick, bp. July 13, 1739 ; Cornelis, b. Nov. 1, 1741 ; Jannetie, bp. Oct. 27, 1743, and was buried in the church Jan. 27, 1755.

GLEN, Johannes, m. Catharina Veeder, May 24, 1759. Ch : Jacob "Gedoopt op Schonechdate, Jan. 25, 1761. See *Schenectady Families.*

GLEN, Cornelis, of Watervliet, and Elizabeth ..... He made his will Aug. 28, 1809, and speaks of wife Elizabeth, brothers John and Henry, sister Jane Cuyler, [w. of Abm. Cuyler] nephews and neices but not of his own children. He d. Mar. 21, 1810, a. 69 y., leaving a considerable estate ; his widow d. Nov.— 1812.

Goarley (Gourley ?) James, and Annatie Schuyler. Ch : James, bp. Sept. 3, 1772.

Goes (Hoes), Jan Tysse of Kinderhook, son of Matthys Jansse, who was in Beverwyck, in 1661 ; m. first Brechje Maryns, widow of Claes Cornelise Van Voorhout ; she was deceased Feb. 1, 1663, leaving two Ch : Maryn and Jacob Van Voorhout ; he m. secondly Styntje Janse Van Hoesen : he d. May 31, 1705 ; made will Feb. 9, 1696-7, and mentions the following Ch : Tys, Jan, Dirk, Anna, w. of Isaac Vosburgh, Teuntje w. of Thomas Winne, Judith w. Isaac Hendrickse Burger, Mayke and Jacobus bp. May 1, 1687.

GOES (Hoes), Dirk Janse of Kinderhook, and Lybetje Luykasse Wyngaart. He made will June 1, 1732,..... Proved Aug. 5, 1732, and speaks of the following Ch : Johannes bp. May 12, 1700 ; Anna, bp. Feb. 13, 1704, m. Tobias Van Buren ; Luykas bp. June 22, 1707.

GOES (Hoes), Matthys (Tys) Janse of Kinderhook, m. Cornelia Mattheuise (Teuisse) Van Deusen, Oct. 21, 1685,..... Ch : Jan, bp. Aug. 7, 1687 ; Mattheus, bp. Mar. 9, 1690 ; Johannes, bp. May 8, 1692 ; Breechje, bp. Jan. 20, 1695 ; Dirk, bp. May 16, 1697 ; Lena, bp. Jan. 7, 1700 ; Herbert, bp. July 5, 1702 ; Christina, bp. Aug. 6, 1704 ; Tryntje, bp. Sept. 1, 1706 ; Ephraim, bp. Jan. 9, 1709 ; Maritje, bp. Feb. 17, 1712.

GOES, Mattheus, and Jannetie Bries. Ch : Cornelia, bp. Feb. 15, 1710 ; Angenietje, bp. Oct. 14, 1711 ; Mattheus, bp. Aug. 7, 1713 ; Cornelia, bp. Oct. 20, 1717 ; Johannes, bp. May 18, 1721.

GOES, Johannes (Jan), of Claverak, m. first Margarita Wyngaard, "Weduwe Van Emanuel, Van Schaick," secondly, Jannetie,.... (bans Feb. 10, 1712). Ch : Jan Tyssen, bp. Feb. 21, 1714 ; Anna, bp. April 8, 1716 ; Styntje, bp. Feb. 26, 1719 ; Jannetie, bp. Aug. 28, 1726 ; Catalyna, bp. Feb. 12, 1727.

GOES, Jan Tyse, and Eytie .... Ch : Jannetie, bp. April 20, 1718 ; Barent, bp. June 12, 1720.

GOES (Goest), Johannes, and Geertruy Van Buren. Ch : Jannetie, bp. Jan. 12, 1746 ; Marten, bp. July 24, 1748 ; Pieter, bp. May 27, 1753.

GOES (Hoes), Jurriaan, and Cornelia Van Buren. Ch : Maria, bp. Dec. 7, 1746.

GOES (Hoes), Johannes, and Maria Quackenbush. Ch : Dirk, b. Jan. 1, 1777.

GOES (Hoes), Jurriaan, and Judike Van Buren. Ch : Cathalina, b. Dec. 26, 1786.

Goewey, Salomon Abelse, b. in Amsterdam, carpenter in his life time in Beverwyck. He had the following Ch : Philip ; Jacob living in 1668 in Albany ; Jan living in 1668 in Albany ; David ; Lysbet living in 1668 ; Sara, wife of Cornelis Teunise Van Vechten, in 1668.

GOEWEY, Jacob Salomonse, owned a house and lot in Albany, in 1775.

GOEWEY, Jan Salomonse, and Caatje Loockermans. His house lot was on the east side of Broadway next south of Bleecker Hall. He was buried Sept. 28, 1731. Ch : Annetie, bp. Sept. 23, 1683, and m. Thomas Doksi of Long Island, Dec. 9, 1704 ; Lysbeth, bp. Aug. 26, 1685 ; Salomon, bp. April 17, 1687 ; Hilletje, bp. Feb. 20, 1689 ; Pieter, bp. May —, 1691 ; Jacob, bp. Sept. 10, 1693 ; Cateleyntje, bp. March 31, 1695 ; Cateleyntje, bp. Jan. 10, 1697 ; Johannes, bp. Feb. 22, 1699 ; Rebecca, bp. April 13, 1701.

GOEWEY, Johannes, m. Jannetie Van den Bergh, Oct. 30, 1726. Ch : Geertruy, bp. July 27, 1729 ; Maria, bp. Sept. 5, 1731 ; Johannes, bp. Jan. 23, 1734 ; Catalyna, bp. March 7, 1736 ; Barent, bp. Dec. 3, 1738 ; Andries, bp. May 7, 1741.

GOEWEY, Salomon, m. first Alida .... And secondly Margarita .... June 15, 1728. His first wife was buried Oct. 17, 1726. Ch : Benjamin, bp. March 28, 1714 ; Elizabeth, bp. June 28, 1716 ; Johannes, bp. July 7, 1721 ; Johannes, bp. Dec. 15, 1723 ; Alida, bp. June 9, 1729 ; Catharina, bp. Aug. 2, 1730, and buried, May 30, 1743 ; Pieter, bp. June 10, 1731, and buried Nov. 4, 1756 ; Anna Catharina, bp. Nov. 27, 1732 ; Johanna Catharina, bp. Nov. 4, 1733 ; Margarita, bp. May 15, 1735 ; Sara, bp. Feb. 6, 1737.

GOEWEY, Benjamin, m. Catharina Vanden Bergh, Oct. 2, 1743. Ch: Alida, bp. Jan. 4, 1745 ; Annatie, bp. April 25, 1746 ; Alida, bp. June 12, 1748 ; Annatie, bp. Jan. 6, 1751 ; Solomon, bp. Aug. 23, 1752 ; Maria, bp. July 22, 1754 ; Gerrit Vanden Bergh, bp. Feb. 26, 1758 ; Elizabeth, bp. Jan. 4, 1760 ; Gerrit, bp. Oct. 11, 1761 ; Johannes, b. Feb. 13, 1764 ; Catharina, b. Dec. 4, 1766.

GOEWEY, Johannes and Elizabeth Young. Ch : Solomon, bp. Sept. 2, 1753 ; Elizabeth, bp. March 15, 1761.

GOEWEY, Pieter, m. Maria Young, May 5, 1753. Ch : Margarita, bp. March 24, 1754 ; Daniel, bp. Dec. 28, 1755 ; Daniel, bp. Dec. 25, 1757 ; Solomon, bp. Dec. 3, 1758 ; Elizabeth, bp. March 15, 1761 ; Pieter, b. Aug. 16, 1763 ; Daniel, bp. Nov. 17, 1765 ; Annatie, b. March 14, 1768 ; Johannes, bp. May 6, 1770 ; Alida, b. March 30, 1772.

GOEWEY, Johannes, Jr., m. Maria Van Ivere, Nov. 26, 1757. Ch : Jannetie, b. Oct. 15, 1758 ; Jannetie, b. May 8, 1760 ; Barent, b. Dec. 4, 1762 ; Cornelia, b. Feb. 15, 1764 ; Pieter, b. Sept. 12, 1767 ; Sara, b. Nov. 19, 1769 ; Geertruy, b. Oct. 4, 1771 ; Maria, b. Dec. 3, 1774.

GOEWEY (Goey), Barent, m. Rachel Van Ostrander, March 24, 1765. Ch : Johannes, b. Jan. 26, 1766 ; Maria, b. June 9, 1768 ; Willem, b. Jan. 2, 1771 ; Jannetie, b. Feb. 1, 1774 ; Geertruy, b. May 31, 1777 ; Caharina, b. Aug. 13, 1780.

GOEWEY, Andreas, m. Florena (Glorena), Young, (Gyoung), May 22, 1766. Ch: Jannetje, b. June 26, 1767 ; Johannes, b. April 27, 1772.

GOEWEY, Solomon, and Elizabeth [Van] Santvoord. Ch : Johannes, b. Oct. 6, 1776 ; Salomon, b. April 23, 1788.

GOEWEY (Goey), Johannes, m. Pietertje Jeralymon, May 25, 1788. Ch : Catharina, b. Nov. 30, 1788 ; Jannetie, b. Feb. 21, 1790 ; Alida, b. Jan. 8, 1792 ; Nicolaas, b. Oct. 18, 1793 ; Benjamin, b. Dec. 15, 1796 ; Hannah, b. Oct. 31, 1798 ; John, b. Dec. 17, 1801 ; Solomon and Nelly, b. June 7, 1808.

GOEWEY (Gui), Gerrit, m. Aagie Look, May 28, 1787. Helena, b. Sept. 9, 1790 ; Catharina, b. Aug. 21, 1793 ; Benjamin and Jacob, b. Oct. 23, 1796 ; Rachel, b. Dec. 22, 1800.

GOEWEY (Guyer), John, and Christina Roff. Ch : Annatie, b. Sept. 24, 1790 ; Rebecca, b. July 1, 1796.

GOEWEY (Goey), Peter, and Mary Milk. Ch : David b. Feb. 17, 1795.

GOEWEY (Goey), John A., m. Rebecca De Foreest, Aug. 11, 1797. He d. June 25, 1828, a. 56 y. 1 m. 28 d. She d. May 11, 1820, a. 50 y. 4 m. 18 d. Ch : John, b. July 10, 1798.

Gonsaulus, Gunsaulus, Consaulus, Gonsaul.

GONSAULUS (Consaulus), Johannes of " Nistigioene," m. Machtelt Heemstraat, April 20, 1765. Ch : Sara, bp. Nov. 3, 1765 ; Johannes, bp. in Schenectady,

Nov. 5, 1767 ; Bastiaan, b. Nov. 16, 1769 ; Francyntje, b. Feb. 2, 1772 ; Engeltie, b. Jan. 16, 1774 ; Bata, b. Jan. 31, 1776 ; Mattheus, b. June 16, 1780 ; Emanuel, bp. in Schenectady, May 4, 1783 ; Machtelt, b. July 31, 1785 ; Annatie, b. Aug. 29, 1787.

GONSAULUS, John, and Dirkse (Durchie), Hogan. Ch : Isaac Hogan, b. Nov. 23, 1793.

Goodair, Benjamin, and Jannetie Adley. Ch : Hannah, b. Aug. 4, 1783.

Goodbrood, Willem, and Barbara Coen. Ch : Bastiaan, b. Oct. 21, 1780.

Gordon, William, and Rebecca ..... Ch : Mary, bp. Jan. 22, 1749.

Gourley, James, m. Lany, (Lana) Bromley, Sept. 10, 1799. Ch : Annatie, b. Oct. 4, 1799 ; Maria, b. Dec. 27, 1801.

Gow, see Vyselaer.

Graham, John, m. Maria Fryer, Nov. 9, 1777, Ch. Sara, b. Jan. 31, 1779 ; Annatie, b. Sept. 26, 1780.

GRAHAM, John, major in the Revolutionary army, m. Debora Staats, Nov. 8, 1778. Ch : Sara, b. May 12, 1780, and still living at Schenectady (Feb., 1871) ; Debora, b. March 1, 1786, and d. Feb., 1866, at Schenectady.

GRAHAM, John, and Gertrude Hilton. Ch : Sarah, b. Nov. 14, 1799.

Grant, James, and Elizabeth ..... Ch : Richard, bp. April 24, 1737.

GRANT, Gregory, and Margaret Echad. Ch : Jany, b. Mar. 18, 1778.

GRANT, Louis, m. Margaret, (Majory), Frasier (Frayer), July 20, 1778. Ch. Simon b. May 2, 1779.

GRANT, John, and Mary Cumming. Ch : James, b. March, 6, 1797.

Grauw, Leendert Arentse, and .... Ch. Gysbertje, bp. May 19, 1689.

Gray, Robert, m. Susanna LaGrange (Grant), May 7, 1777. Ch : Gerrit, b. Oct. 29, 1779 ; Jellis, b. Jan. 2, 1790 ; Susannah, b. Oct. 26, 1797.

GRAY, Robert, and Elizabeth Drummer. Ch : John, b. March 16, 1779.

GRAY, John, and Catharine Osburn. Ch : Catharine, b. Aug. 10, 1797 ; William, b. Dec. 2, 1800 ; Sarah, b. Jan. 31, 1804.

Greedy, Darby, and Arlaantje Symense. Ch : Margriet, bp. Sept. 12, 1736.

Greefraad (see Greveraad).

Green (Groen), Edmund, and Antje .... Ch : William, bp. Nov. 6, 1720.

GREEN (Groen, Groom), Willem, and Sara Coddington. Ch : Edward, bp. Aug. 5, 1744 ; Ytje, bp. Jan. 12, 1746.

GREEN, Willem, and Elizabeth .... Ch : Anna, bp. Dec. 11, 1760.

GREEN (Groen), Willem, and Cathalyntje Borns. Ch : Johannes, b. May 16, 1772.

GREEN, James, and Margarita Smith. Ch : Magdalena, b. Oct. 31, 1773 ; William, b. Oct. 22, 1778 ; Thomas, b. March 26, 1781.

Gregrl (Gregory), James (perhaps same as last), and Margarita Smith. Ch : Margarita, b. July 28, 1771.

Gregory, Philip, and Margaret Herring. Ch : Jane, b. Sept. 19, 1778.

Grennel (see Crannel).

Gremmer, Hannes, and A. Margarita.... Ch:
Elize Barber, bp. Aug. 14, 1714.

Greveraad (Greefraadt), Henricus, "Van New
York, en Sara Sanders Van Nieuw Albany," m. May
4, 1686. Ch: Lysbeth, bp. Dec. 25, 1686; Marytje,
bp. in New York, July 25, 1697; Henricus, bp. in New
York, July 30, 1699.

GREVERAAD, Isaac, m. Alida Gerritsen, Nov. 11,
1727. Ch: Sara, bp. June 9, 1728, and was buried,
Nov. 14, 1746; Maria, bp. Aug. 23, 1729; Maria, bp.
July 2, 1731; Maria, bp. Feb. 4, 1733; Elsie, bp.
May 5, 1734; Elbert, bp. Nov. 21, 1736; Hendrik,
bp. Dec. 26. 1737; Annatie, bp. Aug. 8, 1739; Anna,
bp. Nov. 16, 1740; Alida, bp. July 10, 1743; Gerrit,
bp. April 21, 1745.

Greveradt, Hendrik, m Marytje Van Driessen,
March 2, 1772. Ch: Alida, b. May 24, 1773.

Grewell, see Cribel.

Griffith, John, and Jannet. Ch: James, bp.
Jan. 14, 1759.

Groen, see Green.

Groenendyk, Pieter, and .... Ch: baptized
in New York, Cornelis, July 9, 1673; Johannes,
March 24, 1675; Maritie, April 14, 1677; Pieter,
April 28, 1680; Abraham, May 13, 1682; Petrus, b.
Aug. 16, 1685.

GROENENDYK, Johannes, sheriff of Albany county,
1698–9; later was trader in Schenectady, where he
was buried in the church, Dec., ... 1739; his wife
continued his business there some years longer. He
m. Delia Cuyler (Huylers) in New York, Sept. 19,
1694. Ch: Mary bp. in New York, Sept. 16, 1696; Sara,
bp. April 28, 1700; Pieter, bp. Sept. 7, 1701; Henrick,
bp. Sept. 19, 1703; Anna.

Groenwout, Juriaen Janse, in Albany, 1662–77;
a licensed butcher in 1670; bought and sold divers
houses and lots. He m. Maritie Thomase Mingael
widow of Cornelis Teunise Bos, *alias* Van Westbroeck. Her dau. Wyntie Cornelise Bos, m. Pieter
Bogardus. J. J. Groenwout probably left no children.

Groesbeck (*alias* Van Rotterdam), Nicolaas
(Claes) Jacobse 1662 carpenter; on the 10th Oct., 1696,
he deposed that he was about 72 yrs. old; he then
had a house and lot on the west side of Pearl street,
the second north of Maiden Lane; his wife was
Elizabeth .... ; made a will Jan. 3, 1706-7, and mentions the following children, Jacob, Catrine, late wid.
of Jacob Teunise [Van Woert]; Willem; Barber,
w. of Gysbert Marcelis; Rebecca, wife of Dominicus Van Schaick; Johannes; Stephanus.

GROSBECK, Willem Claase, and Geertruy Schuyler.
He was buried Dec. 23, 1722. Ch: Catalina, bp. Oct.
21, 1685; David, bp. June 17, 1688; David, b. March
17, 1692, and d. Feb. 3, 1763; Elizabeth, bp. Jan. 4,
1699; Jacobus, bp. Oct. 5, 1701.

GROSBECK, Stephanus, trader, m. Elizabeth Lansing, July 16, 1699; he was buried July 17, 1744.   Ch:
Catharina, bp. April, 28, 1700; Johannes, bp. March
26, 1703: Catharina, bp. Jan. 10, 1705; Elizabeth, bp.
Aug. 17, 1707; Gerardus, bp. Oct. 23, 1709.

GROSBECK, Johannes Claase, m. Geertje Quackenbos, Dec. 17, 1699. She was buried March 14, 1747.
Ch: Lysbeth, bp. March 26, 1701; Neeltje, bp. Sept.
5, 1703; Catharina, bp. Nov. 18, 1705; Wouter, bp.

Aug. 15, 1708; Nicolaas, bp. Oct. 28, 1710, and was
buried June 30, 1746; Wouter, bp. Oct. 19, 1712;
Jacob, bp. May 27, 1715; Catryna, bp. Oct. 13, 1717;
Joannes, bp. Dec. 11, 1720.

GROESBECK, Nicholas, of Schachtekook, m. first
Marytje Quackenbos; secondly, Agnietje de Wandelaer, April 23, 1732. His first wife, Maria, was buried
Dec. 30, 1728. Ch: Willem, bp. Feb. 17, 1712;
Wouter, bp. Aug. 29, 1714; Geertruy, bp. Dec. 21,
1716, and was buried June 24, 1746; Pieter, bp. Nov.
29, 1719; Jacobus, bp. Feb. 17, 1723: Neeltie, bp.
June 13, 1725; Maria, bp. Jan. 1, 1729; Hannes, bp.
May 27, 1733; Johannes, bp. Feb. 18, 1735; Harmen
bp. March 2, 1737; Wouter, bp. Sept. 29, 1739; Pieter,
bp. Oct. 11, 1741; Pieter, bp. April 24, 1743; Jacob,
bp. Aug. 25, 1745.

GROESBECK, David, son of Willem Claese G., m.
Maria Van der Poel, Nov. 10 (8) 1724; he d. Feb. 3,
1763; she d. Jan. 18, 1757. Ch: Willem, b. Aug. 2,
bp. Aug. (*sic*) 1, 1725 and d. Oct. 3, 1752; Catrina, b.
Dec. 24, 1726, and d. Jan. 1, 1732; David, b. Aug. 5,
1728 and d. March 30, 1795; Mary, b. April 30, 1730,
and d. Jan. 26, 1732; Melgert, b. April 13, 1732, and
d. Sept. 18, 1748; Johannes, b. Feb. 23, 1734, and d.
Jan. 23, 1737; Abraham, b. April, 1736; Catharyna,
b. May 8, 1737; Geertruy, b. April 30, 1739, d. Aug.
25, 1745; Johannes, b. July 12, 1741: Catelyna, b.
March 12, 1745, and d. Jan. 6, 1756. Abraham, bp.
Nov. 6, 1743.

GROESBECK, Jacobus (Jacob), m. Sara Van Vechten,
Feb. 17, 1738. His wife was buried April 25, 1751.
Ch: Willem, bp. Sept. 17, 1738; Alida, bp. Feb. 8,
1741; Willem, bp. Oct. 16, 1743; Geertruy, bp. July
26, 1746. [Jacobus G., m. Catharina Yates, Oct. 18,
1740.]

GROESBECK, Gerardus, m. Maria Ten Broeck, March
8, 1739. Ch: Elizabeth, bp. July 8, 1739; Stephanus,
bp. May 9, 1742; Margrieta, bp. June 10, 1744; Margarita, bp. Jan. 10, 1746; Dirk, bp. May 29, 1748;
Johannes, bp. Feb. 18, 1750; Anna, bp. Dec. 1, 1751;
Johannes, bp. Nov. 11, 1753; Catarina, bp. Sept. 26,
1756; Catarina, bp. April 8, 1759.

GROESBECK, Wouter, m. Jannetje Bogaard, Dec.
14, 1739. Ch: Maria, bp. July 26, 1741; Pieter, bp.
Aug. 14, 1743; Rebecca, bp. April 19, 1745: Pieter,
bp. July 26,1746; Pieter, bp Oct.23, 1748; Geertruy,
bp. July 29, 1753; Geertruy, bp. Sept. 24, 1758.

GROESBECK, Wouter N., of Halve Maan, m. first
Maria Bogardus, Oct. 18, 1739, and secondly, Alida
Quackenbos, June 5, 1761. Ch: Johannes, bp. Feb.
14, 1742; Jannetje, bp. July 31, 1743; Jannetje, bp.
April 21, 1745; Anthony, bp. June 5, 1748; Nicolaas,
bp. May 6, 1750; Nicolaas, bp. Jan. 31, 1762;
Pieter, b. May 27, 1763; Jacob, b. July 24, 1764
Meinard, b. June 28, 1767; Harmen, b. July 10, 1769;
Wouter, b. Aug. 8, 1771.

GROESBECK, Willem, m. Catharina Van Nes, June
21, 1738. He was buried April 21, 1746; made his
will April 17, 1746 .... proved Jan. 15, 1755. Ch:
Maritie, bp. Dec. 23, 1739; Gerrit, bp. Feb. 28, 1742;
Nicolaas, bp. June 17, 1744; Willem, bp. July 26,
1746.

GROESBECK, David, Jr., m. first, Catrina Vedder,
Dec. 23, 1752, she d. Dec. 15, 1754; secondly, Sara
Winne, Sept. 28, 1765, she d. April 20, 1818. He d.
March 30, 1795. Ch: Willem, b. June 17, 1753; Cor-
nelis, b. Nov. 30, 1754, and d. 1811, a. 57 y.

GROESBECK, Hannes, and Elizabeth Van Brakel, "beide van Schagtekook," m. Nov. 22, 1752. Ch: Neeltie, bp. Aug. 20, 1754; Geertje, bp. Aug. 21, 1757; Gysbert, b. May 9, 1760: Johannes, b. Sept. 15, 1762; Gerrit, b. Feb. 17, 1765; Neeltie, b. Feb. 28, 1768.

GROESBECK, Johannes N., of Schachtekook, m. Maria Viele, July 28, 1755. Ch: Catarina, bp. Dec. 21, 1755; Hugo, b. Dec. 13, 1762; Willem, b. June 23, 1764; Jacob, b. June 10, 1771. [Johannes G., and Maria Groesbeck, of Schachtekook, m. Feb. 23, 1764]

GROESBECK, Johannes D., m. Aaltie Van Arnhem, July 13, 1765. Ch : Maria, b. July 5, 1766 ; Claartje, b. July 23, 1768; Claese, b. March 12, 1770; Jan, b. April 29, 1772.

GROESBECK, Harmen, of Schachtekook, m. Maritie Benneway (Benoit), Sept. 29, 1763. Ch: Agnietje b. July 23, 1768.

GROESBECK, Anthony, m. Cathalyntje [De] Foreest. Feb. 26, 1769. He d. June 11, 1812, a. 63 y. 11 m. 17 d. She d. June 27, 1813, a. 62 y. 6 m. 27 d. Ch: Wouter, b. May 11, 1771; Rachel, b. Jan. 5, 1775; Marytje, b. June 7, 1779 ; Cathalyna, b. Jan. 12, 1782; Annatie, b. Dec. 20, 1785 ; Jannetje, b. Aug. 6, 1787 ; Eleanor, b. Nov. 20, 1790.

GROESBECK, Nicolaas, m. Geertje Waldron, Oct. 17, 1766. Cornelis, b. Nov. 15, 1771 ; Willem, b. Nov. 20, 1773.

GROESBECK, Gerrit, m. Jannetie Van Slyck, Nov. 3, 1765. Ch: Willem, b. Jan. 30, 1771 ; Catharina, b. May 9, 1775.

GROESBECK, Willem, and Catharina Van Deusen. He d. July 6, 1802, a. 49 y. 19 d., for many years clerk of the church, and was succeeded by his sons Cornelis and David the last of the *voorzangers;* she d. Nov. 3, 1821, a. 72 y. Ch: David, b. March 29, 1772 ; Cornelis, bp. Nov. 9, 1777, and d. April 16, 1865, a. 88 y. ; Catharina Van Deusen, b. May 21, 1779 ; Maria, b. Feb. 27, 1781, and d. at Little Falls, Nov. 18, 1831; Lucretia, b. Jan. 14, 1783 ; Willem, b. Sept. 17, 1784, and d. June 25, 1835.

GROESBECK, Johannes D., and Cathalyna Van Schaick. Ch: David, b. Nov. 24, 1774 ; Johannes, b. July 27, 1776; Johannes, b. July 28, 1778 ; Aeltie, b. April 21, 1781 ; Willem, b. March 26, 1784 ; Jacob, b. Feb. 28, 1786; Catrina, b. April 28, 1788 ; Margaret Pool, b. Oct. 29, 1791; Sarah, b. Oct. 5, 1795.

GROESBECK, Pieter W. m. Alida Van Arnhem (Van Allen), July 4, 1779. She d. Feb. 2, 1854, a. 97 y. Ch: Annatie, b. May 15, 1780 ; Wouter b. Oct. 14, 1781 ; Abraham, b. Dec. 2, 1786; Abraham, b. Oct. 7, 1788 ; Isaac Fonda, b. March, 1792 ; Jannetie b. Nov. 23, 1794 ; Isaac Fonda, b. Nov. 18, 1796.

GROESBECK, Gysbert, m. Cornelia Van Valkenburgh, Jan. 1, 1784, and secondly Elizabeth Graff, about 1786. Ch : Cornelia, b. Nov. 10, and bp. Nov. 27, 1784 ; the mother then "overleden ;" Cornelia, b. Oct. 2, 1787 ; John, b. May 24, 1789.

GROESBECK, Cornelia, m. Annatie Van Antwerp. Dec. 4, 1783. He d. Oct. 29, 1811, a. 57 y. Ch: Catharina, b. Jan. 3, 1785 ; Johannes, b. Feb. 17, 1787 ; Rebecca, b. Jan. 18, 1791.

GROESBECK, John, and Cornelia Batt. Ch : Gerrit, b. Aug. 5, 1791.

GROESBECK, Walter, m. Hannah (Ann) Rykman, Jan. 16, 1793. Ch: Catalyntje, b, Oct. 16, 1793 ; Elizabeth, b. Sept. 3, 1795 ; Maria, b. Sept. 20, 1797 ; Cornelia, b. Oct. 8, 1799.

GROESBECK, David, m. first, Elizabeth Burton, who d. Sept. 29, 1804, a. 30 y. 22 d. ; secondly, Ann Willet, who d. May 6, 1810, a. 33 y. 2 m. 27 d. [David W. G. d. in New York, Dec. 9, 1857, a. 36 y.] Ch : Catharine, b. July 18, 1793 ; Eliza, b. .... 1810 ; and d, May 26, 1833, a. 22 y. 7 mo. 11 d. ; Saly Ann, who m. Jas. A. Hewson, and d. March 16, 1842, a. 33 y.

GROESBECK, David F. (T) ?) and Hannah (Harriet) Crannel. Ch : John, b. Aug, 18. 1799, and d. Aug. 16, 1800, a. 11 mo. 29 d. ; John, b. 1801, and d. ; Jan. 31, 1804, a. 2 y. 11 mo. 27 d. ; Maria, b. Sept. 12, 1803 ; (?) Catalina, b. April 7, 1804, and d. Sept. 23, 1806, a. 1 y. 8 m. 14 d. ; Catalina, b. March 11, 1807, and d. Sept. 25, 1807 ; a. 6 mo. 14 d. ; Harriet, b. July 13, 1808 ; Alida, b. July 17, 1810.

Groom, see Green.

Groot, Symon Symonse, senior, a servant of the West India Company, was at Beverwyck in 1654. He became one of the first settlers of Schenectady.

GROOT, Symon Symonse, Junior, m. Geertruy Janse Rinckhout. Ch : Rebecca, bp. July 3, 1692; Susanna, bp. March 21, 1697 ; Lysbeth, bp. Feb. 24, 1706. See *Schenectady Families.*

GROOT, Abraham Symonse, m. Hester Visscher in Schenectady, July 9, 1699. Ch : Harmanus, bp. July 13, 1707 ; Cornelis, bp. Oct. 23, 1709. See *Schenectady Families.*

GROOT, Dirk Symonse, and Lysbeth Vander Volgen. Ch : Nicolaas, bp. Oct. 23, 1709 ; Symon, bp. May 2, 1714. See *Schenectady Families.*

GROOT, Symon, of Schenectady, and Bata Clute. Ch: Elizabeth, bp. Feb. 20, 1739. See *Schenectady Families.*

GROOT, Cornelis, m. Maria Ryckse Van Vranken, Nov. 24, 1752. Ch : Dirk, bp. Sept. 29, 1753 ; Elizabeth, bp. Jan. 9, 1757 ; Dirk, bp. Dec. 31, 1758 ; Rebecca, b. Feb. 11, 1771. See *Schenectady Families.*

GROOT, Eldert, and Alida Gerritsen. Ch : Hendrick, bp. April 26, 1780. See *Schenectady Families.*

Gruum, Edmund, and Aaltie .... Ch : Jacob, bp. Jan. 24, 1723.

Gruwel, see Cribel.

Guest, Thomas, and Gertrude Schuyler. Ch : Sarah Jordon, b. Nov. 12, 1795; Dirk, b. Aug. 20, 1798; Margaret, b. Aug. 30, 1800 ; Mary Ann, b. Sept. 24, 1803 (?) ; Margaret Van Der Werken, b. Oct. 10, 1804 ; Thomas, b. Sept. 25, 1807 ; Schuyler, b. Jan. 22, 1810; John, b. July 28, 1811.

Guest, John, Junr., and Sarah Williams. Ch : Hannah, b. Feb. 9, 1799.

Gui, see Goewey.

Gunner, Arè, and Mary .... Ch : Mary, bp. April 4, 1725.

Gunsaulus, see Gonsaulus.

Guyer, see Goewey.

Haak, Frederick, and Margarita Scheffer. Ch : Laurens, b. Jan. 1, 1782.

Haan, Zacharias Hendrick, of Niskatha, m. Anna Hezy, Sept. 2, 1764. Ch : Harmanus, b. April 22 1767.

HAAN (Hall), Hannes and Catharina Boossen. Ch: Margarita, b. May 20, 1767; Elizabeth, b. March 6, 1769.

Haas, Simon, and Anna Rosina .... Ch : Johannes, b. Aug. 5, "op nooten Hoek" and bp. Nov. 11, 1716, at Klinkenberg.

HAAS, Zacharias, m. Geesje (Geefie, Geetje) Witbeck, Sept. 28, 1737. Ch: Symen, bp. June 18, 1738; Lena, bp. Aug. 31, 1740; Anna, bp. Aug. 1, 1742; Anna, bp. Oct. 21, 1744; Catharina, bp. Aug. 23, 1747.

Hagedorn, Dirk, m. Maritie Matyssen, Aug. 28, 1714. Ch: Anna, bp. April 24, 1715; Johannes Appel, bp. June 30, 1718; Hans Hendrickse, bp. Sept. 18, 1720; Maria, bp. Jan. 6, 1723; Catharina, bp. Feb. 3, 1725.

HAGEDORN, Samuel, of Schenectady, and Sofia Rees. Ch: Jonathan, b. Oct. 8, 1770; Lea, b. April 11, 1774. See *Schenectady Families.*

Haight, Henry, and Margarita Smith. Ch: Maria, b. Dec. 19, 1776.

Hainer, see Heiner.

Haines, see Heens.

Hale, Daniel, and Cathalyna Dyckman. Ch: Richard, b. Dec. 20, 1784.

Halenbeck, Caspar Jacobse, was in Beverwyck in 1654, made his will Sept. 9, 1685, and d. about Aug. 1703, leaving two sons Isaac, and Jan.

HALENBECK, Isaac Casperse, and Dorothee Bosch (Vos, Ten Bosch). He made his will Nov. 14, 1708... proved March 28, 1728, and mentions his wife, Dority, and the following children. He owned a tract of land on the Beaver kil within the present limits of the city; d. in 1709 (?); his widow d. Feb. 4, 1744, and was buried in the Lutheran church yard, Feb. 7, 1744. Ch: Jacob, bp. Oct. 19, 1684, m. Maria, daughter of Nanning Harmense Visscher; Maritie, bp. April 24, 1687, m. Wouter Vrooman; Hendrick, bp. March 13, 1692; Lysbeth, bp. June 23, 1695; Rachel, bp. Feb. 6, 1698; Gerrit, bp. May 12, 1700; Anna, bp. March 24, 1706, m. Benj. Bogart, and d. Oct., 1749.

HALENBECK, Jan Casparse of Coxsakie, and Rachel Willemse. He made his will May 6, 1725,... proved April 23, 1735, in which he spoke of his wife, Rachel, and the children following, except Johannes and Jurriaen. He was buried Dec. 28, 1730. Ch: Willem Janse Casparse, the eldest son; Caspar Janse; Elizabeth, wife of Jan Evertsen; Rachel, wife of Jan Jacobse Van Hoesen; Maritie, wife of Jurriaen Clauw; Rebecca, wife of Jan Van Loon; Johannes, bp. July 29, 1694; Johannes, bp. May 10, 1696; Jurgen or Jurriaen, bp. May 23, "op Kockshagki," and bp. at Klinkenbergh, Nov. 21, 1714.

HALENBECK, Willem Janse Casperse, of Claverak, m. first, Feitje Dirkse Van Vechten, May 23, 1697; and secondly, Cornelia Hoes, June 8, 1723. Ch: Rachel, bp. Nov. 14, 1697; Dirrick, bp. Sept. 10, 1699; Jan, bp. April 27, 1701; Samuel, bp. June 13, 1703; Caspar, bp. Jan. 7, 1705; Michiel, bp. March 9, 1707; Abraham, bp. Jan. 9, 1709; Jannetie, bp. July 5, 1713; Sara, bp. Sept. 4, 1715.

HALENBECK, Casper Janse, of Loonenburgh [Athens], and Magdalena .... He made his will, July 26, 1754. Ch: Jan Casparse, b. Sept. 1, 1712, at Kockshagki; Maria, b. "op de flakte Loonenburgh" Dec. 13, 1713, m. Johannes Klauw; Martinus, b. "op de flakte Loonenburgh" Dec. 19, 1715; Cornelia, b. in April "op de flakte Loonenburgh," and bp. at Gospel hoeck, April 26, 1722; Willem; Rachel, m. Jacob Halenbeck.

HALENBECK, Jacob Jacobse (Isaacse), of Catskil, m. Maria Visscher, Nov. 18, 1715. Ch: Jacobus, b. Dec. 6, and bp. at Klinkenbergh, Dec. 9, 1716; Alida, bp. July 20, 1718; Nanningh, bp. Sept. 11, 1720; Hen-

rick, b. March 18, 1722; Maria, bp. March 8, 1724; Geertruy, bp. Aug. 8, 1732.

HALENBECK, Hendrick, of Albany, m. Susanna Bratt, Dec. 7, 1718. He made his will Nov. 19, 1764, mentioned wife Susanna, and children, Isaac, Dorothy, Elizabeth, Daniel, Gerrit, Jacob, Anthony, and Bernardus then living. He d. July 7, 1766. Ch: Isaac, bp. April 12, 1719; Elizabeth, bp. Feb. 5, 1721; Dorothea, bp. July 14, 1723; Elizabeth, bp. Oct. 3, 1725; m. Willem Helling; Daniel, bp. Dec. 10, 1727; Susanna, bp. April 18, 1730; Gerrit, bp. April 2, 1732; Hendrick, bp. July 29, 1734; Gerrit, bp. Oct. 24, 1736; Anthony, bp. Dec. 20, 1738; Willem, bp. June 28, 1741; Bernardus, bp. April 15, 1744; Jacob.

HALENBECK, Caspar Jacobse, and Maria.... Ch: Hendrikje, b. in Albany, Nov. ...., 1720, bp. in the Lutheran church there, Jan. 1, 1721.

HALENBECK, Jan Casparse. and Willempie.... Ch: Jannetie, b. in Coxsackie June ...., bp. in Lutheran Church in New York, Sept. 24, 1721.

HALENBECK, Dirk, and Commetie.... Ch: Fytje, bp. June 9, 1723.

HALENBECK, Hannes, and Neeltie.... Ch: Jacobus, b. April 24, 1712, " op de flakte Loonenburgh," Maria, b. Sept. 28, 1714; Hanna, b Oct...... 1716.

HALENBECK, Jan, of Catskil, and Catharina .... Ch: Fytje, bp. Oct. 3, 1725.

HALENBECK, Isaac, m. Gerritje Van Woerd (Van Woerden, Woert) Dec. 20, 1741. He is mentioned in his father Hendrick's will (1764) as being then absent. He never returned. His three children were also mentioned. Ch: Hendrik, bp. June 24, 1744; Hendrick, bp. July 7, 1745; Nicolaas, bp. Dec. 20, 1747; Daniel, bp. Nov. 19, 1749.

HALENBECK, Daniel, m. first, Hendrikje Hilten; and secondly, Catharina Quackenbos; his first w. was buried Sept. 6, 1755. Ch: Susanna, bp. March 18, 1753; Maria, bp. June 22, 1755; Maria, bp. Nov. 15, 1760; Hendrick, b. July 18, 1762; Elizabeth, b. Aug. 12, 1765; Dorothea, b. March 30, 1768, m. Spencer Stafford; Johannes, b. Nov. 22, 1771.

HALENBECK, Bernardus, m. Neeltie Clark, March 22, 1766. Ch: Hendrick, b. Oct. 11, 1766; Cornelia, b. Oct. 23, 1768; Isaac, bp. Dec. 20, 1770; also Dorothea; Mary; Bernard; Catalina.

HALENBECK, Anthony, m. Cornelia Cooper, Dec. 12, 1766. She d. Feb. 23, 1840, a. 91 y. 2 mo. 11 d. Ch: Hendrik, bp. Sept. 14, 1767, d. Nov. 2, 1789, a 22 y. 1 mo. 12 d.; Josina, b. Aug. 19, 1769, and d. young; Jacob, b. Feb. 22, 1771, d. Jan. 7, 1789, a. 18 y. 1 mo. 15 d.; Susanna, b. March 26, 1773, m. Willem Fonda, and d. March 18, 1850. a. 76 y. 11 mo. 23 d.; Josyna, b. Dec. 8, 1774, m. Gerrit Roseboom; Gerrit, b. Nov. 24, 1776, d. Nov. 1849, a. 73 y.; Obadia, b. Jan. 8, 1779, d. March, 29, 1850, a. 77 y. 2 mo. 14 d.; Anthony, b. Nov. 21, 1780, m. .... DeGraaff and d. Dec. 25, 1803, a. 65 y. (?); Thomas, b. May, 9, 1783, d. Nov. 6, 1784; Dorothea, b. Feb. 16, 1786, m. William Austin, and d. Sept. 7, 1854, a. 68 y. 6 mo. 22 d.; Daniel, b. Aug. 23, 1788, m. Elizabeth Helling; in 1867 resided in New Hartford.

HALENBECK, Nicolaas, and Jannetie Willet (Willis) Ch: Isaac, b. Dec. 10, 1771; Marytje, b. March 25, 1775. [Nicolaas H. and Maria Shutt, m. June, 5, 1787].

HALENBECK, Nanning, m. Alida Ten Eyck, Dec. 25, 1767. Ch: Maria, b. Nov. 22, 1772.

HALENBECK, James (Jacob), m. Ytje Bratt, Sept. 28, 1772. Ch: Anthony, b. Feb. 2, 1776; Gerrit, b. July 20, 1779; John, b. Oct. 20, 1791.

HALENBECK, Abraham, m. Maria Pruin, Aug. 24, 1776. Ch: Samuel, b. Dec. 11, 1779.

HALENBECK, Casparus, and Hilletje Sharp. Ch: Andries, b. Jan. 5, 1780; Hendrickje, b. Jan. 14, 1784.

HALENBECK, Daniel, Junr., and Geertruy Snyder. Ch: Abraham and Jacob, b. May 1, 1785.

HALENBECK, Henry B., m. Rachel Winne, July 29, 1790. Ch: Eleanor, bp. March 3, 1792; Sike, b. Jan. 18, 1794; Bernardus, b. March 2, 1796; Rachel, b. July 27, 1798; Jellis Winne, b. Jan, 21, 1801; Margaret, b. May 5, 1804; Dorothy, b. Sept. 2, 1806.

HALENBECK, John, m. Ann LaGrange, June 30, 1796. Ch: Christiaan LaGrange, b. Aug. 20, 1799; Hilletie, b. Jan. 15, 1802.

Hall, Joseph, and Johanna Patterson. Ch: John, b. June 16, 1777; Debora, b. July 2, 1779; John, b. July 15, 1781.

HALL, Matthew, and Jane Young. Ch: Samuel, bp. March 29, 1778.

HALL, Thomas, and Mary Helledice. Ch: Philip Hooker, b. March 15, 1797.

Ham, Caspar, m. Anna Leych, Oct. 31, 1721, he was naturalized Feb. 14, 1716. Ch: Johannes, bp. Feb. 20, 1723; Catharina, bp. Nov. 29, 1724; Geertruy, bp. Feb. 23, 1726; Petrus, bp. March 16, 1729; Maria, bp. Sept. 10, 1732.

HAM, Petrus, of Colonie, m. Marytje Mitchel (Michel), May 27, 1768. Ch: Annatie, b. July 9, 1769; Casparus, bp. Dec. 27, 1771; Andries, b. May 13, 1774; Annatie, b. May 12, 1776; Catharina, b. Aug. 21, 1778.

HAM, Coenraad, and Anne Morris. Ch: Elizabeth, b. Dec. 19, 1774.

Hamilton, Alexander, m. Elizabeth Schuyler, Dec. 9, 1780, she d. at Washington, D. C., Nov. 7, 1854, a. 97 y. Ch: Philip, b. Dec. 22, 1781.

Hansen. This is the surname assumed by the desendants of Capt. Hans Hendrickse, who early came to Beverwyck as a trader. His house lot was on the east side of Broadway next north of Bleecker Hall. He made his will Feb. 12, 169¾, and was deceased in 1697. He m. Eva Gillise, daughter of Jellis Pieterse, Meyer of Beverwyck, April 26, 1643, in New Amsterdam, and left the following Ch: Hendrick; Margareta, w. of Frederick Harmense Visscher; Johannes; Elsje.

HANSEN, Hendrick, merchant, m. Debora Van Dam, Sept. 21, 1692. In 1706, he occupied the lot next north of Bleecker Hall on Broadway, lying between the lots of Jacobus Schuyler and Dominie Lydius. He was mayor, 1698-9; made will Sept. 2, 1723, spoke of sons Nicolaas and Hans, and was buried in the church Feb. 19, 1724; his wife Debora was buried in the church, Nov. 5, 1742. Ch : Debora, bp. Aug. 20, 1693; Hans, bp. June 30, 1695; Maria, bp. April 18, 1697; m. David Schuyler; Nicolaas, bp. Sept. 25, 1698, settled at Tribes Hill before 1725; Pieter, bp. April 28, 1700; Rykaart, bp. Aug. 15, 1703; Jefie, bp. Oct. 14, 1705, d. early.

HANSEN, Johannes, m. Sara De Foreest, March 22, 1702. Ch: Margarita, bp. Dec. 25, 1702; Hanse, bp. July 14, 1706; Philippus, Oct. 23, 1709; Henrick, bp. Feb. 10, 1712; Isaac, bp. Sept. 12, 1714.

HANSEN, Hannes, and Neeltie Cornelise .... Ch: Annatie, bp. April 20, 1712.

HANSEN, Johannes (Hans), m. Sara Cuyler, April 25, 1723. He was mayor of Albany 1731-2, and 1754-6; made will March 10, 1756; two sons Johannes, and Pieter, then living; was buried Dec. 6, 1756. Ch: Hendrick, bp. Oct. 20, 1723; Elsie, bp. March 21, 1725; Johannes, bp. Aug. 13, 1727; Johannes, bp. Jan. 12, 1729; Debora, bp. Feb. 3, 1731; Johannes, bp. Sept. 10, 1732; Pieter, bp. Feb. 21, 1735, "Hans Hansen's little son Pieter was buried Jan. 23, 1737; " Pieter, bp. Oct. 6, 1737.

HANSEN, Richard, m. first, Sara Thong in New York, May 14, 1727, and secondly, Catharina Ten Broeck, July 5, 1738. His first wife was buried in the church, Oct. 25, 1733. Ch: Hendrick, bp. March 17, 1728; Walter, bp. Dec. 12, 1730; Pieter, bp. May 13, 1733; Debora, bp. Jan. 17, 1739; Johannes, bp. May 26, 1740; Pieter, bp. Oct. 18, 1741; Dirk, bp. April 24, 1743; Debora, bp. Jan. 6, 1745; Jeremie, bp. Aug. 17, 1746; Debora, bp. July 17, 1748; Hendrick, bp. May 20, 1750; Catarina, bp. Sept. 29, 1751; Maria, bp. March 3, 1754.

HANSEN, Philip, m. Geertruy Van Nes, Feb. 16, 1740. Ch: Sara, bp. Sept. 7, 1740; Jan, bp. March 28, 1742; Catahlyntje, bp. March 11, 1744; Magarietje, bp. Feb. 16, 1746; Annatie, bp. Feb. 18, 1750; Henderick, bp. Nov. 24, 1751; Catarina, bp. Oct. 28, 1753; Hendrick, bp. July 16, 1758.

HANSEN, Hans, Junr., m. Margarita Kip in New York, July 20, 1740. Ch: Johannes, bp. Apr. 24, 1741.

HANSEN, Isaac, m. Maria Bratt, Dec. 11, 1742. Ch: Johannes, bp. Oct. 16, 1743; Magdalena, bp. Jan. 4, 1745; Magdalena, bp. Feb. 16, 1746; Benjamin, bp. Oct. 25, 1747; Sara, bp. Aug. 20, 1749; Albert, bp. July 14, 1751; Magdalena, bp. July 8, 1753; Willempje, bp. Sept. 8, 1754; Margarita, bp. April 10, 1757.

HANSEN, Johannes, m. Geertruy Slingerland, Oct. 14, 1764. Cornelia, b. Sept. 19, 1765; Magdalena, b. Dec. 10, 1767; Isaac, b. Jan. 20, 1771; Isaac, bp. Dec. 7, 1776; Tennis, b. Aug. 17, 1781; Benjamin, b June 26, 1784, d. in Albany, April 28, 1863, a. 79 y.

HANSEN, Jan, m. Elizabeth Vander Heyden, Dec. 13, 1771. Ch: Elizabeth, b. April 30, 1774.

HANSEN, Albert, m. Engeltie Hansen, Dec. 7, 1778. Ch: Margarita, b. Nov. 29, 1778; Maria, b. Aug. 14, 1783.

HANSEN, Dirk, m. Lena Low, July 1, 1781. Ch: Catharine, b. May 26, 1782; Debora, b. June 7, 1787; Richard, b. Nov. 6, 1790.

HANSEN, Pieter, and Rachel Fonda. Ch: Hendrick. b. July 6, 1782.

Hansikker, Jurriaan, m. Anna Smith, Sept. 27, 1777. Ch: Adam, b. Jan. 22, 1778.

Hanway, John, and Hester Ham. Ch: John, b. Dec. 27, 1777.

Hardenbergh (Herttenberch), Gerrit Janse, was in Albany as early as 1667 ; in 1690, owned the sloop, Royal Albany ; he and wife Jaepie Schepmoes, made a joint will in 1678, their children are mentioned but not by name; one named Barendine, bap. Oct. 28, 1683.

Harding, Frank, of Claverac, and Catrine Janse Van Hoesen. He made will Dec. 19, 1737, . . . proved Nov. 3, 1742, and mentioned the following children : but not his wife : Jan, eldest son ; Willem ; Sara, wife of Jonathan Reese; Gerritje, bp. Jan. 17, 1692, m. Justus Valkenaer, both deceased at date of will; Volkie, m. Leendert Rees.

Harding (Hardick, Hardinks), Jan, of Clavarac, m. Maria Beckker, Dec. 22, 1706. Ch: Franciscus, bp. Sept. 28, 1707; Anna, bp. Jan. 22, 1710; Catharina, b. Dec. 12, 1711, "op Klaverack" and bp. at Loonenburgh, Jan. 13, 1712; Hilletje, b. Feb. 18, 1715; Elsia or Elizabeth, b. July 29, 1720.

Harenstrong, Jan, and Catharyn.... Ch: Jan, bp. April 22, 1736.

Hark, Jurriaen, and Jannetie Van Buren. Ch: Daniel, b. Aug. 12, 1778.

Harrick (Harwich ?), Andries, and Elizabeth Warner. Ch: Johannes Juriaan, b. Oct. 4, 1784.

Harrington (Harring), James, m. Christina Coens, Feb. 9, 1773. Ch: Maria, b. Nov. 6, 1774.

Harris, Jan (John), "geboren in Oude Engeland," m. first, Lysbet Claese; and secondly, Moeset Tassama "geboeren in Nieuw Engeland" May 3, 1701. Ch: Maria, bp. Nov. 22, 1685; Willem, bp. April 7, 1689; Willem, bp. Sept. 6, 1691; Lysbeth, bp. June 22, 1701; Tames, bp. Jan. 27, 1703; Jacob, bp. June 2, 1707; Francyntje, bp. July 4, 1708.

Harris, Willem, and Elizabeth .... Ch: James, bp. Oct. 24, 1756.

Harssen, or Harzen.

Harzen, Barnardus, m. Catharyna Pruyn, Feb. 12, 1737. [Bernardus H. m. Sara Myer, in New York, April 5, 1735.] Ch: Jacob, bp. Feb. 22, 1738; Anna, bp. March 15, 1741; Frans, bp. Jan. 19, 1752; Frans, bp. Feb. 24, 1754.

Harzen, Jacobus (Jacob, Junr.), m. Maria Pruyn Bruin), May 8, 1740. Ch: Cornelia, bp. March 1, 1741; Margarita, bp. June 5, 1743; Margarita, bp. April 27, 1746; Margarita, bp. Jan. 10, 1748; Aaltie, bp. Aug. 12, 1750; Maria, bp. April 15, 1753.

Harssen, Jacob, m. Alida Groesbeck, June 4, 1764. Ch: Sara, b. May 13, 1765.

Harssen, Mattheus, and Bregje Van Hoesen. Ch: Volkert, b. June 19, 1773: Robert, b. April 19, 1776; Alida, b. Sept. 3, 1784.

Harssen, Arent, m. Aaltie Quackenbush in New York, May 1, 1768. Ch: Jannetie, b. Oct. 21, 1775; Arent Leendert, bp. Nov. 29, 1778.

Harssen (Harsingh), Frans, m. Rebecca Spoor, July 10, 1779. Ch: Bernardus, b. Sept. 19, 1780; Catharina, b. Oct. 14, 1783; Catharina, b. Feb. 24, 1785; Gerrit, b. May 16, 1787; Bernardus, b. Feb. 1, 1790; Magdalene, b. July 8, 1795.

Harssen, Isaac, and Maria Roller. Ch: Geertruy, b. Jan. 5, 1787.

Harster, Zacharias, and Rebecca Spoor (See Frans Harssen above). Ch: Johannes, b. Dec. 1, 1792.

Hart, Nicholaas, and Margarita .... Ch: Phœbe, bp. Dec. 26, 1768.

Hart, Henry, m. Elizabeth Visscher, Oct. 25, 1782. Ch: Ezekiel, b. March 22, 1783; Harmen Visscher, bp. Sept. 21, 1784.

Hartgers, Pieter (Van Vee), came over in 1643, and settled at Manhattans, removed in 1654 to Beverwyck and became one of the magistrates; m. Sytje Roeloffse, daughter of Anneke Janse, and had two daughters: Jannetie, bp. in Manhattans, Sept. 5, 1649; and Rachel. He returned to Holland and d. in 1670.

Harten, William, and Any Dody (Doty ?). Ch: Elizabeth, b. Jan. 1, 1781.

Hartley, William, and Frances .... Ch: Thomas, bp. Feb. 20, 1757.

Hartwell, John, and Mary Holiday. Ch: Hannah, b. Oct. 28, 1778.

Hartwich, John, and Rachel Archer. Ch: Catharine, b. July 12, 1784.

Harwich, Joost, m. Christina Philips, Aug. 24, 1766. Ch: Jacob, b. April 11, 1768; Christina, b. July 8, 1777.

Harwich, Philip, and Susanna Walton. Ch: Elizabeth, b. July 18, 1777.

Harwig, Coenraad, m. Magdalena Meyer, Nov. 23, 1770. Ch: Catharina, b. March 23, 1778; Magdalena, b. Aug. 6, 1780.

Hash, Hannes, and Catharina Possing (Bussing ?). Ch: Johann Pieter, b. June 27, 1764.

Haslet, Thomas, and Margaret Gibson. Ch: Thomas, b. April 21, 1781; Mary, bp. March 30, 1783.

Haswell, John, and Mary Halliday. Ch: John, b. Jan. 1, 1780.

Haswell, Robert, m. Sarah Mark, Nov. 24, 1780. Ch: Mary, b. March 1, 1781.

Haswell, Joseph. m. Mary Mark, Oct. 14, 1779. Ch: John, b. Sept. 27, 1781.

Haswell, Arthur, m. Mary Coughtry (Cofftree), Aug. 19, 1781. Ch: Elizabeth, b. May 12, 1782; Mary, b. Oct. 24, 1784.

Hatfield, Edmund, and Jane Ranken. Ch: John, b. Nov. 30, 1797; Mary Anna, b. Oct. 16, 1798.

Haver, Christiaan, and Engeltie Vander Werken. Ch: Geertruy, bp. June 2, 1751; Christiaan, bp. June 3, 1753.

Hawks (Hawx), Christophel, and Mary Pase singer. Ch: Andrew, b. Oct. 5, 1796; Anna Maria, b. Dec. 24, 1800.

Hay, Udny, and Margariet Smith. Ch: Jane-Ann, b. Jan. 2, 1778.

Haylingh, William, and Jenny .... Ch: William, bp. June 9, 1723.

Hayner, see Heiner.

Heaton, John, and M. .... Ch: Rebecca, bp. May 16, 1736.

Heener, see Heiner.

Heemstraat (Van Heemstraaten), Takel Dirks and Maritie .... Ch: Dirk; Jannetie, bp. Dec. 7, 1784.

Heemstraat (Van Heemstraaten) Dirk Takelse of "Halve Maan," m. Claartje (Catharina) Quackenbos, Nov. 3, 1700. Ch: Taakel, bp. May 4, 1701: Johannes, bp. Oct. 25, 1702; Machtelt, bp. April 16, 1704; Maritje, bp. Dec. 25, 1706; Johannes, bp. Jan. 12, 1709; Tryntje, bp. Sept. 27, 1713; Jacob, bp. Aug. 11, 1717.

Heemstraat, Dirk, and Maria Barrois (Barreway). Ch: Bata, bp. May 12, 1754; Carel, bp. March 21, 1756; Johannes, bp. Nov. 20, 1757; Hannes, bp. Jan. 18, 1761; Jacob, b. July 11, 1762.

Heemstraat, Hannes, Junr., of Nistigeoenen, m. Elizabeth Bovie, Dec. 30, 1757. Ch: Machtelt, bp. Oct. 15, 1758; Bata, bp. March 12, 1761; Bata, b. July 20, 1764; Catharina, b. March 3, 1767; Frances, b. July 23, 1769; Annatie, bp. Nov. 4, 1773; Johannes, b. May 24, 1779.

HEEMSTRAAT, Jacob, m. Cath. Duret, Nov. 5, 1763. Ch: Johannes, b. March 31, 1765; Annatie, b. July 27, 1766; Bata, b. July 6, 1768; Clara, bp. in Schenectady, July 22, 1772; Teunis, bp. in Schenectady, Sept. 1, 1778.

HEEMSTRAAT, Carel, m. Geertruy Van der Werken, Aug. 5, 1779. Ch: Dirk, b. March 2, 1781; Albert, b. Aug. 2, 1782; Arent, b. March 8, 1784; Jacob, bp. Sept. 17, 1786; Alida, bp. June 7, 1789.

Heene, Jacob, and Magdalena Creller. Ch: Cornelis, b. March 15, 1770.

Heens, or Haines.

HEENS (Haines ?), Arent, and Elizabeth Freelig. Ch: Annatie, b. Sept. 11, 1777.

Haines, Lodewick, and Margaret Arnold. Ch: Annatie, b. Dec. 21, 1788.

Heffenaar, Valentine, and Catrina .... Ch: Rachel, bp. Oct. 20, 1754.

Hegerman, Christofer, and Elisabeth Copper. Ch: Abraham, b. Nov. 25, 1767.

Heidely, Johannes, and Catharina Zegerin. Ch: Juriaan, b. Jan. 1, 1770; Michael, b. Jan. 2, 1773.

Heiner, Heener, Hainer, Hehner.

Heiner (Hegher), Samuel and Rebecca Feller, Ch: Catharina, " 4 weken oud" bp. July 3, 1763; Jacob, bp. Oct. 5, 1766.

Heiner, Philip, and Eva Trever (Dryver). Ch: Anna, b. Nov. 18, 1764; Philip, bp. Feb. 5, 1767; Petrus, b. March 25, 1770.

Heener, Johannes, m. Catharina Theter, Nov. 14, 1769. Ch: Wilhelmus, b. July 28, 1770.

Heiner (Hayner), Wilhelmus (William), and Elizabeth Muller. Ch: Margarita, b. June 10, 1787; Jonas, b. Dec. 13, 1790.

HEINER (Haines), Jacob, and Elizabeth Kinter. Ch: Catharine, b. April 19, 1790.

Hehner, see Heiner.

Heller, Jacob, and Elizabeth Hellering. Ch: Belthazar, b. July 30, 1763; Maria Catharina, b. Sept. 3, 1766.

Hellingh, William, and Geertruy .... Ch: Jeems, bp. April 11, 1725.

HELLINGH, William, and Elizabeth Halenbeck. Ch: Willem, bp. July 9, 1749; Susanna, bp. Oct. 27, 1751; Hendricus, bp. July 29, 1754; Jannetie, bp. Nov. 6, 1757.

Holmer, Johannes, and Catharina Muller. Ch: Margarita, b. Oct. 3, 1783.

Hendrickse, Andries (*alias de heele*), of Kinderhoek, born in Otmars in Twent, made will Jan 5, 1680-1, made Cornelia Arentse Vanden Bergh, wife of John Gilbert, his heir; she was his sister's daughter.

HENDRICKSE, Hendrick [Van Harstenhorst] was in Beverwyck in 1656, a baker by trade: he was deceased Sept. 23, 1662, when his widow, Geertruy Barentse Dwingelo, made a contract of marriage with Jacob Hevick or Gevick, promising to reserve out of her estate 100 gl. for her two children, Lysbet, aged 6 years, and Judick, aged 3 years, by her late husband.

Henry, Robert, and Elizabeth Vernor. Ch: Maria, b. Jan. 26, 1777.

Herbertsen, Andries, see Constapel.

HERBERTSEN, Marten, see Marten Gerritse Van Bergen.

Herder, Michael, and Maria Rees. Ch: Benjamin, bp. Aug 26, 1752; Maria, bp. April 5, 1756.

Herman, Jacob, and Barbara Vos. Ch: Coenraad, b. March 3, 1764; Willem, b. Aug. 23, 1766.

Hermans, Wilhelmus, and Antje Simssin (?). Ch : Andries, b. Oct. 14, 1780.

HERMANS, William, and Mary Scott. Ch: Abraham, b. April 7, 1796.

HERMANS, Andrew N., and Eleanor Van Bergen. Ch: William Van Bergen, b. Feb. 29, 1796.

HERMANS, John, and Eleanor Sheffer. Ch: John, b. Aug. 27, 1796.

Herrick, Juriaan, and Jannetie Van Buren. Ch: Tanneke, b. May 1, 1780.

Herring., Abraham, and Elizabeth Ivers, Ch: Mary, b. March 30, 1798; Abraham, b. June 12, 1799.

Herttenberch, see Hardenbergh.

Herty, John Jacob, and Margarita Pieterse. Ch: Johannes, bp. June 24, 1753.

Hesty, William, and Margarita .....Ch: Robert b. May 8, 1762.

Hesselingh, Dirk, was in Albany in 1666, subsequently at Schenectady where he bought, in 1671, a bouwery of Juriaen Teunise Tappen, which he sold the following year to Harmen Vedder. He also bought land at Lubberde's land [Troy]. In 1667 he m. Eytje Hendrickse, who with her three sisters had been taken prisoners by the Indians at Yonkers in 1655. Her sister Albrechtie was rescued in 1667 and brought into New Haven.

Hevick (Gevick), Jacob, b. at Mecklenburgh, made a marriage contract with Geertruy Barentse Dwingelo widow of the late Hendrick Hendrickse Van Hartstenhorst, in which they agree to reserve half the bride's estate for her children: Lysbet a. 6 y. andJudick a. 3 y., by said Hendrick H. V. H. In 1666 in company with Reyndert Pieterse he bought Pieter Bronck's house, lot, and brewery.

Hyer, Gerrit, and Jannetie Van Slyck. Ch: Tabatha, b. March 19, 1778; Elizabeth, b. Dec. 27, 1781; Jannetie, b. March 6, 1783; Lydia b. June 13, 1785; Lydia, b. Sept. 16, 1787.

Hickson, James, and Elizabeth Van Slyck. Ch: Richard, b. June 14, 1795.

Hieralyman, see Jeroloman.

Hiesoor, Stephanus of Kinderhook, and Sarah Hoorbeck. Ch: Neeltie, bp. Jan. 9, 1709.

Hilbing, William, Jr., and Susanna Halenbeck. Ch: Dorothy b. April 9, 1789.

Hillebrand, Wendell, m. first, Geertruy Visbach June 9, 1764; and secondly, Annatie Hillebrands [in 1787] : Ch: Annatie, b. Dec. 29, 1764; Annatie, bp. Sept. 27, 1767; Jacob, b. Jan. 25, 1770; Johannes, b. Aug. 29, 1777; Geertruy, b. Jan. 9, 1779; Johannes, b. April 5, 1781; Elsie, b. Oct. 27, 1783; Elizabeth, b. April 26, 1788.

Hilten (Hilton), Willem, " Weduwnaer Van Sara Ebb," m. Anna Berkhoven (Barko, Beekhoven), April 6, 1693. [Wm. Hilton, buried Feb. 12, 1749]. Ch: Sara, bp. April 9, 1693; Anna, bp. Jan. 23, 1695; Elizabeth, bp. Dec. 10, 1696; Mary, bp. Nov. 20, 1698; Richard, bp. March 2, 1701; Elizabeth, bp. Feb. 10, 1703; Jacobus, bp.Aug. 19, 1705; William, bp. May 16, 1708.

HILTEN, Reykert, m. Maria (Molly) Bennewe (Bennoit), Dec. 17, 1726. Ch: Anna, bp. Sept. 24, 1727; Petrus, bp. Nov. 10, 1728; Hendrikie, bp. May 17, 1730; Willem, bp. March 8, 1732 [Willem Hilten "a young man" was buried Oct. 24, 1755]; Geertruy, bp. June 23, 1734; Maria, bp. Jan. 12, 1737; Jacob, bp. Sept. 14, 1740. [Richard Hilten d. Jan. 1, 1795, in his 97th y., the "oldest man in the city."]

HILTEN, Jacobus, m. first, Judith Marten, Nov. 11, 1733; secondly, Sarah Barnton, April 4, 1762. Ch: Willem, bp. Aug. 18, 1734, d. June 19, 1825, a. 91 y.; Maria, bp. Nov. 7, 1736; Pieter, bp. Feb. 20, 1739; Adam, bp. Aug. 9, 1741; Annatie, bp. Feb. 26, 1744; Robert, bp. Feb. 16, 1746; Sara, bp. June 28, 1747; Robert, bp. Oct. 22, 1749, d. in Bethlehem June 13, 1829 in 80th y.; Jacobus, bp. March 18, 1753, a revolutionary soldier, d. Dec. 7, 1836, a. 84 y.; Dirk, bp. Nov. 30, 1755.

Hilton, Willem, Junr. (R.) m. Maria (Margr:) Jones, Oct. 31, 1736; secondly, Elizabeth Brooks [in 1758.] Ch: Elizabeth, bp. Oct. 30, 1737; Willem, bp. Feb. 3, 1740; Thomas, bp. May 16, 1742; Pieter, bp. Feb. 17, 1745, d. in Guilderland, Jan. 26, 1836, a. 92 y.; Richard, bp. Dec. 20, 1747; Ryckert, bp. June 24, 1759; Jan, bp. Dec. 25, 1761; Phœbe, b. Feb. 23, 1768.

HILTON, Benjamin, m. Mary Price, Sept. 24, 1742. Ch· Benjamin, bp. Sept. 3, 1749; William, bp. Oct. 27, 1751.

HILTON, Petrus, m. first, Machtel Wyngaert; and secondly, Anna Broecks [about 1756.] Ch: Ryckert, bp. July 1, 1753; Johannes, bp. Sept. 29, 1754. His first w. was buried Sept. 25, 1754. Machtelt, bp. Sept. 9, 1756; Jonathan, bp. March 26, 1758; Jonathan, bp. Nov. 7, 1761; Maria, b. July 24, 1764; Pieter, b. Sept. 13, 1766; Rebecca, b. Jan. 23, 1771.

HILTON, Pieter, and Judith Berrit (Bareuth). Ch: Jacobus, b. Dec. 29, 1769; Maria, b. Nov. 9, 1770; Margarita, b. Oct. 1, 1782.

HILTON, Robert, and Elizabeth Burges (Bortjes). He d. at Bethlehem, June 13, 1829, in his 80th y. Ch: Maria, b. Sept. 7, 1775; Sara, b. Nov. 23, 1777.

HILTON, Jacob, and Sara Barrington. Ch: Petrus, b. Oct. 15, 1776; William Barrington, b. May 26, 1779; Elizabeth, b. Jan. 19, 1782; Folkert Douwe, b. Jan. 27, 1787.

HILTON, William B., and Margarita Gladdon. Ch: Maria, b. Feb. 13, 1778.

HILTON, Pieter, and Elizabeth Eights. Ch: Willem, b. Aug. 31, 1778.

HILTON, Thomas, and Nancy Cadoghan. Ch: Anna, b. Aug. 14, 1779.

HILTON, Jonathan, m. first, Cornelia Van Antwerp, April 27, 1783; secondly, Catharine Hansen [about 1789.] His last wife d. Dec. 16, 1838, a. 85 y. 1 m. 22 d. Ch: Elizabeth, b. July 9, 1784, d. Aug. 6, 1855, a. 70 y.; Philip, b. Oct. 25, 1789; Simon Van Antwerp, b. Feb. 6, 1792.

HILTON, Philip, and Sara Barrington (see *Philip* Hilton above). Ch: Johannes Ten Eyck, b. Oct. 10, 1784; d. Sept. 7, 1858, a. 74 y.

HILTON, Jonathan, and Maria Baldwin. Ch: Pieter, b. Nov. 19, 1786.

HILTON, John W., m. Elizabeth Black, Aug. 15, 1784 [John Hilton d. July 18, 1853, a. 92 y.] Ch: Elizabeth, b. March 28, 1786; Hannah, b. Aug. 17, 1790; Rebecca, b. Aug. 1, 1792; John, b. June 29, 1799; Rebecca, b. July 24, 1800; John, b. July 21, 1803.

HILTON, James (Jacobus), m. Caty Fryer, Sept. 6, 1789. He d. Dec. 7, 1836, a. 84 y. Ch: James, b. Jan. 7, 1790, d. Nov. 2, 1838, a. 49 y.; Hannah, b. Dec. 9, 1792; Hannah, b. May 10, 1797; William, b. Sept. 10, 1799.

HILTON, Richard J., m. Elizabeth Norton, Dec. 9, 1792. [Richard H. d. April 15, 1846, a. 87 y.]. Ch: Sarah, b. Feb. 9, 1794; Jacob, b. Dec. 23, 1800 (?); Maria, b. Feb. 11, 1803.

HILTON, Dirk, and Mary Van Deusen. Ch: Catharine, b. Jan. 11, 1796.

HILTON, Benjamin, and Jemima Van Valkenburgh. Ch: John, b. Aug. 2, 1799; John, b. Feb. 28, 1802.

Hinde, John, and Annatie Thomas. Ch: John, bp. Aug. 9, 1747.

Hindermond, see Hoendermont.

Hindern, Jacob, and Margaret Philips. Ch: James, b. May 13, 1792.

Hitchcock (Hickok), Humphrey, m. Sara Thomas, widow, Feb. 20, 1742. Ch: Willem, bp. Jan. 30, 1743.

Hock, John, and Ellie Dunbar. Ch: Henry, b. Oct. 8, 1792.

Hodick, Thomas, and Catharina Conny. Ch: Anna, b. June 11, 1783.

Hoendermont, Johannes Henrich, and Anna Catharina ..... Ch: Dorothee, bp. Sept. 7, 1755.

Hoenderman, Henrich, and Catarina Margarita .... Ch: Janney, bp. March 12, 1758.

Hoendermond, Hendrick, and Baatje Smith, Ch: Marytje, bp. Nov. 9, 1777; Hendrick, bp. April 16, 1780.

Hoes, see Goes.

Hoesie (Huzzon), Daniel, and Mary .... Ch: Simon, bp. March 7, 1736; Ann, bp. Aug. 14, 1737.

Hoffman, Marten, sadler, of Revel, m. first, Lysbet Hermans of Ootmorsen, March 31, 1663; and secondly, Emmerentje De Witte of Emberland, in Manhattans, May 16, 1664; in Albany, 1662-76; owned a house and lot in New York.

HOFFMAN, George, and Maria Carnin. Ch: Barbara, bp. Aug. 21, 1757.

HOFFMAN, Philip, and Elizabeth Clerk. Ch: Martin Jacob, bp. Feb. 14, 1757.

HOFFMAN, Hermanus, and Catharina Douw. Ch: Martinus, b. April 8, 1772.

HOFFMAN, Marten, and Mary Van Benthuysen. Ch: Catharine, b. Aug. 1, 1792.

Hoffmeyer, Willem, in 1656, was fined 500 guilders and to be imprisoned until the fine be paid, and banished three years from Manhattans for conveying beer up the river and selling it to the Indians. He retired to Beverwyck where in 1657, Jochem Wesselse Backer brought an action against him for possession of a house; the defendant alleged that plaintiff being his stepfather made him a present of the premises on his wedding day; plaintiff puts in a special agreement and gains the cause.

Hogen, Hogan, Hoogen, Hoghing, Hoghil, Hogh, Hog, etc.

HOGEN, Harmanus, and Margriet Dirckse. Ch: Dirk, bp. June 19, 1692.

HOGEN (Hoogen), Jurriaen, m. Maria Beeckman, Nov. 9, 1714. Ch: Joannes, bp. March 2, 1718; Anna, bp. April 3, 1720; Martha, bp. April 8, 1722; Eva, bp. Jan. 22, 1727; Eva, bp. Oct. 20, 1728; Margarita, bp. April 4, 1731; Alida, bp. Jan. 20, 1734; Maria, bp. Dec. 4, 1737; Susanna, bp. Feb. 24 1740.

HOGEN, Willem, innkeeper, "Van Bor in Yrlandt in de Kings county," m. Martena (Anna) Bekker. Sept. .... 1692. She was buried July 5, 1736. Ch: Jurriaen, bp. April 9, 1693; Daniel, bp. March 10, 1695; Maria, bp. June 6, 1697; Margariet, bp. Aug. 4, 1700; Judith, bp. Feb. 28, 1703.

HOGEN, Willem, Junr., and Pietertje Dow. Ch: Neeltie, bp. July 31, 1734; Hendricus, bp. Oct. 3, 1736; Martinus, bp. Dec. 24, 1738; Margarieta, bp. Jan. 31, 1748.

HOGEN (Hogan) Hendrick, and Alida .... Ch: Franciscus, bp. July 26, 1736. (See also Logen.)

HOGEN (Hogh) Johannes and Catharyna .... Ch: Johannes, bp. May 28, 1738; Francis, bp. June 29, 1740; Juliana, bp. Oct. 31, 1742.

HOGEN, Willem, Jr., m. Susanna Lansing, Jan. 17, 1740. Ch: Maria, bp. July 16, 1740; Isaac, bp. Nov. 14, 1742; Juriaan. bp Aug. 25, 1745; Jannetie, bp. Dec. 13, 1747; Martina, bp. Nov. 4, 1750; Elsje, bp. April 1, 1753; Marten, bp. Sept. 21, 1755; Gerrit, bp. July 29, 1759.

HOGEN (Hogel), Edward, m. Maria Egmond, June 14, 1742. Ch: Elizabeth, bp April 17, 1743; Jacob, bp. Oct. 25, 1747; Anna, bp. March 10, 1751; Franciscus, bp. Nov. 14, 1756; Nicholaas, bp. Nov. 23, 1760.

HOGEN (Hogil. Hogh, Hog), Pieter, and Catrina Vosburgh. Ch: Francis, bp. Oct. 25, 1747; Abraham, bp. Aug. 20, 1749; Elizabeth, bp. Aug. 25, 1751; Geertje, bp. Aug. 12, 1753; Johannes, bp. Dec. 11, 1757; Isaac, b. March 25, 1760; Annatie, b. May 27, 1762; Maritie, bp. July 22, 1767; Janneke, b. Nov. 12, 1770.

HOGEN, Marten, and Rachel Slingerland. He was buried June 7, 1750. Ch: Maria, bp. Oct. 22, 1749.

HOGEN, Barent, of Hosauck m. Geertje Huyck, June 15, 1750. Ch: Franciscus, bp. Dec. 8, 1754; Elizabeth, bp. Dec. 25, 1756; Pieter, bp. July 26, 1761; Cornelis, "4 weken oud" bp. July 3, 1763; Marytje, b July 18, 1770.

HOGEN (Hoghil), Franciscus, of Steen Rabie, and Sara Young. Ch: John, bp. Dec. 6, 1761; William, b. Sept. 28. 1763; Elizabeth, b. Dec. 26, 1764; Catharina, b. Feb. 8, 1771; Hendrik, b. May 5, 1773.

HOGEN (Hoghil) Hannes of Hosac, m. Elisabeth Leek, Nov. 14, 1764. Ch: George, b. Nov. 7, 1766; Jacobus, b. Aug. 1, 1771.

HOGEN (Hoghing) Isaac, m. Maritie Gerritsen, Nov. .... 1767. Ch: Willem, b. March 11, 1768; Dirckie, b. Sept. 30, 1769; Hendrik, b. Nov. 8, 1771.

HOGEN (Hoghing) Jurriaen, and Annatie White. Ch: Willem, b. May 6, 1779; John, b. March 7, 1781; Gerrit, b. July 29, 1783, d. July 16, 1848. a. 65 y.; John b. Aug. 23, 1786; Mary Ann, b. Oct. 2, 1791; Eetie, b. Dec. 8, 1794.

HOGEN (Hoghil), Francis, m. Cornelia (De) Foreest, Feb. 6, 1780. Ch: Edward, b. Nov. 10, 1780; Johannes, b. June 23, 1787.

HOGHIL, Nicolaas, m. Catharina (Van) Valkenburgh, Aug. 22, 1784. Ch: Edward, bp. June 12, 1785; Jacob, b. June 21, 1787.

HOLBROOK, Ephraim, and Esther Johnson, Ch: Caty, b. Oct. 2, 1781; Johnson, b. May 29, 1783.

HOLLAND, Henry, and Jenny Sehly. Capt. Henry Holland had command of the garrison at Albany, in 1732, when he was incapacitated " by the Providence of Almighty God." In 1713-17 his residence was on west corner of Broadway and Beaver street. Ch: Mary, bp. Feb. 9, 1701; Edward, bp. Sept. 6, 1702; Henry, bp. March 1, 1704; Sealy, bp. Jan. 5, 1707.

HOLLAND, Edward, mayor of Albany 1733-41; his first wife was Magdalena March 26, 1737. Valentine says he married Frances, dau. of William Nicolls. Ch: Magdalena Mary, bp. June 4, 1727; Ann, bp. Oct. 15, 1732.

HOLLAND, Henry, m. Alida Beekman, Dec. 14, 1728. Ch: Eva, bp. June 27, 1736.

HOLLAND, Hitchen, his first wife was Mary .....Ch: Henrietta, bp. Oct. 31, 1736. His second wife was Margarieta Collins. Ch: Margarieta, bp. May 28, 1749; John Collins, bp. Nov. 24, 1754.

HOLLAND, Thomas, and Christina Barheit. Ch: James, bp. May 10, 1752.

HOND (Hont, Hunt ?) Willem, "geboren tot London in oude Engelandt," m. Geertury Gerritse Van Schoonhoven, Oct. 27, 1700. Ch: Gerrit (Geurt) bp. Jan. 12, 1701; Elizabeth, bp. Nov. 4, 1702; Maria, bp. June 18, 1704; Elizabeth, bp. Dec. 22, 1706.

HONDECOUTRE, Daniel, a trader from New York in Beverwyck, 1661-73.

HOOGEBOOM, Cornelis Pieterse, tile and brickmaker, was in Manhatans in 1656; at New Amstel, on the Delaware, in 1657, at which time he had a son in the same trade at Beverwyck; in 1660-1 at Beverwyck; associating with himself, Jan Andriese De Graaf, he attempted brickmaking at Manhatans in 1661, but with indifferent success. In 1664, he engaged to make tiles at Beverwyck for Gerrit Van Slichtenhorst, from January to November for 60 beavers, half in tiles. In 1675 he was at Kingston, where he probably resided till his death. In 1719, Pieter Hogenboom, Ruleif Elting, Cornelis Elting, Thomas Noxon and Jacobus Brown, petition for a survey of the *Great Vly* in Kingston, come to them by the decease of Cornelis Hogenboom and Janite his widow and Severyn Tenhout, late of the county of Ulster.

HOOGEBOOM, Bartholomeus (Meuwis, Mees), Pieterse, probably came to New Netherland with his brother Cornelis, about the year 1656. In 1657, he had an affray in Beverwyck with Jacob Loockermans, who drew a knife and wounded him severely in the face for which he was sentenced to pay 350 guilders. At that time Hoogeboom was servant of Claes HendrickseVan Utrecht. In 1685, he was fined 12 shillings and costs of court for burying his negro in a private and suspicious manner. In 1680, he was a skipper on the Hudson, plying between New York and Albany. He died Feb. 15, 1702; his wife Catryn .... in 1707. Ch: Bartholomeus, bp. Dec. 30, 1683; Pieter; Dirk ?.

HOOGEBOOM, Pieter Meese of Claverac, m. Jannetje Muller, Jan. 26, 1698. He made his will June 20, 1747... ; proved, Feb. 23, 1758; in it he mentioned the following children, except Cornelis and Annatie. Ch :

Catharyntje, bp. Sept. 3, 1699, m. Philip Conyn; Cornelis, bp. Jan. 5, 1701; Bartholomeus, bp. May 10, 1702; Hilletje, bp. Jan. 8, 1704, m. Jochem Radcliff; Ariaantje, bp. May 13, 1705, m. Lourens Van Allen; Maritie, bp. March 23, 1707, m. Jochem Van den Bergh; Johannes, bp. July 4, 1708; Geertruy, bp. Jan. 22, 1710, m. Willem Van Nes; Jeremias, bp. Oct. 14, 1711; Annatie, bp. Oct. 9, 1712.

HOOGEBOOM, Dirk of Claverac, and Maria Delmont, Ch: Catharina, bp. Aug. 21, 1709; Maria, bp. May 30, 1725.

HOOGEBOOM, Bartholomeus, and Hendrikje .... Ch: Anna, bp. Oct. 3, 1730.

HOOGEBOOM, Jeremias, and Jannetje .... Ch: Jannetje, bp. Feb. 6, 1743.

HOOGEBOOM, Pieter, and Heyltje Van Deusen. Ch: Cornelis, bp. Jan. 22, 1754.

Hoogen, see Hogen.

Hooghkerke (Van Hooghkerke), Lucas Lucase, m. first, Henderikje Janse, Feb. 10, 1686; secondly, Judik Marselis, Nov. 23, 1692; the last was buried Aug. 19, 1734. Ch: Anneken, bp. Jan. 23, 1687; Maria, bp. Oct. 27, 1689; Hendrikje, bp. Aug. 20, 1693; Annetje, bp. Dec. 4, 1695; Maria, bp. July 10, 1698; Elizabeth, bp. May 11, 1701, buried Aug. 26, 1752; Johannes, bp. Jan. 30, 1704; Sara, bp. Sept. 9, 1705; Rachel, bp. March 9, 1709; Lucas, bp. April 20, 1712. [Lucas H. was buried March 13, 1741.]

HOOGHKERKE, Lucas, m. Rebecca Fonda, Aug. 11, 1734. She was buried Nov. 6, 1750. Ch: Lucas, bp. Nov. 17, 1734, buried June 9, 1756; Isaac, bp. March 2, 1737; Judikje, bp. Dec. 31, 1738; Abraham and Jacob, bp. Feb. 1, 1741; Alida, bp. March 14, 1742; Abraham, bp. Oct. 19, 1744; Johannes, bp. July 12, 1747; Jacob, bp. Jan. 7, 1750.

HOOGHKERK, Isaac, m. Rachel Van Santen [Zandt], Oct. 28, 1763; he d. Sept. 12, 1809, a. 72 y. 5 m. 22 d. Ch: Rebecca, b. June 16, 1766; Antie, b. Aug. 25, 1770; Lucas, b. March 22, 1775; Gerrit, b. Aug. 8, 1778.

HOOGHKERK, Abraham, m. Antje Hilton, Oct. 18, 1767. He d. May 12, 1807, a. 63 y. 6 m. 26 d. Ch: Rebecca, b. July 26, 1768; Jacobus, b. Oct. 21, 1770; Lucas, b. Aug. 7, 1773; Maria, b. Nov. 27, 1776; Abraham, b. Oct. 18, 1781; Willem, b. Feb. 22, 1785.

HOOGHKERK, Johannes, m. Margarita (Elizabeth) Meerthen (Marten), Aug. 4, 1776. Margareta, widow of John H., d. Nov 30, 1830, a. 82 y. Ch: Rebecca, bp. Nov. 10, 1776; Elizabeth, b. Aug. 18, 1778; Lucas, b. July 10, 1780; Elizabeth, b. Nov. 30, 1782; Alida, b. March 22, "de Vader overleden," 1785.

HOOGHKERK, Jacobus (James), m. Alida Van Zandt, July 3, 1792. Ch: Ann, b. May 8, 1793; John, b. Oct. 5, 1794; John, b. Oct. 22, 1795; Elizabeth, b. July 28, 1797; Alida, b. Oct. 31, 1800; Abraham, b. Aug. 25, 1802; Alida, b. April 12, 1806; William, b. March 21, 1808; Isaac, b. Aug. 4, 1810.

HOOGHKERK, Lucas, and Eleanor (Nelly, Helen) De Foreest. Ch: Walter, b. May 13, 1797; Ann, b. July 4, 1798; Walter, b. April 25, 1800; Abraham, b. April 4, 1802; Philip, b. Sept. 22, 1804; Alida, b. Feb. 16, 1807.

HOOGHKERK, Lucas J., and Mary Burton. Ch: Rebecca, b. March 17, 1799; Isaac, b. Sept. 2, 1801; Susannah, b. Dec. 26, 1803, d. Sept. 28, 1808, a. 4 y. 9 m. 19 d.; Elizabeth, b. Feb. 28, 1806; Rachel, bp. June 19, 1808.

Hooghstrasser, Paisly (Paulus?), and Elizabeth .... Ch: Paichir (Pieter?) b. Oct. 18, 1765.

HOOGHSTRASSER, Jacob, and Maria E. (Mareillys) Hooghstrasser. Ch: Maria Elizabeth, b. June 10, 1768; Maria, bp. May 19, 1771.

Hooghteeling, Mathys, and Maria Hendrikse. In 1676, M. H. was 32 y. old, he d. 1706. Ch: Coenraad; Jacob (?); Zytje, who m. 1st, Frans Morris, and 2d, Patrick McGregory; Rachel, bp. Dec. 28, 1684; Mathys, bp. April 29, 1694.

HOOGHTEELING, Coenraad Mathys, m. Tryntje Willemse Van Slyck in 1688. Ch: Hendrick, bp. Nov. 17, 1689; Willem, bp. Jan. 17, 1692; Maritje, bp. April 15, 1694; Mathys, bp. June 14, 1696; Pieter, bp. Oct. 9, 1698; Beertje, bp. Dec. 29, 1700; Hendrik, bp. June 20, 1703; Teunis, bp. Sept. 29, 1705; Johannes, bp. June 6, 1708; Jannetje, bp. April 30, 1710; Jonathan, bp. April 20, 1712.

Hooghteling, Jacob, of Kinderhook, and Jannetje . . . Ch: Elizabeth, bp. Jan. 7, 1705.

HOOGHTELING, Willem, m. Lena Uzile, Nov. 9, 1716. Ch: Coenraat, bp. Aug. 25, 1717; Pieter, bp. Oct. 19, 1718; Tryntje, bp. Dec. 25, 1720; Cornelia, bp. Sept. 30, 1722; Maria, bp. July 5, 1724; Elizabeth, bp. April 23, 1727; Mathias, bp. Feb. 19, 1729; Jonathan, bp. Sept. 12, 1736; Willem, bp. Sept. 7, 1740.

HOOGHTELING, Hendrik, m. Hester Pricker (Bricker), Sept. 12, 1729. Ch: Thomas, bp. Dec. 23, 1731; Maria, bp. Feb. 22, 1747.

HOOGHTELING, Teunis, and Dorothea Van den Bergh. Ch: Rykert, bp. Jan. 25, 1744; Catarina, bp. May 19, 1751.

HOOGHTELING, Coenraad, m. 1st, Catharina ....; 2d, Cornelia Bratt. Ch: Catharina, bp. April 15, 1744; Lena, bp. Feb. 22, 1747.

HOOGHTELING, Pieter, and Anna Becker. Ch: Lena, bp. Jan. 1, 1749; Gerrit, b. May 26, 1751; Willem, bp. Dec. 23, 1753; Johannes, bp. May 29, 1757; Dirk, bp. Nov. 25, 1758 or '9; Ariaantje, bp. Dec. 11, 1760; Ariaantje, b. March 14, 1762; Ariaantje, b. May 29, 1764; Jonathan, b. July 19, 1765; Ariaantje, b. Sept. 28, 1766; Elizabeth, b. Feb. 18, 1768; Elizabeth, b. May 20, 1769; David, b. Nov. 31 (*sic*), 1770.

HOOGHTELING, Jonathan, of Niskitha, m. Jannetie Slingerland, Nov. 2, 1754. Ch: Neeltie, bp. Sept. 28, 1755; Coenraad, bp. Nov. 1, 1761; Johannes, b. Aug. 3, 1763; Wouter, b. July 3, 1765.

HOOGHTELING, Matthys, of Niskitha, m. Ariaantje Van der Zee, Jan. 5, 1756. Ch: Storm, bp. May 7, 1758; Lena, bp. May 31, 1761; Eva, "oud 5 weken," bp. Dec. 19, 1762; Willem, b. Dec. 11, 1769.

HOOGHTELING, David, m. Hilletie (Helegonda) Van der Zee, Dec. 31, 1760. Ch: Lena, bp. Nov. 1, 1761; Storm, b. March 2, 1765; Willem, b. Feb. 6, 1768, d. at Coeymans Oct. 18, 1827, a. 60 y.; Ariantje, b. Sept. 19, 1771.

HOOGHTELING, Jacobus, and Gerritje (Charity) Pangburn. Ch: Johannes, bp. July 5, 1767; Emmetje, bp. June 4, 1769.

HOOGHTELING, Teunis, of Niskatha, and Lena Hooghteling. Ch: Neeltie, b. Jan. 10, 1771; Jonathan, b. Oct. 21, 1775; Elizabeth, b. Dec. 14, 1778.

HOOGHTELING, Willem P., of the *Colonie*, m. Marytje Bloemendal, March 2, 1773. Ch: Pieter, b. Jan. 21, 1774; Johannes Bratt, bp. Nov. 3, 1776; Rebecca, b. April 3, 1779; Lena, b. March 8, 1781; Catharina, b. May 15, 1783; Elizabeth, b. Nov. 19, 1784;

Maas, b. April 7, 1787; David, b. June 22, 1789; Cornelis, b. Feb. 19, 1792.

HOOGHTELING, Abraham, m. first, Antje Hilton; secondly, Antje Buys [about 1780.] Ch: Judik, b. May 29, 1779; Anna Margarita, b. Nov. 16, 1780; Matthys, b. Aug. 4, 1783.

HOOGHTELING, Gerrit, m. Annatie Oosterhout, March 7, 1779. Ch: David, b. Oct. 31, 1779; Wilhelmus, b. Jan. 27, 1781; Annatie, b. Nov. 22, 1784; Maria, b. Sept. 28, 1786; Pieter, b. Jan. 19, 1790.

HOOGHTELING, Johannes, m. first, Maria Mason; secondly, Jane Burhans [about 1793.] Ch: Jannetie, b. Jan. 10, 1785; Catharine, b. Oct. 28, 1793.

HOOGHTELING, Wouter, and Jenny (Jannetie) Addringtrawn (Adering), m. March 2, 1784. Ch: Jannetie and Lena, b. Dec. 12, 1786.

HOOGHTELING, James, and Neeltie Palmatier. Ch: Isaac, b. Dec. 9, 1788.

HOOGHTELING, Dirk, and Antje Vander Kar. Ch: Peter, b. Oct. 24, 1793.

Hook, Thomas, and Catharine Crane. Ch: Sarsa b. July 20, 1780; Hannah, b. April 6, 1784; Thoma,, b. March 24, 1786.

HOOK, Frederick, and Margarita Schefer. Ch: Philip and Jacob, b. June 27, 1787.

Hopkins, Benjamin, and Mary Rickeley. Ch: John, bp. Aug. 6, 1758.

Horn, Mathys, and Catharina .... Ch: Joseph, bp. March 15, 1761.

HORN, Johannes, and Catharina Poosen. Ch: Catharine, b. Feb. 27, 1771.

Hosford, David, and Christiana Petrie. Ch: David, b. Feb. 1, 1798.

Hovenback, Benjamin, and Jenneke Oosterhout. Jenneke, b. July 29, 1782.

House, David, and Maria .... Ch: Jan, b. May 20, 1733.

HOUSE, Jacob, and Catharine Snyder. Ch: Elizabeth, b. April 9, 1795; Sarah, b. May 11, 1797; Helena, b. Dec. 9, 1800.

Howell, Chrismas, and Margaret.... Ch: John, bp. June 19, 1758.

Hudson, Ephraim, and Hannah Claus.... Ch: Ann, b. Sept. 10, 1779.

HUDSON, Moses, and Amelia Upham. Ch: William, b. April 22, 1784,

Hughson (Huson), John, and Anna Cock (Koch). Ch: Casparus, bp. July 16, 1758; Annatie, b. Jan. 30, 1767.

Humphrey, Morris, and Margaret ... Ch: Morris, bp. Oct. 4, 1757.

Hun (Van Hun), Harmen Thomase, was from Amersfort, Holland, had an aged aunt named Wendeltie Harmense his father's sister living at Alckmar, Holland. In 1662 he married Catalyntie Bercx widow of Dirk Bensingh. She was daughter of Tryntje Janse of Amsterdam, wife of Cornelis Stoffelse Bul. At the time of her marriage with Hun she had 5 children living by Bensingh. In 1663 Hun and his wife made a joint will. Ch: Thomas, and Wyntje to whom Jan Clute conveyed 20 morgens of land on Murderer's creek in 1681.

HUN, Tomas Harmense, m. Mayke Janse Oothout, Nov. 20, 1692. Ch: Catalyntje, bp. Sept. 3, 1693;

Harmen, bp. Nov. 24, 1697; Cornelis, bp. July 21, 1700; Henrikje, bp. Aug. 20, 1702; Dirk, bp. Sept. 17, 1704; Ruth, bp. March 16, 1707; Adriaan, bp. July 24, 1709; Johannes (?) .

HUN, Johannes, m. Anna Winne, May 4, 1725. Ch: Thomas, bp. June 19, 1726; Elsie, bp. May 15, 1728; Elsie, bp. March 18, 1733; Thomas, bp. Feb. 29, 1736.

HUN, Dirk, and Margarita ..... Ch: Catalyntje, bp. Aug. 13, 1732; Willem, bp. Aug. 28, 1734; Thomas, bp. May 19, 1736; Johannes, bp. Dec. 24, 1738; Pieter, bp. Oct. 2, 1741.

HUN, Dirk, and Elizabeth .... Ch: Mayke, bp. Sept. 5, 1736.

HUN, Harmen, m Elsie Lansing, Dec. 6, 1735. Ch: Jannetje, bp. June 3, 1739; Cathalyntje, bp. April 17, 1743; Cathalina, bp. Dec. 17, 1749; Machtel, bp. May 27, 1753.

HUN, Willem, m. Sara De Foreest, Aug. 18, 1759. Ch: Dirk, bp. Dec. 7, 1760; Cornelia, b. May 28, 1763.

HUN, Thomas, m. Barentje (Bata) Van Deusen, Nov. 29, 1761. Ch: Cathalyntje, b. Aug. 26, 1762; Rachel, b. July 4, 1764; Dirk, b. June 19, 1768; Rachel, b. Oct. 19, 1773.

HUN, Thomas, m. Elizabeth Wendell, Aug. 27, 1761. She d. April 19, 1810, a. 72 y. Ch: Annatje, b. Sept. 15, 1763; Abraham, b. Feb. 7, 1768, d. Jan. 29, 1812, a. 43 y. 11 m. Maria his w. d. Oct. 19, 1813.

HUN, Johannes, and Catharina Diele; he d. April 12, 1825, a. 84 y. Ch: Dirk, b. April 13, 1766.

HUN, Dirk, m. Annatie (Ann, Hannah) Lansing, Dec. 8, 1782. Ch: Cathalyna, b. March 19, 1783; Elsie, b. March 27, 1785; Sara and Geertruy, b. Feb. 24, 1787. Sara, d. at Oyster Bay, Aug. 5, 1863, a 76 y.; Neeltie, b. April 13, 1789; John, b. Dec. 13, 1791; Dirk, b. Dec. 10, 1793.

Hunger, Nicolaas, and Anne Catharina.... Ch: Jacob, bp. May 2, 1762.

Hungerford, Elisha, and Sofia Conger. Ch: Martha, bp. Oct. 4, 1779.

Hunter, Johannes, and Eva Van Aalsteyn. Ch: Jochum, b. July 22, 1767; Elizabeth, b. April 5, 1775.

Hutton, Timothy, and Jane McChesny. Ch: John, b. Dec. 28, 1777; Samuel, b. Jan. 9, 1779; Timotheus, b. Nov. 2, 1780.

Huybertse, Jan, m. Lysbeth Van Klinkenbergh from Ulster county, Jan. 29, 1704. He d. Feb. 24, 1706-7. Ch: Alida, bp. April 8, 1705; Jan, bp. Oct. 5, 1707, "dog de Vader was gestorven."

Huyk (Huygh), Andries Hanse of Kinderhook, and Cathaline (Cateryn) Lammerse Van Valkenburgh. He made his will Aug. 23, 1705; Ch: Johannes; Lambeert; Burger; Catie; Jochem, bp. July 29, 1685; Cornelis, bp. March 11, 1688; Anna; Andries, bp. Dec. 31, 1693; Maritie, bp. Nov. 11, 1696; Margarietje, bp. Jan. 7, 1700.

HUYK, Burger, of Kinderhook, m. Mayke Goes (Hoes), Oct. 2, 1703. Ch: Andries, bp. Aug. 20, 1704; Johannes, bp. Jan. 13, 1706; Catharina, bp. Sept. 26, 1708; Christintje, bp. Oct. 14, 1711; Jacobus, bp. Aug. 19, 1716; Dirk, bp. May 13, 1722.

HUYK, Lambert, of Albany, m. Anna Ratcliffe, Aug. 28, 1707. Ch: Andries, bp. Feb. 27, 1709; Rachel, bp. March 11, 1711; Catryna, bp. Sept. 27, 1713.

HUYK, Andries, m. first, Maria Ouderkerk, April 29, 1713; and secondly, Neeltie, about 1740. Ch: Catryna, bp. Nov. 3, 1717; Anna, bp. March 17, 1723; Andries, bp. Feb. 6, 1726; Pieter, bp. Jan. 11, 1741; Nicolaas, bp. May 29, 1743.

HUYK (Huygh), Cornelis, of Claverac, and Geertruy.... Ch: Isaac, bp. April 21, 1717. [Cornelis H. m. Neeltie Bovie, Nov. 24, 1739.]

Huyk (Huygh), Willem, m. Anna Ouderkerk, Feb. 15, 1725. Ch: Johannes, bp. Oct. 10, 1725.

HUYK (Huygh), Johannes, of Kinderhook, m. Lena (Madalena) Van Vlieren, May 13, 1724. Ch: Hieroon, bp. April 2, 1727.

HUYK (Huygh), Hannes, m. Catharine Bovie (Bevier), Nov. 24, 1739. Ch: Cornelis, bp. June 29, 1740; Nicolaas, bp. Feb. 14, 1742; Andries, bp. May 20, 1744; Cornelia, bp. Feb. 16, 1746; Geertie, bp. April 5, 1751; Catrina, bp. Dec. 31, 1752; Maria, bp. Oct. 27, 1754; Petrus, bp. May 20, 1761.

HUYK, Isaac, m. Neeltie Clute, Feb. 18, 1740. Ch: Geertruy, bp. Aug. 30, 1741.

Huyck, Andries, and Maritie Van Deusen. Ch: Elizabeth, bp. Dec. 21, 1746; Johannes, bp. Oct. 22, 1749.

HUYCK, Johannes, and Engeltie Van Hoesen. Ch: Burger, bp. Dec. 21, 1746.

HUYCK, Andries, and Gerritje Van Valkenburgh. Ch: Cornelis, bp. June 21, 1747; Maria, bp. April 1, 1750.

HUYCK, Andries, and Neeltie Bovie. Ch: Hendrick, bp. April 5, 1751; Cornelia, bp. July 19, 1752.

HUYCK, Andries, and Cornelia Van Deusen. Ch: Maria, bp. May 29, 1752.

HUYCK (?) (Hug, Hog), Barent, and Geertje Huyck. Ch: Johannes, bp. Dec. 31, 1752; Elisabeth, bp. Nov. 12, 1757.

HUYCK, Burger, and Jannetje Hoogeboom. Ch: Burger, bp. May 20, 1753.

HUYCK, Ryckert, and Jacomyntje Van Deusen. Ch: Geesje, bp. Nov. 11, 1753.

HUYCK, Hannes, and Lena Beekman. Ch: Lodewyck, b. July 20, 1775.

HUYCK, Cornelis, and Hester Gardenier. Ch: Henrick, b. June 1, 1781.

HUYCK, Andries, of Hellonberg, and Rachel Carr. Ch: John, b. June....., bp. Sept. 14, 1790.

HUYCK (Huick) Andries, and Rebecca Quackenbush. Ch: Leonard, b. Nov. 24, 1792, John Quackenbush, b. Nov. 6, 1800, (Church: record.) Nov. 23, 1801. (Himself).

Huyter, Christoffel, and Caterina.....Ch: Johan Frederic, bp. Nov. 11, 1753.

Ieton (Iten, Eaton?) John, and Maria Hooghkerk, Ch: Mary, bp. Feb. 3, 1734; Lucas, bp. Dec. 3, 1738.

Ismy, see Esmy.

Jackson, Hendrick, and Sara Clute. Ch: Ariaantje. b. Nov. 9, 1771; James, b. Sept. 29, 1773; Pieter, b. July 10, 1776.

JACKSON, John, and Sarah Lundy. Ch: Margaret, bp. Feb. 5, 1777; John, b. May 12, 1779.

JACKSON, Francis, and Charlotte Glover. Ch: Francis, b. Sept. 17, 1782.

JACKSON, John, and Elizabeth Jackson. Ch: Harry, b. March 5, 1793.

Jacobi, Christiaan, and Margarita Hogen (Hoghing) Ch: Geertruy, bp. Dec. 18, 1757; Magdalena, b. March 19, 1760, Frans, b. July 31, 1762; Magdalena, b. Jan. 28, 1766; Marytje, b. May 13, 1768; Frans, b. Aug. 13, 1770.

Jacobse (Gardenier ?) Hendrick, and ..... Ch: Hendrick, bp. Aug 18, 1686.

Jafesh, Teunis, and Alida Lansing. Ch: Sara, b. March 10, 1791.

Jager, Wendel, and Anna Maria Simmons. Ch: Wilhelmus, b. May 21, 1787.

JAGER (Yager), Salomon, and Sarah Price. Ch: Lydia, b. March 30, 1791.

James, Roger, and Sara .... Ch: Richard, bp. Dec. 16, 1722.

JAMES, Paulus, m. Annatie Crankheid, Nov. 11, 1771. Ch: Willem, b. Dec. 5, 1773.

JAMES, David, and Margarita Van der Werken. Ch: John, b. Dec. 29, 1777.

Janse, Jacobus, at Greenbush 1663, and Judik Franse. Ch: Brant, bp. April 6, 1684; Gerrit, bp. Oct. 24, 1686; Maritje, bp. Sept. 3, 1693.

JANSE (Vander Laen ?), Marten, and Jannetje Mingael. Ch: Maritie, bp. Dec. 27, 1685; Thomas, bp. Aug. 22, 1688; Johannes, bp. Aug. 17, 1691; Dirkje, bp. May 26, 1695; Antje, bp. Jan. 16, 1698.

JANSE, Anneke, see Bogardus.

JANSE, Marten, and Jannetie Cornelise. Ch: Maritie, bp. Feb. 1, 1685; Geertie, bp. Oct. 2, 1687; Lydia, bp. Feb. 5, 1690; Jacob, bp. Dec. 4, 1695; Abigail, bp. Jan. 20, 1695; Abram, bp. July 17, 1698.

JANSE, Broer, and .... Ch: Heyltie, bp. April 19, 1685.

JANSE, De Vroome, Hubert 1667-77 owned lot on Maiden Lane next east of Stanwix Hall. His wife .... in 1670, bound her son Hubertse to Tryntie Jochimse, wife of Major Abram Staas to serve for one year.

JANSE, Gerrit, and Maritie Louys. Ch: Antje, bp. Feb. 12, 1693.

JANSE, Arent, master carpenter, in 1641 in the service of the W. I. Company; 1667 he bought the lot on which Stanwix Hall stands from Hendrick Gerritse Vermeulen; 1668 being about to return to Holland he mortgaged the same.

JANSE, Anthony, 1662, court messenger of colony Rensselaerswyck; 1662-68 an innkeeper in Beverwyck; his house and lot was on the south side of State street east of Broadway; his wife was Orseltie Dirkse, probably from Rotterdam.

JANSE de Boer (Van Hoorn), Pieter, b. in Hoorn, his father was Jan Pieterse de Boer of Hoorn; in Beverwyck 1661, where he bought a house and lot which he sold in 1666, then living in the colony Rensselaerswyck.

JANSE, Thomas, of Kinderhook, and Mayke Bogart. Ch: Magdalena, bp. Jan. 13, 1706.

JANSE, Dirk, m. Maritie Janse (Cornelise), July 17, 1709. Ch: Dina, bp. Oct. 14, 1711; Sara, bp. Jan. 25, 1713; Dirk, bp. March 21, 1714; Pieter, b. Oct. 9, 1715.

JANSE, Evert; his wife was Maria .... Ch: Susanna, bp. Jan. 21, 1728; Jan, bp. Feb. 3, 1731; Ariaantje, bp. June 2, 1735; Debora, bp. Jan. 30, 1743.

JANSE, Evert, see also Evertse.

Jansen, Roeloff, m. Elizabeth Schermerhoorn, Feb. 13, 1728. Ch: Jacob, bp. May 16, 1736.

JANSEN, Johannes, and Jannetie Schermerhoorn, "beide Van Schotack," m. June 28, 1750. Ch: Elizabeth, bp. Jan. 19, 1752; Jacob, bp. Nov. 18, 1753.

JANSEN (Johnson), Isaac, m. Annatie Rumney, Aug. 21, 1773; Ch: Gerrit, b. Jan. 23, 1774.

JANSEN, Pieter, and Elizabeth Huik. Ch: Abraham, bp. June 9, 1777.

JANSEN (Johnson), Evert of Noormanskil, m. Antje LaGrange, July 13, 1770. Ch: Jelles, bp. Jan. 2, 1778; Jelles, b. Sept. 1, 1779; Annatie, bp. Feb. 20, 1785; Ariaantje, b. Aug. 8, 1788; Angeltie, b. Feb. 5, 1791.

JANSEN, Jacques, and Catharine Beekman. Ch: Jacobus Van der Veer, b. Aug. 27, 1785.

Jenkins, Richard, and Margaret Norton. Ch: Richard, bp. Aug. 27, 1749.

JERALOMON (Jeronymer, Hieralomon), Nicolaas, m. Jannetie Waldron, May 14, 1770. Ch: Pietertje, b. Oct. 8, 1770; Neeltie, b. March 13, 1772; Elizabeth, b. Feb. 18, 1774; Jannetje, b. Nov. 29, 1775; Nicolaas, b. April 22, 1778; Susanna, b. Sept. 24, 1780; Annatie, b. March 27, 1784; Isaac Lansing, b. Jan. 15, 1787; Pieter, b. Aug. 26, 1789.

JERALOMON, Nicolaas (probably same as last), m. Eva Becker, Feb. 4, 1797. Ch: Gerrit, b. Feb. 3, 1805; Isaac Lansing, b. Aug. 6, 1812.

Johannes, Jan, ... Ch: Lysbeth, bp .... 1685.

Jochemse, Hendrick in Beverwyck 1654-69. He was lieutenant of the Burgher Company; owned a lot on east corner of Broadway and State street, part of the Exchange lot, which his attorney sold in 1669, to his brother-in-law, Abram Staats.

Johnson, Peter, and Susanna.... Ch: Thomas, b. Aug. 29, 1779.

JOHNSON, William, and Margarita Frets. Ch: Sara, b. May 30, 1780.

JOHNSON, John, m. Helena Lotteridge, Aug 14, 1789. Ch: Eleanor, b. Oct. 21, 1790; William, b. Nov. 2, 1794; Eleanor, b. July 21, 1796.

JOHNSON, Reuben, and Ann Hartwick. Ch: Reuben, b. March 21, 1796.

JOHNSON, Rev. John B., became minister of the Reformed Dutch Church of Albany, colleague of Rev. Mr. Westerlo, March 23, 1796, removed to Brooklyn in Sept., 1802. and d. in Newtown, Aug. 29, 1803. He m. Elizabeth Lupton. She d. in April, 1803. Ch: Maria Laidlie, b. Aug. 30, 1798; William Lupton b. Sept. 15, 1800. [Rev. Wm. L. Johnson, D.D., rector of Grace Church, Jamaica, d. Aug. 4, 1870, in his 70th year.]

JOHNSON, William, and Rebecca Hickson. Ch: Sarah Eliza, b. Nov. 5, 1799.

JOHNSON, John and Elizabeth Marshall. Ch: George, b. Nov. 5, 1798; John, b. June 1, 1802.

JOHNSON, see Jansen.

Jones, TJans, SJans, Shawns, Schauns, etc.

JONES, Pieter, m. Abigail Winne, Oct. 30, 1748. Ch: Thomas, bp. March 4, 1750; Johannes, bp. June 24, 1753; Thomas, bp. Oct. 15, 1758; Thomas, bp. Oct. 7. 1759; Pieter, b. Aug. 3, 1766; Pieter, b. Sept. 17, 1768.

JONES, Samuel B., and Anna Bohannan. Ch: Samuel, b. Oct. 22, 1797.

JONES, Andrew, and Hannah Barnham. Ch: Mahala, b. Oct. 12, 1799.

Joons (JONES?) Ryer, and Mary.... Ch: Annatie, bp. July 30, 1735.

Jordan, Martin, and Sara.... Ch: Pieter, bp. Feb. 8, 1738.

Jordens, Pieter, and Elizabeth Drersaus. Ch: Simon, bp. Nov. 9, 1760.

Kaatsbah (Katiebach, Katienbach), Hendrick, and Eva Devoe. Ch: Christopher, bp. Nov. 11, 1760; Abraham, "5 weken oud," bp. May 8, 1763; Alletteke, bp. Aug. 4, 1768; Johannes, b. April 30, 1771.

Kane, Elisha, and Alida Van Rensselaer. Ch: Robert Van Rensselaer, b. Aug. 20, 1797. [Elisha Kane, d. in Philadelphia, Dec. 4, 1834.]

KANE, Elias, m. Debora Van Scherluyne, Oct. 29, 1797. Ch: Elizabeth, b. Oct. 17, 1798; Mary, b. Oct. 17, 1799; Cornelius Van Scherluyne, b. Aug. 6, 1801; Louisa, b. May 31, 1803; Theodorus, b. June 24, 1808; Matilda, b..... 1812, d. March 3, 1819, a. 6 y. 3 m. 22 d.

Kannick, Jonathan, and Margarita Perry. Ch: Alida, b. May 22, 1779.

Kartritch, Jan, and Catharyna.... Ch: Charles, bp. Feb. 5, 1738.

Katleback, see Kaatsbah.

Kaye, see Van Oosanen.

Keating, John, and Jane Duryea. Ch: Jane Maria, b. Sept. 21, 1796.

Keller, Christiaan, and Elizabeth Boeckes (?). Ch: Frederick, bp. Nov. 11, 1760.

Kellinin, Patrick, and Susanna Raw. Ch: Mary, b. Sept. 9, 1779.

Kemmel, see Campbell.

Kennall, William, and Margarita.... Ch: Hendrikje, b. Nov. 19, 1729.

Kerchener, Willem, and Christina Harmsin. Ch: Johannes, bp. Nov. 10, 1754.

Kercher, Hendrik, and Maria B. Schultren. Ch: Jacob Hendrik, bp. Dec. 30, 1778.

Kerel, Kl: and Judikie Irtsin. Ch: Susanna, "oud omtr. 6 jaaren," bp. Aug. 1, 1771.

Kerhart, Christiaan, and Anna Barbara Walfin. Ch: Susanna Catarina, bp. July 1, 1759.

Kerkenaar, Ryckert, and Annatie Van Alsteyn. Ch: Sofia, b. Dec. 23, 1780.

Kernel, John, and Susanna.... Ch: Johan Jury, b. May 2, 1777.

Kerner, Philip, and Margarita.... Ch: Willem, b. May 1, 1785.

KERNER, Philip, and Hannah Crannel. Ch: George, b. March 4, 1800.

Kernryk, Juriaan, and Margarita Rockenfeller. Ch: Zacharias, b. March 14, 1771.

Kersten, Roeloff.... Ch: Roeloff, "geboren naa des Vaders doodt," bp. Dec. 13, 1685.

Ketelhuyn, (Kettel, Kittle), Joachim, from Cremyn, came to Rensselaerswyck in 1642, the first settler of the name. His lot was on the west corner of Broadway and Maiden Lane. The following sons had families: William, David, Daniel.

KETELHUYN, Willem, had a lot on north side of Beaver St., second E. of Green street. He was buried Aug. 26, 1746. About 1683 he m. Hilletie Van der Zee, w. of Storm Van der Zee, Ch : Joachim, bp. Nov. 9, 1684 ; Storm, bp. July 24, 1687 and Gerrit Van der Zee.

KETELHUIN, David, m. Johanna (Anna) Brat, Jan. 31, 1695. Ch : Anna, bp. Dec. 8, 1695, d. April 23, 1705; Barent, bp. Feb. 21, 1697; Susanna, bp. Aug. 18, 1700 ; Margarita, bp. Feb. 19, 1704 ; Marytje, bp Feb. 23, 1707.

KETELHUYN (Kitkel), Daniel, of Schaatkooke, m. Debora Viele " op Schenegtade" Aug. 16, 1695. Ch : Anna, bp. Sept. 13, 1696 ; Greetje, bp. March 16, 1698 ; Cornelis, bp. Nov. 3, 1700 ; Cornelis, bp. Dec. 6, 1702; Suster, bp. Jan. 30, 1704 ; Joachim, bp. Aug. 12, 1705 ; Douw, bp. Oct. 5, 1707 ; Douw, bp. Dec. 19, 1708 ; Cornelis, bp. in Schenectady, March 6, 1711 ; David, bp. Oct. 19, 1712; Grietje, bp. April 24, 1715 ; Margarita, bp. Jan. 24, 1722.

KETELHUYN, Joachem, of Schaachtekooke, m. Eva Vrooman of Schenectady, June 25, 1730. Ch : Daniel, bp. Jan. 5, 1737; Debora, bp. Sept. 10, 1738 ; Maria, bp. June 14, 1740. See *Schenectady Families.*

KETELHUYN, Douwe, m. Nelletje Brouwer, Sept. 9, 1738. Ch : Maria, bp. July 15, 1739 ; Willem, bp. June 14, 1740.

KETELHUYN (Kittle), Daniel, and Catarina Van Valkenburgh. Ch : Lea, bp. Jan. 22, 1749.

KETELHUYN (Kettel), Daniel, of Schenectady, m. Sara Van Schaick in Schenectady, July 11, 1761. Ch : Joachem, b. July 20, 1765. See *Schenectady Families.*

Keyser, Henderick, and Catarina Tzellerin. Ch : Johannes, bp. March 26, 1758.

Kidney (Cittene), Jan (John) "Van Barbados" m. Maritie Roeloffse Van den Werke (dau. of Roeloff Gerritse V. D. W.), May 1, 1698. Letters of administration were issued to his wife Maritie, June 8, 1722. Ch : Roeloff, bp. June 7, 1700; Johannes, bp. July 9, 1704; Jacobus ; Robert, bp. July 6, 1708.

KIDNEY, Roeloff. m. Engeltie Burger, June 18, 1721. He had a lot in 1729, on west side of Pearl south of Beaver street. Ch : Maritie, bp. Dec. 31, 1721 ; Rebecca, bp. May 5, 1723, m. Jas. Elliot and d. Feb. 18, 1809, a. 85 y. 9 m. 13 d ; Johannes, bp. Sept. 20, 1724 ; Nicolaas, bp. April 16, 1727 ; Geertruy, bp. Feb. 2, 1729 ; Geertruy, bp. Jan. 6, 1731 ; Nicolaas, bp. March 18, 1733 ; Jacobus, bp. March 3, 1735 ; Andries, bp. April 3, 1737 ; Roeloff, bp. July 15, 1739 ; Lena, bp. June 13, 1742; Margrietje, bp. July 1, 1744 ; Elizabeth, bp. April 3, 1748.

KIDNEY, Johannes, and Geertie Van der Werken. 1730 he owned a lot (?) on north side of Hudson, east of Pearl street. Ch : Maritie, bp. Nov. 20, 1736; Catarina, bp. June 7, 1747.

KIDNEY, Jacob, m. Annatie Hagedorn Oct. 23, 1737. Jacob K., many years high constable, d. Aug. 19, 1795. Ch : Johannes, bp. Sept. 17, 1738; Marytje, bp. Sept. 23, 1739 ; Annatie, bp. Sept. 12, 1742.

KIDNEY, Jan, and Phœbe .... Ch : Jonatan, bp. Dec. 11, 1760 ; Roeloff, b. Jan. 27, 1766.

KIDNEY, Jonathan, and Hannah Van Zandt. He d. March 20, 1849; she d. Dec. 30, 1833. Ch : Celia, b. Feb. 18, 1794; Rebecca, b. Nov. 21, 1795 ; William, b. Oct. 10, 1797 ; Angelica, b. June 2, 1800.

Kierstede, Cornelis, and Sara Elswaert. Ch : Johanna, bp. Dec. 24, 1704.

Kim, Jacob, and Elizabeth Fort. Ch : Maria, bp. July 30, 1780.

Kimmel, see Campbell.

King, Thomas, and Jannetie Krankheid. Ch : Annatie, bp. July 4, 1781.

KING, John, and Rebecca .... Ch : Ann Mary, b. April 17, 1799.

Kinney, Jacob, and Elizabeth Fort (see Kim). Ch : Debora, b. March 3, 1786.

Kinter, Joseph, and Maria Ering. Ch : Magdalena, b. June 11, 1773.

Kip, Abraham, m. Geesie Vander Heyden, Oct. 16, 1687; in 1714 his house was on the south corner of Maiden Lane and Pearl street. His w. was buried Feb. 9, 1748. Ch : Isaac, bp. Nov. 18, 1688; Anna, bp. Dec. 20, 1691; Anna, bp. June 17, 1694 ; Catelyntie, bp. Aug. 8, 1697; Jacob and Cornelia, twins, bp. July 20, 1701; Geertruy and Catharina, twins, bp. June 24, 1705.

KIP, Jacob, and Rachel Swartwout. Ch : Catalyntie, bp. Feb. 18, 1705.

KIP, Isaac A., m. Nelletie Bratt, Nov. 12, 1752. Ch : Anthony, bp. Jan 27, 1754 ; Benjamin, bp. Jan. 16, 1757.

KIP, Ignas, of Schachtekooke, m. Annatie Van Vechten, Jan. 29, 1767. Ch : Margarita, b. Oct. 27, 1772.

KIP, Abraham, and Saartje Hansen. Ch : Geertruy, bp. Dec. 16, 1778.

Kirchner, Wilhelm, and Justina .... Ch : Johannes Christopher, b. May 2, 1762.

KIRCHNER (Carkner), George, and Margaret Wediman. Ch : William, b. Nov. 29, 1793.

Kirk, Gerrit, and Mary Pritchard. Ch : William, b. Sept. 9, 1799.

Kitchel (Ketelhuyn ?), Nicholaas, and Catharina .... Ch : Elizabeth, bp. Jan. 7, 1722; Daniel, bp. March 1, 1724 ; Margarita, bp. Nov. 6, 1726.

Kitkel, see Kettelhuin.

Kitsholt, Jacob, of Steenrabie, and Femmetie Van Yeveren. Ch : Jacob, b. Oct. 8, 1771.

Kittle, see Ketelhuyn.

Klauw, see Clauw.

Klerk, see Clark.

Kleyn, Elderick (Ulderick), in Beverwyck, 1657, with his wife ; brought an action against Eldert Gerbertse, Cruyff for saying his wife was branded and whipped, on the scaffold in Amsterdam : 1667-9, he was the town herder of cattle.

KLEYN, Johannes, of Schenectady. m. a dau. of Ludovicus Cobes, secretary of that town, Ch : Weyntje, bp. Jan. 23, 1684 ; Baatje, bp. April 2, 1686.

Klein, Nicolaas, m. Elizabeth Coughter (Cougler, Coochler, Kohler, Kogly), Feb. 1, 1767. Ch : Elizabeth, b. Nov. 29, 1767; George, b. Nov. 17, 1769 ; Margarita, b. Aug. 5, 1772 ; Christina, b. Oct. 23, 1774 ; Nicolaas, b. Dec. 5, 1776 ; Nicolaas, b. Aug. 14, 1778 ; David, b. Oct. 26, 1780.

KLEIN (Clyne), Joseph, and Hannah Tolhammer. Ch : Peter, b. July 29, 1783.

Klock, Hendrik, and Jacomyntie..... Ch: Magdalena, bp. June 9, 1728.

KLOCK, Jacob, and Rachel..... Ch: Egje, bp. Aug. 9, 1761.

Knikkelbakker, Van Wye, Harmen Janse, of Dutchess county, and Lysbeth Janse Bogaart. He made his will Jan. 7, 1707-8, in which he mentioned the following children Johannes, Lourens, Cornelia, Evert, Pieter, Jannetie widow of Hendrick Lansing, Jr., Cornelia. The following children were baptized in the church of Albany. Cornelis, bp. Sept. 2, 1688; Cornelis, bp. Jan. 6, 1692; Cornelia, bp. July 21, 1695; Evert, bp. Sept. 3, 1699; Pieter, bp. April 19, 1722.

KNIKKELBAKKER, Johannes Harmense, of Schaatkooke, m. Anna Quackenbos, Sept. 27, 1701. Ch: Lysbeth, bp. Nov. 1, 1702; Neeltie, bp. June 30, 1706; Harmen, bp. Dec. 25, 1709; Wouter, bp. Oct. 19, 1712; Cornelia, bp. Oct. 21, 1716; Johannes, bp. March 24, 1723.

Knickerbacker, Wouter, m. Elizabeth Fonda, Jan. 9, 1735. He d. at Saratoga, Aug. 8, 1797, a. 94 y. 9 m. Ch: Anna, bp. Nov. 9, 1735; Isaac, and Alida, bp. Nov. 20, 1737; Elizabeth, bp. March 25, 1739; Elizabeth, bp. Sept. 28, 1740; Johannes, bp. April 3, 1743; Johannes, bp. Nov. 16, 1746; Rebecca, bp. June 18, 1749.

Knickerbakker, Harmen, and Rebecca De Wandelaar. Ch: Johannes, bp. May 25, 1746.

Knickerbacker, Johannes, and Rebecca Fonda. Ch: Johannes, bp. March 24, 1751, d. in Schaghticoke, Nov. 10, 1827, a. 76 y. 9 m. 19 d.; Anna, bp. March 11, 1753; Neeltie and Elizabeth, bp. Nov. 24, 1754.

KNICKERBACKER, Harmen, and Judith Marl (Morrell). Ch: Daniel, b. Aug. 27, 1765.

KNICKERBACKER, Johannes, m. Elizabeth Winne, March 1, 1769. Ch: Willem, b. Dec. 11, 1771.

Koch, Hendrik, and Maria Young. Ch: Anna, b. Oct. 15, 1777; Sara, b. June 23, 1780.

KOCH, Zephyrinus, and Elizabeth Hall. Ch: Elizabeth, b. Nov. 25, 1780.

Kodman, Tames, and Margarita Yvens. Ch: Betty, bp. May 24, 1708.

Koeler, Matthias, and Anna..... Ch: George Matthias, b. Feb. 23, 1763; Johanna and Wendell, twins, b. Oct. 19, 1764.

Koen, Jurriaen, and Anna (Androsina) Erhart. Ch: Coenraad, bp. June 26, 1743; Simon, bp. Aug. 14, 1748; Johannes, bp. May 26, 1751.

KOEN, Johannes, m. first, Hilletje Zeger, Sept. 28, 1751; secondly, Christina Bratt, about 1772. Ch: Margarita, bp. Nov. 12, 1752; Johannes, bp. Sept. 8, 1754; Coenraad, bp. Feb. 13, 1757; Neeltie, bp. Dec. 20, 1761; Elizabeth, bp. May 6, 1764; Margarita, b. 1767; Bregje, b. May 17, 1770; Annatie, bp. May 9, 1773; Susanna, b. April 12, 1776.

KOEN, Adam (Arent), m. Maria Van den Hoff (Hoeven). Ch: Jacob, bp. March 5, 1758; Coenraad, b. Sept. 8, 1767; Maria, bp. Aug. 13, 1769.

KOEN, Petrus, and Marytje Welch. Ch: Coutina, b. Sept. 14, 1771 [Pieter Koens, and Catharina Soill, m. Aug. 17, 1775].

KOEN, Petrus, and Lydia Duitscher. Ch: Catharina, b. Dec. 29, 1789; Elizabeth, bp. Aug. 14, 1791; Margaret, b. Sept. 11, 1794.

Koens (Kuhns), Philip, and w. Maria Elizabeth.. Ch: Catharina, b. Feb. 6, "op Taghkanick," and bp. at Claverack, Feb. 28, 1721.

KOENS (Coens), Abraham, and Annatie Hegeman. Ch: Christoffer, b. Dec. 27, 1774.

KOENS, Coenraad, and Anna Stafford. Ch: Annatie, b. Oct. 8, 1778; James, b. Dec. 11, 1782.

KOENS (COOLS, Conse), Adam, and Margaret Snyder. Ch: Catharine, b. Sept. 12, 1792.

Kool, Jacobus, of Ulster county, m. Jannetie Witbeck, of Albany county, Oct. 22, 1762. Ch: Abraham, b. Oct. 19, 1763; Jannetie, b. March 1, 1766; Maria, b. July 10, 1768; Jacobus, b. July 31, 1775.

KOOL, Jacob, and N. .... Ch: David and Petrus, *tweegebroeders,* bp. Aug. 13, 1769.

Koolbrat, Willem, and Hester Van Deusen. Ch: Catharina Van Deusen, b. July 8, 1779..

Koolhamer, Stefanus, and Anna B. Freelich. Ch: Anna Maria, bp. May 13, 1764.

Koorenbeurs, Jacob, and .... Ch: Catalyntje, bp. Aug. 26, 1683.

Koorn (Coorn), Nicolaas, came to Beverwyck, in 1642, was appointed *wachtmeester* for the Patroon, in 1644, and fortified Beeren island to command the river, for his master. He created great excitement in the Province by firing upon the *Goet Hope* on her way down for refusal to lower her colors. On the retirement of Van der Donck in 1644, he succeeded him as sheriff of Rensselaerswyck. *O'Callaghan's History N.N.* I.

Krankert, Judlof, and Neeltie Gardenier. Ch: Pieter, b. Jan. 26, 1781.

Kregier (see Cregier).

Krimer (see Cremer).

Kruck (Crook), William, m. Margriet Anderson, Feb. 22, 1738. Ch: Hilletie, bp. May 27, 1739; Robert, bp. May 26, 1740.

Kruel, Franciscus, and Annatie Bulsing, Ch: Rachel, b. May 1, 1762.

Kulerman, see Gerrit Claes Van Vranken.

Kuyper, Evert Janse, in Albany 1675-1725.

Kuyskerk, Pieter, and Elizabeth.... Ch: Elise Margarita, bp. Aug. 14, 1714.

Kwee, Alexander, and Margarita.... Ch: Johan Andreas, b. April 18, 1767.

Labagh, Nicholas, and Eleanor Wilsie. Ch: Jan, b. Oct. 28, 1792.

Labatie (Labaddie), Jan, a native of France came to Beverwyck previous to 1634, subsequently commissaris to the Patroon of Rensselaerswyck, afterwards held a like office at Fort Orange under the W. I. Company. *O'Callaghan's Hist. N. N.* I, 434. He bought and sold various lots of ground in Albany and Schenectady. His wife was Jillesje Claes [Swits] aunt of Claes and Isaac Cornelise Swits of Schenectady, and widow of Surgeon Harmen Myndertse Vander Bogart. It is not known that he left any children.

Lady, John, and Catrina Oliford (Alvord?) Ch: Thomas, bp. Aug. 25, 1751.

La Fort, see Fort.

LaGrange, and LaGranzie, see De la Grange.

Lancaster, Samuel, and Sara Warren. Ch: Elizabeth, bp. Feb. 21, 1780.

Lanck, Philip, and Madalena.... Ch; Anna Maria, bp. March 31, 1717; Jacob, bp. May 4, 1718; Anna Maria, bp. Oct. 2, 1720. (See also Leen).

Lange, Christiaan, and Beertie (Dorothea). Ch: Madalena, bp. June 23, 1734; Tryntje, bp. Feb. 8, 1736; Lena, bp. April 3, 1738; Johannes, bp. Sept. 26, 1742.

Lang, William, of Saratoga, and Betsey Johnson, Ch: Drew, b. May 5, 1787.

LANG, Hannes, and Christina (Stina) Bratt. Ch: Christina, b. March 1, 1763; Adam, b. Aug. 22, 1764; Coenraad, b. Oct. 16, 1766; Lydia, b. Sept. 22, 1768; Beertje, b. Jan. 16, 1771; Geerit, b. Dec. 4, 1773; Pieter, b. Nov. 2, 1774; Susanna, b. May 24, 1780.

LANG, John, of Saratoga, and Elizabeth Rob. Ch: John, b. Sept. 22, 1786; Jane, b. June 19, 1788.

Langburn, Edmund, and Maria Van Oostrander. Ch: Catharine, b. April 27, 1780.

Lansing (Lansinck, Lansingh), Gerrit, from Hassell near Swoll in Overyssell, was deceased before Oct. 3, 1679. He left the following children: Gerrit; Hendrick; Johannes; Aeltie, w. of Gerrit Van Slicktenhorst; Gysbertje, w. of Hendrick Roseboom; and Hilletie, widow of Storm Van der Zee.

LANSING, Hendrick, son of Gerrit L., was in Albany as early as 1666; d. July 11, 1709. His wife was Lysbet .... Ch: Alida, bp. July 3, 1685; Jacob; Maria, wife of Huybert Gerritse? Henrick?

LANSING, Gerrit (son of Gerrit), baker and trader, resided at different times in Albany, Schenectady and New York; m. secondly, about 1692, Catryntje Sanderse Glen, widow of Cornelis Barentse Van Ditmars, who was killed at the burning of Schenectady, in 1690; and thirdly, about 1696 (?), Elsie .... The name of his first wife is not known. Perhaps he d. July 20, 1708. Ch: Elizabeth, bp. Jan. 20, 1689; Gerrit, bp. Aug. 20, 1693, perhaps buried Jan. 26, 1736; Johannes, bp. March 10, 1695; Anna, bp. in N. Y., March 28, 1697; Elsie, bp. in N. Y., March 12, 1699; Sander, bp. in N. Y., April 20, 1701; Susanna, bp. in N. Y., Jan. 5, 1703; Evert, bp. Dec. 31, 1704; Jacob, [Jacobus?] bp. Dec. 22, 1706; Abraham, bp. Feb. 27, 1709; Isaac (?); Jacob (?).

LANSING, Johannes (son of Gerrit), merchant, m. in 1678, Geertie Goosense Van Schaick, widow of Hendrick Coster; naturalized in 1715; d. and was buried in the church, Feb. 26, 1728. Ch: Elizabet, b. 1679, m. Stephanus Groesbeck, in 1699; Geertruy, bp. Nov. 2, 1684, m. Ryer Gerritse; Johannes, bp. Sept. 4, 1687; Engeltie, bp. Aug. 17, 1690; Gerrit (?); Abraham (?).

LANSING, Jacob (son of Hendrick), m. Helena Pruyn, Sept. 27, 1701. [Jacob L. "was buried by [near] his house," Oct. 17, 1756]. Ch: Alida, bp. July 26, 1702; Henrick, bp. Dec. 1, 1703; Elizabeth, bp. June 30, 1706; Franciscus, bp. July 18, 1708; [Note: the following baptisms and those under Jacob *Gerritse* which follow cannot be placed with *certainty*, owing to ambiguity in the Record.] Gerrit, bp. March 4, 1711; Jacob, bp. July 12, 1714; Anna, bp. July 15, 1716; Johannes, bp. Oct. 19, 1718; Abraham, bp. Nov. 13, 1720.

LANSING, Jacob (son of Gerrit), baker, 1711, owned the lot on west corner of Steuben St. and Broadway, and was then about to make "a considerable arrectment thereon," subsequently he had a "boulting house" there; in 1715, petitioned for addition to his lot. His wife was Helena (?) .... Ch: Gerrit, bp. Oct. 7, 1711; Jacob, bp. Oct. 29, 1713; Johannes, bp. Dec. 23, 1715; Catryna, bp. Sept. 7, 1718; Abraham, bp. April 24, 1720; Isaac, bp. Jan. 28, 1722; Sander, bp. Aug. 18, 1723, d. April 3, 1807, a. 84 y.; Elsie and Isaac, bp. Oct. 24, 1725.

LANSING, Isaac [son of Gerrit ?], m. Jannetje (Johanna) Beekman, June 27, 1703. Ch: Maghtel, bp. Dec. 12, 1703; Gerrit, bp. Dec. 12, 1705; Johannes, bp. Sept. 11, 1709, buried Sept. 16, 1745; Susanna, bp. Nov. 13, 1715; Jacob, bp. April 27, 1718; Neeltje, bp. March 31, 1723.

LANSING, Abraham [son of Johannes], in 1710 had lot on south corner of Chapel and Steuben Sts.; m. Magdalena Van Tricht, Nov. 28, 1703. He was buried June 20, 1745. Ch: Abraham, bp. May 14, 1704; Gerrit, bp. Nov. 28, 1705; Johannes, bp. May 16, 1708; Jacobus [Jacob ?], bp. April 23, 1710 [Jacob, son of Abraham L., was buried May 12, 1745]; Elsie, bp. March 8, 1713; Elizabeth, bp. Nov. 10, 1717; Myndert, bp. Jan. 24, 1722; Susanna, bp. Aug. 9, 1724; Margarita, bp. April 7. 1728, buried July 31, 1747.

LANSING, Henrik, Jr. [son of Henrik ?], m. Jannetie Knikkelbakker, March 4, 1704. Ch: Lysbeth, bp. Aug. 5, 1705.

LANSING, Johannes Gerritse, had a lot on north side of State by the river side; m. first, Helena Sanders, Sept. 20, 1704; secondly, Catalyna .... about 1726. Ch: Gerrit, bp. Sept. 9, 1705; Robert, bp. Jan. 12, 1707; Elsie, bp. July 4, 1708; Maria, bp. Oct. 7, 1711; Joannes, bp. June 30, 1718; Sander, bp. 1724; Thomas, bp. Sept. 24, 1727, d. March 4, 1811, a. 83 y. 5 m. 2 d.

LANSING, Gerrit, Junior [son of Johannes ?], m. Elizabeth Bancker, dau. of Evert B., Oct. 27, 1715. Ch: Neeltie, bp. Nov. 4, 1716; Neeltie, bp. April 11, 1718; Geertruy, bp. Dec. 26, 1719; Johannes, bp. Oct. 9, 1724; Johannes, bp. April 24, 1726; [a Gerrit L., was buried Jan. 26, 1736.]

LANSING, Johannes [son of Johannes and Geertie], m. Geertruy Schuyler, dau. of Pieter S., June 13, 1714. [The wife of Johannes L., was buried June 23, 1744.] Ch: Johannes, bp. April 7, 1715; Maria, bp. Dec. 4, 1717; Pieter, bp. Aug. 6, 1721, d. May 13, 1807, a. 86 y.; Gerardus, bp. Sept. 29, 1723, d. March 24, 1808, a. 84 y.; Geertruy, bp. Jan. 1, 1727; Philip, bp. Feb. 23, 1729; Geertruy, bp. Jan. 7, 1733.

LANSING, Gerrit, Junior, [son of Gerrit ?]. He had a lot in 1736, in the rear of Bleecker Hall, between Dean St. and the river, 75 feet front and rear; m. Engeltie Van Deusen, dau. of Rutger Melgertse V. D., Oct. 23, 1718. [Gerrit G. L.'s wife was buried Oct. 6, 1745.] Ch: Gerrit, bp. July 26, 1719; Rutgher, bp. March 25, 1722; Johannes, bp. Aug. 28, 1726.

LANSING, Johannes Gerritse, m. Jannetje Van Vechten, May 12, 1729; she was buried March 19, 1752. Ch: Catharina, bp. June 5, 1730; Catharina, bp. Nov. 22, 1732; Maria, bp. Jan. 22, 1737; Cathalyntje, bp. May 16, 1742.

LANSING, Abraham Gerritse, m. first Ryckie, dau. of Goosen V. Schaick; she was buried May 18, 1732; secondly, Helena Van Deusen, dau. of Harpert V. D. April 21, 1733; she d. before the baptism of her son Harpert, Sept. 7, 1740; thirdly, Catharine De Foreest widow, April 20, 1741. Ch: Goosen, bp. April 16, 1732; Catharina, bp. April 11, 1734; Lena, bp. Feb. 29, 1736; Annatie, bp. May 28, 1738; Harpert, bp. Sept. 7, 1740.

LANSING, Gerrit Jacobse; in 1732, he had a lot on the north corner of Hudson and Green streets 60 ft. square; m. Ida Van Wie, dau. of Jan V.W., Aug. 1734; He was buried Aug. 1, 1746; She was buried Aug. 4, 1743. Ch: Helena, bp. June 8, 1735; Catharyna, bp. Aug. 28, 1737; Jacob, bp. June 10, 1741.

LANSING, Robert [son of Johannes] m. first, Margarita Roseboom, Dec. 5, 1734, who was buried Sept. 5, 1746; secondly, Sarah Van Schaick about 1748, who was buried May 14, 1749; and thirdly, Catarina Ten Broeck, widow of Ephraim Van Vegten of Claverack, June 27, 1752. Ch: Maria, bp. Nov. 2, 1735; Hendrik, bp. Dec. 23, 1737; Helena, bp. March 27, 1743; Helena, bp. Oct. 6, 1745; Sarah and Margarita, bp. April 16, 1749.

LANSING, Gerrit Jacobse, m. Marytje Evertsen, Nov. 29, 1734, she was buried Jan. 27, 1741. Ch: Jacob, bp. April 4, 1736; Maria, bp. Oct. 6, 1737; Alida, bp. Sept. 7, 1738.

LANSING, Henrik, [son of Jacob ?], m. Annatje Ouderkerk. Ch: Lena, bp. Aug. 29, 1736; Isaac, bp. May 6, 1739; Jacob, bp. April 4, 1742; Mayke, bp. Jan. 4, 1745.

LANSING, Evert. [son of Gerrit], m. Annatie Cooper. Ch: Gerrit, bp. June 30, 1736; Cornelia, bp. Jan. 11, 1738; Obedia, bp. Feb. 4, 1739; Obedia, bp. June 29, 1740; Catharina, bp. Feb. 14, 1742; Johannes, bp. May 1, 1743; Annatie, bp. Feb. 22, 1756.

LANSING, Franciscus [son of Jacob], m. Maria Lieverse (Laviense), "op de Halve Maan" Jan. 6, 1737. Ch: Jacob and Helena, bp. April 30, 1738; Catharina, bp. Sept. 28, 1740; Rachel, bp. June 19, 1743; Anna, bp. Feb. 16, 1746; Rachel and Anna, bp. July 19, 1747; Rachel, bp. July 7, 1750; Lavibus, bp. June 23, 1754.

LANSING, Jacob Jacobs, m. Huybertje Yates, May 13, 1738 [Col. Jacob L. Jr. d. Jan. 18, 1791, a. 76 y.] Ch: Jacob, bp Nov. 4, 1739; Christoffel, bp. Jan. 30, 1743; Henderick, bp. March 20, 1748; Catalyntje, bp. May 6, 1753; Helena, bp. Jan. 1, 1758.

LANSING, Gerrit Isaacse, m. Ariaantje Beeckman, March —, 1740, and was buried Oct. 2, 1748. Ch: Isaac, bp. Nov. 2, 1740; Hester, bp. July 17, 1743; Jannetie, bp. Jan. 1, 1747; Gerritje, Nov. 6, 1848.

LANSING, Gerrit Johannese or Janse, m. Elsie Lansing, May 14, 1740, and was buried Aug. 27, 1757. Ch: Helena, bp. Dec. 13, 1741; Abraham, bp. May 5, 1745; Elsie, bp. Oct. 1, 1749.

LANSING, Abraham [son of Abraham], m. Catharina Lansing. Ch: Jacob, bp. Feb. 6, 1743; Magdalena, bp. Nov. 16, 1746; Magdalena, bp. June 2, 1750; Abram, bp. July 26, 1752, d. at Cherry Hill, Feb. 21, 1822, a. 70 y.

LANSING, Jacob Jacobse. He resided in the ancient house on the corner of Broadway and Quackenbush street; commanded a regiment at the battles of Stillwater and Saratoga: m. Marytje Egbertse (Ebberts), Nov. 6, 1742. Ch: Lena, bp. Feb. 6, 1743; Benjamin, bp. Jan. 3, 1745; Annatie, bp. July 26, 1746; Elsie. b. July 28, 1748, d. July 27, 1811, a. 62 y. 11 m. 20 d.; Benjamin, bp. June 31 (*sic*) 1750; Femmitie, bp. July 7, 1751; Jacob, bp. Aug. 19, 1753; Maria, bp. Dec. 7, 1755; Benjamin, bp. July 31, 1757.

LANSING, Abraham Jacobse, m. Elizabeth Cooper, May 20, 1744. Ch: Obadiah, bp. Aug. 5, 1744; Jacob, bp. Jan. 10, 1746; Gerrit, bp. Oct. 25, 1747;

John, bp. Nov. 12, 1749; Elsie, bp. Sept. 22, 1751; Cornelia, bp. May 27, 1753; Lena, bp. July 27, 1755; Abram, bp. Feb. 13, 1757; Isaac, bp. March 18, 1759; Helena, b. Sept. 4, 1760; Annatie, b. May 16, 1762.

LANSING, Johannes Jacobse, m. first, Rachel Lievens, Aug. 14, 1741, who d. May 28, 1742; secondly, Cathalyna, Van Schaick, Oct. 20, 1744; thirdly, Cathalyna Schuyler [about 1747], she d. March 31, 1797, a. 73 y. 7 m. He occupied a house on west side of Broadway the 4th north from Maiden Lane; died April 19, 1808, a. 92 y. 3 m. 19 d. Ch: Goosen, bp. Sept. 8, 1745; Nicolaas, bp. Sept. 11, 1748; Rev. Nicolaas Lansing, d. at Tappan, Sept. 26, 1835, a. 87 y.; Lena, bp. Nov. 4, 1750; Jacob, bp. Aug. 19, 1752; Philip, bp. Nov. 28, 1756; Elsie, bp. July 15, 1759.

LANSING, Abraham Jacobse, and Catharina Lievens. Ch: Levinus, bp. Jan. 12, 1746; Levinus, bp. Aug. 2, 1747; Levinus, bp, Aug. 6, 1749; Cornelis, bp. July 6, 1752.

LANSING, Gerrit Jacobse, and Elizabeth Van Schaick. Ch: Gerrit, bp. Aug. 3, 1746.

LANSING, Johannes Johannese, and Ariaantie Wendell. Ch: Johannes, bp. July 26, 1746; Evert, bp. May 8, 1748; Geertruy, bp. July 22, 1750; Johannes and Engeltie, bp. June 23, 1754; Geertruy, bp. Aug. 1, 1756; Johannes, bp. Aug. 6, 1758.

LANSING, Pieter, and Elizabeth Wendell. He d. May 13, 1807, a. 86 y. Ch: Maria, bp. July 26, 1746; Maria, bp. July 30, 1749; Catalyntie, bp. Nov. 17, 1751; Jeremias, bp. April 22, 1754; Isaac, bp. May 9, 1756; Geertruy, bp. May 2, 1758.

LANSING, Isaac, and Annatie Van Woert Ch: Jacob, bp. Dec. 14, 1746; Hendrikje, bp. Oct. 23, 1748; Helena, bp. Sept. 1, 1751; Jacob, bp. July 14, 1754; d. June 4, 1830, a. 77 y. Sara, bp. Aug. 28, 1757; Sara, bp. Sept. 20, 1761; Hendrick, b. Jan. 30, 1763.

LANSING, Gerrit Junior, and Annatie Yates. Ch: Anna, b. Jan. 12, 1746.

LANSING, Johannes Jacobse, and Maritie Huyck, Ch: Maria, bp. Jan. 24, 1748; Joeh (Job), bp. Jan. 21, 1750; Gerrit, bp. April 26, 1752; Lena, bp. March 12, 1755; Anna, bp. July 24, 1757; Andries, b. Feb. 12, 1760; Rachel, b. Oct. 5, 1762; Johannes, b. April 10, 1765; Hendrik, b. Sept. 29, 1767; Neeltie, b. Oct. 7, 1769; Alida, b. March 30, 1772.

LANSING, Gerardus, and Marytje Wendell. He d. March 24, 1808, a. 84 y. Ch: Geertruy, bp. Nov. 19, 1749; Anna, bp. May 16, 1754.

LANSING, Gerrit J., and Jannetie Waters. She d. March 2, 1810, a. 87 y. Ch: John, bp. March 5, 1749; John, bp. Feb. 3, 1754; Chancellor Lansing disappeared in New York city, Dec. 12, 1829, and was never heard of afterwards; Abraham, bp. Dec. 12, 1756; Sara, bp. July 1, 1759; Gerrit, bp. Nov. 11, 1760, an officer of the Revolution, d. at Oriskany, May 29, 1831, a. 70 y. Sara, b. June 23, 1763, m. Barent Bleeker; Sander, b. Jan. 17, 1767, m. Catharina, eldest dau. of Abm. Ten Eyck, and d. in Manheim, Sept. 19, 1850, a. 84 y. 3mo. 2d.

LANSING, Gerrit Junior, and Wyntie Van den Bergh Ch: Anna, bp. Nov. 4, 1750; Gerrit, bp. Sept. 9, 1753; Catalyntje, bp. Aug. 15, 1756; Gerrit, bp. July 16, 1760.

LANSING, Hendrick, and Anna Ouderkerk. Ch: Abram, bp. June 2, 1750.

LANSING, Philip, and Elsie Hun. Ch : John, bp.
April 2, 1748 ; Johannes, bp. Jan. 4, 1760 ; Jan. bp.
Feb. 15, 1761 ; Annatie, b. June 25, 1762 ; Geertruyd,
b. March 13, 1766 ; Maria, b. July 23, 1771 ; Johannes
Hun, b. April 12, 1774 ; Pieter, b. Dec. 15, 1778.

LANSING, Hendrick R., m. Mary Marcelis, Sept. 19,
1762. Ch : Margarita, b. Sept. 18, 1762 ; Johannes,
geboren desen dag, bp. Nov......, 1764 ; Robert, b.
Nov. 14, 1766 ; Robert, b. Nov. 28, 1767 ; Margarita,
b. Oct. 30, 1770. [Henry R. Lansing, d. Aug. 9, 1819,
a. 81 y. 7 mo.]

LANSING, Harpert (Herbert), and Maritje Visscher.
Ch : Abraham, b. Oct. 14, 1763 ; Gerrit, b. March
4, 1765 ; Johannes, b. April 20, 1777.

LANSING, Johannes, m. Catharyntje Burhans, Oct.
25, 1761. She d. Oct. 27, 1799, a. 61 y. Ch : Lena, b.
Oct. 6, 1763 ; Sara, b. Sept. 6, 1765 ; Meinard, b. Aug.
1, 1767 ; Helena, b. July 2, 1769 ; David and Helena,
bp. March 2, 1773 ; Robert, b. May 19, 1775 ; Hans
Burhans, b. July 25, 1778 ; Gerrit, b. Oct. 31, 1783.

LANSING, Jacob H., and Maria Ouderkerk. Ch : Annatie, b. April 10, 1764 ; Maria, b. Feb. 28, 1766 ; Helena, b. July 21, 1768 ; Elizabeth, b. Dec. 31, 1771 ;
William, b. May 11, 1774.

LANSING, Jacob Franse, of the *Colonie,* m. Jannetie
Visscher, June 27, 1762, [widow Jane Lansing, d. in
Watervliet, Nov......, 1830, in her 92d year.] Ch :
Isaac, b. Aug. 25, 1764 ; Theunis, b. Jan. 10, 1766 ;
Marytie, b. Oct 22, 1767 ; Machtel, b. Sept. 27, 1769 ;
Dirkie, b. April 9, 1775 ; Franciscus, b. Aug. 4, 1774 ;
Helena, b. Nov. 14, 1780.

LANSING, Isaac H., m. Annetie Van Arnhem, June
19, 1761. Ch : Abraham, b. July 24, 1765 ; Jacob, b.
Dec. 26, 1769.

LANSING, Rutger, m. Susanna Van Schoonhoven,
Oct. 27, 1764. Ch : Gerrit, b. Nov. 18, 1765.

LANSING, Christofer, of the *Colonie,* m. Sara Van
Schaick, Jan. 26, 1766. Col. Christopher L., was
quarter master of Col. Schuyler's regiment in the
Revolutionary war ; he built and occupied, in 1766,
the house on north corner of Broadway and North
Lansing street ; d. Oct. 25, 1819, a. 76 y. 8 m. 26 d. ;
his wife b. Nov. 26, 1743, d. April 23, 1788, a 44 y. 4 m.
28 d. Ch : Jacobus, b. June 15, 1766 ; Alida, b. Aug.
14, 1768 ; Johannes Van Schaick, b. May 20, 1771, d.
April 30, 1798, a. 26 y. 11 m. 10 d. ; Hubertje, b. July
26, 1773 ; Cathalyntje, b. Oct. 7, 1778 ; Sara, b. June
18, 1784.

LANSING, Jacob, of the *Colonie,* m. Willempie Brat,
Nov. 2, 1764. Ch : Lena. b. Nov., 1766, m. Dr Van
Zandt of Watervliet ; Jan Van Arnhem, b. June
15, 1769.

LANSING, Jacob A., and Alida Levison. Ch :
Maria, b. Sept. 17, 1768 ; Maria, b. June 27, 1772.

LANSING, Johannes E., and Maria Staats. Ch : Alida, b. Sept. 17, 1769 ; Evert, b. Oct. 27, 1773 ; Abraham, b. March 15, 1777 ; Maria, b. Feb. 25, 1781 ;
Catharina, b. May 20, 1787.

LANSING, Hendrick J., of the *Colonie,* m. Lena
Winne, May 6, 1769. She d. in Watervliet at the
residence of her son Benjamin, Aug. 27, 1827, in her
81st year. Ch : Jacob, b. Aug. 2, 1770 ; Sara, b.
July 20, 1773 ; Benjamin, b. July 10, 1776 ; Christoffer,
b. Oct. 22, 1779 ; Rachel, b. Aug. 28, 1782 ; Rachel, b.
Aug. 9, 1784 ; Hubertje, b. Sept. 11, 1787 ; Levinus,
Winne, b. Feb. 8, 1792.

LANSING, Lavinus F., of the *Colonie,* m. first Catharina Van der Heyden, March 11, 1770 ; secondly,
Marytje Persse (Pearse) Oct. 15, 1780. Ch : Catharina, bp. Oct. 8, 1770 ; Dirk, bp. Jan. 23, 1772 ; Alida,
b. June 4, 1783 ; Franciscus, b. April 15, 1790.

LANSING, Gerrit A., m. first, Agnietie Bratt, Oct. 1,
1771 ; secondly, Catharina Swart about 1776. Ch :
Margarita, b. April 20, 1772 ; Annatie, b. July 15, 1775.

LANSING, Obadiah, of Greenbush, m. first, Cornelia
Van Benthuysen ; secondly, Cornelia Cooper about
1774. Ch : Annatie, b. May, 9, 1773 ; Evert, b. Feb.
6, 1775 ; Jacobus, b. Oct. 27, 1776 ; Gerrit, b. Sept. 4,
1778 ; Jacobus, b. March 15, 1780 ; Sara, b. March 6,
1782 ; Johannes, b. Nov. 8, 1783 ; Obadia, b. Oct. 23,
1785 ; Catharina, b. March 4, 1787.

LANSING, Gerrit J., m. Alida Fonda, June 5, 1773.
Ch : Cornelia, b. Dec. 17, 1774 ; Johannes, b. Feb. 29,
1776 ; Isaac, b. Sept. 19, 1778 ; Marytje, b. Feb. 12, 1781.

LANSING, Abraham A., and Elsie Van Rensselaer.
He d. at Cherry Hill, Feb. 21, 1821, a. 70 y. Ch : Abraham, b. March 18, 1775 ; Ariaantje, b. Nov. 11,
1778 ; Ariaantje, b. April 24, 1781 ; Catharina, b. Aug.
27, 1783 ; Ariaantje, b. July 23, 1785 ; Kilian, b.
May 8, 1787 ; Magdalena, b. Nov. 6, 1789 ; Magdalena,
bp. April 6, 1793 ; Gerrit, b. March 14, 1791 ; Kilian
Van Rensselaer, b. Nov. 23, 1794.

LANSING, Jacob G., m. Femmetie Lansing, Aug.
28, 1774. He d. Nov. 25, 1803, a. 66 y. His wife
Frances, d. March 26, 1807, a. 56 y. [Jacob G. L.,
m. Neeltie Rosenboom, March 14, 1767.] Ch : Gerrit, b. Dec. 24, 1775 ; Maria, b. July 19, 1779 ; Jacob
Sanders, b. Dec. 21, 1781 ; Jannetie, b. May 14, 1786.

LANSING, Johannes A., m. Elizabeth Fryer, Feb. 10,
1776. He d. Jan. 30, 1825, a. 76 y. at 33 South Pearl
street, corner of Hudson. Ch : Abraham, b. Aug. 6,
1776, d. June 2, 1820, a. 44 y. ; Annatie, b. May 13,
1778 ; Annatie, b. Nov. 23, 1779 ; Willem, b. Feb. 23,
1782 ; Jacob, b. March 21, 1784 ; Annatie, b. June 1,
1786 ; Elizabeth and Maria, b. Sept. 5, 1788 ; Gerrit,
b. Feb. 15, 1791.

LANSING, Gerrit A., m. Elizabeth Wynkoop, Dec.
26, 1776. [This or another Gerrit A. L. m. Cathalina Van Aelstyne, Feb. 27, 1768]. Ch : Abraham,
b. Dec. 6, 1777 ; Abraham, b. Jan. 3. 1782 ; James
Wynkoop, b. April 20, 1783 ; James Wynkoop, b.
July 19, 1784 ; Gerrit, b. July 20, 1785 ; Alida, b. Jan.
19, 1787 ; Elizabeth, b. Dec. 30, 1788 ; James, b. April
2, 1791 ; Abraham, b. Feb. 10, 1793 ; Cornelia Wynkoop, bp. Dec. 25. bp. Sept. 10 (*sic*) 1794 ; John,
b. March 10, 1797 ; Robert, b. May 6, 1800 ; Sarah,
b. Sept., 1802

LANSING, Jacob Isaacse, m. Susanna Fonda, Jan.
10, 1778. He d. June 4, 1830, a. 77 y. ; she d. April
25, 1817 ; in her 61st y. Ch : Annatie, b. Dec. 27,
1778 ; Maria, b. Sept. 8, 1780 ; Sarah, b. Nov. 3, 1782 ;
Abraham Fonda, b. Dec. 28, 1784, d. April 8, 1861, a.
77 y. ; Isaac, b. April 8, 1787 ; Jacob and Alida, b.
Oct. 25, 1789 ; Jacob, b. June 17, 1791 ; Alida, b. Dec.
30, 1794 ; Alida, b. May 17, 1796.

LANSING, Abraham, and Annatie Van den Bergh.
Ch : Abraham, b. Sept. 23, 1779 ; Isaac, b. March 26,
1781 ; Annatie, b. Feb. 25, 1786.

LANSING, Abraham G., and Susanna (Sanneke)
Yates, daughter of Abraham Yates. [Dr. A. G. Lansing d. May 15, 1844.] Ch : Jannetie, b. Feb. 18,
1780 ; Abraham Yates, b. Jan. 12, 1782 ; Gerrit, b.
Aug. 4, 1783, d. Jan. 3, 1862, a. 79 y. ; Cornelis De

Ridder, b. Nov. 17, 1785; John, b. March 10, 1788; Antje, b. June 6, 1790; Sanders, b. April 15, 1792; Christopher, b. May 27, 1795; Antie, b. Jan. 26, 1799; Sarah, b. Sept. 5, 1802 (?).

LANSING, Jacob, and Maria Knipp. Ch: Johannes, b. Aug. 9, 1781.

LANSING, Jeremie, m. Lena Wendell, Oct. 1, 1780. She d. Oct. 11, 1829, a. 69 y. Ch: Pieter, b. April 13, 1781; Hermanus, b. Nov. 6, 1783; Elizabeth, b. Aug. 14, 1786, d. March 23, 1865; a. 79 y. at No. 80 North Pearl street; Pieter, b. Jan. 18, 1790; Jacob Jeremiah, b. Nov. 27, 1792; Barbara, b. June 19, 1800.

LANSING, Johannes, Jr., late chancellor, lived on north corner of Broadway and Steuben street in 1805; disappeared in New York, Dec. 12, 1829, and never heard from afterwards. He m. Cornelia Ray, April 8, 1781. Ch: Robert, b. July 13, 1783; Jane b. Jan. 27, 1785; Sara, b. Feb. 12, 1787; Robert Ray, b. Nov. 8 1788; Frances, b. June ...., bp. June 26, 1791; Elizabeth, b. July 5, 1793, d. Oct. 21, 1834; Sara and Cornelia, b. Jan. 17, 1795; Sara, b. Aug. 19, bp. Aug. 15, (*sic*), 1797; Mary, b. Sept. 16, 1800.

LANSING, Abraham, Junior, m. Maria Bloodgood, Feb. 8, 1784. Ch: Abraham, b. June 8, 1785; Annatie, b. Dec. 15, 1787; Jacobus Stoutenburgh, b. Jan. 1, 1791.

LANSING, Jacob J., and Jannetie Heyer. He d. June 21, 1794, a. 40 y. Ch: Geertruy, b. April 5, 1784; Catharina, b. April 30, 1786; Helena, b. Sept. 1, 1793.

LANSING, Andries, and Annatie Van den Bergh. Ch: Johannes, b. March 4, 1787; Evert, b. Dec. 4, 1790. [See also *Abraham* L., and Annatie V. D. Bergh, above.]

LANSINGH, James (Jacobus), and Rachel Verplanck. Ch: Lydia, b. March 1, 1788; Sara, b. July 5, 1790.

LANSING, Gerrit J., m. Maria Van Aernham (Van Deusen), April 21, 1787. Ch: Lea, b. June 26, 1788; Helena, b. Jan. 21, 1790.

LANSING, Gerrit R., m. Alida [De] Foreest, Sept. 2, 1787. Ch: Susanna, b. Aug. 26, 1788; Isaac De Foreest, b. June 17, 1790.

LANSING, John Van Aernhem, m. Ariaantie Verplanck, July 9, 1788; he d. Nov. ....., 1863, in Watervliet, a. 94 y. Ch: Maria, b. Feb. 13, 1789; Abraham Verplanck, b. Nov. 12, 1790; Jacob, b. Dec. 16, 1793; Willempie, b. Feb. 13, 1795; Gerluyn Verplanck, b. April 27, 1797; John, b. Aug. 18, 1899; Helena; Harriet.

LANSING, Johannes Jr., and Annatie Marshall. Ch: Maria, b. Sept. 26, 1789.

LANSING, Sander (son of Gerrit J. L.), was a lawyer; removed to Little Falls, in 1820; many years a Land agent there; one of the judges of Herkimer county; removed to Manheim where he died Sept. 19, 1850, a. 84 y. 3 m. 2 d. He m. Catharina Ten Eyck, eldest daughter of Abraham T. E., Dec. 9, 1789; she d. Sept. 23, 1850, four days after her husband. Ch: Jane Ann, b. Aug. 19, 1790; Abraham Ten Eyck, b. Aug. 12, 1792, d. at Manheim, Feb. 10, 1842, a. 47 y.; Maria, b. Jan. 10, 1797; Robert, b. Feb. 2, 1799; Maria, b. Feb. 21, 1801; Frances (*sic*.), b. April 3, 1803; Frederic, b. May 30, 1806; Edward, b. June 18, 1808.

LANSING, Jacob Jacobse (son of Col. Jacob J. L., and Marytje Egbertse), m. Annatie Quackenbush, Jan. 21, 1790. Ch: Margarita, b. Nov. 5, 1790; Jacob, b. Dec. 17, 1792. He was born in the ancient Dutch house on the north-east corner of North Pearl and Columbia streets, graduated at Middleburg College; practiced law in Albany; was judge of the Court of Common Pleas; and d. March 20, 1858. Ch; Elizabeth, b. Dec. 1, 1794.

LANSING, Jacob, and Alida Douwe. Ch: Mary, b. April 26, 1793; Andries Douwe, b. Feb. 29, 1796, Gen. Andries D. L., d. July 26, 1864, a. 68 y.; James b. Sept. 22, 1799; Volkert Douwe, b. April 3, 1804: Volkert Douwe, b. Feb. 10, 1807.

LANSING, Myndert, m. Mary Usher, daughter of Rev. John U. of Bristol, R. I., June 3, 1791. He d. April 10, 1814, in his 40th y., she d. March 7, 1845, a. 78 y. Ch: Catharine, bp. Feb. 5, 1792; Ann Usher, b. Feb. 24, 1794; Pieter R., b. 1796, d. Sept. 22, 1809; George Dunbar, b. Aug. 11, 1798; George Dunbar Usher, b. Aug. 26, 1799; Myndert, b. Feb. 9, 1801, d. April 24, 1842, a. 43 y.; Sarah, b. Nov. 11, 1804; Sally Usher, d. Sept. 10, 1842, a. 38 y.

LANSING, Gerrit, and Christal Hoffman. Ch: Mary, b. Nov. 5, 1794. [Gerrit L. d. April 29, 1860, a. 86 y.]

LANSING, John, and Ariaantie Lansing. Ch: Helena, b. Oct. 23, 1801.

Lant, Johannes, and Sara Winne. Ch: Michael, bp. Aug. 26, 1752.

Lantman (Landman), Pieter, and Elizabeth.... Ch: Stephanus, bp. Dec. 8, 1736; Abraham, bp. Jan. 10, 1739; Elizabeth, bp. Feb. 15, 1741.

LANTMAN, Michael, of Hosack, m. Maria Brouwer, Oct. 6, 1751. Ch: Elizabeth, bp. Nov. 19, 1752; Catharyntje, *oud* 4 *weeken* 1 *dag*, bp. March 4, 1762; Abraham, b. July 31, 1763; Neeltie, bp. Sept. 8, 1765; Catalyntje, b. May 6, 1773.

LANTMAN (Landman), Hannes, and Santje Litger. Ch: Hendrick, *oud* 6 *weken*, bp. Oct. 2, 1763; Abraham, b. Aug. 12, 1765.

LANTMAN (Landman), Pieter, and Sara Van Santen. Ch: Susanna, b. Dec. 15, 1776.

Lappary, see Lappius.

Lappius, William, m. Alida Van Dewsen, May 26, 1776. Ch; Johannes, b. June 5, 1778.

LAPPIUS (Lappary), Abraham, and Maria (De) Foreest. Ch: Tanneke, b. Jan. 25, 1787; Elizabeth, b. Jan. 3, 1789; Susanna, b. March 29, 1791 (?), bp. April 25, 1791.

Larraway, Willem, m. Sara Wynkoop, June 12, 1779. Ch: Catharina, b. Oct. 12, 1781.

Larwee (see Le Roy).

Lasher (Leycher, Lisser, Lisjer, Litzert, Lygher, Lycher), Mark, and Elizabeth Kilmer. Ch: Catharine, b. June 10, 1793.

Lassingh, Pieter Pieterse, in 1659, ran away from his master, Volckert Janse Douw, who sent after him to Hartford, Connecticut; in 1675, in company with Goosen Gerritse Van Schaick, he purchased the brewery of Harmen Rutgers standing on the casterly half of the Exchange lot; subsequently he sold his half interest in it to Sybrant Goosense Van Schaick; in 1685, he was at Esopus.

LASSINGH, Pieter, Jr., born at Albany, and dwelling at *het lange rak* [Poughkeepsie?] married Cornelia Rees of Claverak, Oct. 28, 1704, at Albany.

9

Lath, Willem, and Nancy Jackson. Ch: John b. Aug. 11, 1780.

Lattimore, Francis, and Geertruy [Van] Esch [Ness]. Ch: Elizabeth, b. Dec. 27, 1787.

Lauer, Michael, and Janneke Van Buren. Ch: Margarita, b. Aug. 16, 1771; Catharina, b. April 1, 1773; Catharina, b. Dec. 5, 1775.

Lawrence, William, m. Maria Perry, March 6, 1796. Ch: Andrew McNeally, b. April 25, 1799.

Leek, Nicolaas, and Marytje Snyder. Ch: Cornelis, b. Jan. 12, 1768.

Leen (Lanck), George, m. Mary Shaw, May 11, 1765. Ch: James, b. Jan. 16, 1771; Cornelis, b. Jan. 6, 1773.

Leendertse, Jan, and Eliaan Janse. Ch: Timotheus, bp. April 30, 1710.

Leenert (Lingert, Leonert), Johannes, m. Cornelia Richter (Rechteren), Aug. 29, 1767. Ch: Johannes, b. Oct. 1, 1770; Margriet, b. April 26, 1777; Nicholas, b. March 19, 1779; William, b. Oct. 18, 1792;

Le Foy, Abraham, and Anna Maria Forer. Ch: Catharina, bp. Feb. 18, 1705.

Legged (Legate), John, and Bata .... Ch: Cornelis, bp. Jan. 20, 1742.

Le Maitre, Cornelis of Esopus, and Margarita Van Steenbergen. Ch: Anna Catharina, bp. Jan. 28, 1708.

Lent, Jacob, and Hannah Odell. Ch: Catharine Odell, b. Dec. 1, 1798.

Leonard, Enoch, and Maria Van Vechten. Ch: Anna, b. Oct. 19, 1785; Cornelius Van Vechten, b. July 28, 1791; Miriam, b. Jan. 15, 1794; Herman, b. Oct. 11, 1797; Richard, b. March 10, 1800; Helena Maria, b. Dec. 20, 1803.

Leonard, John, and Maria Van Vechten [perhaps the same as the last.] Ch: Reuben, bp. July 12, 1788.

Le Roy, Larraway, Larwee, Lerway, Lerrday, &c.

Le Roy, Jonas (Jonathan), of Esopus, and Maria Usile. Ch: Blandina, bp. Feb. 1, 1708; Jonas, bp. Sept. 19, 1714; Jonas, bp. June 24, 1716; Jan, bp. Oct. 19, 1718; Maria, bp. June 4, 1721.

Lerway (Larraway?) Isaac, m. Sara Heemstraat, Jan. 28, 1779. Ch: Teunis Van der Volgen, b. April 20, 1796. See also Le Roy.

Leycher, Johannes Hendrickse, and Elizabeth .... Ch: Margarita, bp. March 28, 1756; Marytje, bp. April 9, 1758; Hendrik, b. Sept. 6, 1766.

Lisser, Hendrick, and Annatje Huyck. Ch: Susanna, bp. May 28, 1737; Geertruy, bp. Feb. 18, 1739; Catharina, bp. June 7, 1741; Marytje. bp. Jan. 11, 1744; Christina, bp. May 29, 1752; Johannes, bp. March 19, 1757.

Lespinard, Antony (Anthoine), baker, hired the bakery of Jan Rinckhout in 1670, with permission to bake for both Christians and Indians; made a will April 2, 1685, and spoke of his wife Abeltie and children: Johannes, aged 10 y.; Cornelia: Margarita; and Abeltie, aged about 6 mos. (bp. Sept. 21, 1684). He gave to the poor of Albany 8 beavers or the value thereof in silver money. His son Antony, bp. Oct. 31, 1683, was probably not living at the date of his will; he had another son of the same name who settled in New York, where he married Elisabeth DeKleyn, Nov. 3, 1705.

Letteson (Liddeson), William, and Maritie: [Wm. Letteson, m. Elisabeth Bouman, Dec. 16, 1720.] Ch: Jems, bp. June 30, 1717.

Levy, Asser, a Jewish trader of New Amsterdam, who owned a house and lot, and did business in Albany from 1661 to 1665.

Lewis (Luwes), Tames, and Mary French. Ch; Tames, bp. Nov. 19, 1707.

Lewis, Anthony, and Jannetje Morenes. Ch: Barent, bp. March 4, 1711; Johanna, bp. in New York, April 10, 1715; Barent, bp. in New York, Feb. 17, 1717; David, bp. in New York, Oct. 7, 1719.

Lewis, Barent, and Catharina Van Slyck. Ch: Jannetie, bp. Dec. 16, 1741; Jannetie, bp. Jan. 12, 1746; Annatie, bp. Nov. 10, 1751.

Lewis, John, and Hillegont .... Ch: Mary, bp. July 8, 1744.

Lewis (Louis), Hendrick, m. Marytje Davids, Feb. 3, 1771. Ch: Johannes, b. Dec. 6, 1771; Elizabeth, b. Sept. 22, 1774; Elizabeth, b. May 9, 1776. [Hendrick Lewis and Jannetie Helling, m. Aug. 16, 1778.]

Lewis, Neimy, and Maria Davis. Ch: Magdalena, b. Sept. 2, 1789.

Liethers, John, and Maria .... Ch: Richard, bp. May 21, 1731.

Lievens (Lievense, Liverse, Lieverse, Levison), Janse, in 1657 conveyed to Andries Andriesen a house and plantation consisting of 25 morgens lying in the town of Newtown, adjoining Hellgate; about this time he probably removed to Beverwyck. He had at least two children, Harmen and Annatie, who married Goosen Gerritse Van Schaick in 1657.

Lievense, Harmen (perhaps son of the above), and Maritje Teunise. He had a farm on Van Schaick's island at the mouth of the Mohawk river, in 1681. His wife was a widow in 1700. Ch: Tomas, bp. Feb. 24, 1684; Egbertje, bp. April 2, 1686; Pieter, bp. Dec. 15, 1689; Rachel, bp. Jan. 13, 1692, buried, Aug. 21, 1746; Livinus? Teunis? (probably son of the last), m. Catryna Van den Bergh, Oct. 26, 1713. Ch: Maritie, bp. March 26, 1714; Wilhelmus, bp. Jan., 1716; Harmen, bp. Jan. 28, 1718; Cornelis, bp. July 15, 1720; Catharina, bp. March 6, 1723; Rachel, bp. March 27, 1726; Pieter, bp. Sept. 7, 1729. Teunis Harmense (probably son of Harmen Lievense above), m. Rachel Gansevoort, Nov. 6, 1714. Ch: Harmen, bp. Aug. 27, 1715; Maria, bp. Oct. 6, 1717; Rachel, bp. April 19, 1719; Agniete, bp. May 13, 1722; Lidia, bp. Jan. 17, 1728.

Lievense, Willem, m. Maria Fonda, Dec. 9, 1742. Ch: Lavinus, bp. May 15, 1743; Alida, bp. Oct. 23, 1748; Levinus, bp. Oct. 6, 1754.

Lieverse, Livinus, and Catharina .... Ch: Livinus, bp. July, 1746. [Levinus Lieverse was buried July 2, 1749.

Lieverse, Harmen, and Anna Van Schoonhoven, *beide van Haalve Maan*, m. Jan. 30, 1752; She was buried Jan. 6, 1757; he m. secondly Catharine Winne (Van den Bergh), Dec. 8, 1760. Ch: Catarina, bp. July 12, 1752; Susanna, bp. Aug. 20, 1754; Geertje, 4 *weken*, bp. Feb. 26, 1764.

Lieverse, Cornelis, m. Cornelia Bratt, March 5, 1757. Ch: Livinus, bp. July 15, 1757; Antony, bp. April 29, 1760.

Lieverse, Pieter, and Maria Fonda. Ch: Douwe, bp. Jan. 4th, 1760 ; Lavinus, bp. Nov. 14, 1761 ; Aaltie, b. Sept. 6, 1763 ; Marytje, b. April 11, 1766 ; Cornelis, b. Sept. 24, 1768 ; Isaac, b. April 14, 1771 ; Maayke, b. Oct. 20, 1774 ; Willem, b. Jan. 4, 1779.

Levison (Lieverse), Douwe, and Annatie Visscher. Ch: Barent, b. Dec. 2, 1786 ; Pieter, bp. Oct., 1788.

Lighthall, Nicolas, of Schenectady, and Elisabeth Wageman. Ch: Margarita, bp. Oct. 21, 1776. See *Schenectady Families.*

Lincoln, Hosea, and Elisabeth Correl. Ch: Josiah, b. Jan. 9, 1777.

Lins, Jur(iaan), and Maria .... Ch: Molly, bp. June 29, 1734 ; James, bp. Dec. 17, 1736.

Liswell, John, and Annatie Lansing. Ch: John, bp. July 3, 1786 ; Abraham, bp. Jan. 13, 1788.

Littelriel, David, and Susanna ..... Ch: Lourens, bp. Dec. 3, 1715.

Livingston, Robert, secretary of Albany, from 1675 to 1721, when he was succeeded by his son Philip; mayor of Albany 1710-1719 ; his house lot was on the north corner of State and North Pearl streets ; m. Alida, widow of the Rev. Nicolas Van Rensselaer; was buried in the church in Albany, April 21, 1725. Ch : Philipina Johanna, bp. Feb. 3, 1684 ; Philippina, bp. July.25, 1686 ; Robert, bp. July 29, 1688 ; Gysbert, bp. March 5, 1690 ; Willem, bp. March 20, 1692 ; Johanna, Dec. 16, 1694 ; Catrine, bp. July 17, 1798.

Livingston, Robert, Jr., cousin (nephew) of the last ; appointed deputy secretary of Albany in 1699 ; m. Margareta Schuyler, Aug. 26, 1697. Ch : Engeltie, bp. July 17, 1698 ; Jacobus, bp. Oct. 21, 1701 ; Jannet, bp. Nov. 24, 1703 ; Pieter, bp. Jan. 6, 1706 ; John, bp. March 6, 1709 ; [Robert, bp. in New York, Aug. 31, 1718.]

Livingston, Philip, eldest son of Robert, senior, admitted to the bar of New York, Dec. 31, 1719 ; in 1720, appointed commissioner for Indian affairs ; 1721, succeeded his father as secretary of the commissioners of Indian affairs, and clerk of Albany county ; called to the Council in 1725, and continued in public life until his death Feb. 4, 1749. He occupied his father's house and lot on the north corner of State and Pearl streets ; m. Catharina, dau. of Pieter Van Brugh of Albany, Sept. 19, 1707. Ch : Robert, bp. Dec. 25, 1708 ; Pieter (Van Brugh), bp. Nov. 3, 1710, m. Maria Alexander in New York, Nov. 3, 1739 ; Pieter, bp. April 20, 1712 ; Johannes, bp. April 11, 1714 ; Philippus, bp. Jan., 1717, d. June 12, 1778 ; Hendrik, bp. April 5, 1719 ; Sara, bp. May 7, 1721 ; William, bp. Dec. 8, 1723 ; Sara, bp. Nov. 7, 1725, m. Gen. Lord Sterling; Alida, bp. July 18, 1728 ; Catharina, bp. April 15, 1733.

Livingston, Pieter, m. Zelia Holland, dau. of Henry H., Nov. 13, 1728. Ch : Robert, bp. July 27, 1729 ; Henry Holland, bp. Sept. 25, 1730 ; Margarita, bp. July 2, 1732 ; Thomas, bp. Oct. 5, 1733 ; Jane, bp. June 18, 1735 ; Margarita, bp. June 23, 1736.

Livingston, Robert, m. Maria Thong in New York, May 20, 1731. Ch : Catharina, bp. Aug. 6, 1732.

Livingston, John, m. Catharyna Ten Broeck, Sept. 6, 1739. Ch : Robert, bp. March 16, 1740 ; Margrieta, bp. Oct. 10, 1742 ; Dirk, bp. Oct. 19, 1744.

Livingston, Philip, Jr., m. Christina Ten Broeck, April 14, 1740. Ch : Philip, b. May 28, 1741 ; Dirk

geboren den 6 *Juny* and bp. June 8, 1743 ; Catharina, bp. Aug. 25, 1745.

Livingston, James, and Elisabeth .... Ch : John, b. May 19, 1777.

Livingston, Jacob, and Sarah House. Ch : Maritie, b. April 7, 1791.

Lock, Claas Hendrickse ; 1665 in Albany ; 1668 owned a sloop ; 1674 valuation of his property was 600 guilders ; 1684 master of the sloop *Sarah* plying between Albany and New York ; in 1671, he m. Cuiesje Hendricks, widow, in New York.

Lodewycksen, Thomas, a carpenter, in partnership with Reynier Wisselpenningh ; in 1658 they brought an action against the church for 270 guilders for building the *doop huysie* (baptistery), and recovered the whole amount ; in 1661 his partner sued him in the matter of fitting out a sloop which they were building together.

Loeck, Coenraad, m. Geertruy Van Deusen, Oct. 6, 1751. Ch : Philip, bp. June 17, 1753 ; Engeltie, bp. May 30, 1756.

Loeck, Johannes, "Van Neskatha," m. Geesje, La Grange, "Van Noormanskil," April 27, 1753. Ch : Philip, bp. Dec. 9, 1753 ; Maria, bp. March 5, 1758.

Loeck (Lock) Jacob, m. Alida Goewey (Hooey), Nov. 2, 1754. Ch : Philip and Salomon, bp. Oct. 23 1755, the mother then being dead.

Loeck, Jacob, m. Rachel Slingerland (widow Hogen), May 28, 1757. Ch : Alida, bp. July 1, 1759.

Loek, Loeck, Louk, Look, Luke, Lock, &c.

Loek (Louk) Philip, and Magdalena .... Ch : Magdalena, bp. Dec. 5, 1726. Philip Louk was buried near his house, April 4, 1751.

Loek, Hendrick, and Neeltie Scherp. Ch : Martinus, bp. June 4, 1763.

Loek (Look) Philip of Niskatha, m. Magdalena Van Wie, July 9, 1772. Ch : Hendrik, b. Nov. 17, 1776.

Loek (Luke) Philip, and Aitie (Eitie) Van der Spaan (Spawn). Ch : Johannes, b. March 10, 1777 ; Catrina, b. May, 1789, bp. Jan. 10, 1790.

Loek, Philip (see above), and Magdalena Van Wie. Ch : Johannes Van Wie, b. Dec. 20, 1779.

Loek (Look) Salomon, and Lena Moock. Ch : Jacob, b. Aug. 10, 1790 ; Maria, b. Jan. 9, 1794.

Loek (Luke) Coenraad, and Elizabeth Hillebrant, m. May 24, 1790. Ch : Magdalena, b. April 7, 1791.

Loockermans. Three brothers of this name were among the first settlers of New Netherland, — Govert Janse, who settled in New Amsterdam, where he m. Maritie Janse, July 11, 1649,—and Jacob and Pieter Janse Loockermans, who settled in Beverwyck. Jacob was in Beverwyck as early as 1657 : the sheriff brought a suit against him for having assaulted Meuwes Hoogeboom and split his face open from his.forehead to his underlip with his knife ; he was fined 350 guilders and ordered to pay for loss of time, board and surgical attendance. In 1664 he was one of the commissioners to negotiate a treaty of peace between the Mohawk and Northern Indians. Pieter Janse Loockermans was a citizen of Beverwyck in 1656 ; in 1658, he was boatswain in the service of the W. I. Company. He had a son Pieter, and daughter Lammertie who married Arien Oothout.

Logen, Hendrick (Andries), *geborte in Irland* [probably intended for Hogen], m. Alida Pruyn, Oct. 29, 1733. Ch: Johannes, bp. July 7, 1734; [Franciscus, bp. July 26, 1736; see Hogen]; David, bp. April 23, 1738; Hendrik, bp. April 20, 1740; Anna, bp. Aug. 1, 1742; Margarita, bp. May 20, 1744.

Long, Adam, and Neeltie Groesbeck. Ch: John, b. June 26, 1789.

Lotteridge, William, and Anna De Wever. Ch: John b. April 4, 1777; Abraham, b. March 9, 1779.

Lottridge, Thomas, m. Mary Bratt, July 13, 1766. Ch: Bernardus Bratt, b. Jan. 19, 1779; John, b. March 9, 1781.

Lottridge, Robert, and Sarah Bloemendal. Ch: William, b. Nov. 21, 1792. [Robert L., d. Oct. 31, 1848, in his 75th y.

Louw, Nicolaas, and Sara .... Ch: Pieter Nicolaas, b. Dec. 23, 1777.

Love, William, and Elisabeth Danielson. Ch: Jennet, bp. Sept. 24, 1780.

Low, William, and Elisabeth Daniels [see the last.] Ch: Pieter, b. Jan. 4, 1779.

Lowe (Loery), Thomas, and Geertruy (Charity)) Vosburgh. Ch: Thomas Witbeck, b. March 25, 1791; Sarah, b. March 11, 1793.

Loveridge, William, hatter. In 1671 he bought a house and lot of Pieter Jacobse Borsboom on the east side of Broadway, bounded north by the king's court house. This lot was taken to extend Hudson street to the river. In 1676 he was accused of having charged the Dutch with supplying the Indians with ammunition, and ordered to be kept in custody until he made good the charge; not proving the same, he was fined 20 beavers. In 1678 he and others were condemned for planting a scandalous tree before the door of Richard Pretty, magistrate; he addressed Capt. Brockhols in extenuation, that it was a custom of the place to set up a tree on the occasion of marriage; notwithstanding, his sentence was confirmed. In 1680 he owned a farm at Catskil, and petitioned for an addition of 40 acres. He had a son William.

Lubbertson, Gerrit, from New York, m. Alida Evertsen, of Albany, March 12, 1684. Ch: Grietje, bp. Jan. 4, 1685; Grietje, bp. Aug. 15, 1686; Rebecca, bp. March 4, 1688.

Lubkins, Georgius (George), and Margaret .... Ch: Johannes, bp. Feb. 27, 1737; George, bp. April 23, 1738; Albertus Meinert, bp. Sept. 9, 1739.

Luke, see Loek.

Lupton, Rev. Brant Schuyler,and Esther Brown. Ch: Elisabeth Schuyler, b. Oct. 6, 1790.

Lush, Richard (Dirk), m. Lyntje Fonda, Dec. 14, 1780. In 1805 he dwelt on the north corner of Broadway and Maiden Lane. Ch: John, b. Oct. 12, 1781; Elsie, b. May 3, 1783, d. June 1, 1843; Mary, b. Feb. 19, 1785; Annatie, b. May 28, 1789; Lyntje Douw, b. April 11, 1791; Gilbert Fonda, b. April 19, 1793, d. Dec. 10, 1828, a. 35 y.; Lydia, b. Feb. 13, 1800.

Lush, Stephen, a native of New York, graduate of Columbia College; admitted to the bar in 1774, at the age of 21 y.: an officer of the Revolutionary war at the close of which he removed to Albany, where he httained eminence in his profession. He m. Lydia, bau. of Doctor Samuel Stringer, d. April 19, 1825. She d. Aug. 10, 1841. a. 82 y. Ch: Samuel Stringer, d. Sept. 7, 1782; Samuel Stringer, b. Oct. 20, 1783; ae was an eminent lawyer and sometime member

of the legislature; d. June 21, 1841, a. 58 y.; William, b. Nov. 6, 1785, d. July 2, 1846; his wid. Margaret Trotter, d. Sept. 1, 1870; Mary b. Jan. 10, 1787, m. Doctor John M. Bradford; Richard, b. June 20, 1798, d. Oct. 25, 1828, in 30th y.; Rachel, .. m. Henry G. Wheaton; Gertrude, —— m. Wm. S. Ross.

Luther, John, and Elizabeth Roller (Rowler). Ch: Jeremiah, b. Aug. 20, 1783; Maria, b. May 6, 1791; Helen and Susanna, bp. Jan. 14, 1793; George, b. July 29, 1795; Elizabeth, b. April 10, 1799.

Luwes (see Lewis).

Luycassen, Evert, baker (perhaps son of Lucas Gerritse Wyngaard), at Beverwyck in 1657; in 1665, purchased land behind Kinderhook of the Indians; sold the same in 1677 to Jacob Janse Gardenier; in 1680, with Lourens Van Alen, he petitions for another tract of land in Kinderhook.

Luyks (Loux), Hendrik, and Anna Elizabeth Coen. Ch: Margariet, bp. May 22, 1743; John Pieter, bp. Aug. 25, 1745.

Lydius, Domine Johannes, arrived in Albany from Holland with Domine Barnhardus Freeman, July 20, 1700, and officiated as minister of the church, until his death on March 1, 1710. He lived in the Parsonage standing on the site of Bleecker Hall. His wife (?) Isabella Staats, and daughters (?) Geertruy Isabella Lydius, and Maria Adrianata Lydius, were naturalized Feb. 28, 1716. The latter was buried in the church, May 4, 1733. Children baptized in Albany: Margarita Johanna, Nov. 19, 1701; Johannes Henricus, July 9, 1704; Susanna Catharina, July 13, 1707, buried in the church, Oct. 2, 1727.

Lydius, Johannes Henricus. Serious charges were brought against him in 1747, by the council of the Province: for abjuring his Protestant religion in Canada; of marrying a woman there of the Romish faith; and of alienating the friendship of the Indians from the English; he d. in Kensington near London, in 1791, having retired to England in 1776. His wife was Genevieve Masse (Mazie, Mazee). Ch: Nicolaas Jacob, bp. Oct. 8, 1732; Maryanus, bp. May 19, 1734; Isabella Margarita, bp. Jan. 14, 1736; Sara Maria, bp. July 7, 1738; Balthazar, bp. March 8, 1740, lived unmarried, on the east corner of State and Pearl streets; an eccentric man, the terror of boys, d. Nov. 17 (19), 1815; Catharina, bp. Sept. 25, 1743.

Lynd, Hannes (Herculeus, Archelaus) and Mary-tje Duivebach. Ch: Johannes, b. Sept. 1, 1762; Antje, b. Nov. 14, 1764; Catharina, b. March 17, 1767; Archelaus, b. May 1, 1768; Antje, b. Oct. 25, 1770.

Lynn, Arent, and Phœbe Woodruff. Ch: Eleanor, b. April 18, 1788.

Maat, alias Van Loosereght, Jacob Hendrickse, an innkeeper, in 1654, became farmer of the excise for 1300 gl.; in 1665 was accused of gambling, and of roughly handling one Steven Janse Conninck.

Maby, Johannes, and Christina .... Ch: Hanna, b. Oct. 12, 1769.

McAdam, Hugh, and Catharina Gerritsen. Ch: Mary, b. Aug. 19, 1780.

McAlpine, James, and Margarita Bratt. Ch: David, b. Dec. 13, 1780.

McBead, Daniel, and Rachel McCantish. Ch: William, b. April 6, 1779.

McBride, William, and Elizabeth Chambers. Ch: Margaret, b. Feb. 20, 1795; George, b. June 17, 1797.

McCanteish, William, and Geertruy Kidney. Ch: Roeloff, b. March 1, 1771.

Macarty, Pieter (Patrick), of Half Moon, m. first, Greefje Rhee, wid., March 7, 1736; and 2dly, Anna .... about 1742. Ch: Philip, bp. Jan. 8, 1736; Catharina, bp. Feb. 6, 1743.

MACARTY, John, and Anna Dorson. Ch: Elizabeth, bp. Feb. 14, 1748.

McCarty, Dennis, and Nancy Homes. Ch: Rachel, bp. Feb. 21, 1780.

McCARTY, Timothy, and Rebecca Patin. Ch: Henry, b. Feb. 15, 1787.

McCasory, James, and Dolly Ramsey. Ch: John, b. July 24, 1781.

McCay, John, and Alida Barheit. Ch: Catalyntje, bp. March 6, 1748.

McCAY, Neil, and Catharine McKinzy. Ch: John, b. Aug. 20, 1781.

McChesney (McChesnut), Hugh, and Joanna Plum (Plumb). Ch: Joseph, b. Aug. 31, 1776; Isaac, b. Nov. 15, 1779; Isabella, b. Oct. 30, 1780.

McCHESNEY (McChesnut), Robert, and Mary Cannum. Ch: William, b. Dec. 11, 1779.

McCHESNEY, Joseph, and Mary Monney (Mullenniche). Ch: Samuel, b. March 14, 1780; William, b. Sept. 15, 1781.

McCHESNEY, John, and Catharina Heens. Ch: Samuel, b. Dec. 5, 1780.

McCHESNEY, John, and Rebecca Hooghkerk, m. Aug. 25, 1796. Ch: John Hooghkerk, b. June 23, 1797.

McClairen, Pieter, and Margaret Thompson. Ch: John, bp. Jan. 8, 1777.

McClellan, Robert, and Jane Williams. Ch: Hannah, b. Feb. 27, 1779 [Robert McClellan, formerly State treasurer, d. Oct. 8, 1817.]

McClesky, John, and Mary Nengels. Ch: Martha, bp. April 24, 1779; James, b. Nov. 31, 1781.

McCloud, Mordar (Mordach), and Christina Rose. Ch: Hugh, b. Nov. 8, 1780; Reynold and Alexander, b. Sept. 4, 1782.

Macluur, John, and Jannetie .... Ch: Johann, bp. Sept. 5, 1731; Andries, bp. Jan 25, 1733; Thomas, bp. Feb. 9, 1735; Margrietje, bp. Dec. 26, 1736; Alida, bp. June 3, 1739; Jannetje, bp. Aug. 21, 1743.

McCoy, William, and Geertje Levison. Ch: Mayke, b. July 25, 1785.

McCoughtry, John, and Elizabeth Seabury. Ch: Jane, bp. May 14, 1793.

McCrea (Carree), John, and Eva Beeckman. Ch: Sara, b. Nov. 1, 1767; Maria, b. June 5, 1772; Johannes Beeckman, b. Aug. 20, 1773.

McCREA (?) (Carray), James, and Maria Hoghing. Ch: Maria, b. Feb. 2, 1771.

McCullogh, Willem, and Elizabeth Bride. Ch: Nancy, July 8, 1781.

McDeerwith, Angus, and Margaret Campbell. Ch: Read, bp. July 4, 1756.

McDole (Doll), George, and Catharina Zeger. Ch: Thomas, b. Jan. 3, 1773; Elizabeth, b. June 24, 1779; Jacob, b. June 22, 1781; Maria Catharina, b. May 21, 1787.

McDOLE, John, and Eleanor Chasley. Ch: William Chasley, b. March 29, 1792.

McDonald, Neil, and Anna Davie. Ch: George, bp. Aug. 26, 1752.

McDONALD, Donald, and Catarine .... Ch: John, bp. Oct. 4, 1756.

McDONALD, James, and Margaret Nevels (Nevins). Ch: John, bp. Sept. 14, 1756.

McDONALD, Jacob (John), Lydia Pangburn. Ch: Jacob, b. March 20, 1781; Joseph, b. April 4, 1782.

McDONALD, Daniel, and Nancy McGrieger. Ch: Christina, b. Sept. 16, 1781.

McDONALD, Norman, and Eleanor .... Ch: William, b. May 9, 1777.

McDougal, Pieter, and Catharina Thompson. Ch: Malcolm, b. July 20, 1781.

McElwayn, Thomas, and Jenny .... Ch: Elizabeth, b. Jan. 21, 1781.

McFarland, Thomas, and Catharina Kincheler (Kinsela?). Ch: Elizabeth, bp. Nov. 2, 1756.

McGinnis, Teddy, and Sarah Coss. Ch: Catharina, bp. April 24, 1748.

McGregory, Patrick, *uyt Schotlandt*, m. Zytje Matthyse Hooghteling *weduwe* of Frank Marrits, May 4, 1697. In 1686, Patrick M. was commissioned ranger general of Staten Island; 1697, he was in Albany and petitioned the city council for his father-in-law Hendrick Marcelis's place as city porter, the latter being then deceased; 1701, he was admitted city carman, provided he take out his "Citty freedom:" not living in 1707. Ch: Tryntje, bp. July 25, 1697; Margriet, bp. May 9, 1700; Rachel, bp. Aug. 16, 1702; Pieter, bp. Aug. 20, 1704.

Magregorie, Pieter, m. Annatie Broedts, Nov. 12, 1733. Ch: Elizabeth, bp. April 13, 1735.

McGriger, Alexander m. Ebbie (Betsey) McVie, Feb. 14, 1779. Ch: Mary and Jannet, b. March 13, 1780; John, bp. Sept. 5, 1782.

Mack, John, and Anna Sudita (?) Mack. Ch: Anna, b. Nov. 25, 1767.

Mackansch, Andries, m. Hagar Pycket, Aug. 18, 1725. Ch: Johannes, bp. Nov. 27, 1726; Maria, bp. Feb. 9, 1729; Patrick, bp. May 4, 1735; Elizabeth, bp. Oct. 16, 1737.

Mackansh, John, and Anna .... Ch: Volkert Van Hoesen, bp. Jan. 26, 1743.

Mackans, Patrick, and Jannetje .... Ch: Joachim, b. May 9, 1762.

McKans, Daniel, and Rachel McKentish. Ch: Alexander, bp. July 22, 1781.

Mackay, (Coy) Charles, m. Mayke Ouderkerk, Feb. 20, 1761. Ch: Willem, b. June 18, 1762; Elizabeth, b. Sept. 4, 1764; Maria, b. Aug. 3, 1781.

McKee, James and Mary Logan. Ch: Elizabeth, and Margaret, b. Dec. 14, 1776.

McKentick, John, and Eleanor McNeal. Ch: Duncan, bp. Aug. 6, 1756.

Mackie (Magee), Jan, m. Catharyna Oliver, Nov. 21, 1737. Ch: James and John, bp. Jan. 14, 1739.

MACKIE, Tobias and Sara Cos. Ch: Elizabeth, bp. Jan. 4, 1745.

McKinney, John and Elizabeth McCarty. Ch: Elizabeth, b. May 19, 1782.

Mackintosh, Anniar and Ebbetje Vanden Bergh, Ch: Catharina, b. Aug. 2, 1766.

McIntosh, John and Mary Smith. Ch: Rebecca, b. Aug. 22, 1788.

McKinsey, Hugh, and Maron McCloud. Ch: Catharine, b. Aug. 29, 1779.

McKinsey, Francis, and Eleanor Watson. Ch: Margaret, b. April 18, 1781.

McKinsy, Henry, and Elizabeth Van Alsteyn. Ch: Jannetje, b. Sept. 30, 1783.

McLean, John. and Catrina Van Deusen. Ch: Isaac, bp. Nov. 24, 1751.

McLean, Cornelius, of Saratoga, and Margaret McLean. Ch: Cornelius, b. Feb. 28, 1789.

MacManus (Meemannus), Cornelius, and Rebecca Northen (Norton). Ch: Hugh, bp. June 14, 1747; Elizabeth, bp. April 9, 1749.

McManus, William, m. Mary Veher (Fare), Jan. 18, 1784. Ch: Rebecca, b. Oct, 19, 1784.

McMichael, Daniel, and Sara Marselis. Ch: James, bp. June, 21, 1752.

McMichael, John, and Engeltie Kidney, Ch: Dirk, b. Feb. 13, 1779; Phebe, b. July 24, 1783; Sara, b. May 14, 1790. Bassett, b. Oct. 14, 1792.

McMullen, Hugh, and Rosanna ..... Ch. John, b. Aug. 9, 1777.

McMullen, John, and Agnes Gordon, Ch: Alexander, b. Dec. 20, 1780.

McNaughton, Hugh, and Judith McDonald. Ch: Daniel, bp. Nov. 2, 1756.

McPherson, Alexander, and Anna McCantish. Ch: Farquard, bp. July 4, 1756.

McPherson, Lewis, and Ann .... Ch: Lewis, bp. Aug. 29, 1758.

McVie, William, and Mary McDonald. Ch: Christina, b. Sept. 19, 1780.

Mahoney (Mohennie), David, and Rebecca .... Ch: Mary, bp. Feb. 13, 1737; Jan, bp. Sept. 10 1737; Rebecca, b. June 14, 1740; William, bp. Jan. 30, 1743.

Maloney, John, and Elizabeth Erskine. Ch: Elizabeth, b. Oct. 22, 1779.

Man, Jacob, and Catharina Smith. Ch: Marytje, bp. Jan, 20, 1773.

Mangelse, Jan, was in Beverwyck as early as 1657; his father-in-law was Pieter Adriaense Soegemackelyk. Ch: Johannes, bp. Jan. 27, 1686.

Mancius, Wilhelmus, m. Annatie Ten Eyck, Dec. 17, 1766. Doctor Mancius, b. Sept. 29, 1739, d. Oct. 22, 1808, a. 70 y.; she d. April 26, 1816, a. 74 y. 7 mo. 16 d. Ch: Georgius Wilhelmus, b. Dec. 13, 1767, d. Dec. 1 (4), 1823; Anna, b. Dec. 12, 1769; Jacob and Anna, b. Jan. 12 1771; Anna, b. April 10, 1773; Anna, b. May 13, 1777, d. in Watervliet, Dec. 20, 1855, a. 79 y.; Jacob Ten Eyck, b. Dec. 10, 1779, d. Nov. 7 (8), 1833, in his 54th y.; John, b. Sept. 9, 1784, d. Jan. 6, 1827.

Manley, John, and Richard (*sic*) Tuttle. Ch: Richard Brewster, b. May 11, 1798.

Mannypenny, John, and Darky Kendy. Ch: Clemens, bp. Dec. 12, 1756.

Marinus, Willem, of Schenectady, and Bata Klein. Ch: Maria, bp. June 19, 1709.

Marinus, Karel, of Schenectady, and Margareta Mambrut (Van Brute). Ch: Willem, bp. Jan. 15, 1749.

Marking, Hendrik, and Frena .... Ch: Hendrik, bp. March 30, 1740.

Marselis, Hendrik, was one of Melyn's colonists of Staten Island, having come over probably with the others in the *New Netherland's Fortune* in 1650. In 1654, he had a grant of a lot in Beverwyck. When Staten Island was attacked by the Indians in 1655, he fled with his wife, two children (daughters), and servant, and removed to Fort Orange, where he made a permanent settlement. In 1673, he dwelt "behind Kinderhook," where his son-in-law Matthys Coenraedse lived. His other daughter m. Patrick McGregory. He acted as city porter in 1697, in which year he died about Nov. 1. His wife was Tryn Van den Bergh.

Marselis, Janse Van Bommel, "born at Bommel in Gelderland," one of the first setlers of Beverwyck and ancestor of those bearing the name of *Marselis*, in this region, was farmer of the excise for several years following 1655. His wife was Annatie Gerritse. In 1690, June 11, he made his will, and was not living in 1700. Ch : Gysbert ; Huybertje, m. Joseph Yates ; Sytje, m. Joseph Janse Van Santen [Zandt] : Judith, m. Lucas Hooghkerk : Ahasuerus settled in Schenectady : Gerrit with wife and child was killed in the massacre at Schenectady, Feb. 9, 1690.

Marselis, Gysbert, shoemaker, in 1680, bought a house and lot of Gerrit Slichtenhorst, on the East corner of Maiden Lane and Pearl street where he was still living in 1714. He was buried June 8, 1740; His first wife was Barber Claase Groesbeck dau. of Claas Jacobse G. Ch: Nicolaas, and Johannes twins, bp. Aug. 5, 1683; Gerrit, bp. Feb. 10, 1686; Annetie, bp. June 30, 1689, d. Nov. 30, 1702; Lysbeth, bp. Jan. 31, 1692; Johannes, bp. May 26, 1695; Gerrit, bp. Feb. 16, 1698; Catharina, bp. Jan. 1, 1701.

Marselis, Ahasuerus, shoemaker, had a lot in 1716, without the *South Gate*, near the corner of Broadway and Hudson street, removed to Schenectady in 1710 ; m. Sara Van Heemstraaten Dec. 8, 1697. Ch : Johannes, bp. June 26, 1698 ; Derrick, bp. Jan. 5, 1700 ; Johanna, bp. Jan. 26, 1701 ; Gysbert, bp. June 4, 1704 ; Gerrit, bp. Sept. 22, 1706 ; Takel, bp. Jan. 1, 1709 ; Annatie, bp. in Schenectady, March 6, 1711 ; Marretie, bp. March 8, 1713 ; Trientien, bp. in Schenectady July 31. 1715 ; Ahasuerus, bp. Dec. 15, 1717 : Abraham, bp. July 8, 1721 ; Isaac, bp. June 29, 1723.

Marselis, Myndert, m. Tytje Oothout, May 23, 1713 she was buried May 30, 1757. Ch : Gerrit, bp. Nov. 13, 1713 ; Alida, bp. May 10, 1715 ; Breghie, bp. June 10, 1717 ; Rebecca, bp. July 3, 1720 ; Elizabeth, bp. Dec. 10, 1727 ; Gerrit, bp. May 10, 1730 ; Andries, bp. Oct. 30, 1732.

Marselis, Johannes, m. Anna (Johanna), Beekman, June 9, 1723. She made her will Aug. 9, 1769, proved Jan. 26, 1780 ; in which she spoke of her Ch : Gysbert, Eva wife of Johannes M. Roseboom ; Barbara, w. of Hendrick I, Bogart ; Maria, w. of Henry Lansingh, and Henderick. ... The following Ch : were bp. in the church. Gysbert, March 29, 1724. Eva, Jan. 1, 1726 ; Barber, Sept. 24, 1727 ; Johannes, Sept. 7, 1729 ; Gerrit, April 7, 1732, made will Feb. 5, 1766, proved May 28, 1766, in which neither wife nor children are spoken of ; Maria, Aug. 31, 1735 ; Hendricus, Sept. 23, 1739 ; Hendricus, Oct. 31, 1742

[Johannes Marselis was buried, Aug. 19, 1747; another Johannes, M. was buried, Jan. 26, 1746.]

MARSELIS, Gerrit, m. Margarita Bleecker, Dec. 22, 1730. Ch: baptized, — Gysbert, Sept. 26, 1731; Gysbert, Nov. — 1732; Johannes, Sept. 22, 1734; Barber, April 31 (*sic*), 1737; Nicolaas, May 25, 1740; Jacob, Sept. 12, 1742; Jacob, March 27, 1748; Anna, April 29, 1750.

MARSELIS, Gysbert, m. Catalina Wendell, Nov. 29, 1751. Ch: bp. — Johanna, June 10, 1753; Johannes, Feb. 1, 1756; Anna, Sept. 17, 1758; Eva, Jan. 18, 1761; Evert, b. Feb. 20, 1764; Eva, Sept. 27, 1767.

MARSELIS, Johannes (Hannes), and Neeltie Gardenier. Ch: Andries, bp. May 9, 1756; Myndert, b. Jan. 13, 1760; Fytje, b. Sept. 4, 1762.

MARSELIS, Gysbert G., Jr., m. Annatje Staats, Feb. 5, 1761. Ch: Gerrit b. June 25, 1762; Gerrit, b. Dec. 8, 1763; Maria, b. Jan. 31, 1766; Margarita, bp. Sept. 11, 1768; Isaac, b. March 21, 1772.

MARSELIS, Nicolaas, m. Margarita Groesbeck, Aug. 9, 1766. Ch: born, Gerrit, Nov. 2, 1767; Maria, Oct. 25, 1769; Anna, Dec. 3. 1771; Gerardus, Feb. 25, 1774; Maria, June 5, 1776; Margarita, June 19, 1780; Stephanus, Oct. 19, 1782; Geertruy, bp. July 6, 1785.

MARCELIS, Johannes, Junr., m. Margarita Van den Bergh, June 8, 1770. Ch: born; Barbara, Aug. 15, 1771; Margarita, Sept. 22, 1772; Annatie, April 12, 1774; Lydia, Oct. 13, 1775.

Marselis, Hendrikus, m. Maria (De) Foreest, Nov. 7, 1766. She d. Jan. 4, 1816. Ch: Johanna *geboren desen dag*, bp. Aug. 21, 1771.

MARSELIS, Evert, m. Sara Van Benthuysen, Aug. 17, 1786. Ch: born; Cathalina, April 16, 1787; Gysbert, June 9, 1792; Mary, Aug. 15, 1802.

MARSELIS, Gerrit G., m. Magtel Visscher, Jan. 31, 1787. Ch: born; Engeltie, May 19, 1788; Engeltie, June 24, 1789; Anna, June 23, 1791; Catalina, Feb. 13, 1796; Gysbert, June 4, 1801.

MARSELIS, Myndert, and Catharine Milderbergh. Ch: born; Eleanor, July 14, 1796; John Milderbergh, May 31, 1798.

Marshall, Pieter Busie, m. Annatie Flensburgh, July 23, 1743. Ch: baptized; Johanna, Jan. 4, 1745; Daniel, Feb. 15, 1747; Franciscus, Jan. 15, 1749; Johanna, Feb. 23, 1752; Johannes, Dec. 7, 1755; Johannes, b. Jan. 6, 1765.

MARSHALL, Franciscus, m. Geertruy Van Deusen, Nov. 23, 1770. Ch: born; Annatie, Sept. 13, 1771; Cornelis, June 5, 1773; Petrus, July 25, 1775; Maria, bp. Feb. 8, 1778; Immetje, Jan. 31, 1780; Lea, March 17, 1782.

MARSHALL, Daniel, and Elizabeth Conchron (Cachron, Cochron). Ch: born; Petrus, Jan. 17, 1773; Petrus, April 20, 1774; Daniel Flensburgh, Feb. 11, 1781; Joseph, May 31, 1784; Franciscus, March 5, 1788; John, Dec. 7. 1795.

MARSHALL, Peter, and Hannah Bacon. Ch: born; Daniel, Aug. 23, 1797; Rebecca, Aug. 9, 1801.

Martense, Jan, see DeWeever.

MARTENSE, Jacob, perhaps brother of Jan Martense DeWeever, and Paulus Martense Van Benthuysen. In 1571 he bought a lot of land behind Kinderhook of Robert Orchard. Ch: baptized; Johanna, April 17, 1685; Maria, Jan. 16, 1687; Ytje, Aug. 22, 1688.

Martin, Patrick, trommelslager onder de compagnie granadiers van de Hon. Richard Ingoldsby

m. Mary Cox, March 15, 1707. Ch: baptized; Elizabeth, July 27, 1707.

MARTIN, Daniel, and Alida ..... Ch: baptized, Jonathan, April 27, 1735; Margrieta, May 15, 1737.

MARTIN, Peter, and Elizabeth Burns. He was buried, Nov. 24, 1755. Ch: baptized; Maria, Feb. 5, 1749; Patrick, June 14, 1752; Margarita, March 31, 1754. [Petrus Meerthen of Hosak and Elizabeth Creller, m. June 17, 1865].

MARTIN, Alexander, m. Annatie Philipse, May 13, 1753. Ch: Alexander, bp. Jan. 27, 1754.

MARTIN, John, and Cath. Beemus. Ch: Geertruy, b. March 23, 1781.

Maryns, ... and Lysbet Tyssen; they had a dau. Brechie Maryns, in 1663, late wife of Claes Cornelise Van Voorhout deceased.

Matthews, Vincent, and Catryna ... . Ch: Catalyna, bp. Aug. 18, 1723,

Matthias, Elias, and Margaret Soor. Ch: Maria, b. Dec. 16, 1792.

Matthison, John, and Margaret Sunderland. Ch: Jenny, bp. Nov. 7, 1756.

Matthysse, Tjerk, of Esopus, and Maria Ten Eyck. Ch: Tjaatje, bp. Jan. 28, 1708.

Meble, Jan Pieterse, of Schenectady, and Antje Pieterse Borsboom. Ch: Pieter, bp. Jan. 20, 1686; Annetje, bp. April 16, 1693. (See *Schenectady Families.*)

Megapolensis, Domine Johannes, came to Beverwyck in 1642, with his wife Machtelt Willemsen; removed to New Amsterdam in 1649. His children were Hillegonda, who married Cornelis Van Ruyven, the colonial secretary; Dirck; Jan, who became a physician and practiced in Beverwyck in 1654, in New Amsterdam 1655, and removed to Holland about 1656; Samuel, educated in Harvard College, and at Leyden, and returned to New Amsterdam.

Meigs (Miggs), Seth, and Jemima Boskerk. Ch: Jenny, b. Dec. 27, 1784.

Meisserger, Hans, and Antje Van den Bergh. Ch: Petrus, bp. Feb. 18, 1776.

Merky, Roeloff, and Catharina Bovie. Ch: Antje, b. Aug. 9, 1765.

Merriday, William, m. Hilletie (Bratt) Lewis widow, Dec. 3, 1748. Ch: Susanna, bp. Aug. 27, 1749.

Metselaer (De Metselaer) Harmen, in Albany 1666; died, Nov., 1667, leaving a widow.

Metselaer (De Metselaer), Marten, in 1657 got into a fight with Pieter Jacobse Borsboom whom he wounded in the head with his dagger, for which he was hauled out of bed and set in the stocks.

METSELAER (De Metselaer) Teunis Teunise, came to Beverwyck in 1641; made his will Aug. 7, 1685, and spoke of his wife Egbertien Egbertse and Ch: Maritie, w. of Harmen Lieverse; Egbert; Gerritje, w. of Andries Hanse; Dirkje, w. of Bastiaan Harmense [Visscher;] Willemtie, a. 23 y.; Anna, a. 21 y; Martyn, a. 19 y.

METSELAER Egbert Teunise, and Maritie Barentse. In 1708—the consistory of the church dealt with him for refusing to pay his seat rent for the benefit of the domine's salary; after standing out for a time he yielded. Ch: baptized; Benjamin, March 28, 1686; Jeremia, Dec. 4, 1687; Susanna, m. Jan. 20, 1689; Gerritje, Dec. 6, 1691.

Meyer, See Gillis Pieterse.

MEYER, Hendrick, m. first, Susanna .... who was buried Sept. 1, 1756 ; 2d, Maria Morry June 1, 1761. Ch : Hendrik, bp. May 18, 1740 ; Johannes, bp. Oct. 27, 1743 ; Susanna, bp. April 21, 1745 ; Johannes, bp. Feb. 1, 1747 ; 1, Johannes, bp. June 11, 1749 ; Susanna, bp. 1752 ; Cornelis, bp. Sept. 20, 1761 ; Elizabeth, bp. Dec, 23, 1764 ; Hendrick b. Jan. 23, 1769.

MEYER, Hendrik, and Maria Snyder. Ch : Johannes, b. May 26, 1766 ; Leendert, b. Nov. 1, 1771.

MEYER, Andries, m. Catharina Ronkel, Jan. 22, 1771. Ch : Andries, b. April 14, 1777.

MEYER, Stephen, and Catharina Bernard. Ch : Susanna, b. March 19, 1781,

MEYER, Abraham, and Geesie Bont. Ch : Theuntje, b. Jan. 15, 1788.

Michel, Pieter, m. Maria Bosch, June 25, 1764. Ch : Maria b. Jan. 27, 1767.

Michel, Hannes and Sarah Church Ch : Hannes b. March 7, 1771.

Michielsen Jan (Van Edam), tailor, came to Beverwyck in 1637 with his boy. His wife Tryntje Jansen died in 1665, when an inventory of her effects was made, amounting to 414 guilders. Willem Janse Shut agreed to take these goods and maintain for life Jan Michelsen, who was to do what work he could.

Middleton, Benjamin, and Elizabeth Owens. Ch : born ; Mary, Aug. 17, 1794 ; Richard, July 5, 1798 ; Joseph, June 27, 1801.

Miller, Richard, and Elizabeth .... Ch : Sjene (Jane ?) bp. Sept. 26, 1736.

MILLER, Robert, and Margaret .... Ch : Mary, bp. Nov. 8, 1747.

Miller, Andries, and Margarita Kets. Ch : Jacob, b. March 11, 1778.

MILLER, Jacob, and Annatie Bratt. Ch : Margarita, b. Aug. 22, 1780.

MILLER, Henry, and Mary McCarty. Ch : William, b. Feb. 9, 1781.

MILLER, John-Ernest-Coonraad-Christian, m. Maritie Van Schaick June 25, 1791. Ch : John Ernest, b. April 14, 1792 ; Gosen Van Schaaick, b. April 13, 1794 ; Augustus Van Schaack, b. April 4, 1796 ; William b. Aug. 8, 1798.

Milligan, James, and Isabella Campbell. Ch : Ann, bp. Jan. 29, 1780.

MILLIGAN, Thomas, m. Catharine Outhout, Nov. 3, 1797. Ch : Robert, b. July 12, 1798 ; Margaret, b. March 17, 1800.

Millington (Willinton), Thomas, *geboren in oud Englandt* public carman, m. Tryntje Wendel, Sept. 17, 1699. Ch : Mayke, bp. April 28, 1700 : Thomas, bp. Jan. 21, 1702 : Anna, bp. April 23, 1704.

Mills, Abraham, and Margaret Britton. Ch : Guy, bp. Aug. 8, 1778.

Milton, Hendrick, m. first, Jannetie Eivens ; secondly, Rachel Naarten (Norton), Dec. 31, 1757. Ch : Johannes, bp. Aug. 2, 1752 ; Hendrick, bp. Nov. 30, 1760 ; Barbara, b. May 16, 1762 ; George, b. July 17, 1768 ; Willem, b. Nov. 5, 1770 ; George, b. June 17, 1776.

MILTON, John, and Rosina Shockat (Chucat, Shoeact, Joucat). Ch : Hendrick, b. June 28, 1780 ; Anna-

tie, b. March 13, 1784 ; Daniel, b. Aug. 15, 1786 ; Cathalina, b. Sept. 24, 1788.

Mingael, Jan Thomase, of New Amsterdam, was deceased Nov. 3, 1642, when his widow Jannetie Martense had the paternal estate settled upon her children.

MINGAEL, Thomas Janse (son of the last) settled in Beverwyck as early as 1654, and married Maritie Abrahamse, daughter of Abraham Pieterse Vosburgh by whom he had at least two sons and one daughter : Capt. Johannes Thomase M. who married Mayke Oothout ; Pieter Thomase M. who married Margarita Rosenboom Nov. 15, 1685 and d. in April, 1706 ; and Anna Thomase. After Thomas Janse Mingael's death in 1662 his widow married (in 1763) Evert Janse Wendel.

MINGAEL, Capt. Johannes Thomase, and Mayke Oothout daughter of Jan Janse O. He lived on the north corner of James St. and Maiden Lane, 1703–14 ; his pasture in 1706 was on the south corner of Hudson and Pearl. Ch : Johannes, bp. Oct. 13, 1696.

Mitchell, James, and Mary Cameron. Ch : Christina, bp. Jan. 21, 1779.

MITCHELL (Mitcher), James, and Mary McGrieger, Ch : James, b. Sept. 29, 1781.

Mol, Jacobus, and Lydia Winne. Ch : all baptized in New York save the first ; Engeltie, April 16, 1704 ; Myndert, May 22, 1706 ; Catharina, Oct. 29, 1707 ; Johanna, July 24, 1709 ; Rachel, April 20, 1712 ; Annatie, Aug. 4, 1714 ; Abraham, July 4, 1716 ; Johannes, Jan. 8, 1718 ; Jacobus, Dec. 9, 1719.

MOL (Mor.), Johannes, and Rebecca Barheit (Borhead). Ch : baptized ; Jacobus, Jan. 12, 1746 ; Wouter, June 14, 1747 ; Thomas, Aug. 6, 1749 ; Rachel, Aug. 25, 1751 ; Engeltie, May 20, 1753.

MOL, Abraham, and Tytie Barheit. Ch : baptized ; Annatie, Sept. 26, 1749 ; Engeltie, Aug. 30, 1752.

MOL, Wouter, and Cornelia Cool. Ch : Johannes, b. March 10, 1778. [Wouter Mol m. Catharina Peek, May 2, 1779.]

MOL, Isaac, m. Jannetie Schermerhorn Feb. 1, 1784. Ch : John, b. Dec. 24, 1785.

Monroe, William, and Hester Blackfield. Ch : John, bp. Nov. 5, 1756.

Montgomery, William, m. Alida Halenbeck, July 10, 1796. Ch : born ; Mary, Aug. 10, 1799 ; Elisabeth, March 26, 1801 ; John, Aug. 21, 1802.

Montour, Andrew, and Sara .... Ch : Nicolaas, bp. Oct. 31, 1756.

Moogh, Jacob (Hannes Jochem) m. first, Frena .... ; secondly, Catharina Claasen Feb. 21, 1761. Ch : Hendrik, bp. June 29, 1740 ; Elisabeth, bp. Jan. 22, 1744 : Ariaantje, bp. Dec. 16, 1753 ; Jacob, bp. Sept. 29, 1761 ; Frena, b. July 10, 1763 ; Susanna, b. Jan. 14, 1766 ; Hendrick, b. Nov. 20, 1771.

Mook, Johannes, and Barber Beekman. Ch : Johannes, bp. Jan. 30, 1757 ; Elisabeth, b. Jan. 3, 1767; Lena, b. June 12, 1770.

MOOK (Mooth), Hendrik, and Elisabeth Keller (Neller). Ch : born ; Ariaantje, July 22, 1780 ; William, Jan 11, 1791.

MOOK, Jacob, and Mary McGee. Ch : John, b. Aug. 10, 1782.

Moon, Jan, and Christina Logen. Ch : Susanna, bp. Oct. 12, 1735 ; Catryn, bp. March 6, 1738.

Moor, Richard, *jong man geboren in West-Indien nu wonende aan 't Claver-rak,* m. Geesje Janse Salsbergen (Salsbury), dau. of Jan Hendr: Van S., Nov. 3, 1700. Ch: baptized; Johannes, March 26, 1701; Jannetie, March 21, 1703; Omphry, Oct. 7, 1705; Richard, Aug. 8, 1708; Ephraim, b. Jan. 15, at Klaverak and bp. at Klinkenberg, April 22, 1711; Jacob, bp. Jan. 10, 1714; Omphrey, bp. June 24, 1716; Anna, b. March 21, at Claverak, and bp. at *gospel hoek* 3 Sondag naa Paschen, 1718 (?)

Moor, John, and Christina McKinley. Ch: Margaret, bp. Jan. 21, 1782.

Morgan, Charles, m. Sara Heger (Neyer, Heyer), Nov. 17, 1788. Ch: born; Gerrit, Aug. 24, 1789; Elizabeth, March 26, 1792; Charlotte, Oct. 25, 1795; Juliana, Sept. 27, 1804.

Morrill (Marl), Daniel, and Alida Doxat (Doxie, Dox). Ch: baptized; Judick, May 27, 1739; Elizabet, Oct. 21, 1744; Samuel, Dec. 23, 1748; Johannes, April 26, 1752.

Morrill (Marl), Thomas, m. Hester De Mes, June 22, 1742. Ch: baptized; Marytje, Dec. 4, 1743; Johannes, June 19, 1748; Elizabeth, July 29, 1750.

Morrill (Marll), m. first, Rachel Gardenier, March 14, 1772; and secondly, Claartje Groesbeck about 1798. Ch: born; Andries, May 11, 1773; Daniel, Feb. 1, 1775; Johannes, Jan. 12, 1777; Nicolaas, Feb. 23, 1779; Harmen, May 1, 1781; Harmen, June 30, 1783; Mattheus, Dec. 23, 1785; Jonathan, March 20, 1788; Jacob, April 18, 1791; Samuel, Dec. 22, 1798.

Morrill (Marsel, Morel), Andrew, and Cornelia Slingerland. Ch: born; Richard, Jan. 12, 1795; Rachel, Sept. 27, 1796; Rachel, April 1, 1798; Christina, Feb. 6, 1800; Samuel, Jan. 18, 1802.

Morris, Frans, and Zytje Matthys Hooghteling. [She m. Patrick McGregory, May 4, 1697.] Ch: baptized; Lysbeth, June 7, 1691; Maria, Oct. 23, 1692.

Morris, John, m. Eva Bratt, Dec. 26, 1736. Ch: John, bp. Oct. 23, 1737.

Morrow, John, and Judy .... Ch: Samuel, bp. Aug. 16, 1724.

Mourisse, Marten, brother of Jacques Cornelise Van Slyck; their mother was a Mohawk woman.

Mowers, Philip, and Hannah Coens (Coons) Ch: born; William, Aug. 1, 1795; John, June 7, 1802.

Muller, Mulder, Miller.

Mulder, Jan Pieterse, a soldier in the service of the West India Company at Beverwyck, 1660-1; in garrison at the Esopus in the village of Wiltwyck in 1663.

Muller, Cornelis Stephense, of Greenbush, 1663; of Claverack, 1720. He owned a large lot, of more than 100 feet front, on west side of Broadway, two rods and ten feet north of Maiden Lane, which passed by will to his sons Jacob and Johannes. He married Hilletje Loockermans, probably dau. of his neighbor Pieter L. Ch: baptized; Jannetie (?) wife of Pieter Meese Hoogeboom; Jeremiah (?); Pieter, Dec. 25, 1683; Cornelis, Oct. 28, 1685; Jacob, Jan. 8, 1688; Johannes, March 9, 1690; Johannes, Oct. 18, 1691; Christoffel, Nov. 19, 1693; Ariaantje, July 19, 1696; Kiliaan, May 12, 1700; Stephen (?).

Muller, Jeremias of Claverac. M. Lysbeth Halenbeck, *wonende op Klinkenberg,* [near Athens], Feb. 10, 1705. Ch: baptized; Cornelis, Feb. 3, 1706; Hendrikje, July 4, 1708; and bp. *op Klinkenberg,* April

22, 1711. Johannes, and Heylie, May 10, 1715; Maria, July 27, 1718; Jannetie, June 11, 1721; Jacobus, b. *op Klaverak,* March 22.

Muller, Johannes, m. Lybetie Halenbeck, June 5, 1715. He was buried March 24, 1727. Ch: baptized; Cornelis, June 9, 1717; Isaac, May 7, 1719; Jacob, July 16, 1721; Jeremias, April 25, 1724; Hendrik, Oct. 2, 1726.

Muller, Jacob, and Agnietje ..... Ch: baptized; Cornelis, Sept. 6, 1719; Philip, July 9, 1721; Heyltie, May 3, 1724; Wyntje, July 23, 1727; Leendert, May 1729; Johannes, March 14, 1731.

Muller, Stoffel, m. Rachel Hallenbeck, Sept. 6, 1719. Ch: baptized; Fytje, Aug. 6, 1721; Jeremias, April 17, 1726.

Muller, Stephen, and Maria ..... Ch: Heyltie, April 15, 1722.

Muller, Isaac, and Elizabeth Kittle. Ch: baptized; Maria, April 25, 1742; Elizabeth, May 27, 1744; Elizabeth, Oct. 23, 1748.

Muller, Cornelis, m. Maria Van Hoesen, Feb. 17, 1743. Ch: baptized; Jacob, May 8, 1743; Geesie, June 10, 1744; Harmanus, May 25, 1746; Philip, Oct. 23, 1748; Angenietie, May 26, 1751; Hendrik, Jan. 7, 1753; Leendert, April 27, 1755; Geesie, March 12, 1758; Volkert, b. Feb. 5, 1760; Johannes, b. April 1, 1762; Lucas, b May 21, 1765; Cornelis, b. April 23, 1768.

Muller, Philip, and Geertruy Goewey. Ch: Heyltie, bp. Aug. 12, 1750; Johannes, bp. March 29, 1752; Jacob, bp. May 22, 1759; Barent, b. Aug. 26, 1762; Agnietje, b. Oct. 10, 1764; Andries, b. June 22, 1766; Jannetie, b Jan. 29, 1774.

Muller, Willem, and Rachel Hallenbeck. Ch: Rachel, bp. Aug. 26, 1752.

Muller, Cornelis J., and Teuntje Van Valkenburgh. Ch: Elizabeth, bp. June 17, 1753.

Muller, Jacob, and Heyltie .... Ch: Heyltie, bp. Jan. 22, 1754.

Muller, Johannes, m. Sara Van Iveren, June 30, 1753. Ch: Barent, bp. July 27, 1755; Angenietje, bp. Aug. 28, 1757; Cornelia, b. Feb. 23, 1760; Barent, b. Aug. 21, 1762; Heiltje, b. Jan. 24, 1764; Jacob, b. April 25, 1767; Reynier, b. Oct. 17, 1769; Cornelis, b. March 23, 1772; Sara, b. Sept. 8, 1778.

Muller (Miller), Leendert, of *Halve Maan,* m. first Maritie Van Nes; and secondly, Maria Strong, April 9, 1784. Ch: Angenietje, bp. Sept. 3, 1755; Angenietje, bp. Dec. 10, 1758; Gerrit, bp. July 12, 1761; Jacob, b. Nov. 7, 1765; Sara, b. June 16, 1768; Marytje, b. Dec. 5, 1770; Johannes, b. June 23, 1773; Petrus, b. Sept. 27, 1777; Cornelis, b. Jan. 9, 1785; Maritie, b. June 12, 1791.

Muller, Isaac, and Geertruy [Van] Driessen. Ch: John Hendrick, bp. July 31, 1757.

Muller (Miller), Hendrick, and Rachel Norton. Ch: Willem, bp. Oct. 22, 1758. [See Hend. Miller.]

Muller, Philip, and Geesie Van Hoesen. Ch: Maria, b. March 29, 1772; Harmen, b. Jan. 31, 1778; Maria, b. March 11, 1783: Cathalina, b. Oct. 13, 1785.

Muller, Jeremiah and Catharina Moor. Ch: Heiltje, b. Nov. 15, 1774; Geesie, b. Dec. 2, 1776; Stephanus, b. Jan. 30, 1780; Ridgard (Richard ?), b. April 19, 1783.

10

MULLER, Hendrick, m. Catharina Van Ostrander, Oct. 6, 1776. Ch: Maria, b. April 12, 1777; Abraham, b. Jan. 16, 1780.

MULLER, Nicolaas, and Cathalina Gardenier. Ch: Isaac, b. Jan. 8, 1781.

MULLER, Barent, and Cornelia Goey (Goewey). Ch: Johannes, b. Oct. 15, 1785: Barent, b. Oct. 4, 1787.

MULLER, Jacob P., m. Geertruy Veeder, Oct., 1783. Ch: Rachel, b. Dec. 23, 1786; Pieter, b. June 4, 1789; Maritie, b. Sept. 28, 1793; Philip, b. Feb. 14, 1797; Cornelis Veeder, b. Nov. 10, 1799: John, b. Feb. 27, 1803.

MULLER, John, and Catharine Strunk. Ch: Hendrick, b. Sept. 1, 1791.

Murphy, Peter, and Catharine Cannel (Connor). Ch: born; Peter, b. Oct. 1, bp. Sept. 21 (*sic*), 1795; Sarah, Jan. 15, 1797; Peter, July 18, 1801; James Jan. 16, 1808.

Myndertse, Barent, master shoemaker, in Beverwyck, as early as 1659; d. about 1689, when Pieter Vosburgh administered on his estate. It is not known that he left any children.

Two brothers, Myndert and Carsten Frederickse, smiths, were among the early settlers of Beverwyck. They came from Iveren. Among other real estate in the village they owned the north corner of State street and Broadway, and had their smith shop without the south gate on the north corner of Broadway and Spanish (now Hudson) street. They were members of the Lutheran church of which Myndert was elder and Carsten deacon, in 1680. The latter died probably about 1690 leaving four children (see Frederickse).

Myndert Frederickse was armorer to the fort in 1697; made his will March 20, 170¾ proved May 1, 1706, in which he spoke of " my house hard by the church in *Cow* street [now Broadway], and of "my [Lutheran] church book with silver clasps and chain." He married first Catharyn Burchharts [Burger], in New Amsterdam, Aug. 5, 1656; and secondly Pietertje Teunise Van Vechten, in 1663. At the date of his will, in 1704, he had five children living, viz: Frederick, b. in 1657; Burger, b. 1660, settled in New York; Neeltie, w. of Hendrick Douw; Reynier; Johannes, who settled in Schenectady.

The unsettled condition of the early Dutch family names is well shown by the descendants of Myndert Frederickse, which follow; some took the surname of *Myndertse*, his Christian name; whilst others took that of *Van Iveren*, the place from whence he came in Holland.

MYNDERTSE, *alias* Van Iveren, m. Saartje Bratt, Sept. 7, 1699. She was buried, Feb. 4, 1756. Ch: baptized; Myndert, April 28, 1700; Susanna, Oct. 5, 1701; Pieterje, Aug. 22, 1703; Barent, Jan. 6, 1706; Johannes, Jan. 4, 1708, buried, May 15, 1746; Antony, June 8, 1710; Reinier, Oct. 12, 1712, buried Feb. 5, 1731; Jacob, Dec. 25, 1714; Susanna, June 31 (*sic*), 1717.

MYNDERTSE, Van Ivere, Johannes of Schenectady, and Geertruy Van Slyck. Ch: Margarita, bp. June 8, 1707; Jacobus, bp. April 22, 1709. See also *Schenectady Families*.

MYNDERTSE, Van Ivere, Frederick, m. Sara De Wandelaer, Oct. 9, 1706. He was buried Feb. 12, 1740; she was buried, Dec. 11, 1732. In 1716, his house was without the south gate on the north corner of Spanish [now Hudson] street and Broadway, and he was granted the privilege of building a blacksmith's shop north of his house keeping 6 feet away from the stockadoes. Ch: baptized; Myndert, April 27, 1707; Sara, June 12, 1709; Johannes, Oct. 7, 1711; Petrus, Feb. 14, 1714; Andries, June.3, 1716, moved to Schenectady; Neeltie, April 12, 1719; Abraham, April 1, 1722; Catharina, Oct. 25, 1724; Marten, April 16, 1727; Hendrik, July 13, 1729.

MYNDERTSE, Harmen, [Vander Bogart ?] and Geertruy. Ch: Harmen, bp. Sept. 13, 1712.

MYNDERTSE, (Van Iveren) Myndert [son of Reynier M. and Saartje Bratt] m. Ariaantje Wyngaart Dec. 2, 1721. Ch: baptized; Sara, March 18, 1722; Hessie, March 5, 1727; Reinier, Dec. 4, 1728; Anna, May 9, 1731; Gerrit, Oct. 7, 1733; Susanna Feb. 20, 1737.

MYNDERTSE, *alias* Van Iveren, Barent [son of Reynier and Saartje Bratt], m. Cornelia Van Aalsteyn, July 8, 1728 He was buried May 12, 1746. Ch: baptized; Reynier, May, 1729; Cornelis, Dec. 12, 1730; Sara, Aug. 10, 1734; Maria, Oct. 3, 1736; Myndert, May 31, 1739; Martinus, Dec. 25, 1741; Barent, July 26, 1746.

MYNDERTSE (Van Ivere), Warner, see Casparse.

MYNDERTSE (Van Iveren), Anthony, [son of Reinier and Saartje Bratt], m. Maria Van Den Bergh May 23, 1740. Ch: baptized; Reinier, Nov. 9, 1740; Cathalyntje, July. 27, 1743; Gysbert, Oct. 19, 1744; Jacob, March 29, 1747; Cornelis, Jan. 21, 1750; Cornelis, July 19, 1752; Sara, July 25, 1756.

MYNDERTSE, *alias* Van Iveren, Johannes [son of Frederick and Sara De Wandelaer] m. Maria Ostrander, May 24, 1740. Ch: baptized; Sara, May 10, 1741; Sara, Dec. 25, 1742; Elizabeth, April 19, 1745, d. Aug. 27, 1823; Frederick, Oct. 25, 1747; Frederick, May 28, 1749; Sara, March 24, 1751; Frederick, April 8, 1753; Rachel, March 21, 1756.

MYNDERTSE, *alias* Van Iveren, Jacob, [son of Reinier and Saartje Bratt], m. Wyntje Van den Bergh, June 16, 1743. He was buried May 12, 1746. Ch: Reinier, bp, Oct. 19, 1744.

MYNDERTSE, Martin (Matthew), (son of Frederick: and Sara Ryckman, Nov. 16, 1751. He d. April 26, 1806, a. 79 y. 6 d.; she d. Feb. 15, 1791, a. 66 y. 1 mo. Ch: Sara, bp. March 29, 1752; Wilhelmus, bp. March 12, 1755; Sara, bp. Oct. 11, 1761; Wilhelmus, b. July 11, 1767.

MYNDERTSE, (Van Yveren), Reinier (son of Myndert, and Ariaantje Wyngaard) m. Debora Filden, (Fielding, Viele). Ch: Sara, bp. Jan. 4, 1760; Catharina, b. July 26, 1762; Meinard, b. Jan. 22, 1765; George, b. June 5, 1768; Ariaantje, b. July 15, 1771; Annatie, b. Sept. 15, 1775.

MYNDERTSE, Abraham (son of Frederic, and Sara DeWandelaer), m first, Catharina Oostrander, who was buried, June 21, 1756; secondly, Catharina Lansing, Oct. 18, 1760. Ch: born; Sara, July 6, 1762; Johannes, Feb. 6, 1764.

MYNDERTSE (Van Yveren), Gerrit (son of Myndert, and Ariaantje Wyngaard), m. Catharyntje Bogart, July 17, 1764. Ch: born; Myndert, Sept. 1, 1764; Hendrikje, Jan. 6, 1766; Ariaantje, Sept. 13, 1767; Catharina, Aug. 18, 1769; Sara, July 19, 1772.

MYNDERTSE, Frederic (son of Andries of Schenectady), m. Elizabeth Waldron, April 23, 1765. Ch: born; Andries, Nov. 10, 1765; Annatie, Dec. 22, 1764; Susanna, July 23, 1768; Susanna, Dec. 24, 1770; Sara, Sept. 9, 1773; Annatie, Aug. 25, 1776; Willem, March 15, 1779; Neeltie, Sept. 25, 1781; Catharina, March 24, 1784; Jannetie, Nov, 5, 1786; Hendrik, Feb. 1, 1790.

MYNDERTSE (Van Yveren), Barent, m. Rebecca Bratt, March 5, 1770. Ch: born; Barent, June. 21, 1770; Wyntie, Aug. 10, 1772; Cornelia, Sept. 18, 1776; Meinard, Jan. 15, 1779; Cornelia, Aug. 24, 1780; Meinard, May 24, 1784; Cornelia, Dec. 1786.

MYNDERTSE (Van Iveren), Reinier, and Annatie Hoghil. Ch: Cathalyntje, b. Feb. 9, 1773.

MYNDERTSE (Van Iveren), Reinier, m. Rebecca De Foreest, Jan. 19, 1777. Ch: Maria, b. Feb. 28, 1778.

MYNDERTSE (Van Iveren), Reinier m. Elizabeth Ostrander, Feb. 1784. Ch: born; Christina, Sept. 12, 1784; Annatie, Feb. 25, 1787.

MYNDERTSE (Van Iveren), Martinus (son of Barent, and Cornelia Van Aalsteyn), m. Cornelia Van Schaick. Feb. 26, 1776. Ch: born; Barent, Oct. 16, 1776; Maayke, Aug. 21, 1778; Gosen, Dec. 28, 1780; Gerrit, July 17, 1784; Cornelia, March 30, 1786; Cornelia, April 1, 1788; Annatie, May 3, 1790.

Mynderse, Frederic (son of Johannes, and Maria Ostrander), m. Machtel Witbeck, Jan. 12, 1777. Ch: born; Maria, Sept. 29, 1777; Gerritje, Feb. 2, 1780; Johannes, Jan. 29, 1783; Jonathan, Nov. 2, 1787.

Naarten (Narden, Norton ?) William, and Rachel ..... Ch: baptized; Margariet, Jan. 7, 1722; Rachel, Jan. 7, 1736.

Nak, Jan, trader and gunstocker, m. Catharina Roomers in New York, Oct. 28, 1663; d. Dec. 12, 1708. Ch: Matthys.

NAK, Matthys, m. first, Susanna Lansing, July 24, 1698; and secondly, Agnietje Schaets *geboren tot Schenectade* daughter of Reinier, son of Domine Gideon S., Dec. 5, 1702. Ch: Johannes, and Gerrit, twins, bp. Feb. 22, 1699; Catharina, bp. Oct. 24, 1703; Catharina, bp. May 20, 1705; Johannes, bp. Jan. 23, 1709; Willemyntje, bp. April 23, 1710; Reinier Schaets, bp. Dec. 6, 1712; Alida, bp. Aug. 13, 1716; Alida, bp. July 26, 1717; Chistina in New York, Oct. 12, 1720.

Neer, Barent, and Mary B .... Ch: Anna Maria, b. Jan. 12, 1765; Johannes, b. June 6, 1767.

Nelber, Johannes, and Anna Maria Folin. Ch: Catarina, bp. May 10, 1752.

Neidhart, Fredrik, and Maria Strongk. Ch: Maria, bp. Feb. 19, 1777.

Nellinger, Coenraat, and Anna Tiel. Ch: Anna, Margarita, bp. June 3, 1753.

Neugel, Daniel and Martha .... Ch: Debora, b. Jan. 6, 1769.

Nevin, Peter, and Elizabeth Caldwell. Ch: Noble Caldwell David, b. Feb. 15, 1791.

Nichols, Rensselaer, and Elizabeth Saltzberg (Salisbury). Ch: William, bp. Feb. 21, 1731; Maria, bp. June 24, 1733; Anna, bp. Jan. 7, 1736; Francis, bp. Dec. 23, 1737; Catharyna, bp. June 17, 1740; Francis, bp. Oct. 31, 1742; Sylvester, bp. Feb. 17, 1745; Frances, bp. April 8, 1750; Rachel, bp. Jan. 1, 1754.

Nicolaas, Michael, and Maria B. Wagenaar. Ch: Jacob, b. Feb. 23, 1768.

Nicolls, Francis, and Margarita Van Rensselaer. Ch: Elizabeth, b. July 21, 1764; Willem, b. April 13, 1766; Hendrick, b. Aug. 13, 1768.

Nieuwkerk, Gerrit, and Anna .... Ch: Elizabeth, bp. Nov. 1, 1719.

Nightingale, John, and Elizabeth Neitthall. Ch: Elizabeth, b. Nov. 3, 1780.

Nin, Michael, and Catharine Power. Ch: Elizabeth, b. May 28, 1793.

Nivin, David, and Margaret Waggener. Ch: Ann. b. Dec. 12, 1790.

Nobel, Willem, and Maritie Pieterse. Ch: Willem, bp. Feb. 14, 1692.

Noble, Thomas, and Catharina Morris. Ch: David, bp. March 8, 1704; Thomas, bp. in New York Oct. 30, 1717; Anthony, bp. in New York Jan. 20, 1720.

Nordman, Tobias, and Maria ..... Ch: Susanna, bp. Nov. 22, 1747.

North, Joshua, and Martha ..... Ch: Joshua, bp. Sept. 21, 1758.

Northen, Norton.

NORTHEN, William, and Rachel ..... Ch: baptized; Richard, Feb. 23, 1724; John, June 19, 1726; Jan, Aug. 12, 1739.

NORTHEN (Norton), William, and Mary Baylie (Malbary). Ch: Christopher, bp. Feb. 11, 1759; Christoffel, *nu 3 weken oud,* bp. March 4, 1762; Maria, b. Feb. 18, 1764; Johannes, b. Oct. 16, 1766; Elizabeth, b. July 7, 1771.

NORTHEN, Henry, of Halve Maan, m. Margarita Van der Werken, Feb. 18, 1762. Ch: William, b. Nov. 3, 1762.

NORTHEN, John, and Elizabeth De Voe. Ch: born, Willem, Sept. 21, 1763; Abraham, June 1, 1766; Margarita, Jan. 11, 1769; Rebecca, bp. Oct. 18, 1778.

NORTHEN, William, and Catharine Livingston. Ch: born; Maria, Aug. 5, 1788; Sarah, Feb. 8, 1791; Elizabeth, Oct. 16, 1793.

Norton, Samuel, and Elizabeth Radley. Ch: John, bp. Sept. 16, 1792; Lambert, and William, b. July 10, 1793; Maria, b. Oct. 28, 1796; William, b. July 28, 1799.

Nottingham, William, trader in Albany, 1674-6; in 1676, he and wife Ann, were residents of Kingston, where he was still living in 1722; 1715, he was captain of the Marbletown company.

Noxon, Tomas, m. Geertruy Hoogeboom, Dec. 23, 1691. Ch: Alida, bp. April 1, 1694.

Oake, Abraham, and Elizabeth De Assigne. Ch: Elsie Lansing, b. Aug. 7, 1797.

Oakey, John, and Jane Williams. Ch: born. Edward, Sept. 12, 1796; Stephen Williams, Feb. 4, 1798.

O'Brien, Louis, and Catharina Rendell. Ch: born; Louis, Dec. 8, 1775; Catharina, bp. Feb. 1, 1778; Joseph, Nov. 1, 1780; Elizabeth, Aug. 3, 1784.

O'BRIEN, John Graham, and Nancy (Hanna) Davenport. Ch: James, b. Sept. 12, 1777; Maria, bp. Oct. 5, 1783.

Oliver (Olivert, Olphert, Olfer).

OLIVER, Charles, and Margaret Schuyler. Ch: Robert, bp. Dec. 7, 1707.

OLIVER, Richard, m. Martha Bennewe, [Bennoit], Oct. 29, 1734. Ch: baptized; Margarita, July 9, 1735; John, Oct. 6, 1738; Thomas, Jan. 18, 1744; Martha, June 7, 1747.

OLIVER (Olivert, Olphert), Jan, and Antje Blom, Ch: bp; Wyntje, Dec. 23, 1737; Frederick Blom, Feb. 24, 1740; Jacobus, Jan. 6, 1742; Arent, Jan. 4, 1745.

OLIVER, Johannes, m. Maritie Sixberry, Jan. 16, 1758. Ch: Johannes, bp. July 30, 1758; Evert, bp. Nov. 11, 1760; Arent, b. Jan. 15, 1763; Elsie, b. May 8, 1767; Jacob, b. August 31, 1773.

OLIVER, Jacob, of Niskitha, m. Annatie Sixby, May 13, 1761. Ch: Antje, bp. Sept. 20, 1761; Nicolaas, *oud* 7 *weeken*, bp. May 15, 1763: Johannes, b. Feb. 13, 1766.

OLIVER (Olfer), Frederick, of Niskitha, m. Catharina Van den Berg Feb. 5, 1763. Ch: born; Johannes, Oct. 7, 1763; Elisabeth, Oct. 7, 1765; Cornelis, April 25, 1768; Arent, April 1, 1771; Antje, bp. Feb. 27, 1774.

OLIVER (Olfer) Johannes, and Catharina Van den Berg, [see the last]. Ch: Cornelia, bp. May 23, 1779.

OLIVER, Evert, m. Rebecca Cooper, June 23, 1781. Ch: born; Catharina, Feb. 3, 1782; Johannes, Nov. 5, 1783.

Oly (Oley), Christoffer, m. first, Eleanor Kern, (Cornelia Kerl); and secondly, Sarah Van Antwerp, about 1798. Ch: born; Rachel, August 8, 1778; Rachel, March 3, 1780; Eleanor, August 16, 1799; Eleanor, August 14, 1800.

Onirold (?) Benjamin, and Cornelia Van Arnhem, Ch: Annatie, bp. March 4, 1761.

Oost, Johan Philip, and Maria Elisabeth .... Ch: Johanna Charlotta, bp. July, 1759.

Oosterhout, Johannes, m. first Agnietje Winne, Oct. 1, 1775; and secondly, Mary Williamson about 1792. Ch: born, Wilhelmus, June 23, 1776; Helena, Oct. 1, 1778; Helena, Oct. 25, 1779: Maria, Nov. 30, 1781; David, August 6, 1783; Elias, Feb. 17, 1785; John, Feb. 20, 1793.

OOSTERHOUT, Hendrik, m. Caty Warner (Catharina Warrant *weduwe Van* James Burnside), Feb. 27, 1785. Ch: Elias, b. Oct. 12, 1785.

OOSTERHOUT, Wilhelmus, and Jane Chrysler (Schuyler). Ch: born; Henry, April 30, 1785; Agnes, March 23, 1791.

Oosterum, Gerrit Willemse, came to Beverwyck in 1631.

Oostrander, Pieter, and Rachel Dingmans. Ch: Petrus, bp. Feb. 6, 1709.

OOSTRANDER, Arent, and Geertruy Van Bloemendaal. Ch: Petrus, bp. Oct. 7, 1711.

OOSTRANDER, Johannes, and Elizabeth Van den Bergh. Ch: baptized; Maria, Jan. 26, 1715: Petrus, Nov. 12, 1716; Rebecca, Aug. 31, 1718; Huibert, Jan. 28, 1722; Lea, Feb. 12, 1724; Gerritje, Jan. 9, 1725; Elizabeth, March 27, 1732; Johannes, Feb. 20, 1734.

OOSTRANDER, Abraham, and Elizabeth Oostrander, of Esopus, m. Jan. 23, 1753. Ch: Maria, bp. Dec., 23, 1753; Elizabeth, bp. July 25, 1756; Teunis, bp. Jan. 21, 1759; Johannes, bp. Aug. 30, 1761; Hubert, b. June 12, 1764; Elizabeth, b. Dec. 18, 1767; Sara, b. March 31, 1771; Teunis, b. Feb. 9, 1773; Petrus, b. Oct. 6, 1775.

OOSTRANDER, Isaac, m. Elizabeth McKans, Sept. 30, 1757. Ch: Andries, bp. Aug. 20, 1758; Rachel, bp. Nov. 2, 1760: Pieter, 2 *maand oud*, bp. May 8, 1763; Johannes, b. Sept. 5, 1765; Annatie, b. May 10, 1770.

OOSTRANDER, Gerrit, m. Christina Van den Bergh, Sept. 25, 1761. Ch: born; Elizabeth, Oct. 2, 1762; Catharina, Feb. 22, 1765; Rachel, March 30, 1767: Maacke, Jan. 22, 1770; Johannes, June 27, 1772; Volkie, March 19, 1775; Christina, Feb. 25, 1780.

OOSTRANDER, Hannes, m. Marytje Van Aalsteyn, June 11, 1763. Ch: born; Folkie, Jan. 2, 1764; Elizabeth, March 28, 1766; Johannes, Oct. 6, 1768; Catharina, Dec. 10, 1771; Cornelia, Oct. 19, 1776; Martinus, Aug. 23, 1779.

OOSTRANDER, Johannes, and Anna Wolffen. Ch: Comfort, b. April 29, 1767; Susanna and Rachel, twins, bp, April 5, 1769; Susanna, b. Dec. 26, 1775.

OOSTRANDER, Hendrick, and Maria Van den Bergh. Ch: born; Andries, March 1, 1772; Johannes, Jan. 29, 1774; Barent; May 1, 1776; Elizabeth, Sept. 9; 1778.

OOSTRANDER, Petrus, and Catharina Ering. Ch: born; Jacob, June 19, 1773; Petrus, April, 14, 1777.

OOSTRANDER, Petrus, and Antje Dienmaker (Denemark). Ch: born; Petrus; Sept. 10, 1777; Geertje, May 1, 1785.

OOSTRANDER (Van Ostrander) Hannes, and Maritie Van Deusen. Ch: Annatie, bp. Feb. 4, 1778; Jacomyntje, b. Jan. 1, 1780.

OOSTRANDER, Jonathan, and Lea.... Ch: Jacomyntje, b. Dec. 3, 1778.

OOSTRANDER (Ostrander), Teunis, and Marytje Van Vliet. Ch: born; Benjamin, Aug. 8, 1786; Catharine Dec. 3, 1800.

OOSTRANDER, Johannes, Jr. and Catharina Witrel, (Wetsel). Ch: Cornelia, bp. March 4, 1787; Mary, b. Oct. 18, 1791; Levy, b. Feb. 1, 1794. [Catharine Oostrander, d. in Tully, Nov. 13, 1847, a. 97 y.]

OOSTRANDER, John, and Mary Scott. Ch: born; Mary, March 29, 1795; Maria, Oct. 31, 1796.

OOSTRANDER, Johannes, and Anna Muir. Ch: Catharina, b. July 2, 1800.

OOSTRANDER, John, and Fanny Consaul. Ch: Anne, b. June 9, 1800.

Oothout (Oothoet), Jan Janse, of Greenbush, brewer, in Albany as early as 1665; made his will March 13, 1687-8; letters of administration to his sons Hendrik and Jan, Jan. 3, 1695-6, gave to son Johannes a red mare; to Hendrick, 3 or 4 years after " my decease" a young horse or an old one; Arien, aged about 12 y. to have two years schooling and a trade, and a red stone horse with a star in his forehead; when 20 years of age a new suit of clothes, and then the remaining property was to be divided equally among his 6 children. His ch. were Johannes, eldest son; Hendrick; Arien; Mayke w. of Capt. Johannes Thomase Mingael; Antje; and Jannetie.

OOTHOUT, Hendrick Janse, in 1700, and succeeding years surveyor of the city; made his will Oct. 11, 1738, proved, April 26, 1740, mentioned the following sons and daughters save Maritie, buried, July 15, 1739. He m. Caatje Volckertse Douw, April 30, 1684. Ch: baptized; Volkert, March 1, 1685; Hendrick, March 10, 1686; Dorothee, Dec. 18, 1687, m. Cornelis Bogard; Maritie, d. before 1738; Volkert, Oct. 23, 1692; Jan, April 7, 1695; Henderickje, May 2, 1697; Henderickje,

Sept. 3, 1699, m. Isaac Bogard ; Margariet, July 13, 1701, m. Domine Johannes Van Driessen ; Anna, Dec. 15, 1703, m. Pieter Wouterse Quackenbos ; Jonas, Dec. 9, 1705.

OOTHOUT, Johannes, m. Aaltie Evertse, widow of Gerrit Lubbertse, May 5, 1689 ; she was buried Dec. 12, 1739 ; he was buried, Feb. 5, 1745. Ch : baptized ; Feitje, April 17, 1693 : Rebecca, Nov. 17, 1695 ; Jan, Jan. 7, 1700 ; Henrikje, Jan. 5, 1707.

OOTHOUT (Ootland), Ariaan (Adriaan), m. Lammertje Loockermans, Nov. 3, 1700 : He was buried, Feb. 26, 1752 ; Ch : baptized ; Johannes Arie, Nov. 29, 1702 ; was buried, Sept. 27, 1756 ; Pieter Loockermans, Dec. 17, 1704 ; Hendrikje, Dec. 15, 1706 ; Maria, Dec. 8, 1708 ; Anna Catryna, March 4, 1711 ; Pieter Loockermans, March 1, 1713 ; Anna, Jan. 1, 1716 ; Catryna, Jan. 11, 1718 ; Mayke, Feb. 10, 1723.

OOTHOUT, Jan (Johannes), m. Catalina Van Deusen, July 15, 1721. Ch : baptized ; Catharina, April 29, 1722 ; Elizabeth, Sept. 27, 1724 ; Maria, May 6, 1727 : Margarita, Feb. 15, 1730.

OOTHOUT, Jan (Johann ese); m. Maritie Wendel June 23, 1729. Ch : baptized ; Johannes, Jan. 6, 1731; Maicke, Sept. 24, 1732 ; Abraham, Dec. 8, 1733 ; Cornelis, Dec. 7, 1735 ; Mayke, April 30, 1738 ; Myndert, April 20, 1740 ; Evert, June 27, 1742 ; Alida, Oct. 19, 1744.

OOTHOUT, Jonas, m. first Elizabeth Lansing, March 30, 1741 ; secondly, Elizabeth Vinhagen, April 13, 1756. The tradition is [not strictly true] that the first child baptized in the old church was Elizabeth Vinhagen, wife of Jonas Oothout ; and that the church bell tolled the last time at her burial, she having died March, 1806, in her 92d year. His first wife Elizabeth Lansing, was buried, March 11, 1754. Ch : baptized, Hendrick, May 16, 1742 ; Abraham, May 27, 1744 ; Volkert, Dec. 26, 1747 ; Volkert, Sept. 2, 1750; Magdalena, July 8, 1753 ; Johannes, Feb. 6, 1757 ; Catarina, May 7, 1758.

OOTHOUT, Johannes (Hannes), m. Elizabeth Van Woert, June 30, 1759. Ch : Marytje, bp. Jan. 18, 1761 ; Alexander, oud 5 weken, bp. Oct. 9, 1763 ; Cornelis, b. Dec. 5, 1766 ; Cornelis, b. Feb. 20, 1769 ; Elizabeth, b. Dec. 14, 1772.

OOTHOUT, Hendrick, junior, m. Lydia Douw, Sept. 1, 1765. Ch : born ; Jonas, Sept. 13, 1766 ; Aaltie, July 24, 1768 ; Jonas, Oct. 12, 1770 ; Volkert Douw, Dec. 4, 1773 ; Abraham, Feb. 7, 1775 ; Andries Jan. 30, 1777 ; Andries, Sept. 26, 1778; Hendrik, Feb. 11, 1781 ; Elizabeth, May 20, 1782 ; Hendrik, March 21, 1785 ; Elizabeth, Dec. 7, 1786.

OOTHOUT, Abraham, m. first, Martha Benneway [Bennoit] May 7, 1769 ; and secondly, Maria Dox about 1776. Ch : born ; Jacobus, Feb. 5, 1770 ; Evert, Oct. 21, 1776.

OOTHOUT, Evert, m. Margarita Davenport, July 20, 1771. Ch : born ; Jan. May 5, 1772 ; Maria, July 13, 1774 ; Catharina, Jan. 17, 1780.

OOTHOUT, Volkert, m. Jannetie Bogart, March 30, 1774. Ch : born ; Jonas, Sept. 18, 1774 ; Engeltie, March 22, 1776 ; Elizabeth, Oct. 21, 1779 ; Hendrik, Oct. 1, 1781 ; Magdalena, Feb. 28, 1784 ; Volkert, Sept. 10, 1786 ; Dorothea, Sept. 26, 1788.

OOTHOUT, Myndert, and Maria Sixby. Ch : born ; Cornelis, Sept. 10, 1777 ; Jan, Dec. 7, 1781 ; Engeltie, Dec. 3, 1787.

OOTHOUT, Henry A. and Eliza Ann ..... Ch : Samuel Nicoll, b. Aug. 25, 1810.

Orchard, see Archard.

ORCHARD, Robert, in 1671, May 31, with Jannetie Donckertse. then his wife, widow of the late Thomas Powell, conveyed diverse parcels of land " behind Kinderhoek" to Hendrice Coenraetse, Lourens Van Alen, Jacob Martense, Dirk Hendricxse Sweed, Andries Hanse [Sharp], and Jan Martense [De Weever or Weever].

Orloop (Orlok, Oorloff, Orlogh), Willem, and Maria Harman (Hartman). Ch : Willem Hendrik, bp. Feb. 7, 1762 ; Jacob, b. June 4, 1766 ; Pieter, bp. May 12, 1771 ; Peter, b. Dec. 18, 1801.

Otten, Helmer, from Isens [Essen ?], Baker. was in Beverwyck from 1663 to 1676, when he died ; among other lots owned by him was the north corner of Pearl and State streets, which he conveyed to Domine Nicolaas Van Rensselaer, in 1675 ; married Ariaantje Arent Bratt, dau. of the first settler of that name in Schenectady ; 1670, purchased a bouwery of 26 morgens at Schenectady of Pieter Adriaense Soegemackelyk ; he left one dau. Catharyna; who married Gerrit Symonse Veeder. After his death Otten's widow married Ryer Schermerhorn.

Ouderkerk, Jan Janse, cooper, in Beverwyck as early as 1664 ; in 1692, lived on north side of Yonker [State] street and was commonly called *Smalle cuyper.*

OUDERKERK, Johannes, m. Neeltie Claase, widow of Hendrick Gardenier, May 20, 1695. Ch : baptized ; Maria, June 21, 1696 ; Annetie, Oct. 30, 1698, d. 1706; Ariaantje, June, 1, 1701 ; Neeltje, July 11, 1703.

OUDERKERK, Isaac, of Kinderhoek, 1709, Half Moon, 1720, m. Mayke Van Nes, May 3, 1696. She was buried, Oct. 30, 1747. Ch : baptized ; Johannes, April 5, 1697 ; Cornelis, Sept. 3, 1699 ; Abraham, Sept. 14, 1701 : Aaltje, Feb. 6, 1704, m. Douw Isaacse Fonda ; Cornelis, Sept. 22, 1706 ; Annatie, Jan. 9, 1709 ; Willem, Oct. 7, 1711 ; Maritie, Sept. 27, 1713 ; Isaac, Sept. 23, 1716 ; Jacob, April 3, 1720.

OUDERKERK, Pieter, of Half Moon, and Alida Clute. Ch : baptized ; Johannes, Jan. 19, 1707 ; Pieter, May 8, 1720.

OUDERKERK, Abraham, of Canistagioene, m. first, Lysbeth Clute, Dec. 1, 1705 ; secondly, Ariaantje Van Nes, Jan. 24, 1724. He was buried, Oct. 24, 1743. Ch : baptized ; Johannes, Jan. 11, 1708 ; Benjamin, Oct. 30, 1710 ; Isaac, May 3, 1724.

OUDERKERK, Eldert, of Half Moon, m. Lena Sophia Knipping, July 24, 1714. Ch : baptized ; Anna, Jan. 23, 1715 ; Sophia, Feb. 27, 1717 ; Maria, May 22, 1718 ; Joannes, April 10, 1720 ; Susanna, April 1, 1722 ; Abraham, May 3, 1724 ; Elizabeth, April 17, 1726.

OUDERKERK, Abraham, and Metty ..... Ch : baptized ; Anna, July 30, 1721 ; Jacob, Oct. 4, 1724 : Jenneke, Sept. 15, 1727.

OUDERKERK, Johannes, m. first Jannetie Viele May 15, 1720 ; secondly, Helena Fonda, July 27, 1735. He was buried, Sept. 30, 1746. Ch : baptized ; Maycke, May 6, 1722, buried, March 19, 1747 ; Maria, May 31, 1724 ; Jacomyna, Oct. 2, 1726 ; Elizabeth, Feb. 8, 1736 ; Jan. Dec. 4, 1737 ; Abraham, Oct. 28, 1739 ; Elizabeth and Maria, twins, Oct. 19, 1744.

OUDERKERK, Willem, of Schachtekook, and Marytje : he was buried, Aug. 26, 1746. Ch : baptized ; Mayke, Feb. 18, 1739 ; Marytje Sept. 13, 1741.

OUDERKERK, Cornelis, m. Catharina Huyck, Jan. 19, 1739. Ch: baptized; Maria, Feb. 1, 1741; Mayke, Dec. 12, 1742; Isaac, Feb. 17, 1745; Anna, March 13, 1874; Andries, Nov. 18, 1750; Alida, March 30, 1755.

OUDERKERK, Isaac, m. first Anna Clute, Feb. 24, 1743; secondly, Hesje Van Arnhem, about 1749; his first wife was buried, Oct. 20, 1748. Ch: baptized; Mayke, Jan. 4, 1745; Antje, June 3, 1750; Abraham, Nov. 17, 1751; Maycke, Dec. 16, 1753; Isaac, Oct. 23, 1755.

OUDERKERK, Jacob, and Neeltie Clute. Ch: baptized; Anna, Jan. 24, 1748; Isaac, Oct. 8, 1749; Jenneke, May 22, 1752; Francyna, March 24, 1754; Abraham, April 4, 1756; Frederic, Aug. 27, 1758; Frederic, b. April 4, 1760.

OUDERKERK, Isaac, and Mary Foster, she was buried, May 7, 1754. Ch: baptized; Abraham, Feb. 17, 1751; Anna, July 1, 1753.

OUDERKERK, Isaac, and Annatie Rodgers. Ch: born; Jacob, March 1, 1772; Neeltie, Dec. 22, 1777.

OUDERKERK, Abraham, m. Alida (Aaltie) Ouderkerk, Sept. 11, 1774. Ch: Isaac, b. Jan. 1776.

OUDERKERK, Andries, and Annatie Fero. Ch: Cornelis, b. Dec. 6, 1779; Margarita, bp April 16, 1780 David, b. Nov. 10, 1781; Maayke, b. Jan. 4, 1788.

OUDERKERK, Johannes [Andries above?] and Annatie Fero. Ch: Maria, b. Sept. 10, 1785.

OUDERKERK, John J. and Mary Sickels. Ch: Johannes, b. Oct. 23, 1799.

Overbach (Oevenbach), Benjamin, and Jenneke Oosterhout. Ch: born; Marytje, Oct. 5, 1774; Sara, March 1, 1777; Catharina, June 25, 1779.

Owen, Thomas, and Elizabeth Norman. Ch: Thomas, bp. Oct. 24, 1756.

Owens (Ojens), John, and Lena ..... Ch: Lena, bp. Julp 27, 1772.

OWENS, Daniel, m. Elizabeth Springsteen, May 2 1779.

Owen, John, and Ariaantje Hegerman. Ch: Lena, b. Dec. 19, 1784.

Owens, Owen (Oyje Oyjens), *geboren tot Cork in Ierland*, m. Maria Wendel, June 10, 1704. Ch: baptized; Henrik, Nov. 29, 1704; Anna, Feb. 2, 1707.

Paal (Pawl, Paul or Powell?) James and Ann McEwen (Cowen). Ch: Robert, and Duncan, bp. April 25, 1779; James, b. Jan. 17, 1781; Margaret, b. July 30, 1782.

Palmentier, Damin, and Elizabeth Bertley. Ch: Peter, b. Nov. 22, 1782.

Pammerton, see Pemberton.

Pangburn, Pengburn, Bengburn.

PANGBURN (Bengburn), William, and Elizabeth Bogart (Van der Bogart). She died Jan. 18, 1827, a. 87 y. 4 m. Ch: born; Johannes, Aug. 12, 1764; Maria, Oct. 10, 1766; Lydia, Sept. 10, 1768; Neeltie, Oct. 13, 1770; Elizabeth, May 7, 1775; David, March 14, 1777; Margaret, June 18, 1779.

PANGBURN (Pengburn), Richard, of Niskatha, m. Cathalyntje Van Etten, Sept. 28, 1769. Ch: born; Willem, Oct. 6, 1771; Hilletje, Jan. 8, 1772; Benjamin, Feb. 24, 1777; Isaac, Aug. 12, 1791.

PANGBURN, Stephen, and Sarah Seger. Ch: Gerrit, b. July 15, 1797.

Papendorp, Adriaen Gerritse, probably came to colony Rensselaerswyck, in 1634; served many years as magistrate; his wife was Jannetje Croon; made a will, Oct. 7, 1688, in which he did not speak of any children.

Pars, (Puis), Matthys, of Kingston 1701; of Kinderhook, 1706; m. Tanna Winne, Nov. 1, 1701. Ch: Adam, bp. Jan. 13, 1706

Parse, see Pearse.

Paree, (Pary, Pareois), Johannes, and Annetie,.... Ch: baptized; Johannes, April 5, 1719; Nicolaas, June 18, 1721; James, August 7, 1762.

Parker, Sergeant William, owned lot on the hill which he sold in 1670-1, to Dirck Albertse Bratt, and Ryck Claese [Van Vranken.]

Passage, John, and Margarita Cramm. Ch: Lena, b. May 15, 1780.

PASSAGE, Henry, and Elizabeth Claus. Ch: Elizabeth, b. Sept. 5, 1793.

Pastoor, Frans Barentse, in 1654, one of the magistrates of Fort Orange; a brewer, and owned among other property a lot on east side of Broadway next north of Bleecker Hall, which with house, garden and brewery he sold to Hendrick Andriese Van Doesburgh, for 3630 guilders. It is not known that he left any children.

Patridge, Thomas and Mary McGuire. Ch: Nancy, b. Jan. 8, 1778.

Patterson, David, and Phebe Cox. Ch: George b. Dec. 29, 1778.

PATTERSON, William, and Mary McEntee, Ch Peter, b. April 13, 1782.

Pearse, Persen, Peers, Parse, &c.

PEARSE, Nehimiah, in 1675 bought house and lot on the hill of Evert Janse Wendel, which in 1676 he soid to Samuel Holman.

PEARSE (Parse), Jacobus, m. Maritie Van den Bergh, Nov. 18, 1781. Ch: born; Abraham, Jan. 14, 1788; Rachel, May 28, 1800.

Persen (Peers), Jacob, of Nistagieone in 1720, and Jannetje ... Ch: baptized; Annatie, April 20, 1712; Geertruy, April 5, 1719; Johannes, Nov. 27, 1720; Elizabeth, Oct. 7, 1722.

PEERSEN (Pearse), Johannes, m. Alida Van Vranken in Schenectady, Nov. 8, 1745. He was buried Oct. 26, 1756. Ch: baptized; Ryckart, March 24, 1751; Abraham, Jan. 17, 1753; Johannes, August 5, 1754; Maria, in Schenectady, March 6, 1757; Jacob; Annatie.

Pearson, George and Gitty Huyck. Ch: Catalyna, b. Dec. 10, 1796.

PEARSON, George, m. Judith Van Vechten, Dec. 12, 1808. Ch: Ann Van Vechten, b. Feb. 10, 1818.

Peck, Abraham, and Mary Hammond. Ch: Sarah, b. July 14, 1790.

Peebles, Thomas, of *Halve Maan*, and Elizabeth Bratt. Ch: born; Gerrit, March 28, 1769; Gerritje, Sept. 12, 1771.

Peck (Peeck), Jan, innkeeper of New Amsterdam; in 1655, sold two houses in Fort Orange, to Joannes Dyckman for 1627 guilders. The creek at Peekskil, takes its name from him. He m. Maria Volchers widow of Cornelis Volckertse, in New Amsterdam, Feb. 20, 1650. Ch: baptized in New York. Anna,

Oct. 15, 1651 ; Johannes, Oct. 12, 1653 ; Jacobus, Jan. 16, 1656 ; Maria, March 6, 1658. See *Schenectady Families.*

Peek, Jacobus of Schenectady, and Elizabeth Teunise. Ch : baptized ; Ludovicus, July 14, 1686 ; Margriet, March 27, 1692. See also *Schenectady Families.*

Peek, Abraham, m. Catarina Van Santen [Zandt], Aug. 22, 1752. Ch : Johannes, bp. March 18, 1753 ; Joseph, bp. April 13, 1755 ; Maria, bp. Dec. 12, 1756 ; Gerrit, bp. April 5, 1759 ; Tryntje, bp. July 5, 1761 ; Joseph, b. March 13, 1764 ; Elizabeth, b. Aug. 30, 1765 ; Abraham, b. July 17, 1768 ; Joseph, b. Feb. 14, 1771.

Peelen, Brandt, Van Nieuwkerk, came to Fort Orange in 1630 ; his second (?) wife was Maritie Pieterse widow of Claas Sybrantse of New Amsterdam, whose daughter Aaltie Claese, m. Claes Calff. Brandt Peelen died in 1644, leaving at least three children : Lysbet, Gerritje, w. of Goosen Gerritse Van Schaick, deceased in 1657 ; and Cornelis Brantse Van Nieuwkerk. His descendants in Albany county are said to pass by the name of Brandt.

Peeren, Wilhelm, and Lysbeth Sickell. Ch : Maria, bp. March 1, 1693.

Peesing (Beesinger) Andries, of Niskitha, m. Jannetje Bratt, Nov. 1762. Ch : born ; Annatie, Dec. 5, 1763 ; Pieter, June 11, 1765 ; Andries, June 5, 1769 ; Isaac, Aug. 16, 1774 ; Catharina, March 10, 1780.

Peesinger, Zepherinus (Sobrinus), m. Maritie Young, Oct. 18, 1773. Ch : born, Willem, Oct. 30, 1776 ; Johannes, April 1, 1779 ; Daniel, May 1, 1789.

Pels, Evert, Van Steltyn, settled in Rensselaerswyck in 1642, was a brewer and erected a brewery in the Colonie ; lived on Mill creek in Greenbush ; also owned a sloop an the river and a lot in Broadway Manathans, which he sold in 1656. In 1657 he sent down to New Amsterdam 2100 beaver skins. His son Evert Evertse, m. Breechtje Elswaerts in New York Aug. 13, 1670.

Pels, Evert [Evertsen, grandson of the first settler ?] m. Grietje Van Deusen in New York, Sept. 29, 1695. Ch : baptized in Albany, Breechje, and Evert twins ; June 7, 1696 ; baptized in New York, Bregie, and Engeltie, July 25, 1697 ; Bregje, Feb. 4, 1700 ; Rachel, March 29, 1702 ; Evert, July 2, 1704 ; Annatie, Aug. 24, 1706 ; Abraham, March 28, 1708, buried Sept. 1, 1754 ; Rachel, Dec. 9, 1711 ; Annatie, April 17, 1715.

Pemberton (Pammerton), Jeremiah, and Maritie In 1730, he had a lot on the " Plain " north side of Hudson east of Pearl street. Ch : baptized ; Andries, March 28, 1730 ; Andries, and Willem, May 14, 1732 ; Andries, May 13, 1733 ; Willem, Aug. 26, 1735.

PEMBERTON, Jeremiah, and Susanna Bratt. Ch : Adam, b. Dec. 6, 1776.

Pendell, Thomas, m. Jannetie Salsbury, July 17, 1776. Ch : Jannetie, bp. July 17, 1776.

Pender, Christiaan, and Elizabeth Cramer, Ch : Sara, b. Oct. 10, 1780.

Penniman, James, bought John Cornell's lot for 70 pounds Boston money, and sold the same in 1677, to Andries Teller.

Pepper, William, and Elizabeth Simpson. Ch : born ; William, Aug. 22, 1795 ; John, Aug. 14, 1797 ; Magdalena, Aug. 24, 1799 ; John, Oct. 24, 1801.

Perry, Johannes ; of Claverac, m. Francyntje Clute, Jan. 9, 1748. Ch : baptized ; Emmetie, Nov. 7, 1752 ; Marytje, Dec. 21, 1760.

PERRY, William, and Elizabeth Gardenier. Ch : John, bp. Feb. 19, 1754.

Pest (Pess), Jacob, and Annatie Jaart (Shaat), Ch : born ; Annatie, July 22, 1764 ; Margarita, Feb. 9, 1767.

PEST, Jacob of Hosac, m. Catharina Mellingtown (Mellendon, Mellery), Jan. 26, 1766. Ch : born ; Ja cob, Nov. 9, 1768 ; Thomas Oct. 12, 1770.

PEST, Jacob, and Jannetie Vredenburgh. Ch : Nelly, b. May 16, 1777.

Petit, Jonathan, and Agnes Riddle. Ch : born ; James, April 13, 1777 ; George, Jan. 13, 1780.

Philips, Michael, m. Margarita Wyngaart, Nov. 28, 1748. Ch : baptized ; Maria, Sept. 24, 1749 ; Michael, Aug. 16, 1752 ; Machtelt, Nov. 24, 1754.

Philip, Willem, and Eva Church. Ch : baptized ; Jurrie, Aug. 26, 1752.

Pieterse, Meyer, Gillis, carpenter of Gouda, m. Elsie Hendrickse of Amsterdam, in New Amsterdam July 6, 1642. Valentine says he resided on the site of Wall street where it joins Pearl ; on his decease in 1676, his son Hendrick Gillise, purchased the interest of his brothers-in-law, Capt. Hans Hendrickse and Johannes Wendel, in said lot. He received a patent for a house lot in Beverwyck in 1654. Ch. baptized in New Amsterdam : Eva, April 26, 1643, m. Capt. Hans Hendrickse of Beverwyck ; Pieter, Nov. 20, 1644 ; Tryntje, April 22, 1647 ; Tryntje, July 4, 1648 ; Hendrick, March 6, 1650, cordwainer in New York, 1702 ; Maria, Jan. 21, 1652 ; m. Johannes Wendel, of Beverwyck.

PIETERSE, Reyndert, in 1662, with Jacob Gevick, bought Pieter Bronk's brewery, lot, etc., he died in 1673.

Pieterse, William, and Lena Van Eps. Ch : Sophia, bp. Sept. 28, 1745. See *Schenectady Families.*

PIETERSEN, Petrus, and Rebecca Montagne. Ch : Geertruy, bp. Dec. 7, 1760 ; Petrus, b. Dec. 18, 1762.

Pikkart, Bartholomeus, *jong man Van Lester schier in out Englandt,* m. Aagje Claase, *Van Schenegtade,* Nov. 12, 1698. In 1716, he purchased a parcel of ground at the *Verreberg* on the north side of the highway (to Schenectady) over against the house of Isaac Valkenburgh. Ch : Rachel, bp. Jan. 29, 1709.

Pitman, Nicolaas, and Anna Margarita Pit. Ch : Sophia Christina, bp. Feb. 22, 1756.

Plank, Jacob Albertse Sheriff of Rensselaerswyck, 1630-8.

PLANCK, see also Verplanck.

Plass, Evert Emmerick, of Claverack, made his will April 8, 1745, proved July 15, 1752, spoke of wife Agneta Flora, and " my only daughter Elizabeth wife of Henderick Plass " and " my grandson John Emmerick Plass."

Ploeg, Pieter, and Aaltie Pels. Ch : Catharina, bp. Jan. 25, 1708.

Poel, Willem, and Elizabeth .. .. Ch : Elizabeth, bp. Feb. 21, 1714.

POEL, Mattheus, m. Elizabeth Shutter, Nov. 18, 1777. Ch : born ; Catharina, May 17, 1779 ; Catharina, May 7, 1781 ; Barbara, June 12, 1783 ; Gerrit, Nov. 24, 1787.

POEL, Johannes, and Geertruy Van Buren. Ch: Pieter, b. Aug. 27, 1780.

POEL, Johannes, and Isabella (Elizabeth) Douglas. Ch: born; Abraham, Feb. 21, 1783; John, Sept. 11, 1784; Margarita, March 2, 1787.

POEL, Isaac, and Maria Van Buren. Ch: Catharina, b. June 4, 1785.

POEL, Gerrit, and Caty Cowenhoven. Ch: Pieter, b. Dec. 26, 1786. [Gerrit Poel, and Margarita Wilson, m. April 8, 1780.]

Poentie, Young, an *alias* for Theunis Cornelise [Van Vechten?]

Poin, Johannes, and Maria Geertruy ..... Ch: Anna Catharina, bp. Feb. 11, 1739.

Pootman [now Putman], Victor, of Schenectady, m. Grietje Mebie, Dec. 13, 1706. Ch: baptized, Cornelia, Aug. 3, 1707; Antje, April 25, 1709. See *Schenectady Families.*

POOTMAN, Arent of Schenectady, and Lysbeth Akermans. Ch: Jannetje, bp. June 12, 1709. See *Schenectady Families.*

POOTMAN, Lodowyck, of Johnston, and Elizabeth Soets. Ch: Elizabeth, bp. Aug. 29. 1754.

Potman, Adam, and Catharina Myers. Ch: Salomo, b. Oct. 20, 1778.

Pork, Joh. Thys, and Catharina Keveling. Ch: Jacob, b. July 2, 1763.

Possi, Henri, *geboren in Engelandt te Boorton*, m. Antje Hoogeboom, Sept. 10, 1695. Ch: Catrine, bp. Jan. 12, 1696.

Post, Simon Janse, m. Jannetie Paulusse, Feb. 11, 1685. Ch: baptized; Jan, Nov. 14. 1686, Jan, Jan. 8, 1688; Maritie, Aug. 10, 1690.

POST, Elias, from Amsterdam, m. Catalyntje Coninck, of New Albany, May 6, 1671, in New York, again Elias P. widower m. Maritie Cornelise, June 13, 1674; in New York.

POST or Poest, Jan Barentse, see J. B. Wemp.

POST, Johannes, m. Frena Meyer, July 7, 1751. Ch: Jacob, bp. April 19, 1752; Anna, bp. April 14, 1754; Catrina, and Margarita twins b. Feb. 8, 1760.

POST, Benjamin, and Catharina Van Norden (Northen). Ch: born; Margarita, Oct. 14, 1776; Catharina, July 16, 1779; Benjamin, Oct. 8, 1787.

Potton, J. and R. .... Ch: William, bp. Oct. 5, 1733.

Powell (Poulussen), Thomas, baker, was sergeant in the W. India company's service in Brazil, from 1641 to 1653; in 1657 he was in Beverwyck where he remained till his death in 1671. Besides several lots in Beverwyck he owned a parcel of land behind Kinderhoek and between Kinderhoek and Neutenhoek, which his widow, Jannetie Donckertse, and Robert Orchard conveyed to diverse persons in 1671.

Powell, William, and Charity Brown. Ch: Jacob b. July 5, 1798.

Pretty, Richard, in 1677 was collector of the excise; 1678-90 sheriff of the county: He owned a lot on west corner of Pearl and State streets which in 1673 he conveyed to Mrs. Salisbury wife of Capt. Silvester Salisbury.

Price, Seth, of Hellenbergh, and Mary Gold. Ch: Elizabeth b. May 1, 1790.

PRICE, Gould, and Hannah Wally. Ch: Hannah, b. March, 1795.

Primmer, Hannes, and Mary Powell. Ch: Jacob, b. Feb. 20, 1771.

Proper, Jacobus, and Eva Althouser. Ch: Jacobus, b. May 10, 1776.

Prout, Albert, and Magdalena Lang. Ch: Hadriaan, b. August 14, 1765.

Provoost, Johannes, clerk in Fort Orange under Johannes DeLa Montagne and notary public from 1656 to Nov. 1664, when he became secretary of Albany until August, 1665, and again from Oct. 1673, to August, 1675: Sheriff of Albany 1678; died 1696. He had three wives; by the first, a son Isaac, bp. in Albany Sept. 23, 1683; he married secondly, Sarah Webber, widow of L. Vander Speigle, June 26, 1685; they made a joint will Nov. 3, 1685; letters of administration were granted on her estate Dec. 23, 1685; thirdly, he m. Anna widow of Domine Van Neuwenhuysen, July 18, 1687. In 1696, the sheriff of Albany, was directed to expose his goods at public sale and "pay his debts so far as it will goe." He or one of the same name was called *schoonsoon* of Elizabeth Bancker, in her inventory made in 1693.

PROVOOST, Abraham of Catskill, and Jannetie..... Ch: Isaac, bp. Oct. 10, 1718. [Abraham P. m. Janneke Meyer in New York, May 27, 1701, and had 6 Ch: bp. there from 1703 to 1715.]

Pruyn, Frans Janse, tailor, was in Albany as early as 1665, previously in New Amsterdam where most of his Ch: were born. In 1699, he could not take the oath of allegiance, &c., because he was a Papist. His wife was probably Alida,.... Ch: bp. in New York, Tryntie, Nov. 24, 1641; Jannetie April 9, 1656; Lysbeth, Sept. 14, 1659; Johannes, Jan. 5, 1663; bp. in Albany, Samuel, Helena (?) w. of Jacob Lansing, Maria, w. of Elbert Gerritse; Christina (?); Frans, Sept. 28, 1683; Barentje, April, 11, 1686; Arent, May 24, 1688.

PRUYN, Samuel, blacksmith, m. Maria Bogart, Jan. 15, 1704; made will March 27, 1752, proved Jan. 26, 1753, and spoke of wife Maritie, and Ch. Francis: Johannes; and Jacob, buried June 27, 1752. Ch: bp.; Franciscus, March 15, 1704; Alida, Nov. 17, 1706; Jacob, Feb. 10, 1712; Maritie, Sept. 20, 1713; Johannes, July 14, 1723.

PRUYN, Johannes, m. Emilia Sanders, Sept. 1705. He was buried Aug. 23, 1749. Ch; bp.; Alida March 23, 1707; Johannes, June 12, 1709; Elsie, Feb. 14, 1714.

PRUYN, Frans, and Margarita .... Ch: bp.; Christina, May 23, 1715; Maria, March 8, 1719; Magdalena, Jan. 11, 1721; Antje, March 24, 1723; Elisabeth, June 13, 1725; David, Oct. 6, 1727; Franciscus, June 8, 1731; Hendrick, Dec. 30, 1733.

PRUYN, Arent, m. Catryna Gansevoort, Nov. 21, 1714. Ch: bp.; Alida, March 11, 1716; Maria, May 31, 1719; Christina, and Lydia, Jan. 24, 1722; Franciscus, Feb. 2, 1724; Harman, Oct. 18, 1727.

PRUYN, Frans S., m. first, Anna ....; secondly, Alida Van Yveren, July 15, 1726. Ch: bp.; Franciscus, Jan. 16, 1717; Anna, Oct. 30, 1726; Samuel, Oct. 6, 1727; Samuel, Sept. 15, 1728; Anna, April 16, 1732; Casparus, May 19, 1734; Johannes, Dec. 23, 1739, d. March 23, 1815, a. 75y. 2m. 21d.; Jacob, July 22, 1744.

PRUYN, Johannes S., and Jannetie Van Aalsteyn. Ch : bp. ; Jacob, Jan. 22, 1749 ; Maritie, Nov. 4, 1750 ; Samuel, Nov. 19, 1752 ; Johannes, April 27, 1755 ; Reinier, May 22, 1757 ; Pietertje, March 15, 1761 ; Franciscus, b. Oct. 1, 1764.

PRUYN, Samuel, m. Neeltie Ten Eyck, Feb. 7, 1756. Ch : b. ; Franciscus, bp. July 10, 1757 ; Maria, Jan. 22, 1760 ; Anna, Aug. 2, 1762, d. Feb 3, 1833, a. 70 y. 6 m. ; Jacob, June 28, 1765, d. at Lafayette, N. Y., July 20, 1836, a. 72 y. ; Johannes, Nov. 1, 1768.

PRUYN (Pruim), Casparus, m. Catharina Groesbeck, Dec, 1762. He d. Oct. 8, 1817. Ch : b. ; Maria, April 12, 1763 ; Alida, Jan. 12, 1764 ; Franciscus, bp. Sept. 27, 1767 ; Franciscus, July 19, 1769 ; David, Aug. 24, 1771 ; Willem, March 11, 1776.

PRUYN, Jacob, Jr., and Hendrickie Van Buren. Ch : b. ; Alida, Jan. 20, 1775 ; Cathalyna, April 24, 1778 ; Franciscus, Jan. 31, 1781 ; Margarita, Dec. 10, 1783 ; Annatie, Aug. 22, 1786 ; Debora, April 13, 1790.

PRUYN, (Pruin) Samuel, m. Neeltie Horsford (Hasevaet, Eleanor Horsefield), dau. of Reuben H. of Schenectady, June 11, 1775. Ch : born, Johannes Nov. 17, 1776 ; Reuben. in Schenectady, Jan. 25, 1778 ; Dirk, April 2, 1786 ; Jannetie, Sept. 30, 1790.

PRUYN, (Pruin) Johannes J. and Ariaantje Verplanck. Ch : born, Johannes, April 13, 1783 ; Johannes, April, 1, 1785 ; Willem, March 31, 1787 ; Teunis, August 6, 1789 ; Rynier, August 7, 1793.

PRUYN, (Pruin), Reiner, m. Jannetie Goey, (Goewey,) Oct. 3, 1786. Ch : born, Jannetie, August 27, 1787 ; Loreina, May 31, 1789 ; Maritie, August 18, 1791.

PRUYN, (Pruin) Jacob J. m. Neeltie De Foreest, March, 17, 1786. Ch : born, Isaac, Feb. 3, 1788 ; Johannes, May 28, 1790, d. July 12, 1862, a. 72y. ; Alida, Sept. 4, 1792 ; Jacob, Dec. 12, 1794 ; Jannetie, August 3, 1796.

PRUYN, (Pruin), Francis C. m. Cornelia Dunbar, August 30, 1791. Ch : born, Casparus, May 26, 1792, d. Feb. 11, 1845 a. 54y. ; Catharine, Jan. 30, 1794 ; Levinus, Oct. 4, 1796 ; David and Margaret, Jan. 26, 1799 ; David, Nov. 20, 1801 ; Gertrude, Oct. 19, 1802 ; Maria, June 5, 1808 ; Cornelia, Dec. 12, 1810.

PRUYN, (Pruin) John S. m. Margaret Lansing, April 4, 1795. He d. May 8, 1816, a 47y. 6m. 8d. ; she d. Oct. 15, 1839, a. 67y. 5m. 25d. Ch : born ; Sarah, Sept. 26 1795 ; Alida Ten Eyck, Nov, 23, 1797 ; Samuel, Feb, 25, 1800, d. Feb. 18, 1862, a. 63 y. ; Agnes, June 15. 1807.

PRUYN, David, and Hubertie Lansing. He d. Jan., 1843 ; she d. Sept. 2, 1855, a. 83 y. Ch : b. ; Sara, Aug. 5, 1796 ; Catharine, Feb. 14, 1803 ; Casparus, April 2, 1809 ; John Van Schaick Lansing " June 22, 23, 12 o'clock," 1811.

Purnel, John, and Joanna .... Ch : John, bp. Aug. 7, 1748.

Putnam, Elisha, m. Esther Johnson, Dec. 25, 1792. Ch : b. ; Laina, Jan. 4, 1798 ; Stephen, June 14, 1800.

Quackerbos, Pieter, brickmaker, in 1668, bought Adriaen Van Ilpendam's brickyard ; had the following sons probably : Wouter ; Reinier ; and Johannes.

Quackenbos, Wouter Pieterse, m. first, Neeltje Gysbertse, and secondly, Cornelia Bogart, dau. of Lourens B., Oct. 4, 1696, buried Nov. 21, 1736. Ch :

bp. Martje, May 7, 1684 ; Pieter, March 18, 1688 ; Maritje, Sept. 13, 1691 ; Neeltje, Aug. 22, 1697 ; Cornelia, Sept. 3, 1699 ; Maria, April 19, 1702 ; Pieter, June 9, 1706 ; Johannes, Nov. 13, 1709.

QUACKENBOS, Johannes, of Niskayuna, m. first, Magtelt Janse Post ; secondly, Anna Clute, Oct. 20, 1700. Jan and Reyer [Reinier ?] Q. owned farms on the north side of the Mohawk river in the present town of Clifton Park, which were extended north one mile by patent, April 22, 1708. Ch : bp. Geertruy, May 10, 1684 ; Magtelt, Feb. 13, 1687 ; Abraham, March 23, 1690 ; Isak, Feb. 19, 1693 ; Jacob, Nov. 17, 1695 ; Bata, Dec. 7, 1707 ; Abraham, Nov. 3, 1710 ; Isaac, Jan. 25, 1713 ; Jacob, Oct. 30, 1715.

QUACKENBOS, Reinier Pieterse, from Oestgeest, Holland, m. first, Lysbet Janse of Flushing, New Netherland, March 2, 1674, in New York ; and secondly, Claesje Jacobse, Sept. 13, 1692. Ch : bp. in Albany ; Livertje and Claas, Dec. 9, 1685 ; Claas, Sept. 15, 1689 ; bp. in New York : Jacob, June 4, 1693 ; Marritie, Feb. 16, 1696 ; Johannes, Jan. 22, 1699 ; Abraham, Feb. 25, 1705.

QUACKENBOS, Adriaan of Schaatkooke, m. Catharina Van Schaick, dau. of Sybrant V. S., Jan. 18, 1699. Ch : bp. Maghtel, Jan. 7, 1700 ; Sybrant, June 14, 1702 ; Adriaan, Dec. 6, 1704 ; Adriaan, Aug. 17, 1707 ; Johannes, Oct. 28, 1710 ; Gosen, Oct. 19, 1712 ; Gideon, Dec. 25, 1714, buried Sept. 13, 1747 ; Anthony, Oct. 13, 1717, an innkeeper in Kinderhoek, by the river, in 1755 ; Elisabeth, Oct. 28, 1719.

QUACKENBOS, Pieter, m. Neeltie Marens (Marinus) of Schenectady, Nov. 1, 1701. In 1733 he bought lands on the Mohawk river, of Edward Collins ; was buried July 20, 1748. Ch : bp. ; David, June 21, 1702 ; Abraham, Nov. 19, 1704 ; Maghtelt, Dec. 30, 1705 ; Abraham, Sept. 19, 1708 ; Jeremias, Oct. 26, 1713 ; Rachel, Jan. 22, 1716.

QUACKENBOS, Johannes, m. Elizabeth Rumbly, Dec. 22, 1730. Ch : bp. ; Johanna, August 30, 1730 ; Adriaan, Nov. 17, 1734 ; Catharina, Oct. 26, 1735 ; Elizabeth, Sept. 10, 1738 ; Goosen, May 27, 1744.

Quakkenbos. Jacob, m. Geertruy Van der Werke, Sept. 20, 1719. Ch : bp. ; Abraham, May 14, 1721 ; Gerrit, March 15, 1724 ; Isaac, April 21, 1728 ; Maria, Oct. 2, 1731 ; Jacob, April 13, 1735 ; Machtelt, May 28, 1737.

QUAKKENBOS, Sybrant, m. Elizabeth Knickerbacker, Feb. 8, 1725. Ch : bp. ; Catharina, Sept. 5, 1725 ; Anna, Feb. 25, 1728 ; Johannes, May— 1729 ; Adriaan, March 18, 1732 ; Annatje, Jan. 8, 1735 ; Elizabeth, Sept. 11, 1737 ; Harmen, Dec. 6, 1738 ; Neeltie and Elizabeth, Feb. 28, 1742.

QUAKKENBOS, Johannes Wouterse, and Margarita, Ch : bp. ; Wouter, Sept. 3, 1732 ; Nicolaas, August 28, 1734 ; Pietertje, Dec. 8, 1736 ; Cornelia, June 17, 1740 ; Johannes, March 7, 1742 ; Cornelis, June 27, 1744.

QUACKENBOS, D., and Anna.... Ch : Abraham, bp. Feb. 5, 1732.

QUACKENBOS, Pieter, m. Anna Oothout, Dec. 27, 1733. Ch : bp. ; Wouter, August 18, 1735 ; Jan, April 11, 1742. The wife of Pieter Q. was buried Feb. 1, 1757.

QUACKENBOS, Jacob, and Geertruy Huyck. Ch : bp. ; Johannes, Feb. 16, 1746 ; Cornelis, Nov. 18, 1753.

QUACKENBOS, Hannes (Johannes), and Rachel Gardinier. Ch : bp. ; Pieter, August 17, 1746 ; Nicolaas, Jan. 21, 1750.

11

QUACKENBOS, Adriaan, m. first, Elizabeth Clute; secondly, Volkie Vanden Bergh, July 9, 1757. Ch: bp. Jacob, August 14, 1748; Machtel, July 7, 1751; Machtel, August 31, 1755.

QUACKENBOS, Gerrit, of Saratoga, m. Catharina De Voy (Voe?) of Half Moon, Feb. 6, 1750. Ch: bp.; Magtel, August 16, 1752; Hannes, August 20, 1754; Jacob, Jan. 18, 1756; Abraham, Oct. 16, 1757; Catarina, July 29, 1759; Isaac, March 15, 1761; Gerardus, June 28, 1762; Ariaantje, b. June 10, 1763.

QUACKENBOS, Abraham, and Bata Ouderkerk. Ch: Lena, bp. July 7, 1754.

QUACKENBOS, Jacob, m. Catharina De Voe, Feb. 3, 1776. Ch: b.; Rachel, Nov. 19, 1777; Isaac, July 3, 1786.

QUACKENBOS, Jacob, and Catarina Huyck, Ch: Cornelia, bp. Dec. 14, 1755; Cornelia, bp. July 30, 1758; Geetruid, b. June 13, 1762; Bata, b. May 3, 1764; Willempie, bp. Jan. 26, 1767.

QUACKENBOS, Johannes S., m. Jannetie Viele, Dec. 9, 1758. Ch: Elizabeth, bp. July 1, 1759; Teunis, bp. Oct. 25, 1761; Rebecca, b. Nov. 20, 1767; Annatie, b. Nov. 1. 1769; Sybrand, b. Nov. 17, 1771.

QUACKENBOS, David, (Jacob? see above) and Catarina Huyck; Ch: Isaac, b. May 19, 1760.

QUACKENBOS, Harmen of Schaagtekook. and Judith Marl (Morrell), Ch: Elizabeth, bp. Sept. 20, 1761; Sybrant, bp. Sept. 29, 1763; Jacob, b. Nov 15, 1772.

Quackenbusch, Wouter, of the *Colonie,* m. Bata Clute, Oct. 29, 1763. Ch: Pieter, b. Sept. 3, 1764.

QUACKENBUSCH, Hendrik and Margarita Oothout, Ch: b.; Annatie, Jan. 30, 1765; Cathryna, Sept. 16, 1766; Catharina, Sept. 11, 1768; Margarita, March 17, 1770.

Quackenbush, Johannes P., and Cornelia Quackenbush. Ch: b.; Pieter, Nov. 7, 1771; Johannes, Oct. 14, 1773; Wouter, Sept. 20, 1775; Anna, Dec. 18, 1779; Hendrik, July 20, 1782; Johannes, Oct. 31, 1784; Margarita, June 6, 1788; Walter, Nov. 6, 1791; Henry, Nov. 22, 1793.

QUACKENBUSH, Pieter J., and Maria Shisley (Shipfield, Sheffield). Ch: b.; Johannes, April 24, 1776; Willem, Nov. 27, 1778; Willem, Nov. 21, 1780; Petrus, Feb. 16, 1783; Petrus, Nov. 9, 1784; Maria, April 17, 1787.

QUACKENBUSH, Isaac, and Catharina (Althumne?) Gardenier. Ch: b.; Catharina, July 16, 1784; Andries, June 16, 1786; Jacob, Jan. 18, 1793; George Clinton, Oct. 1, 1795; John, Dec. 14, 1790; Nicholas, March 5, 1797; Cataline, Jan. 29, 1799.

QUACKENBUSH, Isaac A. and Catharine Bancker (Baker). He was a lawyer and d. in Schenectady (late of Erie, Penn.), April 26, 1841, æ. 74y. She was dau. of John (?) B. of Normanskill, and d. at Erie, Pa, April 8, 1850, æ. 96 y. Ch: b. John Bancker, Dec. 12, 1790; Magdalene, May 3, 1793; Anthony, August 7, 1795; Esther, Feb. 4, 1803.

QUACKENBUSH, Nicholas A., and Annatie Gansevoort. He was counsellor at law; d. Jan. 26, 1823, æ. 49 y.; She d. Dec. 16, 1828. Ch: b.; Catharine, Nov. 16, 1793; Nicholas, Feb. 29, 1796; Margaret, May 27, 1807.

QUACKENBUSH, Abraham, and Caty Radliff. Ch: b.; Lawrence, July 3, 1795; John, Aug. 5, 1797; Peter, March 7, 1800; Abraham, June 1, 1802.

QUACKENBUSH, Gerrit, and Elisabeth Banker. Ch: Ann, b. March 1, 1797.

Quilhot, Harry, and Mary Lansing. Ch: Philip, b. Sept. 11, 1795.

Quin (Quint) Christopher, and Elizabeth Carlin. Ch: bp.; Catarina, May 28, 1749; Eva, Feb. 17, 1751.

Raaf, Frederic, and Elisabeth Daalhamer. Ch: Maria, b. Nov. 28, 1764.

Raca (Riker?) Jeremiah, and Ann McMillen. Ch: Andrew Truex, b. Nov. 14, 1790.

Radcliffe, Rateliffe; Ratle; Rattelief: Redliff; Redley, &c.

RADCLIFFE (Redley, &c.), Jan, was appointed city porter in place of Hendrick Marcelis, in 1697, and *klockluyer* instead of Hend. Roseboom, in 1703. His wife, Rachel Lambertse Jochemse Van Valkenburgh, was a widow in 1727, and was buried April 7, 1748. Ch: bp.; Anna, Jan. 10, 1686, buried April 24, 1741, then being the widow of Billy Sixberry. who d. Jan. 19, 1740; Rykert, July 15, 1688; Lambert Sept. 6, 1691; Johannes, Aug. 19, 1694; Jochem, Nov. 24, 1697; Willem, Nov. 3, 1700, buried Feb. 12, 1734; Jacobus, Sept. 12, 1703; Margarita, June 9, 1706.

RADCLIFFE, Joannes, m. first Selia Yates, March 24, 1717, secondly, Geertruy Bratt, Jan. 21, 1744. His first w. was buried Jan. 10, 1741; he was buried Jan. 19, 1757. In 1719, he had a lot 35 by 120 ft., at the foot of Gallows Hill on the west side of Pearl, south of Beaver street. Ch: bp.; Johannes, June 31 (*sic*), 1717; Anna, Nov. 30, 1718; Joseph, Dec. 23, 1720; Rachel, Dec. 9, 1722, buried April 7, 1749; Marytje, Feb. 17, 1725; Rykert, June 30, 1728; Catalyna, Nov. 1, 1730; Johannes, Jan. 4, 1745; Wyntje, July 12, 1747; Andries, Aug. 20, 1749; Celia, Feb. 17, 1751.

Rattelief, Willem, m. Martha Bennewe (Bennoit), Feb. 13, 1725. He was buried, Feb. 12, 1734. Ch: bp.; Rachel, April 11, 1725; Pieter, Jan. 21, 1728; Johannes, Oct. 24, 1730; Rachel, Oct. 1, 1732.

RATTELIEF, Samuel, and Anna .... Ch: Johannes, bp. Jan. 17, 1725.

RATTELIEF, Lambert, m. Antie Van Santen, Jan. 4, 1724. In 1733, he had an acre of land on Gallows Hill for a brickyard. Ch: bp.; Maria, Oct. 30, 1726; Rachel, Oct. 13, 1728; Johannes, Nov. 8, 1730,; Anna, Dec. 24, 1732; Margarita, Jan. 18, 1735.

Rettelief (Radclif), Jacob (Jacobus), and Catharina Bovie. In 1729, he had a lot 30 x 120 ft., at the foot of Gallows Hill, on west side of Pearl and south of Beaver St. Ch: bp.; Rachel, Feb. 19, 1729; Mattheus, Oct. 3, 1730; Catharina, Nov. 21, 1731; Johannes, Jan. 6, 1734; Philip, Oct. 26, 1735; Willem, April 16, 1738; Willem, Dec. 23, 1739; Willem, July 12, 1741; Maria, Feb. 26, 1744; Elisabeth, Aug. 16, 1747,

RETTELIEF, Jochem, and Hilletie ... Ch: Johannes, bp, Feb. 22, 1730.

Radclief, Joseph, m. Margriet Bratt, Feb. 19, 1743. Ch: Johannes, bp. Oct. 2, 1743.

Radcliff, Johannes, Jr., m. Anna Macans, May 16, 1752. Ch: bp.; Celia, March 8, 1753; Margarita, Aug. 12, 1754; Geertruy, Feb. 15, 1756; Andries, Nov. 4, 1757.

RADCLIFF, Johannes, Jr. [perhaps the same as the last] m. Margarita Passage, Oct. 18, 1760. Ch : Jacobus, bp. Aug. 2, 1761; Hendrik, b. Nov. 13, 1763; Nicolaas, b. Oct. 25, 1765; Johannes, bp. March 2, 1768; Willem, b. March 26, 1770; Sofia, b. Feb. 24, 1772.

RADCLIFF (Redlof), Ryckert, of Niskitha, m. Maria Oliver (Olfer), Jan. 5, 1755. Ch : Johannes, bp. May 16, 1756; Arent, bp. April 23, 1758; Willem, *oud 5 weken*, bp. June 5, 1763; Antje, b. Sept. 3, 1765; Ryckert, b. Aug. 22, 1768; Jacobus, bp. Aug. 18, 1771.

Redley, .. , and Cathalyntje ..... Ch : Martha, bp. June 22, 1761.

Radcliff, Johannes, and Catharina Van .... Ch : Annatie, bp. June 22, 1761; Jacobus *oud 4 weken*, bp. June 26, 1763; Philip, b. Oct. 9, 1765; Ryckert, b. April 10, 1768; Catharina, b. Feb. 13, 1772.

RADCLIFF (Redly), Johannes L., and Elizabeth .... Ch : Thomas, b. Sept. 13, 1762.

Redliff, Johannes, and Elisabeth Wilkeson. Ch : b. ; Elisabeth, Nov. 24, 1763, m. Samuel Norton, d. April 30, 1841, a. 77 y.; Lambert, April 18, 1766; Lambert, April 17, 1767.

Redley, Joseph, and Geertruy ... Ch : Johannes, bp. Sept. 10, 1769.

Redliff, Johannes, and Marytje Egmond. Ch : b. ; John, Nov. 5, 1774; Jacob, Feb. 5, 1776; Andries, Nov. 18, 1778.

Redlif, Jacobus, m. Mary Otman, Nov. 9, 1783. He d. May 16, 1831, in 72d y. Ch : b. ; Margarita, Oct. 7, 1784, d. July 2, 1865, a. 82 y. ; Catharine, May 21, 1790 ; John, May 26, 1792.

REDLIF, Hendrik, m. Elizabeth Jacobs, May 4, 1784. Ch : Margarita, b. March 5, 1785.

REDLIF, Jacobus, m. Susanna Claasen, Nov. 10, 1784. Ch : Margarita, b. Oct. 8, 1785.

Redly (Raidley), Philip, m. Nancy (Newman, Hesbe, Naomi) Hall, Feb. 23, 1786. Ch : b. ; Jacobus, March 14, 1787 ; William, Jan. 21, 1792 ; Thomas, Nov. 30, 1794.

REDLY, Philip, and Susanna Seger. Ch : Mary, b. June 11, 1790.

Radley, William, and Margaret Cline. Ch : b. ; Nicolaas, Jan. 4, 1794; Nicholas Kline, Jan. 18, 1800 ; William, August 24, 1802.

Radney, Jonathan, and Hannah Van Zandt. Ch : b. ; John, May 29, 1792.

Ramter, Adam, and Magdalena.... Ch : Catharina Barbara.

Ramert, Francis, and Carolina Beever. Ch : Mary, b. July 15, 1780.

Richter, Nicolaas, of Niskitha, m. Maria Hindermond, (Hoenemond), Feb. 27, 1762. Ch : Margarita, b. May 30, 1762 ; Elsie, bp. March 4, 1764 ; Catharina, bp. Dec. 8, 1765 ; Cornelia, b. June 1, 1767 ; Maria, b. April 11, 1769 ; Johannes, b. June 26, 1771 ; Cathalyna, bp. August 22, 1779.

Reddeines, Peter and John (?) Lodowic. Ch : Jane, b. Nov. 28, 1794.

Rees, Willem, of Claverac 1720, m. first Catrina Janse, and secondly Maria Goewey. Ch : Cornelis, Sept. 16, 1685 ; Benjamin, Feb. 7, 1694, *nota d' ouders vande Luysersche kke synde soo hebden de getuygen belooft om het kint in de belydenisse ouser-*

kke op-te-brenze ; Henderick, Feb. 16, 1696; Willem, Oct. 31, 1703.

REES, Andries, of Claverac, m. Ariaantje Andries Scherp, Jan. 1, 1697. Ch : bp. ; Jonathan, Jan. 26, 1690 ; Johannes, in New York Feb. 12, 1696; Catryntje, May 9, 1697 ; Andries, April 9, 1699 ; Neeltje, July 6, 1701; Lysbeth, June 18, 1704 ; Geertruy, May 11, 1707 ; Willem, Jan. 22, 1710.

REES, Jan, of Kinderhoek, 1709, Claverac, 1720, m. Maria Janse Goewey, Oct. 9, 1702. Ch : Catelyntje, b. Nov. 8, 1706 ; Andries, bp. Jan. 9, 1709.

REES, Johann, and Catharina.... Ch : Catharina, b. Oct. 5, at Claverack, and bp. Jan 15, 1721.

REES, Benjamin, and Geertruy.... Ch : Wilhelm, b. April 9, and bp. by the Lutheran minister, Falkner, at Claverac, April 30, 1721 ; Catharina, bp. May 19, 1723.

REES, Ephraim, and Margarita.... Ch : Christoffel, b. at Taghkanick and bp. at *Gospel-hoek* in Claverac, 22 naar Trinit : 1721.

Reese, Philip, and Eleanora Callingon, (Calligan) Ch : John, b. July 21, 1779.

REESE, George, and Anna Bullocks. Ch : Nicolaas, b. Dec. 27, 1779.

Reisdorp, Lourens, and Margarita,.... Ch : Lena, b. June 28, 1762.

REISDORP, Leendert, and Jannetie (De) Foreest, Ch : b. Marten, Sept. 11, 1788; Lourens, July 21, 1790 ; Philip, Oct. 3, 1800.

Reims, Edward, victualler, made will Sept. 14, 1702, spoke of his wife Elizabeth, also of Daniel Wilkeson to whom he gave 10 pounds, " for his care of me in sickness;" John Taylor drummer in Capt. James Weem's company to whom he gave £5; and of Capt. Henry Holland, whom he made his executor ; letters of administration issued Sept. 24, 1702.

Rendel, Timothy Van Dyck, and Catharina Van Antwerpen, Ch : Willem, b. March 1, 1762.

Rendell (Rundle) Jeremiah and Geertruy Gardenier, Ch : b. Tempe, b. May 7, 1784; Henrika (?) July 20, 1795 ; Anna, March 24, 1797 ; Abigail, Sept. 15, 1799.

Reur, Hendrick Jansen, in Beverwyck and the *Colonie* 1656-64 ; owned land at *Lubberde's* land (Troy) which after his decease in 1664 was let to wife of Marcelis Janse.

Reydt, Hendrick, and .... Ch : Jonathan, bp. June 30, 1689.

Reyerse, Gerrit, and Jannetie Van Slyck. Ch : Hendrick, b. August 13, 1775.

Reyersen, Jan, came to Beverwyck in 1637, and succeeded Ryckert Rutgersen in the possession of the Bethlehem Island, in 1652, and gave his name to it. *O'Callaghan's Hist. N. N.,* I. 437. He died in 1665.

Reyndertsen, Barent, smith, purchased a house and lot in Beverwyck in 1657, and continued to live there until his death in 1682. He bought and sold diverse lots of ground in the village among which was one in Yonker (State) street which was conveyed in 1682 to his son in law Joachim Staats.

Reynlie (Raily, Reyley), John and Lena (Magdalena) Barber. Ch : bp. ; Maria, July 24, 1743 ; Hendrik, June 8, 1747 ; Daniel, May 8, 1748 ; Lena, May 28, 1749 ; Thomas, March 3, 1751 ; Magdalena, March 22, 1752 ; Jannetie, Dec. 22, 1754.

Reyley, Philip, of Schenectady, and Jannetie Van Slyck. Ch: Jacobus Van Slyck, bp. Oct. 25, 1761; Harmanus, b. Aug. 22, 1766. See *Schenectady Families.*

REYLEY, Johannes, of the *Colonie,* m. Cathalyntje Van Den Berg, Jan. 7, 1769. Ch: b.; Thomas, July 8, 1769; Willem, June 4, 1772; Reinier, Feb. 15, 1780; John, Aug. 23, 1785; Jacob, June 3, 1788.

Reynolds, James, and Margaret Jackson. Ch: Ephraim, b. May 22, 1799.

Rham (De Rham), Johan Otto, m. Catharina Hoogstrasser, March 6, 1765. Ch: b.; Jacob, Feb. 12, 1768; Elisabeth, May 25, 1771; Hendrik, Feb. 8, 1777; Catharina, May 2, 1779.

Richards, John, m. Elisabeth, dau. of Hendrik Van Rensselaer, April 24, 1731. She d. April 13, 1779, a. 78 y. Ch: Stephanus, bp. July 9, 1732.

RICHARDS, Hendrick, and Annatie Huyck. Ch: Margarita, Sept. 21, 1755.

RICHARDS, Ozia, and Hannah Sickels. Ch: Elisabeth and Abraham, b. Oct. 26, 1792.

Rickert, Jurriaan, and Eva Staring. Ch: Geertruy, b. April 6, 1766.

Riddeke (Riddeker), Hendrik, m. Elisabeth Clute (Wells), Nov. 17, 1765. Ch: Ariaantie, bp. June 17, 1770; Pieter, bp. May 14, 1775; Nicolaas, b. April 31 (*sic*), 1777; Sofia Regina, bp. Feb. 2, 1781.

Riddeker (Ridecker), Nicholas, m. Hannah (Alida) Bulsen, July 15, 1796. Ch: b.; a child, name not given, June 22, 1797; Geertruy, Aug. 15, 1799; Elisabeth, March 1, 1802.

RIDDEKER, Peter, m. first, Elisabeth Suatt, and secondly, Mary Clute, about 1803. Ch: b.; Henderick, Dec. 30, 1791; Elisabeth, May 22, 1804.

Riddle, John, and Mary Creaton. Ch: Jean, bp. June 28, 1756.

RIDDLE, Walter, and Margaret Brown. Ch: Henry, bp. Oct. 4, 1757.

Rightmeyer, Coenraet, m. Catharina Hoogtmensch (?), Oct. 24,1728; who was buried April 8,1783; secondly, Elisabeth Houst, about 1835. Ch: bp.; Johannes, April 20, 1729; Coenraat, Nov. 25, 1730; Jacobus, March 31, 1733; Elisabeth, Aug. 22, 1735; Eva, Nov. 14, 1736; Jurriaan, April 23, 1738; Christiaan, April 20, 1740; Elisabeth, Oct, 27, 1743; Elsje, Jan. 12, 1746; Heyltie, April 17, 1748.

Rine, (Ryan?) Michael, and Josina Clerk. Ch: Margarita, bp. Jan. 24, 1754.

Rinckhout, Daniel, was in Beverwyck as early as 1653; had a house and lot on the south corner of Exchange street and Broadway, which his brother Jan inherited after his death in 1662. He was born in Pomeren, Holland, and in 1662 was 32 yrs. old; then made a will giving to his brother Jan his house and all his property, save 25 guilders bequeathed to his brother Aertman of Pomeren, if living. His brother Jan was a baker, and in 1670 his wife Elizabeth Drinckvelt leased his bakery to Antony Lespinard.

Roberts, Ebenezer (Abner), of New England, m. Geertie, (Caatje, Catharina) Vosburg of Hosack, Dec. 30, 1751. He lived in "Steen Rabie" in 1771. Ch: Abraham, bp. Sept. 29, 1753; Sara, bp. Nov. 22, 1755; Abner, bp. Jan. 18, 1757; Sara, b. May 7, 1771.

Robertson, Hendrick, and Ann Weeger. Ch: Mary b. Sept. 3, 1790.

Robinson, Joseph, and Susanna.... Ch: Maria, *oud* 9 weeks, bp. June 19, 1763.

ROBINSON, John, and Geertje Van Petten. Ch: David, b. April 10, 1784.

ROBINSON, William, m. June (?) (Jaranah, Elhanah) Fryer, Dec. 9, 1789. Ch: b.; Jane, March 16, 1789; James, June 16, 1795; Elizabeth, March 25, 1797.

Rock, Adam, and Maria Van der Hoef. Ch: Margarita, bp. August 3, 1760.

Rodey, Hendrik, and Maria Smith. Ch: Margarita, b. June 24, 1784.

Rodgers, William, *soldaat onder de compagnie van* Capt. James Weems, m. Mary Johnson *geboren tot* Boston in Niew Engeland, July 3, 1706. [Wm. Rodgers and Susannah Foreest, m. Feb. 7, 1721.] Ch: Susanna, bp. Feb. 19, 1707; Mary, bp. Feb. 11, 1708; William, bp. Dec. 4, 1709.

RODGERS, (Radtgeert), William, Jr., m. Mary White (Weith) Feb. 19, 1738. Ch: bp.; Susanna, Oct. 21, 1744; John, August 9, 1747.

RODGERS, George, and Eleanor Murray (Morry). Ch: Jane, bp. May 11, 1776; George, b. Sept. 27, 1778; Elizabeth, b. Jan. 22, 1781.

Rolantsen, Adam, schoolmaster in Beverwyck in 1639, afterwards in New Amsterdam.

Roeloffse (De Goyer), Jan, son of the noted Anneke Janse by her first husband. See Bogardus.

Roej, Thomas, and Catharina Tarrant. Ch: Susanna, b. March 6, 1779.

Roeso (Rousseau ?), Frans, *geboren in Flanderen,* m. Maria Palsin, *geboren in de Palts,* April 11, 1758, Ch: Maria, bp. Nov. 19, 1758.

Roman, Barent, m. Maria Wendell, March 8, 1761. Ch: Pieter, b. Jan. 16, 1762.

ROMAN, Pieter, and Catharine Van Deusen. Ch: b.; Lea, Jan. 24, 1787; Robert, Oct. 4, 1790; Mary, July 14, 1792; Margaret, March 26, 1794; Gertrude, Jan. 12, 1796; Hubertus, June 29, 1797; Gertrude, April 22, 1800.

Romville, Antoine, *geboren tot Vienne in Dauphine,* m. Heyltie Dekker, Feb. 8, 1707. Ch: Margarita, bp. Jan. 30, 1709.

Ronckel, Hendrik, and Margarita Toeper. Ch: Margarita, b. March 18, 1785.

Roos (Reus), Johannes, and Cornelia .... He d. in 1695, leaving his three children to the care of his father, Gerrit Janse Roos. Ch: bp.; Catarina, Oct. 7, 1683; Cornelia, May 6, 1688; Jacobus, March 29,1 689.

Roos, Frans, and Maritie Bonns [perhaps same as Frans Roeso above.] Ch: Frederick, bp. July 12, 1761.

Roos, Daniel, and Baatie Ponk (Bank ?). Ch: Marten, bp. Jan. 26, 1777.

Roos, Samuel, and Elizabeth Rees. Ch: Johan Pieter, b. Feb. 11, 1780.

Rosa, Isaac, m. Marytje Van Vranken, Nov. 22, 1763. Ch: b.; Johannes, Aug. 13, 1764; Annatie, Aug. 18,1766; Ryckert, Dec. 17, 1769; Machtel, April 20, 1772. See *Schenectady Families.*

Roseboom, Hendrick Janse, trader, was the *Voorlezer* and sexton of the church; in 1674, he brought a suit to recover his fees from a man who had employed the grave-digger of the Lutheran church, styled an interloper; judgment for the plaintiff 18 guilders. His house and lot originally Pieter Bronck's was on the east side of North Pearl street, 162 Rynland ft. north of Maiden Lane, and in 1677, the stockades passed through it and the gate (called Roseboom's gate) and the burgher blockhouse were situated there; this was one of the best business places in the village because the Indians entered chiefly through this gate. He was for many years farmer of the slaughter excise. His first wife was Gysbertje Lansing; in his old age he married Tryntje Janse Van Breestede, widow of Rutger Jacobsen; d. Nov. 4, 1703. Ch: Johannes; Gerrit (?); Henderik; Myndert (?); Margarita, w. of Pieter Thomase Mingael.

ROSEBOOM, Johannes, trader, m. Gerritje Coster, dau. of Hendrick Coster, Nov. 18, 1688. He was buried in the church Jan. 25, 1745. Ch: bp.; Hendrick, Aug. 4, 1689; Johannes, April 23, 1692; Johannes, April 29, 1694; Gerrit, Feb. 17, 1697; Elisabet, April 28, 1700; Geertruy, Dec. 27, 1702; Margarita and Anna, April 21, 1706.

ROSEBOOM, Gerrit, trader, m. Maria, dau. of Robert Sanders, Nov. 24, 1689. He was buried Dec. 21, 1739. Ch: bp.; Robert, May 21, 1693; Elsje, Sept. 15, 1695; Gysbert, Dec. 15, 1697; Ahasuerus, April 28, 1700; Johannes, March 22, 1702: Elizabeth, July 23, 1704.

ROSEBOOM, Henderick, Jr., m. Debora Staats, Nov. 1, 1694; she was buried Oct. 2, 1749. Ch: bp.; Jacob, July 14, 1695; Elisabeth, June 6, 1697; Rykje, Oct. 13, 1700; Hendrik, March 3, 1703; Catharina, June 16, 1706; Margarieta, Oct. 19, 1712; Abraham, Jan. 9, 1715.

ROSEBOOM, Myndert, m. Maria Vinhagen. He was buried Oct. 22, 1722. Ch: bp.; Hendrik, Sept. 21, 1707; Maria, Oct. 23, 1709; Margarita, Oct. 7, 1711, buried April 9, 1741; Alida, Sept. 20, 1713; Joannes, Jan. 15, 1716.

ROSEBOOM, Jacob, m. Geertruy Lydius, Aug. 12, 1716. She was buried July 27, 1757. Ch: bp.; Sara, Jan. 13, 1717, buried. Feb. 16, 1733; Joannes, Feb. 4, 1719; Hendrik, May 28, 1721; Hendrick Jacobus, Sept. 4, 1726; Geertruy, living in 1764.

ROSEBOOM, Gysbert, and Catharina .... He was buried Oct. 29, 1749. Ch: bp.; Maria, Nov. 20, 1721; Anthony, July 23, 1727; Elisabeth, Oct. 24, 1731; Catharina, Oct. 7, 1733; Catharina, June 28, 1738; Elsie, May 13, 1741. [Gysbert R., and *Christina* (Catharina?) Bries, m. Dec. 4, 1720.]

ROSEBOOM, Ahasuerus, m. Maritie Bratt, Nov. 25, 1725. She was buried Nov. 30, 1745. Ch: bp.; Maria, Sept. 25, 1726; Gerrit, Jan. 9, 1732, d. July 7, 1787, a. 54 y. 5 m.; Hendrik, June 3, 1734.

ROSEBOOM, Hendrick, m. Elsie Cuyler, Oct. 25, 1724, Ch: bp.; Johannes, Jan. 19, 1726; Elsie, Dec. 17, 1727; Elisabeth, June 14, 1730; Elisabeth, March 8, 1732; Gerritje, July 26, 1738, buried in the church, Nov. 23, 1746. [Hendrik Roseboom, buried Oct. 29, 1754.]

ROSEBOOM, Hendrik Hendrikse, m. Cathalyna Schuyler, April 3, 1729. He was buried Aug. 15, 1746. Ch: bp.; Debora, June 21, 1729, buried, July 20, 1746; Jacobus, Aug. 8, 1731; Susanna, June 6, 1733; Jacobus, Nov. 20, 1736; Hendrik, Sept. 2, 1739; Elisabeth, June 2, 1742; Jacobus Schuyler, April 19, 1745.

ROSEBOOM, N. ...., and M. .... Ch: Johannes, bp. Dec. 31, 1732.

ROSEBOOM, Hendrik Myndertse, m. Maria Ten Eyck, Oct. 29, 1734. Ch: bp.; Myndert, May 26, 1735; Barent, Oct. 24, 1736; Johannes, Oct. 14, 1739; Neeltje, Nov. 15, 1741; Maria, July 26, 1746.

ROSEBOOM, John Jac., m. Magtel Ryckman, May 25, 1740. Ch: Jacob, Nov. 23, 1740.

ROSEBOOM, Jacob, Jr., m. Hester Lansing, Jan. 20, 1763. She d. 3 (30) Nov. 1826, in 84th y. Ch: b. Geertruid, July 30, 1763; Johannes, April 8, 1766; Geertruy, April 28, 1768; Ariaantje, Oct. 2, 1770; Johannes, March 25, 1773; Johannes, July 17, 1774; Johannes, Sept. 15, 1776, d. at Cherry Valley, March 15, 1829, a. 54 y.; Gerrit, August 7, 1778; Lena, April 18, 1781; Lena, and Johannes, twins, Dec. 6, 1783.

ROSEBOOM, Meinard, m. Geertruy Swits, July 24, 1765. Ch: Maria, b. June 1, 1766.

ROSEBOOM, Jacob G., and Neeltie.... Ch: Gerrit, bp. Sept. 11, 1768.

ROSEBOOM, Dirk, and Rhoda Dowey. Ch: Gerrit, b. March 11, 1791.

ROSEBOOM, Gerrit, m. Josina Hornbeck (Halenbeck) Jan. 28, 1798. Ch: b.; Jacob, August 22, 1798; Cornelia, Sept. 24, 1800; Hester, Nov. 15, 1802.

Rosenberg (Rosevelt) Jacob, and Regina Tzisesa. Ch: Johannes, bp. Dec. 29, 1751; Hans Tjerk, bp. Oct. 21, 1753.

Rosie, Jan, an early settler of Albany, was buried in 1709; another of the same name (his son?) was buried Nov. 1, 1737.

Ross, John, and Mary Russell. Ch: Sara, bp. Feb. 20, 1780.

Roube, Coenraad, and Sara.... Ch: Frany, b. Nov. 18, 1763.

Roul, Nicolaas, and Ann Dorothe Margarita .... Ch: Christiaan Willem, bp. May 25, 1713.

Rous, Johannes, of Halve Maan, and Alida Van Etten. Ch: Lena, b. Jan. 29, 1787.

Rouw, Wilhelmus, m. Geertruy Schnuk (Schup), Sept. 25, 1778. Ch: Annatie, b. Jan. 4, 1780.

Ruger, Frans, *op Saratoga,* and Jennet Jewel. Ch: Elizabeth, b. Sept. 18, 1787; Johannes, b. June 13, 1789.

Ruiler, Harmanus, and Barbara Marcelis. Ch: Anna, bp. Feb. 7, 1762.

Rumney, (Rumbly), Jonathan, *geboren in London in oud England* m. Johanna Van Corlaar, Nov. 17, 1707. He d. Sept. 16, 1722. Ch: Robert, bp. Oct. 30, 1709.

Rumney, John, m. Rachel Meinersse, August 28, 1784. Ch: b.; Benjamin, Oct. 2, 1785; Maria, Dec. 18, 1787.

Rumple, Hendrick, and Margaret Hooper. Ch: Sarah, b. Aug. 31, 1790.

Russell, Benjamin, and Rachel Bank. Ch: Thomas, b. Nov. 22, 1782.

Rutgers. Two brothers, Rutger and Teunis Jacobse Van Schoenderwoert or Van Woert were among the early settlers of Beverwyck and originated two families, distinct in name and locality. Rutger Jacobsen's descendants assumed the surname of *Rutgers*, and were later found in New York and vicinity: his brother Teunis's descendants took the surname *Van Schoenderwoert,* or simply, *Van Woert* and settled chiefly in Albany county. [See *Van Woert.*]

94 *Genealogies of the First Settlers of Albany.*

Rutger Jacobsen, *alias* Rut Van Woert, was a man of considerable repute and wealth in the little village in which he served as magistrate many years, probably until his death in 1665. His business was varied; he owned a sloop upon the river which he sometimes commanded himself; at other times, Abraham De Truwe [Truax now] was his skipper; he was a considerable dealer in village lots and farming lands, among which was the island called Pachonakellick or Mohicander's Island, "obliquely over against Bethelehem," owned in partnership with Andries Herbertsen Constapel, and hence sometimes called *Constapel's* island : In 1654, he bought Jacob Janse Van Noorstrant's brewery and lot in Beaver street nearly opposite the present Middle Dutch church, which was inherited by his son Herman; he m. Tryntje Janse Van Breestede in New Amsterdam, June 3, 1646; her sister Dorotee subsequently m. Volckert Janse Douw. After Rutger Jacobsen's death, his widow in her old age, m. Hendrick Janse Roseboom, Dec. 5, 1695. She is said to have d. at her son's in 1711 at a very great age. It is not known that Jacobsen had more than three ch : two daughters, Margaret, who m. Jan Janse Bleecker; and Engel, bp. in New Amsterdam, April 10, 1650; and one son, Harmen.

RUTGERS, Harmen, son of Rutger Jacobsen Van Schoenderwoert last mentioned, was probably b. in Beverwyck soon after his father moved there; he was still living in 1720. He was a brewer, his brewery, which he sold in 1675 to Goosen Gerritse Van Schaick, and Pieter Lassingh, being on the east half of the present Exchange Block; in 1678, Richard Pretty, collector of the excise complained of him for defrauding the excise and selling beer to the Indians, but after considerable litigation the complaint was dismissed. He had two sons, Anthony and Harmen, who settled in New York.

RUTGERS, Anthony, baker, admitted freeman in New York, in 1699, m. Hendrickje Vandewater, of N. Y., Dec. 30, 1694. Ch : bp. ; in New York; Harmanus, Nov. 5, 1699 ; Petrus, May 4, 1701 ; Catryna, Dec. 20, 1702 ; Anneke, March 31, 1704 ; Catharina, Nov. 21, 1705 ; Anthony, Feb. 9, 1707 : Catharina, Oct. 27, 1708 ; Anthony, April 29, 1711.

RUTGERS, Hermanus, brewer, admitted freeman in New York, in 1696, m. Catharina Myer, in N. Y., Dec. 25, 1706. He d. Aug. 9, 1753 "at an advanced age." Ch : bp. ; in New York, Harmen, May 2, 1708 ; Elsie, Feb. 1, 1710 ; Hendrik, Feb. 24, 1712 ; Catharina, Feb. 21, 1714 ; Maria, April 11, 1716 ; Anthony, June 8, 1718 ; Eva, Aug. 30, 1719.

Ruyter (Ruiter), Frederic, m. Engeltie Vander Werken Feb. 6, 1738. [Frederic Ruyter, Jr., was buried, May 19, 1746.] Ch : bp. ; Margriet, May 27, 1739 ; Elisabeth, Oct. 5, 1740 ; Hendrik, Sept. 26, 1742 ; Johannes, Feb. 26, 1744 ; Catharina, Jan. 10, 1746.

RUYTER, Philip, m. Geertruy Vander Werken, March 20, 1741, was buried June 1, 1746. Ch : bp. ; Hendrik, Feb. 14, 1742 ; Johannes, April 24, 1743.

RUTTER (Ruiter), Hendrick, of Hoosac, m. Rebecca Dooth (Doth, Staats), Aug. 16, 1763. Ch : b. ; Gertruid, April 12, 1764 ; Johannes, June 16, 1768 ; Elisabeth, Sept. 8, 1770.

RUTTER, Johannes, of Hoosac, m. Elisabeth Pest, Nov. 14, 1764. Ch : Annatie, b. Sept. 23, 1768.

Ruyting, Gerrit Janse, and .... Ch : Louys, bp. June 22, 1690.

Ryan (Reyel), James, and Elizabeth .... Ch : bp. ; William, Sept. 5, 1736; Anna, Sept. 9, 1739 ; Sara, Oct. 11, 1741 ; Philip, Oct. 2, 1743.

Ryckensen (Richardson?), Samuel, and Catryna .... Ch : Johannes, bp. Oct. 7, 1759 ; Johannes, bp. Oct. 14, 1759.

Ryckers, Michael, and Maria .... Ch : Johannes, bp. Oct. 5, 1766.

Ryckman, Harmen Janse, was a resident in Albany, from 1666 to 1677.

RYCKMAN, Jan Janse, of Beverwyck, d. before 1663, at which time his widow, Tryntje Janse, had become the wife of Eldert Gerbertse Cruyff. She then had one son living named *Albert Janse Ryckman.*

RYCKMAN, Capt. Albert Janse, brewer, had his brewery on the east side of Broadway on or near the south corner of Hudson street and Broadway heretofore the property of Pieter Bronck. He was mayor of Albany, 1702-3; made his will, Dec. 23, 1736, proved May 1, 1739; was buried Jan. 12, 1737. In his will he spoke of the heirs of his son Johannes, of Margaret, w. of Samuel Kip ; of Magdalena, wife of Benjamin Bratt ; of Tryntje ; Pieter ; Harmanus ; of the two ch. of his dau. Maria, who m. Barent Bratt, and of Tobias. His wife Neeltie Quackenbos, was buried Oct. 17, 1738. Ch : Johannes, deceased in 1736 ; Albert, buried Oct. 8, 1722 ; Tryntje ; Pieter ; Harmanus ; Margaret ; Catharina, wife of Anthony Bries ; Maria, bp. Aug. 26, 1683, w. of Barent Bratt, d. about 1729 ; Magdalena, bp. May 13, 1685 ; Tobias, bp. Oct. 27, 1686 ; Magdalena, bp. March 24, 1689 ; Rachel, bp. Dec. 18, 1692.

RYCKMAN, Pieter, tailor, [son of Albert] m. Cornelia Keteltas in New York, May 6, 1696. He made will in 1747, proved Oct. 21, 1749, and spoke of his children Wilhelmus and Petrus, and of his grand dau. Cornelia, dau. of his son, Wilhelmus. Ch : Wilhelmus, bp. in N. Y., June 18, 1699 ; Lelletie, bp. in N. Y., July 8, 1702 ; Petrus, bp. in N. Y., July 21, 1706 ; Petrus, bp. in Albany, Nov. 14, 1708.

RYCKMAN, Harmen [son of Albert], made his will August 28, 1750, proved Oct. 11, 1756, spoke of his brothers Tobias, John, and Pieter, and of sisters Margaret, Maria, and Magdalena, also of his father, but not of any wife or children. He was buried Nov. 3, 1755.

RYCKMAN, Tobias [son of Albert], in 1745 had a house on the dock near " Gansevoort's Point" [foot of Maiden Lane ?]. He m. Helena Beekman, August 18, 1715. She was buried August 26, 1744. Ch : bp. Nelletie, June 3, 1716 ; Machtelt, August 22, 1719 ; Lena, Sept. 29, 1723.

RYCKMAN, Pieter [son of Pieter], m. Catharyna Kierstede, was buried Sept. 4, 1748. Ch : bp. ; Cornelia, Dec. 15, 1734 ; Ariaantje, April 3, 1737.

RYCKMAN, Tobias, Junior, and Marytje.... Ch : Aafje, bp. Jan. 12, 1737.

RYCKMAN, Wilhelmus, and Anna Vander Heyden. Ch : Rachel, *in ondertrouw zynde,* bp. June 18, 1721 ; Nilletje, bp. June 28, 1741 ; Ariaantje, bp. June 29, 1744.

RYCKMAN, Pieter, m. Lydia Vanden Bergh, Nov. 28, 1758. He d. Jan. 22, (15) 1811, in his 80th year. Ch : Wilhelmus, bp. April 8, 1759 ; Margarita, May 3

1761; Gerrit, b. July 31, 1762; Albert, b. Jan. 3, 1765; d. August 24, 1841; aged 77; Margarita, b. July 7, 1767, d. August 2, 1840, a. 72; Pieter, b. Oct. 23, 1769; Cornelis, b. June 14, 1777.

RYCKMAN, Gerrit, m. Elizabeth Van Buren, Dec. 5, 1769. Ch: b.; Wilhelmus, April 29, 1770; Anna, May 16, 1772; Teuntje, Feb. 28, 1774; Pieter, March 19, 1776; Pieter, Feb. 22. 1777; Elizabeth, April 20, 1779; Cornelia, Nov. 10, 1781; Sarah, Dec. 15, 1784; Cornelis, bp. Jan. 6, 1786; Hester, b. Dec. 13, 1788; Henry, b. May 2, 1791.

RYCKMAN, Wilhelmus G. [P. ?] m. Maria Fonda, d. Sept. 16, 1840, a. 81 y. Ch: b.; Gerrit, Jan. 26, 1798; Catalina, Nov. 22, 1799; Lawrence Fonda, Jan. 29, 1806; Peter, Oct. 6, 1806.

Ryerse, Gerrit, probably son of Reyer Elbertse, (see Gerritse). Ch: bp.; Wouter, August 12, 1683; Barent, Oct. 14, 1683, [1684 ?]; Goosen, March 7, 1686; Barent, June 4, 1688.

Ryverdingh, Pieter, in 1654–5 clerk and court messenger at Fort Orange and Beverwyck.

Saffin, George, and Jennette Stewart. Ch: James, bp. Nov. 6, 1756.

Salisbury, Capt. Sylvester, was commissioned, July 13, 1670, to be lieutenant of the governor's company of foot and commander of the fort at Albany, D. Lovelace, ensign. In 1673, he was sheriff of Rensselaerswyck; and was continued in the office of commander of the fort, until his death about 16₴. In 1682, his wid., then w. of Doctor Cornelis Van Dyck, administered on his estate. His son Francis settled in Catskill, where his descendants were numerous.

SALISBURY, Francois, of Catskil, m. Maria Gaasbeek. Ch: William, bp. Jan. 30, 1709; Abraham (?). (See also *Catskill Families*).

SALISBURY, William, m. Teuntje Staats, March 27, 1740. Ch: bp.; Sylvester, Jan. 27, 1741; Barent, Staats, April 3, 1749; Elisabeth, May 12, 1751. (See also *Catskill Families*).

SALISBURY, Francis, m. first, Lydia ....; secondly, Elsie Staats, Jan. 27, 1772. Ch: William, b. June 17, 1772. (See also *Catskill Families*).

SALISBURY, Joseph, and Margaret Oversandt. Ch: Margaret, b. March 12, 1793.

SALISBURY, James, and Catharine. Ch: David, b. Oct. 1, 1798.

SALISBURY, John, and Alida Martin. Ch: Gertrude, b. Sept. 10, 1798.

Sanders, Thomas, smith, of Amsterdam, m. Sarah Cornelise Van Gorcum, in New Amsterdam, Sept. 16, 1640. She d. in Albany, in Dec. 1669. He received a patent from Gov. Kieft for a house and 25 morgens of land on Manhattan island. In 1654, he owned a house and lot in Beverwyck, which he sold to Jan Van Aecken. He probably returned to New Amsterdam. Ch: bp. in New Amsterdam; *Robert*, Nov. 10, 1641; Cornelis, Nov. 25, 1643; Cornelis, Nov. 17, 1644; *Thomas*, July 14, 1647.

SANDERS, Thomas, bolter, of New York, son of the last, had the following ch. bp. in New York: Robert, Oct. 4, 1696; Styntje, Dec. 26, 1697; Robert, Jan. 1, 1700; Jacob, Oct. 19, 1701; Elsie, Oct. 27, 1703; Anneke, Jan. 30, 1706; Maritie, May 13, 1708; Jacob, June 9, 1712; Beatrix, Sept. 25, 1715.

SANDERS, Robert, son of Thomas and Sarah Van Gorcum, smith, 1667, merchant, 1692, settled in Albany as early as 1665. In 1691, he and Harmanus Myndertse Van der Bogart, received a patent for a mile square of land in Dutchess county, including the site of the city of Poughkeepsie. His first w. was Elsie Barentse; the second was Alida .... Ch: Helena, wife of Johannes Lansing; *Barent*; Maria, w. of Gerrit Roseboom; Sara (?), w. of Hendrik Greefraadt; Elsje, bp. July 13, 1683, buried, Dec. 31, 1732.

SANDERS, Barent, mayor, 1750–4, m. Maria, dau. of Evert Wendel, Sept. 19, 1704. He was buried in the church, June 22, 1738; She was buried in the church, Nov. 21, 1757. Ch: bp.; *Robert*, July 15, 1705; Maria, Dec. 3, 1707; *Johannes*, July 12, 1814.

SANDERS, Robert, merchant, m. first, Maria Lansing, Dec. 6, 1740; secondly, Elisabeth Schuyler, Jan. 11, 1747. His first w. was buried in the church, Feb. 15, 1743, and the second d. about 1763. He made a will May 7, 1765, proved June 6, 1765, and spoke of "my only son Pieter;" dau. Maria; Catharina; Debora; Elisabeth; and "my late wife." Ch: bp.; Barent, Feb. 6, 1743; Maria, Aug. 23, 1747; Maria, Aug. 23, 1747; Maria, Oct. 22, 1749; Catharina, Feb. 23, 1753; Barent, Dec. 16, 1753, buried Oct. 6, 1756; Pieter, Dec. 7, 1755; Debora, Feb. 9, 1758; Elisabeth, b. July 9, 1760; Elisabeth, bp. Dec. 20, 1761.

SANDERS, Johannes, m. Debora Glen, of Schenectady, Dec. 6, 1739. She was the only child and heir of Col. Jacob Glen, of *Scotia*. In 1765, by the purchase of the interest of John Glen, of Albany, and John Glen, Jr., of Schenectady, for £4,000, Johannes Sanders and w. became sole owners of the Glen estate in the present town of Glenville. He made a will Jan. 27, 1779, proved Feb. 11, 1783; in it he mentions his only son, Johannes; w. Debora, living; and daughters, Maria; Sarah; Elsje; and Margaret. He d. Sept. 13, 1782; she d. March 8, 1786. Ch. all b. in Schenectady; Maria, bp. June 14, 1740, w. of Johannes Beekman of Albany; Sarah, bp. Feb. 20, 1743, m. her cousin Jno. Sanderse Glen, of Scotia; Barent, b. Aug. 6,1744, d. Nov. 21,1746; Elisabeth, b. Sept. 19, 1746, d. Sept. 19, 1747; Elisabeth, b. Dec. 5, 1748, d. Feb. 5, 1776; Barent, b. Dec. 22,1750, d. Sept. 5, 1758; Elsje, bp. April 5, 1752, m. Schuyler Ten Eyck, of Schenectady; Jacob Glen, b. April 5, 1755, d. Sept. 18, 1765; Johannes, bp. Oct. 23, 1757, m. his cousin Debora, dau. of Robert Sanders, of Albany; Barent, b. Dec. 26, 1759, d. Dec. 31, 1759; Margaret, bp. June 24, 1764, m. Kiliaan Van Rensselaer, of Claverack.

SANDERS, Johannes, Jr. (son of the last), m. first, Debora Sanders, of Albany, Feb. 24, 1777, and secondly, Albertina Ten Broeck, of Clermont, Columbia county, in 1799. His first w. d. Nov. 28, 1793, the second d. July 30 (23), 1840, a. 79 y.; he d. March 30, 1834. Johannes Sanders, Jr.,inherited his father's estate, and resided in the ancient Glen house at Scotia. Ch. b. at S.; Elisabeth, Dec. 20, 1777, m. Doct. William Anderson, d. June 21,1850; Barent, Jan. 12, 1779, d. June 5, 1854, a. 75 y.; Robert, Sept. 8, 1781, d. Oct. 25, 1783; Sarah, Aug. 28, 1783, m. Peter S. Van Rensselaer, d. Aug. 13, 1869, a. 86 y.; Catharina, Oct. 10 (11), 1785, m. Gerard Beekman, of New York; Robert, July 18, 1787, d. Nov. 5, 1840; Jacob Glen, April 20 (22), 1789, d. March, 1867; Peter, Feb. 17, 1792, d. May 12, 1850; John, Dec. 27, 1802; Theodore (or Derrick Wessels), Oct. 20, 1804.

SANDERS, Barent, of Albany, m. Catalina Bleeker, June 9, 1810, d. June 5, 1854, a. 75 y. Ch: John, b. Feb. 1, 1812 ; Debora, b. Feb. 9, 1814.

Sans, Hendrick, and Catarina Ham. Ch: bp. ; Annatie, Feb. 19, 1754 ; Catarina, July 11, 1756.

Santhagen, Frerik, and Charlotte Roff. Ch: Johannes Frerik, b. Jan. 14, 1779.

Schaats, Domine Gideon, became the second minister of the church in Beverwyck, in 1652. Having become incapacitated by age to perform the duties of his office Domine Dellius became his coadjutor in 1683. He died in 1690 in his 83d year. The name of his first wife is not known ; on the 22d of August, 1683, he married widow Barentje Hendrickse in New York, he being then 75 years old ; she d. in 1688. Three of his children reached mature age ; Reynier, the eldest son ; Anneke, who married Thomas Davidtse Kikebell, of New York, with whom she had some disagreements which were finally amicably arranged ; and Bartholomeus who passed over to Holland, in 1670 and on his return settled in New York as a silversmith. According to the church records, he, with Catalyntje Schaats, [perhaps his wife] *abiit cum testimonio Neo Eboraca* in 1706. He is said to have died about 1720, leaving a son Reynier from whom are descended all of the name now in this country. *O'Callaghan's Hist. of N. Netherland.* He had a daughter Antje, bp. in N. Y. Feb. 27, 1715. [Bartholomeus Schaats m. Jacoba Kierstede, widow, in N. Y., April 21, 1734].

Schaets, Reynier, "Chyrurgion," eldest son of Domine S., was an early settler at Schenectady, where he was appointed justice of the peace by Leisler in 1689. He and a son were killed on the 9th of Feb. 1690, at the massacre and burning of the village by French and Indians. His widow Catrina Bensing, m. Jonathan Broadhurst, in Albany, April 23, 1696. Reynier Schaets left two children, a son Gideon, and dau. Agnietie, who m. Matthys Nak of Albany.

Schans (Schyaensch), Christiaen, m. Catharina Van Buren, Nov. 8, 1719. Ch: bp. : Catharina, Feb. 12, 1721 ; David, March 24, 1723 ; Andries, August 1, 1725 ; Maria, Jan. 8, 1727 ; Hendrik, June 14, 1749 ; Margarita, April 30, 1732 ; Anthonie, Sept. 22, 1734 ; Jeremias, Sept. 5, 1736.

SCHANS, Hendrick, and Catharina Ham. Ch : Andries, bp. Sept. 24, 1758.

Schants, David, m. Maritie Immerick, June 22, 1744. Ch: Christiaan, bp. May 5, 1745.

Schauns, see Jones.

Scheer, Petrus, of *Halve Maan,* m. Catharina (Maria) De Voe, Feb. 23, 1773. Ch : b. : Elizabeth, April 27, 1777 ; Isaac, August 3, 1780.

Schefer, Johannes, and Elizabeth Daniels. Ch : Jacob, bp. August 9, 1747.

Schenklin, Andrew, and.. Ch : Joseph Jan, and Elizabeth, *drielingen !* bp. Mar. Jan. 11, 1782.

Schermerhooren, Jacob Janse, brewer and trader was born in 1622, it is said in Waterland, Holland ; in 1654, his father was living in Amsterdam. He came out to Beverwyck, in 1636, and became a prosperous trader. He made his will May 20, 1688, and soon after died at Schenectady. He left a large estate for the time, amounting to 56,882 guilders. He married Jannetie Segers, dau. of Cornelis Segerse Van Voorhoudt, and had nine children : Reyer, Symon, Helena, w. of Myndert Harmense Vander Bogart

Jacob, Machtelt, w. of Johannes Beeckman, Cornelis, Jannetie, w. of Caspar Springsteen, Neeltie, w. of Barent Ten Eyck, and Lucas.

SCHERMERHOOREN, Reyer Jacobse, born in Beverwyck, in 1652, settled in Schenectady and became a prominent and influential citizen there. He m. in 1676, Ariaantje Arentse Bratt, widow of Helmer Otten, baker, of Albany. He made his will April 5, 1717, and d. Feb. 19, 1719. He had the following Ch ; Jan, bp. ; Oct. 14, 1685 ; Catalina, w. of Johannes Wemp ; Janneke. w. of Volkert Symonse Veeder, Jacob, and Arent, bp., Jan. 1693.

SCHERMERHOOREN, Symon Jacobse, was born in 1658. At the burning of Schenectady, Feb. 9, 1690, he rode to Albany by way of Niskayuna to carry the news of the massacre, although shot through the thigh and his horse wounded. His son Johannes, together with his three negroes, were killed on that fatal night. In 1691 he removed to New York where he died about 1696, leaving a widow and one son Arnout. He married Willempie Viele, probably dau. of Arnout Cornelise V. and had the following ch. bp. in Albany : Johannes, July 23, 1684, killed in 1690 ; Arnout, Nov. 7, 1686 ; Maria, bp. in N. Y., 1693 ; Jannetic, bp. in N. Y., March 24, 1695.

SCHERMERHOOREN, Jacob Jacobse, resided in the manor of Rensselaerswyck and was master of the sloop *Star* plying between New York and Albany, in 1681-4. He was buried at Papsknee, below Albany, June 20, 1743. He married Gerritie Hendrickse, [Van Buren] and had the following Ch: bp. ; in Albany ; Jacob, Dec. 27, 1685 ; Hendrik, Oct. 16, 1687 ; Cornelis, Sept. 22, 1689 ; Magtelt, Jan. 3, 1692 ; Jannetie, May 6, 1694 ; Elizabeth, August 28, 1698 ; Johannes, July 21, 1700 ; Reyer, Feb. 21, 1702.

SCHERMERHOOREN, Cornelis Jacobse, was living in the of Manor Livingston, near Kinderhook, in 1720. He had previously been master of the sloop *Star*. He married first ; Maritie Hendrickse Van Buren, Jan. 21, 1695 and secondly. Margarita, Albertse, Feb. 6, 1713. Ch: bp. : in Albany Jacob, Oct. 4, 1696 ; Hendrik, in N. Y., Sept. 9, 1699 ; Hendrik, Feb. 23, 1701 ; Cornelis, Sept. 9, 1705 ; Lysbeth, Feb. 16, 1707 ; Jannetie, April 23, 1710 ; Jannetie, May 24, 1719 ; Jacobus, July 3, 1720.

SCHERMERHOOREN, Lucas Jacobse, settled in Raritan, N. J., and is said to have married Elizabeth Dame, in 1700. He had two Ch: bp. ; in N. Y., Jannetie, Oct. 29, 1701 ; Sophya, April 7, 1703.

SCHERMERHOOREN, Arnout, son of Symon Jacobse, of New York, had the following Ch : bp. there ; Catharina, May 10, 1711 ; Willemyntje, Oct. 14, 1713 ; Johannes, July 13, 1715 ; Aeltie, May 19, 1717 ; Jannetie, Sept. 20, 1719.

SCHERMERHOOREN, Arent, of Schenectady, m. Antje Fonda, April 16, 1714. Ch : Catalyntje, bp. Oct. 10, 1714. See also *Schenectady Families.*

Schermerhoorn, Jacob, m. Margarita Tillery, Nov. 20, 1715.

SCHERMERHOORN, Jacob, and Susanna.... Ch : Catryna, bp. ; July 10, 1715.

SCHERMERHOORN, Jacob Cornelise, and Antje.... [A Jacob Schermerhoorn, and Agniete Van Vechten, were m. in Albany June 23, 1714 ; another Jacob S. m. Johanna Beekman, May 4, 1718.] Ch: bp. : Maria, March 6, 1717 ; Marretie, Oct. 12, 1718 ; Cornelis, Jan. 1, 1719 ; Marten, Sept. 11, 1720 ; Reyer, April 9, 1721 ;

Cornelis, Sept. 23, 1722; Maria, Jan. 30, 1723; Gerritie, Oct. 11, 1724; Hendrik, Sept. 25, 1726; Johannes, May 13, 1727; Jannetie, Feb. 25, 1728; Philip, April 17, 1737.

SCHERMERHOORN, Hendrik, and Elsie.... Ch: Gerritje, b. Nov. 24, *op de flakte* Loonenburgh, and bp. in the Luth. Church, at Klinkenberg, Dec. 16, 1716; Johannes, bp. August 31, 1718; Geesie, bp. Nov. 27, 1720; Elizabeth, bp. May 5, 1723; Jacob, bp. June 13, 1725; Roeloff, bp. Jan. 15, 1727.

SCHERMERHOORN, Reyer, blacksmith of Rhinebeck, [son of Jacob Jacobse] m. Geertie Ten Eyck, July 4, 1724. He made a will July 16, 1759, proved May 26, 1768; in which he spoke of wife *Maritie*, brother-in-law Johannes B. Ten Eyck, and children Barent, Jacob, Jan the youngest, Johannes, Jannetie, Catharine, and Gerritie, w. of Gerrit Harmenci; of these Ch: the following were bp. in Albany, Barent, May 17, 1725; Gerritie, April 2, 1727; Reyer, June 5. 1737.

SCHERMERHOORN, Johannes, [son of Jacob Jacobse], and Engeltie ... Ch: bp.; Gerritie, April 30, 1732; Jacob, May 16, 1736; Samuel, July 2, 1738; Dirk, March 23, 1740; Gerritje, March 7, 1742.

Schermerhorn, Jacob, Jr., of manor of Livingston [son of Jacob Jacobse,] and Cathalyntje . .. He made will Nov. 19, 1760, proved July 21, 1761, in which he mentioned ch: Cornelis; Jacob; Teunis; William; Hendrick; Marten; Neeltie, w. of Johannes Radclift; and Polly, w. of Jeroo Halenbeck, of Claverack: of these ch., Jacob was bp. Nov. 1, 1741; and Cornelis, April 24, 1743.

SCHERMERHORN, Cornelis, m. Maria Winne, Oct. 22, 1742. Ch: bp.; Jacob, June 12, 1743; Philip, Jan. 28, 1750; Dirkie, June 14, 1752.

SCHERMERHORN, Jacob, Jr., m. first, Elisabeth Whitaker, and secondly, Annatie Stroop, about 1773. Ch: b.; Neeltie, Nov. 11, 1767; Rebecca, March 6, 1770; Maria, Dec. 3, 1773.

SCHERMERHORN, Jacob C. and Gerritje Schermerhorn. Ch: bp.; Marytje, Dec. 17, 1769; Marytje, Aug. 16, 1778; Cathalyna, Jan. 20, 1782; Gerritje, b. Feb. 5, 1787.

SCHERMERHORN, Ryer, and Dirkie Van Buren. Ch: Antie, b. June 26, 1776.

SCHERMERHORN, Johannes, and Margarita Folksby. Ch: Jannetie, bp. June 23, 1777.

SCHERMERHORN, John W., and Cathalyntje (Van) Valkenburg. Ch: Cornelis, bp. March 1, 1778.

SCHERMERHORN, Hendrik, and Cornelia Lansing. Ch: Cornelia, b. July 1, 1778.

SCHERMERHORN, Ryer B., of Albany Co., m. Marytje Beveers, Feb. 2, 1775. Ch: Willem, b. April 11, 1779.

SCHERMERHORN, Jacob, and Geertruy .... Ch: Barent, b. April 19, 1779.

SCHERMERHORN, Dirk, and Cathalyntje .... Ch: Susanna, b. March 20, 1779.

SCHERMERHORN, Daniel, and Maria Van Der Poel, Ch: Jacob, b. Jan. 7, 1780.

SCHERMERHORN, Johannes, and Bata Van Valkenburgh. Ch: Neeltie, b. Dec. 25, 1781

SCHERMERHORN, Jacob J., and Aaltie Schermerhorn. Ch: Cornelia, b. April 15, 1783.

SCHERMERHORN, Jacob, and Annatie Kenneda. Ch: Samuel, b. April 17, 1787.

SCHERMERHORN, Cornelius, and Catharina Van Rensselaer. Ch: b.; Henry Rensselaer, March 24, 1797; Alida, Dec. 30, 1799.

Scherp, see Sharp.

Schever (Scheber, Schiever), Hendrick, and Marytje .... Ch: Catharyna, bp. Dec. 17, 1738; Christina, bp. June 7, 1741; Philip, bp. Jan. 26, 1743.

SCHEVER, Diederich, and Maria Margarita Hendrich. Ch: Annelse, bp. Aug. 22, 1756.

Scholtus, Johannes, and Elisabeth Doth. Ch: Hendrik, b. July 20, 1768.

Schoon, Jan Willemse, farmer in colony Rensselaerswyck, in 1660.

Schoonmaker, Jan Barentse (Van Edam) came to Beverwyck in 1636, and was still there in 1665.

SCHOONMAKER, Harmen, owned a house lot in Albany, in 1676.

SCHOONMAKER, Michael, and Catharina Oatner. Ch: Anna, bp. March 11, 1754.

SCHOONMAKER, Johannes, and Aaltie (Alida) Burhans. Ch: Hendrikus, bp. May 21, 1775; Abraham, b. Oct. 20, 1777; Margarita, b. Margrita, b. May 27, 1780; Cornelis, b. Jan. 14, 1783.

SCHOONMAKER, Tjerk, and Cornelia Acker. Ch: Johannes, b. March 17, 1786.

SCHOONMAKER, John, Jr., m. Magdalena Honser (Hansen), Oct. 5, 1790. Ch: John, b. July 22, 1791; Maria, b. Dec. 18, 1792.

Schouten, Gerrit Jacobse, of Kinderhook, m. Lysbeth Arnoutse (Arnolds) Eli [Viele?], June 17, 1693. Ch: bp.; Abigail, Jan. 20, 1695; Meesje, June 28, 1696; Cornelis, Jan. 8, 1699; Dorothee, Feb. 5, 1701.

Schouter (Schoute, Shuter?), of Niskayuna, and Cypjen .... Ch: bp.; Jurriaen, March 23, 1684; Jan, April 18, 1686; Jacob, March 2, 1690.

Schram, Johannes, and Eva (Van) Valkenburgh. Ch: Abraham, b. Jan. 7, 1774.

Schreydel, Jan Lod: m. Neyltie (Heyltie) Van Woerd, Oct. 31, 1727. Ch: Eva, bp. July 14, 1728.

Schufeldt, (Schoufeld, Zoufeld) Adam, and Neeltje Freer. Ch: b.; Annatie, Jan. 8, 1764; Theunis, Nov. 20, 1766; Willem, Sept. 9, 1768: Elisabeth, Nov. 10, 1769; Zacharias, Feb; 23, 1772.

SCHUFELDT (Zoufeld), Hannes, and Sara (Elisabeth) Freer. Ch: b.; Petrus, July 22, bp. June 30 (*sic*), 1765; Maria, Jan. 2, 1767; Neeltie, April 14, 1770.

Schut (Schuidt) alias Dommelaer, Willem Janse, tailor, was in Beverwyck, 1657-68.

Schuyler. Two brothers of this name, David and Philip Pieterse Schuyler, were among the early settlers of Beverwyck, and were the progenitors of the numerous families bearing this name in Albany and vicinity. They came from Amsterdam.

SCHUYLER, David Pieterse, m. Catalyn, dau. of Abraham Verplanck, Oct. 13, 1657, in New Amsterdam. On the 29th Nov., 1692, he lived near the northeast corner of the city walls by the water side, on the south corner of Broadway and Steuben street, and in 1699 she petitioned for an addition of 14 feet to the north side of her lot, which was refused by the city authorities, because "it will reach too near ye Citty Stockadoes." This lot was occupied in 1709 by Jacobus and Abraham, his sons. His sons who lived to maturity and had families in Albany were : *Pieter ; Jacobus ; Abraham ; David ;* and *Myndert.*

SCHUYLER, Pieter Davidtse, was a trader and in 1694, lived in Claverack ; in 1685, he was commissioned judge of the court of Oyer and Terminer for Albany county ; in May, 1696, he was lately deceased. He m. Alida Van Slichtenhorst, widow of Gerrit Goosense Van Schaick, and dau. of Brant Arents Van S. Ch : Gerrit (?) Johannes, bp. Dec. 3, 1684 ; Catalina, bp. Oct. 10 1686 ; David, bp. Dec. 26, 1688 ; Alida, bp. Jan. 21, 1693 ; Philip, bp. Oct. 28, 1694 ; Pieter, bp. Aug. 9, 1696.

SCHUYLER, Jacobus, Davidtse, lived on the lot now on the south corner of Broadway and Steuben street. He d. March 22, 1706-7. His first wife was Catalyntje Wendel ; he m. secondly Susanna Wendel, June 3, 1704, and had one Ch : Catalyntje, bp. April 21, 1706.

SCHUYLER, Abraham Davidtse, in 1709, resided upon the lot which his father had occupied on the south corner of Broadway and Steuben street. In 1684 he was master of the sloop *Hopewell* plying between New York and Albany. In his will, made Dec. 15, 1709, he speaks of the five following children, and of his wife and his brothers-in-law Wessel and Samuel Ten Broeck. He m. Geertruy Ten Broeck, Nov. 11, 1691. Ch : David, bp. Nov. 30, 1692 ; Christina, bp. July 21, 1695 ; Dirk, bp. July 28, 1700 ; Abraham, bp. Aug. 27, 1704 ; Jacobus, bp. March 23, 1707.

SCHUYLER, David Davidtse, was mayor of Albany, 1706-7. He m. first, Elsje, dau. of Harmen Rutgers (?) Jan. 1, 1694 ; and secondly, Elizabeth Marschalk in New York, May 3, 1719. She d. Sept. 24, 1722. Ch : Catrina, bp. Nov. 25, 1694 ; David, bp. April 11, 1697 ; Hermanus, bp. July 21, 1700 ; Catharina, bp. Dec. 19, 1703 ; Myndert, bp. Oct. 7, 1711 (admitted freeman of N. Y. city, 1734, m. Elizabeth Wessels, June 21, 1735) ; Anthony, bp. Oct. 30, 1715 ; Elizabeth, bp. in N. Y. , March 6, 1720.

SCHUYLER, Capt. Myndert (Davidse), merchant ; mayor of Albany, 1719-21, and 1723-5. In 1703, he occupied a lot on the south side of State street, formerly Gerrit Bancker's, the third east from South Pearl street. He was buried in the church, Oct. 21, 1755. He m. Rachel Cuyler in New York, Oct. 26, 1693 ; she was buried in the church, July 24, 1747. Ch : Anna, bp. Feb. 28, 1697, m. Johannes DePeyster ; Rachel, named in her father's will.

Col. Philip Pieterse Schuyler, the better known of the two brothers of this name who first settled in New Netherland, is usually recognized as the ancestor of all the Schuylers of Albany and vicinity. Like his brother David, he had a numerous family, who became connected by marriage with some of the most respectable families of the Province. He was a trader and farmer and resided on a bouwery, at the *Flats* below the present village of West Troy ; died March 9, 168¾, and was buried on the 11th in the church. His wife, Margareta Van Slichtenhorst, dau. of Brant Aertse Van S., he m. Dec. 12 (22), 1650. Ch : Guysbert, b. July 2, 1652 ; Geertruy, b. Feb. 4, 1654, m. Stephanus Van Cortlandt, of N. Y., Sept. 10 (Oct. 3), 1671 ; Alida, b. Feb. 28, 1656, m. first, Rev. Nicolaas Van Rensselaer, and secondly, Robert Livingston ; Pieter, b. Sept. 17, 1657 ; Brant, b. Dec. 18, 1659 ; Arent, b. June 25, 1662 ; Sybilla, b. Nov. 12, 1664, d. aged 4 weeks ; Philip, b. Feb. 8, 1666 ; Johannes, b. April 5, 1668 ; Margareta, b. Jan. 2, 1672.

SCHUYLER, Col. Pieter (Philipse), merchant of Albany, was the first mayor of the city, 1686-1694. In 1703, he occupied a house and lot on the east side of Broadway at the "Great bridge," across the *Rutten Kil* just south of State street. His lot extended back to the river. He m. first, Engeltie Van Schaick ; and secondly, Maria Van Rensselaer, Sept. 14, 1691. He was buried Feb. 22, 1724. Ch : baptized ; Philippus Oct. 1684 ; Anna, Sept. 12, 1686 ; Geertruy, Aug. 17, 1689 ; Maria, May 8, 1692 ; Geertruy, Feb. 11, 1694, m. Johannes Joh. Lansing ; Philippus, Jan. 15, 1696 ; Jeremias and Pieter, twins, Jan. 12, 1698.

SCHUYLER, Brandt (Philipse), lived in Broad street, New York, in 1686. He m. first, Cornelia Van Cortlandt, July 12, 1682 ; and secondly, Margarita Van Wyck, April 16, 1741 ; d. Aug. 15, 1752. Ch : baptized in New York, Philippus, Nov. 6, 1683 ; Oloff, Dec. 12, 1686 ; Johannes, Jan. 15, 1690.

SCHUYLER, Arent (Philipse), trader, was admitted freeman of New York city in 1695 ; before 1725, he was probably settled on the *Second* or Passaic river, at Belleville, N. Y. He m. 1st, Janneke Teller, Nov. 26, 1684 ; 2d, Swantie Dyckhuyse about Jan. 1703. Ch : baptized in Albany, Margareta, Sept, 27, 1685 ; Philippus, Sept. 11, 1687 ; Maria, Oct. 6, 1689 : Judik, March 13, 1692 ; Casparus in N. Y., May 5, 1695 ; Wilhelmus, June 2, 1700.

SCHUYLER, Philip (Philipse), m. Elizabeth De Meyer of New York, August 24, 1687. Ch : Nicolaas, bp. Sept. 21, 1692, in N. Y.

SCHUYLER, Capt. Johannes, trader, youngest son of Philip Pieterse, held a captain's commission in 1690, at the age of 22 yrs, and led an expedition into Canada ; he had great influence with the Indians ; was mayor of Albany, 1703-6 ; in 1712, his house lot was 55 ft. wide (Rynland measure) on the south corner of Pearl and State streets, running back to the *Rutten kil.* He d. July 25, 1747. His wife Elisabeth Staats, widow of Johannes Wendel, was m. April 25, 1695 ; buried in the church June 5, 1737. Ch : bp. ; Philip, Dec. 25, 1695, killed by the French at Saratoga, Nov. 28, 1745 ; Johannes, Oct. 31, 1697 ; Margarita, the "American Lady," Jan. 12, 1701 ; Catalyntje, March 5, 1704, m. Cornelis Cuyler.

SCHUYLER, Gerrit or Gerardus [son of Pieter and Alida Van Slichtenhorst], was admitted freeman of New York city in 1702, and m. Aagje De Grood, there Sept. 28, 1703. Ch : bp. ; in N. Y. Alida, Nov. 19, 1704 ; Janneke, Jan. 29, 1707 ; Aegje, Jan. 25, 1710 ; Pieter, Jan. 9, 1712 ; Aegje, March 20, 1715 ; Johanna Gouda, June 2, 1717 ; Maria, Feb. 10, 1720.

SCHUYLER, Col. Philip [son of Pieter and Maria Van Rensselaer], m. his cousin Margarita ["Aunt Schuyler"] dau. of Johannes Philipse. He lived on the *Flats* [West Troy] and d. Feb. 16, 1758.

SCHUYLER, Philip [son of Brandt S., of N. Y.?], m. Ann Elisabeth Staats, dau. of Dr. Samuel S., of N. Y., Aug. 28, 1713. Ch. bp. in N. Y. : Johanna, Oct. 17, 1714 ; Brandt, July 21, 1717 ; Samuel, June 7, 1719.

SCHUYLER, Jr., Philip [son of Arent?], m. Sara Roselevelt, in N. Y., Feb. 28, 1718. Ch : Sara, bp. in N. Y., Aug. 19, 1719.

SCHUYLER, Nicolaas [son of Philip and Elisabeth De Meyer], was a surveyor, m. Elsie Wendel, Dec. 2, 1714, was buried July 8, 1748. Ch : bp. ; Elisabeth, Sept. 18, 1715 ; Philip, Oct. 27, 1717 ; Harmanus ?

SCHUYLER, David [son of Abraham, and Geertruy Ten Broeck], had a lot in 1735 on the south corner of Broadway and Steuben street; m. first, Anna Bratt, July 17, 1720, who d. Sept. 24, 1722ǁ and secondly, Maria ...., about 1734. Ch: bp.; Alida, Feb. 12, 1721; Pieter, March 10, 1723; Abraham, Nov. 15, 1734; Abraham, Dec. 25, 1735.

SCHUYLER, Pieter, Jr. [son of Pieter and Maria Van Rensselaer], m. first, Catharina Groesbeck, Nov. 4, 1722, and secondly, Geertruy Schuyler, dau. of Johannes S. He was buried at the *Flats* Sept. 2, 1753. Ch: bp.; Pieter, Feb. 20, 1723; Elisabeth, Jan. 3, 1725; Maria, Jan. 22, 1727; Stephanus, Oct. 3, 1728; Stephanus, Dec. 13, 1729; Stephanus, April 2, 1732; Philip, April 22, 1736; Col. Philip P. Schuyler d. June 3, 1808, a. 73 y.; Maria, Dec. 20, 1738; Maria, May 7, 1741; Johannes, Aug. 14, 1743; Cornelia, July 26, 1746; Johannes, Dec. 10, 1749.

SCHUYLER, Jeremias [son of Pieter and Maria Van Rensselaer], in 1728, lived on the east side of Broadway in the first ward, by the bridge over the *Rutten* kil, just south of State street, He m. Susanna ....; was buried at the *Flats*, Dec. 10, 1753; she was buried June 17, 1747. Ch; bp.: Magdalena, Nov. 3, 1723; Maria, April 17, 1726; Pieter, Sept. 22, 1728; Thomas, Nov. 15, 1734; Margrieta, Sept. 3, 1738.

SCHUYLER, Harmanus [son of David and Elsie Rutgers], was admitted freeman of N. Y. city in 1728; m. Jannetie Bancker in Albany, Dec. 1, 1722. Ch. bp. in Albany: David, Feb. 7, 1725; Evert, Aug. 28, 1726.

SCHUYLER, Johannes, Jr. [son of Johannes, and Elizabeth Staats], m. Cornelia Van Courtlandt of N. Y., Oct. 18, 1723. [He or another of this name was mayor of Albany, 1741-2.] Ch: bp.; Geertruy (?) w. of Pieter Schuyler, Jr.; Catharina, July 14, 1728; Philip, Oct. 17, 1731; Philip [Maj. Gen.] Nov. 11, 1733; Cortlandt, July 9, 1735; Stephanus, Aug. 14, 1737; Elizabeth, Oct. 8, 1738; Oliver, Feb. 22, 1741. [Johannes Schuyler, Jr., was buried at the *Flats* Nov. 6, 1741; another Johannes S. was buried in the church March 2, 1747; Johannes S., Jr., was buried in the church Nov. 7, 1746; and another Johannes S. was buried in the church July 22, 1740.]

SCHUYLER, Abraham, [son of Abraham, and Geertruy Ten Broeck,] m. Catharine Staats, Sept. 7, 1732. Ch: Christina, bp. June 20, 1733.

SCHUYLER, Abraham A. [perhaps same as last] and Maria .... Ch: Hendrick, bp. Feb. 8, 1738.

SCHUYLER, Jacobus [son of Abraham and Geertruy Ten Broeck,] m. Geertruy Staats, Nov. 12, 1735. Ch: Geertruy, bp. May 2, 1736; Geertruy, bp. Oct. 21, 1737; Dirk, bp. March 16, 1740; Neeltie, bp. Aug. 15, 1742; Anna, bp. April 21, 1745; Neeltje, bp. Nov. 22, 1747; Barent Staats, bp. Feb. 18, 1750; Christina, bp. Dec. 24, 1752.

SCHUYLER, Harmanus [son of Nicolaas, and Elsie Wendel], m. Christina Ten Broeck of Claverack, Sept. 4, 1754. Ch: Nicolaas, bp. June 22, 1755; Samuel, bp. Nov. 20, 1757; Elsie, bp. March 9, 1760; Dirk, bp. Dec. 6, 1761; Johannes *geboren gisteren*, bp. Aug. 1, 1763; Maria, b. Feb. 1, 1766; Philip, b. Dec. 12, 1767; Maria, b. April 25, 1769; Philip, b. Aug. 22, 1771.

SCHUYLER, Gen. Philip, Jr., [son of Johannes and Cornelia Van Cortlandt,] m. Catrina Van Rensselaer dau. of Johannes V. R., Sept. 7, 1755, d. Nov. 18,

1804, a. 71y. Ch: Engeltie, bp. Feb. 22, 1756; Elizabeth, b. Aug. 7, 1757, m. Alexander Hamilton, Dec. 9, 1780, d. in Washington, Nov. 7 (?), 1854; Margarita, bp. Sept. 24, 1758, m. Stephen Van Rensselaer; Cornelia, bp. Aug. 1, 1761; John Bradstreet, bp. Oct. 8, 1763; John Bradstreet *in huis gedoopt* July 23, 1765; d. in Saratoga Aug. 19, 1795; Philip Jeremias, b. Jan. 20, 1768, d. Feb. 21, 1835, in N. Y.; Rensselaer b. Jan. 29, 1773; Cornelia Lynch b. Dec. 22, 1776, m. ...Morton, d. in Philadelphia, July 5, 1808; Cortlandt, b. May 15, 1778; Catharina Van Rensselaer, b. Feb. 20, 1781, m. first Samuel Malcolm son of Gen. Malcolm, and secondly Maj. James Cochrane, son of Surgeon Gen. Cochrane of the Revolutionary army, and d. in Oswego, Aug. 26, 1857.

SCHUYLER, Stephanus [son of Pieter, ·Jr., and Catharina Groesbeck], m. Engeltie Van Vechten. Ch: Pieter, bp. May 14, 1758; Geertruy, bp. Jan. 4, 1760; Reuben, bp. Jan. 10, 1762; Philip, b. Aug. 21, 1763; Catharina, b. Oct. 9, 1765; Johannes, b. May 23, 1768; Jeremie, b. Sept. 27, 1771.

SCHUYLER, Stephen or Stephanus, J. [son of Johannes and Cornelia Van Cortlandt], m. Lena Ten Eyck, April 29, 1763. Ch: born; Johannes, b. Jan. 4, 1764; Tobias, b. Nov. 27, 1765; Philip, b. Jan. 24, 1768; Hendrick Ten Eyck, Dec. 31, 1772; Philip Cortland, July 30, 1775; Cornelia, Nov. 1, 1777; Barent, April 12, 1780; Stephen Van Rensselaer, Oct. 3, 1783; Cortlandt, bp. Sept. 24, 1786, d. July 31, 1858, a. 72 y., and was buried from his residence in Tivoli Hollow.

SCHUYLER, Abraham [son of David and Maria ....], m. Eva Beeckman, Dec. 2, 1763, d. May 27, 1812, a. 76 y.; she d. July 17, 1803, a. 69 y. 5 mo. 3 d..... Ch: born; Maria, Dec. 18, 1764; Martin Beeckman, March 2, 1767; David, March 31, 1769; Maria, Feb. 14, 1771; Geertruy, July 16, 1773; Hendrik, Sept. 8, 1775.

SCHUYLER, Col. Philip Pieterse [son of Pieter, Jr. and Catharina Groesbeck], m. Annatie Wendel, April 21, 1765, d. June 3, 1808, a. 73. Ch: b.; Catharina, March 23, 1766; Elizabeth, May 4, 1771; Geertruy, June 26, 1773; Pieter, July 15, 1776; Maria, Sept. 11, 1778; Stephen, Nov. 17, 1780, d. Feb. 5, 1845, a. 66 y.; Ariaentje, Sept. 15, 1782; Lucas, March 9, 1785.

SCHUYLER, Dirk, [son of Jacobus and Geertruy Staats], m. Maria Van Deusen, in N. Y, April 26, 1764. Ch: b.; Jacobus, July 29, 1768; Catharina, Nov. 20, 1770; Willem Van Deusen, May 9, 1773; Geertruy, July 25, 1775.

SCHUYLER, Pieter, Jr., m. Geertruy Lansing, Jan. 17, 1767. Ch: Anna, b. Feb. 6, 1769.

SCHUYLER, Reuben, [son of Stephanus and Engeltie Van Vechten], m. Sara Foss. Ch: Sara, b. March 8, 1785.

SCHUYLER, John Bradstreet, [son of Gen. Philip, and Catrina Van Rensselaer], m. Elizabeth Van Rensselaer, Sept. 18, 1787, d. in Saratoga, August 19, 1795. Ch: Philip, b. Oct. 26, 1788; Stephen Van Rensselaer, b. May 4, and d. May 25, 1790.

SCHUYLER, Pieter S. [son of Stephanus, and Engeltie Van Vechten], m. Caty Cuyler, Dec. 2, 1789. Ch: b.; Engeltie, Sept. 8, 1790; Angelica, Jan. 30, 1794; Angelica, Oct. 1, 1798, m. Sander Lansing, Jr., and d. March 24, 1863, a. 67 y. buried at West Troy; John Cuyler, Dec. 1, 1801.

SCHUYLER, Harmanus P., [son of Philip P. and Annatie Wendell ?], m. first, Mary Staats, Oct. 2, 1790; and secondly, Maria Dean, about 1800. [Harmanus P. S., and Hester Beeckman, m. Feb. 16, 1797.] His first wife d. March 24, 1794, a. 20 y.; his wife Mary Dean d. Dec. 28, 1810, a. 33 y. 2 mo, 28 d.; he d. in Niskayuna, Oct. 13, 1822, a. 53 y. Ch: born; Mary, July 8, 1791; Philip, Jan. 26, 1793; Mary Anna, July 27, 1800.

SCHUYLER, John S., [son of Stephen J., and Lena Ten Eyck], m. Catharine Cuyler; she d. at Watervliet, Sept. 28, 1855, a. 92 y. Ch : born; Stephen, Nov. 26, 1793; Stephen, June 30, 1797; Helena, Jan. 16, 1803.

SCHUYLER, Philip S., [son of Stephanus, and Engeltie Van Vechten ?], m. Rachel Van den Bergh, July 1, 1789. Ch: born; Stephen, Oct. 27, 1794; a child name not registered, Dec. 12, 1796; Abraham, Sept. 5, 1799; Lucas Van Vechten, Nov. 20, 1801.

SCHUYLER, Jeremiah, [son of Stephanus and Engeltie Van Vechten ?], m. Jane Cuyler. She d. at Watervliet, Feb. 15, 1832. Ch: Cornelius, b. July 1, 1795; Anne Jane, b. May 28, 1797.

SCHUYLER, Philip S. [son of Stephen, and Lena Ten Eyck ?], m. Cynthia Carpenter. Ch: b. ; John Carpenter, Oct. 2, 1801; Helena, Aug. 30, 1803.

Schyarch (Church), William and Mary .... Ch: Jeremias, bp. May 2, 1725.

Scott, Robert, m. Agnietje Williams, May 23, 1736. Ch: bp. ; Jan, Jan. 26, 1737; Hilletje, Nov. 8, 1738; Margarieta, Dec. 14, 1740.

SCOTT, Matthew, and Mary Hue. Ch: Marytje, bp. Aug. 17, 1746.

SCOTT, John, and Mary .... Ch: Elisabeth, bp. Jan. 15, 1749.

SCOTT, David, and Marytje Wendell. Ch: b. ; Alexander, Nov. 16, 1765; Claartje (?), June 18, 1768; Susanna, July 7, 1771; Claartje, July 25, 1773.

Seaton, William, and Cathy Connick. Ch: Alida, b. April 21, 1775.

Seaman, Isaac, and Margaret .... Ch: Mary, b. Jan. 11, 1795.

See, David, and Leentje Snyder. Ch: Joseph, bp. Jan. 6, 1782.

Segers is the surname of a family in Albany which in earlier times was called *Van Voorhoudt*. Cornelis Segerse Van Voorhoudt, the first settler, came to Beverwyck in 1642, " and succeeded Vander Donck on the farm called Welysburgh, on Castle Island." His wife was Bregie Jacobsen; she d. April, 1667. In 1663, they made a joint will, she being then indisposed, and mentioned the following ch., all living save Claas : Cornelis, Claas, Seger, Jannetje, w. of Jacob Janse Schermerhoorn; Neeltje, w. of Hans Carelse Noorman; and Lysbeth, w. of Francis Boon.

[SEGERS,] Seger Cornelise, m. Jannetie, dau. of Teunis Dirkse Van Vechten.

[SEGERS,] Claas Cornelisse, m. Bregje Maryns, and was accidentally killed in a brawl by Andries Herpertsen in 1662. After his death his widow m. Jan Tyssen Goes and d. in 1663. In 1663, the following ch., of Claas Cornelise Van Voorhoudt were living: Maryn, a. 12 y. ; Jacob, a. 10 y. ; Lysbeth, a. 8 y. ; Tryntje, a. 5 y.

SEGERS, Johannes, m. Breechie Wielaars [Wheeler ?], June 19, 1719. In 1730, he bought a lot on the east side of South Pearl next to Jacob Egmont's lot

105 ft. north from Hudson street. Ch : bp. Evert (?) : Hilletie, Jan. 20, 1723; Hendrik, April 25, 1724; Thomas, Jan. 16, 1726, d. March 25, 1809, a. 84 y. ; Roeloff, Aug. 13, 1727; Johannes, Nov. 9, 1729; Albertus, Oct. 21, 1733; Hilletic, Jan. 8, 1735; Jacob, Oct. 31, 1736; Josyntje, July 31, 1738.

SEGERS, Staats, m, Susanna Bratt, Dec. 6, 1740, Ch: bp. Gerrit, March 22, 1741; Pieter, Dec. 5, 1742; Frederic, June 10, 1744; Johannes, Jan. 24, 1748; Adam, Feb. 25, 1750; Maria, May 29,1752; Adriaan, Jan. 5, 1755: Staats, May 30, 1756.

SEGERS, Evert, [son of Johannes and Brechie Wielaars], m. Sara Orchert [Orchard], April 21, 1744. Ch: bp. ; Johannes, Feb. 17, 1745 ; Brechie, Nov. 22, 1747; Thomas, Dec. 11, 1748; Wyntje, March 17, 1751; Josina, March 8, 1752; Hendrick, Sept. 15, 1754; Jacobus, Nov. 25, 1759; Brechie, b. May 14, 1762; George, May 30, 1765.

SEGERS, Thomas, [son of Johannes and Brechje Wielaars], m. first, Josina Wheeler, and secondly, Judith Hoogland, about 1758. His first wife was buried, Sept. 13, 1753; he d. March 25, 1809, a. 84 y. Ch: Johannes, June 26, 1748; Bregie, bp. Oct. 15, 1758; Adriaanus Hogeland, b. July 27, 1762; Hadrian Hoogeland, b. Feb. 29, 1764.

SEGERS, Johannes, [son of Johannes and Breghie Wielaars ?]. Ch: bp. ; Maria, March 27, 1748 ; Pieter, Feb. 20, 1751; Gerrit, June 24, 1753; Johannes, Dec. 7, 1755; Maria, April 2, 1758; Lydia, *geboren voor* 6 *weken*, May 6, 1764; Frederic, b. Aug. 20, 1767.

SEGERS, Roeloff, [son of Johannes and Breghie Wielaars], m. first, Margarita Arnold, who was buried, March 9, 1752; and secondly, Lidia Harty, Feb. 25, 1754. Ch: Margarita, bp. Feb. 23, 1752; Jacobus, bp. Oct. 20, 1754; Johannes, bp. Feb. 4, 1767.

SEGERS, Johannes, and Catarina Pieterse. She was buried June 17, 1757. Ch: Johannes, bp. March 30, 1755 ; Thomas, bp. June 5, 1757.

SEGERS, Hendrick [son of Johannes and Breghie Wielaars], m. first, Elizabeth Haver, who was buried Sept. 2, 1757; and secondly, Margarita Koen, April 16, 1761. Ch : Johannes, bp. Aug. 28, 1757; Elizabeth, b. Oct. 15, 1762; Elizabeth, b. April 1, 1767; Juriaan, b. March 20, 1769; Bregtje, b. July 25, 1771; Simon, b. March 26, 1781.

SEGERS, Gerrit, m. Wyntje Oliver, July 15, 1757; Ch: Antje, bp. June 15, 1758; Maria, bp. Aug. 5, 1759; Jan, bp. Oct. 11, 1761; Lydia, b. Jan. 9, 1764; Lydia, b. Sept. 13, 1766; Sara, b. March 11, 1769.

SEGERS, Gerrit, [son of Staats, and Susanna Bratt ?] m. Mary Pengburn (Bengwood), Dec. 11, 1766. Ch: William, b. Feb. 10, 1770; Marytje, b. Oct. 12, 1771; Adam, b. March 5, 1773.

SEGERS, Johannes E. [son of Evert and Sara Orchard], m. first, Sara Brook; and secondly, Sara Pengburn about 1771. Ch : Sara, b. Aug. 16, 1770; Susanna, b. May 1, 1772; Adam, b. July 25, 1783.

SEGERS, Pieter, [son of Staats and Susanna Bratt,] m. Annatje Howk (Huik). Ch: Susanna, bp. March 3, 1771; Marytje b. Aug. 24, 1780.

SEGERS, Johannes [son of Evert, and Sara Orchard ?] Ch: Evert, b. Aug. 10, bp. Sept. 31 (*sic*) 1774. [A Johannes S., m. Rebecca Witbeck, Oct. 6, 1782.]

SEGERS, Jacob [son of Roeloff, and Lydia Harty ?], m. Maria Crosby. Ch: Lydia, b. Sept. 7, 1778.

SEGERS, Alexander, and Mary Potter. Ch: Alexander, b. April 23, 1778.

SEGERS, Hendrik [son of Evert, and Sara Orchard.] and Annatie. Ch: b.; Sara, Sept. 14, 1780; Sara, Oct, 17, 1785.

SEGERS, George [son of Evert, and Sara Orchard.] and Catharine Van der Williger [Terwilliger.] Ch: b.; Dirk, Feb. 28, 1790; Jane, March 16, 1792.

SEGERS, William [son of Gerrit, and Mary Pengburn,] m. Annatie Brant. Ch: Gerrit, b. Jan. 18, 1793.

Sequa, Jacob, and Margarita Dunbar. Ch: Elisabeth Roe, b. March 25, 1790.

Sharp, Scharp, Scherp, Schaap, &c.

Scharp, Andries Hanse, in Beverwyck, as early as 1660; in 1671, bought a farm behind Kinderhook. He had sons; Johannes and Gysbert; Laurens.

SCHARP, Johannes Andriese [son of the last], of Kinderhoek, and 1720, of Claverack, m. Geertruy Rees, Nov. 25, 1694. Ch: bp.; Jannetie, Sept. 8, 1695; Andries, Jan. 5, 1701; Willem, July 10, 1698; Andries, Jan. 8, 1704; Neeltie, July 6, 1707; Cornelis April 30, 1710; Catryna, Aug. 2, 1713.

SCHARP, Gysbert Andriese, of Kinderhoek, m.Lysbert Janse Goewey Oct. 21, 1701. Ch: bp.; Andries, Aug. 30, 1702: Catharina, Aug. 20, 1702; Jan Salomon, March 24, 1706; Cornelis. May 3, 1708; Philip, Oct. 30, 1710; Laurens, Oct. 19, 1712; Maria, May 23, 1723.

SCHARP, Laurens [son of Andries Hanse (?) and Hilletie Janse Goewey.] Ch: bp.; Andries, May 16, 1714; Salomon, Dec. 16, 1716; Catalyna, Aug. 24, 1718; Cornelia, Sept. 4, 1720; Pieter, Oct. 20, 1723; Jacob Salomonse, April 3, 1726.

SCHARP, Thomas, m. Maria De Warran, Nov. 13, 1720; she was buried Nov. 3, 1748. Ch: bp.: Jacobus, Aug. 12, 1722: Thomas, Sept. 27, 1724; Thomas Scherp's son "Tommie" was buried April 18, 1741; Anna, Aug. 7, 1726; Maria, July 3, 1747.

SCHARP, Jurriaan, and Barbara .... Ch: bp. ; Coenraad, Sept. 10, 1738; Augustinus, May 13, 1744; Jurrie (?) ; Pieter (?).

SCHARP, Andries, Jr. [son of Lourens and Hilletie Goewey?], m. Elizabeth dau. of Salomon Goewey, Aug. 31, 1739. Ch: Laurens, bp. June 22, 1740.

SCHARP, Jurrie, Jr., [son of Jurriaan and Barbara] ....m. Catharina Fleegring (Fliegery). Ch: Jurrie, bp. May 28, 1758; Catharina bp. June 13, 1761; Jacob, *geboren Pinxter-dag*, bp. June 19, 1763; Marytje, b. May 3, 1766; Barbara, b. April 20, 1768; Christina, b. Sept. 29, 1770.

SCHARP, Jacobus [son of Thomas and Maria De Warran?] and Annatje McGinnis. [James Sharp, m. Hanna Wendell, widow, of Albany, March 12, 1763]. Ch: Maria, b. Sept. 28, 1763.

SCHARP, Pieter, Jr., [son of Jurriaan and Barbara?] ....m. first Catharina Berringer, Nov. 1762, and secondly Mary Donneway, about 1778. Ch: b. ; Barbara, Oct. 6, 1765; Frederic, July 22, 1769; Margarita, Dec. 6, 1776; William, Oct. 20, 1778; Mary, June 12, 1781.

Sharp, Willem, and Neeltie Suydam (Zerdam), Ch: Johanna, b. Sept. 15, 1767.

SHARP, Nicolaas, m. Lena Hoogeboom, Jan. 31, 1767. Ch: b. Jacob, March 30, 1767 ; Bartholomeus, April 1, 1769 ; Jurriaan, Dec. 7, 1771 ; Barbara, June 25, 1776; Margarita, April 9, 1779.

SHARP, Lourens, and Geesie Schermerhorn. Ch: Hendrik and Gerritje, twins, bp. March 14, 1769.

SHARP, Augustinus, m. Maria Van Alsteyn, Dec. 10, 1767. Ch: b. ; Maria, August 17, 1769; Barbara, Oct. 29, 1775; Jurriaan, March 30, 1780; Jannetie, April 22, 1788.

SHARP, Coenraad, [son of Juriaan and Barbara....,] and Elizabeth Staats. Ch: Jurriaan b. April 9, 1776; Jurriaan, b. Aug. 25, 1778; Catharine, b. March 30, 1786; Catharina, b. May 12, 1790.

SHARP, Johannes, and Jerusha (Jerisia) North (Noth). Ch: Elizabeth, b. Feb. 6, 1779; Abraham, b. March 3, 1786.

SHARP, Salomo, and Rachel Halenbeck. Ch: Johannes, b. June 25, 1781; Hilletje, b. Nov. 15, 1784.

SHARP, Abner, and Cornelia Halenbeck. Ch: Sible, b. Jan. 22, 1788; Henry Halenbeck, b. Nov. 15, 1799.

SHARP, Jacob, m. Ariaantje Van Iveren [Everen], April 9, 1789. Ch: Catharine, b. Sept. 22, 1789; Elizabeth, b. Aug. 12, 1791.

SHARP, Gilbert, m. Annatie Schoenmaker, b. May 28, 1792. Ch: Peter, b. March 8, 1793.

SHARP, Jacob, and Geertruy Wing. Ch: Samuel, b. March 22, 1800.

Shaw, Joseph, and Sara Duischer. Ch: Thomas, b. March 1, 1769; Catharina, b. Feb. 25, 1771.

SHAW, Benjamin, and Antje .... Ch: Benjamin, b. Sept. 10, 1769.

Sherman (Shairman), Job, and Anna (Any) Conger. Ch: Lydia, b. Jan. 3, 1781.

Shever, Carel, m. Sara (Celia) Redly, May 25, 1776. Ch: Johannes, b. March 1, 1779.

Shewdy (Shoudy), Johannes, and Catharina Keizer. Ch: Barbara, b. Aug. 22, 1790; John, bp. Feb. 13, 1793.

Shuckburgh, Richard and Mary .... Ch: John, bp. March 15, 1747.

Shutter, Hendrick, m. Jannetie Hindermond, March 29, 1779. Ch: b.; Margarita, May 20, 1783; Temperance, May 10, 1787.

Shutter, Abraham, and Geertruy Vosburgh. Ch: Barbara, bp. May 2, 1784.

Sibry (Sibree), William, m. Rebecca Yates, May 30, 1779. Ch: b.; Maria, Sept. 28, 1783; Johannes Yates, April 28, 1786.

Sickels, Zikkels, Zichelson.

SICKELS, Van Weenen, Zacharias, was for many years in the West India Company's service as corporal, first at Curaçoa, and from 1656-9 at Fort Orange and New Amsterdam. In 1693, he removed from Albany to New York. In the years 1670-1-2 and 1681-2-3 he was the town's herder, and contracted to perform this duty for the season at 18 guilders a head. In 1689, he was *Rattel watch* for the village. He had the following ch: Lambrecht, b. 1666; Zacharias, b. 1670; Grietje, bp. May 17, 1684; Lea, bp. May 8, 1687; Robert (?); Thomas (?).

SICKELS, Robert [son of Zacharias the first settler] m. Geertruy Ridderhaas April 5, 1686. Ch. bp. in Albany : Maria, March 11, 1688; Sophia, July 27, 1690; Henricus, bp. in New York, Aug. 14, 1692; Elizabeth, bp. in N. Y., Aug. 13, 1707.

12

SICKELS, Lambert (Lambrecht) [son of Zacharias the first settler.] Ch. bp. in N. Y.: Johannes, Dec. 18, 1692; Alida, May 9, 1703.

SICKELS, Lea, [dau. of Zacharias the first settler.] had a dau. Martha, bp. in N. Y., Aug. 25, 1706.

SICKELS, Zacharias [son of Zacharias the first settler], m. Maryhen Janse in N. Y., Aug. 29,·1693. and had the following ch. bp. there: Johannes, July 29, 1694; Jacobus, Nov. 17, 1695; Zacharias, Sept. 4, 1698; Zacharias, June 12, 1700; Thomas, March 28, 1703.

SICKELS, Thomas, [son of Zacharias the first settler], had Ch bp. in N. Y.: Zacharias, Aug. 30, 1702; Zacharias, Feb. 23, 1704; Hendrikje, Oct. 7, 1705; Johannes, May 16, 1707; Thomas, March 6, 1709; Thomas, Sept. 24, 1710; Wilhelmus, April 13, 1712; Maritie, Sept. 13, 1713; Robert, Nov. 2, 1715; Annatie, June 2, 1717; Jannetie, Nov. 30, 1718; Jannetie, Sept. 18, 1720.

SICKELS, (Zikkels, Zilchelson) Zacharias, [perhaps son of Lambert], m. Annatie Wyngaard, July 4, 1728. She was buried August 6, 1746. Ch. bp. in Albany: Maria, June 21, 1729; Jacobus, May 19, 1731; Elizabeth and Annatie, August 8, 1733; Lammert, July 30, 1735; Abraham, June 5, 1737; Gerrit, Feb. 17, 1740; Christina, August 7, 1743; Christina and Margareta, Sept. 8, 1745.

SICKELS, Abraham, [son of Zacharias and Annatie Wyngaard], m. Maria Cannel, (Kanner, Conner), April 16, 1767. She d. 27 (28,) May 1829, a. 89 y. Ch: b.; Annatie, August 16, 1767; Daniel, Sept. 14, 1769; Marytje, August 25, 1771; Jacobus, Dec. 31, 1773; Elizabeth, May 26, 1776; Willem, June 24, 1778; Catrina, Oct. 26, 1779; Johannes, Sept. 6, 1785.

SICKELS, Zacharia, m. Catharina Sheers (Cheir, Sheerum, Sharer, Shaver) June 19, 1777. Ch: b.; John, May 16, 1778; Rachel, Nov. 9, 1780; Letty, April 6, 1784; Jane, Oct. 28, 1793.

SICKELS, Christoffer, and Neeltie Fynhout. Ch: Debora, b. Sept. 7, 1778.

SICKLES, Thomas, and Mary Norwood. Ch: Richard, b. July 9, 1780; John Brazier, bp. Oct. 11, 1782.

SICKELS, Daniel, and Jane Dox (Jennet Dunse). Ch: born; Alexander, Oct. 27, 1796; Marian, Jan. 4, 1800.

SICKKET, Lodewyck, m. Christina Vretje (Fratien), Nov. 23, 1765. Ch: Jacob, b. Feb. 20, 1768.

SILL, Richard, m. Elizabeth Nicolls, May 2, 1785. Ch: born; William Nicolls, March 25, 1786; John Lea, Aug. 13, 1787.

Silverssen, Pieter, and Jannetje Van Schaick. Ch: Francis, b. July 22, 1767.

Simmons, Benjamin, and Annatie Manley. Ch: John, b. July 20, 1783.

SIMMONS, Jonas, and Elsie Strunk (Strong). Ch: Pieter, b. Dec. 6, 1788.

Simpson, John, and Catharine Douglass. Ch: born; George, May 17, 1797; Christiaan, Aug. 25, 1799; John, Oct. 24, 1803.

Sinhoo, Jacob, and Matnamskidaa. Ch: Johannes, bp. July 26, 1724.

Sitzer, Andries, and Sara Allen. Ch: Pieter, b. Oct. 14, 1781.

Siverse, Siwerts, Siversend, Syberse, Siwers, Snoerts, Swart, &c.

SIVERSE, Claas, was nephew of Marten Gerritse Van Bergen, his sister's son.

SIVERSE (Sywertsen), Jurriaan, of Catskil 1732-5, m. Elizabeth Groot of Schenectady, Feb. 5, 1727, in S. Ch. baptized in Albany: Nicolaas, May 30, 1728; Anna, June 18, 1730; Gertrand in Catskill, March 26, 1732; Syme in Catskill, Jan. 27, 1735.

Sixberry, Nicolaas, and Mary. .... Ch: Nicholaas, bp. June 10, 1722.

SIXBERRY, Evert, and Elsie Egmond. Ch: bp.; Marytje, Oct. 22, 1738; Anna, Jan. 11, 1741; Catharina, April 3, 1743; Nicholaas, July 18, 1744; Catarina, Jan. 10, 1748; Gerrit, May 19, 1751; Willem, July 22, 1754; Evert, May 2, 1756.

SIXBERRY, Willem, m. Anna Radcliff, Dec. 9, 1738, "Billy Sixberry" was buried Jan. 19, 1740. Ch: Nicolaas, bp. Aug. 19, 1739. Billy Sixberry's child was buried, April 1, 1740.

SIXBERRY, Abraham, and Eva Backes (Baccis, Eegie Ackers). Ch: Maria, bp.· March 19, 1758; Abraham, b. Oct. 15, 1766.

SIXBERRY, Nicholaas, m. Cornelia Cooper, March 7, 1773. Ch: born; Elsie, Feb. 7, 1774; Evert, Feb. 5, 1776; Catharina, Dec. 12, 1777; Annatie, Sept. 14, 1779; Maritie, April 13, 1782; Jacob, Nov. 8, 1786; Elizabeth, Jan. 6, 1789; Elizabeth, March 26, 1790.

Sixsby, Johannes, and Lea Davenport, Ch: born; Abraham, July 6, 1780; Johannes, Sept. 22, 1782. [Johannnes Sixby, and Alida Bont, m. Feb. 28, 1776.]

Skidmore, John, and Ann Clark. Ch: b.; Jane, Nov. 13, 1794.

Skinner, Jared, and Mary Drew. Ch: Mary Ann, b. July 2, 1798.

Slickoten, Willem Janse, in 1661, was the husband of Neeltie Frederickse, widow of the late Claas Hendrickse Van Schoonhoven, deceased.

Slingerland, Teunis Cornelise, m. first, Engeltie Albertse Bratt, and secondly, Geertie Fonda widow of Jan Bikker, April 9, 1684. Of his children, the following reached maturity and left families: Arent, Albert, and Cornelis; Elizabeth, wife of Thomas Eeckars, of New York.

SLINGERLAND, Arent, m. Geertruy Cobuse Van Vorst (Vosch), his second wife, Oct., 1688. In his will made Jan. 28, 171¾, he speaks of Ch: Engeltie, Teunis, Gerrit, and Sara. Ch: baptized: Johannes, May 10, 1685; Engeltie, Nov. 10, 1689; Teunis, March 18, 1694; Gerrit, May 2, 1697; Sara, July 21, 1700; Albertus, Jan. 2, 1704.

SLINGERLAND, Albert, of "Niscothaa" and Hester Brikkers (Bekkers). In his will made July 7, 1725, proved July 18, 1781, he mentions his wife, and the following children: Johannes, bp. July 19, 1696; Engeltie, bp. July 10, 1698, m. Andries Witbeck, Jr.; Teunis, bp. Dec. 8, 1700; Tennis, bp. Dec. 21, 1701; Thomas, bp. March 5, 1704.

SLINGERLAND, Cornelis, of Schenectady, m. Eva Mebie, May 28, 1699, in S. [Cornelis S., was buried in Niskatha, Sept. 3, 1753.] Ch: Catharina, bp. April 28, 1710; Eva, bp. July 12, 1714. See also *Schenectady Families.*

SLINGERLAND, Teunis [son of Arent,] m. first, Elizabeth Vanderzee, Oct. 4, 1719; and secondly, Cornelia Kip, July 5, 1724; he was buried June 29, 1746; his wife, March 16, 1745. Ch: Arent, bp. April 24, 1720; Wouter, bp. Nov. 4, 1722; Hester, bp. Jan. 19, 1729;

Abraham, bp. Nov. 29, 1730 ; Albert, bp. Nov. 27, 1732 ; Isaac, bp. Aug. 14, 1734 ; Geesie, bp. Sept. 12, 1736 ; Engeltie, bp. Dec. 25, 1738 : Anna, bp. Feb. 22, 1741 ; Geertruy, bp. Sept. 25, 1743.

SLINGERLAND, Johannes (Hannes), son of Albert] m. his cousin Anna, dau. of Cornelis S., of Schenectady, Jan. 24, 1724. Ch : Hester, bp. July 26, 1724 ; Egie, bp. Jan. 22, 1727 ; Engeltie, bp. April 6, 1729 ; Albert, bp. May 20, 1731 ; Albert bp. March 7, 1733 ; Eggie, bp. Sept. 14, 1735 ; Cornelis, bp. May 7, 1738 ; Maria, bp. Sept. 26, 1742 ; Maria, bp. Sept. 28, 1745.

SLINGERLAND, Arent, [son of Teunis,] m. Jacomyntje Van der Volgen, dau. of Teunis V. D. V. of Schenectady. Ch : Teunis, bp. Aug. 24, 1746 ; Sara, bp. Feb. 17, 1751 ; Wouter, bp. Feb. 24, 1754 : Nicolaas, bp. March 7, 1756 ; Antony, bp. Feb. 26, 1758 ; Elizabeth, b. Oct. 14, 1764.

SLINGERLAND, Teunis Cornelise [son of Cornelis of Schenectady,] m. Angenitje Witbeck. Ch : bp. ; Maria, Dec. 25, 1747 ; Eechie, May 13, 1750 ; Cornelis, Feb. 2, 1752 ; John, March 10, 1754 ; Petrus, Sept. 19, 1756 ; Petrus, Feb. 25, 1759 ; Eytje, June 7, 1761 ; Hendrik, b. Aug., 1765 ; Albert, bp. Oct. 8, 1769.

SLINGERLAND, Wouter [son of Teunis, and Elisabeth Van der Zee,] m. Hester, dau. of Johannes Slingerland. Ch : bp. ; Teunis, Nov. 4, 1750 ; Arent, March 22, 1752 ; Isaac, May 21, 1756 ; Wouter, b. Feb. 9, 1770.

SLINGERLAND, Anthony, m. first, Claartje Clute, Sept. 21, 1751 ; and secondly, Saartie Clute, about 1766. Ch : bp. ; Elieabeth, July 26, 1752 ; Gerrit, April 7, 1754 ; Dirk, Jan. 7, 1759 ; Wouter, b. April 12, 1767.

SLINGERLAND, Abraham [son of Teunis,] m. Rebecca Viele, Dec. 4, 1756. Ch : b. ; Teunis, bp. Oct. 2, 1757 ; Petrus, March 4, 1760 ; Abraham, Dec. 13, 1762 ; Catharina, May 10, 1765 ; Cornelia, Aug. 28, 1767 ; Maria, Dec. 15, 1769 ; Albert, Dec. 24, 1773 ; Stephanus, Oct. 23, 1775.

SLINGERLAND, Gerrit T., of Niskitha [son of Teunis, and Elisabeth Vanderzee,] m. Egie Vanderzee, Nov. 16, 1757. Ch : b. : Elisabeth, bp. May 28, 1758 ; Storm, Sept. 28, 1764 ; Lena, April 28, 1767 ; Lena, Aug. 5, 1769 ; Teunis, June 5, 1774.

SLINGERLAND, Isaac, [son of Teunis and Elizabeth], m. Eva Van Woert, Dec. 27, 1760. Ch : b. ; Cordelia, bp. Nov. 14, 1761 ; Jacob, Feb. 18, 1763 ; Teunis, Nov. 10, 1764 ; Johannes, July 4, 1766 ; Johannes, August 24, 1769 ; Hendrikje, Sept. 22, 1771 ; Hendrikje April 6, 1774 ; Isaac, bp. May 5, 1776 ; Petrus, Dec. 21, 1778.

SLINGERLAND, Albert, [son of Johannes and Anna], m. Elizabeth Moke (Mook), Dec. 26, 1760. Ch : b. ; Annatje ; Maria, Oct. 2, 1763 ; Hester, Dec. 25, 1765.

SLINGERLAND, Albert, [son of Teunis and Cornelia], m. Christina Van Vranken, Sept. 31, (sic) 1763. Ch : b. ; Maria, May 20, 1766 ; Ryckert, March 26, 1768 ; Teunis, March 27, 1770 ; Annatje, March 30, 1772 ; Cornelia, Dec. 7, 1775 ; Teunis, Feb. 2, 1779 ; Abraham Trouex, July 1, 1781.

SLINGERLAND, Teunis W. [son of Wouter and Hester], m. first, Rachel Bogart, May 31, 1777 ; and secondly, Rachel Davis about 1792 ; she d. June 26, 1833. Ch : b. ; Hester, Oct. 22, 1778 ; Douwe, April 4, 1781 ; Douwe, April 4, 1782 ; Isaac, Feb. 19, 1784 ; Isaac, April 25, 1793 ; Annatie Drett, Oct. 22, 1797.

SLINGERLAND, Teunis [son of Abraham and Rebecca], m. first, Margarita Hansen, April 18, 1779 ; secondly, Maritie Malice (Nenlie), 1791. Ch : born ; Abraham, Nov. 28, 1780 ; Maria, March 2, 1782 ; Maria, Nov. 25, 1783 : Rebecca, Jan. 5, 1786 ; Maritie, Feb. 2, 1792 ; Maritie, Oct. 13, 1793.

SLINGERLAND, Arent W. [son of Wouter and Hester], m. Annatie Aarnouds (Arnold), Jan. 3, 1786, Ch. b. ; Hester, Dec. 25, 1786 ; Elizabeth Feb. 5, 1790 ; Jacob, July 8, 1793 ; Angeltie, Sept. 5, 1804.

SLINGERLAND, Storm [son of Gerrit and Eegie], and Annatie Halenbeck. Ch : Gerrit, b. July 22, 1786.

SLINGERLAND, Pieter [son of Abraham and Rebecca], m. first, Mary Vander Veer ; and secondly, Mary Waldron about 1789. Ch : Rebecca, bp. Feb. 3, 1788 ; Hendrick, b. Aug. 14, 1790.

SLINGERLAND, Francis, and Rachel Davis. Ch. : Jannetie, b. Jan. 9, 1790.

SLINGERLAND, Abraham [son of Abraham and Rebecca], m. Sarah Schoenmaker, March 18, 1790. Ch : b. Rebecca, April 18, 1791 ; Jannetie, Feb. 9, 1793.

SLINGERLAND, Wouter [son of Anthony and Claartje], m. first Jacomyntje Halenbeck ; and secondly, Henrietta Slingerland about 1801. Ch ; b. ; Claartje, Feb. 14, 1792 ; Esther Rebecca, Nov. 10, 1801.

SLINGERLAND, Peter [son of Abraham and Rebecca,] m. Maritie Van der Werken, Jan. 2, 1785. Ch : Abraham, b. May 20, 1793.

SLINGERLAND, Jacob [son of Isaac and Eva], m. first, Catharine Van everen, May 23, 1790 ; and secondly, Cornelia Van Alsteyn about 1799. Ch : born ; Isaac, Sept. 2, 1790 ; Debora, Nov. 16, 1792 ; Catharine, Oct. 14, 1795 ; Stephen Van Rensselaer, April 19, 1800.

SLINGERLAND, John [son of Isaac and Eva], and Susannah Evertsen. Ch : born ; Martina, Dec. 15, 1796 ; Isaac, Jan. 8, 1800.

Slover, Isaac, and Alida (Antje) Whitlock. Ch : born ; Eleanor, March 25, 1799 ; Isaac, March 18, 1801.

Sluyter, Willem, and Sarah .... Ch : Cornelia, bp. March 1, 1713 ; Edward, Oct. 20, 1714.

SLUYTER (Sleighter), Bartholomew and Catharine Boyle. Ch : Maria, bp. Dec. 22, 1779.

Smit, Rem Jansen, in New Amsterdam 1643-51 ; in Beverwyck, 1655-60 ; at Waleboght, 1663-85, in which places he owned several houses and lots. In 1663, he was complained of by Adriaen Hegeman for carrying off a ploughshare, was ordered by the court to replace it in the spot where he found, and if he had any claim to prosecute it at law. His w. was Jannetie Joris Rapaille.

Smith, Thomas, and Maria Barret (Bergen). Ch : bp. ; Elsie, June 14, 1747 ; Margarieta, July 2, 1749 ; Barentje, May 18, 1755.

SMITH, Bennoni, and Mary Springer. Ch : Daniel, bp. March 18, 1750.

SMITH, Jacob, and Mary .... Ch : Wilhelmus, bp. April 15, 1764.

SMIT, Coenraad, and Jannetie Hoogeboom. Ch : Jeremias, bp. Jan. 22, 1764.

SMIT, Jacob, Van Saratoga, m. Maria Barbara Smit, Oct. 14, 1753. Ch : bp. ; Johannes, Feb. 10, 1754 ; Rachel, Jan. 15, 1758 ; Jacob, Aug. 17, 1762 ; Margarita, b. July 10, 1769.

SMIT, Wilhelmus, m. Annatie (Hanna) Bratt, Dec. 6, 1761. Ch : born; Elizabeth, Nov. 6, 1762 ; Barent, *oud* 4 *weken*, bp. April 7, 1765 ; Annatie, Sept. 8, 1767 ; Albert, Oct. 30, 1770 ; Elizabeth, Dec. 14, 1773; Cornelia, Dec. 7, 1776.

SMIT, Johannes H., of Niskatha, m. first, Margarita Weitman ; and secondly, Margarita Peesinger, Oct. 8, 1765. Ch : Zacharias, *oud* 6 *weken*, bp. May 15, 1763; Andries, b. July 1, 1766 ; Elizabeth, bp. Oct. 19, 1768 ; Sabina, bp. Feb. 17, 1771.

SMITH, Jacob, and Barbara Crafter. Ch : Nicolaas, b. Oct. 16, 1764.

SMITH, Alexander, and Rachel .... Ch : Catharina, b. Feb. 2, 1768.

SMITH, Hannes, and Neeltie Larraway. Ch : Saartie, b. April 7, 1768.

SMITH, Jacob, and Elizabeth Vinkel. Ch : Jurriaan, b. March 13, 1770.

SMITH, David, and Any Smith. Ch : David, b. July 12, 1773.

SMITH, James, and Elizabeth Allen. Ch : James, b. Jan. 31, 1778.

SMITH, Willem, and Mary Corker. Ch : Willem, bp. May 2, 1778.

SMITH, Elisha, m. Alida Bulsing, April 5, 1778. Ch : Helena, b. May 10, 1778.

SMITH, Theodorus, and Caty Simson. Ch : Nicolaas, b. April 18, 1780.

SMITH, Charles, and Margaret Asurine (?) Ch : Margarita, bp. April 14, 1782.

SMITH, John, of Saratoga, and Mary McDole. Ch : Abijah, b. April 28, 1789.

SMITH, Richard, and Sophia Muller. Ch : Jeremia and Geesie *tweelingen in huis ge doopt wegens ziekte*, June 7, 1790 ; Elizabeth, b. April 11, 1796.

SMITH, Barent, m. Hannah Bel, March 21, 1790. Ch : born ; Margaret, Dec. 1, 1790 ; Jeremiah, March 7, 1793 ; Anna, Sept. 23, 1795 ; Elizabeth, Sept. 28, 1798 ; Elizabeth, April 3, 1801.

Snoet, Johann Matthys, and Geertruy Rees. Ch : Anna, b. Jan. 30, 1788.

Snyder, Jacob, and Anna ..... Ch : Pieter, bp. May 25, 1713. [Jacob Snyder m. Elizabeth Feek, June 9, 1722.]

SNYDER, Willem, and Barber Clapper. Ch : Margarita, bp. Jan. 22, 1754.

SNYDER, Andries, and Annatie Harris. Ch : Annatie, b. June 23, *by de Fonteine en op weg gedoopt*, Aug. 13, 1769.

SNYDER, Johannes and Maria Cool. Ch : Lydia, bp. July 4, 1773.

SNYDER, Lourens, and Elizabeth Heggerry. Ch : Christiaan b. Aug. 12, 1774.

SNYDER, John and Mary Deerstine. Ch : Henry, b. Feb. 17, 1793.

SNYDER, Nicolaas, and Femmetie Van Sinderen. Ch : Ulpianus, b. Dec. 12, 1788.

Soesbergen, Reyer Cornelise, miller, in 1660, hired a horse mill and gears of Arent Van Curler and Willem Bout for three years.

Soegemakelyk, *alias* Van Woggelum. Two brothers of this name, Pieter and Jacob Adriaense, with their mother, were early settlers of Beverwyck; both were inn keepers. In 1660, their mother Anna

Pieterse Soegemakelyk was a widow by the death of her second husband, Barent Janse Bal ; she d. in Dec. 1669. Pieter Adriaense was apprehended by the revenue officer, Johan De Dekkere, for refusing to pay the excise on his sales of wine, beer, &c., but escaped ; he denied the right of the officer of Fort Orange to collect this excise in the Colonie where he lived and in this he was sustained by the Patroon. In 1664 he received a patent for a bouwery and home lot at Schenectady, which he sold in 1670, to Helmer Otten for 35 beavers ; after Otten's death his widow married Reyer Jacobse Schermerhorn, and this bouwery thus acquired has remained in this family until the present time. He had at least three children, Pieter, Jan, and a daughter who m. Jan Mangelse. The first, Capt. Pieter Pieterse Van Woggelum, in 1669 had a lot and garden at *Lubberde's land* [a part of Troy] and in 1672 he bought of Myndert Janse Wemp of Schenectady his father's bouwery lying upon and south of the Poestenkil, for 250 beavers ; subsequently he sold this land to Dirk Van Der Heyden from whom it passed to his three sons, Jacob, David, and Matthys. Capt. Van Woggelum was a skipper, and in 1684 was master of the open boat *Unity* plying between New York and Albany. Jan Pieterse Adriaense Soegemakelyk, the brother of Pieter, was also an inn keeper in 1655, and because he lived without the village of Beverwyck, in the *Colonie* refused to allow the excise collector to gauge his liquor casks. He is sometimes called Jacob Adriaense Van Utrecht (?)

Sornberger, David, and Christina Louwer. Ch : bp. ; Jurrie Jacob, Jan. 1, 1754 ; Coenraat, May 20, 1759.

Soul (Sool), William, m. Margaret Wyngaard (widow Philips), June 2, 1758. Ch : Robert, bp. Jan. 21, 1759 ; Martha, Dec. 21, 1760 ; Hannes Wyngaart, b March 14, 1763 ; Elizabeth, bp. March 29, 1767.

Soup, Dirk, and Mary Couverd. Ch : Mary, b. Nov. 8, 1791.

Sperry, Jan, and Francyntje Clute. Ch : Antje, bp. Oct. 23, 1748.

Speulman, Johannes, and Christina Huyck. Ch : Christina, bp. June 26, 1757.

Spitsbergen, Teunis, see Vander Poel.

Spoor, *alias* Wybesse, Jan, of Niskayuna ; in 1662, Jan Wybesse Van Harlingen, farm servant, bought of Christoffel Davidts 16 morgens of land over the kil at Catskil, lying next Eldert Gerbertse Cruiff's land. In 1698, he owned land at Niskayuna, which he sold to Johannes Schuyler for £120. His wife was Anna Maria Hanse. Ch : bp. ; Antje ; she was killed and burnt at Schenectady by the French and Indians Feb. 9, 1690 ; Saartje, Dec. 3, 1684 ; Nicolaas, April 27, 1690 ; Annetje, June 7, 1691 ; Rebecca, April 22, 1694 ; Rachel, Jan. 31, 1697.

SPOOR, Johannes, of Kinderhoek, joined the church of Albany in 1700, *met attestatie Van Kingstowne* ; his wife was Maria Singer. Ch : bp. ; Henricus, Jan. 13, 1707 ; Abraham, Aug. 3, 1707 ; Dirk, April 30, 1710.

SPOOR, Gerrit, and Mary Gilbert, were m. before 1700. He made his will May 26, 1719, proved June 3, 1720, and mentioned his wife Mary and the following Ch : Ann ; Mary ; Cornelia, bp. April 20, 1712 ; Johannes, bp. Nov. 29, 1713 ; Willem or Wilhelmus, Feb. 12, 1716 ; Abraham, Feb. 2, 1718.

Spoor, Hendrik, and Rebecca Van Valkenburgh.
Ch : bp. ; Hieronymus, Sept. 9, 1739 ; Rebecca, Aug.
5, 1744 ; Abraham, June 11, 1749.

Spoor, Johannes, m. Magdalena Bogart, June 18,
1757. Ch : Rebecca, bp. Feb. 11, 1759 ; Maria, bp.
Dec. 7, 1760 ; Maria, b. Feb. 1, 1764 ; Gerrit, b. Dec.
8, 1767.

Springer, Dennis (Daniel) and Mary .... Ch :
bp. ; Abigail, Jan. 12, 1737 ; Dennis, Sept. 10, 1738 ;
Benjamin, June 14, 1740.

Springer, J., and A. .... Ch : John, bp. March 3,
1737.

Springer, Hendrik, and Frena Keyser. Ch : bp. ;
Jacob, May 8, 1743 ; Elizabeth, Aug. 17, 1746.

Springer, David, m. Margarita Oliver, Oct. 26,
1754. Ch : Maria, bp. March 8, 1761.

Springer, Benjamin, and Hendrikje Oliver (Olfer).
Ch : Vincent, b. Dec. 14, 1767.

Springer, Hannes, and Jannetje Bont. Ch : born ;
Theuntje, Jan. 10, 1771 ; Alida, April 1, 1778.

Springer, Jacob, m. Marytje Snyder, Feb. 10, 1771.
Ch : born ; Hendrik, July 26, 1771 ; Frina, Feb. 10,
1776.

Springstede, Joseph, and Elizabeth Matthews.
Ch : Jeremiah, b. Dec. 23, 1781.

Springsteen, Caspar, miller, of Schenectady,
1707, m. first, Wyntje Jurcx in New York Aug. 9,
1693 ; and secondly, Jannetje Jacobse Schermerhoorn
in N. Y., July 28, 1695. Ch : bp. in N. Y., Melle,
Jan. 31, 1694 ; Jannetje, June 13, 1697 ; Jacob, May
14, 1699 ; Simon, June 19, 1709, in Albany. See also
Schenectady Families.

Springsteen, Abraham, and Antie .... Ch : Machtelt, bp. May 16, 1736.

Springsteen, Reyer, m. first, Mary Borner (Tor-
ner), Nov. 21, 1735 ; secondly, Helena.... about 1751.
Ch : bp. ; Caspar, Aug. 1, 1736 ; Jannetie, May 6,
1739 ; Willem, Oct. 26, 1740 ; Jannetje, Nov. 6, 1743 ;
Jacob, April 27, 1746 ; Isaac, Aug. 30, 1752.

Springsteen, Simon, m. Maria Seger June 1, 1744.
Ch : bp. ; Casparus, July 7, 1745 ; Gerrit, June 5,
1748 ; Magtel, May 27, 1751 ; Jannetje, April 15, 1753 ;
Staats, Jan. 5, 1755.

Springsteen, Jacobus (Jacob) m. Rachel Cole
(Cool) Aug. 15, 1779. Ch : Jacob, b. July 4, 1780.

Springsteen, Daniel, of Greenbush, and Annatie
Schermerhorn. Ch : Cornelia, b. March 23, 1787.

Sprong, Cornelis, and Margarita Schans
(Schawns ; l"Jaans, Jones ?) Ch : Johannes, bp.
March 24, 1754 ; Catarina, bp. July 25, 1756 ; Johan-
nes, bp. June 25, 1760 ; David, b. Feb. 14, 1763 ; Chris-
tiaan, b. Oct. 7, 1764 (?) ; Christina, b. Jan. 18, 1768 ;
Elisabeth, b. Oct. 18, 1770 ; Volkert, bp. May 16, 1773 ;
Marytje, b. Sept. 2, 1775.

Sprott, William, of Saratoga, and Margaret Mc-
Grieger. Ch : James, b. Sept. 21, 1788.

Squince, John, and Jane Nixon. Ch : John, b.
March 19, 1778.

Staats (Staes), Maj. Abram, surgeon, came to
Rensselaerswyck in 1642, with Dominie Megapolensis ; in 1643, he became one of the council and president of the board in 1644, at a salary of 100 florins ;
he obtained a license to trade in furs [in 1657, he sent
to N. Amsterdam 4200 beaver skins], and had also a
considerable bouwery, besides pursuing the practice
of his profession (*O'Callaghan's Hist., N. N.*). For

many years he was a skipper on the North river, com-
manding the sloop *Claverack,* plying between New
York and Albany, in 1684. He m. Catrina Jochemse
[dau. of Jochem Wesselse.] He had four sons who
reached maturity (and perhaps a daughter), Jacob ;
Abraham, b. in 1665 ; Samuel, and Jochem.

Staats, Jochem, m. Antje, dau. of Barent Reyn-
dertse ; she d. in 1707. Ch : bp. ; Barent ; Tryntje,
Jan. 7, 1685 ; Isaac, Jan. 15, 1688 ; Tryntje, Sept. 8,
1689 ; Isaak, June 28, 1691 ; Reynier, in New York,
July 29, 1696 ; Richard, in New York Aug. 10, 1698 ;
Isaak, July 20, 1701 ; Elisabeth, in New York, June
18, 1712.

Staats, Samuel, "chirurgeon," is said to have
learned his profession in Holland, and on his return
to have settled in New Amsterdam. When the Province surrendered to the English in 1664, he returned
to Holland where he remained until the Prince of
Orange ascended the English throne in 1688, when
he returned to New York. During Leisler's administration of the government he was a prominent leader
and councillor. His death occurred in 1715. *Valentine's Man.*, 1864.] The name of his first wife is not
known ; May 7, 1709, he m. Catharina Hawarden,
in New York. Of the 9 children, which he had in
1703, the first five were probably b. in Holland ; the
four, bp. in New York, were Catalina, June 16, 1689 ;
Anna Elizabeth, Dec. 21, 1690, m. Philip Schuyler ;
Joanna, Jan. 31, 1694 ; Tryntje, April 5, 1697.

Staats, Jacob, surgeon, eldest son of Maj. Abram
Staats, resided in Albany ; was master of the sloop
Unity plying between New York and Albany in 1684 ;
justice of the peace, 1690 ; surgeon to the garrison at
Albany, 1698–1708. His wife Ryckie, d. in Sept. 1709.
It is not known that he left any children.

Staats, Abraham, of Claverack, was b. about 1665 ;
m. Elsje, dau. of Johannes Wendel, July 3, 1696 ;
made his will Sept. 24, 1731, proved Jan. 30, 1739–40,
in which the following Ch. are mentioned : Abraham,
bp. May 30, 1697 ; Maria, bp. Oct. 23, 1698 ; Abraham,
bp. July 28, 1700 ; Catharina, Nov. 1, 1702 ; Johannes,
Sept. 24, 1704 ; Sara, June 2, 1706 ; Isaac, Sept. 26,
1708 ; Jacob, bp. Oct. 7, 1711, d. Feb. 16, 1735 ; Elisabeth, bp. Jan. 4, 1713 ; Jochem, bp. May 20, 1716 ;
Elsje, bp. June 30, 1718 ; Samuel.

Staats, Barent [son of Jochem], m. Neeltje Gerritse Van den Berg, Dec. 15, 1701. Ch : bp. ; Joachim,
May 3, 1702 ; Anna, Dec. 24, 1703 ; Ariaantje, May 13,
1706 ; Catharina, Dec. 12, 1708 ; Geertruy, March
11, 1711 ; Jannetie, Feb. 22, 1713 ; Joachim, Sept.
15, 1717 ; Teuntie, March 31, 1720 ; Gerrit, June 3,
1722 ; Elisabeth, Oct. 3, 1725.

Staats, Abraham and Maria .... Ch : bp. ; Pieter,
Jan. 7, 1713 ; Barent, March 20, 1717.

Staats, Isaac [son of Jochem], m. Maria Van
Deusen, June 23, 1728. Ch : bp. ; Joachim, April 20,
1729 ; Elisabeth, April 16, 1731 ; Anna, Oct. 22, 1733 ;
Willem, May 2, 1736 ; Barent, June 3, 1739 ; Hendrik,
Sept. 20, 1741.

Staats, Joachem [son of Barent], m. Elisabeth
Schuyler, May 12, 1739. Ch : bp. ; Neeltje, Aug. 12,
1739 ; Barent, Nov. 29, 1741 ; Nicolaas, Oct. 2, 1743 ;
Elsie, Oct. 25, 1747 ; Neeltie, Feb. 18, 1750 ; Gerrit,
March 29, 1752 ; Philip, Aug. 12, 1754 ; Johannes,
Nov. 20, 1756 ; Annatie, Jan. 4, 1760.

Staats, Barent [son of Abraham], m. Magdalena
Schuyler, Nov. 2, 1743. He was buried at the *Hooge-
bergh*, July 28, 1752 ; she was buried June 16, 1749.
Ch : bp. ; Maria, Oct. 19, 1744 ; Susanna, Nov. 16, 1746.

STAATS, Samuel [son of Abraham,] m. Neeltie Staats, Jan. 8, 1742. Ch: bp.; Neeltie, Feb. 16, 1746; Elsie, June 4, 1749; Anna, May 17, 1752.

STAATS, Gerrit [son of Barent,] and Debora Beekman. Ch: bp.; Jacob, July 3, 1748; Neeltie, May 3, 1750; Debora, May 10, 1752, m. Maj. John Graham; Anna, Sept. 29, 1754; Jacob, Nov. 20, 1756; Neeltje, March 25, 1759; Barent, b. May 16, 1762; Hendrik, b. July 27, 1764.

STAATS, Jochem [son of Barent ?], and Geesie Vedder. Ch: Maria, b. May 7, 1767.

STAATS, Barent J., m. Antje Winne, August 24, 1767. She d. in Bethlehem, April 11, 1829, a. 81 y. Ch: b. Joachim, April 27, 1769; Daniel, Sept. 19, 1771; Cathalyna, Jan. 11, 1774; Gerritje, April 18, 1777; Elisabeth, May 3, 1779.

STAATS, Gerrit, and Catharina Cunningham. Ch: born, Joachim, bp. Jan. 4, 1769; Joachim, b. Feb. 6, 1771; Margarita, Nov. 19, 1773; Hendrick, Dec. 8, 1775; Willem, April 19, 1778; Johannes, Sept. 25, 1780; Annatie, Nov. 2, 1784.

STAATS, Hendrick, and Maria Du Mont. Ch: b. Hendrik Du Mont, Dec. 1, 1771; Maria, May 10, 1773; Catharina, Feb. 1, 1776; Hendrik Du Mont, Dec. 13, 1777.

STAATS, Hendrick, and Antje Lott; Anna, wid. of Henry S., born on Long Island, d. Feb. 25 (26), 1829, a. 82 y. Ch: Cathalina, b. August 29, 1787.

STAATS, Willem, m. Annatie (Hannah) Yates, May 1, 1771. He d. May 22, 1825, a. 89y. 15 d.: his widow d. June 3, 1829, a. 79 y. 5 mo. 11 d. ; Ch: born, Isaac, Nov. 1, 1772; Rebecca, Nov. 9, 1774; Johannes Yates, Sept. 6, 1776, d. at his bro. Willem's, 195 N. Market St. April 21, 1830; Hendrik, Oct. 21, 1778; Catharina, May 18, 1783; Elisabeth, Sept. 20, 1786; Isaac, June 1, 1789; Willem, Oct. 16, 1791.

STAATS, Nicolaas, and Maria Salisbury. Col. Nicholas S. of Schodac, d. May 7, 1816, in his 78d year. Ch: born; Willem, June 16, 1773; Jochem, Jan. 25, 1777; Joachim, Aug. 25, 1778.

STAATS, Abraham, m. Cornelia Lansing, Feb. 6, 1774. Ch: b. Isaac, Jan. 7, 1775; Gerrit, Nov. 29, 1780.

STAATS, John, m. Jenny McClellan, Sept. 24, 1780. Ch: b. Joachim, July 5, 1781; John, April 15, 1784.

STAATS, Gerrit, Jr., m. Elizabeth Low (Yates), Nov. 22, 1779. Ch: b. Cornelis, Aug. 1, 1780; Maria, Feb. 22, 1781; Elizabeth, April 16, 1782; Samuel Provost, Sept. 6, 1784.

STAATS, Gerrit, and Ann Lowe. Ch: Nancy, b. March 20, 1793.

STAATS, Barent, and Antje Winne. Ch: b.; Joachem, bp. Aug. 1782; Dirkje, b. Nov. 28, 1785; Gerritje, b. Feb. 5, 1789.

STAATS, Barent G, merchant, on west sidd of Broadway one door south of Maiden Lane, m. Catharina, dau. of Jacob Cuyler, March 25, 1789. He d. Aug. 25, 1840, a. 78 y. his widow d. Sept. 16, 1852, a. 86 y. Ch: born; Willem, March 22, 1790, d. at Haverstraw about April 1, 1830, a. 30 y. (?); Catharine Cuyler, July 13, 1799; John, Nov. 15, 1795; Gerrit, March 1, 1798; Richard Cuyler, July 16, 1800; Henry, Jan. 17, 1802; Richard Henry, Oct. 6, 1803; Cuyler, 1806, d. Jan. 24, 1832, a. 25 y. 5 mo. 18 d.; Edward, Jan. 31, 1810; Lydia, May 8, 1814.

Stalker, Joseph, *van de Presbyteriansche gemeente*, m. first, Elisabeth Boils; she d. 1767; secondly, Hannah Albrechts, about 1780. Ch: b.; Alexander, Nov. 13, 1767; William, April 16, 1781.

Staring, Nicolaas, and Catryna. Ch: bp.; Joseph and Catryna, April 11, 1714.

Stater, Jurian Henrich, and Maria Rosina Renitsin. Ch: Johan Philip, bp. June 24, 1759; Elisabeth, b. July 18, 1766.

Stavast, Gerrit, and Claas Janse, left New York about 1672, and came to Albany; the former d. about 1676, and his wid. m. Pieter Meese Vrooman. Soon after the death of his brother, Claas returned to New York, and in 1686, was living with his w. Eefie Gerritsen, in Stone street.

Steele, Daniel, m. Elisabeth Van Benthuysen, April 15, 1797. Ch: Daniel, b. Jan. 24, 1798.

Steen (Sting), Juriaan, and Lea Van der Hoef (Van Roef): Ch: born; Johannes, Jan. 17, 1762; Leona, July 15, 1764; Michael, Jan. 29, 1767; Maria, bp. August 13, 1769; Lydia, Feb. 19, 1772; Rachel, April 17, 1774; Johannes, May 24, 1780.

Stenhouse (Steenhuysen), James, m. Anna Margarita Vedder, Sept. 16, 1732. She was buried April 9, 1748. Ch: bp.; Anna, Oct. 5, 1733; Margarita, Jan. 12, 1737; Johannes, June 17, 1739; Robert, Dec. 13, 1741; Seth, March 27, 1748.

Sterrevelt, Cornelis Cornelise, owned a house and lot in Beverwyck, 1657-60.

Stevenson (Stevens), James, m. Sara Groenendyck, Dec. 9, 1729. He was buried in the church June 6, 1744. Ch: bp.; Sara, Dec. 12, 1736; Pieter, June 28, 1741.

STEVENSON, John, and Magdalena Douw. He d. April 24, 1810, a. 75 y. Ch: Catharina, b. Jan. 6, 1779.

Still, Francis, and Rosino Fero. Ch: Francis, b. April 20, 1786.

Stooner, Pieter, of Hellenbergh, and Mary Steely, Ch: Geertje, bp. Sept. 14, 1790.

Stol, *alias* Hap, Jacob Janse, came to Beverwyck, in 1630 and succeeded Hendrick Albertsen as ferrymaster, About 1657, he bought land at Esopus of Kit Davidts and removed thither. He was an active man in the management of affairs there, frequently corresponding with the Governor in relation to the Indians. His wife was Geertruy Andriese, sister of Hendrick Andriese Van Doesburgh. After her husband's death in 1661, she lived in Esopus.

Stoll, Willem Janse, probably brother of the last, sold a house in the Fort [Orange] to Arent Vandenbergh for 1100 guilders. In 1661, he was the husband of the widow of the late Claas Hendrickse Van Utrecht.

Stoppelbeen, Hendrick, and Elsie Smith. Ch; Maria, bp. Jan. 22, 1754.

Story, Robert, trader in 1676, bought two houses and lots of William Nottingham, on the north corner of Maiden Lane and Pearl street.

STORY, Thomas, and Helena (Eleonora) .... Ch: bp.; Catryn, Dec. 9, 1722; Maria, Feb. 26, 1724.

STORY, Frans, and Catharina De Wever. Ch: Magdalena, b. April 2, 1785.

Stover, William, m. Elisabeth Halenbeck, Oct. 1, 1789. Ch: Mary, b. Dec. 24, 1790.

Streel, Johannes, and Margarita .... Ch : Margarita *geboren voor 3 weken,* bp. Oct. 2, 1763; Mattheus, bp. Nov. 12, 1769.

Streler (Strell), John, and Marytje Elva. Ch : Eva, *oud 5 weken,* bp. Aug. 25, 1765 ; Elizabeth, b. Dec. 24, 1767.

Stridles, Gabriel Tomase (Gabriel Thompson Strudles), in 1662,, hired himself to Thomas Powell for two years at breadmaking, for 22 beavers [$70.40] a year and found ; 1665, hired Jochem Ketelhuyn's house ; 1670, bought a house and lot of Jan Clute ; 1684, was master of the sloop Hopewell, plying between New York and Albany. About 1690, he removed to New York, and in 1701, was an innkeeper there ; 1718, Gerrit Van Laer of New York, baker, petitioned for administration on the estate of Gabriel Thompson Strudles. He was brother-in-law of Richard Pretty, and had the following children bp.: Jannetje, Aug. 19, 1683 ; Thomas, Sept. 28, 1684; Dirk, Jan. 31, 1686 ; Elisabeth, May 12, 1689 : Johannes, in New York, May 7, 1693 ; Fytje, in New York, Feb. 14, 1694.

Stringer, Samuel, and Rachel Vander Heyden. Doctor S. was a native of Maryland, settled in Albany at the conclusion of the French war ; d. July 11, 1817, in his 83d y. His house was on the west side of Broadway, the 9th north from Maiden Lane, and his office was next north of the house. Ch: David, b. March 23, *in huis gedoopt wegens zietke,* March 24, 1765 ; Lydia, m. Stephen Lush ; Gertrude, m. Richard S. Treat, and d. March, 1837.

Strobel, Emanuel, m. Helena Burn, wid. Oct. 15, 1758. Ch : Johannes, bp. June 24, 1759.

Stroop (Strook), Johannes, and Dorothea Canner. Ch : Christina, bp. Feb. 1, 1761; Willem, b. Oct. 31, 1763 ; Frederic, b. Jan. 13, 1768 ; Catharina, b- Aug. 24, 1770.

Stronk (Strunck ; Strong) Hendrick, *geboren in Dutschland,* m. Elsie Harwich (Harbich), Nov. 23, 1756. Ch : Maria, bp. Oct. 2, 1757: Catharina, b. March 1, 1762 ; Elsie, b. Jan. 29, 1766 ; Christina, bp. Jan. 10, 1768 ; Jacob, bp. Dec. 24, 1769 ; Johannes, b. Nov. 21, 1776 ; Johan Joost, b. July 25, 1779.

Strunk, Philip, and Elisabeth Cooper. Ch : Henry, b. Nov. 5, 1799.

Stuart (Stewart) Jan, bought a lot on the hill in 1670, of John Conell, which his administrators sold to Laurens Van Alen in 1675.

STUART. James, and Jenny .... Ch : Thomas, bp. June 15, 1778.

STUART, John, and Jane Campbell. Ch : Nancy, b. May 27, 1779 ; Jenny, b. June 14, 1781.

Studevant, James, and Mary Devenant. Ch: Caleb, b. Sept. 22, 1758, bp. Sept. 28, 1796.

STUDEVANT, Caleb, and Sarah Chandler. Ch: born ; Susanna, April 29, 1783, bp. Sept. 28, 1796; Sarah, b. Feb. 25, 1788, bp. Sept. 28, 1796.

Stuip, Frans, and Catharina DeWever. Ch: born ; Maria, March 20, 1774; Abraham, Aug. 16, 1776 ; Karel, June 16, 1779 ; Annatje, April 3, 1782.

Sturges, Isaac, m. Sally Hardy (Smith), Nov. 6, 1777. Ch : Elizabeth, bp. July 8, 1779.

Suidam, Tennis Pieterse, and Margariet Lawrense. Ch : bp. Pieter, Jan. 28, 1694 ; Lourens, June 13, 1703 ; Samuel, Aug. 12, 1705 ; Catharina, Jan. 30. 1709.

Sulliman (Sullivan ?) Charles, and Dorothea Luther. Ch : Angenita, bp. Dec. 26, 1757.

Sullivan, John. and Elizabeth Cooper. Ch : Dorothea, bp. ; May 8, 1773 ; Maria, b. April 11, 1775 ; Abraham, b. June 25, 1779.

Sutherland, William, and Elizabeth. Ch : Elizabeth, bp. July 3, 1759.

Swart, Gerrit, was appointed *schout fiscal* or sheriff of Rensselaerswyck in 1652; in 1670 he was succeeded by Capt. Salisbury : the magistrates, appointed four schoolmasters for the village in 1676, of whom he was one : at this time he owned land at *Lub-berde's land* [Troy] and a lot on the mill road [now upper Broadway], 80 ft. wide next to Barent Pieterse Coeymans. In 1661, he and his wife Anthonia Van Ryswyck, made a joint will ; they had then no child living ; she died Feb. 15, 1700.

SWART, Cornelis, of Schenectady, eldest son and heir of Teunis Cornelise S. and Elizabeth Van der Linde, was born in 1652 ; in 1715, he was a resident of Ulster county tho' owning land at Schenectady. Ch : bp. Abigail, Sept. 16, 1685 : Elizabeth, Nov. 13, 1687 ; Geertruy, April 27, 1690.

SWART, Esaias Teunise of Schenectady, son of Teunis Cornelise S. m. Eva Teunis Van Woert. Ch : bp. ; Sara, Dec. 16, 1696 ; Jesaias, Oct. 30, 1709. See also *Schenectady Families.*

SWART, Adam Antonise " Van Schenegtade " 1690, Kinderhoek, 1706 ; m. Metie Willemse Van Slyck " Van Nieuw Albanie " Jan. 15, 1690. Ch : Johanna, bp. Jan. 13, 1706.

SWART, Dirk, m. Jannetie Van der Zee, July 22, 1758. Ch : Teunis, bp. Jan. 4, 1760.

SWART, Jacobus, and Nelly Whitaker. Ch: born ; Edward, Jan. 10, 1771 ; Dirk, Oct. 20, 1773 ; Elizabeth, Nov. 26, 1775.

Swartwout, Roeloff, a resident and freeholder of Beverwyck, until 1660, when he was appointed first sheriff of Wiltwyck, at the Esopus ; 1663, suspended from office on account of an insolent letter, on making an apology restored ; 1689–90 appointed justice and collector of the grand excise of Ulster county. He m. Eva Albertse, dau. of Albert Andriese Bratt, and widow of Antony de Hooges, of Beverwyck.

SWARTWOUT. Barnhardus of Esopus and Rachel Schepmoes. Ch : bp. ; Eva, Feb. 18, 1705 ; Jacob, Feb. 1, 1708.

Swits, Isaac Cornelise, of Schenectady, and Susanna Groot. Ch : bp. ; Isaac, July 28, 1691 ; Jacob, Oct. 29, 1693. See also *Schenectady Families.*

SWITS, Cornelis, *geboren en wonende tot Schenechtade* in 1702, m. Hester Visscher, Oct. 9, 1702 ; she was buried Nov. 14, 1757. Ch : bp. ; Isaac, July 2, 1703 ; Femmetje, Jan. 13, 1705, buried June 8, 1725 ; Isaac, Sept. 22, 1706 ; Tjerk Feb. 29, 1708 : Anna Oct. 19, 1712, Tjierk, Harmense, August 14, 1714, buried Angust 25, 1740 ; Arisantje, April 15, 1716 ; Cornelis, August 30, 1719.

SWITS, Isaac, m. Maria Vrooman, Feb. 25, 1728 ; Ch : bp. ; Femmetie, August 22, 1735 ; Cornelis, April 23, 1738 ; Geertruy, Jan. 10, 1742 ; Catharina, Jan. 10, 1746. See also *Schenectady Families.*

SWITS, Cornelis, m. Catharina Schuyler, in New York, Jan. 15, 1762. Ch : b. ; Maria, August 7, 1763 ; Margarita, Sept. 20, 1765 ; Isaac, Oct. 19, 1767 ; Johanna, Jan. 2, 1771 ; Brand Schuyler, Sept. 11, 1772;

Femmetie, August 17, 1774 ; Catharina, August 21, 1776.

Swits, Brandt Schuyler, m. Alida, dau. of Col. Goosen Van Schaick, Oct. 13, 1797. She d. April 1, 1823, a. 52 y. then a widow. Ch : Schuyler, b. August 15, 1798, d. April 15, 1799.

Nov. 21, 1695, Lancaster Simms, and Katharine his wife petitioned for a confirmation of a tract of land on the boundary line between New York and New Jersey, and between Hudson's river and Overpeck's creek, formerly granted by the governor of New Jersey to Balthazar De Haart.

Symes, Lancaster, Jr., m. Mrs. (Mary) Lydius, Jan. 15, 1729. Ch : Lancaster, bp. Nov. 19, 1729.

Symonse, Willem, servant of Volkert Janse Douw, in 1659 ; with his fellow servant Pieter Pieterse Lassingh ran away to Hartford, Conn.; his master empowered Paulus Schrik, merchant there to apprehend and send them back.

Symonse, Pieter, Van Oostsanen, a tobacco planter at Beverwyck, in 1661.

Tack, Aert Pieterse, born at Etten in the barony of Breda, in Brabant, where he had a brother Cornelis, living ; in 1660, a resident of Beverwyck.

Tappen, alias Glasemaecker, Juriaan Teunise, innkeeper, 1654–1677. He was a large dealer in real estate, comprising village lots and farms. In 1670, he exchanged a house and lot in Albany for the farm of Cornelis Cornelise Viele in Schenectady, which was purchased two years later by Harmen Vedder, and in 1671 he received a conveyance from Jeronimus Ebbingh, husband of Johanna De Laet, who inherited one-tenth of Rensselaerswyck from her father, of a bouwery lying between the *Wynant's* and *Poesten* kils ; the next year Capt. Philip Pieterse Schuyler bought this bouwery for 600 beaver skins. Juriaan Teunise and his wife Wybrecht Jacobse Dochter made a joint will in 1661 ; at this time they had no children living.

Teabear (Taber?), Joseph, and Debora Smith. Ch : Maria, bp. Feb. 19, 1777.

Talbot (Tarbird), William, m. Annatie (Johanna, Hannah), Young, March 16, 1777. Ch : b. ; Robert, Sept. 28, 1779 ; Maria, Sept. 9, 1781 ; Hannah, Jan. 8, 1784 ; ... (no name written), Jan. 8, 1797 ; Susanna, Feb. 2, 1799 ; Margaret, Nov. 28, 1801.

Tannson, Jan, m. Maria Huygh, Jan. 20, 1717. Ch : Anna, bp. July 13, 1717.

Taylor, James, and Rachel Hooghkerk. Ch : Jacobus, bp. June 10, 1753.

Taylor, John, and Susanna Baxter. Ch : William, bp. Nov. 6, 1756.

Taylor, John, and Sara Wilry. Ch : Phœbe, b. Sept. 12, 1768.

Taylor, Robert, *op de Halve Maan,* and Emmetje Hendrickse. Ch : born ; Willem, Sept. 19, 1768 ; Johannes, Jan. 2, 1770.

Taylor, John, and Claartje Clute. Ch : Phœbe, b. June 19, 1770.

Taylor, Lucas, and Celia Bratt. Ch : b. Rachel, Jan. 8, 1777 ; Lydia, Sept. 20, 1779.

Taylor, Alexander, of Saratoga, and Jenny Brisby. Ch : Jane, bp. Feb. 5, 1789.

Taylor, John, and Eleanor Naggy. Ch : Hugh, b. March 28, 1793.

Teller, Willem, the first settler, merchant of New York, aged about 78y. in a deposition made July 6, 1698, said that he arrived in this Province in the year 1639, was sent to Fort Orange, by Kieft, served there as corporal, and then was advanced to be *Wachtmeester* of the fort ; that he had continued his residence at Albany, from 1639, to 1692, with some small intermissions upon voyages to New York, Delaware and one short voyage to Holland. He was a trader for about 50 years in Albany from whence he removed to New York in 1692, with his sons ; he died in 1701. In his will made March 19, 1869, proved 1701, he spoke of but 6 of his 9 Ch : as then living, viz, Andries, Helena, Elizabeth, Willem, Johannes and Jannetie, and though a prosperous merchant the inventory of his property amounted only to £910 10s. 2p. There is reason to believe that he had distributed most of his property among his children before his death. He was one of the early proprietors of Schenectady, in 1662, though probably never a resident there, and one of the 5 patentees mentioned in the first patent of the town in 1684. His first wife was Margaret Donchesen ; she d. before 1664, in which year, he made a marriage contract with Maria Varleth, widow of Paulus Schrick ; she died in 1702, when an inventory of her estate was made amounting to £1275 12s, 9p. His Ch : were Andries, b. 1642 ; Helena, b. 1645, m. first Cornelis Bogardus, and secondly Francis Rombouts ; Maria, b. 1648, m. first Pieter Van Alen, secondly.... Loockermans ; Elizabeth, b. 1652, m. first Abraham Van Tricht, and secondly, Melgert Wynantse Van der Poel ; Jacob, b. 1655 ; Willem b. 1657 ; Johannes, b. 1659 ; Caspar ; and Jannetie, m. Arent Philipse Schuyler.

Teller, Andries, merchant and for many years magistrate in Albany ; m. Sophia dau. of Oloff Stevense Van Cortlandt, May 6, 1671, in New York, to which place he soon after removed ; made his will Dec. 16, 1702, and he spoke of his ; Andries, and Margarita, he likewise had a son Oliver Stephen, bp. in Albany, Nov. 29, 1685.

Teller, Oliver [son of Andries], m. Cornelia De Peyster, in New York, Oct. 12, 1712. Ch : bp. in New York, Margareta, March 18, 1713 ; Johannes, Aug. 21, 1715 ; Margareta, Dec. 25, 1716 ; Cornelia, March 29, 1719.

Teller, Andries [son of Andries,] resided in New York ; made will Sept. 3, 1702, and spoke of son Andrew ; brother Oliver ; sister Margaret ; and mother Sophia. His son Andries probably m. first, Catharine Vandewater, Sept. 15, 1722, and secondly, Maria Marius, Nov. 15, 1730 ; made will Feb. 15, 1730–31, and spoke of w. Mary ; dau. Catharina ; and Uncle Oliver.

Teller, Jacob [son of Willem T., senior], of New Albany, m. Christina Wessels, of New York, Oct. 24, 1683, in N. York. In 1686, he lived in Whitehall street. He was master of the sloop Hopewell, plying between N. York and Esopus ; made will Aug. 8, 1696, and spoke of w. Christina ; and dau. Anna Margarita ; his wid. made will Sept. 17, 1698, also spoke of dau. Anna Margarita. Ch : bp. in New York ; Willem, Dec. 22, 1689 ; Anna Margarita, Aug. 1, 1694.

Teller, Willem, Jr, [son of Will T., senior], of New Albany, m. Rachel Kiersted, of New York, Nov. 19, 1686 ; soon after removed to New York ; made will June 25, 1710. Ch : bp. in New York ; Margarita, Aug. 17, 1687 ; Willem, Sept. 1, 1689 ; Willem, Dec. 25, 1690 ; Hans, March 12, 1693 ; Margariet, Feb.

2, 1696; Jacobus, April 18, 1699; Andries, Jan. 25, 1702; Jacobus, Aug. 29, 1703. [Willem Teller and Maria Van Tricht received a license to marry Jan. 19, 1706.]

TELLER, Willem, probably son of the last, had a son Willem, bp. in New York, March 21, 1714.

TELLER, Hans [son of Willem T., Jr.], m. Catharina Van Tilburg, April 23, 1719. Ch: Willem, bp. in New York, May 26, 1720.

TELLER, Johannes [youngest son of Willem T., Senior], settled in Schenectady, and m. Susanna Wendel, August 18, 1686. Ch: bp.; Margarita, Feb. 19, 1693; Willem, Oct. 4, 1695; Jacobus, July 15, 1698. See also *Schenectady Families.*

TELLER, Johannes, and Elizabeth.... Ch: John, bp. Feb. 21, 1725.

Ten Broeck, Major Dirk Wesselse, born in 1642, was a servant of Pieter Van Alen in Beverwyck, as early as 1662; soon after, he began to trade for himself, and for many years was largely engaged in Indian and other public affairs at Albany. Some years he exported as many as 5,000 beaver skins. In 1686, he became the first recorder under the charter of the city; 1696-8, he served as mayor. The following notice of his death is recorded in an ancient Bible owned by one of his descendants: 1717, *Den 13 Sept. in Roeloff Jansen's kil is myn vader Dirk Wesselse in den Heere gerust op syn bouwery op Roeloff Jansen's kil. De Heere geve hem een zalige opstandinge.* He married Christina Cornelise Van Buren. In his will made Feb. 4, 1714-5, proved Feb. 6, 171¾ he mentioned the following children: Wessel; Elsje, w. of Johannes Cuyler; Catalyntje, w. of Johan Lisajer; Cornelia, w. of Johannes Wyncoop; Geertruy, w. of Abraham Schuyler; Christina, w. of Johannes Van Alen; Elisabeth w. of Antony Coster; Lidia, w. of Volkert Van Vechten; Samuel; Johannes; Tobias, bp. Feb. 20, 1689; besides these, Manasse and Ephraim, twins were bp. Nov. 21, 1681. Maj. Ten Broeck bought of the heirs of the famous Anneke Janse, soon after her death in 1663, the lot on the east corner of State and James streets, which he retained till his death. Besides this he owned a bouwery on the Roeloff Jansen's kil. [Hendrick Wesselse Ten Broeck, of New York, 1686, and Jochem Wesselse, of Beverwyck, were probably his brothers.]

TEN BROECK, Wessels, baker, m. Caatje Lookermans, April 2, 1684. In his will, made June 10, 1723, proved Jan. 29, 1752, he spoke of his w. Catharyna, dau. and heir of Jacob Lookermans, late of Albany, deceased, of his ch: Dirk; Jacob; Christine; Cornelis; and Anna Catharina. He d. May 27, 1747. In 1678, he and Cornelis Van Dyck bought land of the Indians on the east side of the Hudson river. The following ch. were bp. in Albany: A child, name omitted, April 26, 1685; Dirk, Dec. 5, 1686; Christina, Oct. 20, 1689; Jacob, Feb. 28, 1692; Christine, June 17, 1694; Elisabeth, Aug. 23, 1696; Maria, June 26, 1698; Jacob, Aug. 18, 1700; Cornelis, March 10, 1706.

TEN BROECK, Samuel, of Claverack, m. Maria, dau. of Hendrick Van Rensselaer, and Catharine Van Brugge, Nov. 7, 1712. She d. April 4, 1756, in Albany, a. 74 y. 7 m. and was buried in Greenbush. Ch: bp.; Christina, Feb. 7, 1714: Dirk Wesselse, May 1, 1715; Hendrik, March 24, 1717; Johannes, Sept. 4, 1720, d. Oct. 23, 1793; Cathrina, d. May 18, 1753; Jeremias, Feb. 1, 1727, d. Oct. 24, 1802; Christina, Jan. 7, 1730.

TEN BROECK, Dirk, mayor of Albany, 1746-8; m. Margarita Cuyler, Nov. 26, 1714, was buried in the church Jan. 7, 1751. Ch: bp.; Catryna, Sept. 4, 1715; Anna, June 9, 1717, was buried Dec. 30, 1731; Christina, Jan. 1, 1719; Maria, April 23, 1721; Wessel, April 28, 1723; Sara, May 30, 1725; Margarita, March 26, 1727: Abraham, April 6, 1729; Margarita, Oct. 10, 1731; Abraham, May 19, 1734; Dirk, May 16, 1736; Dirk, July 26, 1738.

TEN BROECK, Tobias, of Claverack, m. Maritie Van Stry, Oct. 24, 1714. 1724 *Den 8 Juny, Is Tobyas Ten Broeck in den Heere gerust op syn bouwery op Roeloff Jansen's Kil. De Heere geve hem een zalige opstandige.* Ch: bp.; Catryna Johanna, Sept. 26, 1715; Dirk, April 14, 1717; Christina, May 17, 1719; Elisabeth, Jan. 8, 1721.

TEN BROECK, Johannes, m. [first, Elisabeth Wendel, June 18, 1709, and secondly] Catryna Van Rensselaer, Dec. 29, 1714. Ch: bp.; Dirk Wesselse, Oct. 30, 1715; Catryna, Jan. 6, 1717; Hendrik, March 9, 1718; Johannes, Sept. 20, 1719; Ephraim, Jan. 15, 1721; Christina, March 18, 1722; Jeremias, Jan. 18, 1724; Christina, Sept. 5, 1725; Cornelis, May 22, 1727; Pieter, Nov. 17, 1728; Abraham, June 18, 1730; Maria, Nov. 21, 1731; Ephraim, Aug. 15, 1733.

TEN BROECK, Jacob, and Christina .... Ch: bp.; Catharina, June 4, 1727; Johannes, Feb. 9, 1729; Christina, Feb. 15, 1738; Maria, March 30, 1740.

TEN BROECK, Cornelis, m. Maria Cuyler, Oct. 12, 1733. Ch: bp.; Catharyna, May 19, 1737; Johannes, July 30, 1740, d. Dec. 26, 1822, a. 83 y.

TEN BROECK, Hendrick, m. Annatje Van Schaick, Oct. 14, 1743. Ch· bp.; Antony, Nov. 1, 1747; Antje, July 7, 1754.

TEN BROECK, Dirk Wesselse, m. Catarina Conyn June 26, 1743. Ch: Leendert, bp. Feb. 11, 1753. [Dirk Ten B. m. Annatje Douw, Nov. 25, 1761.]

TEN BROECK, Johannes, m. Sara Gansevoort, June 12, 1762, d. Dec. 26, 1822, a. 83 y. Ch: born; Cornelis, Feb. 23, 1763; Magdalena, May 8, 1765; Harmen, March 25, 1767; Maria, Nov. 11, 1768; Johannes, March 26, 1771; Petrus, bp. May 9, 1773; Leendert, Jan. 24, 1775; Sara, Feb. 2, 1778; Catharina, Nov. 20, 1779; George, Dec. 23, 1781; Wessel, Sept. 25, 1783.

TEN BROECK, General Abraham, mayor of Albany, 1779-83 and 1796-99; d. Jan. 19, 1810, a, 75 y. He m. Elizabeth Van Rensselaer. Ch: born; Dirk, and Elizabeth, twins, Nov. 3, 1765; Elizabeth, Aug. 25, 1772; Margarita, July 18, 1776; Maria Van Rensselaer, Feb. 23, 1779.

TEN BROECK, Dirk, and Cornelia Stuiversand [Stuyvesant]. Ch: b.; Abraham, July 13, 1788; Margaret Stuyvesant, July 24, 1790; Petrus Stuyvesant, Jan. 26, 1792; Elisabeth Maria, May 20, 1795; Cornelia, April 23, 1798.

Ten Eyck, Coenraad, of New Amsterdam, a tanner and shoemaker. Ch. bp. in New York: Margariet, August 20, 1651; Tobias, Jan. 26, 1653; Coenraad, Nov. 22, 1654; Hendrick, April 30, 1656; Matthys, March 30, 1658; Margriet, Oct. 22, 1659; Andries, Jan. 15, 1662; Metje, April 11, 1664; Jacob; Dirk.

TEN EYCK, Coenraad, Jr., of New York, m. Beletie Hercks, May 19, 1675. Ch: bp. in New York: Coenraad, Dec. 13, 1675; Samuel, July 24, 1678; Maritie, Nov. 3, 1680; Wyntje, Jan. 15, 1684; Belitie, Feb. 23, 1687; Johannes, Nov. 28, 1690; Jacob? Sam-

uel, Sept. 6, 1704; Beletie, Sept. 11, 1706; Elisabeth,
April 2, 1710; Jacobus, Feb. 20, 1712.

TEN EYCK, Jacob Coenraetse, shoemaker, of Albany, m. Geertje Coeymans, who was b. April 23,
1654, and d. Feb. 2, 1736, a. 82 y. She made her will
Sept. 6, 1716, proved July 10, 1736, then a widow, and
spoke of the following ch. except Andries; d. Feb.
27, 1735-6. Ch: Coenraat, b. April 9, 1678; Barent;
Mayken, b. April 2, 1685, m. Andries Van Petten, of
Schenectady, Dec. 26, 1712; Andries, bp. March 25,
1688; Anneken, bp. August 20, 1693, m. Johannes
Bleecker, and d. Dec. 9, 1738.

TEN EYCK, Barent, m. Neeltje Schermerhooren,
Sept. 30, 1700. He d. Jan. 20, 1710-1. The following
ch. were spoken of in their grandmother's will as
living in 1716, except the first. Ch: bp.; Jannetie,
March 23, 1701; Geertje, August 30, 1702; Jacob, Feb.
6, 1704; Jannetje, Dec. 12, 1705; Maria, May 30, 1708;
Johannes, Nov. 27, 1709.

TEN EYCK, Coenraad, silversmith, m. Gerritje Van
Schaick, Sept. 24, 1704, (church rec.) Oct. 10, 1703,
(Family Bible). He was buried Jan. 23, 1753. Ch:
Jacob, b. April 21, 1705; Maria, b. Jan. 3, 1707, m.
Gerrit Bratt; Gerritje, b. July 1710; Antony, b.
Sept. 17, bp. Sept. 13 (*sic*) 1712; Barent, b. Sept. 29,
1714, d. March 1 (Feb. 27), 1795, a. 81 y. (Effie, w. of
Barent Ten Eyck, d. Nov. 27, 1791, a. 63 y. 2m. 1d.);
Catrina, b. Jan. 29, 1716-7, d. Nov. 11 (Oct. 15),
1741; Andries, b. Dec. 18, bp. Dec. 17 (*sic*) 1718;
Anna Margarita, b. Feb. 12, 1721; Tobias, b. May
18, 1723; Gerritje, b. August 19, bp. July 18 (*sic*)
1728, m. Pieter Gansevoort.

TEN EYCK, Henrik, baker, m. Margarita Bleecker,
Nov. 28, 1706. Ch: bp.; Jacob, Jan. 25, 1708; Johannes, Oct. 28,1710; Geertie, Jan. 18,1713; Margarita,
May 10, 1715; Tobias, August 18, 1717. [See *Schenectady Families.*] Henrik, May 8, 1720; Barent, Sept.
9, 1722; Hendrik, Sept. 5, 1725.

TEN EYCK, Jacob, m. Alida Visscher, June 17,
1728. Ch: bp.; Neeltje, Jan. 15, 1729, m. Samuel
Pruyn, and d. April 14, 1817, a. 88 y. 2 m. 22 d. Alida,
Nov. 15, 1730; Alida, Sept. 15, 1732; Barent, Sept.
22, 1734; Geertje, Jan. 11, 1736, m. Johannes F.
Pruyn, and d. May 16, 1807, a. 70 y. 3 m. 27 d.; Barent, Sept. 24,1738; Barent, Sept. 7,1740: Maria, Feb.
27, 1743.

TEN EYCK, Jacob H. m. Annatje Wendel, Nov.
30, 1737. Ch: bp.; Margarita, Oct. 1, 1738; Anna,
Aug. 31, 1740; Anna,.Sept. 12, 1742; Hendrik, Oct.
9, 1744; Harmanus, March 29, 1747; Harmanus, Jan.
14, 1750.

TEN EYCK, Jacob C. m. Catharyna dau. of Abraham Cuyler, Aug. 1, 7136. He was judge of the court
of common pleas, and mayor 1748. Ch: b.; Conraad,
Nov. 27, 1741-50, d. Sept. 9, 1793, a. 88 y. She d.
Nov. 22, 1790, a. 81 y. Ch: b.; Coenraad,_ Nov. 27,
1741; Abraham, Nov. 29, 1743; Catharina, March 14,
1746; Anthony, Sept. 17, 1739.

TEN EYCK, Barent Henderickse, merchant, m. Lena
Ryckman, April 21, 1745. Ch: bp.; Lena, Sept. 8,
1745; Hendrick, Nov. 8, 1747. [Barent Ten E. and
Elsie Cuyler, m. Jan. 29, 1759.]

TEN EYCK, Johannes H. and Sarah Ten Broeck.
He d. July 31, 1794, a. 83 y. 11 m. 10 d. ; she d. Feb.
16, 1801, a. 70 y. Ch: bp.; Hendrick, April 17, 1748;
Hendrick May 28, 1749; Hendrick, June, 23, 1754;
Margarita, April 16, 1758.

TEN EYCK, Andries, and Anna Margarita Coeymans. Ch: bp.; Pieter, b. Oct. 29, 1749; Maria, and
Charlotte, Jan. 30, 1752: Coenraad, Aug. 20, 1754;
Pieter Coeyman, July 15, 1759; Andreas (?), Charlotte.

TEN EYCK, Tobias C., of Albany, m. Judithje Van
Buren of Schotack, Feb. 6, 1756. Ch: bp.; Coenraad,
May 31, 1757: Eytje, Dec. 31, 1758; Johannes, Nov.
1, 1761; Gerritje, b. March 15, 1765.

TEN EYCK, Hendrik, Jr., m. Margarita Douw, May
22, 1767. Ch: born; Anna, Sept. 17, 1768; Lyntje,
March 28, 1770; Catharina, Sept. 7, 1772; Geertruy,
June 15, 1774, d. at Cazenovia, June 17, 1839, a. 64 y.;
Elsie, June 4, 1777; Elsie, Feb. 19, 1779; Jacob,
Dec. 8, 1785.

TEN EYCK, Abraham, m. Annatie Lansing, April
14, 1769. He d. Nov. (Oct). 7, 1824; she d. Nov. 7,
1824, a. 76 y. 6 m. Ch: born; Catharina, Nov. 17,
1769; Jacob, Feb. 17, 1772, m. Magdalena Gansevoort,
March 6, 1795; Maria, June 28, 1774; Abraham, Oct.
23, 1767; Lena, Aug. 26, 1779; Coenraad, July 17, 1782;
Jeremiah Van Rensselaer, May 13, 1785; Lena, June
13, 1787; Jeremiah Van Rensselaer, April 3, 1790.

TEN EYCK, Barent, and Sara Codwies. Ch: Maria,
b. Sept. 6, 1769.

TEN EYCK, Hendrick B., and Catharina Sanders.
She was dead at the baptism of her child. Ch: Robert Sanders, b. July 25, bp. July 28, 1771.

TEN EYCK, Anthony, of Schodac, was a member of
the convention in 1787, which ratified the constitution
of the United States; first judge of Rensselaer county
until 60 years of age, and member of the senate for 8
yrs. He m. Maria Egbertse, Feb. 18, 1776. Ch: b.;
Catharina, Dec. 14, 1776; Egbert, April 18, 1779; Anthony, July 9, 1783; Anthony, Dec. 23, 1784.

TEN EYCK, Coenraad. m. first, Charlotte Ten Eyck;
secondly, Geertje Ten Eyck, Feb. 18, 1781. Ch: Jacob, b. Jan. 10, 1778.

TEN EYCK, Harmanus, m. Margarita Bleecker,
March 30, 1776; he d. Jan. 27, 1828, a. 71 y. at No.
362 N. Market St.; she d. Sept. 1, 1834, a. 79 y.
Ch: b.; Cathalyna, May 24, 1777; Cathalyna, Oct. 12,
1778; Jacob, Feb. 9, 1781; Anna, March 16, 1783;
Hendrik, Feb. 21, 1786; Margarita, April 30, 1788;
Margariet, July 22, 1791; Catharine Van Ingen, Feb.
10, 1796.

TEN EYCK, John De Peyster, son of Tobias Ten E.,
of Schenectady, m. Maria Douw, Jan, 20, 1782. Ch:
John De Peyster b. May 3, 1788.

TEN EYCK, George, and Magdalena Upham. Ch:
b.; Andreas, Sept. 10, 1789; Hendrick, June 30, 1795;
Hendrick, Nov. 12, 1797 (?); Susanna, July 11, 1801.

TEN EYCK, Barent, m. Annatie Hoffman, July 18,
1790. She m. secondly, Dr. McClelland. Ch: b.;
Catharine, April 7, 1791, m. Barent Mynderse, of
Schenectady; Harmen Hoffman 1793 (?)

TEN EYCK, Andreas, and Luetie Van Esh. Ch:
Sarah, b. May 28, 1791. [Andrew Ten E., and Lucy
La Grange were m. March 10, 1797.]

TEN EYCK, Jacob,m. Magdalene Gansevoort, March
6, 1795; he d. at Whitehall, near Albany, July 26,
1862, a. 90 y. 5 m. 9 d.; she d. at same place, May 14,
1863, a. 86 y. Ch: b.; Hester Gansevoort, Jan. 4,
1796; Abraham Cuyler, July 6, 1797; Anna, Jan. 3,
1800; Leonard Gansevoort, Oct. 12, 1801; Jacob Lansing, Dec. 20, 1803; Harmen Gansevoort, Jan. 17,
1806; Peter Gansevoort, Dec. 19, 1809.

Terwillegen, Simon, and Jannetie Coen. Ch: Saartie, b. June 28, 1789.

Teunissen, Gerrit, and Geertruy Groesbeck. Ch: Jacobus, b. Nov. 1, 1776.

Teunisse, Juriaan, see Tappen.

Thiel, Bastiaan, and Catarina Ruyter. Ch: bp.; Henderick, April 20, 1753; Catarina, April 20, 1755.

Thing (Tingy, Tingly, Tinky), John and Mary Lucy (Luitz, Louths). Ch: b.; William, Nov. 11, 1768; Catharina, August 14, 1770; Johannes, July 17, 1773; Maria, August 29, 1780; Susanna, March 21, 1787.

Thomas, Evan, and Catharine.... Ch : Willem, and Susanna, twins, bp. April 19, 1767.

Thompson, William, an d Mary.... Ch: William, b. March 27, 1777.

THOMPSON, John, and Jannet Wilson. Ch: Christina, b. August 4, 1778. [John T. and Janny McFarson, m. Jan. 21, 1781.]

THOMPSON, Robert and Agnes Webner. Ch: Nancy, b. Nov. 15, 1779.

THOMPSON, Alexander, and Nelly Grant. Ch: Ann, b. June 31 (*sic*) 1781.

THOMPSON, James Elliott, and Gertrude Conner. He d. August 28, 1825. Ch : a child, no name registered b. Feb. 14, 1789; Margaret, b. May 8, 1791: Archibald, b. August 2, 1799.

THOMPSON, George, and Elisabeth Bratt. Ch: Jane, b. Oct. 18, 1789.

Thomson, Capt. Gabriel, see Stridles.

Thorn, Jan, *geboren tot N. Y.*, m. Geertje Bresser, *geboren tot Kingstown*, Jan. 23, 1706. She d. Oct. 23, 1707. Ch : Nicolaas, bp. Sept. 21, 1707.

Thousek, Caspar, and Elizabeth.... Ch: Catharina, bp. March 7, 1769.

Tiets, Willem, and. Maria M. Cregeler. Ch: Catharina, b. July 5, 1780.

Tietsoort, Willem Abrahamse, of Schenectady, removed to Dutchess county. He m. Neeltje Swart. Ch : Ariaantje, bp. August 2, 1685.

Tilman, Christopher, and Lucy Tracy. Ch : Christopher William, b. July 29, 1790.

Tilton, Pieter, and Margaret, Yhl (Ehle). Ch : Petrus, b. Dec. 20, 1782.

Timmel, Jan, a resident of Greenbush in 1671.

Toinel, Anthony, a trader of Beverwyck. In 1661, Mrs. Sophia Van Wyckersloot, wife of Mr. Toinel, sold certain goods to arrive from Holland to Asser Leevi, a Jewish trader, at 75 pr. ct. advance and freight. In 1662, he acknowledged a debt of 60 guilders and two beavers to Philip Pieterse Schuyler, for his fare from Holland, which he promised to pay when he returned from Holland, next year. His wife was the widow of Didrick Van Hamel late secretary of Rensselaerwyck.

TJans, see Jones.

Tjerkse, Isaac, and .... Ch: Willem, bp. May 23, 1686.

Toll, Carel Hansen, of Schenectady, and Lysbet Rinckhout, Ch: bp.; Neeltje, June 20, 1686; Daniel, Aug. 11, 1691; Neeltje, July 7, 1695; Simon, May 8, 1698. (See also *Schenectady Families*).

TOLL, Carel H., of Schenectady, m. Marytje Kittel at S., Oct. 2, 1759. Ch: Maria, b. Oct. 5, 1771. (See also *Schenectady Families*).

TOLL, Jesse, of Saratoga, and Maria Viele. Ch : Anna, b. Dec. 31, 1786.

Tomase, Jacob, and .... Ch : Rutgert, bp. April 17, 1687.

TOMASE, Cornelis, and .... Ch: Agniet, bp. April 10, 1687.

Tortler, John, and Elisabeth Cribble. Ch: Anna Maria, b. July 3, 1791.

Teunsel, James, and Rachel Gardenier. Ch: James, b. May 6, 1776.

Towhay, Timothy, and Elisabeth Jones. Ch : Jacob, bp. June 21, 1747.

Treal, Hannes, and Elsie Mucret. Ch: Catarina, bp. Feb. 7, 1762.

Treat, Richard S., and Gertrude Stringer. Ch : b.; Elisabeth, Jan. 30, 1795; Samuel Stringer, Dec. 30, 1796; Samuel Stringer, April 27, 1798; Rachel Stringer, Jan. 15, 1800; Richard Joseph, May 30, 1802.

Trephagen, Johannes, and Aagie Winne. Ch: Willem, bp. Jan. 8, 1706; Alida, bp. in N. York, Oct. 10, 1708.

Trotter, John, and Annatie Hogen. Ch: Marten, bp. Sept. 16, 1750; Matthew (?)

TROTTER, Gen. Matthew, and Margaret Wendell. He d. Dec. 9, 1830; she d. July 23, 1849, in her 80th yr. Ch: b.; John, Oct. 17, 1789; Henry, Dec. 11, 1792, d. March 25, 1825, at 488 South Market St.; Margaret, Sept. 3, 1796, m. William Lush, and d. Sept. 1, 1870; Anna Maria, Aug. 2, 1803, d. Dec. 2, 1815.

TROTTER, John, merchant, m. Sarah Ten Eyck, dau. of Dr. Elias Willard; she d. Oct. 22, 1830, in her 41st y. ; he d. Dec. 31, 1862, a. 75 y. Ch: John; Edward Willard; and ....

Trowbridge, Luther, m. Elisabeth Tillman, March 15, 1778. Ch: b.; Margaret, June 14, 1796; Ann Maria, Sept. 7, 1798; Charles Christopher, Dec. 29, 1800.

Truex, a corruption both in pronunciation and spelling from *De Trieux*. Philip Du Truy, an early settler in New Amsterdam, was court messenger there. His sons were Isaac, bp. in N. Amst., April 21, 1642; Jacob, bp. in N. Amst., Dec. 7, 1645, and Abraham (?) and dau. Sara; Susanna; Rachel; and perhaps Rebecca.

TRUEX, Isaac, of Schenectady, m. Maria Willemse Brouwer. Ch : Isaac, bp. March 2, 1690; Lysbeth, bp. July 3, 1692; Johannes, bp. Dec. 11, 1696. (See *Schenectady Families*).

TRUEX, Abraham, of Schenectady, m. Christina La Grange. Ch: bp.; Joanna, Sept. 20, 1713; Anna, April 14, 1717; Abraham, Feb. 21, 1728.

TRUEX, Isaac Jacobse, of Schenectady, m. Maria Wyngaart, June 16, 1750. Ch: bp.; Jacob, April 21, 1751; Petrus, March 19, 1762; Maria, Nov. 2, 1766; [Isaac T. of the Normanskil, m. Christina Pelleger, Jan. 21, 1769.] (See *Schenectady Families*).

TRUEX, Jillis, and Ariaantje Jansen. Ch: Jacob, bp. June 26, 1755.

TRUAX, Gillis, and Nancy McKinney. Ch: Andries, b. Nov. 2, 1775.

TRUEX, John W., of Schenectady, and Magdalena Huyser. Ch: Isaac, b. June 13, 1779. (See *Schenectady Families*).

112   *Genealogies of the First Settlers of Albany.*

Truex, Andries, of Schenectady, and Cathalyna Wyngaard. Ch: Elisabeth, b. March 4, 1780. [Andries T., and Cathalyntje Maris, m. Feb. 13, 1770.] (See *Schenectady Families*).

Truex, Jacob I, and Catharina Dochsteder. Ch: b.; Jacob, Jan. 8, 1780; Caty, July 23, 1783; Elisabeth, Dec. 16, 1786; John, Dec. 28, 1790.

Truex, Isaac, m. Jenneke Bleecker, March 16, 1788. He d. Oct. 12, 1812, a. 53 y. 5 m. 9 d.; she d. March 26, 1811, a. 47 y. 5 m. 11 d. Ch: b.; Hendrick Roseboom, March 30, 1789; Ann Bleecker, April 7, 1791; Isaac, July 21, 1793; Gerritie, Aug. 29, 1795; John Bleecker, Dec. 14, 1798, d. May 9, 1817, a. 18 y. 4 m. 25 d.

Truex, Henry, m. Ann Yates, Nov. 9, 1789. He d. Dec. 15, 1834, in his 74th y.; she d. Nov. 23, 1845, in her 77th y. Ch: b.; Catharine Waters, June 26, 1791, d. Aug. 15, 1791; Catharine Waters, July 25, 1792, d. May 19, 1794; Susanna, Oct. 15, bp. Sept. 18 (*sic*), 1795; Catharine Waters, Feb. 28, 1800, d. July, 1826.

Truex, Isaac P., and Ann Bovie. Ch: b.; Sarah, Ann, Oct. 24, 1805; Isaac Van Santvoord, April 17, 1808; Elisabeth Maria, June 5, 1816. (See *Schenectady Families*).

Truax, Isaac Isaacse, of Schenectady, m. Susanna Roseboom. Ch: b.; Cathalyna, Nov. 9, 1770; Cornelis, April 9, 1773. (See *Schenectady Families*).

Tuck, William, and Ruth ... Ch: b.; Routh, Dec. 9, 1722; Mary, April 4, 1725.

Turk, Jacobus, of Kinderhook, high sheriff of Albany county, 1703, m. first, Catharina Van Benthusen, who d. Feb. 4, 1705; and secondly, Tryntje (Teuntje) Hoes, wid. of Thos. Winne, Oct. 27, 1705. Ch: bp.; Jacob, Oct. 14, 1683; Jacobus, Jan. 1, 1685; Johannes, May 16, 1687; Alida, June 16, 1689; Alida, Nov. 27, 1692; Sara, April 7, 1695; Ahasuerus, Nov. 14, 1697; Augustinus, July 21, 1700; Thomas, June 22, 1707; Catharina, Jan. 9, 1709.

Turk, Thomas, and Eva Van Valkenburgh. Ch: bp.; Margarita, Jan. 23, 1740; Johanna, April 25, 1742; Johannes, and Eva, twins, Oct. 21, 1744.

Turk, Jeronimus, Jr., and Elizabeth Bussing. Ch: b.; Timothy, Sept. 24, 1796; Angelica, Feb. 12, 1799.

Turner, William, of Kinderhook, *geboren in oude Engeland*, m. Abigail Bogart, Nov. 7, 1702. Ch: bp.; Jacobus, Oct. 17, 1703; Helmer Johannes, Jan. 7, 1705; Jacobus, b. Nov. 1, *op de Vlakte Klinkenbergh*, and bp. there Dec. 12, 1708; Geisbert, b. *op de flakte Loonenburgh* Feb. 28, and bp. there March 4, 1711.

Turner, Robert, and Rebecca Gardenier. Ch: William, bp. Feb. 19, 1754.

Tuttle, Stephen, and Mary Graham. Ch: Guy, b. Jan. 23, 1778.

Tymensen, Cornelis, of Niskayuna, and Maritie Ysbrantse; in 1713, she willed to the church of Albany £20, for the poor of said church. Ch: Tymen, bp. Dec. 13, 1691; Eldert.

Tymensen, Eldert Cornelis, of Nistigioene, m. Hester Visscher, Nov. 7, 1709. Ch: bp.; Marytje, Oct. 30, 1710; Dirkje, April 20, 1712, m. Hendrick Gerritse; Cornelis, July 26, 1713; Anna, Jan. 5, 1715. (See also *Schenectady Families*).

Tymensen, Bastiaan, m. Mayke Ouderkerk, July 7, 1743. Ch: bp.; Eldert, bp. in Schenectady, July

1, 1744; Eldert, July 26, 1746; Maria, Aug. 14, 1748; Eldert, Sept. 2, 1750; Hester, April 26, 1752; Johannes, Oct. 3, 1756; Jacomyna, Nov. 10. 1758 (?)

Tymensen, Cornelis, and Maria Lieverse. Ch: bp.; Petrus, June 26, 1748; Teunis, March 11, 1750; Rachel, May 10, 1752; Eldert, Oct. 14, 1753; Rachel, March 28, 1756.

Tymensen, Pieter, and Geertruy Cregier. Ch: Cornelis, b. March 12, 1772.

Urlub, Willem Henry, and Maria Aug. Hartman. Ch: bp.; Hendrik, and Anna Margarita, Sept. 15, 1754; Catarina, Sept. 4, 1759.

Usile, Pieter, of Esopus, and Cornelia Dame. Ch: David, bp. Feb. 1, 1708.

Usile, Pieter, Jr., m. Anna Ackerson, June 4, 1724. Ch: bp.; Cornelia, July 5, 1724; Anna, March 7, 1733.

Uzile, David, and Engeltie .... Ch: bp.; Pieter, Jan. 14, 1733; Cornelia, Sept. 1, 1734; Geertruy, Feb. 28, 1736; Adam, Feb. 8, 1738.

Valk, Johannes, and Lysbet .... Ch: Hendrik, bp. Dec. 17, 1738.

Valk, Isaac, and Maritie Warner. Ch: bp.; Maritie, May 28, 1758; Cornelia, Aug. 16, 1761.

Van Aecken, Jan Coster, a trader in Beverwyck, 1654-1672, and perhaps later; a considerable dealer in houses and lots. His w. was Elsie Janse.

Van Alen. There were two persons of this name at Beverwyck, Pieter and Lourens, sons perhaps of Lourens Van Alen.

Van Alen, Pieter, trader and tailor, in Beverwyck, 1658-1674. He d. Jan., 1674, and two years later his bouwerie at Kinderhook was sold to Harmen Janse. He m. Maria Teller, dau. of Willem T. In 1676, his wid. was called Maria Loockermans. Ch: Willem, and Johannes.

Van Alen, Willem [son of the last], of manor Rensselaerswyck, m. Maritie Van Petten, Nov. 4, 1694. Ch: bp.; Maritie, June 21, 1695; Eva, Nov. 7, 1697; Rachel, July 21, 1700; *Pieter*, April 12, 1702; Gerrit Cornelise, May 21, 1704; Nicolaas Frederickse, Aug. 18, 1706; Catharina, Sept. 14, 1707; Claas Frederick, Feb. 5, 1710.

Van Alen, Johannes [son of Pieter], m. Christina Ten Broeck, 1701. He was buried April 12, 1750: she was buried Oct. 6, 1744. Ch: bp.; Maria, Feb. 7, 1703; Christina, April 16, 1704; Pieter, Aug. 18, 1706; Lena, Sept. 19, 1708; Dirk Wesselse, Oct. 28, 1710.

Van Alen, Lourens, in Beverwyck 1630 (?) — 1673; resided in Pearl street, east side between Steuben and Maiden Lane. He probably had a son Lourens.

Van Alen, Lourens [son of the last], of Kinderhook 1673-1699. In 1677, he owned a lot on the west side of Broadway between Steuben and Maiden Lane, which he conveyed in 1684, to Jacob Loockermans; 1690, commissioned justice of the peace; 1703, elected one of the trustees of Kinderhook. His w. was Elbertje Evertse. Ch: bp. a child name not registered Nov. 7, 1686; Lourens, Feb. 6, 1689; Jacobus, Oct. 23, 1691; Johannes, Stephanus, Pieter.

Van Alen, Johannes Lourense, of Kinderhook, had a lot near west corner of Broadway and State 1714; m. Sara Dingman, July 3, 1697. Ch: bp.; Mauris, Nov. 6, 1698; Adam, July 21, 1700; Jacobus, Oct. 8, 1702; Elbertje, Jan. 7, 1705; Alida, Feb. 5, 1707;

Lysbeth, April 25, 1709; Catharina, b. Dec. 12, 1711, bp. at Klinkenbergh, by Domine Falkner the Lutheran minister, Jan. 20, 1712.

VAN ALEN, Stephanus [son of Lourens], of Kinderhook, m. Maria Cornelise Muller (Mulder), July 2, 1702. Ch: bp.; Lourens, Oct. 3, 1703; Heyltje, April 8, 1705; Ephraim, Oct. 3, 1708; Jacobus, Oct. 19, 1713; Ephraim, Oct. 5, 1718; Jannetie, Dec. 26, 1720.

VAN ALEN, Pieter [son of Lourens], of Kinderhook, m. Josina Dingman, Dec. 30, 1704. Ch: bp.; Lourens, May 19, 1706; Adam, August 21, 1709; Elbertje, Feb. 17, 1712;' Alida, August 29, 1714; Lucas, April 21, 1717.

VAN ALEN, Pieter [son of Willem], m. Anna Van Wie, April 11, 1727. He was buried Sept. 17, 1749. Ch: bp.; Willem, Dec. 8, 1728; Agnietje, April 18, 1731; Gerrit, Dec. 16, 1733; Johannes, [mother, Anna Van Benthuysen], Oct. 6, 1733; d. Dec. 30, 1797, a. 63 y. 3 m.; Jenneke, May 26, 1736; Barent, Oct. 1, 1738, d. Oct. 1, 1799; a. 61 y. 3 d.; Dirk, Nov. 28, 1742; Pieter, [mother, Anna Van Benthuysen], August 21, 1743; Christina, Nov. 16, 1746; Pieter, [mother, Anna Van Benthuysen] Nov. 5, 1749. [Perhaps these Ch. belong to two families.]

VAN ALEN, Jacobus, of Kinderhook, and Helena Van Alsteyn. Ch: bp.; Maria, July 3, 1737; Johannes, Oct. 21, 1744.

VAN ALEN, Dirk, andCatharina Johanna. Ch: bp.: Johannes, Jan. 24, 1739; Maria, Jan. 21, 1741.

VAN ALEN, Adam, and Catharyna.... Ch: Jacobus, bp. Jan. 20, 1742.

VAN ALEN, Gerrit, m. Catharina Van Wie, June 25, 1742. Ch: bp.; Willem, June 12, 1743; Willem, Jan. 4, 1745; Johannes, March 13, 1748; Maria, Oct. 8, 1749, d. Oct. 30, 1805, d. 56 y. 4 m.; Catarina, August 2, 1752; Eva, June 22, 1755.

VAN ALEN, Lourens, and Cornelia.... Ch: Elbertje, bp. July 31, 1743.

VAN ALEN, Adam, and Annatie Vosburgh. Ch: Pieter, bp. Jan. 11, 1747.

VAN ALEN, Evert, and Margarita Vergerls. Ch: Johannes, bp. June 19, 1748.

VAN ALEN, Adam, weduwnaar van Kinderhook. m. Maria Roseboom, June 20, 1752. Ch: Gysbert, bp. April 16, 1758.

VAN ALEN, Johannes, and Maria Lansing. Ch: Annatie, b. Jan. 15, 1776. ·

VAN ALEN, Johannes, m. Maria Look, March 8, 1778. Ch: b.; Gerrit, June 11, 1779; Geesie, May 12, 1783.

VAN ALEN, Willem [Gerrit], m. Magdalena Van Wie, wid. of Philip Look, Sept. 26, 1789. Ch: Gerrit, b. August 1, 1790.

VAN ALEN, John J., and Mary Diamond. He d. June 25, 1801, a. 28 y. 8 d. Ch: b. Thomas Diamond, April 15, 1794 ;. Anna Fitch, Feb. 4, 1796; George June 29, 1798, d. Feb. 3, 1802, a. 3 y. 7 m.; Margaret, Sept. 28, 1800, d. July 25, 1801, a. 9 mo. 27 d.;

VAN ALEN, Gerrit and Ann Moody. Ch: Margarita, b. Oct. 23, 1795.

Van Alstyn, Isaac Janse, of Kinderhook, m. first, Maritie Abbedie (Vosburgh), Oct. 20, 1689; and secondly, Jannetje Jochemse Van Valkenburgh, Feb. 20, 1698. Ch: bp.; Pieter, June 16, 1695; Jochem, Jan. 8, 1699; Harmen, Nov. 10, 1700; Bartholomeus,

May 19, 1702; Dirkje, Feb. 13, 1704; Eva, June 9, 1706; Maria, Oct. 31, 1708; Lammert, April 30, 1710.

VAN ALSTYN, Abraham Janse, of Kinderhook, m. first ....; and secondly, Maritie Van Deusen, Jan. 17, 1694. Ch: bp.; Janneke, March 15, 1685; Jan, May 22, 1687; Jacob, Sept. 8, 1689; Johannes, August 26, 1694; Mattheus, June 14, 1696; Dirkje, Dec. 4, 1698; Sander, Jan. 5, 1701; Abraham, August 15, 1703; Lena, Nov. 18, 1705; Isaac, Jan. 28, 1708; Dirkje, April 30, 1710; Catryntje, Oct. 12, 1713; Jacobus, April 21, 1717; Marten, May 3, 1719.

VAN ALSTYN, Thomas [Lambert? see the next], of Kinderhook, and Jannetje Mingael. Ch: bp. Annatje, July 28, 1700.

VAN ALSTYN, Lambert Janse, and Jannetie Mingaal. He d. Oct. 16, 1703. Jan. 31, 1713–4, she (then a widow) contracted marriage with Jochem Van Valkenburgh. Ch: Pieter, bp. August 9, 1702.

VAN ALSTYN, Cornelis Martense, m. Maria Van Den Bergh, May 15, 1703. Ch: bp.; Martinus, Dec. 15, 1703, buried May 12, 1746; Cornelia, August 4, 1706; Cornelis, Feb. 27, 1709; Jenneke, April 20, 1712; Gysbert, May 13, 1716; Abraham, Jan. 21, 1719; Isaac, Feb. 1, 1721; Jacob, Dec. 18, 1723.

VAN ALSTYN, Marten Janse, m. first, Jannetie Cornelise; secondly, Cornelia Van Den Bergh, Nov. 10, 1705. Ch: bp.; Isaac, June 20, 1703; Martinus, Sept. 22, 1706, was buried August 4, 1755; Cornelis, Sept. 26, 1708; Johannes, March 11, 1711; Cornelia, Sept. 20, 1713; Gysbert, Dec. 3, 1716; Jannetie, August 22, 1719; Goosen, April 8, 1722; Abraham, Oct. 11, 1724.

VAN ALSTYN, Pieter and Margarita.... Ch: bp. Isaac, April 17, 1720; Jochum, Sept. 9, 1722; Isaac, April 11, 1725.

VAN ALSTYN, Thomas, of Kinderhook, m. Maria Van Alen, Dec. 12, 1718. Ch: bp.; Jannetie, March 6, 1720; Willem, Dec. 10, 1721; Lambert, Oct. 4, 1724; Maria, Nov. 18, 1733; Pieter, May 16, 1736.

VAN ALSTYN, Harmen, m. Dorothe Van Slyck, Nov. 12, 1721. Ch: bp.; Isaac, Sept. 9, 1722; Eva, Jan. 15, 1724; Jannetie, July 3, 1726.

VAN ALSTYN, Jacob, m. Pietertje Van Iverin, Oct. 10, 1723. He was buried Nov. 4, 1730. Ch: bp.; Jannetie, Nov. 22, 1723; Reynier, April 4, 1725; Sara, June 4, 1727; Maria, July 27, 1729.

VAN ALSTYN, Marten, m. Catharina Van Den Bergh, March 6, 1727. Ch: bp.; Cornelis, Sept. 24, 1727; Volkie, Jan. 5, 1729; Volkie, Sept. 13, 1730; Wynant, August 13, 1732; Isaac, June 2, 1735; Isaac, July 31, 1737; Volkert, May 18, 1740; Maritie, and Cathalyntje, March 3, 1743.

VAN ALSTYN, Isaac, m. Maritie Van Den Bergh, March 23, 1728. He was buried July 6, 1746; she was buried Oct. 24, 1756. Ch: bp.; Jannetie, Nov. 10, 1728; Jannetie, June 18, 1730; Volkie, April 22, 1733; Marten, Feb. 8, 1736; Wynant, April 28, 1738; Johannes, Dec. 19, 1739; Willem, July 21, 1742; Maria, April 19, 1745.

VAN ALSTYN, Jan, and Elizabeth ——, he was buried Sept. 27, 1738. Ch: Maria, bp. April 6, 1729.

VAN ALSTYN L., and M——. Ch: Isaac Valk, Sept. 1, 1734.

VAN ALSTYN, Alexander, and Elbertje ——. Ch: Abraham, bp. Sept. 3, 1738.

VAN ALSTYN, Bartholomeus, and Agnietje ——. Ch: Johannes, bp. June 3, 1739.

13*

VAN ALSTYN, Cornelis C., m. Catharina Wendell, Feb. 21, 1742. Ch: bp.; Cornelis, Sept. 19, 1742; Abraham, Jan. 10, 1746. [Cornelis Van A. and Teuntie Fort, m. March 19, 1738.]

VAN ALSTYN, Gysbert, and Annatie Gardenier. He was buried May 3, 1746. Ch: Rachel, bp. May 25, 1746. [Gysbert Van A. and Annatie Ridders, m. June 11, 1744.]

VAN ALSTYN, Reinier, m. Cornelia Van Den Bergh, Nov. 5, 1748. Ch: bp.; Jacob, May 28, 1749; Catalyntje, March 17, 1751; Mattheus, June 3, 1753; Pietertje, b. Aug. 31, 1760.

VAN ALSTYN, Harmanus, and Anna Catrina Pesinger (Besinger). Ch: bp.; Eva, July 4, 1754; Anna Rosina. July 15, 1759; Jannetie, Jan. 13, 1762. Ch: born; Elizabeth, Nov. 15, 1764; Lydia, Oct. 25, 1766; Zeferinus, Sept. 18, 1768; Catharina, Dec. 26, 1770; Dirkje, May 31, 1774; Harmanus, April 7, 1779.

VAN ALSTYN, John, and Lena Scharp. Ch: born; Maria, Dec. 1, 1763; Barbara, April 29, 1765; Marytje, March 13, 1767; Isaac, Jan. 23, 1769. [See Johannes Van A. below.]

VAN ALSTYN, Wynand, m. Margarita Bendor (Reisdorp) Oct. 10, 1767. Ch: b.; Isaac, March 27, 1769; Margarita, Aug. 29, 1771,

VAN ALSTYN, Willem, of Halve Maan, and Catharina Hogeboom. Ch: Isaac, b. Aug. 28, 1771.

VAN ALSTYN, Johannes, and Lena Scherp, m. Sept. 31 (*sic*) 1763. Ch: Isaac, b. Oct. 5, 1771. [Same as John Van A. above?]

VAN ALSTYN, Cornelis, and Maria Goeway. Ch: b.; Daniel, Nov. 9, 1777; Benjamin, Dec. 8, 1779; Cornelis, Aug. 31, 1782; Salomon, May 30, 1784; Gerrit, Dec. 7, 1788.

VAN ALSTYN, Jacob, and Annatie Lansing. Ch: Cathalyntje, May 9, 1779.

VAN ALSTYN, Hans, m. Dirkje Winne, Jan. 12, 1775. Ch: Adam Winne, b. Dec. 6, 1780.

VAN ALSTYN, Mathys, m. Rachel DeForeest, March 31, 1782. Ch: b.; Marten, July 19, 1784, d. March 23, 1849, a. 65 y.; Cornelia, Feb. 4, 1788.

VAN ALSTYN, Isaac, and Barbara Scharp. Ch: Petrus, b. May 31, 1790.

Van Antwerpen, Daniel Janse, of Schenectady, and Maritie Groot. Ch: bp.; Neeltie, July 27, 1690; Rebecca, Dec. 25, 1692. [*See Schenectady Families.*]

VAN ANTWERPEN, Simon Danielse, of Schenectady, and Schaaghtekooke 1720, m. Maria Peek, Dec. 22, 1706. Ch: bp.; Lysbeth, Jan. 15, 1710; Sara, May 13, 1716; Margarita, Oct. 1, 1721; Jacobus, May 17, 1724; Johannes, Jan. 22, 1727; Lowys, Feb. 25, 1731. [*See Schenectady Families.*]

VAN ANTWERPEN, Arent Danielse, of Schenectady, and Sara Van Eps. Ch: bp.; Maria, Dec. 25, 1706; Neeltie, April 28, 1710. [*See Schenectady Families.*]

VAN ANTWERPEN, Jan Danielse, of Schenectady, and Agnietie (Annetie) Vedder. Ch: bp.; Neeltie, April 23, 1710; Rebecca, March 2, 1715. [*See Schenectady Families.*]

VAN ANTWERPEN, Daniel S., of Schenectady, m. Rebecca Van Antwerpen in Schenectady, Oct. 21, 1738. Ch: bp.; Angenietie, Dec. 2, 1750; Annatie, Jan. 23, 1757. [*See Schenectady Families.*]

VAN ANTWERPEN, Johannes, of Schenectady, m. Catarina Vedder (Veeder) in Schenectady, Aug. 11,

1750. Ch: bp.; Simon, March 24, 1751; Engeltie, April 15, 1753. [*See Schenectady Families.*]

VAN ANTWERPEN, Lewis, of Schactekook, and of *Halve maan* 1771; m. Hendrikje Fonda (Van Buren), Nov. 27, 1754. Ch: Simon, bp.; March 30, 1755; Douwe, bp. July 24, 1757; Johannes, b. Jan. 12, 1760; Alida, b. March 16, 1762; Louys, b. Aug. 17, 1771.

VAN ANTWERPEN, Simon D., m. Maria Dunbar, Nov. 20, 1761. She d. April 11, 1826, a. 87 y. 11 m. Ch: born; Rebecca, Sept. 19, 1762; Cornelia, Jan 30, 1764; Saartie, Jan. 4, 1771; Sara, Jan. 27, 1774.

VAN ANTWERPEN, Arent, of Nisthigioone, m. Hester Cregier, Nov. 29, 1764. Ch: Geertruid, b. Oct. 6, 1765; Neeltie, b. Feb. 26, 1767; Hermanus, bp. April 18, 1770.

Van Antwerp, Daniel, m. Dirkie Winne, Dec. 5, 1766. Ch: b.; Gerrit, Dec. 11, 1767; Willem, Jan. 23, 1770.

VAN ANTWERP, Daniel, m. Gerritje Witbeck, m. Oct. 27, 1772. Ch: Andries Witbeck, b. Jan. 30, 1774.

Van Arnhem, Jan Janse, m. Hester Fonda, Oct. 14, 1696. He d. April 1, 1708. Ch: bp.; Sara, August 15, 1697; Abraham, April 28, 1700; Rebecca, March 25, 1702; Isaac, May 7, 1704; Rachel, Nov. 17, 1706; Jan Dirk, Oct. 17, 1708.

VAN ARNHEM, Abraham, m. Alida Lansingh, July 11, 1721. She was buried July 11, 1755. Ch: bp.; Johannes and Jacob, Dec. 17, 1721; Helena, Sept. 20, 1724; Hester, April 17, 1726, buried Feb. 23, 1753; Jacob, August 30, 1730; Sara, April 10, 1732; Elisabeth, Nov. 10, 1734; Jacob, April 4, 1736; Anna, Sept. 23, 1739; Isaac, April 19, 1745.

VAN ARNHEM, Isaac, m. first, Jannetie Salisbury, Nov. 2, 1722; and secondly, Elisabeth .... about 1729. Ch: bp.; Hester, August 16, 1724; Johannes, Feb. 1, 1730.

VAN ARNHEM, Jacob, m. first A........ and secondly, Margarieta .... about 1739. Ch: bp.; Jacob, Oct. 30, 1732; Johannes, Nov. 25, 1739.

VAN ARNHEM, Jan D., m. Elisabeth Lansingh, July 18, 1729. Ch: bp.; Hester, Feb. 14, 1735; Hendrik, July 23, 1738; Abraham, Sept. 28, 1740; Isaac, Feb. 26, 1744; Isaac, August 25, 1745; Abram, Nov. 19, 1749.

VAN ARNHEM, Johannes, m. Alida Van der Heyden March 4, 1756. Ch: bp.; Abraham, August 14, 1757; Alida, Jan. 7, 1759; Jacob, May 3, 1761. Ch: b.; Hester, April 10, 1763; Abraham, June 3, 1766; Elisabeth, Nov. 10, 1768; Dirk, Nov. 20, 1770.

VAN ARNHEM, Jacob, m. Anneke Van Vranken, Nov. 18, 1757. Ch: bp.; Alida, June 11, 1758. Ch: b.; Rykert, May 28, 1760; Abraham, Oct. 30, 1762; Annatie, Dec. 3, 1764; Elisabeth, Nov. 9, 1766; Helena, March 9, 1771; Jacob, April 18, 1773.

VAN ARNHEM, Hendrick, m. Susanna Winne, May 13, 1761. Ch: Susanna, bp. Nov. 21, 1761; Johannes, b. Oct. 4, 1763; Helena, Oct. 8, 1767; Lavinus, Feb. 7, 1770; Jacob and Elisabeth, March 25, 1773; Hester, bp. Nov. 24, 1776.

VAN ARNHEM, Isaac J. m. Catharina Van Wie, August 24, 1768. Ch: b.; Alida, Oct. 9, 1769, Alida, April 18, 1771; Alida, July 5, 1779; Jan Dirksen, Jan. 30, 1779; Andries, August 19, 1781.

VAN ARNHEM, Isaac, and .... Runnels. Ch: Hester, b. April 8, 1777.

VAN ARNHEM, Abraham (J.), and Anneke Bogert. Ch : b. ; Jan Dirkse, March 5, 1780 ; Jacob Bogert, April 4, 1785.

VAN ARNHEM, Jacob, and Maria Van Deusen. Ch : Alida, b. Nov. 12, 1782.

VAN ARNHEM, Abraham, and Maritie Lansing. Ch : Lansing. b. Oct. 9, 1799.

Van Arsdalen, Dirk, and Gysbertje DeGrauw. Ch : bp. ; Gerrit, Feb 5, 1749 ; Gerrit, June 21, 1752.

Van Baal, Jan Hendrickse, free trader in Beverwyck 1661-78 ; beside houses and lots in the village, had a patent for a large tract of land on the Normanskil, which was sold to Omy LaGrange and Johannes Symonse Veeder for £250. He had an only son Hendrick who died before 1716, and four daughters, Hannah *non compos mentis ;* Maria, who m. Isaac DePeyster, merchant of N. Y., Dec. 27, 1687 ; Margaret, who m. Nicolaas Evertsen, mariner of N. Y., and Rachel, who m. Henry Wileman of N. Y.

Van Benthuysen, Paulus Martense (*rademaker of raemmaker*), an early settler at Fort Orange and Beverwyck, became a considerable owner of real estate in the village among which was the lot on the south corner of Broadway and Maiden Lane, which he sold in 1677, to Harme Gansevoort.. He had three sons, who arrived at maturity : Balthus ; Barent ; and Marten of Schenectady.

VAN BENTHUYSEN, Balthus (Balthazar), merchant, m. Lidia Dealy (Daily) in N. Y., Feb. 22, 1707. He made a will Nov. 5, 1720, proved March 31, 1725, in which he spoke of the following children, and his brothers, Marten and Barent. Ch: bp. ; Johannes, Sept. 19. 1708 ; Catrina, Oct. 27, 1710 ; Jacobus Perreker [Parker] ; Elizabeth, June 30, 1718 ; Maria, July 16, 1721.

VAN BENTHUYSEN, Gerrit, m. Maria Van Alen, July 12, 1729. She was buried Jan. 16, 1738. Ch : bp. ; Johannes, Feb. 5, 1732 ; Pieter and Jenneke, Jan. 30, 1734 ; Christina, May 15, 1735 ; Maria, Jan. 11, 1738.

VAN BENTHUYSEN, Jacobus P. (James Parker), m. Sara Cooper, Feb. 6, 1741. Ch: bp. ; Balthazar, March 28, 1742 ; Obadiah, June 17, 1744 ; Cornelia, April 7, 1748 ; John, Nov. 4, 1750 ; Dorothea, May 13, 1753 ; Annatie, Sept. 5, 1756 ; Willem, June 19, 1760 ; Hendrick, b. Oct. 12, 1762, d. June 8, 1834, a. 72 y. ; Thomas, b. Sept. 5, 1767.

VAN BENTHUYSEN, Baltus, m. first, Sara Viele and secondly, Elizabeth Rumney, Dec. 31, 1768. Ch: born ; Jacobus, Jan. 1, 1764 ; Hugo, July 1, 1766 ; Sarah, July 31, 1769 ; Maria, March 3, 1772 ; Cornelia, July 1, 1774 ; Anna, Aug. 1, 1776 ; Benjamin, Nov. 20, 1778, d. March 3, 1848, a. 70 y. ; Hendrik, July 20, 1781 ; John, Nov. 14, 1783 ; Maria, Feb. 1, 1786.

VAN BENTHUYSEN, Obadiah, and Annatie (Hannah, Johanna) Rumney (Rumley). She d. July 17, 1825, a. 75 y. Ch : born ; Annatie, Feb. 5, 1769 ; Maria, bp. ; July 17, 1770 ; Jacobus Parker, Oct. 1, 1772 ; d. May 10, 1835, a. 62 y. ; Annatie, Sept. 12, 1774 ; Elizabeth, bp. March 12, 1777 ; Cornelia, Jan. 24, 1780 ; Benjamin, March 13, 1782 ; Sara, Oct. 16, 1784 : Obadia, July 13, 1787, d. Aug. 15, 1845, a. 59y ; Magdalena, Sept. 15, 1791, d. at Geneva, May 15, 1863, a. 72 y.

VAN BENTHUYSEN, Johannes, m. Geesie Van Hoesen, Dec. 9, 1770. Ch: b. Jacobus, June 28, 1771 ; Alida, Nov. 8, 1773 ; Sara, Sept. 14, 1776 ; Johannes, May 29, 1782 ; Folkert, Oct. 23, 1785 ; Annatie, Aug. 8, 1790.

VAN BENTHUYSEN, Willem, and Margarita Conklin (Cochran). Ch : b. ; Evert Swart, Jan. 10, 1781 ; John, Dec. 16, 1784 ; Jacobus, Aug. 9, 1788 : William, Jan. 20, 1791 ; Dorothea, Aug. 22, 1793 ; Eliza, June 4, 1796.

VAN BENTHUYSEN, Hendrick, m. Cathalyntje Hun, Dec. 14, 1785. He d. June 8, 1834, a. 72 y. She d. Aug. 13, 1841, a. 79 y. Ch : born ; Elizabeth, Nov. 3, 1786 ; Jacobus, Sept. 27, 1788 ; Thomas, March 9, 1791 ; Sara, July 4, 1793.

VAN BENTHUYSEN, Thomas, and Nancy (Ann) Enax (Enochs). He d. July 24, 1832, a. 67 y. Ch : b. ; Sara, Oct. 14, 1788 ; Mary, Oct. 16, 1789 ; Sara, March 1, 1791 ; Godfrey Enoch, March 17, 1794 ; Cornelia, June 20, 1800.

VAN BENTHUYSEN, James, and Elizabeth Herman. Ch : b. ; William Belshazar (Balthazar ?) Oct. 1, 1791 ; Thomas, Oct. 26, 1793 ; Annatie, Oct. 10, 1795.

VAN BENTHUYSEN, James, and Mary .... Ch : Geesie, b. May 5, 1795.

VAN BENTHUYSEN, James P., and Hannah Van Benthuysen. Ch : b. ; James Parker, Nov. 17, 1795 ; Parker, April 6, 1797 ; Benjamin, Dec. 14, 1798.

Van Bergen, Capt. Marten Gerritse, in 1668, had a lease of Castle Island called after him, Marten Gerritsen's Island, and in 1690, he lived south of that Island on the west side of the river. [*O' Callaghan's Hist. N. N.*]. In 1662, the island opposite the kil at Coxsackie was also called Marten Gerritsen's Island ; 1669, he bought 69 morgens and homestead at Catskil [Coxsackie] of Jan Andriesse the Irishman ; 1670, purchased more land at Coxsackie of Jan Clute and others ; 1673-85, a magistrate of the county ; 1685, commissioned captain of a company of foot. He m. first, Jannetie Martense, and secondly, Neeltie Myndertse, Jan. 21, 1686. Letters of administration were issued to his wife, Dec. 3, 1696 ; on Oct. 3, 1697, she m. Hendrick Douw. Ch: bp. ; Gerrit, Nov. 27, 1687 ; Myndert, Sept. 1, 1689 ; Marten, March 28, 1692 ; Pieter, Feb. 21, 1694 ; Johannes, Oct. 4, 1695.

VAN BERGEN, Gerrit, of Catskill, 1720, and Anna, Ch : bp. Debora, Oct. 16, 1715 ; Marten Gerritsen, April 13, 1718 ; Anna, May 15, 1720 ; Wilhelmus, May 13, 1722 ; Petrus, July 26, 1724 ; Neeltie, March 5, 1727.

VAN BERGEN, Marten, of Catskill, 1720, m. Catryna Meyer, June 7, 1715. Ch: bp. ; Marten Gerritsen, June 3, 1716 ; Wilhelmus, Jan. 11, 1718 ; Hendrickus, Sept. 27, 1719 ; Catharina, Jan. 22, 1724 ; Neeltie, Oct. 24, 1725 ; Elisabeth, May 13, 1727 ; Anna Maria, Dec. 8, 1728.

VAN BERGEN, Pieter (Petrus), m. first Christina Coster, Nov. 10, 1724 ; and secondly ? Jan. 28, 1731. Ch: bp. ; Marten Gerritse, Oct. 10, 1725 ; Elisabeth, July 23, 1727 ; Anthony, Jan. 7, 1730 ; Elisabetha, Jan. 1, (?) 1734 ; Neeltie, Sept. 18, 1737 ; Petrus, June 13, 1742.

[*The following Van Bergen families are copied from the Catskill church records.*]

VAN BERGEN, Gerrit, and Debora Van Bergen. Ch : Petrus, bp. August 26, 1753.

VAN BERGEN. Gerrit, and Catharine Van Bergen. Ch : bp. ; Maria, Feb. 24, 1771 ; Catharina, March 21, 1773 ; Hendrick, Sept. 6, 1774 ; Willem, April 19, 1777.

VAN BERGEN, Wilhelmus, and Annatie.... Ch : bp. ; Anna Maria, Jan. 16, 1754 ; Annatie, May 15, 1756 ; Gerrit, Jan. 27, 1758 ; Anna Maria, May 16, 1761.

VAN BERGEN, Marten Gerritse, and Maritie Van Dyck. Ch : bp. ; Elisabeth, Jan. 25, 1756 ; Elisabeth, July 10, 1763.

VAN BERGEN, David, and Catharina... Ch : bp., Jan, July 1, 1781 ; Marten Gerritsen, April 25, 1783 ; Gerrit, Sept. 12, 1784; Jeems, April 16, 1786 ; Maria, Jan. 2, 1791.

VAN BERGEN, Petrus, and Annatie.... Ch : bp., Marten Gerritsen, Feb. 4, 1781 ; Maritie, Jan. 9, 1787.

VAN BERGEN, Gerrit, and Elisabeth Van Dyck. Ch : bp.; Gerrit, Dec. 24, 1789; Jan. August 28, 1791 ; Annatie, Feb. 18, 1794 ; Marten Gerritsen, Feb. 16, 1796 ; Peter, May 11, 1800.

Van Berger, Peter, m. Elisabeth Fryer, March 8, 1797. Ch : b. ; Peter, July 1, 1797; Henry, March 31, 1803. [Mrs. Elisabeth Van Bergen, d. Dec. 11, 1848, a. 82y. 11 mo.]

Van Bloemendael, see Bloemendael.

Van Boeckhoven, Claas Janse, in 1672-7 in company with Ryck Claase Van Vranken, bought land over the river in Niskayuna. In 1662, he owned a lot on the *Vossen kil* in Beverwyck. In 1683, his wife was Volckertje Janse ; about 1691, he m. Catalyntje De Vos, dau. of Andries De Vos and widow of Arent Andriesse Bratt. He probably died about 1712, leaving no children ; his property passed to the children of his last wife.

Van Rommel, Harmen Janse, perhaps brother of *Marcelis* Janse Van B. Ch : bp. ; Lourens, Jan 1, 1686 ; Cornelis, ... 1688.

Van Breuckelen, (Brackelen) Cornelis Teunise, *raedts-person,* in Beverwyck, 1631-62. A Van Brakel family early settled in Schenectady.

Van Brakel, Gerrit Gysbertse [Gysbert Gerritse ?] widower of Reyntie Stephens m. Elisabeth Janse widow of Jan Van Eps, July 23, 1693. Ch : bp. ; Anneke, Dec. 6, 1685 ; Gerrit, July 15, 1688. [See *Schenectady Families.*]

VAN BRAKEL, Gerrit Gysbertse, of Schenectady, and Catharina Van Der Volgen. Ch : bp. ; Maria, Feb. 15, 1710 ; Claas, Oct. 12, 1712. [See *Schenectady Families.*]

VAN BRAKEL, Gysbert, of Schenectady, and Maria, Van Antwerpen. Ch : bp. ; Rebecca, Sept. 28, 1745 ; Neeltie, July 16, 1749 : Sara, Aug. 5, 1753. [See *Schenectady Families.*]

Van Bremen, Jan Dirkse, in Beverwyck. 1655-62 ; in 1662, contracted to deliver 400 logs for Frans Pieterse Clau, on the banks of the *Flodder's* kil [in Columbia county.]

Van Brugh, See Verbrugge.

Van Buren, Cornelis Maas, came out in the ship Rensselaerswyck, and had a farm at Papsknee. He and his wife died in 1648, and *beide op eenen dagh zyn begraaven.* Teunis Dirkse Van Vechten, *Poentie,* and Cornelise Van Vechten were trustees of his estate, and guardians of his children in 1657. His wife was Catalyntje Martense. Ch : *Hendrick,* eldest son ; *Marten ; Maas ;* Styntje, w. of Dirk Wesselse Ten Broeck, in 1663 ; Tobias ; all these children were living in 1662.

VAN BUREN, Hendrick, and ..... Ch : *Maas ; Cornelis, Henrik.*

VAN BUREN, Marten Cornelise, alias Black Marten, in 1660, deposed that he was born at Houten, in the Province of Utrecht. In 1662, he owned a barn,

house, &c., " this side of Bethlehem," which he sold to Gysbert Cornelise Van Den Bergh ; 1675, leased half of *Constapel's* island below Albany ; made his will April 10, 1703, proved June 7, 1710, and spoke of his w. Maritie, and the following Ch : Tobias, son of his eldest son Cornelis deceased, whose widow, Ariaantie Gerritse, m. Coenraad Elmendorf, June 28, 1693 ; Cornelia, w. of Robert Van Deusen ; *Pieter ; Marten ;* Maria, w. of Cornelis Gerritse Van Den Bergh ; Catalina, w. of Jonathan Janse Witbeck ; Magdalena. He d. Nov. 13, 1703.

VAN BUREN,. Maas Cornelise, and Josine (Jacomyntje) Janse Gardenier. He d. Nov. 22, (27) 1704 ; she d. July 1701. Ch : bp. ; Cornelis, Feb. 6, 1684 ; Jan, Dec. 20, 1685 ; Jacob, Feb. 19, 1688 ; Geertruy, June 22, 1689 ; Evert Wiler [Wheeler ?] 1692 ; Jacob, April 6, 1701.

VAN BUREN, Pieter Martense, of Kinderhook, 1720, m. Ariaantje Barentse, Jan. 15, 1693. Ch : bp. ; *Cornelis,* May 14, 1693 ; *Barent,* Jan. 20, 1695 ; Maritie, March 8, 1696 ; *Tobias,* Nov. 7, 1697 ; Eytje, Jan. 7, 1700 ; Marten, Dec. 28, 1701 ; Cornelia, Aug. 24, 1707 ; Ephraim, March 11, 1711 ; Maria, Dec, 18, 1715.

VAN BUREN, Maas Hendrickse, of Manor Rensselaerswyck, 1720, m. first, Ariaantje Van Wye, Sept. 17, 1699, who d. Feb. 3, 1706 ; and secondly, Magdalena Bogard, about 1711. He made his will April 7, 1733, proved June 1, 1733, and spoke of w. Magdalena, and the three children following : He was buried at Schoodac, April 14, 1733. Ch : bp. Henderick, Jan. 7, 1700 ; Henrik, Dec. 28, 1701 ; Johannes, Aug. 13, 1704 ; Catalyntje (Catryntje ?) April 20, 1712.

VAN BUREN, Marten Martense, and Judikje Barentse. He was buried near his own house, Oct. 23, 1740. Ch : bp. ; Maritje, Jan. 1, 1701 ; Barent, Sept. 6, 1702 ; *Marten Cornelise,* July 15, 1705 ; Ida, June 13, 1708 ; Tobias, April 30, 1710 ; Jannetie, April 20, 1712 ; Petrus, June 13, 1714.

VAN BUREN, Cornelis Henrikse, of *Halve Maan,* m. Hendrikje Van Nes, Dec. 26, 1702. Ch : bp. ; Lysbeth, April 23, 1704 ; *Willem,* July 28, 1706 : Aaltie, April 25, 1709 ; Catalyntje, Feb. 10, 1712 ; Henrik, March 1, 1713 ; Jan. Sept. 4. 1715 ; Catalyna, Dec. 11, 1717 : Maria, July 2, 1721 : Maria, Feb. 24, 1725 ; Cornelis, May 30, 1728.

VAN BUREN, Pieter [son of Henrik], m. Geertruy Vosburgh, May 20, 1707. She was buried, April 21, 1748. Ch : bp. ; *Henrik,* Dec. 26, 1708 ; Jannetje, Nov. 5, 1710 ; Pieter, Feb. 22, 1713 ; Tobias, May 13, 1716 ; Elizabeth, Jan. 11, 1718 ; Cornelie, Dec. 7, 1721 ; Maas and Madalena, June 26, 1725 ; Catalyna, March 14, 1731.

VAN BUREN, Marten [son of Pieter Martense], m. Maria Van Den Bergh, July 14, 1719. Ch : bp. ; Geertruy, Jan. 14, 1720 ; Cornelia, Oct. 1, 1721 ; *Petrus,* Dec. 26, 1723 ; Johannes, Nov. 21. 1725 ; Maria, Dec. 6, 1727 ; *Benjamin,* Oct. 24, 1731 ; Tobias, May 22, 1737.

VAN BUREN, Tobias [son of Pieter Martense], m. Anna Goes, Jan. 10, 1721 ; Ch : Pieter, bp. July 16, 1721.

VAN BUREN, Barent [son of Pieter Martense], m. first Maria Winne, Dec. 29, 1719 ; secondly, Margarita Van Vechten, Dec. 23, 1737, buried at Papsknee, Aug. 11, 1743 ; and thirdly, Catalyntje Schermerhorn, about 1747. Ch : bp. ; Ariaantje, Nov. 8, 1724 ; Elsie, Oct. 23, 1726 ; Marten Cornelise, Oct. 22, 1738 ; Maria, May 11, 1740 ; Marytje, July 22, 1741 ; Margarita, Nov. 1, 1747 ;

Hendrikje, Oct. 15, 1749; Judikje, Dec. 9, 1753; Elizabeth, March 1, 1756; Willem, May 27, 1759.

VAN BUREN, Cornelis [son of Pieter Martense], m. Maria Litser, Sept. 8, 1724. Ch: Pieter, bp. May 30, 1725.

VAN BUREN, Marten Cornelise, Jr. [son of Marten Martense], m. first, Th. Van den Bergh, March 28, 1730; and secondly. Lena Hus (Hoes), about 1745. Ch: bp.; *Barent*, March 14, 1731; Marten, April 25, 1746.

VAN BUREN, Hendrick Maase [son of Maas Hendrickse] m. Aaltie Winne, Oct. 7, 1731, Ch: bp.; Ariaantje Aug. 6, 1732; Dirkie, June 9, 1734; Maas, June 13, 1736; Maas, June 6, 1736. (*sic*): Daniel, Aug. 31, 1740; Johannes, Nov. 6, 1743; Ariaantje, Feb. 1, 1747; Johannes, May 17, 1752.

VAN BUREN, Johannes [son of Maas Hendrickse], m. Ida (Eytje)Van Buren, Oct. 18, 1732; Maas, Oct. 28, 1733; Judickie, Ap. 13, 1735; Johannes, Oct. 6, 1745.

VAN BUREN, Willem [son of Cornelis Hendrickse], and Teuntje Van den Bergh. He was buried at Papskesee Aug. 17, 1752. Ch: bp.; Cornelis March, 7, 1736; Ebbetje Ap. 2, 1738; Gerrit, May 4, 1740; Hendrikje, June 20, 1742; Maria, Feb. 17, 1745; Elizabeth, July 19, 1747; Hendrick, Feb. 4, 1750; Hendrick, Feb. 2, 1752.

VAN BUREN, T, and Maritie .... Ch: Harmen, bp. Jan. 7, 1736.

VAN BUREN, Marten, and Dirkie .... Ch: Abraham, bp. Feb. 27, 1737.

VAN BUREN, Hendrick, [son of Pieter], m. Annatie Van Saltzberg, Nov. 13, 1736. Ch: bp.; Pieter, Sept. 14, 1740; Tobias, Feb. 17, 1745; Tanneke, Nov. 1, 1747; Johannes, Dec. 3, 1749; Cornelis, Sept. 22, 1751; Geertruy, March 10, 1754; Harmanus, Feb. 8, 1756.

VAN BUREN, Pieter, and Elbertje .... Ch: Christina, bp. Jan. 23, 1743.

VAN BUREN, Jan. m. Angenietje Conyn, Mar. 10, 1740. Ch: Hendrikje, Aug. 3, 1746.

VAN BUREN, Pieter M. [son of Marten], and Marytje Van Der Poel. Ch: Anatje, bp. Feb. 22, 1747; Maria, bp. Jan. 8, 1749; Marten, bp. Jan. 5, 1752; Abraham, b. March 25, 1764; Benjamin, b. July 19, 1769.

VAN BUREN, Jan, and Sara Bronck. Ch: bp.; Leendert, July 7, 1751; Cornelis, Sept. 29, 1753.

VAN BUREN, Barent, [son of Marten C.] and Ariaantje Van der Poel. Ch: Marten Cornelise, bp. Feb. 9, 1752; Marten Cornelise, bp. Ap. 8, 1753; Antje, bp. Nov. 30, 1755; Abraham, bp. Aug. 12, 1759; Teuntje, b. Jan. 29, 1762; Judikje, b. Sept. 1, 1765; Johannes, b. June 3, 1769.

VAN BUREN, Benjamin, [son of Marten], and Cornelis Salisbury. Ch: Marten, bp. Nov. 30, 1755; Jobje, b. June 13, 1770.

VAN BUREN, Cornelis, m. Maicke Hun, Dec. 23. 1758. Ch: Elsie, bp. Nov. 25, 1759.

VAN BUREN, Maas, and Catalina Van Den Bergh. Ch: Eytje, bp. July 29, 1759; Jacob, b Jan. 8, 1761; Catharina, b. Nov. 4, 1763; Ariaantje, b. Aug. 27, 1768; Johannes, b. May 29, 1771.

VAN BUREN, Marten, m. Hendrikje Van Buren, Sept. 10, 1761. Ch: b. Barent, Aug. 29, 1762; Margarita, June 3, 1765; Teunis, May 3, 1769.

VAN BUREN, Hannes, and Marytje Briesch. Ch: Marten, b. Dec. 8, 1762.

VAN BUREN, Tobias, and Catalyntje Witbeck. Ch: b.; Maria, June 20, 1765; Machtel, Nov. 18, 1768.

VAN BUREN, Gerrit, m. Maria Witbeck, Feb. 22, 1765. Ch: b. Willem, Dec. 26, 1765; Catharina, July 15, 1767.

VAN BUREN, Maas, m. Rebecca Bogart, Feb. 14, 1767. Ch: b.; Douwe, May 29, 1771; Marytje, April 18, 1777.

VAN BUREN, Marten, m. Jannetie Holliday, Aug. 8, 1774. Ch: b. Maria, July 21, 1774; Abraham, April 16. 1782.

VAN BUREN, Hendrick, of Saratoga, m. Annatie Van Schaaick, Sept. 22, 1773. Ch: b. Geertje, Feb. 11, 1774; Teuntje, May 3, 1776.

VAN BUREN. Cornelis, and Molly Ojens (Maria Owens). Ch: b. Geertruy, March 4, 1775; Magdalena, Aug. 15, 1779; Jannetie, June 10, 1783.

VAN BUREN, Johannes, and Annetie Van der Poel. Ch: b. Catharina, Aug. 6, 1776; Jannetie, Aug. 10, 1778.

VAN BUREN, Johannes, and Jannatie..... Ch: Tanneke, b. Feb. 5, 1777.

VAN BUREN, Cornelis, and Jannetie Van der Poel. Ch: b.; Gerrit, Dec. 10, 1776: Catharina, Feb. 17, 1779; Catharina, March 31, 1784; Pieter, April 23, 1786, d. Sept. 26, 1862, a. 76 y.

VAN BUREN, Pieter, m. Dorothea Shutter (Poel), March 2, 1778. Ch: b.; Abraham, March 13, 1781; Cornelis, Nov. 31 (*sic*), 1783.

VAN BUREN, Hendrick, and Hilletje Shutter. Ch: Pieter, b. Feb. 4, 1785.

VAN BUREN, Marten C. m. Theuntje Van Buren, Dec. 2, 1787. Ch: Maria, b. Dec. 29, 1787.

Van Cleef, Lourens, and Cathalyntje Jackson. Ch: Hendrik, b. Feb. 5, 1779.

Van Coppernol, Claas Willemse, of Schenectray. He m. a Mohawk woman who after Van Coppernol's death m. Jonathan Stevens, of Schenectady. In 1678 he and his w. contracted to serve Jan Conell on his bouwery at Catskil for one year for 42 beavers. Ch: Willem, bp, May 22, 1691. [*See Schenectady Families.*]

Van Covelens, [Van der Coulen ?] Jacob Joosten, owned a house in Beverwyck which in 1657 he sold to Jan Dareth for 570 guilders; in 1669 his house stood 40 ft. south of the court house on or near the south corner of Broadway and Hudson street. In 1671 his w. Adriaentie Cornelise Van Velpen sold his house and lot to Jan Conell.

Van Corlaer, Bennony, glazier, master of the sloop *Endeavor* from N. Y. to Esopus in 1684; m. Elizabeth Vanderpoel, wid. of Sybrant Van Schaick, June 2, 1686; d. in 1704. Ch: bp.: Johanna, May 1, 1687; Maria, July 11, 1693; Arent, April 19, 1696, d. at Mapletown, March 1, 1795, a. 99 y.; Gideon, Aug. 15, 1700.

Van Curler, Arent, m. Anthonia Slaghboom widow of Jonas Bronck, about 1643, d. 1667, *sine prole*. After his death his wid. resided in Schenectady until her death, Jan. 15, 1676-7. See also *O'Callaghan's Hist. N. N.* I, 322.

Van Dam, Claas Ripse, carpenter, in Beverwyck, 1657-93, resided in *Bergh* [Chapel] street: m. Maria Bords. Ch: Rip, b, in Beverwyck, about 1660; Debora, who m. Hendrick Hansen.

VAN DAM, Rip [son of the last] *knecht van* Robert Story in 1681, removed to New York about 1684, and became a merchant. He was president of the Provincial council ; m. Sara Van der Spiegle of N. Y., Sept. 14, 1684, and had the following children bp. there. He d. June 10, 1749, "in extreme old age." See *Valentine's Manual*, 1865, and *Hist, N. Y.* Ch : bp. ; Maria, July 15, 1683 (1685 ?) ; Sara, Oct. 31, 1686 ; Nicolaas, Nov. 4, 1688 ; Maria, Nov. 16, 1690 ; Catharina, Nov. 27, 1692 ; Rip, Oct. 7. 1694 ; Margarita, Nov. 10, 1695 ; Elizabeth, who m. .... Kierstede ; Isaac, "yesterday, Dec. 10, 1749, died here Mr. Isaac Van Dam, merchant, the last surviving son of the late Hon. Rip Van Dam." *Valentine's Manual*, 1865.

Van den Bergh, Arent, corporal in the West India Company's service at Fort Orange, 1654: still there in 1666. His w. was sister of Andries Hendrickse, and her dau. Cornelia m. John Gilbert, and was Andries Hendrikse's heir.

VAN DEN BERGH, Claas Cornelise, in Beverwyck, 1660-5. Ch : *Cornelis*.

VAN DEN BERG, Gysbert Cornelise, 1660-7. In 1662, he bought a house, barn, &c., "lying this side of Bethlehem," of Marten Cornelise Van Buren. Ch : *Cornelis ; Willem ; Gerrit ;* Frederick, *Adelborst*, or corporal in the W. I. Company's service, at Fort Orange in 1661 ; Maritie, bp. July 5, 1685.

VAN DEN BERGH, Gerrit (Gysbertse), ...1663, a servant on the Bouwery of the late Jan Barentse Wemp. Ch : *Barent ; Gerrit*.

VAN DEN BERGH, Cornelis Gysbertse, of Manor of Rensselaerswyck, made his will March 3, 1714, proved July 6, 1717, m. first Cornelia Wynantse Van der Poel, and secondly, Maria Van Buren, widow of Teuwisse Van Deusen, Nov. 21, 1702. Ch : bp. ; and all mentioned in the father's will, 1714 ; Maritie, March 8, 1685, w. of Cornelis Van Alstyn : Cornelis (Cornelia in will), Oct. 2, 1687 ; w. of Marten Van Alstyn ; *Matthys*, March 23, 1690 ; Geertie, Dec. 20, 1691 ; *Wynant*, June 24, 1694 ; Goosen ; *Gysbert ;* Gerrit, bp. Sept. 19, 1703 ; Tryntje, w. of Pieter Waldron.

VAN DEN BERGH, Willem Gysbertse, carman, and Catryn Wynantse Van der Poel. Ch : bp. ; *Gerrit; Wynant; Cornelis ;* Willem, July 5, 1685 : Willem, May 16, 1687 ; Catharina, Oct. 13, 1689 ; *Wilhelmus,* June 12, 1692 ; Geertie, April 10, 1698.

VAN DEN BERGH, Frederick Gysbertse, and w. Maria Lubbertse ; 1661, *adelborst*, or corporal, in Fort Orange ; 1663-86 in New Amsterdam.

VAN DEN BERGH, Barent Gerritse of manor Rensselaerswyck, m. Geertruy Janse Witbeck (Lansing 1695), March 16, 1687. Ch : bp. Jan. Oct. 6, 1689 ; Gerrit, Oct. 18, 1691 ; Marietje, Jan. 21, 1694 ; Teuntje, May 26, 1695 ; Geertruy, Dec. 27, 1696 ; Ariaantje, March 26, 1699 ; *Andries*, Jan. 1, 1701 ; Jannetje, Dec. 25, 1702 ; Catharina, March 17, 1706 ; Neeltie, Jan. 28, 1708 ; *Benjamin*, Nov. 13, 1709 ; *Johannes*, Feb. 14, 1714.

VEN DEN BERGH, Cornelis Claase, [of Westchester Co. 1699], m. Susanna Ouderkerk, Dec. 13, 1693, and was buried in his orchard, Feb. 14, 1738; she was buried, Aug. 13, 1744. Ch : bp. ; *Claas*, July 1, 1694 ; Ariaantje, in N. Y. Nov. 14, 1697 ; Susanna, Jan. 18, 1702 ; *Pieter*, April 25, 1703 ; Sara, May 13, 1705 ; *Cornelis*, April 23, 1710.

VAN DEN BERGH, (Van der Berk), Richard Janse, m. Tryntje Hooghteling, Nov. 13, 1699. Ch : bp. ;

Maria, May 12, 1700 ; Antje, May 17, 1702 ; Jan, Sept. 19, 1703 ; *Matthys*, Jan. 15, 1706 ; Racheltje, Feb. 22, 1708 ; Dorotea, Oct. 30, 1710 ; *Hendrick*, Oct. 19, 1712 ; Lidia, April 24, 1715 ; *Robert*, June 31 (*sic*) 1717.

VAN DEN BERGH, Cornelis Willemse, carman and millwright; made his will, Nov. 24, 1706, proved, April 18, 1707, spoke of his eldest son Willem. Ch : bp. ; Willem, Sept. 7, 1701 ; Adam, Sept. 5, 1703 ; Cornelis, June 8, 1707.

VAN DEN BERGH, Wynant Willemse, brickmaker, m. Volkie Volkertse Van Hoesen, Dec. 4, 1700, made his will, May 8, 1749, proved, Aug. 8, 1759, in which he spoke of " my brothers Gysbert, and Wilhelmus." His w. was buried, April 14, 1747. Ch : bp. ; Catharina, Oct. 26, 1701 ; Volkert, Dec. 17, 1704 ; Willem, Oct. 3, 1708 ; Maria, April 23, 1710 ; Wilhelmus, Jan. 18, 1713 ; Cataline, Oct. 27, 1716, m. Hendrick Van Hoesen; Volkie, Nov. 27, 1720 ; Volkie, March 10, 1723, buried, Jan. 27, 1743.

VAN DEN BERGH (Bey), Cornelis, [son of Gerrit ?] and Maria Van Buren. Ch : Gerrit, bp. .... 1703.

VAN DEN BERGH, Gysbert, [son of Cornelis Gysbertse ?] m. first Diewertje Masten, *geboren en wonende tot Kingstown*, Oct. 20, 1700 ; and secondly, Catalyntje, ... about 1720. Ch : bp. ; Cornelis, May 10, 1702 ; *Willem* (?) ; Volkert, Oct. 12, 1712 ; Maria, Oct. 19, 1718 ; Catharina, June 18, 1721 ; Catharina, May 23 ,1723, buried, June 30, 1757 ; Volkie, Feb. 27, 1726.

VAN DEN BERGH, Gerrit Gerritse, m. first Egbertje Harmense ; and secondly, Maria, about 1729. Ch : bp, Teuntje, April 20, 1712 ; Maria, Jan. 1, 1715 ; Gerardus, Sept. 1, 1717 ; Rachel, Feb. 26, 1721 ; *Gerrit*, Sept. 26, 1725 : Cornelis, Feb. 4. 1730.

VAN DEN BERGH, Gerrit Cornelise, and Tryntje..... He was buried, Oct. 14, 1731. Ch : bp. ; Cornelis, Sept. 23, 1716 ; Breghie, Jan. 1, 1719 ; Harmanus, March 1, 1721 ; Gysbert, April 28, 1723 ; Cornelia, May 15, 1726 ; Abraham, Nov. 10, 1728 ; Volkert, Aug. 23, 1729 ; Wynant, May 7, 1732.

VAN DEN BERGH, Wilhelmus [son of Willem], m. Geertie Van Den Bergh, Oct. 24, 1716. Ch : bp. ; Wilhelmus, Jan. 16, 1717 ; Cornelis, Feb. 24, 1720 ; Cornelis, April 23, 1721 ; Cornelia, June 29, 1723 ; Catharina, Oct. 24, 1725 ; Cornelis, Nov. 3, 1728 ; Gerrit, Sept. 5, 1731.

VAN DEN BERGH, Matthias [son of Cornelis], m. Cathalyna Van Deusen, May 21, 1717 : buried Dec. 22, 1745. Ch : bp. ; Cornelis, April 13, 1718 ; *Cornelis*, Oct. 9, 1719 ; Wyntje, Dec. 17, 1721 ; Cornelia, May 24, 1724 ; *Rutgert*, Aug. 28, 1726 ; Gysbert, May, 1729 ; Engeltie, May 17, 1730 ; Gerrit, Dec. 24, 1732 ; Catalyna, Aug. 18, 1735 ; Cathalyna, Oct. 3, 1736.

VAN DEN BERGH, Wynant [son of Cornelis], of *Halve maan*, 1720, m. first Aaltie Van Nes, Nov. 21, 1715 ; secondly, Anna Wendel, March 20, 1721 ; thirdly Catharina Van Nes, widow Groesbeck, Aug. 25, 1750 ; she was buried, Dec. 21, 1754. Ch : bp. ; Cornelis, July 20, 1718 ; Cornelia, March 11, 1722 ; *Abraham*, Aug. 25, 1723 ; Cornelia, June 6, 1725 ; *Cornelis*, May 13, 1727 ; Maycke, July 27, 1729 ; Aaltie, Nov. 13, 1731 ; Anna, Nov. 1732 ; Wynant, June 1, 1735 ; *Evert ?* ; Gysbert, and Catharina, July 15, 1744 ; Catalina, May 5, 1751.

VAN DEN BERGH, Claas [son of Cornelis Claase], m. Antje Hooghkerk, Jan. 16, 1719. Ch : bp. ; Cornelis, Oct. 4, 1719 ; Cornelis, Sept. 11, 1720.

VAN DEN BERGH, Gerrit W. [son of Willem], m. Alida Van Wie, June 25, 1722. Ch: bp. ; Agniete. Jan. 30, 1723 ; Catharina, Sept. 20, 1724 ; Anna, Dec. 13. 1726 ; *Willem*, Dec. 8, 1728 ; Maria, Feb. 21, 1731 ; Maria, Nov. 1732 ; Gerrit, March 30, 1735 ; Alida, Nov. 6, 1737 ; Hendrik, April 27, 1740 ; Cornelis, Oct. 16, 1743.

VAN DEN BERGH, Adam [son of Cornelis Willemse], m. Maria Spoor, Dec. 15, 1724. Ch: bp. ; Maritie, Aug. 16, 1725 ; Cornelis, Feb. 10, 1728.

VAN DEN BERGH, Gerrit [son of Barent Gerritse], and Engeltie ... Ch: bp. ; Barent, March 6, 1725 ; Rachel, Dec. 5, 1726 ; Geertruy, Sept. 7, 1729 ; Engeltie, May 7, 1732 ; Barent, Dec. 1, 1734 ; Cornelis, Feb. 20, 1736.

VAN DEN BERGH, Johannes, m. Maria, Van Nes Jan. 26, 1726. Ch: bp. ; Cornelis, Nov. 6, 1726 ; Marretie, Dec. 13, 1729 ; Gerrit, March 18, 1733 ; Nicolaes, Nov. 23, 1735 ; Marritie, Feb. 12, 1738 ; Susanna, June 7, 1741 ; Johannes, July 28, 1742 ; Petrus, Oct. 19, 1744 ; Willem, July 26, 1746 ; Abraham, Jan. 8, 1749 ; Alida, June 2, 1751.

VAN DEN BERGH, Folkert [son of Wynant Willemse], and Catharina Huyck. Ch: bp. ; Maycke, Aug. 2, 1730 ; Volkie, Aug. 28, 1734 ; Volkie, Aug. 3, 1735 ; Christina, April 23, 1738 ; Burger, Aug. 3, 1740 ; Catharina, March 20, 1743 ; Rachel, July 5, 1745 ; Rachel, May 15, 1748.

VAN DEN BERGH, Gerrit C. [son of Cornelis Gysbertse], m. Margarita Van Vechten, July 15, 1729. Ch: bp. ; Volkert, Aug. 22, 1731 ; Volkert, March 25, 1733 ; Maria, May 4, 1735, d. July 5, 1836, a. 101 y; Lydia, Aug. 10, 1737 ; Margarieta, Sept. 23, 1739 ; Gerrit Teunise, June 6, 1742 ; Christina, June 17, 1744 ; Elizabeth, May 28, 1749.

VAN DEN BERGH, Pieter, [son of Cornelis Claase(?)] and Maria ..... Ch: bp. Cornelis, May 19, 1731 ; Egbertie, April 31 (*sic*) 1737 ; Gerrit, Nov. 4, 1739 ; Petrus, Aug. 14, 1748.

VAN DEN BERGH, Andries, [son of Barent Gerritse], and Maritie (Margarita) Vinhagel (Pinhaarn). Ch: bp. Barent, July 23, 1732 ; Johannes, May 19, 1734 ; Geertruy, Jan. 9, 1737 ; Abraham, April 15, 1739 ; Gerrit, April 25, 1742 ; Maria, Feb. 17, 1745.

VAN DEN BERGH, Turuf (?) and Maritie .... Ch: Cornelis, bp. Sept. 30, 1733.

VAN DEN BERGH, Cornelis M. (?) [son of Cornelis Willemse(?)], m. Rachel (De) Ridder, March 13, 1733. Ch: bp. ; Cornelis, Feb. 14, 1735 ; Autie, Sept. 5, 1736 ; Cornelia, Sept. 17, 1738 ; Marytje, March 21, 1742 ; Kiliaan, Aug. 17, 1746 ; Kiliaan, June 11, 1749.

VAN DEN BERGH, Mattys [son of Richard Janse], m. Rebecca Hendrickse .... 1733. Ch: bp. ; Rachel, Sept. 5, 1736 ; Ryckert, Jan. 6, 1742, m. Hanna Bronck ; Rebecca, June 21, 1752.

VAN DEN BERGH, Cornelis, [son of Cornelis Claase], m. Anneke Ryckse Van Vranken, June 1, 1737. Ch: bp. Cornelis, May 7, 1738 ; Anneke, March 23, 1740 ; Maas, April 11. 1742 ; Susanna, Oct. 23, 1748 ; Nicolaas, Dec. 9, 1753.

VAN DEN BERGH, Willem G. [son of Gysbert], m. Zantje (Susanna), Van Iveren, Jan. 26, 1739. Ch: bp. Cathalyntje, Aug. 8, 1739 ; Sara, May 2, 1742 ; Gysbert, July 5, 1745 ; Gysbert, Aug. 7, 1748 ; Reynier, Jan. 6, 1751 ; Catalina, June 17, 1753 ; Volkert, Oct. 23, 1755 ; Jacob, May 6, 1759.

VAN DEN BERGH, Johannes [son of Barent Gerritse?] and Catharina ..... Ch : Barent, bp. May 15, 1743.

VAN DEN BERGH, Benjamin [son of Barent Gerritse], m. Anna (Johanna) Vinhagen, Nov. 20, 1741. Ch : bp. ; Geertruy, March 27, 1743 ; Maria, Jan. 12, 1746 ; Barent, March 25, 1750 ; Neeltie, June 17, 1759.

VAN DEN BERGH, Hendrick [son of Richard Janse], m. Catharina Hoogteling, Nov. 21, 1743. Ch: bp. ; Catharina, Jan. 4, 1745 ; Lena, Dec. 21, 1746 ; Ryckert, June 24, 1753.

VAN DEN BERGH, Wilhelmus, Jr., and Angenietje Van Den Bergh. Ch: bp. ; Cornelis, Jan. 3, 1748 ; Alida, May 20, 1750 ; Cornelia, Aug. 30, 17:2 ; Gerrit, Dec. 9, 1753 ; Cornelia, Nov. 21, 1756 ; Geertje, Nov. 28, 1761.

VAN DEN BERGH, Gerrit Gerritse [son of Gerrit Gerritse], and Agnietje Lieversen. Ch: bp. ; Teunis, Oct. 23, 1748 ; Ebbertie, and Rachel, twins, Nov. 4, 1750 ; Gerrit, June 30, 1754 ; Maria, and Teunis, Oct. 16, 1757 ; Maria, June 25, 1760.

VAN DEN BERGH, Cornelis Matthys, m. secondly, Cornelia Van Den Bergh, in New York, Feb. 13, 1747. Ch: bp. ; Rachel, May 28, 1749 ; Annatie, March 17, 1751 ; Matthews, Nov. 24, 1754 ; Matthys, Aug. 13, 1758 ; Cathalyntje, Nov. 15, 1760 ; Wynant, b. March 17, 1764 ; Gysbert, May 19, 1766.

VAN DEN BERGH, Robert [son of Richard (?)], and Brando. Ch : Wilhelmus, bp. July 29, 1750.

VAN DEN BERGH, Abraham [son of Wynant (?)], m. Rachel Lieverse, Nov. 22, 1751. Ch: bp. ; Anna, July 12, 1752 ; Catharina, July 22, 1754 ; Catharina, March 27, 1757 ; Maritje, April 1, 1759 ; Lavinus, Feb. 15, 1761 ; Cornelia, b. April 4, 1767.

VAN DEN BERGH, Cornelis J., and Catarina De Ridder. Ch: bp. ; Gerrit, Dec. 31, 1752 ; Marytje, Sept. 24, 1758 ; Annatie, Dec. 26, 1768.

VAN DEN BERGH, Cornelis W. [son of Wynant (?)], and Maria Viele. Ch: Annatie, bp. Nov. 3, 1754 ; Elizabeth, Aug. 7, 1757 ; Wynant, b. June 14, 1760 ; Philippus, b. April 30, 1763 ; Maria, b. Oct. 11, 1765 ; Helena, b. Feb. 13, 1769.

VAN DEN BERGH, Wynant, and Catarina Van Nes. Ch : Gysbert, bp. Dec, 15, 1754.

VAN DEN BERGH, Wynant [son of Wynant], and Maria (De) Ridder. Ch: Annatie, bp. March 15, 1761 ; Gerritje, b. Sept. 8, 1762 ; Wynant, b. March 4, 1764 ; Cornelis, b. Nov. 11, 1765 ; Johannes, Sept. 13, 1774.

VAN DEN BERGH, Cornelis, and Elizabeth Pieterse, Ch: Annatie, bp. Oct. 13, 1754.

VAN DEN BERGH, Cornelis G., and Elizabeth .... Ch: Gysbert, bp. Oct. 11, 1761.

VAN DEN BERGH, Rutger [son of Matthys], m. Maria Van Den Bergh, July 6, 1754. Ch: Cathalyntje, bp. March 12, 1755 ; Matthys, bp. April 17, 1757 ; Matthys, bp. June 17, 1759 ; Alida, bp. Oct. 11, 1761 ; Cathalina, b. Jan. 18, 1764 ; Gerrit, June 29, 1766 ; Gerrit, b. Sept. 8, 1768 ; Alida, b. April 8, 1771 ; Alida, b. Oct. 16, 1773.

VAN DEN BERGH, Evert [son of Wynant (?)], m. Annatie Lansing, Sept. 18, 1756. Ch: Wynant, bp. Aug. 7, 1757 ; Abraham, b. June 4, 1762 ; Annatie, July 28, 1764 ; Annatje, b. Sept. 15, 1765.

VAN DEN BERGH, Folkert G., m. Neeltie Waldron, May 10, 1755. Ch: bp. ; Gysbert, March 20, 1758 ; Gysbert, Nov. 25, 1759; Willem, Jan. 31, 1762. Ch : b. ; Elizabeth, Sept. 13, 1763 ; Willem, Oct. 5, 1764; Willem, Sept. 29, 1765 ; Elizabeth, July 28, 1767 ; Willem Waldron, Oct. 8, 1770 ; Catharina, Oct. 19, 1773.

VAN DEN BERGH, Gerrit Johannese, of *Halve Maan,* m. first Alida Gerritse Van Den Bergh (Alida Van Nes). Sept. 28, 1758 ; secondly, Rebecca Fonda, Nov. 30, 1769. Ch : bp. ; Maria, Jan. 14, 1759 ; Gerrit, July 5, 1761 ; Ch : b. Marytje, Oct. 25, 1770 ; Petrus, Sept. 9, 1774 ; Isaac, Nov. 11, 1776 ; Alida, March 20, 1781 ; Gerrit, April 23, 1786 ; d. Aug. 16, 1860, a. 75 y.

VAN DEN BERGH, Wynant Folkertse, m. first, Marritie Van Den Bergh, Sept. 28, 1758 ; and secondly, Francyntie Clute, about 1768. Ch : bp. ; Volkert, June 24, 1759 ; Catharina, Nov. 23, 1760. Ch : b. ; Maria, Oct. 3, 1768 ; Gysbert, April 8, 1770 ; Maria, Feb. 20, 1772.

VAN DEN BERGH, Willem, and Marytje ..... Ch : Maria, b. Jan. 22, 1763.

VAN DEN BERGH, Willem, m. Annatje Van Der Werken, Nov. 21, 1761. Ch : Wynant, b. Jan. 30, 1763.

VAN DEN BERGH, Willem, and Annatie Vosburgh. Ch : Abraham, b. Nov. 18, 1767.

VAN DEN BERGH, Evert, and Marytje Van Der Werken. [Evert V. D. B. m. Marytje Ouderkerk, Aug. 31, 1764.] Ch : b. ; Rachel, April 2, 1765 ; Kiliaan, Oct. 11, 1767 ; Cornelis, June 10, 1770.

VAN DEN BERGH, Cornelis, and Maicke Ouderkerk, m. June 29, 1765. Ch : b. ; Cornelis, Sept. 3, 1766 ; Annatie, Jan 29, 1769 ; Maas, Nov. 8, 1771 ; Susanna, April 27, 1777·

VAN DEN BERGH, Johannes F., of *Halve Maan,* m. Maayke Ouderkerk, May 20, 1770. Ch : b. ; Hester, Sept. 7, 1770 ; Johannes, June 6, 1773.

VAN DEN BERGH, Richard, m. Hanna, dau. of John Bronck, Dec. 24, 1763. Ch : b. ; Matthew, July 8, 1772 ; Teddy, April 21, 1773 (?) ; Rebecca, Oct. .... 1774; John, Nov. 3, 1776 ; Abraham, May 5, 1779. [*Van Den Bergh Bible.*]

VAN DEN BERGH, Johannes, and Eva Van Alstyn. Ch : Harmanus, bp. Aug. 13, 1774 ; Cornelis, b. Nov. 16, 1778.

VAN DEN BERGH, Jellis, and Marytje Ouderkerk. Ch : Isaac, b. Sept. 17, 1774.

VAN DEN BERGH, Gerrit A. m. Annatie Jones (SJans), June 22, 1775. Ch. b. ; Andries, May 14, 1776 ; Catharina, March 15, 1779 ; Hendrik, April 4, 1782.

VAN DEN BERGH, Reinier, m. Elizabeth Vinhagen (Van Allen), Jan. 11, 1778. Ch : b. ; Neeltie, June 4, 1779 ; Susanna, April 17, 1782 ; Wilhelmus, July 3, 1784.

VAN DEN BERGH, Evert, and Jannetie Van Schaick. Ch. b. ; Cornelia, Dec. 24, 1778 ; Maria, Nov. 16, 1780.

VAN DEN BERGH, Cornelis, and Rebecca Fonda. Ch : Cornelis, b. Dec. 3, 1778.

VAN DEN BERGH, Cornelis, and Cathalyntje Bogart. Ch : b. ; Agnietje, May 31, 1781 ; Jacob, and Agnietie, Oct. 22, 1782; Wilhelmus, July 28, 1784.

VAN DEN BERGH, Gysbert. m. Jannetie Witbeck, Nov. 24, 1771. Ch. b. ; Eva, Jan, 16, 1780 ; Catryntje, Oct. 18, 1787.

VAN DEN BERGH, Nicolaas, and Catharina Waldron. Ch : Marytje, b. Aug. 5, 1781.

VAN DEN BERGH, Nicolaas, and Hannah Clute. Ch : Annatie, b. Jan. 17, 1788.

VAN DEN BERGH, Volkert, m. Marytje Vinhagen, Nov. 21, 1779. Ch : Catharina, b. Jan. 16, 1781.

VAN DEN BERGH, Wynand, m. Annatie Cooper, May 28, 1780. Ch : b. ; Evert, July 4, 1771 ; Catharina, Dec. 22, 1787.

VAN DEN BERGH, Maas, and Catharina Sheer. Ch : Andries, b. March 19, 1781.

VAN DEN BERGH, Matthias, and Annatie Yates. Ch : b. ; Cornelis, June 7, 1785 ; Catalina, March 22, 1788 ; Wynand, Nov. 16, 1792.

VAN DEN BERGH, Wynand, and Maria Hickson. She d. June 22, 1846, a. 79 y. Ch : b. ; Willem, Sept. 2, 1788 ; Abraham, May 17, 1790, d. Feb. 28, 1811, a. 20 y. 9 m. 22 d. ; Wynant, July 26, 1796 , Sarah, Oct. 19, 1798 ; James, Feb. 7, 1801 ; James, Jan. 31, 1803 ; Abraham, Dec. 1, 1811 ; Stephen, Feb. 2, 1814.

VAN DEN BERGH, Teunis, and Marytje Becker. Ch : Gerrit, b. May 16, 1789.

VAN DEN BERGH, Nicolaas, of Saratoga, and Jannette Waldron. Ch : Cornelius, May 8, 1789.

VAN DEN BERGH, Lavinus, and Elizabeth Anthony. Ch : Rachel, b. Jan. 29, 1790.

VAN DEN BERGH, Cornelius, m. Annatie Ten Eyck, Sept. 15, 1795. Ch : Henry, b. June 29, 1795 [1796 ?].

VAN DEN BERGH, Matthew R., m. Caty Ray, Nov. 14, 1795. Ch : b. ; Richard, Feb. 13, 1796 ; William, Dec. 24, 1799 ; Hanna, Sept. 27, 1801 ; John, M. Aug. 31, 1803. [*Van Den Bergh Bible.*]

Van Den Uythoff, Wouter Albertse, baker, in 1657, owned a lot bounded east and south by the river and the [*Rutten*] kil, and north by the [Staats's] alley, now State street. He was living as late as 1674.

Van Der Baast, Joris Aertse, surveyor, of Schenectady, where he was killed by the French and Indians on the night of Feb. 8, 1690.

Van Der Bogart, Cornelis, d. in Albany, about July 10, 1666.

VAN DER BOGART [Boghardij] Harmen Myndertse, came to the province in 1631, as a surgeon in the W. I. Company's ship *Eendraght,* and was appointed commissary of Fort Orange ; he came to a violent death in 1647 or, 8. His wife Gillisje Claese Schouw [Swits (?)], of Zierickzee, after his death, m. Jan Labatie. Ch : Frans, bp. in New York, Aug. 26, 1640 ; Myndert, bp. in New York, May 3, 1643 ; Lysbeth, who m. Harmen Janse Knickelbakker.

VAN DER BOGART, (Uyt Den Bogaardt), Myndert Harmense, gunstocker, 1689, trader, 1692, resided on the south side of *Yonker* street [State] west of Pearl ; about 1686, he removed to Dutchess county where in company with Robert Sanders, he obtained a patent of land one mile square including the site of the present city of Poughkeepsie one half of which he mortgaged to Abraham De Peyster, of New York, for £116–6–6. He m. Helena Schermerhoorn. Ch : bp. ; Johannes, Jan. 18, 1685 ; Cornelis, Dec. 15, 1686 ; Elizabeth, Sept. 30, 1688 ; Catarina, Aug. 10, 1690 ; Reyer and Francis twins, June 5, 1692.

VAN DER BOGART, Claas Franse, of Schenectady, m. Barbara Heemstraat, in Schenectady, Dec. 31, 1699. Ch : Grietje, bp. Feb. 9, 1709. [See also *Schenectady Families.*]

VAN DER BOGART, Nicolaas, tailor, of Jerico, Albany district, corporal in the first New York Regiment, having served " faithfully " 7 y. and 3 m. received a bounty of 600 acres of land from the state of New York. He m. Margarita Flensburgh, Dec. 29, 1782. Ch: Catharina, b. May 23, 1784.

Van Der Heyden, Jan Cornelise, b. at Sevenbergen in Brabant, trader, in Beverwyck, 1663, m. Aeltie Janse Wemp, dau. of Jan Barentse Wemp, of *Colonie* Rensselaerswyck. They made a joint will, Sept. 1, 1663, at which time they had no children living.

VAN DER HEYDEN. Jacob Tyssen, tailor, came from New Amsterdam to Beverwyck in 1654. He was over 60 y. old in 1676. July 25, 1655, he m. Anna Hals, in Amsterdam, Holland. They had one son *Dirk.*

VAN DER HEYDEN, Dirk, "tapper," of manor Rensselaerswyck, m. Rachel Jochemse Ketelhuyn, March 9, 1687. He purchased a bouwery of Pieter Van Woggelum, at *Lubberdes* land [now Troy] which in 1731 from love to his three sons, Jacob, David and Matthys, he conveyed to them. He was buried Oct. 13, 1738. Ch: bp.; Agniet, Aug. 28, 1687; Anna, Jan. 1, 1689; Jacobus, Aug. 3, 1690; Jacob, April 23, 1692, m. Hester, dau. of Nanning Harmense Visscher, Dirk, Jan. 7, 1694; David, May 19, 1695, m. Geertruy, dau. of Nanning Harm. Visscher; Matthys, Jan. 10, 1697; Anna, March 26, 1699, d. July 10, 1709; Jochem, Sept. 15, 1700; Rachel, Sept. 19, 1703; Johannes, March 2, 1707.

VAN DER HEYDEN, Dirk, m. Egbertie Bratt, April 22, 1716. Ch: Rachel, bp. July 29, 1716, m. Harmen Visscher.

VAN DER HEYDEN, Jacob, m. Hester Visscher, May 3, 1720. He was buried, April 10, 1746. Ch: bp.; Dirk, June 19, 1720; Nanningh, Nov. 25, 1721; Jacob, March 6, 1725; Alida, Oct. 27, 1727.

VAN DER HEYDEN, Johannes, m. Rachel Van der Heyden, Jan. 16, 1724. She was buried at the flats, Jan. 3, 1754. Ch: bp.; Johannes, Nov. 14, 1725; Rachel, Nov. 19, 1727; Dirk, Jan. 19, 1729; Jacob, May 15, 1731; Maria, Sept. 16, 1733; Rachel, May 2, 1736; David, April 27, 1740; Mattheus, Dec. 1, 1742; Janneke, May 8, 1748.

VAN DER HEYDEN, Jochum, of Schenectady, m. first Anna Ketelhuyn, Jan. 8, 1725; and secondly, Bata Clute, in Schenectady, July 10, 1730; she was buried June 19, 1746. Ch: bp.; Dirk, Oct. 24, 1725; Johannes, Nov. 7, 1731; Rachel, Aug. 24, 1735; Jacobus, Feb. 8, 1738. [See also *Schenectady Families.*]

VAN DER HEYDEN, David, merchant, m. Geertruy Visscher, Dec. 26, 1725. He made a will Feb. 7, 1770, proved Aug. 13, 1770, in which the following children are spoken of except Nanning. Sept. 5, 1766, he leased in perpetuity of the city a lot of land for a family burial place on the west side of Swan street north of Washington street at a rent of $2.50, which was commuted in 1856; on this lot a vault was erected called "the Stringer vault," from his dau. Rachel Stringer. Ch: bp.; Dirk, Oct. 30, 1726; Nanning, who was buried, Sept. 23, 1739; Rachel, Aug. 22, 1730; David, Nov. 19, 1732; Alida, Aug. 28, 1734; m. Domine Barent Vrooman, of Schenectady: Jacob, March 3, 1737; Rachel, July 16, 1740; m. Samuel, Stringer, M.D.

VAN DER HEYDEN, Matthys, m. first Geertruy ...., and secondly, Marg. Bratt, Dec. 17, 1730. Ch: bp.; Nanning, Oct. 20, 1728; Dirk, May 14, 1732; Johannes, Dec. 12, 1733; Johem Bratt, June 20, 1736; Matthys, Nov. 25, 1739; Mattheus, Feb. 14, 1742; Maria, Jan. 10, 1746. [Matthys V. D. Heyden's two children were buried Aug. 31, 1743.]

VAN DER HEYDEN, Johannes, Jr., and Catryna Van Brakelen. She was buried, Feb. 22, 1754. Ch: bp.; Elizabeth, April 2, 1738; Johannes, Jan. 14, 1750. [See also *Schenectady Families.*]

VAN DER HEYDEN, Johannes, and Catrina Brown. Ch: Adam, bp. Nov. 9, 1755.

VAN DER HEYDEN, Dirk, and Elizabeth Wendel. Ch: bp.; Elizabeth, Nov. 16, 1746; Elizabeth, Feb. 19, 1749; Hester, Aug. 12, 1750; Catarina, Jan. 5, 1752; Jacob and Alida, July 14, 1754; Susanna, and Jacob, Nov. 5, 1758; Susanna, Oct. 24, 1762.

VAN DER HEYDEN, Jacob, and Maria Halenbeck. Ch: bp.; Jacob, Dec. 3, 1749; Nanning, Sept. 29, 1751; Nanning, Feb. 24, 1754; Dirk, Jan. 7, 1759; Maria, Nov. 1, 1761.

VAN DER HEYDEN, Dirk Jochemse *van de draagplaets*, m. Margarita Kittle *van Schagtekook*, Feb. 28, 1754. Ch: bp.; Annatje, Sept. 8, 1754; Joachim, April 25, 1756; David, Feb. 26, 1758; Ch: b.; Daniel, Feb. 22, 1760; Eva, March 3, 1762; Jacob, May 17, 1765.

VAN DER HEYDEN, Jacob, and Lea Brouwer. Ch: Johannes, bp. March 12, 1754.

VAN DER HEYDEN, Dirk Matthyse, m. Sara Wendel, July 15, 1758. Ch: bp.; Margarita, June 17, 1759; Mattys, Sept. 9, 1760; Johannes, Oct. 18, 1761; Ch: b.; Dirk, June 3, 1763; Abraham, April 25, 1767.

VAN DER HEYDEN, Abraham, of *Steen Rabie* [Lansingburgh], and Annatie Boorhais [Burhans ?]. Ch: b.; Anny, Dec. 13, 1769; Jochum, March 3, 1771; Barent, July 12, *in huis gedoopt*, Oct. 5, 1775.

VAN DER HEYDEN, Johannes, and Annatie Price. Ch: Maria, b. March 16, 1779.

VAN DER HEYDEN, Jacob, and Jennet Livingston. Ch: b.; Jennet, Nov. 22, 1779; David, Aug. 19, 1784.

VAN DER HEYDEN, Jacob Dirkse, m. Jannetie Yates. He was buried from his residence No. 85, North Pearl street, Sept 24, 1820. She d. at the same place Dec. 21, 1823. He purchased of the Beekman family in 1788 the "Van Der Heyden palace" in North Pearl street; after the death of his wife in 1823 the family left it: it was demolished in 1832 and the Pearl street Baptist church was erected on the site; this in 1870 was turned into stores. Ch: Dirk b. Dec. 23, 1781; Jan Gerritsen, Nov. 5, 1786, d. at Troy, Jan. 5, 1829, a. 42 y.; Samuel: "d. at Troy, Nov. 27, 1823 Samuel V. D. H. son of the late Jacob D." Van Der Heyden, and one of the proprietors of Troy;" Henry, d. in Brunswick, Rensselaer Co. May 21, 1831, a. 42 y.

VAN DER HEYDEN, Nanning, and Catharina Levison. Ch: Annatie, b. Jan. 22, 1782.

VAN DER HEYDEN, Abraham, and Maritie Sharp. Ch: Margaret, b. Aug. 4, 1790.

VAN DER HEYDEN, Matthias, and Mary Denker. Ch: Margaret, b. Feb. 3, 1791.

Van Der Hoeven, Jan Cornelise, of Kinderhook, and Dorothe Janse, Ch: bp.; Cornelis, Sept. 16, 1683; Johannes, May 9, 1686; Geertruy, March 29, 1688; Gysbert, Jan. 20, 1692; Isaac, and Jacob twins, Dec. 9, 1694.

VAN DER HOEVEN, Cornelise, m. Metie Beeckman; Cornelis was buried Jan. 10, 1689-90. Ch: bp.; Marten, March 1, 1685; Susanna, May 5, 1687; Johannes, 1689.

Van Der Kar, Jan. m. Madalena Baart, Sept. 25, 1718. Ch: bp.; Hendrik, Oct. 30, 1720; Dirk, Oct. 20, 1723: Engeltie, Feb. 27, 1726; Jannetie, July 13,

14

1729; Jannetie, Dec. 12, 1731; Hendrik, May 5, 1734; Johannes, Feb. 28, 1736; Abraham, Sept. 3, 1738; Nicolaas, July 8, 1744.

VAN DER KAR (Kerre), Jan (Dirk), m. Feytje Claase Van Schaick, of Kinderhook, in 1687. Ch: bp.; Janneke, June 10, 1688; Ariaantje, Jan. 8, 1690; Claas, May 6, 1694; Salomon, June 28, 1696; Arent, and Lourens, twins, Dec. 25, 1698; Ariaantje, Sept. 7, 1701; Jannete, Aug. 15, 1703; Neeltje, May 17, 1705; Emanuel, Oct. 16, 1709; Elizabeth, Oct. 14, 1711.

Van Der Karr, Arent, and Charlotte. Ch: bp; Fytje, June 5, 1730; Hendrik, Nov. 4, 1733; Maria, and Elizabeth, Dec. 12, 1736; Geertruy, Feb. 18, 1739; Dirk, May 2, 1742.

VAN DER KARR, N. and A ..... Ch: Maria, bp. June 16, 1736.

Van Der Kar, Abraham, of *Halve Maan,* m. Margarita De Voe, Aug. 6, 1759. Ch: Dirk, b. Feb. 1760; Abraham, bp. Aug. 9, 1761; Johannes, b. Nov. 3, 1764; Hendrik, b. Feb. 27, 1767; Daniel, b. June 21, 1769.

VAN DER KAR, Dirk, and Fytje ..... Ch: Charlotte, b. Nov. 25, 1764.

VAN DER KAR, Dirk A., and Hilletje Muller. Ch: Hilletje, bp. Aug. 6, 1775.

VAN DER KAR, Hendrik, and Antje Williams. Ch: Rebecca, b. Jan. 24, 1781.

Van Der Koek, Michael, and Cornelia Van Nes. Ch: Cornelia, bp. Sept. 13, 1761.

VAN DER KOEK, Michael, and Maria Allen. Ch: Sara, b. July 9, 1769.

VAN DER KOEK (Van Der Loek), Simon, m. Laryntie Van Der Hoef, *op de Halve Maan,* June 1, 1773. Ch: Peter, b. Nov. 24, 1790.

Van Der Lyn, Pieter, and Geertruy ..... Ch: bp.; Petrus, March 13, 1726; Elizabeth, April 14, 1728; Jacobus, Sept. 25, 1730.

Van Der Mark, John, and Cornelia Van Den Bergh. Ch: Evert, b. Aug. 13, 1797.

Van Der Meulen, Hendrick Gerritse, master tailor in Beverwyck, 1662, then owned a house on E. side Broadway nearly opposite Beaver street.

Van Der Poel, Teunis Cornelise, *alias* Spitsbergen, in Beverwyck, 1660-87; he owned half of *Constapel's* island opposite *Paerde Hoeck*; 1671 was one of the magistrates of Albany; made his will June 17, 1687, and spoke of his wife Catrine Janse Croon, to whom he left a house and lot in Amsterdam, which she devised to her three daughters: Elisabeth w. of Bennony Van Corlaer (late wid. of Sybrant Van Schaick); Maria w. of Anthony Van Schaick; and Johanna w. of Barent Lewis.

VAN DER POEL, Wynant Gerritse; in 1674 he bought of Geertruy Pieterse, wid. of the late Abraham Vosburgh half a saw-mill on the east bank of the Hudson opposite Capt. Philip Schuyler's bouwery, on the creek on the south side of Jeronimus Ebbingh's bouwery; since which time this creek has been called *Wynant's* kil. W. G. Van Der Poel, "late of Albany now of New York," made his will Feb. 29, 1695, proved April 17, 1702, in which he spoke of his w. Tryntje Melgers, licensed *vroedvrouw* of Albany, eldest son Melgert, and son-in law, Willem Van Den Bergh, who was named his executor. He was deceased in 1699.

VAN DER POEL, Melgert Wynantse, gunstocker, m. first, Ariaantje Verplanck; and secondly, Elizabeth, dau. of Willem Teller, senior, and wid. of Abraham Van Tricht, June 29, 1692. His and his father's house fronted the fort, in 1675, probably on the south side of State street. He was not living Sept. 19, 1700. Ch: *Melgert;* Maria; Trinke; *Abraham; Wynant,* bp. Oct. 14, 1683; Gelyn, bp. May 17, 1685; Jacobus, March 9, 1687; Henderick, June 2, 1689; Wilhelm, March 19, 1693; Ariaantje, Nov. 17, 1695.

VAN DER POEL, Gerrit Wynantse. m. Catryn Van Santen (Zandt). Her house in 1708 was on the E. corner of State and Pearl streets; she d. April 8, 1709. Ch: bp.; Wynant, in New York, Aug. 27, 1690; Wynant, Oct. 11, 1691.

VAN DER POEL, Melgert, Jr., of Kinderhoek, 1720, m. Catharina Van Alen, May 17, 1696. Ch: bp.; Elbertje, Feb. 3, 1697; Ariaantje, Sept. 3, 1699; *Lourens,* Jan. 26, 1701; Maria, Jan. 10, 1703; Johannes, March 4, 1705; Abraham, Feb. 9, 1707; *Jacobus,* April, 17, 1709; *Isaak,* Oct. 14, 1711; Catryna, Dec. 16, 1716.

VAN DER POEL, Wynant [son of Melgert], m. Catharina De Hoogen [Hooges], of Ulster Co. Aug. 17, 1706. Ch: bp.; *Johannes,* Aug. 3, 1707; Abraham, Feb. 13, 1709; Melchert, March, 4, 1711; Ariaantje, March 1, 1713; Margarieta, Dec. 25, 1714; Antony, Aug. 18, 1717; David, Aug. 30, 1719; David, Sept. 27, 1721; Maria, Nov. 4, 1722.

VAN DER POEL, Abraham [son of Melgert], m. Antje Van Den Bergh, Jan. 3, 1713. Ch: bp.; *Melchert,* Feb. 7, 1714; Ariantje, Sept. 23, 1716; Teuntje, Aug. 3, 1718; *Gerrit,* June 11, 1721; Teuntje, Nov. 3, 1723; Maria, Nov. 21, 1725; Ariaantje, June 9, 1729.

VAN DER POEL, Lourens [son of Melgert, Jr.], m. Ariaantje Van Den Bergh, Oct. 29, 1726. Ch: bp.; Catharina, March 5, 1727; Jacobus, July 3, 1737; Jan, March 30, 1740.

VAN DER POEL, Jacobus [son of Melgert, Jr.], m. Neeltie Huyck, Oct. 16, 1740. Ch: bp.; Marytje, Oct. 11, 1741; Catharina, Dec. 10, 1749; Catarina, May 10, 1752.

VAN DER POEL, Isaac [son of Melgert, Jr.], and Anna ... . Ch: bp.; Catharina, May 2, 1742; Abraham, Aug. 10, 1746.

VAN DER POEL, Johannes [son of Wynant?] widower, m. secondly, Annatie Staats, May 5, 1743; Ch: bp.; Isaac, Dec. 25, 1747; Margarita, April 22, 1750.

VAN DER POEL, Melgert [Eldert, son of Abraham?] and Margarita Vinhagen. Ch: bp.; Abraham, July 10, 1748; Maria, June 21, 1752; Jacobus, May 27, 1759; Gerrit, b. March 26, 1762; Maria, b. May 1, 1766.

VAN DER POEL, Gerrit [son of Abraham], and Catarina Hoes (Hus), Ch: bp.; Jannetie, Feb. 9, 1752; Abram, May 27, 1753; Mattheus, Sept. 22, 1754; Melchert, Nov. 30, 1755; Pieter, b. March 6, 1767.

VAN DER POEL, Abraham, and Dorothea Shutter. Ch: b.; Margarita, Oct. 31, 1775; Margarita, May 1, 1778.

VAN DER POEL, Abraham, and Marytje Becker. Ch: Dorothea, b. March 25, 1778.

VAN DER POEL, Abraham, and Catharine Brasie. Ch: Geertruy, bp. Aug. 15, 1784.

VAN DER POEL, Gerrit, m. first, Margarita Wilson, and secondly, Cornelia Muller, about 1785. Ch: Antje, bp May 21, 1780; Margarita, b. May 3, 1786.

VAN DER POEL, Jacobus, m. Marytje Muller, Jan. 27, 1783. Ch: b.; Margarita, Feb. 25, 1784; Catharina, April 9, 1786; Jeremie, Feb. 26, 1788.

VAN DEN POEL, Malachi, and Annatie Seger. Ch: Gerrit, b. Nov. 29, 1788.

VAN DER POEL, John, m. Geertruy Van Buren, April 10, 1780. Ch: John, b. May 27, 1795.

Van Der Volgen, alias Van Purmerent, Claas Lourentse, of Schenectady, and Marytje Swart. Ch: bp.; Lysbeth, May 9, 1686; Nicolaas, Aug. 7, 1687; Ariaantje, May 18, 1690; Ariaantje, Feb. 12, 1793. [See also *Schenectady Families.*]

VAN DER VOLGEN, Teunis, of Schenectady, and Sara Harmense. Ch: bp.; Claas, June 26, 1709; Neeltie, Oct. 12, 1713, [See also *Schenectady Families.*]

Van Der Voort, Jacobus, and Nancy Krups. Ch: Geertruy, Jan. 31, 1785.

VAN DER VOORT, James and Annatie (Mary) Schuyler. Ch: b.; Johannes, Oct. 1, 1787; Daniel, June 2, 1792; Charles, July 20, 1794; Anna Gourlay, June 18, 1798.

VAN DER VOORT, James, and Annatie (Nancy) Neghs (Meggs, Neggs). Ch: b.; Margarita, March 4, 1790; Richard, April 30, 1797; Henry, Jan. 8, 1802.

Van Der Werken, Roeloff Gerritse, of *Halve Maan,* had a farm on "*Cahoos* Island," above the 4th fork of the Mohawk river, as early as 1677; in 1680, bought 7 morgens adjoining his land on the west and north of the 4th fork, also 2 morgens on *Haver* island, of Annetie Lievens, widow of Goosen; Gerritse Van Schaick. He m. Geertruy Jacobse. Ch: bp.; *Gerrit; Albert; Hendrick; Nicolaas; Maritie,* w. of John Kidney; Jannetie, Jan. 21, 1685, Catarina, Jan. 12, 1687; *Johannes,* Sept. 30, 1688; Elizabeth, Jan, 1, 1692; Jacob. Aug. 20, 1693.

VAN DER WERKEN, Gerrit Roeloffse, and Maritie Janse De Voe (De Vooer). He was buried Feb. 2, 1756. Ch: bp.; Geertruy, Jan. 5, 1700; Jannetje, Sept. 27, 1702; Catharina, May 6, 1705; Gerardus, March 4, 1711; Johannes, June 13, 1714.

VAN DER WERKEN, Albert Roeloffse, m. Dirkje Van Alstein, July 15. 1704. Ch: bp.; Roeloff Gerritse, Oct. 14, 1705; Martinus, May 16, 1708; Johannes, Jan. 29, 1710; Roeloff, Feb. 10, 1712; Johannes, Jan. 31, 1713; Abraham, July 30, 1715: Jacobus, April 21, 1717; Jacob, May 3, 1719; Albert, March 1, 1721.

VAN DER WERKEN, Hendrik Roeloffse, of *Halve Maan,* and Marytje ..... Ch: Geertruy, bp. March 1, 1713; Maria, March 31, 1716; Catharina, Jan. 1, 1721.

VAN DER WERKEN, Nicolaas [Roeloffse], and Maria ..... Ch: Elizabeth, bp. April 13, 1718.

VAN DER WERKEN, Joannes Roeloffse, m. Margarita Baart, Jan. 8, 1715. Ch: bp.; Engeltie, Nov. 20, 1715; *Roeloff,* Feb. 10, 1717; Geertruy, Nov. 1, 1718; *Hendrick,* Oct. 30, 1720; *Jacob,* Nov. 11, 1722; Johannes, Feb. 10, 1725; *Albert,* May 22, 1727; Gerrit, June 5, 1730; buried, June 26, 1746; *Johannes,* Jan. 16, 1734.

VAN DER WERKEN, Johannes [son of Gerrit Roeloffse?] m. Christina Pruyn, March 1, 1737. Ch: bp.; Margarita, Feb. 8, 1738; Frans, Jan. 24, 1739; Elizabeth, Oct. 5, 1740; Barent, May 23, 1742; Gerardus, May 20, 1744; Marytje, April 25, 1746; Johannes, March 27, 1754; Barent, Aug. 31, 1755; Alida, Feb, 26, 1758; Johannatje (Jannetie), Oct. 19, 1760.

VAN DER WERKEN, M[artinus?] and Margarita .... Ch: bp.; Johannes, Feb, 22, 1730; Dirckje, March 8, 1732; Roeloff, May 5, 1734.

VAN DER WERKEN, Roeloff, Jr., [son of Johannes Roeloffse], and Annatie Vosburgh. Ch: bp.; Margarita, Jan. 10, 1746; Abraham, Jan. 3, 1748: Johannes, Feb. 5, 1749; Margarita, Oct. 7, 1751; Geertruy, Sept. 15, 1754; Abraham, Nov. 20, 1757.

VAN DER WERKEN, Roeloff [son of Johannes Roeloffse ?], and Geertruy Fonda. Ch: bp.; Hendrik, Jan. 10, 1746; Johannes, April 17, 1748.

VAN DER WERKEN, Albert, of *Halve Maan* [son of Johannes Roeloffse], m. Maria Qackenbos, Oct. 3, 1751. Ch: bp.; Margarita, Nov. 26, 1752; Rachel, Sept. 8, 1754; Geertruy, Sept. 19, 1756; Machtelt, Nov. 12, 1758; Machtelt, June 21, 1761; Johannes, b. April 21, 1764.

VAN DER WERKEN, Jacob [son of Johannes Roeloffse], and Maria ..... Ch: Willem, bp. Dec. 30, 1753.

VAN DER WERKEN, Johannes, Jr. [son of Johannes Roeloffse] of *Halve Maan,* m. Marytje De Voe, Dec. 26, 1754. Ch: Engeltie, bp. Nov. 30, 1755; Margarita, bp. April 30, 1758; Marya, b. April 25, 1760; Johannes, b. Oct. 4, 1762; Geertruy, bp. Dec. 23, 1764: Elizabeth, b. March 13, 1767; Annatie, b. July 24, 1768; Abraham, April 15, 1771; Roeloff, bp. Feb. 7, 1774.

VAN DER WERKEN, Hendrick [son of Johannes Roeloffse], m. Maria Viele, March 13, 1756. Ch: Margarita, bp. July 17, 1757; Johanna *geboren den lesten* Aug., 1762; Johannes, b. Sept. 6, 1764; Teunis b. Sept. 2, 1767; Hendrick, b. Oct, 11, 1772.

VAN DER WERKEN, Hendrick [son of Johannes Roeloffse] of *Halve Maan.* Marytje De Voe,Dec. [Eights or Yates?] Ch: Andries, b. July 27, 1774.

VAN DER WERKEN, Johannes, and Dirkje Van Aalsteyn. Ch: Jacobus, bp. June 24, 1759; Elizabeth, b. Sept. 1, 1764.

VAN DER WERKEN, Albert, m, Annatje Van Den Bergh (Winne), May 13, 1758. Ch: Annatje, bp. Feb. 11, 1759: Margarita, bp. Dec. 21, 1760; Cornelia, b. Jan. 2, 1763; Wynand, bp. July 16, 1768; Wynand, b. April 4, 1772.

VAN DER WERKEN, Roeloff M., m. Cornelia Van Alsteyn. Ch: Margarita, bp. Sept. 15, 1764.

VAN DER WERKEN, Albert, and Marytje Quackenbosch. Ch: b.; Jacob, Sept. 17, 1766; Hendrick, June 15, 1769.

VAN DER WERKEN, Martinus, of Saratoga, m. Marytje Winne, July .... 1771. Ch: Annatje, b. Aug. 30, 1773.

VAN DER WERKEN, Martinus, and Geertje Van Den Bergh. Ch: Annatie, b. Dec. 19, 1776.

VAN DER WERKEN, Johannes, and Annatie Bogardus. Ch: Roeloff, b. Feb. 28, 1774.

VAN DER WERKEN, Willem, of *Halve Maan,* m. Marytje Bogardus, Feb. 10, 1777. Ch: Jacob, b. Dec. 16, 1777.

VAN DER WERKEN, Hendrick, of *Halve Maan,* and Catharina Kremer. Ch: Johannes, b. Jan. 14, 1787.

VAN DER WERKEN, Johannes H., m. Catharina Slingerland. Feb. 12, 1786. Ch: b. Abraham, Sept. 28, 1789; Rebecca, Nov. 28, 1793; Hendrik, May 3, 1795.

Van Der Wilge, Joannes, m. Catryna Heyps, Sept. 6, 1717. Ch: bp.; Margriet, May 18, 1718;

Alida, May 8, 1720; Philip, Dec. 17, 1721; Maria, Jan. 22, 1724.

Van Der Willege, Dirk, and Saartje Larraway [Le Roy.]   Ch: Johannes, b. Jan 25, 1769; Johannes, bp. April 9, 1775.

Van Der Vort, see Fort.

Van Der Zee, Storm, son of Albert Andries Bratt "de Noorman" came to Rensselaerswyck in 1630. The tradition is that one of Bratt's children was born on shipboard on the passage out in the midst of a heavy storm, in consequence of which, he was called Storm Vanderzee. *O'Callaghan's Hist. N. N.* That Van Der Zee was an *alias* for Bratt in early times is certain; in an old deed Storm's son Wouter is called "Wouter Storm Bratt, *alias* Wouter Van Der Zee." Storm Van Der Zee was a trader, and in 1661, was complained of for smuggling in New Amsterdam. He m. Hilletje, dau. of Gerrit Lansing, and had at least two sons who lived to maturity, ... Albert, and Wouter.

VAN DER ZEE, Wouter Storm, m. Jannetje Swart, July 2, 1695. Ch: bp.; Storm, April 5, 1696; Elizabeth, July 10, 1698: *Storm,* Aug. 3, 1701 ; *Antony,* Jan. 5, 1704; Hilletje, Aug. 25, 1706 ; Catharina, Jan. 1, 1709 ; *Albert,* May 20, 1716 ; Wouter, Nov. 29, 1717.

VAN DER ZEE, Albert Storm, m. Hilletje Gansevoort, Jan. 20, 1706. Ch: bp.; Ariaantje, May 22, 1707 ; *Storm,* June 26, 1709 ; *Harmen,* March 4, 1711.

VAN DER ZEE, Storm [son of Albert], m. Lena Slingerland, Nov. 4, 1734. Ch: bp ; Ariaantje, June 2, 1735 ; Echie, Jan. 5, 1737 ; Hilletje, Jan. 9, 1740. [Storm V. D. Z. m. Eva Slingerland, Nov. 11, 1737.]

VAN DER ZEE, Storm [son of Wouter], m. Elisabeth Slingerland, Sept. 5, 1735. Ch: bp. ; Wouter, July 26, 1736 ; Aegie, Dec. 17, 1738 ; *Cornelis,* Oct. 5, 1740 ; Albert, April 10, 1743; Tennis, Aug. 24, 1746.

VAN DER ZEE, Anthony [son of Wouter], m. first Marytje De Ridder, Oct. 12, 1735, who was buried July 31, 1744; secondly, Annatie .... who was buried Dec. 25, 1749, and thirdly, Annatie Van Ness, May 10, 1752. Ch: bp.; Jannetie, Sept. 18, 1737 ; Antje, Jan. 16, 1740 ; Elizabeth, April 4, 1742 ; Antje, March 4, 1744; Wouter, April 11, 1747 ; *Wouter,* Feb. 4, 1753 ; Marytje, Dec. 7, 1755; Catalyntje, April 9, 1758

VAN DER ZEE, Harmen [son of Albert], and Eva .... Ch: bp.; Aalbert, June 28, 1738; Cornelis, Aug. 10 1740 ; Storm, July 11, 1742.

VAN DER ZEE, Albert [son of Wouter], m. Antje Van Wie, May 1, 1741. Ch: bp.; Jannetie, April 18, 1742: Hilletje, Feb. 26, 1744 ; Jannetie, Aug. 2, 1747 ; Hendrikje Van Wie, March 4, 1750; Elizabeth, July 22, 1754.

VAN DER ZEE, Albert [probably same as last], and Marytje Van Der Kar. Ch: b. ; Annatje, March 25, 1765 ; Annatje, April 8, 1766 ; Wouter, June 9, 1768.

VAN DER ZEE, Cornelis [son of Storm ?] of Niskatha, m. Annatie Veder, Nov. 20, 1766. Ch: b.; Hester, Sept. 3, 1769 ; Margarita, Dec. 17, 1780 ; Rachel, Aug. 9, 1782 ; Wouter, March 11, 1784; Engeltie, Oct. 8, 1786.

VAN DER ZEE, Wouter [son of Anthony], m. Marytje Peek (Beck), May 18, 1776. Ch: b. ; Anthony, Feb. 23, 1777 ; Marytje, July 7, 1779 ; Isaac, March 1, 1790.

Van Deusen, Abraham .... Ch: *Melgert; Mattheus* or *Teuwis; Jacob ;* Pieter, who settled in New Amsterdam.

VAN DEUSEN, Teuwis Abrahamse, in Beverwyck, 1657-1700. His wife was Helena ...   Ch: *Robert; Jan ; Isaac.*

VAN DEUSEN, Jacob Abrahamse, cooper, m. Catalyntje Van Eslant, of Amsterdam, Holland, in New Amsterdam, Sept. 23, 1663. In 1677 being about to return to Holland to collect certain legacies due her there, the commissarissen of Albany gave her a certificate that she was the dau. of Claes Van Eslant deceased, undertaker in New Amsterdam, and that her mother's name was Willemtie Harpers Van Der Linde. Her husband, Van Deusen, and her brother Claes also gave her power of attorney to collect the legacies left them by their uncle Harmanus Antonides Van Der Linde, minister in his life time at Naerden. Ch. bp: in New York. *Willem; Herpert,* Oct. 9, 1665 ; *Abraham,* Jan. 11, 1667 ; Adriaen, May 30, 1668 ; Adriaen, March 13, 1670 ; Isaac, Nov. 5, 1671 ; Aeltie, Oct. 7, 1674 ; Jacob, Sept. 13, 1676 ; Maryken, Nov. 27, 1678.

VAN DEUSEN, Melgert Abrahamse, m. Engeltie Rutgertse [dau. of Rutger Jacobsen ?], she was buried July 11, 1728 ; he was buried at Papsknee, Jan. 6, 1742. Ch: *Herpert ; Martin ; Rut ; Caspar ;* Magdalena, bp. May 3, 1685 ; Engeltie, May 22, 1687 ; *Abraham,* July 14, 1689 ; Catalyntje, Sept. 20, 1691, d. Sept. 26, 1704.

VAN DEUSEN, Robert Teuwise, of Claverac, 1720, m. Cornelia Martense [Van Buren]. Ch: bp. ; *Johannes,* July 13, 1690 ; Mattheus, Nov. 1, 1691 ; Marten, Feb. 21, 1694 ; *Tobias,* Aug. 16, 1696 ; Robert, Sept. 1, 1700. [Robert Teuwise, m. Geertruy Van Benthuysen, Aug. 21, 1718.]

VAN DEUSEN, Willem Jacobse, m. Elizabeth Rosenboom, Jan. 13, 1692. His house was on the north corner of Maiden Lane and Pearl street in 1711. He was buried Sept. 8, 1731. Ch: bp. ; Jacob, Sept. 4, 1692 ; Margriet, April 14, 1695 ; Catalyntje, Nov. 21, 1697 ; Marytje, Sept. 1, 1700 ; Elizabeth, March 21, 1703 ; Henrik and Elizabeth, twins, Dec. 25, 1705.

VAN DEUSEN, Rut Melgertse, linen weaver, m. Wyntje Harmense, Sept. 11, 1692. Ch: bp.; Catalyntje May 14, 1693 ; Engeltie, March 22, 1696, m. Gerrit Lansingh, Jr.

VAN DEUSEN, Jan Teuwise, m. Maritie Martense Van Buren, March 14, 1695. His wid. m. C. G. Van Den Bergh, Nov. 21, 1702. Ch: bp., *Mattheus,* Jan. 19, 1696.

VAN DEUSEN, Herbert (Herpert) Jacobse, of Claverac 1707, Albany, 1720, m. Maritje Gerritse (Reyertse,) Jan. 24, 1695. He was buried in the church, July 6, 1742. Ch: *Tryntje,* Aug. 9, 1696; Tryntje, Aug. 22, 1697; Gerrit, Jan. 5, 1700, buried Jan. 29, 1741; Jacob, Nov. 19, 1701 ; Jacob, Oct 3, 1703; Henrik, Sept. 29, 1705; *Abraham,* Nov. 17, 1706 ; Anna, March 16, 1709: Catalina. Feb. 10, 1712 ; Maretie, Nov. 13, 1715.

VAN DEUSEN, (?) [Van Der Poel ?] Caspar Melgertse, and Jannetje Schermerhooren. Ch: Casper, bp. April 20, 1701.

VAN DEUSEN, Abraham [son of Jacob ?], m. Jacomyntje Van Schoonhoven, May 23, 1697. Ch: bp. ; Guert Hendrickse, Sept. 27, 1702 ; Isaac, Dec. 24, 1704 ; Henrik, June 15, 1707.

VAN DEUSEN, Isaac, of Claverac, 1720, Kinderhoek 1740: *geboren en wonende aan Claverack,* m. Baata Van Ysselsteyn, *selver plaatsen,* Oct. 9, 1706. He made will May 24, 1740, proved Oct. 8, 1742, in which he mentioned his w. Baata, and the following children: *Mattheus*, bp. Aug. 3, 1707; Cornelia, bp. July 3, 1709; Batha; Cornelis Andriese, bp. April 22, 1716; Isaac, bp. June 2, 1718; Marietie, bp. May 15, 1720; Tryntje, bp. Sept. 23, 1722; Elizabeth, bp. Aug. 9, 1724; Annatie; Sarah, bp. Jan. 4, 1730; Johannes; Helena, bp. Sept. 29, 1734.

VAN DEUSEN, Harpert [son of Melgert], of Claverac 1707, Albany 1720, m. first, Helena Van Deusen, Nov. 7, 1707, who was buried June 27, 1728; and secondly. The; Van Alsteyn, May 23, 1732. Ch: bp.; Helena, w. of Abm G. Lansing Jr. (?); Melchert, Oct. 19, 1713; Engeltie, Dec. 25, 1714; Tryntje, June 9, 1717: *Melchert*, Dec. 27, 1719; Mattheus, March 24, 1723; Rutgert, June 30, 1728.

VAN DEUSEN, Johannes [son of Robert], of Kinderhook, m. Styntje (Christina) Van Alen, Aug. 16, 1712. Ch: bp.; Robert, Sept. 27, 1713; Elbertje, May 8, 1715; Elbertje, Dec. 16, 1716; Catharina, Aug. 20, 1720; Maria, May 3, 1722.

VAN DEUSEN, Mattheus [son of Jan Teuwise], m. Engeltie Slingerland, June 2, 1716. Ch: bp.; *Johannes*, Feb. 27, 1717; *Arent*, April 19, 1719.

VAN DEUSEN, Mattheus [son of Isaac], and Rachel .... Ch: Bata, bp. Jan. 21, 1741.

VAN DEUSEN, Marten [son of Melgert], m. Elbertje Van Der Poel, Dec. 25, 1719. Ch: bp; Catharina, Oct. 14, 1722; Melchert, April 17, 1726; Milihert [Melgert?] Feb. 22, 1738.

VAN DEUSEN, Abraham [son of Melgert?] and Catharina .... Ch: Hartman, bp. Jan. 7, 1722.

VAN DEUSEN, Tobias [son of Robert], and Ariaantie .... Ch: *Robert*, bp. April 17, 1726.

VAN DEUSEN, Hendrik [son of Willem], and Ariaantje Staats. Ch: bp.; Elizabeth, March 12, 1732; Neeltie, May 22, 1834; Willem, April 11, 1736; Neeltje, Nov. 12, 1738.

VAN DEUSEN, Abraham [son of Herpert], and Rachel Pels. Ch: bp.; Marritie, March 3, 1734; Margarita, July 11, 1736; Tryntje, Jan. 10, 1739; Margarietje, July 23, 1740; Marritje, July 17, 1743.

VAN DEUSEN, Melgert [son of Herpert], and Neeltie Quackenbosch. Ch: bp.; Harpert, Jan. 12, 1746; Lena, Feb. 4, 1750.

VAN DEUSEN, Hannes [son of Mattheus], carpenter, m. Marytje Winne, April 19, 1745. Ch: bp.; Mattheus, Feb. 16, 1746: Pieter, Nov. 22, 1747: Arent, May 13, 1753.

VAN DEUSEN, Arent, mason [son of Mattheus], m. Catharyntje Waldron, April 20, 1745. Ch: bp.; Engeltie, Feb. 22, 1747; Elizabeth, Jan. 22, 1749; Engeltie, Oct. 27, 1751.

VAN DEUSEN, Robert [son of Tobias], and Catharina Van Alen. Ch: Pieter, bp. May 20, 1753.

VAN DEUSEN, Cornelis, and Lea Ostrander. Ch: bp.; Geertruy, Feb. 4, 1753; Arent (?) Dec. 28, 1750; Wilhelmus, Dec. 3, 1758; Jannetje, b. Dec. 13, 1768.

VAN DEUSEN, Wilhelmus, and Christina Kittle (Ketelhuyn). Ch: b.; Cornelis, March 14, 1764; Lena, Aug. 24, 1766.

VAN DEUSEN, Jacob, m. Elsie Lansing, May 19, 1771. Ch: b.; Marytje, Jan. 19, 1773; Marytje, July 18, 1775; Rachel, and Elizabeth, July 18, 1778; Abraham, Dec. 22, 1780; Jacob Lansing, July 17, 1785; Rachel, June 6, 1788; Cornelia, Jan. 9, 1791.

VAN DEUSEN, Pieter, m. Catharina (Lena) Van Wie, Dec. 10, 1769. Ch: b.; Maria, Dec. 29, 1774: Rachel, June 8, 1782; Philip, May 12, 1793.

VAN DEUSEN, Mattheus, and Cornelia Van Wie. Ch. b.; Maria, Feb. 2, 1775; Catharina, Sept. 3, 1779.

VAN DEUSEN, Arent, m. Margarita McCloud, Feb. 23, 1777. Ch: b.; Elizabeth, bp. Dec. 12, 1777; Cornelis, b. April 23, 1780; Lea, April 10, 1782; Annatie, Oct. 30, 1784; Robert, April 7, 1787.

VAN DEUSEN, Harpert, m. Geertje Witbeck, July 25, 1779. Ch: Annatje, b. Aug. 7, 1783.

VAN DEUSEN, Wilhelmus, and Rachel Pieterse .... Ch: b.; Simon, Aug. 25, 1782; Johannes, Oct. 5, 1783; Lea, July 1, 1785.

VAN DEUSEN, John, m. Antje Witbeck, July 13, 1789. Ch: b.; Pieter, Oct. 4, 1790; Walter, Oct. 24, 1792.

VAN DEUSEN, Robert, and Geertruy Yager. Ch: Maria, b. May 3, 1792.

VAN DEUSEN, Peter, and Lidia Brewslin (Brewster). Lydia relict of Peter Van D. d. April 26, 1832, a. 69 y. Ch: b.; Sidney Lewis, Feb. 4, 1793; Abraham Samuel Whittlesea, Sept. 12, 1795; Isaac Gilbert, Jan. 2, 1801; Peter, Dec. 3, 1805.

Van Doesburgh, Hendrick Andriese, *alias* Hendrick Driessen, was in Beverwyck as early as 1654, ... deceased 1664. His wife was Maritie Damen, widow of Dirk Van Eps; by her he had one daughter Jannetie, (11 y. old March 14, 1664), who m. Martinus Cregier, Jr., son of Capt. Martinus C. of New Amsterdam, and settled at Niskayuna, where their descendants may still be found. After Hendrick Andriese's death his widow m. Cornelis Van Nes, in 1664. Van Doesburgh was a considerable dealer in real estate. His sister Geertruy was w. of Jacob Janse Stol, *alias* Hap.

Van Driessen, Dominie Petrus, Jr, m. first, Eva Cuyler, Aug. 26, 1712 (by Do. Petrus Vas); he was buried in the church Feb. 3, 1738; she was buried in the church Aug. 10, 1756. He came to Albany in April, 1712. His brother, Dominie Johannes Van Driessen, m. at Albany, Margarita Van Stryer, July 8, 1727. Ch: bp.; Petrus, Jan. 17, 1713; resided for a time at Schenectady; Hendrick, Oct. 30, 1715. "This my son Hendrick was the first child baptized in the new Church;" Johannes, Sept. 29, 1717; Anna, Nov. 15, 1719; Maria, Sept. 16, 1722.

VAN DRIESSEN, Cornelis, and Lea Van Ostrander. Ch: b.; Maria, June 10, 1762; Catharina, April 11, 1765; Elizabeth, July 5, 1771.

Van Dwingelo, Geertruy Barentse, in 1663, widow of the late Hendrick Hendr: Harstenhorst and now wife of Jacob Hevick; being then about to depart for *Patria* she mortgaged her house and lot in Beverwyck for the security of 100 guilders reserved from her property for her two children by said Harstenhorst.

Van Dyck, Hendrick, came from Utrecht in 1645. He was *schout fiscaal* under Stuyvesant who dismissed him from office on which account he appealed to the states-general for redress. In 1652 he states that he had served the West India Company and the states-general 13 y. both as ensign commandant and as *fiscaal*; at this time he says he was burthened with a wife — Duvertje Cornelise — and four children of whom two were *Cornelis*; and Lydia w. of Nicolaas De Meyer. He d. in 1688.

Van Dyck, Cornelise [son of Hendrick V. D., the *fiscaal*,] received a chirurgeon's certificate in 1661 from Jacob D'Hinsse with whom he studied medicine four years. He m. first, Elizabeth Lakens; and secondly, Elizabeth Beck wid. of Capt. Sylvester Salisbury; after Van Dyck's death about 1687, she m. Capt. George Bradshaw, Oct. 29, 1691; — in 1692 she was again a widow, and was deceased in 1701. Ch: *Hendrick; Jacobus;* Alida, bp. April 20, 1684; Elizabeth, bp. Aug. 22, 1686.

Van Dyck, Hendrick, chirurgeon, resided on the east corner of Broadway and State street; in 1717 his widow Maritie, owned this lot. He was drowned April 11, 1707. He m. Maria Schuyler, Feb. 3, 1689. Ch: bp.; *Cornelis*, Nov. 17, 1689; Elizabeth, April 23, 1692; *David*, Nov. 26, 1693; Catalina, Oct. 6, 1695; Pieter, Nov. 7, 1697; *Arent*, Jan. 5, 1700; Maria, Sept. 28, 1701; Lidia, July 16, 1704.

Van Dyck, Jacobus [son of Hendrick], of Schenectady, chirurgeon, m. Jacomyntje Glen, Oct. 25, 1694. Ch: Cornelis, bp. Aug. 28, 1698. [*See also Schenectady Families.*]

Van Dyck, David [son of Hendrick], m. Christina Ten Broeck, April 10, 1718; Ch: bp.; Hendrick, May 3, 1719; Catharina, March 1, 1721; Maria, Feb. 17, 1723; Wessel, Oct. 11, 1724; Elizabeth, Sept. 11, 1726; Dirk, June 28, 1728; Christina, April 4, 1731; Christina Sept. 10, 1732.

Van Dyck, Cornelis [son of Hendrick], m. Maria Bries, July 9 (?) 1721. He was buried, June 21, 1747; she was buried April 8, 1756. He made his will March 26, 1747, proved Sept. 6, 1768; mentioned his w. Maria and cousin John De Peyster.. Ch: bp.; Maria, June 17, 1722; Anthony, Aug. 25, 1723, buried Jan. 4, 1740; Catharina, March 30, 1725; *Hendrick*, Oct. 2, 1726; David, April 20, 1729; Catharina, Sept. 5, 1731; [Cornelis Van D.'s two daughters were buried, Jan. 16, 1740.]

Van Dyck Arent [son of Hendrick], m. Heyltie Van Alen, Nov. 16, 1722. Ch: bp.; Maria, Jan. 26, 1724; Stephanus, Dec. 13, 1726; Lourens, Dec. 20, 1738.

Van Dyck, Henricus, Doctor [son of Cornelis,] m. Margarita Douw, Dec. 21, 1752. Ch: bp.; Cornelis, Dec. 9, 1753; Maria, March 21, 1756; Anna, Nov. 5, 1758; Petrus Douw, b. 29, May (April (?) bp. May 5, 1760,

Van Eeckelen, Jan Jansen, in Beverwyck, 1657-67; schoolmaster in Flatbush, 1691; the minister and elders of the church there desired his removal from office because he had been an active partisan of Leisler.

Van Imburg (Emburgh), Johannes, m. Annatie (Hannah) Flensburgh (Flansburgh,) May 14, 1780. Ch: b.; Elizabeth, Sept. 23. 1781; Anthony, Jan. 8, 1785; Elizabeth, April 20, 1787; a child, name not registered, Sept. 30, 1789; Matthias, Jan. 31, 1793; John, June 22, 1798.

Van Eps, Jan Dirkse. In 1664 he bought the house, brewery, mill house, etc. of the late Philip Hendrickse Brouwer; 1667 his stepfather Cornelis Van Nes conveyed to him a bouwery, house, lot and garden at Schenectady. His sister Lysbet, m. Gerrit Bancker.

Van Eps, Evert, of Schenectady, m Eva Toll in Schenectady, July 8, 1705. Ch: Johannes, bp. April 28, 1710. [See also *Schenectady Families.*]

Van Eps, Jan Baptist, of Schenectady, m. Helena Sanderse Glen, in Schenectady; July 9, 1699. Ch: Jan Baptist, bp. Sept. 27, 1713. [See also *Schenectady Families.*]

Van Eps, Johannes, of Schenectady, m. Neeltie Toll in Schenectady; Oct. 28, 1720. Ch: Eva, bp. Feb. 25, 1728. [See also *Schenectady Families.*]

Van Esselsteyn, see Esselsteyn.

Van Etten, Jacobus, and Annatie Pangburn (Pengbang). Ch: Jacobus, b. July 16, 1765.

Van Etten, Benjamin, and Heiltie Vredenburgh. Ch: Jacobus, b. April 6, 1768.

Van Etten, Benjamin, and Catharina Earl (Erl, Ell). Ch: b.; Isaac, August 31, 1776; Catharina, August 26, 1778; Jacob, March 14, 1780; Benjamin, May 1, 1788; John, May 24, 1791.

Van Etten, Hannes, and Geertruy Redliff. Ch: Heiltje, b.; June 16, 1783.

Van Etten, Isaac, and Celia Radley. Ch: William, b. Jan. 1, 1793.

Van Frank, Van Franken, see Van Vranken.

Van Gansevoort, Gansevoort.

Van Gudsenhoven, Jan Bastiaanse, a trader in Beverwyck as early as 1659, owned a house and lot in Broadway opposite the Court House; he was deceased in 1667.

Van Gysling, Elias, of Schenectady, came over in 1659 in the Ship *Bonte koe* from Zeeland; purchased Bastiaan De winter's *plantatie* in Schenectady in 1670; d. before April 13, 1695, when his widow Tryntje Claase, m. Willem Hall. Ch: bp.; Jacomyntje, April 11, 1686; Myndert, Oct. 25, 1691. [See also *Schenectady Families.*]

Van Hamel, Didrick, secretary of Rensselaerswyck in 1657; bought Madam Johanna De Hulter's house and lot for 2,100 guilders. His wife was Sophia Wyckersloot; in 1661 she was w. of Antony Toinel.

Van Heemstraat, see Heemstraat.

Van Hoeck, Arent Isaackse, master shoemaker in Beverwyck, 1659; had a son *Bennony.*

Van Hoeck, Bennony Arentse, of Schenectady, m. Jaquimina Swart, wid. of Pieter Cornelise Viele. He was killed Feb. 9, 1689-90 in Schenectady, by the French and Indians. Ch: Gerritje, bp. Jan. 24, 1686.

Van Hoesen (Hoesem), Jan Franse, an early resident of Fort Orange and Beverwyck; 1662 bought land at Claverac of the Indians; d. about 1667. His w. was Volkie Jurriaanse, sister of Annatie Jurriaanse, w. of Andries Herbertsen *Constapel*; after his death she m. Gerrit Visbeeck. Letters of administration were issued to his son Jurriaan, Aug. 2, 1703. The following children were living in 1694: *Jurriaan* eldest son : *Jacob ; Volkert ; Johannes* (an old man in 1724); Anna w. of Luykas Gerritsen ; Styntje, w. of Jan Tys Goes ; Marya, w. of Hendrick Coenraetse ; Catharina, w. of Frank Hardingh. [The Van Hoesens were Lutherans, hence but few of their children were registered in the Reformed church *Doop Boek.*]

Van Hoesen, Jurriaan Janse, came to Beverwyck, probably with his father, Jan Franse, in 1745. Ch: *Jan; Caspar* (?).

Van Hoesen. Volkert Janse, m. Maritje Bensing; was buried Aug. 30, 1725. Ch: Reiner, bp. Jan. 10, 1692; *Jan.*

VAN HOESEN, Jacob Janse, of Claverac, 1720, m. Judik Franse Clauw. Ch: *Jan*; Elsje, bp. Feb 12, 1696; Maria, bp. Nov. 22, 1702; Jacob, b. *op Klaverak*, Sept. 3, 1707, and bp. in the Lutheran church, Albany, May 23, 1708. [Luth. Ch : Rec., Athens.]

VAN HOESEN, Johannes or Hannes, of Kinderhoek, Claverac 1720, m. first Jannetie Janse De Ryk, and secondly, Willempie Viele, wid. of Livinus Winne June 19, 1709. Oct. 24, 1724 he conveyed certain property to "my two sons Gerrit and Jacob who have dutifully assisted and supported me in my old age" he spoke also of "my father Jan Franse Van Hoesen" and my brother Jurriaan V. H." Ch : *Jan* (?) Johannes (?) ; Harmen (?) ; Gerrit ; Jacob, bp. Jan. 8, 1699 ; Jacob, bp. Jan. 5, 1701 ; Franciscus, bp. June 13, 1703 ; Maria, bp. Jan. 7, 1705; Gerritje, b. in Albany the last of April and bp. in the Lutheran church, Aug. 20, 1710. Nicolas b. at Klaverak, Feb. 11, and bp. at Loonenburgh, Feb. 17, 1712.

VAN HOESEN, Jan Jurriaanse, and Jannitie or Janje Ch : Catharina, b. at Claverac, Nov. 26, 1704, and bp. in the Lutheran church at Albany *op den Sondagh Trinit*, 1705 ; Jurgen, b. at Klaverak *koort voor Paaschen van dit jaer*, and bp. at Klinkenbergh, May 26, 1706 ; Elizabeth, b. Feb. 26, and bp. *in onse (Lutheransche) vergaderinge op Klinkenbergh* Aug. 5, 1709 ; Cornelis, b. at Claverac the last of July and bp. at Klinkenbergh, Nov. 7, 1714 ; Cornelia, b. Sept. 27, and bp. at *Gospel-hoeck*, Nov. 12, 1721.

VAN HOESEN, Caspar [son of Jurriaan ?], of Claverac 1720, m. Racnelje Slingerland, Jan. 10, 1701. Ch : bp. ; Catharina, Nov. 2, 1701; Johannes, Jan. 2, 1704; Maria, July 14, 1706 ; Jurriaan, April 10, 1709 ; Teunis, Oct. 7, 1711 ; David, Oct. 13, 1717 ; Anna, Sept. 13, 1719.

VAN HOESEN, Jan Jacobse, m. Rachel, dau. of Jan Casparse Halenbeck, and w. Rachel .... Ch : Jan Casparse, b. last fall at Coxsackie, and bp. at same place Dec. 7, 1710 ; Judith, b. Aug. 19, at Coxsackie, and bp. at Klinkenbergh, Nov. 11, 1716 ; Caspar, b. Feb. 5, at Coxsackie, and bp. *in onser kerke in myn huys op* Claverack, Feb. 26, 1721.

VAN HOESEN, Jan Volkertse, shoemaker, of Claverac 1720, m. first, Jannetje Cornelise Van Schaick, Nov. 7, 1702 ; and secondly, Engeltie Janse, of Coxsackie, Jan. 1, 1706. Ch : Sara, bp. June 13, 1703 ; Maria, b. Aug. 21, 1706 *op de flakte* Loonenburgh, and bp. June 2, 1707, in the Lutheran church, Albany.

VAN HOESEN, Johannes Hannessen [son of Johannes or Hannes ?] and Elizabeth .... Ch : Jannetie, b. in Oct. last and bp. in *Camp Queensburg* Dec. 3, 1721.

VAN HOESEN (Husum), Jan Hannesen, of Claverac, [son of Johannes or Hannes ?] and wife Danike or Tannike. Ch: .... Johannes, b. Dec. 20, 1712 at Claverak, bp. at Klinkenbergh, Jan. 7, 1713 ; Henrikus, b. Dec. 21, 1714; Petrus, b. Jan. 22, 1721 ; Jacob, b. Nov. 17, 1722.

VAN HOESEN, Harmen [son of Johannes (?) and Geesie ; she was buried in the Lutheran church yard April 11, 1746. Ch : Jan. buried Aug. 28, 1754; Volkert ? Reiner ? Hendrick ? Lucas, bp. April 24, 1726.

VAN HOESEN, W. B., and Dirkie .... Ch : Jacob, bp. Jan. 22, 1730.

VAN HOESEN, Volkert [son of Harmen ?] m. Alida Marcelis, April 30, 1738. Ch: bp. ; *Harmen*, Sept. 24, 1738; Bregje, Nov. 9, 1740 ; *Myndert*, Feb. 20, 1743 ;

Geesje, April 21, 1745 ; *Reinier*, Sept. 2, 1750; Gerrit, Oct. 13, 1754 ; *Johannes*.

VAN HOESEN, Hendrick [son of Harmen], m. Catalyntje Van Den Bergh, July 2, 1744. Ch : bp. ; Geesje, Aug. 10, 1746 ; *Hendrick*, Nov. 6, 1748.

VAN HOESEN, Reinier [son of Harmen ?] and Cornelia Becker. He was buried Jan. 3, 1749. Ch: bp. ; Harmen, July 26, 1746 ; Sara, July 17, 1748.

VAN HOESEN, Johannes J., and Sara Rees. Ch : Sara, bp. April 5, 1756.

VAN HOESEN, Harmen, Jr. [son of Volkert], m. Catharyntje Witbeck, Sept. 10, 1763. Ch : b. ; Volkert, Aug. 22, 1764 ; Eva, Oct. 31, 1766 ; *Volkert*, April 1, 1769 ; Alida, Aug. 13, 1771; Engeltie, Sept. 21, 1776 ; Geertruy. Aug. 6, 1780 ; Gerrit, Nov. 12, 1782 ; Alida, Dec. 5, 1787.

VAN HOESEN, Myndert [son of Volkert], m. Geertruy Vinhagel, May 30, 1765. Ch : b. ; Volkert, March 16, 1766; Johannes, Nov. 24, 1768 ; Neeltie, Aug. 3, 1770 ; Alida, Oct. 18, 1776 ; Maria, May 20, 1779; Elizabeth, July 19, 1781.

VAN HOESEN, Johannes [son of Volkert], and Engeltie Van Deusen. Ch: bp. ; Catharina, April 16, 1774 ; Volkert June 15, 1778 ; Alida, May 9, 1781 ; Alida, Aug. 4, 1784 ; Alida, June 20, 1786.

VAN HOESEN, Hendrick [son of Hendrick], m. Elizabeth Evertsen. Oct. 30, 1773. Ch : b. Hendrick, Oct. 4, 1775 ; Catharina, Feb. 24, 1778 ; Wynand, Aug. 21, 1780; Cathalyntje, Jan. 26, 1785.

VAN HOESEN, Midbury (Milbury, Mulbury), and Antje Bevings (Bevens). Ch : b. ; Geertruy, May 12, 1777 ; Isaac, July 30, 1781 ; Cornelia, March 8, 1782 ; Cornelis, Sept. 15, 1784 ; Maria, Sept. 16, 1787 ; David, Sept. 8, 1790.

VAN HOESEN, Reinier [son of Volkert], and Engeltie Cool. Ch: b. ; Volkert, Nov. 6, 1773; Alida, Oct. 26, 1778 ; Maria, July 28, 1781.

VAN HOESEN, Volkert, and Jane Young. Ch: Harmen, b. Dec. 17, 1799.

Van Hooghkerk, see Hooghkerk.

Van Hun, see Hun.

Van Ilpendam, Adriaen Janse, settled in New Amsterdam, in 1645, and for some years taught a School: —notary public in Albany, 1669-85 ; committed suicide in 1685 by hanging. Jacobus De Beavois was his uncle and heir.

Van Ingen, James [son of Doctor Dirk Van Ingen of Schenectady,] m. first, Catharine Bleecker, who d. April 4, 1798, a. 29 y. ; secondly, Elizabeth Schuyler, who d. Feb. 28, 1801 a. 29 y. ; and thirdly Gertrude, who d. Dec. 21, 1825, a. 52 y. He d. Feb. 22, 1843. Ch : b. ; Catharine, Jan. 26, 1800; Philip Schuyler, Feb. 9, 1801, d. at Bethany, Va., March 20, 1847, a. 46 y. ; William Henry, Oct. 9, 1806 ; Margaret ... 1809, d. Sept. 6, 1810, a. 1 y, 1 m. 6 d.

Van Iveren, see Mynderlse.

Van Loon, Jan, blacksmith of Loonenburgh 1699, Coxhackie 1720. He was from Luyck in Holland ; owned land at Coxsackie 1684 ; m. Maria, Albertse in New York, Feb. 23, 1676. Ch : *Jan* ; Elsie who m. first Omy La Grange ; and secondly, Barent Egbertse in 1727 ; *Albert*, bp. Oct. 31, 1683 ; Nicolaas in N. Y. Oct. 14, 1694 ; Mattheus, bp. Dec. 10, 1696.

VAN LOON, Jan, Jr. and Rebecca .... Ch : Maria, b. *op Kogshagki*, the last of Oct. and bp. at Loonenburgh, Nov. 25, 1711; Elsie, b. Sept. 8, at Loonenburgh, bp. at Klinkenberg, Nov. 15, 1713; Johannes, b. at Loonenburgh, Sept. 18, bp. at Klinkenbergh, Nov. 13, 1715; Catharina, b. Jan. 17, at Loonenburg, and bp. at *Gospel hoeck*, Jan. 28, 1722.

VAN LOON, Albert, and Maria .... Ch: Maria, b. Nov. 12, at Loonenburgh, and bp. at Klinkenbergh, Dec. 5, 1714.

VAN LOON, Jacob, of Albany, m. Cathalyntje (Christina) Schuyler, Sept. 27, 1772. Ch: b.; Petrus, March 24, 1773; *Petrus*, Jan. 10, 1775; Jacobus, Dec. 23, 1777; Jacobus, April 4, 1780; Dirkje, June 24, 1782; Dirkje, Oct. 8, 1783, m. Ephraim De Witt, and d. July 8, 1810, a. 25 y. 9 m.; Johannes, Feb. 25, 1787; Barent, Oct. 15, 1789; Barent, July 29, 1791; Barent, June 26, 1791 (*sic*); Cathalina, Oct. 24, 1798.

VAN LOON, Pieter, and Sara Wendell. She d. March 23, 1852, a. 76 y. Ch: b.; Catalyntje, Nov. 11, 1798; Jacob, June 30, 1803. [Peter Van Loon, and Catharine Lusher, m. May 28, 1799.]

Van Marcken, Jan Gerritse, and wife Geertie Huybertse (Guybertse) sister of Fred. Gysbertse Van Den Bergh, came over in the Ship St. Jacob; in 1657 he received a patent for a lot at Fort Casimir; banished from New Amstel in 1657; came thence to Beverwyck and for several years was farmer of the excise of wine, beer and spirits; 1673, appointed a schout of Schenectady.

Van Marle, Barent, trader in Beverwyck, 1661-4 when he d.

Van Neck, Lambert Albertse, in Beverwyck, 1655-65, when he removed to New York.

Van Nes, Cornelis Hendrickse [Hendrick Gerritse Van Nes from Emberland, m. Anneken Wessels, from Colen, in New Amsterdam, April 19, 1654], m. about 1625, Mayken Hendrickse Burchgraeff, dau. of Hendrick Adriaense; her mother Annatie Janse, of Laeckervelt, in 1630, left her a legacy of three morgens of land in Scherpenwyck. Cornelis V. N. and wife in 1625, lived upon the Havendyck in Holland; they then made a joint will; no children mentioned. His first w. d. previously to 1664, when he m. Maritie Damen widow first of Dirk Van Eps; secondly, of Hendrick Andriese Van Doesburgh: Van Nes was a brewer and came to Beverwyck in 1642; had a house, lot, and brewery in Greenbush. Ch: *Hendrick; Jan; Gerrit*: Gerritje, w. of Roeloff Cornelise Van Houten; Hendrickje, w. of Jan Janse Oothout; Grietje, w. of Pieter Claese, of Amersfort, L. I.; Simon (?).

VAN NES, (Esch) Jan, of Greenbush 1663; *Cahoos* island 1681; *Halve Maan* 1700; [son of Cornelis], and Aaltie ... Ch: bp.; Hendrikje, Nov. 2, 1684; Johannes, Nov. 7, 1686; Maria, March 3, 1689.

VAN NES, Hendrick, [son of Cornelis], m. first Annatie Evertse, and secondly, Catryn Van Dam, Nov. 25, 1688. Ch: *Jan: Gerrit*; .... 1681; Maria, bp. April 6, 1692; Anna. bp. Dec. 16, 1694.

VAN NES, Simon [son of Cornelis (?)]. and Rachel Melgertse .... Ch: Anna, bp. March 26, 1693.

Van Ness, Gerrit [son of Cornelis] b. in 1645, resided in Greenbush; m. first, ... secondly, Maria Pieterse Loockermans, widow of Pieter Van Alen, in 1677. He made his will Dec. 6, 1707, and spoke of son Willem, mariner, who was to have the effects of his late mother deceased and former wife of Gerrit Van Ness; provided his (Willem's); sister, wife of

Lourens Van Schaick, late by name Jannetie Oothout have the value thereof in other clothing; all the remainder of the property to go to said Jannetie and Willem, share and share alike: he had other children, Gerrit, b. in 1681; and *Cornelis; Evert* ?

Van Nes, Cornelis [son of Gerrit], of *Halve Maan* 1720, m. Maritje Gerritse Van Den Bergh, July 17, 1695. Ch: bp.; Aaltje, Jan. 6, 1697; *Gerrit*, Dec. 20, 1702: Maria, March 10, 1706.

VAN NES, Evert of *Halve Maan*, 1720 [son of Gerrit?] m. Geertje Gerritse Van Den Bergh, Oct. 27, 1700. She was buried July 2, 1747. Ch: bp.; Johanna, March 19, 1701; Ariaantje, Oct. 31, 1703; Hanna, July 14, 1706; Teuntje, Oct. 28, 1710; Jannetje, April 5, 1713; Marretie, April 15, 1716.

VAN NES, Jan [son of Hendrick], m. Catalyntje Groesbeck, Nov. 17, 1706. He was buried Aug. 12, 1747. Ch: bp.; Henrik, Nov. 23, 1707; Henrik, Nov. 7, 1708; Willem, March 4, 1711; *Cornelis*, March 22, 1713; Geertruy, Sept. 18, 1715; Anna, Dec. 8. 1717; Catalyna, April 10, 1720; Rachel, Sept. 16, 1722; Jan, Sept. 5, 1725; David, Feb. 25, 1728.

VAN NES, Gerrit [son of Hendrick], m. Cathalyntje De Foreest, June 12, 1709; she was buried, March 27, 1743. Ch: bp.; Anna, Oct. 30, 1710; Catryna, Oct. 19, 1712; *Hendrik*, Jan. 30, 1715; Philippus, Dec. 8, 1717; Sara, Sept. 11, 1720; Catalyna, Sept. 16, 1722; Mayke, Sept. 20, 1724.

VAN NES, Gerrit Cornelise, m. Sara Van Den Bergh, Aug. 20, 1724. Ch: bp.; *Cornelis*, Jan. 19, 1726; *Jan*, Oct. 1, 1727; Sartie, Feb. 9, 1729; Petrus, Jan. 23, 1732; Marritie, April 25, 1736; *Abraham*, Dec. 20, 1738; Aaltie, Aug. 23, 1741; Nicolaas, June 17, 1744.

Van Ness, Cornelis [son of Jan], m. Susanna Swits, Dec. 2, 1738. Ch: bp.; Johannes, June 17, 1739; Tierk Harmense, Oct. 25, 1741; Cornelis, April 15, 1750: Willem, July 27, 1755.

VAN NES, Philip [son of Gerrit,] and Margarita ..... Ch: Gerrit, bp. Jan. 12, 1742.

VAN NES, Cornelis [son of Gerrit], and Alida Van Woert. Ch: bp.; Gerrit, Jan. 13, 1751; Jacob, June 13, 1753; Sara, March 12, 1755; Sara, Nov. 6, 1757; Johannes, Nov. 25, 1759; Petrus, b. Jan. 21, 1766; Petrus, bp. May 15, 1768.

VAN NES, Jan [son of Gerrit], and Maycke Van Den Bergh. Ch: Sara, bp. March 17, 1754.

VAN NES, Hendrick Gerritse, m. first Margarita Winne, who was buried Dec. 28, 1754; and secondly, Magdalena Vrooman, Aug. 15, 1759. Ch: bp; Catalina, Dec. 26, 1747; Catalina, July 30, 1749; Pieter, Oct. 27, 1751; Maria, Oct. 19, 1760; Gerrit, b. Sept. 5, 1765; Cathalyntje, Dec. 24, 1767.

VAN NES, Abraham, of *Halve Maan* [son of Gerrit], m. Annatje De Ridder, Jan. 27, 1762. Ch: b. Annatie, Oct. 12, 1762; Gerrit, March 7, 1766: Sara, Nov. 1, 1767; Maria, May 28, 1773.

VAN NES, Philip [son of Gerrit?], and Lena Ten Broeck. Ch: b; Sara, Dec. 21, 1762; Catalyntje, Nov. 22, 1770.

VAN NES, John, and Hester Gerritsen. Ch: Dirkie, b; Feb. 21, 1766.

VAN NES, Gerrit [son of Cornelis], and Eva Scnerp. Ch: b.; Alida, Jan. 31, 1771; Maria, Nov. 22, 1772.

VAN NES, John' (D. ?) m. Margaret Van Woert, Nov. 7, 1773. Ch: b.; Hendrick, Jan. 20, 1775; Jacob, April 5, 1776; Johannes, Sept. 8, 1777; Rebecca, Jan. 3, 1779; Rebecca, Feb. 8, 1780; Petrus, March 22, 1782.

VAN NESS, Johannes, of Claverack, 1777, m. Neeltie De Foreest, June 29, 1777. Ch: Jesse, b. June 12, 1782.

VAN NESS, Henry, and Christina Shelly. Ch: John Ouderkerk, b. Nov. 21, 1797 (?); George, b. July 16, 1803.

VAN NESS, John, and Mary Sicker. Ch: b.; John, Sept. 29, 1800; Anna Helena Ouderkerk, Oct. 18, 1802; Elijah, Oct. 8, 1808.

Van Nest (1st), Hendrick, m. Maria Ten Eyck, May 4, 1785. Ch: b.; Sara, Sept. 21, 1785; Andries (?) Sept. 29, 1787.

Van Nieuwkerk, Cornelis Brantse (probably son of Brant Peelen Van Nieuwkerk,) was about departing for Holland in 1664 with Gerrit Hendrickse Reis.

Van Noortstrant (Van Oostrand) Jan Jacobse, had a farm on Cahoos island 1677, bought from Annetie Lievens w. of Goosen Gerritse Van Schaick and sold to Roeloff Gerritse Van Der Werken, in 1680; 1685, of Coxsackie and bought land at Niskayuna. He m. Agniette..... She departed for New York in 1703. Ch: Margariet, bp. Jan. 11, 1688; Jan, Jr., who was killed in 1702, by the falling of a tree.

VAN NOORTSTRANT, Pieter, senior of Kinderhook, and Rebecca Trephagen. Ch: Pieter (?); Jacob, bp. Jan. 13, 1706.

VAN NOORTSTRANT (Oostrande), Willem, and Marytje De Hoogen (Hooges.) Ch: Johannes, bp. Sept. 19, 1708.

VAN NOORTSTRANT, Jr., Pieter, of Kinderhook, m. Rachel Dingman, of Kinderhook, May 31, 1704. Ch: Rebecca, bp. Jan. 13, 1706.

VAN NOORTSTRANT (Oostrand) Johannes, and Elizabeth..... Ch: bp.; Huybert; Catharina, Dec. 10, 1727; Gerrit, Dec. 13, 1729; Rachel, May 23, 1736; Hendrik, Aug. 12, 1739.

Van Oostrander, see Oostrander.

Van Olinda (Van Der Linde), Pieter Danielse, tailor, m. Hilletie Cornelise, sister of Jacques Cornelise Van Slyck. She was a half breed, her mother being a Mohawk woman, her father Cornelis Antonissen Van Slyck. She was for many years interpreter for the province. The Mohawk sachems gave to her the Great Island in the Mohawk at Niskayuna, in 1667 which in 1669 Van Olinda sold to Capt. Johannes Clute. The Mohawks also gave her land at the Willow Flat (below Port Jackson), and at the Boght in Watervliet. She d. in 1707. Van Olinda, in his will made .... spoke of the following children: *Daniel* eldest son: *Jacob*; Matthys (*non compos.*)

VAN OLINDA (Van Der Linde) Daniel, of *Halve Maan,* 1720, m. Lysbeth Kregier, June 11, 1696. Ch: bp.; *Pieter,* Nov. 8. 1696; Johannes, Sept. 3, 1699. *Marten.* [See also *Schenectady Families.*]

VAN OLINDA, Jacob, and Eva De Graaf. Ch: Pieter, bp. Feb. 17, 1712. [See also *Schenectady Families.*]

VAN OLINDA, Marten [son of Daniel], m. Jannetie Van Der Werken, April 8, 1724. Ch: bp.; Elizabeth, Jan. 24, 1725, buried, March 20, 1756; Gerardus, March 5, 1727; Maria, April 27, 1729; Geertruy, July 2, 1731;

Gerardus, March 6, 1734; Daniel, April 31, (*sic*) 1737; Martinus, Jan. 16, 1740.

VAN OLINDA, Pieter, m. Susanna Leischer, July 27, 1736. Ch: bp.; Daniel, July 17, 1737; Jacob, Feb. 20, 1739.

VAN OLINDA, Jacob, and Elizabeth Schermerhorn. Ch: b.; Abraham, June 6, 1766; Cornelis, June 24, 1768: Jacobus, Sept. 10, 1770; Dirk, Jan. 8, 1773; Neeltie, April 19, 1777; Catharina, Nov. 7, 1780.

VAN OLINDA, Daniel, of *Halve Maan,* m. Marytje Van Der Werken, Dec. 1, 1764, Ch: b.; Johannes, Nov. 29, 1771; Elizabeth, April 25, 1777,

VAN OLINDA, Gerardus, of Hosak 1770 [son of Martin,] m. Catharina Van Oostrander, March 14, 1770. Ch: b.; Jannetie, Jan. 5, 1771; Martinus, Dec. 15, 1775.

VAN OLINDA, Pieter, and Susanna Anthony. Ch: Elizabeth, b. April, 1789.

Van Oort, see Van Woert.

Van Petten, Claes Frederickse, of Schenectady, and Aeffie Arentse Bratt. She d. Jan. 23, 1728, a. 78 y..... he d. Oct 3, 1728, a. 87 y. 5 m. Ch: bp.; Andries, Sept. 10, 1684; Geertruy, April 17, 1687; Claas, April 6, 1690: Geertruy, July 28, 1692. [See also *Schenectady Families.*]

VAN PETTEN, Arent, *wonende tot* Schannechtade, m. Jannetje Conyn, of Koxhakki, April 17, 1703. Ch: Weyntje, bp. Oct. 30, 1709. [See also *Schenectady Families.*]

VAN PETTEN, Nicolaas, of Schenectady, and Rebecca Groot. Ch: Frederick, bp. April 20, 1712. [See also *Schenectady Families.*]

VAN PETTEN, Andries, of Schenectady, m. Mayke, dau. of Coenraet Ten Eyck, silversmith, of Albany, Nov. 25, 1712. He d. Sept. 25, 1748, a. 64 y. Ch: Nicolaas, bp. Oct. 8, 1713. [See also *Schenectady Families.*]

VAN PETTEN, Johannes, of Schenectady, and Wyntje Clute. Ch: Dirk, b. Nov. 18, 1778. [See also *Schenectady Families.*]

Van Ravensteyn, Elias, in Albany 1666–1696, when he d. on Feb. 9.

Van Rensselaer, Killiaan, merchant of Amsterdam, m. first, Hillegonda Van Bylet; and secondly, Anna Wely, who d. in Amsterdam, June 12, 1670, having survived her husband 24 years. Ch: Johannes, child of the first wife; heir to his father's estate, d. without issue. Ch: of the second wife, Maria, d. unmarried; *Jeremias,* m. Maria, dau. of Oloff Stevense Van Cortlandt; Hillegonda, d. unmarried; Jan Baptist, m. Susanna Wely, the first of the family to visit the *Colonie,* d. Oct. 18, 1678; Eleanora; Susan, m. Jan de La Court; Nicolaas a clergyman, for a time Director of Rensselaerswyck, m. Alida Schuyler, d. Nov. 1688: Ryckert, m. Anna Van Beaumont.— *O' Callaghan's Hist. N. N.*

VAN RENSSELAER, Jeremias [son of Kilaan], succeeded his brother, Jan Baptist, as director of the colony in 1658, d. Oct. 12, 1674. He m. Maria, dau. of Oloff Stevense Van Cortlandt, July 12 (April 27), 1662. She d. Jan. 29, 1689, in the 44th year of her age leaving 5 children, the eldest of whom, *Kiliaan,* was the first Lord of the manor of Rensselaerswyck. He conveyed the Claverac, or "Lower manor," to his brother *Hendrick;* from these two proceed the numerous members of this wide-spread family in this country. Jan Baptist survived his brother Jeremias 4 y., having d. Oct. 18, 1678, and Do. Nicolaas, d. the following month.— *O' Callaghan's N. N.*

VAN RENSSELAER, Hendrick [son of Jeremias], m. Catharina, dau. of Johannes Pieterse Van Brugh and Catharina Roeloffse (widow of Lucas Rodenburgh), dau. of the celebrated Anneke Janse, in New York, March 19, 1689 (1688?). She d. in Greenbush, Dec. 6, 1730; he d. in Greenbush, July 2, 1740, and was buried, July 4. Ch : bp. ; Maria, in New York, March 29, 1689, m. Samuel Ten Broeck ; Catarina, Jan, 1, 1692 ; Anna, Oct. 1, 1693 ; Anna, Feb. 2, 1696 ; Elizabeth, May 8, 1698 ; Elizabeth, July 21, 1700 ; Helena, Oct. 4, 1702 ; Jeremy, April 29, 1705, buried, Oct. 5, 1730; *Johannes*, Jan. 11, 1708 ; *Hendrick*, April 20, 1712 ; *Kiliaan*, Nov. 27, 1717.

VAN RENSSELAER, Kiliaan [son of Jeremias], first lord of the manor of Rensselaerswyck, m. Maria, Van Cortlandt, Oct. 15, 1701, in New York. Ch : bp. ; Maria, Aug. 2, 1702 ; Geertruy, Oct. 10, 1703 ; Jeremy *[the Patroon]*, March 25, 1705, buried May 8, 1745 ; *Stephanus*, March 23, 1707; Johannes, Dec. 12, 1708 ; Jacobus, April 3, 1713 ; Geertruy, Oct. 3, 1714 ; Jan Baptist, Feb. 3, 1717 ; Anna, Jan 4, 1719.

VAN RENSSELAER, Stephanus, the third *Patroon* [son of Kiliaan], m. Elizabeth Groesbeck, July 5, 1729, buried at "the mills," July 1, 1747. She was buried Dec. 31, 1756. Ch : bp.; Kiliaan, Dec. 8, 1729 ; Maria, Aug. 13, 1732 ; Elizabeth, July 12, 1734; Kiliaan, April 17, 1737 ; Maria, Aug. 19, 1739 ; *Stephanus*, June 2, 1742.

VAN RENSSELAER, Johannes [son of Hendrick], m. Engeltie Livingston, Jan. 3, 1734. She was buried in the church, Feb. 23, 1747. Ch : bp. ; Catharyna, Nov. 3, 1734 ; Margarieta, Oct. 3, 1736 ; *Jeremias*, Aug. 27, 1738 ; Robert, Dec, 26, 1740 ; *Hendrik*, Oct. 24, 1742 ; *James*, Feb. 1, 1747.

VAN RENSSELAER, Col. Kiliaan [son of Hendrick], m. first, Ariaantje Schuyler, who d. Oct. 17, 1763. She was b. at Schenectady, March 16, 1720; secondly, Maria, dau. of Col. John Low, "*van de Jarseys.*" She d. July 11, 1807, a. 82 y. He d. Dec. 28, 1781, a 64 y. Ch : bp. ; *Hendrick*, Aug. 5, 1744 ; *Philip*, June 7, 1747, d. at Cherry Hill, March 12, 1798 ; Catharina, July 23, 1749 ; Nicolaas, June 30, 1751 ; Catarina, Feb. 16, 1753, m. Wm. H. Ludlow, d. April 29, 1772, a. 19, y. ; *Nicolaas*, Dec. 26, 1754; Elsie, Feb. 26, 1758 ; Maria, Oct. 19, 1760, m. Leendert Gansevoort ; *Kiliaan*, b. June 9, 1763.

VAN RENSSELAER, Hendrick [son of Hendrick], m. Elizabeth Van Brugg, Oct. 16, 1735, in New York. Ch : bp. ; Hendrick, Jan. 22, 1737 ; Catharina, Feb. 15, 1747 ; Pieter, Feb. 2, 1752.

VAN RENSSELAER, Lt. Gov., Jeremiah [son of Johannes], m. Judith Bayard (Basert), July 3, 1760, in New York. He d. Feb. 19, 1810, a. 69½ y. Ch : *Johannes*, b. Dec. 10, 1762.

VAN RENSSELAER, Col. Hendrick [son of Kiliaan], m. Alida Bratt, Oct. 7, 1764. He was a colonel in the Revolutionary war, and desperately wounded in the battle at Bemis's Heights, Sept. 9, 1816, a. 73 y. Ch : b. ; *Hendrikus*, June 20, 1765 ; Killaan, bp. Feb. 25, 1769 ; Catharina, b. June 2, 1772 ; *Salomo* Van Vechten, Aug. 9, 1774 ; Philip, May 27, 1777 ; Johannes, Aug. 28, 1779.

VAN RENSSELAER, Stephanus [son of Stephanus], the 4th patroon, of Rensselaerswyck, m. Catharina, dau. of Philip Livingston, Jan. 23, 1764, in New York. He d. in 1769; in 1775, his widow m. Domine Wes-

terlo. Ch : b.; *Stephen*, Nov. 1, 1764, in N. Y.; Philip, April 15, 1766, mayor several years, m. Ann Van Cortlandt, and d. Sept. 25, 1824, a. 58 y. 5 m., she d. Jan. 10, 1855, a. 89 y. Ch : Elizabeth, b. Aug. 15, 1768.

VAN RENSSELAER, Hendrick [son of Johannes], m. Rachel Douw, Nov. 17, 1765. Ch : b.; Johannes, March 8, 1768 ; Engeltie, July 21, 1770 ; Anna, Jan. 31, 1773.

VAN RENSSELAER, Philip [son of Kiliaan], m. Maria, dau. of Robert Sanders, Feb. 24, 1768. Ch : b. ; Ariaantje, Dec. 5, 1768; Elizabeth, Aug. 28, 1770 ; Robert Sanders, Jan. 20, 1773 ; Ariaantje, Sept. 17, 1775 ; Pieter Sanders, June 16, 1777 ; Pieter Sanders, July 16, 1778 ; Kiliaan, Oct. 24, 1780, d. at Cherry Valley, at his mother's, April 3, 1829 ; Philip, Jan . 20, 1783, d. in Bethlehem, Feb. 17, 1827, a. 44 y. ; Maria Matilda, April 20, 1786 ; Maria Matilda, May 10. 1787 ; Schuyler, April 14, 1790, d. at Marietta, O., May 5, 1836.

VAN RENSSELAER, Col. Nicolaas [son of Kiliaan], m. Elsie Van Buren, Nov. 20, 1780. She d. in Greenbush, Sept. 28, 1844. Ch : b. ; Kiliaan, May 8, 1782; Maayke, Feb. 10, 1785. Col. Nicolaas V. R., a soldier of the Revolution, d. March 29, 1848, a. 94 y. He was with Montgomery, at the storming of Quebec, at Ticonderoga, Fort Miller, Fort Ann, and Bemis's Heights, and was deputed to convey the intelligence of Burgoyne's surrender to the citizens of Albany.

VAN RENSSELAER, Stephen [son of Stephanus], 5th Patroon, m. first, Margarita, 3d dau. of Gen. Philip Schuyler, and secondly, Cornelia, dau. of Judge Wm. Patterson, of New Jersey, May .... 1802. She d. in New York, Aug. 6, 1844, a. 64 y. Ch : b. ; Catharine Schuyler, bp. Aug. 9, 1784 ; Stephanus, b. June 6, 1786 ; Stephen, March 29, 1789 ; Catharine, Oct. 17, 1803 ; William Patterson, March 6, 1805 ; Philip, Oct. 14, 1806 ; Cortlandt, May 26, 1808, d. at Burlington, N. J., July 26, 1860 ; Henry Bell, May 14, 1810, d. at Cincinnati O. March 23, 1864 ; Cornelia Patterson, July 8, 1812 ; Alexander, Nov. 5, 1814 ; Euphemia White, Sept. 25, 1816 ; Margaret Schuyler, May 12, 1819 ; Westerlo, March 14, 1820, d. July 8, 1844.

VAN RENSSELAER, Maj. James, and Cathalyna Cortlandt. He d. at Bethlehem, Jan. 25 (Feb. 1), 1827, a. 80 y. Ch : Engeltie, b, Nov. 5, 1784.

VAN RENSSELAER, Johannes Jeremiah, and Catharina Glen. He d. in Greenbush, Sept. 27, 1828, a. 66 y. Ch : b. ; Catharina Glen, bp. March 31, 1785 ; John Jeremiah, June 6, 1790 ; Jeremiah, Aug. 4, 1793, d. in New York, March 7, 1871, a. 77 y. ; Glen, June 22, 1795 ; Elizabeth Bayard, Sept. 15, 1797 ; Cornelius Glen, July 27, 1801 ; Archibald, Feb. 6, 1803.

VAN RENSSELAER, Hendrick, and Cornelia Van Alsteyn. Ch : Stephen, b. June 11, 1787.

VAN RENSSELAER, Kiliaan [son of Kiliaan], m. Margaret, dau. of John Sanders, of Schenectady. He was a lawyer of prominence, and represented his district in congress five terms, d. June 18, 1845, a. 82 y. She d. April 21, 1830, a. 66 y. Ch : b. ; John Sanders, April 10, 1792, m. Ann Dunkin, d. 1868 ; Debora Sanders, Sept. 27, 1795, d. young ; William, b. 1797, d. 1856 ; Richard S., b. 1799, m. first, Elizabeth ; secondly, Matilda F., daus. of Solomon Van Reusselaer ; Barent Sanders, Jan. 12, 1801.

VAN RENSSELAER, Gen. Solomon [son of Hendrick], and Harriet Van Rensselaer. He d. April 23, 1852, a. 78 y. She d. Feb. 3, 1840, a. 65 y. Ch : b. ; Alida, Nov.

3, 1797; Elizabeth, Dec. 26, 1799; Rensselaer, March 29, 1802; Van Vechten, April 26, 1806; Rufus King, Feb. 3, 1809; Margarita, April 1, 1810; Stephen, Oct. 13, 1812; Harriet Maria, Feb. 22, 1816; Catharine Visscher, Dec. 23, 1817.

Van Rotterdam, Jan Janse, of Schenectady. Ch: bp.; Rachel, Jan. 20, 1686; Sander, June 8, 1690.

VAN ROTTERDAM, Claas Jacobse, see Groesbeck.

Van Salsbergen (Salsbury) Jan Hendrickse. In 1673, he and Gerrit Van Slichtenhorst, received a conveyance from Gerrit Visbeeck of a tract of land at Claverack, extending from the river to the *Stone kil*; Nov. 1, 1675, he conveyed to Gerrit Van Slichtenhorst, half a tract of woodland, at Claverack, on Maj. Abraham Staats's kil. He d. in Oct. 1706. He m. first Emmeke Luycasse; and secondly, Tanneke Janse, widow of Ryk Riddersen, Jan. 30, 1693. Ch: Hendrick, eldest son; Harmen; Lucas; Jan, b. 1673.

VAN SALSBERGEN, Lucas Janse, m. Marrietje Evertse, April 4, 1689. Ch: Lucretia, bp. March 5, 1693. *Nota. De vader is op den 17 feb. tegen syn vyandt doodt gebleven.*

VAN SALSBERGEN, Henrik Janse, of Claverac 1720, in 1699, bought a farm at C., of his father, Jan Hendrickse V. S. He m. Cornelia Claase Van Schaick, widow of Hans Jurriaanse, Nov. 6, 1698. Ch: bp. Jan. 1700; Jannetie, July 6, 1701; Lucas, June 13, 1703; Jobje, Jan. 31, 1705; Cornelis, Nov. 2, 1707; Herman, b. *op* Klaverak, Aug. 9, and bp. *op* Klinkenbergh, Aug. 13, 1709; Emmetie, Jan. 10, 1713.

VAN SALSBERGEN, Harmen Janse, of Kinderhook, in 1695 mortgaged his bouwery, in K., to the heirs of Pieter Van Alen, for 201 beavers, for the purchase money of said bouwery; also his house and lot then inhabited by him in Albany. He m. Tanna Conyn, Nov. 19, 1703. Ch: bp.: Johannes, Aug. 13, 1704; Alette, Jan. 13, 1706; Caspar, May 30, 1708; Harmanus, Jan. 22, 1710.

VAN SALSBERGEN, Jan, and Cath. .... Ch: Hendrick, bp. Nov. 6, 1726.

VAN SALSBERGEN, Harmanus, and Tanneke Carich (Carik). Ch: Johannes, bp. June 17, 1753; Alettetia, b. March 19, 1770; Jonathan, b. Sept. 6, 1776.

VAN SALSBERGEN, Cornelis, and Catharina .... Ch: Lucas, bp. May (?) 26, 1733; Nelch, bp. April 6, 1735. [*From Catskil Church Rec.*]

VAN SALSBERGEN, Tobias, and Margarita Bout. Ch: Lena, bp. Jan. 31, 1762; Joan, b. Oct. 19, 1764.

VAN SALSBERGEN (Salsbury), Cornelis, and Fytje .... Ch: b.; Catharina, April 8, 1769; Neeltje, Aug. 13, 1774; Tanneke, May 1, 1777; Johannes, April 10, 1779.

VAN SALSBERGEN (Salsbury), Lucas, m. Marytje Van Buren, July 12, 1768. Ch: b.; Pieter, April 29, 1769; Johannes, Aug. 27, 1771; Marten, June 20, 1777; Gerrit, Aug. 27, 1780; Lucas, May 16, 1783.

VAN SALSBERGEN (Salsbury), Johannes, and Immetje —— Ch: b.; Catharina, Nov. 19, 1769; Jobje, Oct. 4, 1776; Cornelia, Dec. 28, 1778; Hendrik, Aug. 4, 1784.

VAN SALSBERGEN, Jacobus, and Jannetie .... Ch: Tobias, b. April 4, 1774; Caspar, b. Dec. 31, 1776.

VAN SALSBERGEN, Harmen, m. Alida Scherp, May 21, 1774. Ch: b.; Andries, Aug. 14, 1780; Margarita, July 14, 1786.

VAN SALSBERGEN, Joseph, and Margarita Oetersans. Ch: Hermanus, b. Feb. 9, 1784.

Van Salsdyke [Schaick?] Emmanuel, of Kinderhook, and Rebecca Westfaeling, Ch: Marytie, bp. Jan. 9, 1709.

Van Sant, or Santen, see Van Zandt.

Van Santvoord, Cornelis, and Anna Staats, dau. of Johannes Staats of Staten Island. He was the fifth minister of Schenectady where he d. Jan. 6, 1752, aged 52 years. [See *Schenectady Families.*] Ch: *Cornelis Staats;* Zeger: Jacoba; Geertje, w. of Ryk Vanderbilt on the Raritan; Anne.

VAN SANTVOORD, Staats, gunsmith, second son of Domine Van S., settled in Albany about 1747, and m. Willempie Bratt of Albany, Dec. 31, 1747. Ch: bp.; Antje, May 28, 1749; Rebecca, Jan. 6, 1751; Anthony, Feb. 2, 1752; Rebecca, March 24, 1754; Cornelis, May 22, 1757; Teunis, b. March 10, 1760.

VAN SANTVOORD, Cornelis, eldest son of Domine Van S., removed from Schenectady to Albany about 1747, and m. Ariaantje Bratt, Dec. 31, 1747. He and his brother Staats m. sisters, dau. of Anthony Bratt, upon the same day. He lived in 1761, on the site of the present Delavan House. Ch: bp.; *Cornelis,* Dec. 31, 1749: Rebecca Jan. 5, 1752; Antje, April, 22, 1754; Anthony, Oct. 16, 1757; Willempie, Nov. 19, 1758; *Antony,* Sept. 20, 1761.

VAN SANTVOORD, Cornelis, Jr. [son of the last], m. Cornelia Van Wie. Ch: b.; Cornelis, April 4, 1776; Hendrik, July 29, 1779; Ariaantje, Feb. 2, 1783; Catharina, April 16, 1786. *Antony* (?)

VAN SANTVOORD, Capt. Anthony [son of Cornelis], m. first, Maria Roff (Ross, Rhoff), Sept. 15, 1786. She d. Nov. 16, 1800, a. 22 y. 4 m. 16 d.; secondly, Rachel Groesbeck about 1806; she d. in the Middle Dutch Church, March 8, 1835, a. 60 y. 2 m. 3 d. He d. Feb. 17 (March 17), 1852, a. 90 y. 5 m. 3 d. Ch.: b.; Adriaantje, May 15, 1787; John, Oct. 12, 1788, d. March 1, 1811, a. 22 y. 4 m. 16 d.; Hadrian, Aug. 23, 1790, d. at Kendall, Sept. 6, 1870, a. 80 y. 14 d.; Hosiah, Jan. 16, 1793; Christina Louisa, March 2, 1796; Rebecca, Sept. 7, 1799; Anthony Groesbeck, Oct. 13, 1806.

VAN SANTVOORD, Anthony [son of Cornelis, Jr.?] m. first, Catharine Groesbeck, Oct. 3, 1807, and secondly, Sarah —— about 1815. Ch: b.; Anna Maria, June 12, 1808; Cornelia, March 12, 1810; Cornelius, March 11, 1813; Catharine Groesbeck, Nov. 29, 1815.

Van Schalck, Capt. Goosen Gerritse, brewer, 1649, m. first, Geertie Brantse Peelen Van Nieuwkerk, who d. about 1656; and secondly, Annatie Lievens, or Lievense, in 1657. In 1664, he and Philip Pieterse Schuyler had permission to purchase the *Halve Maan* of the Indians to prevent " those of Connecticut " purchasing it; 1664 he bought a lot 6 R. by 4 R. of his stepfather Reyer Elbertse, on the north corner of Columbia street and Broadway; 1675 he and Pieter Lassingh purchased Harmen Rutger's brewery on the Exchange block. He d. about 1676. In 1657 being about to marry his second wife, he made a contract in which he reserved from his estate 6000 guilders for his four eldest children by the first wife, that being her separate estate; and in 1668 he and his second wife made a joint will, he being about to depart for Holland, in which the following children were mentioned as then living: Geertie, then the wife of Hendrick Coster, in 1681, the wife of Johannes Lansing; *Gerrit,* b. 1650, then in Holland; *Sybrant,* b. 1653; *Anthony,* b. 1655; Gerritie, b. 1657, m. Capt. Andries Drayer;

Engeltie, b. 1659; Livinus, b. 1661; Cornelis, b. 1663; Margarita, b. 1665, m. Rev. Barnhardus Freerman; Barent, b. 1668.

VAN SCHAICK, Gerrit, eldest son of Goosen, m. Alida, dau. of Brant Arentse Van Slichtenhorst, in 1678 his step-mother conveyed to him a house and lot on the Third kil, probably on the north corner of Columbia street and Broadway. He d. on the 11th of Nov. 1679; his widow afterwards m. Pieter Davidtse Schuyler, whom she out-lived.

VAN SCHAICK, Antony [son of Goosen], merchant, m. Maria, dau. of Teunis Cornelise Van Der Poel. He was buried, Feb. 4, 1737. Ch: *Anthony;* Goosen, bp. Oct. 5, 1684; Gerritje, bp. Sept. 11, 1687, m. Coenraat Ten Eyck; Catharina, bp. in New York, Sept. 21, 1690, m. Samuel Coeymans; Goosen, bp. April 29, 1694; *Goosen,* bp. Feb. 16, 1696; *Sybrant,* bp. May 12, 1700; Anna Margarita, bp. Dec. 6, 1702.

VAN SCHAICK, Sybrant [son of Goosen], m. Elizabeth Van Der Poel; in 1686, she contracted a marriage with Bennony Van Corlaer. He d. about 1685. In 1678 his stepmother agreed to sell him her half of the brewery on the easterly half of the Exchange block for 100 beavers. Ch: *Goosen,* b. 1677: Catharina, b. 1679, m. Adriaan Quackenbos; Anthony, b. 1681; *Gerrit,* bp. Jan. 4, 1685.

VAN SCHAICK, Goosen [son of Sybrant], m. Catharina Staats, Dec. 10, 1699. In 1715, he occupied the south corner of Broadway, and Exchange street; was buried, May 29, 1725. Ch: bp.; Rykje, Sept. 22, 1700; Sybrant, Jan. 11, 1702; Rykje, Dec. 24, 1703, m. Abraham G. Lansing; Elizabeth, Nov. 11, 1705; Debora, May 11, 1707; *Sybrant,* Sept. 19, 1708; Jacob, Oct. 7, 1711; Sara, Nov. 27, 1715; Abraham, May 7, 1719.

VAN SCHAICK, Gerrit Sybrantse, m. Sara Goewey, in New York, Oct. 23, 1705. Ch: bp.; Sybrant, Feb. 20, 1706; Sybrant, Feb. 23, 1707; Sybrant, Feb. 22, 1708; Catharina, Dec. 25, 1709; Joannes, April 20, 1712; *Goosen,* Oct. 17, 1714; Elizabeth, Aug. 4, 1717; Catalyna, June 28, 1719; Jacob, May 12, 1723.

VAN SCHAICK, Antony, Sybrant, *filius,* glazier, m. Anna Catharina Ten Broeck, Oct. 19, 1707. She was buried Dec. 30, 1756. In 1704, his house lot was on the present south corner of Pearl and State streets. Ch: bp.; *Sybrant,* Aug. 1, 1708; *Wessel,* Feb. 10, 1712; Catryna, Sept. 27, 1713, buried May 13, 1736; Elizabeth, Sept. 23, 1716; *Jacob,* March 16, 1718; Livinus, Sept. 4, 1720; Goosen, Sept. 9, 1722; Dirk, April 4, 1725.

VAN SCHAICK, Anthony (son of Anthony], m. first, Susanna Wendell, Dec. 16, 1707; and secondly, Anna Cuyler, May 24, 1712; she was buried in the church, March 9, 1743. In 1720, he had a lot on the east corner of Steuben and Pearl streets. Ch: bp.; Antony, Dec. 6, 1713; Elsie, July 30, 1715; Antony, July 13, 1717; Johannes, Nov. 9, 1718; Elsie, Oct. 15, 1719, buried May 12, 1740; Maria, Feb. 12, 1721; Anna, Oct. 22, 1722; Catharina, Oct. 25, 1724, buried April 19, 1743; Christina, Feb. 12, 1727.

VAN SCHAICK, Goose [son of Antony], m. first, Neeltie Abeel, Sept. 15, 1720, and secondly, Debora Van Schaick, Aug. 30, 1734. Ch: bp.; Antony, May 28, 1721; Catalyna, Jan. 9, 1723; Johannes, April 4, 1725; Johannes, June 19, 1726; Maria, Dec. 2, 1729; Goose, June 4, 1735.

VAN SCHAICK, Sybrant [son of Anthony?], m. Jannetie Bogaart, Aug. 19, 1733. Ch: bp.; Cathlyna,

Oct. 10, 1734; Sara, Oct. 19, 1740; Maria, Jan. 2, 1743; Cathalyntje, Jan. 13, 1751.

VAN SCHAICK, Sybrant [son of Anthony Sybrantse], m. Anna Roseboom, March 20, 1735. Ch: bp.; Anna Catharina, Dec. 7, 1735; Gerritje and Elizabeth, April 23, 1738; Geertruy, March 22, 1741; Anthony, Aug. 25, 1745; Anthony, June 21, 1747.

VAN SCHAICK, Sybrant [son of Goosen], mayor, 1756-61, m. Alida Roseboom, Dec. 11, 1735. Ch: bp.; Goosen, Sept. 5, 1736; Maria, Aug. 27, 1738; Ryckie, Jan. 4, 1741; Myndert, July 27, 1743; Catharina, Sept. 8, 1745; Maria, July 31, 1745, m. Philip Conyn, Coxsackie, and d. March 24, 1835, at the house of her son-in-law, John L. Bronck, in her 87th year; Myndert, May 12, 1751.

VAN SCHAICK, Johannes [son of Gerrit], m. Alida Bogart, July 9, 1736. Ch: bp.; Sara, March 8, 1737; Sara, Feb. 20, 1739; *Jacob,* Oct. 19, 1740; Sara, Nov. 27, 1743; Catalina, May 20, 1753; Catharina, Jan. 25, 1756.

VAN SCHAICK, Wessel [son of Anthony Sybr.], m. Maria Gerritse, Nov. 3, 1743; she d. Jan. 31, 1797, a. 79 y. 7 mo. Ch: bp.; Anthony, Oct. 19, 1744; Maria, July 26, 1746, d. Aug. 10, 1813, a. 67 y. 13 d.; *Jan Gerritsen,* Oct. 23, 1748; Catrina, Aug. 16, 1752; Gerrit, May 28, 1758, d. at Lansingburgh, Dec. 13, 1816.

VAN SCHAICK, Jacob [son of Gerrit], and Geertie De Ridder. Ch: bp.; Gerrit, Aug. 14, 1751; Anna, April 14, 1754; Sarah, Nov. 25, 1758 (1759?); Hendrick, b. March 19, 1763; Sara, b. April 30, 1767.

VAN SCHAICK, Goosen [son of Gerrit], m. Maycke Van Den Bergh, Nov. 6, 1748. Ch: bp.; Annatie, Aug. 27, 1749; Sara, March 31, 1751; Cornelia, June 24, 1753; Gerrit, Nov. 1755; Gerrit, Nov. 13, 1757; *Gerrit,* Nov. 2, 1760; Maria, b. April 21, 1763; Elizabeth, July 12, 1766; *Jacob.* (?).

VAN SCHAICK, Anthony [son of Goosen], m. Christina Van Schaick, Sept. 21, 1751. Ch: bp.; Goosen, June 21, 1752; Anna, July 14, 1754.

VAN SCHAICK, Jacob [son of Anthony], m. first, Catrina Cuyler, Sept. 14, 1751: and secondly, Elizabeth Van Schaick, about 1777. Ch: bp.; Catarina, Nov. 24, 1754; Margarita, Nov. 21, 1756; Ch: b.; Antony, Nov. 22, 1763; Hendrick, March 19, 1767; Catharina, March 17, 1778.

VAN SCHAICK, Hendrick, and Jannetie Holland. Ch: Margarita, b. Oct. 15, 1761.

VAN SCHAICK, Jacob Johannese, m. Marytje Van Buren, Feb. 24, 1765. Ch: b.; Johannes, Feb. 1, 1766: Elizabeth, March 4, 1768; Willem, Sept. 13, 1771; Alida, bp. Feb. 25, 1774; Maria, b. Jan. 31, 1777; Catharina, b. May 6, 1780.

VAN SCHAICK, Jacob G[erritse?], and Geertie (De) Ridder. Ch: Gerrit, b. Feb. 25, 1772.

VAN SCHAICK, Gen. Gosen [son of Sybrant], m. Maria Ten Broeck, in N. York, Nov. 15, 1770. She was b. in New Brunswick, Aug. 11, 1750, and d. in Albany, Jan. 15, 1829. Ch: b.; Johannes, Jan. 1, 1774, d. March 1, 1820, a. 46 y. 2 mo.; Sybrand, May 19, 1776; Tobias, Dec. 9, 1779; Meinard, Sept. 26, 1782; Elizabeth, June 11, 1786; Abraham, July 28, 1787, d. Aug. 8, 1827, a. 40 y. 11 d.

VAN SCHAICK, John Gerritse [son of Wessel], m. Annatie Van Schaick, Aug. 2, 1775. In 1805, he had a house and store on west side of Broadway, next north of the Museum building. He d. on Van Schaick's island, July 7, 1828, in his 80th year. Ch:

b.; Wessel, June 29, 1776, d. at Lansingburgh, July 17, 1833, a. 57 y.; Anthony, April 21, 1779, counselor at law, d. March 9, 1822, a. 43 y.; Maria, Jan. 6, 1782; Christina, Feb. 8, 1790; Henry, Dec. 27, 1795, d. at Lansingburgh, Oct. 7, 1829, a. 33 y.

VAN SCHAICK, Jacob [son of Goosen], and Elizabeth Berry. Ch: b; Gosen, Aug. 20, 1780; Jacob, July 18, 1782; Dirk, Jan. 10, 1785; Elizabeth, Feb. 21, 1787.

VAN SCHAICK, Gerrit [son of Goosen], and Christina Berringer. He d. at Lansingburgh, Dec. 13, 1816. Ch. b.; Maayke, April 20, 1783; Margarita, April 16, 1786.

VAN SCHAICK, Claas, and Jannetie —— (?) Ch: *Dominicus*, b. 1667; *Arent*, b. 1676; *Lourens; Emanuel*.

VAN SCHAICK, Dominicus, of Kinderhook, Catskil, 1720; m. Rebecca Groesbeck, dau. of Claas Jacobse G. Feb. 17, 1699: Ch: bp.; Jannetje, Jan. 7, 1700; *Claas*, July 6, 1701; Stephanus, Jan. 7, 1705; Cornelis, Nov. 16, 1707.

VAN SCHAICK, Arent Claase, of Catskil, 1720, m. Marietje Van Loon, Feb. 22, 1698. Ch: bp.; Claas Dec. 25, 1698; Claas, July 5, 1702; Albert b. *op de Flakte*, July 16, and bp. in New York, Oct. 1, 1704; Marytje, Jan. 28, 1708; Cornelia, b. Dec. 1, *op de Vlakte*, Loonenburgh, and bp. *op* Klinkenbergh, Dec. 17, 1710; Michael, b. Oct. 11, and bp. Nov. 13, 1715, at Klinkenbergh.

VAN SCHAICK, Lourens Claase, of Kinderhook, m. Jannetje Oothout, of Albany, Dec. 4, 1699. Ch: bp.; Henrikje, July 21, 1700; Gerrit, Aug. 30, 1702; Jannetje, March 25, 1705; Claas Lourense, Dec. 28, 1707; Johannes, Jan. 29, 1710; Cornelis, April 20, 1712.

VAN SCHAICK, Emanuel, of Kinderhook, m. Margareta Lucasse Wyngaard, June 11, 1703. He d. Nov. 19, 1706. Ch: bp.; Jannetje, Dec. 15, 1703; Cornelis, Nov. 11, 1705.

VAN SCHAICK, Nicolaas [son of Dominicus], m. Dorothea Witbeck, Feb. 26, 1728. He was buried, Sept. 15, 1750; she was buried June 24, 1740. Ch: bp.; Engeltie, May 15, 1728; *Stephanus*, Feb. 4, 1730; *Andries*, Aug. 13, 1732; *Cornelis*, Nov. 14, 1736.

VAN SCHAICK, Stephanus [son of Nicolaas], m. Jannetje Bratt, March 5, 1753. Ch: bp.; Dorothea, Sept. 22, 1753; Dorothea, Feb. 15, 1756; Nicolaas, Nov. 23, 1760; *Egbert*, b. April 4, 1764; Andries, Aug. 30, 1770.

VAN SCHAICK, Andries [son of Nicolaas], m. Alida Hogen, Aug. 27, 1757. Ch: bp.; Dorothea, March 5, 1758; Maria, Dec. 21, 1760.

VAN SCHAICK, Cornelis [son of Nicolaas], m. Willempje Hanssen, Jan. 11, 1784. He was the bell ringer of the church, and lived on the east side of Pearl street above Maiden lane. Ch: Nicolaas, b. May 5, 1786.

VAN SCHAICK, Egbert [son of Stephanus], m. Maria Winne—1791. He d. May 31, 1816, a. 52 y. 1 m. 25 d.; she d. Feb. 17, 1825, at 60 South Pearl street. Ch: b.; Stephen, Nov. 18, 1792; Livinus, Oct. 10, 1794, d. Feb. 28, 1837, a. 43 y.; Dorothy, July 11, 1797; Benjamin, Oct. 30, 1799; Cornelius, July 27, 1804.

Van Schelluyne, Dirk, and Cornelia Van Buren. He came over in 1650, as notary public; soon removed to Beverwyck; secretary of Albany 1665-

1668; 1667 the Mohawks gave him a tract of land in Niskayuna, for services rendered them, a portion of which he sold to Jan Clute. Ch: *Cornelis;* Tileman; Johannes, bp. in New York, Sept. 14, 1653.

VAN SCHELLUYNE, Cornelis Dirkse, shoemaker, m. Geertje Harmense Visscher. He was buried, May 27, 1728. She was buried, April 14, 1734. Ch: bp.; *Dirk*, July 6, 1684; Hester, July 15, 1686; Tileman, July 29, 1688; Johannes, June 11, 1693, buried Oct. 11, 1746; Cornelia, July 21, 1695, buried Nov. 15, 1734; Wilhelm, Feb. 20, 1698, buried May 4, 1752.

VAN SCHELLUYNE, Dirk [son of Cornelis], m. first, Maria Van Nes, Dec. 22, 1722, who was buried June 22, 1730; secondly, Elizabeth Roseboom, Dec. 25, 1735. Ch: bp.; Geertruy, July 4, 1725; Catharina, Feb. 2, 1729; *Cornelis*, Sept. 11, 1737.

VAN SCHELLUYNE, Cornelis Dirkse, m. Elizabeth Roseboom, Dec. 11, 1767. He d. April 13, (16) 1813, a. 76 y. She d. March 18, 1800, a. 57 y. 9 m. 18 d. Ch: b.; Dirk, Jan. 20, 1769; Theodorus, May 19, 1771; Debora, April 26, 1773; Dirk, May 3, 1774, m. Rachel Gansevoort, and d. July 23, 1823, leaving one son.

Van Schie, Domine Cornelis, was minister of the church in Fishkil, 1731-3; called to the church in Albany, May 11, 1733; was buried Aug. 16, 1744, in the church. He m. Josyna Prys. Ch: bp.; Wilhelmus, Aug. 26, 1733; Elizabeth, Nov. 17, 1734; Maria, July 18, 1736; Wilhelmus, Sept. 11, 1737; Nicolaas, Jan. 28, 1739; Maria, Feb. 22, 1741; Wilhelmus, b. Aug. 1, 1744.

Van Schoenderwoert, see Van Woert.

Van Schoonhoven, Geurt Hendrickse, of *Halve Maan* 1675, carpenter, had a farm on Cahoos island in 1681; made his will Aug. 20, 1700, made his w. executrix; d. Jan. 12, 1702. Ch: Jacobus, eldest son; Hendrick, " *obiit* April 28, 1707;" Margareta; Hendrikje; Geertruy; Jacomyntje.

VAN SCHOONHOVEN, or Van Utrecht, Claas Hendrickse, carpenter, of Fort Orange 1654, a considerable dealer in real estate. His wife Cornelia Frederickse, after his death, m. Willem Janse Stoll. He d. March 15, 1661.

VAN SCHOONHOVEN, Jacobus [son of Geurt], of *Halve Maan*, m. Susanna Bratt, Feb. 17, 1714; he was buried, Jan. 26, 1749. Ch: bp.; Geurt, March 31, 1716; *Geurt*, April 11, 1718; *Dirk Bratt*, Feb. 7, 1720; Maria, Aug. 12, 1722; Anna, Sept. 27, 1724; *Hendrick*, May 6, 1727; Susanna, April 18, 1731.

VAN SCHOONHOVEN, Geurt [son of Jacobus], m. Anna Lansing, Feb. 3, 1743. She was buried in the Lutheran church yard, March 2, 1744. Ch: *Jacobus*, bp. March 4, 1744.

VAN SCHOONHOVEN, Dirk Bratt [son of Jacobus], m. Volkie Van Den Bergh. Ch: bp.; Jacobus, March 27, 1748; Catelyntje, April 23, 1749; Jacobus, Nov. 24, 1751; Gysbert, Dec. 15, 1754; *Jacobus*, July 13, 1757; Gysbert, b. June 3, 1760; Hendrick, and Cornelis, b. Oct. 29, 1762; Dirk Bratt, March 23, 1765; Cornelis, b. July 26, 1767, d. July 4, 1828, a. 60 y. 11 m. 8 d.

VAN SCHOONHOVEN, Jacobus [son of Geurt], of *Halve Maan*, m. Elizabeth Clute *uit de Boght*, Jan. 3, 1765. Ch: b.; Geurt, July 6, 1765; Gerardus, Dec. 14, 1769; Susanna, Dec. 13, 1774; Elizabeth, July 28, 1779; Jacobus, Nov. 4, 1781.

VAN SCHOONHOVEN, Hendrick [son of Jacobus], of *Halve Maan*, m. Aaltie Van Ness (Van Den Bergh),

Sept. 20, 1771. Ch: b.; Susanna, June 9, 1772; Jacobus, July 17, 1774; Jacobus, Dec. 24, 1775; Sara, Sept. 12, 1778.

VAN SCHOONHOVEN, James [son of Dirk Bratt], m. Maria Spoor, April 2, 1789. Ch: b.; Dirk Bratt, Nov. 9, 17o9; Magdalena, Dec. 25, 1791: John, Feb. 17, 1794; Madalena, May 22, 1799: Gerrit, d. June 6, 1831, a. 29 y.; Magdalena, Sept. 25, 1807.

Van Sleents, Caspar, and Jannetie .... Ch: Simon, bp.; June 31 (*sic*), 1717.

Van Slichtenhorst, Brant Arentse, of Nieuwkerk, in Gelderland, was appointed a director of the *Colonie* Rensselaerswyck, in 1646; returned to Nieuwkerk where he d. about 1668. Ch: *Gerrit*; Margaret, m. Col. Philip Pieterse Schuyler; Alida, m. Gerrit, son of Goosen Gerritse Van Schaick, by whom she had no issue; after his death, Nov. 11, 1679, she m. Pieter Davidtse Schuyler.

VAN SLICHTENHORST, Gerrit, came to Beverwyck, in 1646, with his father, and served as *schout fiscaal* for a short time. He was one of the commissarissen of Schenectady, 1672, soon after which he removed to Kingston where he d. Jan. 9, 1684. Besides several house lots in Albany he owned land in Claverac. Ch: Hillegonda; Gerrit; Rachel; Gouda.

Van Slyck, Cornelis Antonissen, *alias* "*Broer Cornelis,*" is said to have m. a Mohawk woman by whom he had several children .... two sons *Jacques Cornelise,* and Marten Mouris, a daughter Hilletie and perhaps Lea. The first, Jacques, settled in Schenectady and had a large family; the second, Marten, was in Beverwyck in 1661 but soon disappeared; Hilletie was interpretress for the province; Lea m. first, Claas Willemse Van Coppernol; and secondly, Jonathan Stevens of Schenectady. "Broer Cornelis" d. in 1676. By reason of his eminent services, rendered in bringing about peace with the natives, he received a patent for a large tract of land at Katskil.

VAN SLYCK, Cornelis Teunise, in Beverwyck 1659-68. He was for a time *raets person* for the *colonie.*

VAN SLYCK, Willem Pieterse, in Beverwyck, in 1655. Ch: *Pieter,* Jacob, Dirk, Teunis.

VAN SLYCK, Jacques Cornelise, owned a half island in the Mohawk river, at Schenectady and land 5 miles above, the gift of the natives. [See *Schenectady Families.*]

VAN SLYCK, Pieter Willemse, of Kinderhook, m. Johanna Barheit, April 9, 1683. Ch: bp.; Willem, Sept. 20, 1685; Hans, Sept. 25, 1687; Lysbeth, Feb. 2, 169o; *Teunis,* Nov. 20, 1692; Johanna, May 26, 1695; Tryntje, Nov. 14, 1697; Pieter, April 28, 1700; Barentje, Jan. 3, 1703; Dirk, Oct. 23, 1705.

VAN SLYCK, Jacob [son of Willem?] and .... Ch: Feytje, bp. Jan. 20, 1686.

VAN SLYCK, Dirk Willemse, m. Anneke Janse .... 1686. Ch: bp.; Willem, Jan. 8, 1688; Marritje, April 27, 1690. Ch. bp. in New York: Hendrick, March 4, 1698; Maritie, March 20, 1700; Maritie, Aug. 10, 1701; Pieter, Oct. 21, 1706.

VAN SLYCK, Teunis Willemse, m. Jannetje Hendrickse Van Wie, Feb, 5, 1696. Ch: bp.; *Hendrick*; Ida, June 28, 1702; *Andries*, Sept. 17, 1704; *Gerrit*, May 19, 1706; *Pieter*, Sept. 26, 1708; Alida, Nov. 5, 1710; Dirk, March 1, 1713; Agnietje, June 19, 1720; *Willem.*

VAN SLYCK, Gerrit Teunise, and Annatje Turk. Ch: bp.; Catharyna, Sept. 3, 1738: Sara, Aug. 15,

1742; Johannes, July 7, 1745; Sara, July 23, 1749; Teunis, Dec. 26, 1751.

VAN SLYCK, Teunis [son of Pieter Willemse], m. first .....,and secondly, Cathalyna Goewey, June 7, 1739. Ch: Johannes, bp. June 29, 1740.

VAN SLYCK, Hendrick [son of Teunis], m. first, Elizabeth Visscher, Oct. 21, 1737; secondly, Elizabeth Van Benthuysen, June 21, 1740. Ch: bp.; Teunis, April 4, 1742; Jannetie, Jan. 8, 1744; Agnietje, Jan. 3, 1748; Baltus, Dec. 31, 1749; Catalyntje, Nov. 10, 1751.

VAN SLYCK, Willem, and Catharina Van Slyck. Ch: bp.; Jannetie, April 12, 1746; Teunis, Dec. 27, 1747; Elizabeth, Nov. 10, 1751.

VAN SLYCK, Andries [son of Teunis], m. Maria, Van Benthuysen. Ch: bp.; Jannetie, March 1, 1747; *Baltus,* Feb. 26, 1749; Lydia, June 9, 1751; Alida, b. May 5, 1765.

VAN SLYCK, Pieter [son of Teunis], m. Anna Ryckse Van Vranken. Ch: bp.; Teunis, Feb. 17, 1751; Marritie, Nov. 12, 1752.

VAN SLYCK, Baltus [son of Andries], m. Anna Conyn. Ch: Elizabeth, b. Sept. 11, 1796.

VAN SLYCK, Cornelis, of Schenectady, m. Claartje Janse Bratt, of New Albany, Feb. 10, 1696. Ch: bp.; Margarlet, Feb. 12, 1696; Maria, May 23, 1697; Antony, Dec. 15, 1706; Geertruy, Oct. 30, 1709. [See also *Schenectady Families.*]

VAN SLYCK, Marten, of Schenectady, m. Margarita Van Franken (Vranken), March 23, 1701, in Schenectady. Ch: bp.; Margarita, Feb. 16, 1707; Petrus, Oct. 30, 1709. [See also *Schenectady Families.*]

VAN SLYCK, Harmen, of Schenectady, m. Jannetie Vrooman, March 26, 1704, in Schenectady. Ch: bp.; Helena, Jan. 15, 1710: Catrina, Sept. 13, 1712. [See also *Schenectady Families.*]

Van Strey, Jan. m. Joanna (Annatje) Van Der Poel, widow in New York, June .... 1694. Ch: Lysbet, bp. Jan. 5, 1700.

Van Thessel (Tassel), Abraham, and Annatie Lansing. Ch: Magdalena, b. Sept. 16, 1788.

Van Tricht, Abraham, m. Lysbeth Teller, dau. of Wm. T., senior; after his death she m. Melgert Wynantse Van Der Poel. Ch: bp.; Magdalena, Oct. 21, 1683, m. Abraham Lansing; Helena, May 30, 1686.

Van Twiller, Johannes; merchant, in Beverwyck, 1654-62.

Van Twiler, Aert Goosense, from Niewkerk Gelderland, in Beverwyck, 1661-3.

Van Utrecht, Claes Hendrickse, see Van Schoonhoven.

Van Valkenburgh, Lambert, and Annatie .... in 1645, he bought a house, and 25 morgens of land in Manhattans; 1654 he was in Beverwyck — not living in 1697: his widow d. Sept. 17, 1704. In 1703 his heirs owned a house and lot in "ye *Voddemark*" bounded west by the burying ground, north and east by the highway [west corner of Green and Beaver streets.] Ch: Jochem, eldest son, bp. in New Amsterdam, Nov. 4, 1646; Lambert, bp. in New Amsterdam, July 21, 1652.

VAN VALKENBURGH, Jochem Lambertse, of Kinderhook 1720, m. first, Eva Hendrickse Vrooman, who d. in 1706: secondly, Jannetie Mingael, widow of Lambert Van Alsteyn, Feb. 23, 1713. Ch: bp.; *Johannes; Hendrick; Abraham; Bartholomeus;*

Lambert ; Isaac, July 4, 1686 ; *Jacobus,* April 4, 1689 ; *Jochem,* June 5, 1692; Engeltie, June 5, 1695.

VAN VALKENBURGH, Lambert Jochemse, of Kinderhook 1720. m. Jannetie Franse Clauw, March 28, 1693. Ch : bp. ; Elsie, Sept. 3, 1693 ; Jochem, Jan. 20, 1695 : Pieter, Nov. 11, 1696 ; Eva, Feb, 19, 1699 ; Frans, Jan. 3, 1703; Maria, Jan. 7, 1705 ; Jurriaan, Feb. 26, 1707; Johannes, July 4, 1708 ; Andries, April 30, 1710 ; Wyntje Franse, Feb. 17, 1712.

VAN VALKENBURGH, Bartholomeus, of Kinderhook, 1720 [son of Jochem], m. Catharina Van Alsteyn, June 14, 1701. Ch : bp. ; Jochem, May 19, 1702 ; Lambert, Oct. 1, 1704 ; Pieter, Jan. 19, 1707 ; Eva, March 20, 1709 ; Thomas, Oct. 12, 1713 ; Abraham, Dec. 25, 1715 ; Jacob, June 19, 1720.

VAN VALKENBURGH, Abraham [son of Jochem], m. Catelyntie Schermerhorn, May 18, 1706. Ch : bp. ; Jacobus, March 16, 1707 : Joachim, Nov. 21, 1708 ; *Abraham,* March 11, 1711 ; Isaac, Oct. 19, 1712 ; Johannes, April 21, 1717; Eva, Jan. 18, 1719 ; Gerritje, Dec. 25, 1720; Cornelis, March 24, 1723.

VAN VALKENBURGH, Isaac [son of Jochem], lived at the *Verreberg,* west of Albany, in 1717 ; m. Lydia Van Slyck. Ch : bp. *Jacob ; Isaac ;* Joachim Lambert, Jan. 15, 1710 ; Margarita, Sept. 27, 1713 ; Harmen, March 2, 1715.

VAN VALKENBURGH, Hendrick [son of Jochem], m. Anna Huyck, bans proclaimed, Dec. 10, 1709. Ch : bp. ; Eva, April 20, 1712 : Jochem, Oct. 6, 1717.

VAN VALKENBURGH, Johannes [son of Jochem], of Kinderhook 1706, m. Margarita Barheit, Feb. 26, 1707. Ch : bp. ; Eva, June 13, 1708; Rebecca, Oct. 30, 1710 ; *Jeroon,* Oct, 19, 1712 ; Jannetie, Oct. 31, 1714 ; Johanna, Sept. 23, 1716 ; Jochum, June 28, 1719 ; Marytje, May 27, 1722 ; *Johannes.*

VAN VALKENBURGH, Johannes, and Elizabeth .... Ch : Dorothea, bp. Oct. 19, 1735.

VAN VALKENBURGH, Johannes, and Eva Van Valkenburgh. Ch : bp. ; Jacobus, Oct. 7, 1739 ; Margarita, April 29, 1744 ; Petrus, June 21, 1752.

VAN VALKENBURGH, Jacobus, m. Christina Winne, July 4, 1713. Ch : bp. ; Eva, Oct. 26, 1713 ; *Thomas,* Sept. 23, 1716 ; Jochum, March 9, 1720 ; Teuntie, April 15, 1722.

VAN VALKENBURGH, Jochum [son of Jochem], and Elsie .... Ch : bp. ; Eva, Oct. 25, 1719 ; Jannetie, July 3, 1720 ; Eva, April 28, 1723 ; Jannetie, Aug. 7, 1726.

VAN VALKENBURGH. Lambert [son of Jochem ?], m. Lea Klauw, Sept. 17, 1725. Ch : Jurriaan, Aug. 7, 1726.

VAN VALKENBURGH, Jacob or Jacobus [son of Isaac], m. Margariet Rettelief, Nov. 30, 1732. Ch : bp. ; Lydia, Oct. 3, 1733 ; Rachel, July 27, 1735 ; Isaac, Sept. 4, 1737 ; Rachel, Oct. 28, 1739 ; Johannes, and Margarieta, Dec. 5, 1742 ; Elizabeth, Aug. 25, 1745 ; Eva, Oct. 23, 1748.

VAN VALKENBURGH, Jacob or Jacobus, and Catharina, Durck or Turk. Ch : bp. ; Jannetie, May 8, 1737 ; Jacob, Jan. 10, 1739 ; Catharyna, June 17, 1740 ; Eva, March 7, 1742 ; Gerritje, April 15, 1744 ; Chrystyntje, April 27, 1746 ; Johannes, April 9, 1749.

VAN VALKENBURGH, Isaac [son of Isaac ?], m. Jannetie Klemet (Clement), May 28, 1737. Ch : bp. ; Lidia, Oct. 21, 1737 ; Annatie, Aug. 8, 1739 ; Eva, Oct. 4, 1741.

VAN VALKENBURGH, Hieronomus [son of Johannes], m. Marytje Van Buren. Ch : bp. ; Ariaantje, June 17, 1739 ; Margarita, July 31, 1743 ; Pieter, June 12, 1748 ; Joachim, Aug. 5, 1753.

VAN VALKENBURGH, Lambert, and Jacomyntje Burns. Ch : bp. ; Debora, June 22, 1740 ; Charles, June 12, 1748.

VAN VALKENBURGH, Thomas [son of Jacob or Jacobus], and Theuntje Barheit. Ch : bp.; Christina, Aug. 16, 1741 ; Rachel, May 8, 1743 ; Jacobus, May 12, 1745.

VAN VALKENBURGH, Thomas [perhaps same as the last], and Rachel Van Den Bergh. Ch : bp. : Engeltie, May 29, 1752 ; Bartholomeus, Oct. 21, 1753.

VAN VALKENBURGH, Abraham, B. [Braam(?) son of Abraham], m. Neeltie Gardenier, July 11, 1740. Ch : bp.; Catharina, Jan. 25, 1744 ; Abram, Dec, 20, 1747 ; Nicolaas, Oct. 22, 1749 ; Abraham, Nov. 18, 1753.

VAN VALKENBURGH, Lambert, and Catharina Van Vechten. Ch : Jacobus, bp. March 1, 1753.

VAN VALKENBURGH, Johannes [son of Johannes], m. Elizabeth Meinderssen, March 25, 1764. Ch ; b. ; Margarita, Oct. 22, 1764 ; Margarita, March 12, 1766 ; Sara, March 9, 1768 ; Johannes, May 12, 1770 ; Jacobus, Nov. 1, 1772.

VAN VALKENBURGH, Isaac, and Annatie Van Den Bergh. Ch : Jacobus, b. Aug. 9, 1766.

VAN VALKENBURGH, Isaac, and Engeltie .... Ch : b. ; Cornelia, Feb. 10, 1769 : Rachel, Aug. 6, 1774.

VAN VALKENBURGH, Jacobus, m. Catharina Sixby, Sept. 23, 1775. Ch : b. ; Elsie, Oct. 23, 1778 ; Gerrit, March 9, 1780.

VAN VALKENBURGH, John, and Caty Tingue. Ch : b. ; John, Oct. 21, 1790 ; Maria, bp. Jan. 6, 1793.

Van Vechten, Teunis, Cornelise [Dirkse ?] succeeded Michael Jansen on his farm in 1646, and lived in 1648, in the south end of Greenbush. *O' Callaghan, Hist. N. N.,* I. In 1662, one Theunis Cornelise is called Young *Poentie.*

VAN VECHTEN, Teunis Dirkse, *alias Poentie,* came out in 1638 with wife, child and two servants, in the *Arms of Norway* and had a farm in 1648 at Greenbush north of that occupied by Theunis Cornelise Van Vechten ; he is referred to in 1663 as an old inhabitant here. *O' Callaghan's Hist. N. N.,* I. Ch. living in 1700. *Dirk Theunise,* eldest son ; *Cornelis ; Gerrit ;* Pietertje, w. of Myndert Frederickse.

VAN VECHTEN Dirk Teunise, of Catskil (Coxsackie 1692), m. Jannetie Michielse ; made his will April 4, 1687, proved March 30, 1703 ; d. Nov. 25, 1702. The following children are mentioned in his will, Jannetie, b. 1660 ; Wyntie, b. 1662 ; *Michiel,* b. 1664 ; Neeltie, b. 1665 ; *Johannes,* b. 1667 ; *Teunis,* b. 1669 ; Annatie, b. 1671 ; Fytie, b. 1672 ; Samuel, b. 1673 ; Sara, b. 1675 ; Abraham, b. 1679.

VAN VECHTEN, Samuel [son of the last] made his will Dec. 3, 1739 ; spoke of his father Dirk Teunise deceased who purchased, Oct. 20, 1681, of Stephen Van Cortland, a tract of land at Catskil, confirmed March 21, 1686, which land was afterwards made over to me and my brother Johannes, deceased, by my brothers Michael, and Abraham deceased, by deed of March 30, 1715, and my brother Johannes' share was made over to me by deed, 9 Aug. 1721, all which I am now seized of, &c. .... gave the use of all his real estate at Catskil to his nephew Teunis, son of his brother Johannes during life ; the said estate to pass to said Teunis's lawful heirs and so on from heir to heir " to the end of the world !" The above will was recorded April 15, 1741.

VAN VECHTEN, Gerrit Teunise, of Colony Rensselaerswyck, m. first, Antje Janse ; and secondly, Grietje Volkertse, dau. of Volkert Janse Douw. In 1678 he and Jan Conell bought Capt. Jan Clute's claim in lands at Catskill : 1680 bought of Gerrit Van Slichtenhorst, a negro man named Dick for 150 pieces of *nooten-hout* ; also another negro named Harry for 200 skipples of Indian corn, two loads of hay and 24 beavers in hogs ; 1697 petitioned the governor in favor of his brother who had accidentally killed a child of Col. Schuyler. In his will made March 8, 1680–1, he spoke of wife Grietje and two sons *Johannes*, by the first w. and *Volkert*, by the second.

VAN VECHTEN,, Cornelis Teunise, *alias Keesoom*, of Papsknee (an island below Albany), m. first, Sara Salomonse Goewey ; secondly, Annatie Leendertse, and thirdly Maria Lucase, wid. of Jacob Claase July 3, 1689. Ch : *Salomon ; Dirks ;* Leendert ; *Reuben (?) ; Lucas*, bp. Feb. 26, 1690 ; Anna, bp. Dec. 26, 1692 ; Jannetje, bp, Feb. 13, 1698, m. Johannes G. Lansing.

VAN VECHTEN, Michiel Dirkse, m. Maria Parker, iu 1686. Ch : bp. ; a child name not registered, Nov. 20, 1687 ; Dirk, Jan. 26, 1690.

VAN VECHTEN, Johannes [son of Dirk Teunise], of Catskill, and Elizabeth (?) .... Ch : *Teunis ;* and *Dirk.*

VAN VECHTEN, Teunis Dirkse, of Loonenburgh (Athens) 1702, m. Caatje Van Petten, Nov. 28, 1694. Ch : bp. ; Dirk, Sept. 29, 1695 ; Eva, May 12, 1700 ; Maria, June 4, 1704 ; Teunis, June 1, 1707. Of the parents of this last child it is recorded that *beide voor den doopdag gesturven.*

VAN VECHTEN, Salomon Cornelise, m. Alida Fonda, Nov. 10, 1699. He was buried Oct. 17, 1750 ; she was buried Jan. 5, 1731. Ch : bp. ; Cornelis, Nov. 3, 1700 ; Sara, May 10, 1702 ; *Douwe*, Oct. 21, 1705 ; Rebecca, Jan. 12, 1709 ; Cornelis, April 20, 1712

VAN VECHTEN, Johannes [son of Gerrit Teunise] m. Maria, dau. of Pieter Bogardus, March 19, 1699. A more than doubtful tradition makes her marry first, Pieter Jacobse Borsboom, of Schenectady. [A Johannes V. V. was buried at Papsknee, June 23, 1734 ; and another July 15, 1742.] Ch : b. : Catharina, Nov. 4, 1699, m. Bernardus Bratt ; Annatje, bp. Jan. 5, 1700 ; Weyntje, b. May 17, 1702, m. Maj. Hendrick Bries ; Margarita, b. Nov. 24, 1705, m. Barent Van Buren ; Gerrit Teunise, b. Oct. 4, 1709, d. Jan. 17, 1710–1 ; a daughter b. Nov. 14, 1711 ; Neeltie, b. Feb. 13, 1713, d. Feb. 22, 1713 ; Neeltie, bp. Feb. 7, 1714.

VAN VECHTEN, Volkert [son of Gerrit Teunise], m. Lydia Ten Broeck, Aug. 26, 1702 ; made a will July 15, 1747, proved April 15, 1749, in which he is said to be *oude van dagen*, and spoke of his wife, of Gerrit Teunise's two children, Volkert, and Agnietie, and of his Ch. Dirk, Margarita, w. of Gerrit C : Van Den Bergh ; Ephraim's dau. Lidia ; and Johannes. Ch : bp. : *Gerrit Teunise*, April 25, 1703 ; Margarita, March 3, 1706 ; *Ephraim and Johannes*, twins, June 12, 1709 ; Dirk, Oct. 19, 1712.

VAN VECHTEN, Dirk Cornelise, of Schagtekock, 1720, m. Margarita Harmense Luwes [Lievense ?] Nov. 20, 1708 ; made will August 17, 1739, proved Oct. 17, 1752, and mentioned the following Ch : ex-

cept Cornelis, and Elbert. Ch : bp. ; *Harmen*, Feb. 16, 1704 ; Cornelis, Dec. 15, 1706 ; Anna, Feb. 10, 1712 ; Elbert, May 27, 1715 ; Philip, Nov. 23, 1718 ; *Benjamin*, Sept. 18, 1720 ; *Teunis*.

VAN VECHTEN, Lucas [son of Cornelis Teunise] m. Tanneke Woedes, April 29, 1716. Ch : bp. ; Eva, June 31, (*sic*) 1717 ; Maria, July 19, 1719 ; Johannes, Dec. 31, 1721 ; Anna, March 1, 1724 ; Antje, Oct. 23, 1726.

VAN VECHTEN, Reuben, of Albany, m. Geertruy Witbeck, May 30, 1718. She was buried in the Patroon's vault, Nov. 8, 1745 ; he d. March 5, 1735. Ch : bp. ; Anna, Jan. 1, 1719 ; Catharina, July 10, 1720 ; Cornelis, August 12, 1722 ; Lucas, Oct. 25, 1724 ; Engeltie, Nov. 6, 1726 ; Phillipus, Feb. 2, 1729 ; Maria, Nov. 29, 1730 ; Johannes, Dec. 10, 1732, buried Dec. 3, 1749.

VAN VECHTEN, Harmen [son of Dirk Cornelise], m. Elisabeth... buried April 23, 1746. Ch : bp. ; Maria, June 9, 1729 ; Dirk, Sept. 13, 1730 ; Dirk, Dec. 13, 1732 ; *Cornelis*, Feb. 9, 1735 ; *Dirk*, May 15, 1737 ; Maria, August 9, 1741.

VAN VECHTEN, Douw [son of Salomon], m. first, Helena ; and secondly Ariaantje. ..about 1738 : she was buried March 8, 1754. Ch : bp. ; Maria, May 19, 1731, d. Jan. 27, 1825, a. 94y. ; Salomon, June 17, 1739.

VAN VECHTEN, Dirk [son of Johannes and Elizabeth] of Catskill, m. Lena Van Vechten. Ch : bp. Elisabetha, July 26, 1733 ; Eva, July 6, 1735 ; Jannetie, Oct. 17, 1738 ; *Hubartus*. [*Catskill Church Rec.*]

VAN VECHTEN, Theunis [son of Johannes and Elisabeth] of Catskill, m. Judikje Ten Broeck. Ch : bp. ; *Samuel*, Oct. 8, 1742 ; Elisabeth, Nov. 5, 1757 ; *Abraham*, b. Dec. 5, and bp. Dec. 27, 1762 ; *Teunis*. [*Catskill Church Rec.*]

VAN VECHTEN, Johannes Jr., [son of Volkert] merchant of Albany, m. Neeltie Beekman, Oct. 29, 1734. He was buried Dec. 25, 1746 ; made his will May 2, 1743, proved April 6, 1749. Ch : bp. ; *Volkert*, August 26, 1735 ; Johannes, June 19, 1737 ; Johannes, June 24, 1739 ; Lidia, Aug. 16, 1741 ; Ephraim, April 24, 1743 ; Eva, May 5, 1745 ; Hendricus, March 29, 1747.

VAN VECHTEN, Gerrit Teunise [son of Volkert], m. Lena Witbeck, Nov. 6, 1739. He was buried March 12, 1747. Ch : bp. ; Volkert, July 27, 1740 ; Agnietje, March 27, 1743 ; *Volkert*, Jan. 10, 1746.

VAN VECHTEN, Ephraim [son of Volkert], m. Catharina Ten Broeck, Jan. 3, 1744. He d. in "Nubronswyck" Dec. 10, 1746. Ch : Lydia, bp. Oct. 19, 1744.

VAN VECHTEN, Teunis [son of Dirk Cornelis], m. Cornelia Knickkelbackker, Feb. 29, 1744 ; buried June 27, 1756. Ch : bp. ; *Dirk*, Feb. 17, 1745 ; Anna, Dec. 6, 1748 ; Johannes, Oct. 23, 1755.

VAN VECHTEN, Benjamin [son of Dirk Cornelise], and Annatie Bogardus. She was buried August 31, 1749. Ch : bp ; Margarita, August 25, 1745 ; *Antony*, Jan. 24, 1748.

VAN VECHTEN, Hubartus [son of Dirk and Lena] of Catskill, m. Maria Spoor. Ch : bp. , Helena, April 11, 1751 ; Dirck, Nov. 8, 1753 ; Lena, August 20, 1758 ; Maria, Jan. 6, 1765. [*Catskill Church Rec.*]

VAN VECHTEN, Dirk [son of Harmen], m. Alida Knickerbacker, Oct. 21, 1758. Ch ; Elizabeth, bp Jan. 21, 1759 ; Elizabeth, bp. Nov. 14, 1761 ; Harmen, b. Aug. 7, 1765 ; Wouter, b. July 2, 1768.

VAN VECHTEN, Col. Cornelis, of Schagtekook, [son of Harmen], m. Annatie Knickerbacker, of Albany, Dec. 10, 1757. Ch: b.; Harmen, bp. May 13, 1761; Elizabeth, b. Aug. 19, 1763; Marytje, Dec. 9, 1765, m. Enoch Leonard, and d. at Lansingburgh, in her 94th year; Elizabeth, Dec. 23, 1767; Harmen, March 1, 1772; Rebecca, Sept. 9, 1773.

VAN VECHTEN, John, of Albany, m. Annatie Williams, Jan. 7, 1762. Ch: Lydia, b. Oct. 30, 1762.

VAN VECHTEN, Volkert [son of Johannes, Jr.], of Albany, m. Jannetje Hun, Dec. .... 1762. Ch: b.; Johannes, Oct. 17, 1763; Neeltie, Sept. 3, 1768.

VAN VECHTEN, Volkert [son of Gerrit Teunise], of Albany, m. Elizabeth Van Den Bergh, June 25, 1775. Ch: John Witbeck, bp. Dec. 11, 1776; Gerrit Teunise, b. Jan. 12, 1780.

VAN VECHTEN, Dirk [son of Teunis], of Schachkook, m. first, Cathalyntje Van Nes, Aug. 5, 1764, secondly, Pietertje Yates, June 27, 1770. [Dirk V. V. m. Catharina Spoor, March 5, 1780.] Ch: b.; Teunis, b. *leste* Nov. bp. Jan. 6, 1765; Margarita, b. Jan. 8, 1767; Cathalyntje, b. Dec. 9, 1771.

VAN VECHTEN, Ephraim, of Albany [son of Johannes, Jr.], m. first, Annatie Wendell, Feb. 6, 1767, and secondly, Susanna Hoghen, Nov. 20, 1774. Ch: b.; Johannes, Aug. 14, 1768; Neeltie, Aug. 28, 1779.

VAN VECHTEN, Antony [son of Benjamin], m. Marytje Fonda. Ch: Benjamin, b. Sept. 22, 1771.

VAN VECHTEN, Teunis [son of Teunis, and Judith Ten Broeck], m. Elizabeth De Wandelaar. She d. Dec. 1, 1831, a. 77 y. 11 m. 14 d. In 1805 he was a merchant on west corner of Broadway and Malden lane. Ch: b.; Judike, Oct. 30, 1777; Pieter, July 10, 1780, d. June 3, 1795, a. 14 y. 10 m. 24 d.; Annatie, Nov. 7, 1782, d. May 31, 1817, a. 34 y. 6 m. 24 d. Theunis, Nov. 4, 1785, nephew of Abraham V. V. the eminent lawyer to whose business he succeeded, mayor 1836 and 1841, d. Feb. 1859, a. 73 y.; John, March 23, 1788.

VAN VECHTEN, Samuel [son of Teunis and Judikje Ten Broeck], of Catskil, and Sara Van Orden. Ch: bp.; Teunis, June 29, 1782; Teunis, Jan. 29, 1784; Jan, Jan. 3, 1786; Jacob, Sept 7, 1788; Benjamin, Dec. 5, 1790; Abraham, Dec. 4, 1791; Pieter, March 16, 1794; Ch: b.; Samuel, Aug. 4, 1796; William Washington, Jan. 13, 1799; Catharine Judith, June 9, 1802.

VAN VECHTEN, Abraham [son of Teunis and Judikje of Catskil], m, Catharina Schuyler, May 20, 1784. She d. Sept. 10, 1820, a. 54 y. 5 m. 18 d.; he d. Jan. 6, 1837, a. 74 y. 1 m. 1 d. He was an eminent lawyer, and held many responsible and honorable civil offices. Ch: b.; Judike, March 9, 1785, d. July 27, 1799; Philip, d. Feb. 14. 1814, a 27 y. 7 m.; Judith, d. June 6, 1800, a. 12 y.; Teunis, d. April 3, 1811, a. 23 y. 3 m. 17 d.; Geertruy, bp.; April 14, 1793, d. Feb. 25, 1794; Samuel A., b. Nov. 28, 1794, d. Dec. 14, 1824; Harmanus, July 29, 1796, d. March 29, 1802; Gertrude, July 1, 1798, m. Abraham Van Vechten of Catskil, d. Dec. 20, 1842; Judith, May 25, 1800; Jacob Ten Broeck, May 10 (14), 1801, d. Jan. 20, 1841, a. 39 y. 8 m. 10 d.; Judith, May 22, 1803, d. June 27, 1825; Maria Harriet, Aug. 28, 1805; d. March 16, 1806; Harriet Marie, March 24, 1807.

VAN VECHTEN, Gerrit Teunise, and Ann Marselis. Ch: Gerrit Teunise, b. May 10, 1797.

16

Van Velsen, *alias* Van Westbroek, Sweer Teunise, m. Maritie Myndertse, widow of Jan Barentse Wemp about 1666. In 1669, he received a conveyance of land from Mad. Johanna [DeLaet] Ebbingh, at *Lubberde's* land [Troy] according to contract with Jan Bar. Wemp; And in 1675, he sold to Jan Cornelise Vyselaer and Lucas Pieterse Coeymans a sawmill and two morgens of land on the *Poesten* kil. He received a patent in 1667, for a lot on the West corner of Van Tromp street and Broadway 9 rods square which he sold in 1678, to Wouter Aertse, having previously removed the house to Schenectady where in 1669, he had built a grist-mill and became a permanent settler. He was killed in 1690, at the sacking of the village of S. His property, which was considerable, passed to his wife's children and to the church of Schenectady.

Van Vlieren, Hieroon (Jeroon), m. Margariet Huygh Dec. 13, 1715. Ch: bp.; Jannetje, July 30, 1721; Andries, June-16, 1723; Catharina, July 25, 1725; Hieroon, July 18, 1728; Lena, April 16, 1738.

VAN VLIEREN, N—— and G——. Ch: Johannes, bp. July 16, 1732.

Van Voorhoudt, See Segers.

Van Vorst, Gillis, of Schenectady m. Lysbeth Van Eps in Schenectady, July 16, 1699. Ch: Douw, bp. Feb. 15, 1710. [See also *Schenectady Families.*]

VAN VORST, Gerrit of Schenectady, m. Sarah Schermerhorn in Schenectady, July 7, 1789. Ch: Mary b. May 31, 1798. [See also *Schenectady Families.*]

Van Vranken (Van Franken, Van Frank), Claas [Gerritse]. Ch: Gerrit; Ryckert.

VAN VRANKEN, Ryckert Claase, owned a lot in North Pearl street: with Claas Janse Van Boekhoven bought land in Niskayuna over the Mohawk River in 1672-75. Ch: Maas; Gerrit; Evert.

VAN VRANKEN, Gerrit Claase, *alias Oulis*, [or perhaps Kulernan], m. Ariaantje Uldrick; she m. Geraldus Cambefort (Comfort), Oct. 16, 1692. Ch: bp.; *Claas; Uldrick*, March 22, 1685; Maritie, Feb. 16, 1690.

VAN VRANKEN, (Van Franke) Gerrit Ryckertse (Ryckse), of Nistagieone, m. Barber Janse, Sept. 27, 1696; she was buried Dec. 21, 1747. Ch: bp.; *Ryckert*, Dec. 12, 1697; Alida, Sept. 3, 1699, buried March 12, 1729; Anna, June 20, 1703; Margarita, April 1, 1705; *Johannes*, Oct. 24, 1708; Hillegonda, Oct. 12, 1711; *Andries*, Aug. 7, 1715.

VAN VRANKEN, Claas Gerritse, of Niskayuna 1720, m. Geertruy Quackenbos in *de Kerke van Schonegtade* Dec. 30, 1704. Ch: bp.; Gerrit, Oct. 7, 1705; Lysbeth, Dec. 25, 1706; *Gerrit*, Oct. 3, 1708; Adriantje, Oct. 30, 1710; Magtelt, April 30, 1712; Sara, Feb. 21, 1714; Rachel, Dec. 25, 1715; Joannes, Oct. 25, 1719; *Petrus*. [See *Schenectady Families.*]

VAN VRANKEN, Maas Rykse, of Nistagieone 1720, m. Anna Winne who was b. Oct. 5, 1687, and d. March, 1778. Ch: bp.; Ryckert, Oct. 7, 1711; Annetie, Oct. 30, 1715; *Adam*, Dec. 8, 1717; Maas, Nov. 11, 1722; Hillegonda, June 19, 1726.

VAN VRANKEN, Evert Ryckse, of Nistagieone, m. Maretje Visscher, Nov. 14, 1709. He was buried May 24, 1748. Ch: bp.; Ryckert, Oct. 28, 1710, buried Feb. 9, 1731; Dirkje, May 17, 1713; Bastiaan, Aug. 7, 1715; *Nicolaas*, Feb. 11, 1719; Harmen, in Schenectady,

Feb. 18, 1721; Anna, March 13, 1723; Hilletie, March 21, 1725; Maria, Jan. 29, 1727.

VAN VRANKEN, Uldrick (Ulryk) [son of Gerrit Claase], m. Geertie Cregier, Aug. 22, 1720. She was buried Oct. 1, 1746; he was buried Jan. 24, 1757. Ch: bp.; Jannetie, May 7, 1721; Ariaantje, March 3, 1723; Ariaantje, Sept. 5, 1725; Gerrit, Jan. 10, 1731. [See *Schenectady Families.*]

VAN VRANKEN, Rykert [son of Gerrit Ryckse], m. Maria Bratt, in Schenectady, Feb. 9, 1723. He was buried May 1, 1746. Ch: bp.; Alida, Dec. 18, 1723; Barber, Sept. 24, 1727; Anna, Oct. 7, 1739; *Abraham ; Gerrit.* [See *Schenectady Families.*]

VAN VRANKEN, Johannes [son of Gerrit Ryckse], m. Anna .... Ch: bp.; Elizabeth, Dec. 12, 1731: Barber, April 25, 1736; Jannetie, Sept. 18, 1737; Gerrit, March 30, 1740.

VAN VRANKEN, Abraham [son of Claas Gerritse], of Niskayuna, m. Dirkje Cregier, Nov. 19, 1742. Ch: bp.; Claas; Maria, Aug. 23, 1747; Samuel, July 23, 1749 : Samuel, Oct. 13, 1754; Samuel, in Schenectady, Feb. 8, 1761. [See *Schenectady Families.*]

VAN VRANKEN, Ryckert [son of Maas], m. first in Schenectady, Annatje Truax, Oct. 14, 1738; she was buried Jan. 4, 1755; secondly, Catharina Dunbar, June 26, 1764. Ch: bp. ; Annatie, May 31, 1739; Christina, Feb. 15, 1741; Hillegonda, Dec. 15, 1742; Jannetie, Nov. 16, 1746; Jannetie and Margarieta, July 10, 1748; Maritie, Nov. 4, 1750; *Maas,* Nov. 12, 1752; Elisabeth, Dec. 26, 1754.

VAN VRANKEN, Gerrit [son of Claas Gerritse], m. Maria Fort, July 7, 1738. Ch: bp.; Gerrit, May 31, 1741; Johannes, Nov. 27, 1743; Barbara, April 27, 1746; Alida, Nov 11, 1753. [See also *Schenectady Families.*]

VAN VRANKEN, Adam [son of Maas], m. Ariaantje Clute, March 8, 1744. Ch: bp.; Maas, April 21, 1745; Geertruy, Sept. 15, 1754. [See also *Schenectady Families.*]

VAN VRANKEN, Gerrit [son of Ryckert], m. first, Susanna Egbertse (Ebbas, Ebberse); and secondly, Alida Reyly, about 1765. Ch: bp. ; Maria, Nov. 16, 1746; Elisabeth, Sept. 10, 1749; Elisabeth, Nov. 7, 1752; Geertruy, Oct. 20, 1754; Elisabeth, Dec. 31, 1758; Ryckert, b. May 14, 1766.

VAN VRANKEN, Pieter [son of Claas Gerritse], of Genistagioene, m. Neeltie Groot, in Schenectady, March 3, 1748–9. Ch: bp. ; Dirk, Jan. 19, 1752. [See also *Schenectady Families.*]

VAN VRANKEN, Andries [son of Gerrit Ryckse], m. in Schenectady, Maria Groot, August 14, 1750. Ch: bp. ; Elisabeth, Dec. 16, 1753; Barber, Sept 4, 1757. [See also *Schenectady Families.*]

VAN VRANKEN, Nicolaas [son of Evert], m. Jannetje Van Vranken. Ch: bp. ; Geertruy, Sept. 5, 1754; Evert, August 8, 1756; Ariaantje, Jan. 28, 1759.

VAN VRANKEN, Jacobus [son of Johannes Claas of Rosendaal], m. Geertje Fonda, Nov. 5, 1775. Ch: b. ; Catharina, August 24, 1778; Alida, Sept. 3, 1782.

VAN VRANKEN, Maas [son of Ryckert], m. Geertruy Veeder, Feb. 23, 1783. He was an active officer of the Revolutionary war, and d March 3, 1816. Ch: b. ; Annatie, Dec. 16, 1783; Simon. Jan. 20, 1787.

Van Vredenbergh, Willem, of Kinderhook, m. Heyltje Van Etten. Ch : Appolonia, b. Jan. 13, 1706.

Van Wagenen, Hendrik, and Annatie Landman. Ch : Albertus, bp. Jan. 31, 1790.

Van Westbroek (see also Bos), Cornelis Teunise, came to Beverwyck in 1631, a trader in 1654, when he shipped 700 beavers to Manathan. Perhaps he was a brother of Sweer Teunise Van Westbroeck alias Van Velsen, who settled in Schenectady.

Van Wie, Wye, Wey, Verwey.

VAN WIE (Wie), Hendrick Gerritse, in Beverwyck 1654–91: made will in 1690; spoke of wife and eldest son, Gerrit. In 1691, Pieter Schuyler petitioned.the governor for the relief of Hendrick Gerritse, a volunteer in the late expedition to Canada, who was desperately wounded at *Prary* in Canada, and was cared for at the house of the widow of Jacob Tys Van Der heyden He died soon after.

VAN WIE (Verwey), Teunis Gerritse, perhaps brother of the last, in Albany 1666.

VAN WIE, Gerrit [son of Hendrick], m. Agnietje (Annatie) Casparse Conyn. He was buried Dec. 20, 1746; she was buried by his house March 20, 1746. Ch : bp.; Alida, April 28, 1700; Anna, 1701; *Henrik,* 1703.

VAN WIE, Jan [son of Hendrick], m. Catharina Huyck. She was buried Sept. 2, 1748. Ch: bp.; Yda, Aug. 21, 1709, m. Gerrit Jacobse Lansingh ; Catrina, Oct. 12, 1711 ; *Hendrik,* Sept. 24, 1713; Agnietje, Jan. 15, 1716 ; *Joannes,* June 30, 1718 ; *Andries,* Nov. 20, 1720; Gerrit, April 28, 1723.

VAN WIE, Hendrik [son of Hendrick], m. Hilletje Becker, March 11, 1715. She was buried Dec. 23, 1744. Ch: bp.; *Hendrik,* Jan. 20, 1717; Antje, June 28, 1719 ; Ariaantje, Nov. 5, 1721; Ariaantje. Jan. 22, 1724 ; Johannes, July 3, 1726 ; Eytje, Sept. 15, 1728 ; Elizabeth, Aug. 8, 1731; Maria, Sept. 1, 1734; Catharyna, May 7, 1738.

VAN WIE, Hendrick, Jr. [son of Gerrit] m. Catharina [Cornelia] Waldron, Oct. 2, 1732; Ch: bp.; Agnietje, Aug. 19, 1733; Agnietje, June 18, 1735 ; *Pieter,* Feb. 27, 1737 ; *Gerrit,* Feb. 20, 1739 ; *Willem,* Oct. 19, 1740 ; *Casparus,* Dec. 5, 1742 ; Tryntje, Jan. 6, 1745 ; Hendrick, Jan. 11, 1747 ; *Cornelis,* April 9, 1749 ; Alida, Nov. 17, 1751 ; Cornelia, April 14, 1754.

VAN WIE, Johannes, Jr. [son of Jan], m. first, Gerritje Wendel, Oct. 14, 1742 : secondly, Magdalena, Loek, Aug. 8, 1759. Ch: bp.; Johannes, July 8, 1744 ; Catharina, Sept. 28, 1745 ; Johannes, Jan. 3, 1748.

VAN WIE, Andries [son of Jan], m. Lena Van Arnhem. Ch. bp.; Johannes, Nov. 23, 1746 ; *Johannes* Oct. 25, 1747; Catharina, July 23, 1749 ; Alida, Feb. 23, 1752 ; *Abraham,* Nov. 18, 1753 : *Isaac,* July 30, 1755.

VAN WIE, Hendrick Hendrickse, m. Johanna Gardenier. Ch: bp. ; Hilletje, Oct. 30, 1748 ; Hilletje, Sept. 16, 1750; Andries, Feb. 23, 1752 ; Johannes, Jan. 5, 1755 ; Anig (Anna ?), Dec. 11, 1760 ; Elizabeth, b. Dec. 19, 1763.

VAN WIE, Hendrick [son of Jan], m. Marytje Loeck (Louk). Ch: bp. ; Catarina, Feb. 17, 1751; Magdalena, April 23, 1753 ; Cornelia, July 27, 1755; Philip, Nov. 4, 1757; Johannes, Nov. 25, 1759 (?); Philip, b. April 7, 1763 ; Agnietje, b. July 12, 1765.

VAN WIE, Gerrit [son of Hendrick], m. Catharina Lansing, Sept. 10, 1762. Ch: b.; Gerrit and Ytje, March 10, 1763; *Hendrick,* May 18, 1765 ; Catharina, Aug. 27, 1767 ; Pieter, Dec. 30, 1769 ; Helena, bp.

July 27, 1772; Cornelis, b. Jan. 20, 1775; Pieter, b. April 6, 1780. [Mary the wid. of Peter G. Van W. d. May 20, 1864, a. 83 y.]

VAN WIE, Casparus [son of Hendrick], m. Jannetje Winne, April 20, 1766. He d. March 17, 1818, a. 75 y. 4 mo. 6 d.; she d. Aug. 16, 1815, a. 75 y. 8 m. 28 d. Ch: b.; Catharina, Jan. 21, 1767: Hendrik, July 11, 1769; *Benjamin*, Aug. 7, 1775; Rachel, Nov. 2, 1777; Agnietje, Dec. 16, 1780.

VAN WIE, Willem [son of Hendrick], m. Jannetie Lansing, May 20, 1767. She d. July 19, 1821, a. 75 y. Ch: b.; Hendrick, Oct. 13, 1767; Gerrit, July 23, 1770, d. June 3, 1842; Pieter, May 30, 1773, d. March 9, 1839; Isaac, Jan. 20, 1776; Isaac, July 11, 1778; Catharina, Jan. 4, 1782.

VAN WIE, Johannes [son of Andries], m. Alida Van Wie, Jan. 27, 1771. Ch: b.; Helena, Aug. 18, 1771; Andries, Dec. 28, 1774; Hendrick, May 31, 1777; Tryntje, May 6, 1780; Johannes, Oct. 30, 1784; Pieter, March 17, 1787; Abraham, July 12, 1789; Gerrit, Oct. 10, 1792.

VAN WIE, Pieter [son of Hendrik], m. Ebbetje (Abigail) Van Den Burgh, Dec. 31, 1774. Ch: b.; Hendrik, Nov. 8, 1776; Gerrit, Dec. 7, 1778; Willem, Sept. 20, 1780.

VAN WIE, Abraham [son of Andries], m. Jacomyntje Burhans, Feb. 22, 1777. Ch: b.; Andries, Dec. 5, 1777; Jannetje, Oct. 3, 1779; Johannes Burhans, Nov. 10, 1783; Gerrit, Nov. 4, 1785: Frederick, Jan. 17, 1788 Abraham, Sept. 24, 1790.

VAN WIE, Hendrick [son of Gerrit], m. Maria Merthen (Martin). Ch: b.; Hendrick, Nov. 27, 1773; Elizabeth, July 7, 1776; Peter Martin, Jan. 23, 1779; Catharina, June 22, 1781; Margarita, March 7, 1784, d. Aug. 22, 1862, a. 79 y.; Gerrit, Jan. 16, 1787; Maria, Nov. 17, 1790.

VAN WIE, Isaac [son of Andries], m. Neeltie (Eleanor) Oosterhout, Aug. 4, 1780. Ch: b.; Helena, April 31 (*sic*), 1781; Wilhelmus, Jan. 17, 1783; Maria, Dec. 26, 1784; Alida, Jan. 4, 1787; Wilhelmus, bp. Jan. 4, 1789; Catharina, b. Oct. 19, 1790; Eleanor, b. Nov. 12, 1793.

VAN WIE, Isaac, m. Christina Kettle. Ch: Jane, b. Nov. 2, 1803.

VAN WIE, Abraham, m. Jannetie Lansingh. Ch: Ariaantje, b. April 7, 1785.

VAN WIE, Cornelis [son of Hendrick Jr.], m. Anna (Nancy) Shanklin, Feb. 12, 1785; Nancy, wid. of Cornelis Van Wie, d. April 25, 1844, a. 77 y. Ch: b.; Catharina, Nov. 6, 1785; Agnieta, May 22, 1787; Jannetie, Oct. 26, 1789; Henry, Feb. 3, 1792.

VAN WIE, Gerrit, m. Mary Slingerland, Jan. 10, 1790. Ch: Jannetie, b. March 12, 1790.

VAN WIE, Benjamin [son of Casparus?], m. Magdalena (Maike, Margaret) Bogert. He d. June 9, 1837, a. 62 y.; she d. April 9, 1844, a. 67 y. Ch: b.; Sarah, June 9, 1797; Hendrick, Oct. 21, 1798; Jane, March 26, 1805; Maria, April 23, 1807; Catharine, May 27, 1810.

Van Witbeck, see Witbeck.

Van Woert, Van Schoenderwoert, Van Oort. Two brothers of this name, Teunis Jacobse, and Rutger Jacobse came out to Fort Orange, about 1640; the descendants of the former remained in Albany county and assumed the surname of *Van Woert*, those of the latter removed to New York and took the name of Rutgers. Teunis Jacobse had a

yearly salary from the patroon of Rensselaerswyck, of 90 guilders for the first 3 years and 100 gl. for the next three years. He m. Sara Denys from England, April 19, 1650, in New Amsterdam. In 1650-1, he was a trader and a *bierwercker* probably for his brother Rutger the brewer. Ch: *Jacob, Goosen?* Eva? m. Esaias Teunise Swart, of Schenectady.

VAN WOERT, Jacob Teunise, m. first Catryn Claase and secondly, Anna Loockerman, wid. of Adam Winne, Oct. 18, 1691. He was buried July 18, 1730. Ch: bp.; *Nicolaas*, June 3, 1684; Ruth; Pieter, Oct. 23, 1692; Sara, Dec. 31, 1693; Jeremias, June 16, 1695; Jeremie, May 17, 1696; Sara, Aug. 1, 1697; *Jacob*, Oct. 30, 1698; Margriet, July 21, 1700; Heyltje, Nov 2, 1701; Catharina, Dec. 24, 1704.

VAN WOERT (?), (Oort) Goosen, shoemaker, m. Maria Peek. He was for a time a resident of Schenectady. Ch: bp.; Margariet, April 14, 1686; Willem, May 16, 1690; Antje, August 14, 1692.

VAN WOERT, Nicolaas [son of Jacob], m. Dirkje, (Gerritje) Barheit, Dec. 15, 1707. Ch: bp.; Jacob, Jan. 8, 1710; Gerritje, April 20, 1712; *Andries*, March 18. 1716; Nicolaas and Catryna, May 11, 1718. She was buried March 18, 1749; Jannetie, Oct. 1, 1721; Rachel, March 15. 1724.

VAN WOERT, Ruth [son of Jacob], m. first, Elizabeth....and secondly, M. Eckbertsen, who was buried July 9, 1755. Ch: bp.; *Jacob*, Jan. 31, 1714; Catryn, March 6, 1717; Christina, Sept. 27, 1719; *Teunis*, Feb. 3, 1725; Elizabeth, Dec. 28, 1727, buried Sept. 21, 1746; *Sander*.

VAN WOERT, Jacob [son of Jacob], m. Hendrikje Oothout, Oct. 17, 1723. Ch: bp.; *Jacob*, Jan. 8, 1724; Johannes, Nov. 7, 1725, buried Aug. 26, 1746; Anneke, Nov. 5, 1727; Alida, Dec. 2, 1729; Sara, Oct. 2, 1731; Fytje, Oct. 14, 1733; *Petrus*, Nov. 16, 1735; *Louis*, Jan. 11, 1738; Mydert, Feb. 17, 1740; Rebecca, May 16, 1742; Eva, March 11, 1744; Myndert, May 25, 1746; Margarieta, Dec. 6, 1748.

VAN WOERT, Jacob Rutsche, m. first, Maria.... ; and secondly, Annatie Ouderkerk, May 13, 1738. She was buried April 3, 1749. Ch: bp.; Nicolaas, March 3, 1735; Maria, Dec. 8, 1736; Elizabeth, Sept. 17, 1738; *Eldert*, July 27, 1740; Rutger, Oct. 30, 1743; Lena, April 27, 1746.

VAN WOERT, Alexander [son of Ruth], m. Elizabeth Becker, Oct. 5, 1735. He was buried Sept. 8, 1746. Ch: bp.; Rutger, Aug. 1, 1736; Antje, March 6, 1738; Elizabeth, Dec. 3, 1740; Johannes, Jan. 5, 1743; Mattheus, Oct. 6, 1745.

VAN WOERT, Andries [son of Nicolaas], m. Elizabeth Van Derwerken, Nov. 1, 1740. Ch: bp.; Dirkje, May 7, 1741; Hendrick, March 29, 1747.

VAN WOERT, Jacob Jacobse, and Elizabet Fort. She was buried May 30, 1756. Ch: bp.; Johannes, June 17, 1750; Jacobus, July 7, 1754.

VAN WOERT, Teunis [son of Rutger], m. Elizabeth Van Deusen. Ch: bp.; Elizabeth, Nov. 24, 1751; Bata, Jan. 14, 1753; Rutger, Sept. 28, 1755; Rutger, Feb. 26, 1758; Elizabeth, b. March 21, 1760; Cornelia, Nov. 16, 1762; Catharina, Oct. 2, 1766.

VAN WOERT, Petrus Jacobse, m. Rachel Ridder, Oct. 25, 1760. Ch: Hendrikje, bp. Aug. 30, 1761; Annatie, b. March 9, 1764.

VAN WOERT, Louis [son of Jacob], m. Catharyntje Van Den Bergh, Oct. 10, 1765. Ch: b.; Hendrikie, Aug. 2, 1766; Catharina, Oct. 22, 1768; Jacob, March

5, 1771; Folkie, June 5, 1773; Rachel, bp. Oct. 28, 1778.

VAN WOERT, Eldert [son of Jacob Rutse], m, Elizabeth Fonda. Ch: b.; Annatie, June 2, 1770; Catharina, Jan. 1, 1772; Helena, Sept. 7, 1773; Alida, Dec. 24, 1775; Jacob, May 8, 1778; Geertje, Jan. 5, 1780; Elizabeth, June 2, 1788.

VAN WOERT, Johannes, Jr., m. Cathalyna Lansing, June 20, 1770. Ch: b.: Elizabeth, Feb. 17, 1772; Jacob Lansing, Jan. 9, 1774; Hubertje, Oct. 15, 1776; Sara, June 8, 1778; Helena, March 22, 1780; Hendrikje, bp. Dec. 3, 1781; Willemple, b. May 25, 1783; Pieter, bp. June 12, 1785; Cathalina. b. Aug. 26, 1787.

VAN WOERT, Hendrik [son of Andries ?], m. Catharina Eights, Henry Van Wie an old Revolutionary officer, d. Feb. 5, 1813, a. 65 y. 10 m.; she d. Oct. 3 (4) 1825, a. 74 y. Ch: b.; Abraham, Feb. 13, 1777; Elizabeth, Aug. 21, 1779; Elizabeth, Feb. 14, 1782; Hendrick, April 3, 1784; William. Sept. 7, 1786; Catharine, April 29, 1788; Catharine, Oct. 19, 1791.

VAN WOERT, Jacob, m. Sara Van Ness, March 30, 1777. Ch: b.; Johannes, Dec. 21, 1781; Pieter, Feb. 15, 1784; Elizabeth, Jan. 12, 1788; Hadriaan, March 16, 1790; Elizabeth, Feb, 18, 1793; Jacob, Nov. 15,1796.

Van Woggelum, see Soegemakelyk.

Van Wurmdrick, Cornelis Laurentse, m. Annatje Van Petten, widow of Claas Sieverse, Feb. 9, 1709. Ch: bp.; Lourens, Nov. 13, 1709; Frederik, April 20, 1712; Anna, Dec. 25, 1714.

Van Yveren or Iveren, see Myndertse.

Van Zandt, Van Santen, Van Sant. [In the oldest records this name is Van Santen.]

VAN ZANDT, Jan, and Jannetie.... Ch : *Johannes ; Joseph.* [This family is of Spanish origin.]

VAN ZANDT (Sant), Johannes [son of Jan], turner, m. Margrieta Vanderpoel, and about 1693, removed to New York, Ch: bp. : in Albany, *Wynant,* Dec. 23, 1683; Jannetje March 17, 1686; Adam, Dec. 18, 1687; Johannes, Aug. 3, 1690; Catarina, Nov 27, 1692; Ch. bp. in New York. Isaac, March 10, 1695; Margariet, Feb. 7, 1697; Maria, Aug. 1698; Cornelia, Aug. 15, 1703.

VAN ZANDT [Van Santen], Joseph Janse, m. Seitje Marcelis, 1688. He was a Spaniard by birth; naturalized Dec. 6, 1715; buried Oct. 16, 1753. Ch: bp.; Jannetje, Aug. 11, 1689; Anna, May 4, 1693; *Gerrit,* Oct. 4, 1695; Maria, Jan. 2, 1698; Anthony, Oct. 27, 1700, buried Sept. 2, 1751; Celia, Aug. 1, 1703; *David,* Aug. 6, 1704 : *Gysbert,* Dec. 22, 1706; Celia, June 12, 1709; *Johannes.*

VAN ZANDT, Wynant, of New York probably m. a dau. of Pieter Praa. Ch. bp. in New York, Pieter Praa, May 30, 1708; Elizabeth, Aug 24, 1712; Margarietje, Sept. 12, 1714; Tobias, May 6, 1716; Tobias, March 23, 1718; Catharina, Oct. 4, 1719.

VAN ZANDT, Joannes [son of Joseph], m. Sara Hilten, May 20, 1718. She was buried Sept. 6, 1743. Ch: bp.; Joseph, July 27, 1718; *Joseph,* Sept. 4, 1720; Anna, Nov. 25, 1722; Sara, March 22, 1724; *Willem,* Sept. 5, 1725; Gerrit, March 5, 1727; *Johannes,* Dec. 8, 1728; Gerrit, Jan. 3, 1731, d. July 16, 1806, a. 76 y.; *Jacobus,* Nov..... 1732; *Gysbert,* March 10, 1734; Elizabeth, Dec. 3, 1738.

VAN ZANDT (Santen), Gerrit [son of Joseph], m. first, Antie Van Den Bergh, Nov. 18, 1727; secondly, Hester Winne about 1755; she d. Aug. 24, 1813, a.

81 y. 8 m. 10 d. Ch: bp.; Maria, April 20, 1729; Rykert, Aug. 22, 1731; Catharina, Jan. 7, 1733; *Rykert,* Nov. 2, 1735; Anna, April 16, 1738; Rachel, Feb. 8, 1741; Sara, Jan. 15, 1744; Joseph, June 21, 1747; Johannes, July 9, 1756; Rachel, May 24, 1759; Sara, b. Sept. 14, 1762.

VAN ZANDT (Santen) Gysbert [son of Joseph], m. first, Margrietje Kaarn (Carel), Feb. 22, 1740. Ch: bp.; *Joseph,* Jan. 11, 1741; *Hendrick,* Oct. 24, 1742: Marytje, Oct. 25, 1747; Elizabeth, April 26, 1752.

VAN ZANDT (Santen) David [son of Joseph], m. first, Rachel Hooghteling, April 20, 1745; she was buried Jan. 11, 1746; secondly, Ariaantje Fort about 1748. Ch: bp.; Joseph, Jan. 12, 1746; Joseph, March 5, 1749; Daniel, June 2, 1751; Anthony, June 17, 1753; Rachel, March 21, 1756.

VAN ZANDT (Santen) Willem, [son of Johannes], m. Alida Smith. Ch: bp. ; Sara, Dec. 25, 1750; Sara, May 6, 1753; Johannes ...., buried April 6, 1756; *Johannes,* Aug. 7, 1757. Ch: b.; Margarita, Feb. 28, 1760; Thomas, Aug. 9, 1763; Willem, Oct. 13, 1767; Annatje, Jan. 12, 1772.

VAN ZANDT (Santen) Johannes, Jr. [son of Johannes], m. Margarita Wilkinson, Aug. 23, 1754. Ch: bp.; Sara, July 13, 1755; Sara, Nov. 27, 1757; Sara, Nov. 4, 1758; Sara, Oct. 18, 1761, d. March 26, 1835, a. 74 y. Ch: b.; *Thomas,* Sept. 23, 1763; Annatie, Jan. 9, 1764; Johannes, Aug. 3, 1766; Maria, Nov. 6, 1767; Johannes, April 3, 1769; Margarita, March 25, 1770; Johannes, Nov. 8, 1771; Alida, Jan. 24, 1773: Celia, June 16, 1775; Johannes, Feb. 1, 1778.

VAN ZANDT (Santen) Joseph [son of Johannes], m. Maria Brouwer. Ch : Sara, bp. May 9, 1756.

VAN ZANDT (Santen) Gysbert [son of Johannes], m. Rebecca Winne, Oct. 25,1759. Ch: b.; *Johannes,* April 30, 1762; Rachel, Aug. 8, 1764; *Benjamin,* May 8, 1767; Gerrit, Sept. 5, 1769; Gerrit, Nov. 8, 1771; Sara, Sept. 19, 1774; Hester, Sept. 14, 1777; Annatie, Feb. 28. 1780.

VAN ZANDT (Santen) Jacobus [son of Johannes], m. Molly (Maria) Broecks, Dec. 24, 1758. He d. Nov. 8, 1795, a. 62 y. 11 m. 19, d. She d. may 29, 1814, a. 75 y. Ch: b.; Rebecca, Oct. 30, 1762; Johannes, March 21, 1767, d. April 28, 1858, a. 91 y.

VAN ZANDT (Santen) Rykert [son of Gerrit], m. Sara Hilten, Jan. 20, 1765. He d. June 6, 1814, a. 78 y. 6 m. 16 d. She d. Dec. 13, 1830, a. 83 y. 5 m. 20 d. Ch: b.; *Jacobus,* May 1, 1765; Antje, Jan. 28, 1768; Gerrit, Aug. 31, 1769; Joseph, July 31, 1773, d. March 9, 1836; a. 64 y.; Willem, bp. Oct. 13, 1776; Antje, b. Sept. 15, 1779; Judike, b. Oct. 1, 1785; Maritie, Oct. 25, 1790.

VAN ZANDT (Santen) Joseph [son of Gysbert], m. Rebecca De Garmo, Nov. 13, 1766. Ch: b.; Gysbert, Oct. 15, 1769; Margarita, June 26, 1772; Hester, May 19, 1774 ;·Johannes, Oct. 17, 1780; Margarita, July 16, 1783.

VAN ZANDT (Santen) Hendrick [son of Gysbert ?] m. Catharine De Garmo. Ch : Peter, b. Sept. 12, 1775.

VAN ZANDT (Santen), Johannes [son of Willem], m. Margarita (Maria) Burgess (Burjhess, Burses), Oct.6, 1782. [Johannes Van S. and Elizabeth Van Santen, m. Nov. 19, 1780.] He d. at Watervliet, May 17. 1829, a. 72 y. Ch : b. ; Willem, Oct. 10, 1783. Elizabeth, May 3, 1786; Willem, May 29, 1788; John May 7, 1791; John, Jan. 11, 1793; Gerrit, April 4, 1794; Mary, Aug. 15, 1797.

Van Zandt (Santen), Benjamin [son of Gysbert], m. Sara Visscher, Aug. 5, 1787. Ch: b.; Rebecca, March 29, 1788; Sarah, Jan. 11, 1790; Barent, Dec. 29, 1792.

Van Zandt (Santen), John G. [son of Gysbert?] m. Leentje (Helena) Lansing, Aug. 30, 1787. Ch: b.; Jacob, June 24, 1788; Willempie, June 13, 1797: John, Sept. 18, 1801.

Van Zandt, Gerrit [son of Rykert], m. Caty Hilten, Dec. 2, 1792 (*sic*). He d. May 5, 1840, a. 72 y. she d. April 13, 1851, a. 79 y. Ch: David, bp. Dec. 1, 1792; Sarah, b. Aug. 3, 1793; Margaret, b. July 2, 1797.

Van Zandt, Thomas [son of Johannes, Jr.], m. Rebecca Hooghkerk, Feb. 25, 1792. Ch: b.; Elizabeth, Jan. 3, 1793; Abraham, Oct. 16, 1795: Margaret, Aug. 2, 1797; John, Oct. 4, 1804.

Van Zandt, James [son of Rykert], m. Mary. Ch: b.; John, Oct. 27, 1793; Gerrit, June 28, 1795; Sarah, Sept. 4, 1796; Margaret, Aug. 28, 1798; Anna, July 5, 1802.

Van Zandt, Jacobus, and Alida ..... Ch: Alida, b. July 22, 1799.

Varley, Barnard (Peter), m. Rachel Bulsen. Ch: John, bp. Jan. 6, 1793; Gertrude, b. Nov. 8, 1795.

Vedder, Harmen Albertse, trader, owned land at Schenectady, *Steen Raby* (Lansingburgh), and several house lots in Albany. His children settled in Schenectady.

Vedder, Arent [son of Harmen] of Schenectady, m. Sara Groot. Ch: Rebecca, Oct. 25, 1691; Agnietje, Feb. 11, 1694. [See also *Schenectady Families.*]

Vedder, Harmanus, Jr., of Schenectady [son of Harmen], m. Margrieta (Jacques) Van Slyck, widow of Andries Bratt, Dec. 10, 1691. Ch: bp.; Antje, March 27, 1792; Harmen, Jan. 1, 1698. [See also *Schenectady Families.*]

Vedder, Albert [son of Harmen] of Schenectady m. Maria Glen, in Schenectady; Dec. 17, 1699. Ch: bp.; Catharina, Dec. 25, 1706; Alexander; Feb. 20, 1709. [See also *Schenectady Families.*]

Vedder, Johannes, m. Maria Fort (Van der Vort), in Schenectady, July 8, 1705. Ch: bp; Hermanus, June 8, 1707; Margarita, April 28, 1710; Anna, June 21, 1713. [See also *Schenectady Families.*]

Vedder, Corset, of *Halve Maan* 1715, Schaatkooke, 1720, m. first, Margarita Barrith, March 3, 1709, *voor'r kinds doopdag gesturven*; secondly, Neeltie Christaianse, March 11, 1711. Ch: bp.; Anna Margarita, Jan. 8, 1710; Isaac, Feb. 10, 1712; Anna, Aug. 7, 1713; Christiaan, Jan. 7, 1720. [See also *Schenectady Families.*]

Vedder, Corset (Gerzet) of Niskayuna, m. Neeltje Borda (Birch). Ch: bp.; Harmanus, March 1, 1762; Marytje, July 13, 1766. [See also *Schenectady Families.*]

Vedder, Arent J., and Jannetie Hoghing. Ch: Susannah, b. July 31, 1776.

Vedder, Harmanus, of Niskayuna, m. Elizabeth Basset, May 19, 1788. Ch: b.; Cornelius Basset, Sept. 8, 1797; Eleanor, June 5, 1796.

Vedder, Cornelius, and Caty V. Duicher. Ch: Peter, b. Oct. 16, 1792.

Veeder, Symon Volckertse, *de bakker*, one of the early settlers of Schenectady. He owned a house and lot at Manathans, in 1654, which he sold for 30 beavers; another in Beverwyck, besides a bouwery at Schenectady, where he settled in 1662. He had four sons, Pieter, Gerrit, Johannes, and Volkert, who left families; also three daughters.

Veeder, Gerrit Symonse, of Schenectady, m. Tryntje Helmerse Otten, Aug. 3, 1690. Ch: bp.; Engeltje, Aug. 27, 1693; Magdalena, April 28, 1710. [See also *Schenectady Families.*]

Veeder, Pieter Symonse, of Schenectady, m. Neeltje Van der Volgen. Ch: bp.; Maria, Feb. 19, 1707; Pieter, June 26, 1709; at the date the last child's baptism the father was not living. [See also *Schenectady Families.*]

Veeder, Johannes Symonse, of manor Rensselaerswick, 1720, m. first, Susanna Wemple in Schenectady Nov. 19, 1697; and secondly, Susanna Wendel, June 3, 1718; she was buried in the church, Nov. 16, 1739. Ch: bp.; Simon b. Oct. 30, 1709; Ariaantje, May 31, 1719. [See also *Schenectady Families.*]

Veeder, Volkert Symonse, of Schenectady, m. Jannetje Schermerhooren, Aug. 6, 1698. Ch: bp; Magdalena, Oct. 30, 1709; Susanna, April 20, 1712; Joannes, May 23, 1714. [See *Schenectady Families.*]

Veeder, Simon, m. first, Geertruy Kip, Dec. 17, 1730; she was buried July 20, 1746; secondly, Annatie Van Antwerpen, about 1749; Ch: bp.; Pieter, Sept. 26, 1731; Geertje, Oct. 28, 1733; Pieter Symonse, Feb. 10, 1737; Abraham, June 20, 1742; Geertruy, Jan. 14, 1750; Johannes, Jan. 1, 1755; Geertruy, Sept. 10, 1758.

Veeder, Myndert, m. Elizabeth Douw, Dec. 19, 1733. Ch: bp.; Johannes, June 29, 1734; Volkert, Oct. 3, 1736; Symon, Feb. 20, 1739; Abraham, Oct. 18, 1741; Susanna, April 20, 1744; Myndert, Dec. 14, 1746; Margarita, Jan. 14, 1753; Jacob, Jan. 14, 1759.

Veeder, Simon Johannese, and Catalyntje Veeder, *beide van Noormanskil,* m. April 9, 1752. He was called "merchant of Albany," 1770. Ch: bp.; Susanna, July 26, 1752; Johannes Simonse, March 12, 1755; Lucas Wyngart, July 24, 1757; Volkert, b. June 14, 1760.

Veeder, Pieter Symonse, of Albany, m. Marytje Van Den Bergh, March 13, 1762. Ch: b.; Geertruit, May 26, 1763; Cornelis, March 12, 1766.

Veeder, Abraham, and Sara Hansen. Ch: bp; Isaac, Sept. 12, 1775; Pieter, July 1, 1787.

Veeder, Abraham, and Neeltje Schuyler. Ch: b.; Elizabeth, July 6, 1781; Geertruy, July 27, 1789; Myndert, July 5, 1793.

Veeder, Johannes, and Catharina Winne [John V. and Catharine De Long. m. June 3, 1797.] Ch: b.; Annatie, April 20, 1787; Frans, Jan. 2, 1789; Rebecca, and Simon, twins, March 4, 1792; Simon, Oct. 16, 1793; Rebecca, March 10, 1797; Ann, Jan. 28, 1799.

Veeder, Arent S., and Jannetie Hoghingh. Ch: Anna, b. Dec. 10, 1787.

Veeder, Jacob, of Normanskil, m. Catharine Spawn, March 4, 1787. Ch: b.; Jochum, Oct. 30, 1789; Jochum, April 1, 1791.

Veeder, Volkert S., and Ann Quackenbush. Ch: b.; Catelyntje, March 18, 1791; Anna, bp. Feb. 15, 1794; d. Aug. 24, 1797, a. 2 y. 12 d.; Anne, b. Aug. 12, 1795, d. July 9, 1795, a. 17 m.; Elizabeth, b. Feb. 16, 1798; Maria, b. Jan. 22, 1801, d. June 13, 1803.

VEEDER, Lucas W., of Schenectady, m. Susanna Bratt. Ch: b.; Elias, Jan. 1, 1794; Volkert, July 8, 1796. [See also *Schenectady Families*.]

VEEDER, Myndert, and Elizabeth Perry. Ch: Rynier, b. Jan. 31, 1797.

Venton, William, m. Annatje Egmond, March 31, 1762. Ch: Maria, bp. Oct. 12, 1766; Jacob, b. April 23, 1768.

VENTON, Robert, and Margaret Adams. Ch: Mary b. Dec. 28, 1779.

Verbeeck, Jan or Johannes, came to Fort Orange, in 1635; probably returned to Holland, and brought over his family in 1648, arriving in Manathans with Anthony De Hooges, Nov. 29, in the ship *King David.* He was b. in 1612, and d. in 1698, a. 86 y. He was a considerable dealer in real estate in the village of Beverwyck; magistrate for many years and orphan master. If he left any children their names do not appear in the records, unless Gerrit Verbeek, who was accidentally killed in 1670, by Jan Roeloffse, was one.

Verbrugge (Van Brugh), Johannes Pieterse, from Haarlem in Holland, was b. in 1624. He was a trader in New Amsterdam and Beverwyck, and in 1657, sent down from B. 300 beaver skins ; m. Catrina Roeloffse, dau. of the noted Anneke Janse and widow of Lucas Rodenburgh, March 29, 1658, in New Amsterdam where all his children were b. and bp. He made his will Dec. 22, 1696, and d. in 1697. [*Valentine's Man.*, 1861, 1864, 1866.] Ch: bp.; Helena, April 4, 1659; Helena, July 28, 1660, m. Teunis De Kay ; Anna, Sept. 10, 1662, m. Andries Grevenraedt; Catharina, April 19, 1665, m. Hendrick Van Rensselaer; Pieter, July 14, 1666 ; Maria, Sept. 20, 1673, m. Stephen Richard; *Johannes.*

VERBRUGGE (Van Brugh), Capt. Pieter [son of the last] ; mayor of Albany, 1699, 1700, 1721–3; had a house lot on the south side of State street west of Pearl and near the stockades, the lot of his father-in-law, Hendrick Cuyler; was buried in the church July 20, 1740. He m. Sara, dau. of Hendrick and Anna Cuyler, of Albany, Nov. 2, 1688, in New York. Ch: Catharine, bp. in New York, Nov. 10, 1689.

VERBRUGGE (Van Brugh), Johannes [son of Johannes], m. Margarita Provoost, July 9, 1696, in New York. Ch: bp. in N. Y., Johannes, May 16, 1697; Johannes, Aug. 6, 1699; Catharina, Aug. 16, 1704 ; David, Sept. 12, 1708; Elizabeth, March 26, 1712.

Vermeulen, Hendrick Gerritse, in Albany, 1667–71, in 1667, bought house and lot of Cornelis Van Nes, on S. corner of Broadway and Maiden Lane, which he conveyed same day to Arent Janse.

Vernoy, Cornelis, and Sara Ten Broeck. Ch: Cornelis, bp. Jan. 6, 1706.

Verplanck (Planck), Abraham Isaacse, of New Amsterdam, m. Maria, dau. of Guleyn Vigne and Adriaantie Cuvilje. She d. in 1671; he d. about 1691. Ch: Abigail, m. A. Van Laets; Catalyna, m. David Pieterse Schuyler of Beverwyck; *Guleyn,* b. Jan. 1, 1637 ; Isaac, bp. June 26, 1641 ; Susanna, bp. May 25, 1642, m. Marten Van Woert; Jacomyntje, bp. July 6, 1644 ; Ariaantje, bp. Dec. 2, 1646 ; Hillegond, bp. Nov. 1, 1648 ; *Isaac,* bp. Feb. 26, 1651.

VERPLANCK, Guleyn [son of Abraham], merchant of New Amsterdam, m. Hendrikje Wessels of Aernhem, June 20, 1668. He d. April 23, 1684, and she m. Jacobus Kip, May 29, 1685. Ch: bp. ; in New York.

Samuel, b. Dec. 16, bp. Dec. 19, 1669; Abraham, bp. Jan. 24, 1674 ; Anna, bp. Sept. 15, 1680 ; Guleyn, bp. June 29, 1684.

VERPLANCK, Samuel [son of Guleyn], of New York, m. Ariaantje, dau. of Balthazar Bayard, Oct. 26, 1691. He d. at sea Nov. 20, 1698. Ch. bp. in New York: Maria. Sept. 2, 1692; Henrica, Aug. 19, 1694; Hendrik, June 17, 1696; Guleyn, b. May 31, 1698.

VERPLANCK, Isaac [son of Abraham], shoemaker, of Albany, m. Abigail Uytenbogart; she was a wid. in 1729. Ch. bp. in Albany: *Isaac; Jacobus;* Abigail, buried Feb. 26, 1729; Jacob, June 21, 1684; Dirkje, Sept. 19, 1686 ; Jacob, Oct. 28, 1688 ; *Guleyn,* June 18, 1693; *David,* April 14, 1695; Catalyntje, Jan. 19, 1698; Rachel, May, 12, 1700, m. —— Winne, and a wid. in 1735.

[VERPLANCK ?] Abraham Isaacse, *fort sluyter*, 1695, Ch: bp. ; Isaac, March 14, 1688 : Marie, Feb. 12, 1690 ; Sacharias, Jan. 10, 1692 ; Jacob, Feb. 18, 1694 ; Jannetje, Nov. 17, 1695.

VERPLANCK, Jacobus 'Isaacse, of New York, m. Margareta Schuyler of Albany, Sept. 8, 1691. Ch: bp. ; Jannetie in Albany, April 13, 1690 ; *Philip* in New York, June 3, 1695.

VERPLANCK, Isaac [son of Isaac], m. Amarencie.... Ch : bp. ; Isaac, Feb. 4, 1715 ; Cornelia, July 29, 1716 ; Abraham, Oct. 19, 1718, buried, Nov. 28, 1742 ; Abigail, Oct. 30, 1720.

VERPLANCK, Philip [son of Jacobus], m. Geertruy.... Ch: bp ; Jacobus, Jan. 15, 1721 ; Johannes, Feb. 20, 1723 ; Margarita, Jan. 20, 1725 ; Johannes, June 4, 1727.

VERPLANCK, Guleyn [son of Isaac], m. Ariaantje Van der Poel, Dec. 11, 1724. He was buried July 7, 1749. Ch: bp. ; Isaac, Oct. 1, 1725; *Willem*, Nov. 19, 1727; Abigail, Dec. 8, 1729; Melchert, Dec. 5, 1731; Elizabeth, July 12, 1734; *Abraham*, May 6, 1739.

VERPLANCK, David [son of Isaac], of Beeren island, m. first, Ariaantje, dau. of Barent Pieterse Coeymans, July 16, 1723, who d. without issue; secondly, ... Brouwer; and thirdly, Catrina Boom, Nov. 10, 1752. Ch: David, bp. Sept. 4, 1748 : Johannes, Oct. 12, 1752 ; Ariaantje, July 1,·1753: Isaac, b. 1759; d. at Coeymans, Feb. 4, 1836, a. 77 y.

VERPLANCK, Willem [son of Guleyn], of Albany, m. Lidia Liverse, July 7, 1759. Ch: bp ; Ariaantje, May 4, 1760 ; Rachel, Oct. 11, 1762; Guleyn, July 16, 1765.

VERPLANCK, Abraham [son of Guleyn], m. first, Marytje Bogart, Aug. 8, 1761 ; secondly, Hendrikje Lansing, July 18, 1772. Ch: b.; Guleyn, Jan. 19, 1763; Ariaantje, May 26, 1768.

Verwey, see Van Wie.

Victory, John, and Mary Pangburn. Ch: b.; Edmund, Feb. 5, 1793; John, Oct. 5, 1790.

Viele, Cornelis Cornelise, owned a lot on the west corner of State and South Pearl streets which he sold to Richard Pretty, in 1673; 1668, bought a bowery in Schenectady, which he sold in 1670, to Jurriaan Theunise Tappen, in exchange for a house and lot on south side of State street west of Pearl. Ch: *Arnout ; Cornelis; Pieter.*

VIELE, Arnout Cornelise, Indian interpreter for many years at all the great meetings held by the natives in Albany, and held in high esteem by them,

THE OLD KOEYMANS MANSION.

Barent Pieterse Koeymans was the original settler, having emigrated to this country from Utrecht, Holland, in 1636, and engaged himself as miller to the first Patroon. He afterwards purchased of the Katskill Indians a tract of land having ten or twelve miles front on the Hudson river and extending westward to the head of the waters falling into the Hudson. A litigation followed between him and the Patroon, which terminated in favor of Koeymans, and in 1714 he obtained a patent from Queen Anne confirming the whole tract to him.

Barent Pieterse Koeymans had five children, and two only remained in Coeymans, the other three settled in other portions of the country. The two who continued to live on the Koeymans patent were Peter and Ariaantje. Peter married twice, but had no male descendants; but left five daughters, all of whom were married. Of the two daughters of his first wife, Mayica married Andreas Witbeck and Elizabeth married Jacob Van Alen. Of the three daughters by his second wife Gerritje married John Barclay; Anne Margaret married Andreas Ten Eyck; Charlotte A. married John Bronck. As we said before, there being no male issue, the family name of Koeymans became extinct in this locality with the death of Peter Koeymans.

Ariaantje Koeymans was married to David Verplank when she was of the age of 47, and died without issue. David Verplank subsequently married and left a large family of children: David inherited Ariaantje's portion of her father's property The property now known as the old Stone House and all that portion that is now owned by the Ten Eyck family came to them from Peter Koeymans — Ariaantje having never owned any property north of Coeymans creek.

Elizabeth Van Dalson, great granddaughter of Peter Koeymans, married Abraham Verplank, and was the only member of the Verplank family related to the Koeymans family.

Major Verplank, to whose memory a monument has been lately erected in the Cemetery, was in no way related to the old Koeymans family.

The original Koeymans mansion, or Castle as it was called, stood on the site of the building now occupied by the family of the late Josiah Sherman. — *Coeymans Gazette.* See also *Annals Albany*, and *Hist. Collections Albany*, for further notices of this family. Also O'Callaghan's *New Netherland*.

m. Gerritje Gerritse, from Amsterdam, in 1677. Ch: Aernout ; Willempie (?) w. of Simon Jacobse Schermerhorn. Aernout was carried away from Schenectady in 1690 by the French and Indians and was absent three years before his return.

VIELE, Pieter Cornelise, bought a bouwery at Schenectady, in 1670

VIELE, Cornelis Cornelise, chirurgeon, admitted freeman of New York city 1698, m. first, ... ; secondly, Catharina Bogardus, in New York, April 24, 1693. Ch: bp. ; Volkert, in Albany, Dec. 1, 1689 ; Sara, in N. Y. April 24, 1695 ; Cornelis, in N. Y. Dec. 16, 1702.

VIELE, Lewis, of Schaatkook, and Maria Freer. Ch: bp. ; *Isaac*, April 28, 1710 ; *Abraham*, Sept. 26, 1715 ; *Jacob*, June 21, 1719 ; *Teunis ; Pieter ; Hugo*.

VIELE, Teunis [son of Lewis], m. Maria Fonda, Oct. 12, 1724. Ch: bp. ; Lowys, Aug. 30, 1725 ; *John*, Sept. 17, 1727 ; Maria, Feb. 1, 1730 ; Rebecca, Oct. 30, 1732 ; Stephanus, June 2, 1735 ; Stephanus, July 1, 1736 ; Jannetie, Nov. 20, 1737 ; Catharina, Sept 28, 1740 ; Pieter, Oct. 21, 1744.

VIELE, Pieter [son of Lewis], m. Catharina Van Schaick, June 23, 1728. Ch: bp. ; Lowys, Jan. 22, 1729 ; Sara, August 2, 1730 ; Maria, June 4, 1732.

VIELE, Hugo [son of Lewis], of Schachtekook, m. first, Catharina Van Woert, Feb. 13, 1728 ; and secondly, Elisabeth Van Vechten, widow, Sept. 17, 1752. Ch: bp. ; Lodewicus, April 20, 1729 ; Jacob, August 2, 1730 ; Maria, May 27, 1733 ; Stephanus, Oct. 26, 1735 ; Maria, May 14, 1737 ; Anna, Feb. 17, 1739 ; Sara, Feb. 14, 1742 ; Pieter, Jan. 12, 1746.

VIELE [probably Veeder], Myndert, and Elisabeth ....Ch: Volkert, bp. Oct. 3, 1736.

VIELE, Isaac [son of Lewis], and Hendrikje....Ch: bp. ; Maria, July 3, 1737 ; Lammetje, Jan. 23, 1740 ; Lodewicus Biblicus Jacobus, April 1, 1743.

VIELE, Jacob [son of Lewis], m. Eva Fort, July 4, 1742. Ch: bp. ; Lodovicus, in Schenectady, Oct. 17, 1742 ; Abraham, August 25, 1745 ; Maria, July 12, 1750 ; *Stephanus*, August 3, 1753 ; Annatje, May 27, 1756 ; Johannes, June 24, 1759. [Jacob Viele and Catarina Coddington, m. Nov. 10, 1757.]

VIELE, Abraham [son of Lewis], m. Francina Fort, Jan. 22, 1739, and was buried June 28, 1746. Ch: Johannes, Jan. 12. 1746.

VIELE, Lewis [son of Teunis], and Annatie Quackenbosch. Ch: bp. ; Maria, Feb. 24, 1754 ; Elizabeth, Jan. 30, 1757 ; Teunis, Aug. 5, 1759 ; Teunis, Feb. 14, 1762 ; Stephanus, b. Feb. 3, 1767.

VIELE, John [son of Teunis], m. Geesje Slingerland, Aug. 15, 1759. Ch: b. ; Cornelia, bp. March 15, 1761 ; Teunis, b. Dec. 15, 1762 ; Maria, Jan. 21, 1764 ; Theunis, Nov. 19, 1765 ; Maria, Dec. 1, 1769.

VIELE, Philip G., and Maria Bratt. Ch: b. ; Catharina, April 11, 1773 ; Barent Bratt, June 7, 1775 ; Gerrit, Dec. 28, 1777 ; Rebecca, Aug. 13, 1780.

VIELE, Philip, and Maria Van Den Bergh. Ch: Alexander,,b. Aug. 24, 1795.

VIELE, Simeon, and Neeltie Palmatier. Ch: b. ; Cornelius, April 30, 1777 ; Ariaantje, June 12, 1779.

VIELE, Stephanus [son of Jacob] of Saratoga, and Sara Toll. Ch: Jacob, bp. in Schenectady, Jan. 30, 1774 ; Ludovicus, b. Oct. 3, 1777 ; Hester, b. June 23, 1789.

Vieling, Memay, and Sarah Stierbrander. Ch: Mary, b. April 11, 1791.

Villeroy, see De Garmo.

Vinhagen, Jan Dirkse, tailor, b. 1633, in Geemen, Holland, in 1669, owned a lot in the Exchange Block fronting State street ; was living in 1708. Ch: *Johannes*.

VINHAGEN, Johannes, Jr., m. Maria Van Tricht, March 21, 1706. Ch: bp. ; Maria, Aug. 15, 1708 ; *Johannes*, Oct. 27, 1710 ; *Abram*, Oct. 19, 1712 ; Elizabeth, Sept. 4, 1715, m. Jonas Oothout ; Johanna, March 2, 1718 ; *Jacobus*, Aug. 20, 1720 ; Margarita, May 12, 1723.

VINHAGEN, Johannes [son of Johannes], m. Neeltie Van Den Bergh, Nov. 16, 1738 ; buried near his house, Oct. 22, 1750. Ch: bp. ; Maria, June 17, 1739 ; Geertruy, Aug. 10, 1740 ; Johannes, Feb. 14, 1742 ; Ariaantje, Dec. 11, 1743 ; Elizabeth, May 12, 1745.

VINHAGEN, Abraham [son of Johannes], m. first, Jannetie Van Buren, Feb. 27, 1741 ; who was buried May 20, 1748 ; and secondly, Catharina Bovie, about 1756. Ch: bp. ; Maria, April 25, 1742 ; Marten, June 17, 1744 ; Maria, April 8, 1748 ; Maria, Sept. 18, 1757.

VINHAGEN, Jacobus [son of Johannes.] .... Ch: *Johannes*.

VINHAGEN. Johannes [son of Jacobus], and Baatje (Van) Valkenburgh. Ch: Jacobus, bp. Sept. 18, 1777 ; Maria, b. Feb. 1, 1786.

Visbeeck, Gerrit, master of a sloop in 1665 ; 1672, conveyed to Jan Hendrickse Van Salsbergen, and Gerrit Van Slichtenhorst, a parcel of land at Claverack called *Preeuwen hoek*, on the east bank of the river.

DeVisser, Visser, Visger, Visselaar, DeVysselaar, DeVisser, Fisher.

Vyselaer, Jan Cornelise, *alias* Gouw, in Beverwyck, 1654-91 ; 1658, drew his knife and wounded squint-eyed Harmen so that Doctor D'Hinese had to be called in ; 1675, in company with Lucas Pieterse Coeymans, *hout saager*, bought of Sweer Teunise a saw mill on the Poesten kil [Troy.]

DeVisser, Frederick [probably brother of Harmen], before 1675, at which date he was deceased, had a *kleyne huyaje* on a corner of Gerrit Van Nes's lot in Greenbush.

Visscher (DeVyselaer), Harmen Bastiaanse, carpenter, born in 1619, was in New Amsterdam as early as 1649 ; and soon after came to Beverwyck. In 1675, his father lived at Hoorn, Holland. He had a garden on the river side below Hudson street, and a house lot on the west side of Pearl street between Maiden Lane and Steuben street. He was the village surveyor in 1666. His wife was Hester Tjerkse. Ch: *Johannes*, b. 1669 ; *Bastiaan ; Nanning ; Frederick ; Tjerk*.

VISSCHER, Bastiaan Harmense, brewer, m. Dirkje Teunise, dau. of Teunis Teunise *de metselaer ;* was buried April 23, 1737. Ch: bp. ; Hester, May 17, 1684 ; Maria, Oct. 10, 1686 : Geertruy, Aug. 20, 1693 ; Anna, April 26, 1696 ; *Hermanus*, Jan. 5, 1700 ; *Teunis*, April 3, 1702.

- VISSCHER, Nanning Harmense, m. Alida Vinhagen, Jan. 6, 1686 ; and was buried April 8, 1730. He was skipper of the Sloop *Mary*, in 1711. Ch: bp. ; Harmanus, Jan. 23, 1689 : Maria, Dec. 4, 1689, m. Jacob, Halenbeck ; Hester, July 21, 1692, m. Jacob Van Der Heyden ; Harmanus, Sept. 2, 1694 ; Geertruy and Alida, twins, March 8, 1696, the former m. David Van Der Heyden ; *Johannes*, Aug. 14, 1698 ; *Harmen*, Dec.

26, 1700; Alida, Aug. 1, 1703, m. Jacob Ten Eyck; *Nicolaas*, Nov. 25, 1705.

VISSCHER, (Visger) Tjerk Harmense, m. Femmetje Janse. He was buried in the church, Feb. 9, 1725. She was buried Oct. 15, 1723. Ch: bp.; Jacob, eldest son and heir, owned a lot in 1716, on north corner of Steuben street and Broadway; Geertruy, July 12, 1691; Helena, June 16, 1695; Harmanus, Dec. 18, 1698.

VISSCHER, Frederick Harmense, m. first, Margriet Hanse, Jan. 13, 1692, who d. Aug. 30, 1701; secondly, Elizabeth Sanderse Glen, widow of Evert Wendel, Jr., Dec. 15, 1705. She was buried Aug. 7, 1739. In 1715, he had a mill on the Beaverkil. Ch: bp.; Eva, July 23, 1693; Hermanus, Aug. 18, 1695; Hester, Sept. 27, 1696; Elsje, Sept. 3, 1699; Harmen, Aug. 24, 1701; Willem, Jan. 1, 1708; *Johannes*.

VISSCHER, Johannes Harmense, b. 1669; m. Elizabeth, dau. of William Nottingham. In 1713-5 he lived on or near the west corner of Steuben and Pearl streets, and was complained of for encroaching upon the lane (*rondweg*) fronting the stockades. Ch: bp.; Anna, Sept. 6, 1696; Harmanus, Nov. 27, 1698; William, May 30, 1703; Hester, Sept. 17, 1704; Elizabeth, Aug. 4, 1706: Hester, Oct. 1, 1708.

VISSCHER, (Visger) Johannes [son of Johannes?], of Schenectady, 1727, merchant m. Bethe (Elizabeth) ..... He was buried May 10, 1749; she was buried Oct. 27, 1754. Ch: bp.: Sara, Oct. 24, 1711; Johannes, Sept. 24. 1713; *Harmen*, Oct. 8, 1721 *Jacobus* (?)

VISSCHER, Johannes [son of Nanning], m. Anna Staats, Feb. 16, 1728. Ch: bp.; Catalyntje, March 31, 1723; Alida, July 18, 1728; Neeltie, March 28, 1730; Anna, Oct. 31, 1731; *Nanning*, Dec. 17, 1732; Alida, March 30, 1735; *Barent*, March 27, 1737; *Johannes*, April 23, 1739; Joachim, Dec. 21, 1740, buried Sept. 10, 1747; Gerrit, Oct. 24, 1742; Lucas, April 19, 1745.

VISSCHER (Visselaar, Fitscherler), Johannes [son of Frederick?) and Maritie....Ch: Margarita, bp. April 9, 1727.

VISSCHER, Nicolaas [son of Nanning], of Niskayuna, m. Annatie Tymesen, in Schenectady, Jan. 18, 1734. Ch: bp.; Nanning, Sept. 26, 1736; Alida, August 31, 1740; Hester, Oct. 25, 1747; Geertruy, August 12, 1750; Eldert, Feb. 11, 1753. [See also *Schenectady Families.*]

VISSCHER, Teunis [son of Bastiaan], m. Machtelt Lansing, Jan. 10, 1727. Ch: bp.; Bastiaan, March 24, 1728; Isaac, Nov. 8, 1730, buried Nov. 16, 1731; Isaac, Sept. 15, 1732; Dirkje, April 4, 1735; Jannetje, Feb. 5, 1738; Teunis, June 17, 1740; Johannes, Feb. 12, 1744; a child, name omitted, Dec. 14, 1746.

VISSCHER (Visser), Harmen [son of Bastiaan], m. Sara Wyngaart, August 4, 1731. She d. about 1764 (?) Ch: bp.; Bastiaan, Jan. 23, 1732; Gerrit, Oct. 6, 1734; Teunis, March 13, 1737; Sara, Dec. 19, 1739; Sara, Sept. 20, 1741; Lucas, Jan. 4, 1745; Dirkje, August 24, 1746; Anna, Nov. 12, 1752.

VISSCHER, Harmen, [son of Nanning], m. Rachel, dau. of Dirk Van Der Heyden, Feb. 24, 1739. He was buried in the church August 24, 1744. Ch: Nanning, bp. Dec. 2, 1739.

VISSCHER (Visger) Harmen [son of Johannes, Jr.], of Schenectady, m. Hester Van Iveren, Feb. 3, 1750. Ch: bp.; Johannes, May 26, 1751; Myndert, Oct. 7, 1753; Elisabeth, August 10, 1755; Elisabeth, June 12, 1757; Reiner, b. June 3, 1760.

VISSCHER, Bastiaan [son of Teunis] m. Engeltie Van Den Bergh, July 24, 1751. He d. May 9, 1809, a. 81 y. 1 m. 9 d.; she d. Nov. 1789, a. 59 y. Ch: bp.; *Matheus*, Dec. 15, 1751; Teunis, Oct. 27, 1754; Teunis, Sept. 11, 1757; Magtel, Sept. 9, 1760; Machtelt, b. July 17, 1762; Isaac, b. June 29, 1768; Cathalyntje, Jan. 27, 1771.

VISSCHER, Harmen F, of Schenectady, and Catarina Brouwer. Ch: Geertruy, bp. August 30, 1754. [See also *Schenectady Families.*]

VISSCHER, Jacobus [son of Johannes?] *van de Rosethans*, m. Rachel Jochemse Van Der Heyden, Oct. 25, 1756. Ch; bp.: Maria, August 21, 1757; Elisabeth, March 4, 1759.

VISSCHER, Nanning [son of Johannes], m. first, Catharyntje Wendell; secondly, Lena Lansing, Nov. 2, 1764. Ch: Johannes, bp. Nov. 15, 1760; Ch: b.; Annatie, Nov. 25, 1765; Marytje, May 16, 1767; Nicolaas, May 17, 1771; Franciscus, Oct, 27, 1777.

VISSCHER, Johannes [son of Johannes?], m. Elizabeth Bratt, May 7, 1763. Ch: b.; Neeltje, Sept. 21, 1763; Hendrikus, Nov. 28, 1764; Johannes, Jan. 18, 1766; Susanna, Jan. 10, 1769: Nanning, March 1, 1771; Rebecca, Sept. 2, 1773; Annatie, Feb. 18, 1779; Alida, April 30, 1782.

VISSCHER, Gerrit T., m. first, Alida Fonda *uit de Boght*, Oct. 29, 1762; secondly, Rachel Van Den Bergh, about 1770; she d. Oct. 5, 1799, a. 49 y. He d. Jan. 5, 1805, a. 66 y. 10 m. 29 d. Ch: b.; Annatie, Nov. 25, 1763; *Theunis*, May 28, 1765; *Hendrik*, Sept. 15, 1768; *Gerrit*, July 27, 1771.

VISSCHER, Teunis [son of Harmen], m. Barbara Fonda. Ch: b.; Annatie, Nov. 9, 1766; Harmen, Aug. 25, 1769.

VISSCHER, Barent [son of Johannes], m. Sara Visscher, April 22, 1765. She d. Aug. 22, 1822, a. 80 y. 11 m. 10 d. Ch: b.; Annatie, Aug. 25, 1766; Sara, Nov. 24, 1767; Johannes, Sept. 6, 1769, d. April 13 (15), 1825, a. 55 y. 7 m. 9 d.; Alida, Nov. 7, 1772; Harmen, Nov. 26, 1774; Alida, Feb. 8, 1777.

VISSCHER, Teunis [son of Teunis], of Niskayuna, m. Marytje Tymessen, in Schenectady, Oct. 22, 1767. [Teunis V., widower, m. Elsje Roseboom, widow, Dec. 31, 1788.] Ch: b.; Teunis, June 26, 1768; Jannetje, March 21, 1770; Johannes, Dec. 5, 1771. [See also *Schenectady Families.*]

VISSCHER, Christoffer, m. Anna (Johanna) Canker, Jan. 5, 1768. Ch: Johann Frederic, b. Sept. 15, 1771.

VISSCHER, Johannes [son of Teunis], m. Annatie Pearse, Oct. 7, 1768. Ch: Machtelt, bp. Aug. 13, 1769. Ch: b.; Johannes, March 2, 1771; Teunis Jan. 6, 1774; Elizabeth, Dec. 13, 1775; Teunis, Feb. 13, 1779; Abraham, Jan. 20, 1781; Bastiaan, Feb. 8, 1783.

VISSCHER, Mattheus, counsellor at law [son of Bastiaan], and Lydia Fryer. He d. Aug. 8, 1793, a. 42 y. She d. April 11, 1841, a. 88 y. Ch: b.; *Bastiaan*, March 13, 1773, d Oct. 2, 1884, a. 52 y.; Annatie, Oct. 25, 1778.

VISSCHER, Nanning, m. Angeniete Van Buren, Dec. 21, 1776. Ch: b.; Catharina, April 18, 1777; Sara, Aug. 24, 1779.

VISSCHER, George, and Maria Ruthen (Reddin). Ch: b.; Frederick, Oct. 15, 1779; Edward, Jan. 11, 1783.

VISSCHER, Nanning H., m. Alida Fonda, April 21, 1785. Ch: Rachel, b. Feb. 7, 1786.

VISSCHER, Teunis Gerritse, m. Alida Lansing. He d. June 19, 1829, a. 64 y. 25 d.; she d. Dec, 3 (4) 1848, a. 82 y. Ch: b.; Alida, June 1, 1787; Alida, Feb. 19, 1789; Gerrit, Feb. 16, 1793; Christopher Lansing, May 3, 1795, d. 1796; Lansing, March 17, 1797, d. Sept. 21, 1840; John Van Schaick, May 11, 1799; Annatie, June 6, 1801; James, Dec. 22, 1803, d. June 23, 1830.

VISSCHER, Teunis, m. Elizabeth Groot. Ch: b.; Catharine, Sept. 3, 1790; Eltie, June 5, 1795; Eva, Jan. 21, 1801.

VISSCHER, Henry [son of Gerrit], m. Rebecca Brooks, June 3, 1792; she d. Dec. 31, 1832, widow of late Henry V. Ch: b.; Gerrit, June 3, 1793; Pieter, June 29, 1797, d. Aug. 19, 1807; Gerrit, Nov. 2, 1799; Frances, Feb. 19, 1802; Henry Fonda, Jan. 2, 1804; Abraham, July 15, 1806; Peter, Sept. 28, 1808; Hannah, April 1, 1811.

VISSCHER, Gerrit Gerritse, and Rebecca Brooks. He d. Dec. 13, 1799, a. 27 y. 3 m. 12 d.; she d. Dec. 4, 1804, a, 30 y. 1 m. 19 d. Ch: b.; Rachel, Sept. 27, 1794; Elizabeth, March 25, 1797; Teunis, July 22, 1799.

VISSCHER, Sebastiaan [son of Mattheus], m. Rosanna Shipboy.; she d. March 5, 1837, a. 65 y. Ch: b.; Anna Matilda, Aug. 31, 1798; Matthew, Sept. 5, 1800.

Vlensburgh, see Flansburgh.

Voert, Frederic, and Debora .... Ch: Abraham, bp. Oct. 7, 1751.

Voetje, Johannes Louis, m. Frena (Trina) McGie, Dec, 3, 1765. Ch: b.; Rachel, Jan. 14, 1767; Margarita, May 5, 1770.

Volansby, see Folansbe.

Voorhees, John, m. Jannetie Van Ist (Nest). Ch: b.; Johannes, Dec. 7, 1774; Jan. June 14, 1778; Jacob, July 25, 1780; Hendrick, Nov. 21, 1783. [John J. V. d. at Newport, Herk. Co., Jan. 1, 1853, a. 83 y.]

VOORHEES, John, m. Susanna Du Mont. Ch: b.; Pieter, Dec. 23, 1787; Joseph, May 21, 1793; Cornelis, Feb. 25, 1791.

VOORHEES, John V. m. Elizabeth Wicoff. Ch: Peter Wicoff, b. Aug. 17, 1795.

VOORHEES, Jeremiah, m. Magdalena Terhune. Ch: Elizabeth, June 30, 1798.

Vos (Vosje *alias* Van Schoenderwoert), Cornelis Cornelise, *de boer*, in Beverwyck 1654-67; owned a sloop running between Beverwyck and Manathans, Reynicks skipper. His first wife was Dirckie Pieterse, who d. in 1665, when her household stuff was sold at auction to pay her funeral expenses. In 1667 Andries De Vos is called his father-in-law.

Vos, Hans, Van Baden, at Beverwyck, 1642; removed to Katskil. In 1658, he and his wife were committed to prison, probably for selling liquor to the Indians. In 1661, he was appointed deputy sheriff.

Vos, *alias* Bogert, or Van de Bogert, Jacob Cornelise, m. Jannetje Quackenbos. Ch: bp.; Cornelis, Sept. 28, 1683; Magdalena, March 8, 1685; Jacob, Sept. 18, 1687; Pieter, Sept. 22, 1689; Abraham, Feb. 18, 1692; Isak, Jan. 23, 1695; Benjamin, March 9, 1698. Cornelis Van de Bogert, perhaps father of the above, *is begraven den* July 28, 1665.

Vosburgh, Pieter Jacobse. Ch: *Abraham.*

VOSBURGH, Abraham Pieterse, carpenter and trader, m. Geertruy Pieterse Coeymans, owned a saw mill on the Wynant's kil, which his widow sold in 1674, to Wynant Gerritse Van Der Poel. In 1654, he sent down 1500 beavers; died about 1660. Ch: *Abraham, Isaac, Jacob, Pieter.*

VOSBURGH, Jacob [son of Abraham], m. Dorothea Janse. In 1681, Jacob V. sold a negro named Jack to Tjerk Harm. Visscher for 37 beavers [$118.40.] Ch: bp.; *Abraham*; *Pieter,* May 23, 1686; Isaac, June 16, 1689; Dirk, Dec. 31, 1693; *Marten,* Jan. 31, 1697.

VOSBURGH, Isaac [son of Abraham] of Kinderhook, 1720, m. Anna Janse Goes, 1686. Ch: bp.; Abraham, Oct. 16. 1687; *Pieter,* Aug. 3, 1690; Geertruy, April 4, 1689; *Jan,* July 28, 1692; Geertruy, Dec. 17, 1694; *Abraham,* March 11, 1696; Styntje, Nov. 7, 1697; Jacob, Sept. 3, 1699; Antje, Jan. 4, 1702; Isaac, Feb. 13, 1704; Marytje, Feb. 22, 1708.

VOSBURGH, Pieter [son of Abraham], of Kinderhook, 1720, m. Jannetje Barentse. Ch: bp.; Eytje, June 11, 1693; *Abraham,* Jan. 20, 1695; *Barent,* Nov. 7, 1697; Myndert, Jan. 4, 1702.

VOSBURGH, Abraham [son of Jacob], m. Claartje Bressy (Brussy). Ch: bp.; Jacob (Jacobus), Sept. 29, 1705; Dorothea, Sept. 7, 1707; Christoffel, April 17, 1709.

VOSBURGH, Pieter [son of Jacob], m. Dirkie Van Alsteyn, Feb. 18, 1717. Ch: Jacob, bp. Oct. 28, 1719.

VOSBURGH, Abraham [son of Isaac], m. Geertje Van Den Bergh, Oct. 11, 1719. Ch: bp.; *Isaac,* July 15, 1720; *Willem,* Dec. 2, 1722; Anna, Nov. 25, 1725; Catharina, April 21, 1728; *Petrus,* Oct. 17, 1730; Geertie, Oct. 2, 1733; Johannes, Oct. 6, 1737; Maritie, Jan. 9, 1740.

VOSBURGH, Pieter [son of Isaac], m. Lena Goes Jan. 30, 1720. Ch: bp.; Anna, Aug. 28, 1720; Matthias, Oct. 7, 1722.

VOSBURGH, Marten [son of Jacob], m. Eytje Van Buren, Oct. 21, 1719. Ch: Ariaantje, bp. Dec. 17, 1721.

VOSBURGH, Johannes [son of Isaac], m. Marretie Van Buren, May 24, 1722. Ch: bp.; Isaac, Nov. 18, 1722; Marten, Aug. 9, 1724.

VOSBURGH, Abraham [son of Pieter] and Elizabeth .... Ch: bp.; Pieter, July 3, 1726; Johannes, Oct. 7, 1739.

VOSBURGH, Barent [son of Pieter], and Jannetje ..... Ch: Meyndert, bp. Feb. 6, 1726.

VOSBURGH, Dirk, and Alida .... Ch: Elizabeth, bp. July 8, 1741.

VOSBURGH, Isaac [son of Abraham], m. first, Catarina Van Woert, who was buried May 2, 1757; and secondly, Catharina Staats (Taat *van oost camp*) Jan. 27, 1759. Ch: bp.; Abram, March 6, 1748; Abraham, July 9, 1749; Elizabeth, Feb. 23, 1752; Geertje, Aug. 5, 1754; Jacob, March 15, 1761; *Johannes,* b. May 14, 1763; Catharina, b. June 10, 1765; Annatie, b. Jan. 11, 1768; Willem, b. Dec. 24, 1772, d. June 15, 1839, a. 66 y.; Hendrik, b. Sept. 3, 1775.

VOSBURGH, Petrus [son of Abraham], and Anna Brouwer, both of Hoosack, m. June 9, 1752. Ch: bp.; Abraham, July 14, 1753; Catharina, April 18, 1756; Catarina, Nov. 6, 1757; Geertruy, b. Feb. 18, 1760.

17

VOSBURGH, Willem [son of Abraham], m. Christina Van Woert. Ch: bp.; Marritje, Dec. 31, 1749; Gerrit, July 6, 1752; Geertje, Sept. 15, 1754; *Abraham*, April 17, 1757; Rutger, Jan, 4, 1760; *Isaac*, Jan. 17, 1762.

VOSBURGH, Barent, m. Annatje Gerritsen, Dec. 26, 1760. Ch: Abraham, bp. Aug. 16, 1761. Ch: b.; Dirkje, Oct. 12, 1763; Hendrick, March 23, 1766; Pieter, Dec. 22, 1768; Meinard, July 10, 1771; Meinert, April 27, 1774; Elizabeth, April 21, 1777; Hester, April 17, 1779.

VOSBURGH, Jacob [son of Isaac], m. Hanna (Annatie) Robbison (Robertson); she d. May 10, 1848, a. 82 y, 5 m. 14 d. Ch: b.; Isaac, May 24, 1786; Barbara Clute, Aug. 20, 1788; Elizabeth, Nov. 5, 1790; Abraham, Oct. 9, 1801.

VOSBURGH, Abraham [son of Willem], m. Saartje Bulsing, Nov. 7, 1787. She d. April 13, 1845, a. 84 y. He d. Dec. 1, 1846, a. 92 y. Ch: b.; Willem, Aug. 19, 1788; Hannah, Feb. 10, 1791; Cornelius, Dec. 11, 1793.

VOSBURGH, Johannes [son of Isaac?], m. Elizabeth Richmond. Ch: b.; Catharina, Sept. 8, 1790; Barbara, March 3, 1793; Elizabeth, Sept. 2, 1795; John, May 1, 1800.

VOSBURGH, Isaac [son of Willem], m. Elizabeth, Barry. Ch: William, b. Feb. 17, 1791.

VOSBURGH, Richard, m. Engeltie (Amilia) Bloemendal. Ch: b.; Maritie, June 15, 1793; Sarah, May 12, 1797; Helena, Jan. 29, 1802.

Vrooman, Bartholomeus. Ch: *Pieter, Jacob, Hendrick.*

VROOMAN, Pieter Meese, m. first ...., and secondly, Volckie Pieterse, widow of Gerrit Janse Stavast by whom she had a son named Jan Gerritse Stavast. In 1677 he lived in Yoncker street near the church; d. in 1684. His widow m. Adriaan Appel, June 28, 1685. P. M. V. had but one son, Matthys, who with his wife Maria Arnoutse Viele made a will in 1684, in which they spoke of one child only, Geertruy.

VROOMAN, Jacob Meese, carpenter, m. Elizabeth, widow of Teunis Cornelise Swart, of Schenectady. He made a will July 20, 1691, proved Sept. 22, 1691; wife Elizabeth executrix: mentioned no Ch: his wife was to occupy " my house by the bridge formerly Domine Schaets " (near the south corner of State street and Broadway).

VROOMAN, Hendrick Meese, in 1670 was living " behind Kinderhook;" same year hired a farm of Robert Sanders for six years, at *Steen Raby* (Lansingburgh); 1677, removed to Schenectady and lived on a lot, the present site of the N. Y. Central R. Road depot: 1690 was killed by the French and Indians in the sack of the village; all the Vroomans of this vicinity are his descendants. [See *Schenectady Families.*]

VROOMAN, Adam [son of Hendrick], of Schenectady, m. first, Engeltie Bloom; secondly, Grietje Ryckman; thirdly, Grietje Takelse Heemstraat, Jan. 13, 1697. Ch: bp.; Christina, Oct. 18, 1685; Johannes, May 30, 1697; Jacob Meese, July 3, 1707. [See also *Schenectady Families.*]

VROOMAN, Jan [son of Hendrick], of Schenectady, m. Geesie Symonse Veeder. Ch: Engeltie, b. Jan. 18, 1693. [See *Schenectady Families.*]

VROOMAN, Hendrick, of Schenectady, m. first, Geertruy ....; and secondly, Marytje Wemp (Glen), about 1709. Ch: bp.; Engeltie, Feb. 15, 1702; Maria, Oct. 14, 1705; Barent, Jan. 15, 1710, buried,

Aug. 14, 1746; Adam, April 20, 1712; Engeltie, Sept. 27, 1713. [See *Schenectady Families.*]

VROOMAN, Wouter, of Schenectady, m. Maria Halenbeck, Sept. 24, 1707. Ch: bp.; Engeltie, June 12, 1709; Dorothea, Oct. 3, 1714. [See *Schenectady Families.*]

VROOMAN, Pieter, of Schoharie, m. Geertie Van Alsteyn, Feb. 2, 1706; made will, Oct. 10, 1768, proved, Dec. 20, 1771. Ch: bp.; Martinus and Barent, twins, June 12, 1709; Engel, Aug. 7, 1713; Jannetie, Feb. 6, 1718; Pieter Meese, June 26, 1720; Isaac, Jan. 30, 1723. [See *Schenectady Families.*]

VROOMAN, Jacob, m. Rachel Van Woert, May 29, 1743. Ch: Nicolaas, bp. Aug. 31, 1746.

VROOMAN, Abraham, m. Marytje Verplanck, Sept. 23, 1735. Ch: bp.; Geertruitje, Feb. 8, 1736; Jacob, June 5, 1737; Jannetje, Dec. 24, 1738; Cornelis, July 52, 1742; Isaac, June 17, 1750; Maria, Jan. 7, 1753.

VROOMAN, Adam, of Schoharie, m. Jannetie Ziele, March 17, 1763. Ch: b.; Annatie, Dec. 31, 1768; Barent, July 2, 1771; Jacob, May 14, 1773.

VROOMAN, Cornelis, m. Magdalena Vrooman (Lena Huyck, Hogh), Dec. 19, 1766. Ch: b.; Maria, Dec. 17, 1769; Lena, Dec. 25, 1770; Abraham, bp. May 9, 1773; Annatie, b. Oct. 6, 1774; Jacobus, Sept. 10, 1780; Geertruy, Oct. 2, 1787; Lena, June 2, 1789; Maria, Aug. 25, 1791.

VROOMAN, Pieter, m. Wyntje Redly (Redlif). Ch: b.; Jacobus, April 15, 1773; Andries, Oct. 8, 1775; Pieter, Feb. 23, 1784.

VROOMAN, Anthony, m. Margarita Arnel (Arnold?) Ch: Hendrick, b. Sept. 12, 1777.

Vrydug, Conrad, m. Christine Deppe. Ch: bp.; Johann Christopher, Nov. 30, 1760; George, Oct. 24, 1770.

Wageman, Michael, and Elizabeth ..... Ch: Philip, bp. May 3, 1761.

Wagenaar, Jacob, and Annatje ..... Ch: Jacob, bp. Jan. 8, 1769.

WAGENAAR, John, and Elizabeth Smith. Ch: Elsie, b. Nov. 12, 1783.

Wakefield (?) (Weekfield), Tomas ..... Ch: Anna, bp. Aug. 25, 1689.

Waldron, Willem, of Amsterdam, m. Engeltie Stoutenburgh, in New York. Feb. 10, 1671. Ch: *Pieter.* bp. in N. Y., June 25, 1675.

WALDRON, Pieter, m. Tryntje Cornelise Van Den Bergh, in N. York, Sept. 9, 1698, and removed to Albany about 1700. He was buried May 3, 1725. Ch: bp.; Engeltie, in N. Y. Feb. 19, 1699; Ch: bp.; in Albany, *Williem*, April 28, 1700; Cornelia, Dec. 2, 1702; *Cornelis*, Nov. 18, 1705; Engeltie, May 23, 1708; Catrina, Oct. 24, 1711; Eva, April 11, 1714; Pieter, July 26, 1717, buried May 29, 1728; Rebecca, Aug. 30, 1719; *Gerrit*, April 7, 1723.

WALDRON, Willem [son of Pieter], m. Elizabeth Beekman, Jan. 19, 1720. Ch: bp.; *Pieter*, July 15, 1720; Neeltie, Aug. 13, 1721; Tryntje, Sept. 23, 1722, buried March 5, 1753; Marten, Nov. 22, 1724; Susanna, Sept. 11, 1726; Cornelia, Jan. 10, 1728; Cornelia, Aug. 22, 1730; Neeltie, Dec. 24, 1732; Anna, June 22, 1735; Anna, Feb. 5, 1738; Elizabeth, Aug. 16, 1741.

WALDRON (Walran), Cornelis [son of Pieter], m. Jannetie Van Nes, Sept. 26, 1732. He was buried May 18, 1756. Ch: bp.; Pieter, June 23, 1734; Evert, May 9, 1736, d. in Half Moon June 20, 1829, a. 94 y.

leaving three brothers, Cornelis, Gerrit, and Willem, the first living at Bethlehem, the second in Waterford, and the third in Half Moon whose united ages amounted to between 200 and 270 y. ; *Gerrit*, June 4, 1738 ; Geertje, March 15, 1741 ; *Cornelis*, June 5, 1743 ; Hendrik, May 12, 1745.; Tryntje, Nov. 29, 1747 ; Willem, March 5, 1749.

WALDRON, Pieter [son of Willem], m. first Neeltie Lansing, Dec. 3, 1743 ; secondly, Antje Ouderkerk, about 1768. Ch : bp. ; Elizabeth, Feb. 17, 1745 ; Jannetie, April 7, 1751 ; Willem, June 17, 1753 ; Willem, April 20, 1755 ; Machtelt, Nov. 27, 1757. Ch : b. ; Susanna, Oct. 7, 1763 ; Cornelia, Feb. 6, 1769 ; Abraham, in *Halve Maan*, Sept. 13, 1771 ; Evert, Oct. 8, 1773 ; Tryntje, June 3, 1785.

WALDRON, Gerrit [son of Cornelis] of *Halve Maan* and Waterford, m. Catharina Van Den Bergh, *uit de Boght*, Nov. 26, 1761. Ch : b. ; Cornelis, Jan. 28, 1763 ; Annatie, Oct. 12, 1764 ; Wynand, Dec. 18, 1766 ; Pieter, Nov. 10, 1768 ; Abraham, April 14, 1771 ; Evert, bp. Oct. 17, 1773.

WALDRON, Cornelis [son of Cornelis], of Bethlehem, m. Alida Goey (Goewey), July 2, 1769. Ch : b. ; Cornelis, March 11, 1770 ; Benjamin, Feb. 1, 1772 ; Hendrik, March 17, 1774 ; Salomon, Aug. 30, 1776 ; Pieter, June 7, 1779 ; Gerrit, Nov. 26, 1781 ; Evert, April 19, 1785.

WALDRON, Hendrick [son of Cornelis] of the *Colonie*, m. Margarita Van Franken, Nov. 26, 1771. Ch : b. ; Cornelis, Dec. 18. 1772 ; Ryckert, Sept. 23, 1774 ; Jannetie, Sept. 20, 1776 ; Maas, March 6, 1779 ; Christiana, May 3, 1788 ; Henry, Dec. 25, 1790.

WALDRON, Willem [son of Cornelis], of *Halve Maan*, m. Margarita Van der Werken, Feb. 10, 1777. Ch : Cornelis, b. Sept. 22, 1778.

WALDRON, Willem, and Catharine Van Der Zee. Ch : Maritie, b. Oct. 25, 1792.

Wales, James, and Annatie Broom (Groem). Ch : bp. ; Maria, Jan. 12, 1746 ; Edward, June 10, 1753.

Walker (Wake), Johannes, and Jannetie.... Ch : Edward, bp. May 3, 1761.

WALKER, John, *op de Halve maan*, m. Jannetie Bonns (Born, Burn), Nov. 7, 1760. Ch : b. ; Samuel, Sept. 5, 1762 ; Benjamin, April 20, 1764 ; Abraham, bp. Feb. 9, 1768 ; Magdalena, July 14, 1771.

Walles (Wels), James and Elizabeth .... Ch : Mettie, bp. July 26, 1724 ; Joseph, Feb. 12, 1727.

Walley, John, m. Anne (Charlotte), Smith, Oct. 15, 1758. Ch : John, bp. Aug. 26, 1759.

WALLEY, John, and Sibylla Appely. Ch : b. ; Maria, April 12, 1778 ; Jacob, Sept. 2, 1779 ; Stephen, July 8, 1784.

Walter, John, and Elizabeth... . Ch : Johannes Casparus, bp. Sept. 12, 1758.

Wand, Ebenezer, m. Marytie Hunter, May 9, 1780. Ch : Elizabeth, b. Sept. 8, 1781.

Ward, John, and Margarita Burnside. Ch : Margarita, b. May 30, 1778.

Warmond, Matthys, and Susanna Heghs (Hiks). Ch : bp. ; Willem, April 13, 1696 Edward, Aug. 14, 1698 ; Anne, June 1, 1701.

Warn, Johannes, and Mary Burnside. Ch : Robert, b. Oct. 5, 1781.

WARN (Waan), William W., and Edith La Grange. Ch : John Ebenezer, b. July 19, 1790.

Warner, Michael, and Margarita Schrey. Ch : b. ; Maria, Nov. 3, 1764 ; George, Dec. 3, 1766.

WARNER, Nicolaas, of Hellenberg, and Geertruy Vosburg. Ch : Maria, b. August 16, 1790.

WARNER, Isaac, and Elsie Van Loon. Ch : Benjamin I. Stephenson, Sept. 24, 1790.

WARNER, Peter, and Susanna Burges. Ch : Peter, b. Nov. 29, 1790.

Warren, James, and Mary Crosby. Ch : bp. ; George, Nov. 26, 1775.

Washburn, Bethuel, and Gerritje Lansing. Ch : b. ; John, Oct. 9, 1779 ; Johannes, April 17, 1787.

Waters (Walters), John, " a professional schoolmaster " m. Sara Winne, Oct. 22, 1721. Ch : bp. ; John, March 6, 1725 ; John August 13, 1727 ; John, Sept. 24, 1732.

WATERS, Samuel, and Catharine Lent. Ch : William, b. Sept. 2, 1792.

Watkins, John, and Judith Livingston. Ch : John, b. June 10, 1781, in the manor of Livingston.

Watson, Thomas, and Catharina Veltman. Ch : Thomas, b. Feb. 14, 1770.

WATSON, Ralph, and Hannah Hart. Ch : Hannah, b. July 23, 1776.

WATSON, Daniel, and Isabella.... Ch : b. ; Lachelin, August 3, 1777 ; Daniel, August 5, 1781 ; both bp. June 2, 1782.

WATSON, Zelotes, and Catharina Wynkoop. Ch : Catharina, b. Jan. 14, 1783.

WATSON, Thomas, and Hannah Trever. Ch : Catharina, b. March 13, 1797.

Way, John, and Hilletie Müller. Ch : b. ; Lavariche, Feb. 16, 1781 ; John, Oct. 3, 1783.

Wayland, Leendert, m. Agnietje Muller, June 14, 1778. Ch : Johannes, b. April 6, 1779.

Weaver, Lewis, and Elisabeth Derick. Ch : Elisabeth, b. Dec. 31, 1796.

Webber, Pieter, and Catharina Warn (Ward). Ch : b. Catharina, March 24, 1778 ; Maria, August 4, 1780.

Wedewaks, Andries, m. Catharina Reisdorp, Nov.....1762. Ch : b. ; Lourens, April 1, 1764 ; Catharina, July 28, 1766 ; Andries, June 26, 1769.

Weever, see De. Wever.

Welch, Richard, and Eva Great. Ch : George, b. Feb. 23, 1779.

Wemp, Jan Barentse, *alias* Poest (?), in Beverwyck, 1657, where he owned several lots ; received a contract from Madame Johanna DeLaet, for a bouwery at *Lubberde's Land* (Troy), which his heirs in 1669-72, conveyed to Pieter Pieterse Van Woggelum, whom Myndert Janse sued in 1775, for the fourth payment of 40 beavers. J. B. W. died in 1663, and in 1664, his widow Maritie Myndertse, m. Sweer Teunise Van Velsen, of Schenectady. Ch : Aeltie, w. Jan Cornelis Van der Heyden ; Myndert, b. 1649 ; Grietie, b. in 1651 ; Anna, b. in 1653, m Capt. Sander Glen ; Barent, b. in 1656 ; Johannes. J. B W, also owned half of the Great Island, west of Schenectady, called Van Slyck's island.

WEMP, Barent Janse, of Schenectady, m. Folkje Symonse Veeder. Ch : bp. ; Johannes, Aug. 24, 1684 : Myndert, Aug. 24, 1691 ; Engeltie, Oct. 29, 1693. [See *Schenectady Families*.]

WEMP (Webb), Dirk, and Rebecca Van Arnhem. Ch: bp. ; Maria, March 31, 1759; Johannatje, June 4, 1761.

Wendel, Evert Janse, cooper, b. in 1615, in Emden, probably resided in New Amsterdam, some years before coming to Albany. His house lot was on the west corner of James and State streets, which after his death, was owned by his son Thomas. He married first, Susanna Du Trieux, July 31, 1644, in New Amsterdam; secondly, Maritie Abrahamse Vosburgh, dau. of Abraham Piet: V. and widow of Thomas Janse Mingael, in 1663. In anticipation of this marriage he made a contract, by which he agreed to reserve out of his first wife's estate the sum of 1,000 guilders, for his 6 ch., by her; viz: Elsie, a. 16 y. ; Johannes, a. 14 y. ; Diewer, a. 10 y. ; Jeronimus, a. 8 y. ; Philip. a. 5 y. ; Evert, a. 3 y. ; Isaac De Foreest and Symon Symonse Groot, were the uncles of these children, on the mother's side. And thirdly, he m. Ariaantje ... He d. about 1702. Ch : *Thomas,* eldest son ; *Abraham ;* Elsie, b. in 1647 ; *Johannes,* bp. in N. Amst., Feb. 2, 1649 ; Dievertje, bp. in N. Amst., Nov. 27, 1650 ; Diewer, b. in 1653 ; *Hieronimus,* b. 1655 ; *Phillip,* b. 1657 ; *Evert,* b. 1660.

WENDEL (Wandel), Thomas (son of Evert), resided in New Amsterdam, until his father's death, 1702; owned a lot on Stone street ; another on Broad street and one on Pearl street between old slip and Broad street.

WENDEL, Evert, Jr., merchant, m. Elizabeth, dau. of Robert Sanders ; after his death which happened June 16, 1702, she m, Frederic Harmense Visscher. He made his will Nov. 24, 1690, proved Feb. 4, 1704-5. His house lot was on the south side of State street near Lodge street. Ch : bp. ; Susanna, b. 1681, d. Jan. 20, 1708-9 ; Robert, bp. Sept. 28, 1683, buried April 17, 1750 ; Maria, March 22, 1685 ; Elsje, Feb. 23, 1687 ; Ephraim, Feb. 17, 1689 ; *Johannes (?) ;* Abraham, April 2, 1693; Ahasuerus, May 11, 1695 ; Cornelis, Aug. 15, 1697 : Cornelis, Sept. 22, 1700.

WENDELL, Capt. Johannes [son of Evert], merchant, m. first, Maritie Jillise Meyer, dau. of Gillis Pieterse M., of New York; she was bp. in New Amsterdam, Jan. 21, 1652 ; and 2ndly, Elizabeth Staats. His lot was on the south side of State street, the third west of Pearl. He was justice of peace 1684; 1685, commissioned captain ; 1690, commissioned with others to treat with the Five Nations and superintend affairs relating to the defense of Albany ; made a will which was proved Feb. 9, 169½ ; Elizabeth his w. executrix. Ch : then living, by 1st w. Elsje ; Maria ; by 2d w. *Abraham ;* Susanna ; Catalyntje ; Elizabeth ; *Evert ; Johannes,* bp. March 2, 1684 ; *Ephraim,* bp. June 3, 1685 ; Isaac, bp. Jan. 23, 1687 ; *Isaac* and Sara, twins, bp. Nov. 11, 1688 ; Jacobus, bp. Aug. 1691.

WENDELL, Hieronimus [son of Evert], shoemaker, m. Ariaantje Harmense Visscher. In 1678, his lot was probably on north side of State street 2d east from Pearl. He was deceased in 1701. Ch : bp. ; *Harmanus* eldest son ; *Johannes,* Jan. 13, 1684 ; Hester, Sept. 19, 1686 ; Elsje, April 28, 1689.

WENDELL, Philip [son of Evert], shoemaker, m. Maria Harmense Visscher, June 17, 1688. He was buried Feb. 13, 1743 ; she was buried Feb. 5, 1735. Ch : bp. ; Evert, June 30, 1689 ; Harmanus, July 11, 1693, made will July 9, 1754, proved, April 5, 1763, spoke of brothers and sisters, but not of wife or Ch. ;

was buried Nov. 12, 1754 ; Hester, March 17, 1695 ; *Evert,* April 11, 1697 ; Elsje, Jan. 7, 1700, buried Dec. 20, 1735 ; Tjerk Harmense, Dec. 21, 1701 ; Johannes, Feb. 19, 1704 : buried, Dec. 7, 1728 ; Ariaantje, March 10, 1706 : Tjerk Harmen, July 18, 1708 ; Jeronimus.

WENDEL, Abraham [son of Evert], m. Mayken Van Nes, April 12, 1698. Ch : bp. ; Evert, Aug. 14, 1698 ; Anna, Jan. 7, 1700 ; Maritje, Sept. 27, 1702 ; Evert, Feb. 27, 1706 ; Henrik, Sept. 19, 1708 ; Maria, Oct. 23, 1709 ; Catrina, March 4, 1711 ; Hendrick, Oct. 19, 1713 ; Susanna, June 31, *(sic)* 1716.

WENDEL, Hermanus [son of Hieronimus], shoemaker, m. Anna Glen, dau. of Jacob Sanderse G. His house was on the south side of State street the second west of Pearl in 1716. He was buried in the church Dec. 15, 1731. Ch : bp. ; Ariaantje, Aug. 25, 1700 ; *Jacob,* Nov. 22, 1702 ; Catharina, Jan. 10, 1705 ; Evert, Jan. 19, 1707 ; Anna, Feb. 9, 1709 ; Johannes, Oct. 7, 1711 ; *Harmanus,* April 11, 1714 ; Abraham, June 24, 1715.

WENDEL, Abraham [son of Johannes], m. Katarina De Kay, in New York, May 15, 1702. Ch : bp. ; in New York. Johannes, May 2, 1702 (3) ; Elizabeth, Aug. 20, 1704 ; Abraham, March 3, 1706 ; Helena, Sept, 21, 1707 ; Catharina, March 27, 1709 ; Jacobus, Aug. 31, 1712 ; Lucretia, July 18, 1714 ; Theunis, June 24, 1716 ; Theunis, Oct. 30, 1717 ; *Hendrikus,* Aug. 3, 1719.

WENDEL, Evert [son of Johannes ?], m. Engeltie Wendel, made will July 29, 1749, proved June 20, 1750, buried May 4, 1750. Ch : bp ; Geertruy, Oct. 7, 1711 ; *Johannes,* June 28, 1718 ; Abraham, April 24, 1715, buried June 30, 1753 ; Ariaantje, May 19, 1717 ; Ephraim, April 5, 1719 ; Evert, Jan. 13, 1723 ; Elizabeth, Nov. 29, 1724 ; Engeltie, Sept. 25, 1726 ; Harmanus, July 2, 1731 ; *Philip,* July 7, 1734.

WENDEL, Evert Philipse, m. Susanna Lansing June 29, 1736. Ch.: bp. ; Marytje, Sept. 18, 1737 ; Catharina, Dec. 19, 1739 ; Philip and Gerrit, March 15, 1741.

WENDEL, Capt. Johannes [son of Johannes], m. Elizabeth Walters. He was buried on "the flats" Jan. 13, 1729. Ch : bp. ; Johannes, Feb. 8, 1708 ; *Robert,* Nov. 27, 1709 ; Susanna, March 11, 1711 ; [Gerritje (?) April 20, 1712] ; Catryna, Oct. 19, 1712 ; *Abraham,* Aug. 14, 1714 ; Jacob, Jan. 22, 1716 ; Catryna, Feb. 16, 1718, buried Aug. 29, 1747 ; Jacob, Sept. 6, 1719 ; Elizabeth, Feb. 12, 1721 ; Maria, Jan. 6, 1723 ; Ephraim, May 16, 1725 ; Sara, Oct. 13, 1728.

WENDEL, Johannes *Hieronymi filius,* m. Susanna Viele, June 5, 1707 ; buried Oct. 21, 1743. Ch : bp. ; Ariaantje, March 6, 1709 ; Elsie, Feb. 13, 1715 ; Joannes, June 28, 1719.

WENDEL, Ephraim [son of Johannes], m. Anna ....., Doctor Ephraim W. was buried at "the flats" July 2. 1731. Ch : bp. ; Ephraim, Nov. 1, 1713 ; Catryna, Feb. 20, 1715 ; Elizabeth, Nov. 10, 1717 ; Catharina, May 8, 1720 ; Maria, July 20, 1722 ; Susanna, Sept. 13, 1724, buried Sept. 1734 ; Catharina, May 13, 1727 ; Hendrik, June 5, 1730 ; Margarita, Sept. 5, 1731.

WENDEL, Isaac [son of Johannes], m. Catalyna Van Dyck, Nov. 28, 1717. Ch : bp. ; Joannes, Nov. 15, 1718, buried in Boston, Mass., Nov. 12, 1755 ; Maria, May 14, 1721 ; Elizabeth, June 29, 1723 ; Cathalyna, Feb. 7, 1725 ; Sara, Nov. 27, 1726 ; *Hendrik,* March 16, 1729 ; Isaac and Sara, Sept. 22, 1734 ; Susanna, Oct. 8, 1736 ; Jacob, April 22, 1736.

WENDEL, Johannes Evertse, m. Anna Kip, Nov. 29, 1716 buried Dec. 18, 1739. Ch : bp. ; Elizabeth, Aug. 25, 1717 : Geesie, Feb. 1, 1719 ; Susanna, Jan. 15, 1721 ; *Evert*, March 6, 1725 ; Abraham, Oct. 8, 1727 ; Anna, Jan. 23, 1732 ; Catharyna, March 10, 1734.

WENDEL, Ahasuerus [son of Evert], of Schenectady, m. Anna Van Eps. Ch : bp. ; Elisabeth, Feb. 12, 1721. [See *Schenectady Families.*]

WENDEL, Ahasuerus [same as above ?], m. Marytje ....; buried July 11, 1752. Ch : Dirk, bp. July 13, 1729.

WENDEL, Jacob [son of Harmanus], m. Helena Van Rensselaer, dau. of Hendrick V. R., Dec. 19, 1728 ; buried at Greenbush, Aug. 5, 1745. Ch : bp. : Harmanus, March 28, 1730 ; *Harmanus*, March 18, 1732 ; *Hendrik*, Oct. 15, 1733 ; Catharina, July 23, 1735 ; Anna, June 5, 1737 ; Maria, April 15, 1739 : Ariaantje, April 10, 1743 ; Elizabeth, Feb. 17, 1745.

WENDEL, Robert [son of Johannes], m. Catharina Wenne, Oct. 6, 1732 : she was buried at " the flats " Jan. 22, 1755. Ch : bp. ; Johannes, May 5, 1734 ; Pieter, Feb. 28, 1736 ; Elizabeth, July 7, 1738 : Abraham, March 23, 1744 ; Marten, March 15, 1747 ; Margarieta, Oct. 23, 1748 ; Catarina, May 12, 1751 ; *Marten*, Dec. 9, 1753.

WENDEL, Abraham [son of Harmanus], merchant, m. first, Geertruy Bleecker, Oct. 24, 1736 ; and secondly, Elizabeth (Annatie) Wendel, Sept. 27, 1740; she was buried May 15, 1757 ; he made a will April 13, 1793, proved Feb. 18, 1800. Ch : bp. ; Elizabeth, April 3, 1738 ; Annatie, April 5, 1741, m. .... Van Vechten ; Johannes, July 18, 1742 ; *Harmanus*, May 20, 1744 ; Tanneke, Jan. 10, 1746 ; Tanneke, Dec. 6, 1747 ; Johannes, Nov. 19, 1749 ; Jacob, May 6, 1753 ; Susanna.

WENDEL, Harmanus, Jr. [son of Harmanus], m. Catharina Van Vechten, March 6, 1742 ; she was buried Sept. 19, 1756 ; he made a will May 31, 1769, proved April 27, 1771, and spoke of the following four sons. Ch : bp.; *Harmanus*, June 6, 1742 ; Geertruy, and Anna, Dec. 7, 1743 ; Cornelis, Sept. 8, 1745 ; Geertruy, Aug. 30, 1747 ; Ariaantje, Nov. 12, 1749 ; *Johannes*, July 6, 1752 ; *Jacob*, Aug. 25, 1754 ; Catarina, Sept. 12, 1756,

WENDEL, Johannes J., and Sara Bergen. Ch : bp. : Johannes, June 30, 1751 ; Francyntje, Nov. 12, 1752 : Joris, Aug. 17, 1755 ; Joris, Jan. 29, 1758.

WENDEL, Hendrick [son of Abraham ?], m. Catalyntje Van Schaick, June 17, 1750. Ch : bp. ; Susanna, April 21, 1751 ; Gerrit, May 30, 1753 ; Sara, Jan. 1, 1756 ; Abraham, Oct. 1, 1758.

WENDEL, Evert, and Elizabeth Van Schaick. Ch : bp. ; Abram, Jan. 13, 1751 ; Sara, Dec. 15, 1754.

WENDEL, Johannes Evertse, of Schenectady, m. Maria Catharina Van Santvoord, in Schenectady, July 16, 1741. He was buried Sept. 19, 1756. Ch : bp. ; Geertruy, Sept. 22, 1751, d. Oct. 23, 1837. [See *Schenectady Families.*]

WENDEL, Harmanus [son of Jacob], m. Barbara Bratt, May 8, 1753. Ch : bp. ; Elizabeth, Dec. 9, 1753 ; Jacob, and Helena, March 6, 1757 ; Helena, Oct. 26, 1760. Ch : b. ; Catharina, Sept. 22, 1762 ; Catharina, Nov. 27, 1765 ; Anna, May 3, 1768, d. Jan. 8, 1829, at house of her sister, Mrs. Helena Lansing, 80 North Pearl street ; Maria, June 6, 1772, d. Dec. 26, 1826 at 80 north Pearl street ; Barent, Aug. 12, 1776.

WENDEL, Hendrick [son of Isaac], m. Anna Maginnis. Ch : bp. ; Catalyntje, Nov. 23, 1755 ; Timothy, March 5, 1758 ; Sara Hendrika, b. Sept. 2, 1706.

WENDEL, Hendrick [son of Jacob], m. Maria Lansing, June 9, 1757 ; made will Oct. 30, 1786, in which he spoke of wife Maria, and children, Jacob, Robert, Harmanus, Hendrick, and Margaret ; d. Oct. 1, 1795 ; his wife and son Jacob were not living in 1796. Ch ; bp. ; Jacob, Aug. 20, 1758 ; Robert, Feb. 15, 1761, m. Agnietje Fonda, and removed to Schenectady where he d. July 7, 1848 ; Harmanus, b. April.16, 1763 ; Harmanus, bp. Sept. 27, 1767. Ch : b. ; Margarita, Jan. 19, 1770, m. Gen. Matthew Trotter; Hendrik, May 17, 1773 ; Abraham, Dec. 7, 1775.

WENDEL, Evert J. [son of Johannes Evertse], made a will May 2, 1763, proved Oct. 6, 1764, mentioned mother, Annatie E. and sisters, Geesie, Elizabeth deceased, Cathalina, w. of Gysbert Marcelis, and Catharina.

WENDEL, Philip [son of Evert], m. first, Cathalina Groesbeck, July 28, 1765 ; and secondly, Geertruy Vosburgh, about 1773 ; he d. Dec. 9, 1808, a. 75 y. Ch : b. ; Evert, March 20, 1766 ; Cathalyntje, Sept. 1, 1773 ; Isaac, Oct. 6, 1775 : Cathalina, Dec, 21, 1777 ; Evert, Aug. 16, 1782 ; Abraham, Sept. 12, 1785 ; David Scot, Sept. 30, 1787 ; Philip, March 9, 1790 ; Catharine, July 11, 1793.,

WENDEL, Cornelis [son of Harmanus], m. Annatie Lansing, Jan. 12, 1769. Ch : b. ; Gerrit, Oct. 19, 1769 ; Catharina, bp. June 28, 1772 ; Wyntie, b. Dec. 8, 1775 ; Harmanus, March 29, 1781, d. July 6, 1837, a. 56 y. ; Johannes Lansing, Jan. 2, 1785, in 1823 elected first Judge of Washington Co. ; 1828 appointed reporter of supreme court and court of errors, d. in Hartford, Conn., Dec. 18, 1861.

WENDEL, Harmanus [son of Abraham], first, m. Christina Van Den Bergh, April 9, 1770 : secondly, Catharina H. Wendell, March 21, 1785. He d. July 15, 1819, a. 75 y. 2 m. 9 d. Ch : b. ; Abraham, July 31, 1771 ; Abraham, July 3, 1773 ; Harmanus, April 19, 1787, d. in Philadelphia, Pa. Feb. 1, 1842 ; Elizabeth, June 21, 1789 ; Philip Van Vechten, May 19, 1791, d. Oct. 21, 1816 ; Catrina, Nov. 9, 1793 ; Catharine, Sept. 23, 1796 ; Ann Susan, Aug. 17, 1798.

WENDEL, Johannes, of *Steen Rabie* (Lansingburgh), m. Elizabeth Young. Ch : Marytje, b. Oct. 12, 1770 ; Willem, bp. May 30, 1773 ; Johannes, bp. Aug. 21, 1776.

WENDEL, Johannes, J., [son of Johannes, J.], m. Alida Hooghkerk. Ch : ; Rebecca, Sept. 9, 1774 ; Sara, aug. 27, 1776 ; John, Jan. 26, 1779 ; Judika, Jan. 5, 1781 ; Alida, Feb. 16, 1783.

WENDEL, Abraham, m. Elizabeth Winne. Ch : Catharina, bp. Dec. 8, 1776.

WENDEL, Johannes W. and Maria Trotter. John W. Wendell, keeper of the hotel in *Court* street d. Feb. 29, 1802, a. 63 y. widow Mary Wendell, d. March 14 1831, a. 77 y. buried from house of James L'Amoreux, 59 Hamilton street. Ch : b. ; Johannes, Sept. 1, 1777 ; Mary, Dec. 23, 1783.

WENDEL, Marten [son of Robert], m. Marytje Winne, Feb. 20, 1779. Ch : b. ; Catharina, Nov. 20, 1779 ; Lavinus, Oct. 27, 1785.

WENDEL, Gerrit, and Machtelt Heemstreet. Ch : Cathalyntje, Nov. 2, 1780.

WENDEL, Gen. Johannes H. [son of Harmanus, Jr.] m. Cathalina Van Benthuysen ; in 1805, occupied

17*

house on west side of Broadway the 6th north from Maiden Lane; d. July 10, 1832, a. 80 y.; his w. d. Jan. 1, 1817, a. 55 y. 11 m. 10 d.   Ch: b.; Hermanus, Sept. 6, 1784; Rachel, April 10, 1786; Catharina, July 23, 1787; Harmanus, Jan. 30, 1790, d. July 11, 1810; Jane, Feb. 3, 1792, d. Nov. 24, 1793; Jacob, Oct. 24, 1794; Jane Maria, Oct. 29, 1796, d. Aug. 23, 1798: Maria Van Vechten, Aug. 1, 1799; Jane Ann, Dec. 31, 1802; Anna, Aug. 31, 1804.

WENDEL, Jacob [son of Harmanus, Jr.], m. Geertruy Lansing; resided on corner of Columbia and North Market streets, d. March 23, 1826, a. 71 y. 5 m. 2 d.; she d. May 18, 1827, a. 68 y. 8 m. 18 d.   Ch: b.; Pieter, June 3, 1786; Doctor P. W. d. Oct. 29, 1849 a. 64 y.; Catharina, Feb. 13, 1789, b. Dec. 11, 1813; Mary Ann, Feb. 13, 1800.

WENDEL, Jacob, and Sara Trotter; he d. before 1796, leaving the following children living: Ch: b.; Maria, June 8, 1785; Ann, Sept. 18, 1788; Margaret, July 17, 1790.

WENDEL, Jacob A. [son of Abraham?], m. Eve Stuart (Swart).   Ch: b.; Abraham, May 5, 1791; John, April 25, 1794; Gertrude, June 10, 1801; Susanna, March 10, 1803.

WENDELL, Philip, m. Sarah Packard (Pecker, Packet); Sarah, widow of Philip W. d. April 20, 1830, a. 58 y. 2 m. 14 d.   Ch: b.; Abraham, March 25, 1796; Elizabeth, Oct. 17, 1797; Philip, Dec. 22, 1799; Eunice, Oct. 21, 1803.

Wennel, Jacob, and Anna.... Ch: Ann, bp. March 11, 1778.

Wens, Willem, and Elisabeth.... Ch: Willem, b. August 27, 1767.

Wentworth, Isaac, and Elisabeth Hauver. Ch: Jacob, b. Oct. 7, 1798.

Welth, (Weydt, White?) Gryfyn and Mary. Ch: Mary, bp. Nov. 23, 1721.

WEITH, [White?] Dirk, and Greesie. Ch : Dirk, bp. June 6, 1743.

Welt, [White] Patrick and Molly .... Ch : Patrick, bp. Dec. 11, 1760.

Welth, Dirk, and Jannetie....Ch : Marytje, bp. Sept. 23, 1761.

Wergsmans, Hannes, and Anna .... Ch: bp.; Susanna, May 18, 1740; Hannes Jacobse, Jan. 23, 1743.

Westercamp, Hendrick Janse, at Beverwyck 1645, d. about 1655, when his widow Femmetie Albertse, sold a portion of her lot to Jan Thomase Witbeck, and in 1667, a house and lot on the Exchange block fronting State street to Daniel Rinckhout ; she then lived at Esopus.

Wesselse, Jochem, *bakker;* his w. was Geertruy Hieronimus. Ch : Tringen (Tryntje), w. of Abraham Staats ; Hendrick, who owned a lot on east corner of State street and Broadway which was sold to his brother-in-law Abram Staets ; Andries Jochemse in Beverwyck, 1663-5. Jochem Wesselse made a will Feb. 9, 1680-1, and d. same year. His house and lot was on the south corner of Broadway and State street, extending east to the river and south to the *Rutten kil.* He also had a lot on the south side of *Yonker* street "upon ye hills there next above Capt. Philip Pieterse Schuyler's" near Lodge street, which in 1674, he sold to Hendrick Cuyler. His wife was the wid. of a former husband ; Jan Casparse was her

son and heir ; in 1657, Willem Hoffmeyer called Jochem Wesselse his step father.

Wesselse, Andries, and Geertruy Clute, m. June 22, 1781. Ch : Lucas, bp. ; Nov. 11, 1781.

Westerlo, Domine Eilardus, b. in Groeningen, came to Albany in 1760; his first recorded baptism being on the 19th Oct., 1760, the last on Nov. 28, 1790, d. Dec. 26, 1790, a. 53 y. He m. Catharina Livingston, widow Van Rensselaer, July 19, 1775 ; she d. April 17, 1810, a. 65 y. Ch : b.; Rensselaer, May 6, 1776, m. Jane Lansing, who d. June 15, 1871, a. 86 y. he was member of congress, and d. April 18, 1851, a. 74 y. ; Catharina, August 23, 1778, m. John Woodworth, and d. Sept. 27, 1846; Johanna, March 13, 1783.

Wheeler, Wiler, Wile, Wielaar, Wyllars, Wieler, etc.

WHEELER, Edward (Evert) *jong man van Nieuw Engelandt,* of Kinderhook, 1720, m. Josine, dau. of Jan Jacobse Gardenier, of Kinderhook, in 1689. Ch : bp. ; *Robert* (?) ; *Jan,* Sept. 11, 1692; Sara, May 27, 1694; Breechje, May 10, 1696; Marietje, June 26, 1698; *Thomas,* Jan. 5, 1700; Jacob, Oct. 12, 1701; *Evert,* Feb. 13, 1704; Helena, b. Sept. 17, 1706; Henrik, bp. Sept. 26, 1793; Dorethe, Nov. 5, 1710 ; *Samuel,* Dec. 13, 1713.

WHEELER (Weeler), Jan, [son of Edward], m. Margarita.... Ch : Ephraim, b. Feb. 21, bp. at Klinkenbergh, April 7, 1715 ; Sebastiaen, b. in Kinderhook, in Nov. last and bp. at *Gospel-hoek,* Jan. 7, 1722. [*Athens Luth. Ch. Rec.*]

WHEELER, Robert [son of Edward?] and Catharina ....Ch : Hendrick, bp. Dec. 25, 1720.

WHEELER (Wielaar), Evert [son of Edward], and Maria .... Ch : bp. ; Josyna, April 4, 1725 ; Arisantje, March 27, 1726 ; Hendrik, Jan. 21, 1741 ; *John* (?)

WHEELER (Wyllars) Thomas [son of Edward], and Catharina .... Ch : Edward, bp., Jan. 20, 1723.

WHEELER (Wielaar), Samuel [son of Edward], and Margarita .... Ch : bp. ; Josyna, August 27, 1738; Hiltje, August 17, 1740.

WHEELER (Wielaar), John [son of Evert ?], and Elisabeth .... Ch : Maria, bp. August 28, 1743.

WHEELER (Wieler), Henrik, of Niskatha, and Seintje Vander Hoef. Ch : Seintje, b. Dec. 10, 1770. [Johannes Van Wieler, of Kinderhook, and Josyna Van Der Hoef, of New York, m. May 11, 1761.]

WHEELER (Wieler), Hendrik, m. Bregje Boom, June, 1773. Ch : Bregje, bp. June 11, 1775.

WHEELER, Johannes, and Marytje Cooper. Ch : Maria, b. Sept. 31 (*sic*) 1778.

WHEELER, Johannes, and Maria Hainer. Ch : Mary, b. Sept. 10, 1791.

Wheger, Everhard, and Magdalena Kenfil (?) Ch : b. ; Anna, Jan. 30, 1767; Willem, Dec. 2, 1772.

WHEGER, Jacob, and Retina B.... Ch : Anna, b. Feb. 11, 1767.

White, see Weit.

Whoop, John, and Haccost Barkley. Ch : Sarah, b. Dec. 12, 1792.

Wibusse, Gerrit, m. Maria Gilbert, June 8, 1706. Ch : Anna Maria, bp. Oct. 19, 1707.

Wideman, Hannes, and Margarita Follevin. Ch : Mattheus, b. Feb. 12, 1762; Nicolaas, bp. Nov. 2, 1766.

Wildin, William, and Mary.... Ch: Nathaniel, bp. Jan. 10, 1748.

Wilding, Robert and Nancy Herrington. Ch: Robert, bp. March 28, 1779.

Wilkinson, Willekens, Wilkes.

WILKINSON (Wilkenson, Willekens), Thomas, and Elisabeth Codman. Ch: bp.; Margariet, Feb. 29, 1736; Elisabeth, Jan. 1, 1738; Maria, June 1, 1740; Thomas, March 29, 1747.

WILKINSON, (Wilkes) John, m. Annatie Marshall, April 4, 1769. Ch: b.; Thomas, Oct. 16, 1775; John, Nov. 12, 1779.

Will, Henry, and Magdalena Hun (Margarita Haan). Ch: b.; Rebecca, Nov. 17, 1776; Catharina, May 27, 1780.

Willard, Doctor Elias, m. Catharina Livingston, dau. of John Livingston of N. Y..... in Boston, in 1778; removed to Stillwater: 1801, to Albany. He d. March 20, 1827, a. 71 y. 2 mos.; she d. Jan. 26, 1827, a. 71 y. 2 m. 7 d. Ch: John, b. March 20, 1781; Mary L., d. Nov. 15, 1840; Anna J., m. Estes Howe, and d. in Buffalo, Dec. 14, 1862, a. 75 y.

Willemse, David, and Rachel Hanse. Ch: Johannes, bp. April 6, 1692.

WILLEMSE, Teunis (Van Woutbergh), b. at Heyvelt, in province of Utrecht, purchased and occupied a farm over the river, at Niskayuna, in 1678; m. Jannetje Hendrickse. Ch: bp.; Beertje, Nov. 15, 1696; Willem, Oct. 23, 1698; Hendrick, Nov. 3, 1700.

Willet, Thomas, "1663, trader, formerly of New England, now here in Beverwyck;" from Bristol, England, originally; m. Sara Cornell, of Essex, Eng., in New Amsterdam, Sept. 1, 1643; d. about 1677; John Savine was his heir.

WILLET, Edward S., and Sara Fryer. Ch: b.; Samuel, Nov. 4, 1775; Annatie, Feb. 9, 1778; Catharine, June 14, 1780; Lydia, Dec. 9, 1782; Edward S. W. d. April 23, 1810, a 59 y. 5 m.; his widow d. Dec. 30, 1831, a. 70 y. 10 m. 8 d.

WILLETT, Isaac, and Elisabeth Van Woert. Ch: b.; Catalina, Sept. 28, 1794; Elisabeth, June 18, 1796; John Van Woert, July 7, 1798; Jacob, June 4, 1800.

Williams, Thomas, *jong man van* New York, m. first. Agnietje Gansevoort, August 7, 1692; and secondly, Hilletie (Helena) Bronck, June 26, 1712; 1699, sheriff of Albany Co.; 1719, had a lot on or near the east corner of Green and Hudson streets, near the "Horse guards" blockhouse and stockades, which lot was formerly Gabriel Thomase's. Ch: bp.; Maria, Sept. 16, 1692; Harmanus, Nov. 4, 1694; Anna, Feb. 17, 1697, m..... Witbeck, buried July 23, 1729; Edward, Sept. 3, 1699; Margrietje, Sept. 28, 1701; Thomas, Nov. 7, 1703; Henrik, Nov. 4, 1705; Margrietje, May 2, 1708; Harmen, May 31, 1713; Agnietje, Jan. 23, 1715; Elisabeth, Sept. 1, 1717; Jan, April 12, 1719; Pieter, April 16, 1721; Philip, March 1, 1724, buried Nov. 1, 1744.

WILLIAMS, Edward [son of Thomas] and Maria .... Ch: bp.; Thomas, Sept. 15, 1732; Martina, May 6, 1739.

WILLIAMS, John [son of Thomas], m. Cornelia Bogardus, Jan. 15, 1744. Ch: bp.; Thomas, Oct. 21, 1744; Jannetje, Nov. 4, 1750; Elisabeth, August 12, 1753; Maria, Feb. 13, 1757.

WILLIAMS, Pieter [son of Thomas], m. first, Sara Van Ivero, Jan. 21, 1744, who was buried April 16,

1752; and secondly, Elisabeth Fonda, Sept. 20, 1755. Ch: bp.; Hilletje, Feb. 17, 1745; Thomas, June 20, 1756; Nicolaas, March 25, 1759; Sara, b. June 30, 1762; Gysbert, Jan. 20, 1766.

WILLIAMS, Thomas [son of Thomas], m. Maria Van Hoesen, March 13, 1742. He was buried Nov. 23, 1752. Ch: bp.; Anna, August 16, 1747; Thomas, Sept. 26, 1749; Harmen, Feb. 4, 1753.

WILLIAMS, Benjamin and Mary. Ch: John, bp.; June 17, 1750.

WILLIAMS, Hendrick, m. Francyntje Clute, June 8, 1753. Ch: bp.; Cornelis, May 5, 1754; Frederic, Feb. 7, 1762.

WILLIAMS, James, and Maria O'Connor. Ch: Benjamin, b. May 17, 1783.

Williamson (Williams), John, m. first, Mary Love, Feb. 10, 1778; secondly, Mary Cross. Ch: b.; Ann, Jan. 24, 1779; Elisabeth, Sept. 30, 1782; Benjamin, Sept. 26, 1784; Maria, Nov. 4, 1786.

Willis (Wilson), Thomas, and Rachel Radcliff. Ch: bp.; Catarina, Jan. 15, 1749; William, Dec. 31, 1752; Esther, August 3, 1755; James, Dec. 18, 1757; Thomas, Oct. 16, 1763; Maria, b. May 3, 1766.

WILLIS, John, and Jane Bratt. Ch: Robert, b. June 28, 1779.

Wills, James, and Elisabeth ...Ch: Johannes, bp. Jan. 8, 1723.

WILLS, James, and Annatie Boom. Ch: James, bp. Jan. 18, 1744.

Wilson, Samuel, merchant of New York, and Albany, owned a house and lot in North Pearl street in 1677, and on Broadway, near Stanwix Hall.

WILSON, James, and Anna.... Ch: John, bp. March 4, 1722.

WILSON, Hugh, and Anna Townsley. Ch: Andries, bp. July 12, 1747.

WILSON, John, m. Barbara Dieppendorp (Diependal, Tievetorp), March 30, 1750. Ch: bp.; Barbara, Sept. 1, 1751; Catarina, March 3, 1754; James, April 7, 1756.

WILSON, James, and Martha Welsh. Ch: Margaret, bp. Aug. 10, 1758.

WILSON, John, and Marytje Bratt. Ch: Susanna, bp. Nov. 10, 1776.

WILSON, Robert, and Catharine Wilsie. Ch: David, b. Dec. 27, 1791.

Wilton, John, and Elizabeth Black. Ch: Rebecca, b. Feb. 16, 1797.

Winne, Pieter, "born in the city of Ghent in Flanders (now living in Bethlehem two miles south of the city of Albany" and Tannatje Adams his wife "born in the city of Leeuwaerden in Vrieslandt" made a joint will July 6, 1684. Letters of administration were issued to Livinus Winne and Caspar Leendertse Conyn, Feb. 22, 1695-6; in 1697 his estate was valued at 860 pieces of 8. In 1677 he bought of Volkert Janse Douw, one half of Constapel's island; same year he bought of Nicolaas Van Rensselaer, a saw-mill in Bethlehem, late the property of Eldert Gerbertse Cruyff. He had the following children living in 1684: Pieter Pieterse, b. 1643, living at Esopus; Adam; Livinus; Frans; Alette, w. of Caspar Leendertse Conyn; Kiliaan; Thomas; Lyntie; Marten; Jacobus; Eva; Daniel; Rachel.

WINNE, Livinus [son of Pieter], m. first, Teuntje Martense; and secondly, Willempje Viele, widow of Symon Schemerhorn, June 20, 1699. He d. Nov. 15, 1706. Ch : bp. ; *Kiliaan (?) ; Petrus*, Dec. 16, 1683 : Marten, July 26, 1685 ; Bata, Sept. 11, 1687 ; Maria, April 28, 1700 ; Sara, Aug. 30, 1702 ; *Benjamin*, Dec. 21, 1705.

WINNE, Adam [son of Pieter], ropemaker, m. Anna Lookerman ; after his death she m. Jacob Teunise *de Metselaar*. Ch : bp. ; Lidia, Aug. 31, 1684 ; Rachel, Nov. 24, 1686 ; Anneken, Oct. 7, 1688 ; Rachel, in New York, Aug. 8, 1690.

WINNE, Frans [son of Pieter], m. Elsje Gansevoort, May 12, 1689. Ch : bp. ; Pieter, May 4, 1690 ; Maria, Oct. 23, 1692 ; Annatje (Tanaatje), Oct. 21, 1694 ; Elsje, Nov. 30, 1696, buried June 2, 1727 ; Lysbet, Jan. 5, 1700 ; Harmanus, June 14, 1702 ; Lyntje, Jan. 31, 1705.

WINNE, Thomas [son of Pieter], m. Teuntje Janse Goes, Oct. 20, 1689, Ch : bp. ; Pieter, May 18, 1690 ; Styntje, Sept. 18, 1692 ; Rachel, in New York, Nov. 7, 1694 ; Rachel, in New York, April 5, 1696.

WINNE (?) Jacob Casparse [probably this should be Halenbeck], m. Hendrikje Hanse Dreeper. Ch : bp. ; Caspar, May 31, 1691 ; Johanna, Jan. 17, 1694 ; Isak, May 23, 1697.

WINNE, Jacob [son of Pieter], of Kinderhook, m. Marietje Bronk, Oct. 7, 1696. He d. Sept. 25, 1706. Ch : bp. ; Pieter, March 6, 1698 ; Pieter, April 25, 1703, Kiliaan, Jan. 13, 1706.

WINNE, Daniel [son of Pieter], m. Dirkje Van Nes, March 16, 1698. Ch : bp. ; *Pieter*, Jan. 1, 1699 ; Jan. Oct. 5, 1701 ; Kiliaan, Jan. 19, 1704 ; *Jan*, Oct. 19, 1707 ; *Frans*, March 8, 1713 ; Willem, April 22, 1716 ; Tanneke, Nov. 1, 1718 ; Maria, Oct. 29, 1721 ; *Adam*, Jan. 12, 1724 ; *Cornelis*, Oct. 23, 1726.

WINNE, Pieter [son of Livinus], m. Maria De Forest, April 21, 1706. Ch : bp. ; *Levinus*, Sept. 22, 1706 ; *Philip*, Nov. 21, 1708 ; Catrina, March 4, 1711 ; Isaac, Jan. 4, 1713 ; Marten, Feb. 13, 1715 ; Isaac, July 19, 1717 ; Margarita, Oct. 25, 1719 ; Benjamin, April 29, 1722 ; *Jesse*, June 28, 1724 ; Abraham, Oct. 1, 1727.

WINNE, Kiliaan [son of Livinus], m. first, Maritie Cool, Feb. 15, 1714 ; secondly, Rebecca Fonda, June 16, 1730. Ch : bp. ; Teuntje, Sept. 4, 1715 ; Livinus, Nov. 22, 1724 ; Livinus, June 19, 1726 ; *Daniel*, April 4, 1731 ; *Jillis*, Nov. 19, 1732 ; *Frans*, Sept. 22, 1734 ; Dirkje, Sept. 24, 1738 ; Rachel, Nov. 23, 1740 ; Douwe, and Pieter, July 3, 1743.

WINNE, Pieter Danielse, m. Rachel Van Alen, Jan. 21, 1720. Ch : bp. ; Daniel, Nov. 20, 1720 ; Maria, Dec. 9, 1722 ; Willem, Nov. 7, 1725 ; Willem, Dec. 8, 1728 ; Tanneke, July 9, 1732 ; Willem, March 23, 1735 ; Dirkie, Oct. 14, 1739.

WINNE, Jan [son of Daniel ?], m. Rachel Verplanck, Jan. 2, 1726. He was buried Aug. 12, 1733. Ch : bp. ; Marritie, Oct. 30, 1726 ; Jonathan, April 23, 1727 ; Abigail, Dec. 1, 1728.

WINNE, Benjamin [son of Livinus], m. Rachel Van Arnhem. Ch : bp. ; Willempie, Sept. 7, 1729 ; Hester, Dec. 12, 1731 ; Sara, July 12, 1734 ; Willempie, Nov. 14, 1736 ; Rebecca, Sept. 17, 1738 ; Jannetie, Nov. 23, 1740 ; Lavinus, Aug, 14, 1743 ; *Levinus*, July 5, 1745 ; Lena, Oct. 25, 1747.

WINNE, Livinus [son of Pieter], m. Susanna Wendel, May 26, 1733. .... Ch : bp. ; Pieter, Jan. 9, 1734; *Johannes (?) ; Pieter*, Oct. 16, 1736 ; *Robert*, Feb. 11,

1738 ; Philip, Jan. 24, 1739 ; Jacob, July 23, 1740 ; Susanna, Aug. 30, 1741 ; Elizabeth, July 3, 1743 ; Jesse, April 27, 1746.

WINNE, H. and D. .... Ch : Douwe, bp. Sept. 5, 1736.

WINNE, Philippus [son of Pieter], of Schachtekook, m. Sara Van Antwerp, Oct. 6, 1736. She was buried Sept. 5. 1747. Ch : bp. ; Marytje, Feb. 11, 1738 ; Simeon, Oct. 12, 1740 ; Pieter, May 27, 1744.

WINNE, Frans [son of Daniel], m. first, Agnietje Van Wie, June 21, 1738 ; and secondly, Marritje Hooghteling (widow Lorway), Sept. 15, 1757. Ch : bp. ; *Daniel*, Jan. 10, 1739 ; Catharina, Dec. 28, 1740 ; Gerrit, July 8, 1744 ; Johannes, Nov. 1, 1747 ; Pieter, June 17, 1750 ; Catharina, March 11, 1753 ; Angenitie, Aug. 27, 1758 ; Cornelis, Dec. 26, 1761 ; Jonathan, 4 *weken oud*, May 22, 1763 ; Adam, b. April 2, 1767.

WINNE, Daniel Pieterse, m. Jannetie De Foreest, June 15, 1744. Ch : bp. ; Pieter, Aug. 25, 1745 ; Rachel, June 12, 1748 ; David, Aug. 25, 1751 ; Pieter, Sept. 9, 1753 ; Willem, Aug. 8, 1756.

WINNE, Willem [son of Daniel], m. Maria De Wandelaar. Ch : bp. ; Dirkje, May 1, 1748 ; Elizabeth, April 12, 1752 ; Catalina, June 23, 1754 ; Catalina, July 21, 1758.

WINNE, Adam [son of Daniel], m. Gerritje Schemerhorn. Ch : bp. ; Antje, Oct. 30, 1748 ; Dirkje, April 26, 1752 ; Daniel, March 12, 1755.

WINNE, Cornelis [son of Daniel], m. Catarina Van Den Bergh. He was buried at Bethlehem, Oct. 13, 1752. Ch : Daniel, bp. Feb. 18, 1750.

WINNE, Jesse [son of Pieter], m. Annatie Van Den Bergh, April 25, 1752. He was buried Aug. 29, 1756. Ch : bp. ; Maria, April 22, 1754 ; Pieter, April 4, 1756.

WINNE, Jillis [son of Kiliaan], m. Fytje Van Woert, May 5, 1754. Ch : bp. ; Kiliaan, Sept. 7, 1755 ; Jacob, July 31, 1757 ; Jacob, July 16, 1758 ; Jacob, b. Feb. 29, 1760 ; Rebecca, bp. Dec. 6, 1761 ; Ch : b. Hendrikje, Nov. 13, 1763 ; Kiliaan, Nov. 26, 1765 ; Meinard, Feb. 5, 1768 ; Daniel, Dec. 12, 1769, d. Jan. 4, 1819 ; Margarita, and Rachel, bp. Dec. 18, 1771 ; Meinard, b. Nov. 18, 1774 ; Sara, b. April 17, 1777.

WINNE, Daniel, and Elisabeth Dox. Ch : Angenietje, bp. Nov. 14, 1756.

WINNE, Daniel, and Jannetie De Foreest. Ch : Johannes, bp. Nov., 1758 (9).

WINNE, Daniel [son of Kiliaan], and Jannetie Bantie. Ch : b. ; Kiliaan, Dec. 18, 1766 ; Jellis, July 8, 1772.

WINNE, Daniel [son of Frans], m. Catharina Hooghteling, August 15, 1761. Ch : b. ; Agnietje, bp. April 3, 1763 ; Coenraad, b. Nov. 19, 1764 ; Franciscus, June 11, 1766 ; Catharina, July 3, 1768 ; Willem, Sept. 20, 1769 ; Johannes, Sept. 14, 1771 ; Catharina, June 7, 1773 ; Helena, August 30, 1775 ; Cathalyntje, Jan. 3, 1778 ; David, Jan. 5, 1781.

WINNE, Lavinus [son of Benjamin], m. Marytje Lansing.[*] He d. in Watervliet, Dec. 6, 1825, a. 80y. : she d. March 29, 1824, a. 76y. Ch : b. ; Benjamin, Sept. 16, 1768 ; Maria, May 3, 1770 ; Johannes, July 30, 1772 ; David, August 23, 1774 ; Rachel, Nov. 17, 1776 ; Hendrick, Jan. 11, 1779 ; Sara, April 14, 1781 ; Lavinus, May 11, 1783 ; Sara, June 22, 1785 ; Jacob, Jan. 12, 1788.

WINNE, Frans, Jr. [son of Kiliaan], m. Anneke Viele, Dec. 2, 1758. Ch : b. ; Kiliaan, bp. Oct. 15, 1758 (9) ; Catharina, b. Feb. 28, 1762 ; Hugo, Sept.

26, 1764; Pieter, Sept. 17, 1766; Rebecca, Oct. 16, 1768; Maria, Feb. 6, 1771; Rachel, July 27, 1773; Jacob Viele, Oct. 10, 1775; Stephanus, Jan. 19, 1779.

WINNE, Pieter [son of Livinus], and Susanna Van Den Bergh. Ch : b. ; Maria, March 10, 1762; Livinus, Jan. 12, 1764: Johannes, bp. April 30, 1769.

WINNE, Robert [son of Lavinus], m. Hillegonda Van Franken, Nov. 1762. Ch : b.; Annatie, June 26, 1764; Ryckert, April 11, 1769; Johannes, March 12, 1771; Pieter, April 21, 1775; Catharina, Sept. 8, 1781.

WINNE, Johannes [son of Lavinus?], m. Santje (De) Ridder, March 4, 1758. Ch : b.; Lavinus, April 4, 1762; Gerrit, March 21, 1764; Lavinus, Nov. 19, 1766; Annatje, June 3, 1769; Gerrit, Jan. 26, 1777.

WINNE, Willem, Jr., m. Hubertje Yates, Sept. 11, 1762. Ch : Hubertje, b. April 15, 1764.

WINNE, Daniel, and Jannetie Bancker. Ch : Willem, March 21, 1769.

WINNE, Pieter Ph., and Cathalyntje Van Den Bergh. Ch: Wynand, b. Aug. 18, 1772. .

WINNE, Daniel C., m. Alida Van Den Bergh, May 20, 1770. Ch : Catharina, b. Aug. 2, 1774.

WINNE, Pieter W., and Ryckie Van Schaick. Ch : Abraham, b. Sept. 26, 1775.

WINNE, Pieter, Jr., m. Maria Oosterhout, May 13, 1775. Ch : b. ; Daniel, Nov. 7, 1775 ; Wilhelmus, Aug. 28, 1777 ; David, Feb. 12, 1779 ; Rachel, Jan. 27, 1784 ; *Pieter*.

WINNE, Jacob, and Susanna Evertse (Hoghseton). Ch: b. ; Jellis, June 17, 1778, d. July 22, 1849 ; Johannes Evertsen, July 22, 1780; Elizabeth, April 7, 1792.

WINNE, David, m. Marytje Spaan. Feb. 28, 1780. Ch: b. ; Jannetje, Nov. 25, 1780 ; Rachel, July 30, 1784.

WINNE, Kiliaan, and Maria Perry (Perny). Ch: b. ; Frans, June 12, 1782 ; Annatie, Oct. 3, 1787. [Kiliaan I. Winne, d. at Cazenovia, Sept. 14, 1829, a. 64 y. Sara, widow of Kiliaan I. W., d. Sept. 19, 1848, a. 80 y.]

WINNE, Kiliaan J. [Same as the last?] and Sara Clute. Ch: b. ; Tietje, April 25, 1790 ; Sara, Oct. 7, 1792 ; John Clute, March 16, 1797 ; Jillis, Jan. 3, 1802 ; Gerrit, Sept. 2, 1804 ; Sarah Ann, July 24, 1806 ; Henrietta, Aug. 3, 1813.

WINNE, David, m. first, Geertruy Groesbeck, July 25. 1780 ; secondly, Alida Van Benthuysen, about 1795. Ch: b. ; Jannetie, Feb. 31 (*sic*), 1784 ; Maria, Aug. 3, 1786 ; Wouter, May 2, 1790 ; Geesie, Nov. 7, 1795 ; Sarah, Feb. 9, 1800 ; Sarah, Nov. 11, 1801.

WINNE, Cornelis, and Elizabeth Van den Bogert. Ch : Franciscus, b. Sept. 5, 1783.

WINNE, Frans, m. Lena Flensburgh, May 16, 1784. Ch : Cornelia, b. Dec. 22, 1784.

WINNE, Willem D., m. first, Marytje Becker (Mary Baker), Jan. 26, 1783 ; secondly, Mary Oosterhout about 1792. Ch: b. ; Daniel, Jan. 20, 1786 ; Dirk, Nov. 23, 1787 ; Peter, April 11, 1790 ; Peter, Oct. 13, 1792.

WINNE, Johannes Danielse, m. Agnietje Van Wie, June 22, 1786. Ch: b. ; Jannetje, March 24, 1787 ; Hendrick, April 28, 1789.

WINNE, Benjamin, m. Elisabeth Bassett (Bussel), April 16, 1787. Ch: b. ; Lavinus, Nov. 20, 1787 ; Lavinus, Jan. 1, 1690 ; Michael Basset, April 28, 1792;

Mary, Oct. 19, 1793; Rachel, bp. March 22, 1795 ; John, b. April 7, 1800.

WINNE, Daniel J. (T.), m. first, Hannah Swits; and secondly, Alida Van Arnhem, about 1795. Ch: b. ; Jellis, April 2, 1790; Cornelius Swits, Feb. 22, 1792, d. Dec. 27, 1825 ; Johanna, July 18, 1796; Catharine, Aug. 12, 1798 ; Tickie, Dec. 6, 1800 ; Isaac, Feb. 12, 1803 ; Myndert, April 29, 1805, d. April 18, 1831 ; Jellis, Aug. 13, 1808 ; Jellis, Nov. 26, 1810.

WINNE, Kiliaan (Guliam) D., m. first, Sara Cornell (Connolly), June 2, 1788 ; secondly, Engeltie Clute, about 1801. Ch: b. ; Jannetie, June 28, 1790 ; Rebecca, June 11, 1792 ; Jellis, Nov. 6, 1801.

WINNE, Adam P., and Christina Lagrange. Ch : b. Ann, Oct. 20, 1790 ; Maria, Oct. 18, 1792,

WINNE, Benjamin, and Annatie Bratt. Ch : Maria, b. Sept. 26, 1792.

WINNE, Jonathan, and Annatie Becker. Ch: David. b. Oct. 6, 1793.

WINNE, Lawrence, and Annatie Chambers. Ch : Hendrik, b. Jan. 3, 1793.

WINNE, Daniel K., and Alida..... Ch: b. ; William Bancker, Sept. 3, 1810: Sarah Catalina, Nov. 16, 1811; William Bancker, Sept. 28, 1813; Ann Maria, Jan. 2, 1816 ; William Vischer, April 7, 1818.

Winnings, Leonard, and Annatie Muller, Ch : b. Maria, Sept. 30, 1789 ; Barent, Feb. 6, 1792.

Wisselpenningh, Reynier, carpenter in Beverwyck, 1654-61. He m. the widow of Symen Root; she was deceased in 1654.

Witbeck, *alias* Van Witbeck, Jan Thomase, b. at Witbeck in Holstein, m. Geertruy Andriese Dochter, b. in New Amsterdam. From 1652 when Beverwyck was laid out to 1678, he was the most considerable dealer in house lots in the village. In 1664 in company with Volkert Janse Douw he bought the whole of *Apje's* island or Schotack and the mainland opposite on the east side of Hudson river, from the *natives*. Ch : *Andries ; Johannes ; Lucas ; Hendrik ; Jonathan ; Thomas ;* Catharina (?) w. of Jacob Sanderse Glen, and in 1696, of Jonas Volckertse Douw.

WITBECK, Andries Janse, m. Engeltje Volkertse [Douw]. Ch : bp. ; *Andries,* April 23, 1684 ; Lucas, Jan. 16, 1687 (6) ; *Jan,* April 24, 1687 (?) Hilletje, June 30, 1689 ; Andries, Jan. 1, 1692 ; Geertruy, Dec. 26, 1694 ; Dorothee, Jan. 1, 1698 ; *Jonas,* Nov, 10, 1700.

WITBECK, Johannes Janse, and Lysbeth Leendertse Conyn. Ch: bp. ; *Philip'(?)* ; Leendert, Aug. 16, 1685 ; *Leendert,* July 3, 1692 ; Tomas, April 15, 1694 ; Benjamin, April 3, 1698 ; *Caspar,* March 23, 1701 ; Andries, Jan. 12, 1704.

WITBECK, Lucas Janse, m. Catrine Melgertse Van Deusen, June 28, 1691 (?) Ch : bp. ; Geertruy, May 11, 1690 (?) ; Geertruy, March 6, 1692 ; Johannes, Nov. 19, 1693, buried Aug. 3, 1744 ; *Abraham,* Aug. 29, 1703.

WITBECK, Hendrick Janse, of Claverac, m. first, Lyntje Winne ; secondly, Lena Bout, Sept. 27, 1707. Ch: bp. ; Jan, Dec. 26, 1691 ; Tanneken, Dec. 24, 1693 : Pieter, Feb. 24, 1695 : Geertruy, April 4, 1697; Marietje, Sept. 3, 1699 ; Lyntje, June 22, 1701 ; Lyntje, Feb. 28, 1703 ; Catharina, Aug. 15, 1708.

WITBECK, Jonathan Janse, m. first, Caatje Martense Van Buren, Jan. 7, 1697 ; secondly, Catharina Van Deusen, about 1705. Ch bp. ; *Johannes,* Dec. 5, 1697; Marten Cornelise, April 25, 1703 ; Tobias, Sept. 20, 1706 ; Jonathan, Oct. 30, 1710 ; Marritje, July 5, 1713.

WITBECK, Thomas Janse, m. Jannetje Van Deusen, Sept. 5, 1702. He was buried at Papsknee, May 6, 1731. Ch: bp. ; Geertruy, Jan. 1, 1704; *Melgert Abrahamse*, Sept. 22, 1705 ; *Johannes*, July 9, 1708 ; *Jacobus (Jacob)*, Oct. 30, 1710 ; Geertruy, March 6, 1717 ; *Lucas*, Feb. 26, 1724.

WITBECK, Jan [son of Andries], m. first, Agnietje Bronck, April 7, 1705; secondly, Maria Williams, Jan. 9, 1726. Ch: bp. ; *Andries*, July 4, 1707 ; Lena, March 27, 1709 ; Jan, Sept. 27, 1713 ; Volckert, Aug. 10, 1718 ; Pieter, May 6, 1722 ; Agnietje, Oct. 8, 1727.

WITBECK, Philip [son of Johannes], m. Anna Williams, Dec. 20, 1720. He was buried Dec. 25, 1742. Ch: Joannes, bp. April 10, 1720.

WITBECK, Andries [son of Andries], and Engeltie .... Ch: bp.; Andries, Aug. 5, 1723 ; Albert, Feb. 24, 1725 ; Johannes, Dec. 17, 1727 ; Engeltie, Feb. 22, 1730 ; Hester, July 2, 1732 ; Geertruy, Jan. 10, 1739.

WITBECK, Jonas [son of Andries], m. Dorothea Douw, Dec. 27, 1728. Ch: bp. ; Andreas, Nov. 9, 1729 ; Engeltie, Jan. 1, 1738.

WITBECK, Abraham [son of Lucas], and Anna Van Deusen. He was buried at *Papsknee*, April 28, 1755. Ch: bp. ; Marretie, June 18, 1730 ; Lucas, Jan. 9, 1732 ; Catharina, Jan. 14, 1733, buried at Papsknee, Sept. 30, 1752 ; Lucas, March 9, 1735 ; *Harpert*, Nov. 6, 1737 ; Johannes, Oct. 12, 1740 : Abraham, Aug. 21, 1743 ; Geertruy, Oct. 19, 1744 ; Catalina, Oct. 25, 1747 ; Abram, Jan. 28, 1750.

WITBECK, Leendert [son of Johannes], m. Catharina Verplanck, Feb. 23, 1734. Ch: bp. ; Elizabeth, Nov. 10, 1734 ; Johannes, June 5, 1737 ; Isaac, June 3, 1739.

WITBECK, Johannes [son of Jonathan ?] m. Rachel Conyn. Ch: bp. ; Maritie, May 19, 1734 ; Marten Cornelise, Oct. 3, 1736 ; Leendert, Jan. 24, 1742 ; [Rachel, dau. of Johannes W., buried August 27, 1748.]

WITBECK, Caspar [son of Johannes Janse], m. Annatie Van Der Zee, Oct. 17, 1735. Ch: bp. ; Johannes Jansen, August 22, 1736 ; Wouter, March 2, 1740.

WITBECK, Jonathan [son of Jonathan Janse], m. first, Magtel Wyngaart, April 1, 1738 ; she was buried Sept. 9, 1746 ; secondly, Gerritje (Margarita) Oostrander, about 1751. Ch: bp. ; Jacobus, Nov. 25, 1739; Cathalyna, August 30, 1741 ; *Martin Cornelise*, July 8, 1744 ; Maria, April 25, 1746 ; *Johannes*, Dec. 29, 1751 ; Machtelt, March 17, 1754 ; Elisabeth, Dec. 15, 1756 ; Jonathan, Oct. 21, 1758. Ch: b. ; Lea, April 10, 1762 ; Tobias, May 1, 1765 ; Maria, August 1, 1767 ; Jacobus, March 18, 1770.

WITBECK, Andries [son of Jan], and Mayke.... Ch: bp.; Elisabeth, July 29, 1739 ; Zelotti, June 28, 1741 ; Agnietje, Sept. 26, 1742.

WITBECK, Johannes Thomase, m. Eva Waldron, May 9, 1740. Ch: bp.; *Thomas*, April 26, 1741; Tryntje, May 1, 1743 ; *Pieter Waldron*, Jan. 10, 1746 ; Abram, Dec. 13, 1747 ; Caspar (?) ; Jannetie, August 16, 1752 ; *Willem*, Jan. 1, 1755 ; Geertruy, April 10, 1757.

WITBECK, Melchert A. [son of Thomas Janse], and Marytje.... Ch: Jannetje, bp. Oct. 24, 1742 ; [Abraham Melgertse W. m. Marytje Van Deusen, Oct. 17, 1741.]

WITBECK, Jacob [son of Thomas], m. Cathalyna Van Deusen, Dec. 25, 1742. Ch: bp. ; Marritie, June 27, 1744 ; *Thomas*, May 13, 1750.

WITBECK, Lucas [son of Thomas], and Geertruy Lansing. Ch: bp.; Elisabeth, Nov. 16, 1746 ; Elisabeth, Jan. 24, 1748 ; Thomas, and *Gerrit*, March 18, 1750; Abraham, Feb. 11, 1753 ; *Samuel ; Johannes*, b. Feb. 5, 1760.

WITBECK, Lucas, and Catarina Carter. Ch: Thomas, bp. August 26, 1752.

WITBECK, Casparus [son of Johannes Thomase ?] and Geertruy Van Den Bergh. Ch: b. ; Johannes, June 30, 1766 ; Gerrit, May 16, 1768 ; Barent, Feb. 2, 1774.

WITBECK, Johannes (Hannes), [son of Caspar], and Engeltie Vrooman. Ch: b.; Martynus, Sept. 8, 1762 ; *Casparus*, August 6, 1764; Martinus, bp. Dec. 7, 1768.

WITBECK, Thomas [son of Johannes Thomase], and Janneke Rees. Ch: Johannes, b. June 26, 1769.

WITBECK, Pieter W. [son of Johannes Thomase], m. Rachel Van den Bergh, Jan. 9, 1768. Ch: b. ; Cornelia, Aug. 29, 1768; Eva, Dec. 27, 1770; Annatie, Oct. 17, 1773 ; Johannes, Sept. 25, 1775 ; Cornelis, Aug. 25, 1784. [Pieter W. Winne, and Maritie Pruyn, m. Dec. 9, 1787.]

WITBECK, Marten C. [son of Jonathan], m. Maria Van den Bergh, July 8, 1772. Ch: Machtel, b. Jan. 7, 1773.

WITBECK, Gerrit [son of Lucas], m. Immetje Perry, May 29, 1774. Ch: b.; John Perry, March 10, 1775 : Lucas, June 23, 1778 ; Antje, Jan. 28, 1781.

WITBECK, Johannes [son of Jonathan], m. Catharina Jones (SJans), April 19, 1776. Ch: b. ; Catharina, Oct. 5, 1776; Jonathan, March 23, 1779 ; Catharina, March 20, 1782.

WITBECK, Johannes [son of Lucas ?] and Lena Van Den Bergh. Ch: Geertruy, b. Nov. 19, 1786.

WITBECK, Samuel [son of Lucas ?] and Rebecca Buys (Buis). Ch: b. ; Geertruy, April 22, 1778; Christina, March 22, 1780.

WITBECK, Willem [son of Johannes Thomase], m. Catharine (De) Foreest, Oct. 17, 1779. Ch: b. ; Eva, April 11, 1781 ; Johannes, Jan. 24, 1785 ; Marten, bp. Nov. 12, 1786.

WITBECK, Harpert [son of Abraham], m. Geertruy Wendell, Oct. 15, 1783. Ch: b. ; Abraham, Sept. 10, 1784 ; Catharina, Dec. 1, 1785.

WITBECK, David, and Santje Fonda. Ch: Dirk, b. April 2, 1785.

WITBECK, Thomas J. [son of Jacob], m. Elizabeth Reisdorp, Sept. 22, 1771. Ch: Maria, b. Oct. 3, 1786.

WITBECK, Isaac, and Elizabeth Van Woert. Ch: Elbert, b. July 11, 1792.

WITBECK, Casparus [son of Johannes ?], m. Cornelia Dunbar, June 5, 1793. Ch: b. ; Martinus, May 17, 1793 ; Gerrit, Jan. 11, 1796.

Withardt, Johannes, owned a house and lot in Yonker street next west of the Elm tree corner. He was a trader in New Amsterdam as early as 1654 ; 1656, he was trading in Beverwick ; probably left the village about 1676, when Jan Janse Bleecker, his attorney, sold his lot.

Witmond, Jan, and Cornelis Cornelise, owned a brewhouse in the *Groenebos* (Greenbush), in 1657 which they sold to Willem Brouwer for 1207 guilders.

Witrel, Jean Georg (Jurriaan) *uit de Boght* 1764 ; m. Maria Barbara Nicolaasen, Dec. 17, 1764. Ch : James, bp. Jan. 16, 1768.

Wood, Samuel, and Marytje Schans (Jones?). Ch: Maria, bp. May 15, 1748.

Wood, Thomas, of New York, m. Catarina Gardenier, March 23, 1752. Ch: Thomas, bp. Dec. 23, 1752.

Woodcock, John, *geboren in Yorkshire in Oude Engelandt,* m. Ariaantje, dau. of Jan Jacobse Gardenier, May 3, 1702. Ch: bp. ; Anna, Oct. 4, 1702 ; John, Feb. 6, 1704 ; Abraham, Oct. 28, 1705 ; Isaac, July 4, 1707.

Woodcock, Dirk, and Sara..... Ch: Ariaantje, bp. Feb. 6, 1743.

Woodruff, Doctor Hunloke, m. Maria Lansing, May 16, 1779. Ch: b.; Ann, Jan. 20, 1780 ; Maria, Lansing, Nov. 22, 1781 ; Hunlock, July 27, 1783 ; Hunlock, July 13, 1785 ; Helen, m. Dr. Samuel Freeman, and d. at Saratoga Springs, March 17, 1863. Doctor Woodruff owned a house on the north corner of North Pearl street and Maiden Lane ; died July 4, 1811, a. 56 y.

Woodworth, Absalom, and Catharine Sprong. Ch: Robert, b. Nov. 22, 1783.

Woud (Wood?) Benjamin, and Elizabeth .... Ch: Richard, bp. Oct. 7, 1722 ; John, bp. June 2, 1723.

Wreight, Andrew, and Elizabeth ..... Ch: b. ; Margarita, May 20, 1767.

Wresch, Hannes, and Maria Riesch. Ch: Susanna, b. Jan. 5, 1770 ; David, b. Aug. 23, 1771 ; Johannes, bp. Sept. 15, 1773 ; Helena, bp. Jan. 28, 1776 ; Pieter, b. Jan. 3, 1778.

Writh (Wright?) Richard, of Schachtekook, and Greesie ...., Ch: Catharyna, bp. Feb. 17, 1739.

Wybesse, see Spoor.

Wyngaart, Lucas Gerritse, baker, and Anna Janse Van Hoesen ; made a will Oct. 30, 1709. Ch: *Gerrit,* eldest son ; Maria, bp. Feb. 15, 1685; *Lucas,* youngest son, bp. Nov. 21, 1686 ; *Johannes ; Jacobus ;* [Evert? see Evert Luycasse.]

Wyngaart, Gerrit Lucasse, trader, m. Sara Harmense Visscher, Nov. 4, 1694. In 1703 he bought a lot on south side of State street, next to Pieter Van Brugh's near Lodge street 30 feet deep if not hindered by the stockades. Ch: bp. ; Anna, Dec. 1, 1695 ; Hester, March 14, 1697 ; Lucas (Gerritse), Feb. 26, 1699 ; Anna, Aug. 24, 1701 ; Ariaantje, Oct. 10, 1703 ; Lucas, Jan. 6, 1706 ; Sara, Feb. 15, 1708 ; Gerritje, Jan. 15, 1710.

Wyngaart, Johannes Lucase, m. Sara Wendel, April 25, 1695. Ch: bp. ; Lucas, April 28, 1695 ; Johannes, Sept. 25, 1697 ; Ephraim, Aug. 11, 1700 ; Lucas, May 7, 1704.

Wyngaart, Jacobus Lucase, m. Maria Quackenbos, Nov. 3, 1700 ; he was buried Sept. 10, 1727. Ch: bp. ; Anna, May 11, 1701 ; *Johannes,* May 30, 1703 ; *Abraham,* July 29, 1705 ; Machtelt, Jan. 28, 1708 ; Gerrit Lucase, Oct. 27, 1710 ; Gerrit Lucase, April 20, 1712 ; Lucas, June 9, 1717 ; Christina, May 17, 1719 ; Lucas, Nov. 30, 1721, buried in the church Dec. 7, 1754.

Wyngaart, Johannes [son of Jacobus], m. Maritje Huysen, Nov. 22, 1725. Ch: bp. ; Elizabeth, Aug. 7, 1726 ; Marretie, Sept. 29, 1728; Machtel, June 14, 1730 ; Margarita, Aug. 6, 1732 ; Cathalyna, May 19, 1734 ; Cathalyna, Aug. 29, 1736 ; Jacobus, June 21, 1738.

Wyngaart, Abraham [son of Jacobus] m. first, Elizabeth Van Franken, Dec. 13, 1729 ; who was buried April 22, 1733 ; and secondly, Lybetje Van Aalsteyn, widow, Aug. 11, 1737. Ch: bp. ; Maria, Nov. 13, 1731 ; Elizabeth, May 22, 1738 ; Petrus, Aug. 16, 1741.

Wyngaart, Gerrit Lucase [son of Jacobus] and Christina Van Woert. Ch: Maria, bp. Jan. 10, 1746.

Wynkoop, Pieter, supercargo of Arms of Renselaerswyck in 1644, sent over by the Patroon ; he remained in the colony for some years.

Wynkoop, Cornelis, supposed to have been the son of the last, was in Beverwyck in 1657, where he purchased a lot and house ; he is said to have removed to Esopus in 1664, where he died in 1674 leaving six children.

Wynkoop, Gerrit, and Hilletje Gerritse. Ch: Nicolaas, bp. Feb. 18, 1705.

Wynkoop, Evert, and Geertje Elmendorp. Ch: Teola, b. Feb. 18, 1705.

Wynkoop, Cornelis, m. first, Annatie Gansevoort, Jan. 2, 1778 ; secondly, Miss Forcey, Dec. 12, 1789. Ch: Harmen Gansvoort, b. Dec. 16, 1785.

Wynkoop, James, m. Cataline Dunbar, Feb. 11, 1791. She d. June, 1838, a. 68 y. Ch: b. ; James, Nov. 1, 1791, d. April 25, 1843 ; John Henry Meyers, Sept. 10, 1796 ; Sarah, Aug. 5, 1806 ; William, Feb. 1, 1809 ; Robert, Aug. 1, 1811. [James Wynkoop, "a merchant of this city," d. May, 1794, a. 75 y.]

Wynkoop, John, and Harriet Bartay. Ch: Helena, b. Jan. 13, 1794.

Yates, Joseph, smith, m. Hubertje Marselis. He was buried May 22, 1730: his wife was buried July 13, 1730. In 1693 he petitioned Gov Fletcher for £20, due him for wood furnished the Fort " this being all he has to look to for support of his wife and *seven* children:" in 1713 he lived on the east corner of Beaver and Green streets. Ch: bp. ; *Christoffel,* April 16, 1684 ; *Robert,* Nov. 11, 1688; Selia, May 7, 1693 ; *Joseph,* March 17, 1695 ; Sara, March 6, 1698 ; Abraham, March 1, 1704. [Abraham Y. m. Hester Drinkwater, in New York, Sept. 10, 1726.]

Yates, Christoffel [son of Joseph], m. Catelyntje Winne, July 12, 1706. He was buried Feb. 26, 1754. Ch: bp. ; Joseph, April 20, 1707 ; *Adam,* August 15, 1708 ; Catalina, Oct. 7, 1711 ; Catalyna, Oct. 19, 1712 ; Huybertje, Nov. 7, 1714 ; *Johannes,* Oct. 14, 1716 ; Anneke, Oct. 5, 1718 ; Maria, April 29, 1722 ; *Abraham,* August 23, 1724 ; *Pieter,* Jan. 8, 1727.

Yates, Robert [son of Joseph], of Schenectady, m. Margriet De Graaf in Schenectady, Feb. 13, 1712. Ch: Joseph, bp. July 12, 1714. [*See Schenectady Families.*]

Yates, Joseph [son of Joseph], m. Hendrikje Hooghkerk, May 28, 1719. She was buried Jan. 19, 1750. Ch: bp. ; Joseph, March 9, 1720 ; Luycas, April 22, 1722 ; Albertus, Oct. 4, 1724 ; Judic, Feb. 12, 1727, d. Feb. 5, 1805, a. 77 y. 11 m. 28 d. ; Johannes, Sept. 7, 1729 ; Abraham, Dec. 20, 1730 ; Abraham, Dec. 24, 1732 ; Huybertje, June 16, 1736.

Yates, Joseph, Jr., of Schenectady, m. Eva Fonda, Jan. 17, 1730. Ch: bp.; Catalyna, Jan. 17, 1731; Rachel, May 7, 1732. [*See Schenectady Families.*]

Yates, Adam [son of Christoffel], m. Anna Gerritse, June 2, 1733 ; she was buried Sept. 15, 1751. Ch: bp.; *Jan Gerritsen,* March 23, 1735 ; Christoffel, April 22, 1739, d. Nov. 8, 1809, a. 71 y. ; Joseph, Jan.

13, 1742; Maria, Oct. 19, 1744 ; Maria, Jan. 18, 1747 ; Annatje, Feb. 19, 1749.

YATES, Johannes G., blacksmith [son of Christoffel], m. Rebecca Waldron, Nov 28, 1737. He made a will Dec. 27, 1775, proved June 4, 1776 ; the following Ch. were then living except Cathalina and Cornelia. Ch: bp. ¡ Christoffel, August 27, 1738; Tryntje, Dec. 28, 1740, m. Antony Bries ; Cathalina, Feb. 12, 1744 ; Cornelia, Jan. 12, 1746 ; *Pieter Waldron*, August 23, 1747 ; Annatje, Dec. 25, 1749, m. Willem Staats ; Engeltie, July 6, 1752, m. Cornelis Van Schaick, Jr. ; Rebecca, Nov. 14, 1756.

YATES, Johannes G. [son of Adam], and Catalyntje Goewey. Ch : Annatie, bp. Jan. 29, 1760 ; Johannetje, b. May 10, 1762 ; Adam, b. May 13, 1764.

YATES, Abraham [son of Christoffel], and Antje De Ridder. Abraham Yates, Jr., mayor of Albany, d. June 30, 1796, a. 73 y.... Ch : bp. ; Christoffel, June 7, 1747 ; Christoffel, July 10, 1748 ; Tanneke, Nov. 4, 1750 ; Cornelis, March 11, 1753.

YATES, Pieter [son of Christoffel], m. Sara Van Aalsteyn. Ch : bp. ; Christoffel, March 18, 1750 ; Pietertje, May 29, 1752 ; Jacob, March 28, 1755, d. at Schaghticoke, Nov. 21, 1831, a. 76. y. ; Abraham, Dec. 25, 1757 ; Cathalina, June 7, 1761 ; Maria, b. April 18, 1764 ; Annatje, March 2, 1767.

YATES, Abraham J. m. Jannetje Bratt, Aug. 22, 1761 ; Ann, w. of Abraham, J. Y. d. Nov. 22, 1804, a. 70 y. 9 m. 25 d. Ch : b. ; Hendrik, Sept. 28, 1763 ; Jannetje, July 17, 1766 ; Hubertje, June 12, 1769 ; Annatie, April 20, 1772 ; Daniel, Sept. 9, 1774, d. June 29, 1802.

YATES, Christoffer, J. [son of Johannes ?], m. Catharina Lansing, July 17, 1761. Ch : b. ; Abraham, Oct. 14, 1763 ; Evert, Oct. 24, 1764, d. at Fultonville, Sept. 10, 1846 a. 82 y. ; Johannes, May 13, 1766 ; Gerrit, April 13, 1768 ; Pieter, Jan. 28, 1770 ; Cathalyntje, Oct. 28, 1771 ; Alexander, Nov. 22, 1773 ; Annatje, July 6, 1776 ; Christoffer, May 10, 1779. Doctor Christopher C. Y. d. at Parishborough, Nova Scotia, Sept. 23, 1848.

YATES, Chief Justice Robert, [son of Joseph of Schenectady], m. Jannetje Van Ness. He d. Sept. 9, 1801. Ch : b. : Maria, Feb. 12, 1767 ; Maria, Oct. 19. 1768 ; William, Sept. 2, 1771 ; Joseph, Nov. 3, 1773 ; John Van Ness, 1779, d. Jan. 10, 1839 a. 60 y. ; Pieter, Aug. 30, 1783.

YATES, Christofer [son of Adam], m. Catharina Waters, July 19, 1766. He d. Nov. 8, 1809 a. 71 y. Ch : bp. ; Annatie, Feb. 10, *in d' avond Kerk gedoopt*, Feb. 11, 1767 ; Annatje, March 27, 1768 ; John Waters, Oct. 25, 1769, cashier of New York State Bank, d. March 29, 1828, a. 58 y. ; Sara, Dec. 14, 1771, d. Feb. 6, 1794 ; Marytje, Feb. 12, 1775 ; Christoffel, and Adam, Feb. 9, 1776.

YATES, Peter Waldron [son of Johannes], m. Ann Margarita Helms (Hellems, Kellens). Mrs. Mary Yates, w. of Peter W. Y., Esq., d. Nov. 23, 1794 a. 45 y. ; Peter W. Y. counsellor at law of Albany, d. at Caughnawaga March 9, 1826. a. 79 y. Ch : b. ; Cornelius Erasmus, July 21, 1768 ; Margarita, Jan. 28, 1770 ; Cornelia, Sept. 27, 1771 ; Cornelia, May 14, 1773 ; Maria, Dec. 23, 1775 ; Rebecca, Aug. 20, 1780, m. John King, and d. in New Lebanon, Sept. 28, 1829 ; Magdalena, Dec. 15, 1782 ; Engeltie, July 12, 1786.

YATES, Peter W. [same as the last ?], m. Mary Ter-Bush (Ter boss), Dec. 19, 1798. Ch : b. ; Elizabeth, May 28, 1800, " it was intended to call this child and

she is called Catharine by her parents ; " Catharine. June 28, 1801.

YATES, Christopher [son of Pieter], and Rebecca Winne. She d. July 11, 1863, a. 68 y. Ch : Pieter, b. July 15, 1784.

YATES, Hendrick [son of Abraham, Jr.] m. Rachel Van Santen [Zandt]. Jan. 19, 1786. She d. April 5, 1846, a. 80 y. 7 m. 27 d. Ch : b. ; Abraham, Feb. 14, 1787 ; Rebecca, Sept. 19, 1788 ; Gysbert, Nov. 20, 1790 ; Henry, Dec. 1, 1792 ; Jane, March 22, 1797 ; Sara, May 9, 1799 ; Sara, March 7, 1801 ; Judith, August 14, (20) 1803.

YATES, Adam [son of Johannes G. ?] and Margaret Cardenright. Ch : Eleana, b. Dec. 21, 1791.

YATES, John, and Geertruy Van Vranken. Ch : John, b. Jan. 4, 1793.

Yonghans, Matthias, and Margarita.... Ch : Hendrik, bp. Feb. 3, 1740.

Yonsen, Daniel, and Mary Barreth. Ch : Thomas, b. Dec. 28, 1771.

Yorck, Daniel, and Mary.... Ch : *David*, bp. August 15, 1737.

York, David, m. Susanna Grelle (Grennell, Creller), Dec. 27. 1761. Ch : b. ; *Daniel, geboren den lesten* August, bp., Sept. 5, 1762 ; Petrus, Dec. 6, 1765.

Young (Jongh), Simon, and Anna Ro (Rowe ?) He was sheriff of Albany 1696. Ch : Elizabeth, bp. Sept. 6, 1696

YOUNG, W., and ... . Ch : Mercy, bp. Nov. 9, 1735.

YOUNG, ,William, and Catharina (Helena) Fonda. Ch : bp. ; Guy, April 23, 1749 ; Maria, March 24, 1754 ; Catarina, Feb. 20, 1758.

YOUNG, Hendrick, m. Catrina Landman, Jan. 24, 1744. Ch : bp. ; Pieter, Nov. 23, 1746 ; Pieter, Dec. 6, 1748 ; Elizabeth, April 28, 1751 ; Johannes, May 20, 1753 ; Catarina, April 6, 1755 ; Abraham, 7 *weken oud*, Oct. 31, 1762 ; Isaac, b. March 14, 1767.

YOUNG, Guy, and Elizabeth ..... Ch : John, bp, March 27, 1748.

YOUNG, George, *van de vlachte*, m. Catarina Litcher, Jan. 29, 1757. Ch : bp. ; Elizabeth, March 5, 1758 ; Henderick, Nov. 25, 1759 ; Elizabeth, b. May 5, 1768.

YOUNG, Philip, m. Annatie Syphes Seckels, Seckens, Dec. 6, 1760. Ch : Annatie, bp. Aug. 16, 1761 ; Ch : b. ; Philip, Nov. 8, 1763 ; Jacobus, June 24, 1766 ; Eva, March 19, 1769 ; Philip, Dec. 2, 1771.

YOUNG, Hendrick, and Maria Lidger (Fletcher). Ch : Daniel, bp. Dec. 13, 1761 ; Ch : b. ; Annatje, Oct. 22, 1763 ; Hendrik, April 22, 1768 ; Marytje, Oct. 6, 1770.

YOUNG, Hendrick, and Catharine Keller. Ch : Henry, bp. Oct. 18, 1770.

YOUNG, Guy, m. first, Dirkie Winne, Nov. 19, 1769 ; and secondly, Maria Lansing, about 1775. Ch : b. ; Cathalyna, Sept. 11, 1771 ; Kiliaan, Oct. 23, 1773 ; William, Nov. 7, 1775.

YOUNG, James, and Anne Snyder. Ch : Anthony, b. May 13, 1775.

YOUNG, Daniel, and Elisabeth Van Der Kar. Ch : b. ; Annatie, August 27, 1778 ; Charlotte, Oct. 27, 1781 ; Willem, Jan. 1, 1783.

YOUNG, John, and Celia.... Ch : Henry, b. Dec. 7, 1779.

YOUNG, Alexander, and Elisabeth Sneed. Ch: Mary, bp. Jan. 24, 1780.

YOUNG, Barent, and Elisabeth Rykers. Ch: Johannes, bp. May 13, 1786.

YOUNG, Pieter, and Eva Moor. Ch: b.; Catharina, August 1, 1786; Peter, Dec. 10, 1790; Margaret, Sept. 30, 1792.

Ysselstyn, see Esselsteyn.

Zabriskie, Johannes, of Hackensack, m. Leentje (Leena) Lansing, of Albany, Jan. 11, 1776. Ch: b.; Sara, Nov. 30, 1776; Johannes Lansing, March 4, 1779.

Zangh, Thomas, and Clara ..... Ch: Pieter, bp. April 20, 1712.

Zebo, Johannes, and Anna M. Rockefeller. Ch: Hendrick, b. May 28, 1771.

Zeller, Johannes, and Catryna ..... Ch: Anna, bp. Oct. 12, 1718.

Ziele, Pieter, and Annatie ..... Ch: Pieter, bp. Feb. 8, 1738.

Zipperlem, Barent of Hosak, m. Margarita Wheger, Nov. 20, 1764. Ch: Catharina, b. Dec. 5, 1767.

Zoup, Frederic, and Maria.... Ch: b.; Margarita, Sept. 25, 1764; Dirk, Nov. 13, 1766.

Zwaertweger,.... and ... Hener. Ch: Lena, bp. Nov. 17, 1776.

18

INDEX.

19

Kierstede, Blandina, 46
Catharyna, 94
family, 68
Jacoba, 96
Kiersted, Rachel, 108
Kierstede, Surgeon Hans, 20
Kikebel,ThomasDavidtse, 4, 96
Kilmer, Elizabeth, 73
Kim family, 68
Kimmel, see Campbell, 68
Kincheler, Catharina, 77
King, Elizabeth, 32
families, 68
John, 156
Kinney family, 68
Kinter, Elizabeth, 61
family, 68
Kip, Anna, 141
Cornelia, 102
families, 68
Geertruy, 141
Jacobus, 142
Margarita, 59
Samuel, 94
Tryntje, 38
Kirchner family, 68
Kirk family, 68
Kitchel (Ketelhuyn?) family, 68
Kitkel, see Kettelhuin, 68
Kitsholt family, 68
Kittel, Anna, 39
Marytje, 111
Kittle, Bata, 81
(Ketelhuyn) Christina, 125
see Ketelhuyn), 68
Margarita, 121
Klauw, see Clauw, 68
Johannes, 58
Lea, 135
Kleermaker, Evert Janse, 7
Jan Pieterse, 9
Klein, Bata, 78
families, 68
Johannes, 32
Klemet (Clement), Jannetie, 135
Klerk, see Clark, 68
families, 68
Jan Cornelise, 3
Kleyn, Pieter Gerritse, 5
Klock family, 69
Knickelbacker, Cornelia, 136
Knickelbakker, Hanna Janse, 120
Knickerbacker, Alida, 136
Elizabeth, 89
families, 69
Knickerbakker,EvertHarmense, 5
Cornelia Harmense, 5
Cornelis Harmense, 5
Jannetje, 21, 70
family, 69
Jannetie Harmense, 5

Knickerbakker, Johannes Harmense, 5
Lourens Harmense, 5
Pieter Harmense, 5
Knipp, Maria, 13
Knipping, LenaSophia, 85
Knoll, Maria, 40
Koch, families, 69
Kock, Jan Gillise, 5
Kodman family, 69
Koeler family, 69
Koen, Barbara, 51
families, 69
Margarita, 100
Koens families, 69
Kool family, 69
Koolbrat family, 69
Koolhamer family, 69
Koorn (Coorn) family, 69
Koorenbeurs family, 69
Koperslager, Maes Cornelise, 4
Krankert family, 69
Kregier (see Cregier) family, 69
Geertruy, 39
Lysbeth, 129
Kremer, Catharine, 123
Krimer (see Cremer), 69
Kromenborch, Jan Janse, 7
Kruck (Crook), family, 69
Kruel family, 69
Krups, Nancy, 123
Kuis, Mary, 46
Kulerman family, 69
Gerrit Claese, 3
Kunst, Jan Barentsen, 3
Kuyper,JacobAbrahamse, 2
family, 69
Hanse Evertse, 4
Jacob Evertse, 4
Johannes Evertse, 4
Kuyskerk family, 69
Labagh family, 69
Labatie (Labaddie) family, 69
Lady family, 69
La Fort, see Fort, 69
La Grange, and La Granzie, see De la Grange, 69
Ann, 59
Antje, 67
Christina, 110, 153
Edith, 147
Elsie, 45
Geesje, 75
Lucy, 110
Omy, 127
Susanna, 47, 55
Lakens, Elizabeth, 126
Lamaker, Pieter Janse, 7
Lambert, Elizabeth, 30
Lancaster family, 69
Lanck family, 70
Land, Margarita, 14
Landman, Annatie, 138

Landman, Catrina, 156
Laner family, 74
Larraway family, 74
Neeltie, 104
(Le Roy) Saartje, 125
families, 70
Magalena, 25, 88
Langburn family, 70
Lange family, 70
Langh, Tryntie, 25
Lansing, Abraham, 38
Abraham G., 132
Abm., G. Jr., 125
Aeltie, Gerritse, 5
Alida, 49, 66, 145
Anna, 46, 133
Annatie, 73, 75, 110, 114, 119, 134, 149
Annatie (Ann, Hannah), 65
Lansing, Annetie Gerritse, 5
Catalyntje, 44
Catarina, 31
Cathalyna, 140
Catharina, 44, 71, 82, 138, 156
Cornelia, 97, 106
Elizabeth, 23, 25, 55, 85
Elsie, 65, 71
families, 70
family, 73
Femmetie, 72
Geertruy, 53, 100, 150, 154
Geertruy Janse, 7
Gerrit Abrahamse, 2
Gerrit Gerritse, 5
Gerrit Isaacse, 6
Gerrit Jacobse, 6
Gerrit Janse, 7
Gerrit Reyerse, 9
Gerritie, 26
Gysbertje, 93
Gysbertie Gerritse, 5
Helen Gerritse, 45
Hendrick, 68
Hendrick Gerritse, 5
Hendrikje, 49
Henry, 78
Hester, 93
Hilletje, 124
Hilletje Gerritse, 5
Hubertie, 89
Jacob, 87
Jane, 150
Jannetie, 139
Johannes, 59, 131
Johannes G., 136
Johannes Jacobse, 6
Johannes Janse, 7
Johannes Johanese, 8, 98
John, Jr., 156
Leentje (Helena, Leena), 141, 156
Lena, 144
Lena (Hanna), 41
Maayke, 31
Machtel, 50, 144

Lansing, Margaret, 89
Maria, 53, 95, 112, 149, 155, 156
Maritie, 115
Maritie Gerritse, 5
Mary, 90
Marytje, 159
Neeltie, 146
Pieter Pieterse, 9
Rachel, 32
Reyer Gerritse, 5
Sander, Jr., 99
Sarah, 19,
Susanna, 63, 83, 148
Lansingh, Alida, 114
Elizabeth, 114
Elsie, 43
Gerrit, Jr., 124
Jannetie, 139
Johannes, 34
Johannes Gerritse, 5
Lantman (Landman), families, 73
Lappany, see Lappius, 73
Lappius family, 73
Larroway, Lydia, 17
Larwee (see Le Roy), 73
Lassen, Pieter Pieterse, 9
Lasher (Leycher, Lissar, Lisjer, Litzert, Lygher, Lycher), family, 73
Lassingh family, 73
Lath family, 74
Lattimore family, 74
Lawrence family, 74
Margariet, 107
Ledyard, Mary Forman,37
Leek, Elizabeth, 63
family, 74
Leen (Lanck) family, 74
(Dennison), Jannetie,37
Leendertse, Annatie, 136
family, 74
Lenert (Lingert, Leonert) family, 74
Le Foy family, 74
Leg, Susanna, 45
Legged (Legate) family,74
Leischer, Susanna, 129
Le Lamater families, 41
Le Maitre, Cornelia, 22
family, 74
Lent, Catharine, 147
family, 74
Lents (Linch),Maria (Malli, Molly ?) 46
Leonard, Enoch, 137
families, 74
Regina Cath., 46
Le Roy (Larraway, Larwee, Lerway, Leuday, &c.) families, 74
Lerway (Larraway) family, 74
Lery, Jacob Hendrickse,6
Lespinard family, 74
Letteson (Liddeson) family, 74
Levison,Alida (Aaltie), 50, 72

21